To Frances

THEORIES OF COUNSELING
AND PSYCHOTHERAPY

THEORIES OF COUNSELING AND PSYCHOTHERAPY

FOURTH EDITION

C. H. PATTERSON
University of North Carolina, Greensboro
University of Illinois, Urbana–Champaign

HARPER & ROW, PUBLISHERS, New York
Cambridge, Philadelphia, San Francisco.
London, Mexico City, São Paulo, Singapore, Sydney

1817

Sponsoring Editor: Susan Mackey
Project Editor: Mary Ward
Cover Design: 20/20 Services, Inc.
Production: Willie Lane
Compositor: ComCom Division of Haddon Craftsmen, Inc.
Printer and Binder: R. R. Donnelley & Sons Company

Theories of Counseling and Psychotherapy,   Fourth Edition

Library of Congress Cataloging in Publication Data

Patterson, C. H. (Cecil Holden), 1912-
   Theories of counseling and psychotherapy.

   Includes bibliographies and indexes.
   1. Psychotherapy.   2. Counseling.   I. Title.
[DNLM: 1. Counseling.   2. Psychotherapy.   WM 420
P317t]
RC480.P38   1986   616.89′14   85-16365
ISBN 0-06-045053-3

85 86 87 88 9 8 7 6 5 4 3 2 1

CONTENTS

6. LEARNING FOUNDATIONS OF BEHAVIOR THERAPY: KANFER AND PHILLIPS   138

7. SOCIAL LEARNING APPROACH: ROTTER   171

8. COGNITIVE-BEHAVIOR MODIFICATION: MEICHENBAUM   190

PART THREE PSYCHOANALYTIC APPROACHES 207

9. PSYCHOANALYSIS: FREUD   211

10. PSYCHOANALYTIC THERAPY: ALEXANDER   233

PART FOUR PERCEPTUAL-PHENOMENOLOGICAL APPROACHES   265

11. PSYCHOLOGY OF PERSONAL CONSTRUCTS AND COUNSELING: KELLY   269

12. TRANSACTIONAL ANALYSIS: BERNE   309

13. GESTALT THERAPY: PERLS   342

PREFACE

Students in counseling or psychotherapy should be exposed early in their preparation to the major approaches or points of view. To expect them to read the original sources of even a half-dozen of these approaches would be unrealistic. But the thumbnail sketches included in introductory textbooks are inadequate. What is needed is a source book that presents comprehensive and accurate summaries in enough detail to give students a grasp of the structure and the organization of the theories, in order that they can compare them and use them as a basis for later reading of original sources for at least some of the theories.

There are a number of ways in which a book such as this may be approached. It is difficult for a single person, with the biases that he or she has, to present various points of view accurately and fairly. One way of minimizing this bias would be to have collaborators representing differing views. The writing of such a book would be difficult, however, and numerous collaborators would be necessary or desirable. A second approach, derived from this difficulty, would be to have a general editor, as well as acknowledged representatives of the various theories, who would present them. Such a book presents problems, however, with regard to bias on the part of the proponents of each theory and the consistency of presentation. Evaluations by others than the representatives or the editor would be desirable. A third approach would be to have a single person present the various theories, who would then have the pertinent chapters read and critiqued by appropriate colleagues or representatives of the theories presented.

The third approach is the one taken in this book. Two variations of this approach are possible. In the first, the theories could be summarized from the writer's point of view, that is, in an expository or openly critical or evaluative manner. In the second, the writer would attempt to present nonevaluative summaries as they are propounded by their originators or representatives. A critique or evaluation could follow each presentation. It is the second variation that I have used.

In each chapter, I have described a given approach, not based on my views of the approach but from the point of view of an adherent. I have attempted to be nonevaluative in the presentation of each approach, and I have aimed at comprehensiveness, completeness, and accuracy in each presentation. In some cases, I have reorganized the original theorists' presentations in the interest of clarity. In each case,

I immersed myself in the writings of the theorist, and in the process, I found myself identifying with the theory; as a result, most, if not all, of the theories are presented in a rather favorable light. Accuracy and clarity have been striven for in each case, however.

That I have been at least fairly successful in avoiding biased presentations is evidenced by the fact that the summaries have been accepted by the authors or developers of each approach in those cases where they were read by the original author or a person identified closely with the approach. This was done for each theory included in the first edition, and suggestions by readers were incorporated in each summary. The following persons read the chapters in the first edition, which are also included here, and I am indebted to them for reading and commenting on the presentations and in some cases for permitting me to reprint case summaries or typescripts: Albert Ellis, Vicktor E. Frankl, Thomas M. French (for Alexander's psychoanalytic psychotherapy), George A. Kelly, Neal E. Miller, Carl R. Rogers, Julian B. Rotter, Frederick C. Thorne, and Joseph Wolpe. Frederick Kanfer read the introduction to Part Two and the chapter on learning foundations of behavior therapy, and Erving Polster read the chapter on Gestalt therapy in the second edition. Donald Meichenbaum read the chapter on cognitive-behavior therapy in the third edition.

The task of selecting a dozen or so theories for inclusion in a book such as this is a difficult one. There are at least twice as many theories as I have presented that would warrant summarizing—a number that would require two volumes. One basis for exclusion was the availability of summaries elsewhere; thus, the theories of Freud, Jung, Adler, Horney, and Sullivan were not included in previous editions. In the second edition, summaries of Salter's conditional-reflex therapy, the Pepinskys' reinforcement theory, and Phillips's interference theory were dropped. The summaries of Wolpe's reciprocal-inhibition therapy and Bordin's psychological-counseling approach were revised to include newer publications, and the chapter on Thorne's eclectic system was rewritten and placed in a different part of the book.

The past ten years have been a period of ferment—perhaps turmoil might be a better word—in the field of counseling or psychotherapy. There has been a proliferation of new or so-called innovative therapies or, more accurately, methods and techniques. An examination of these methods, however, indicates little, if any, conceptual or theoretical foundations for most of them. Interested readers will find thumbnail sketches of over 30 approaches (not all new, however) from *A* (Arica therapy and autogenics) to *Z* (Zuk's family therapy), but not including EST or scientology, in a little paperback by R. A. Harper, *The New Psychotherapies* (Prentice-Hall, 1975). None of these approaches warrants inclusion in a book such as this.

A particularly difficult task was to determine if there was a more appropriate statement of the behavior therapies than that of Kanfer and Phillips. Many new behavior-therapy texts have appeared, and these (not including edited books) were examined, among them M. R. Goldfried and G. C. Davison, *Clinical Behavior Therapy* (Holt, Rinehart and Winston, 1976); K. D. O'Leary and G. T. Wilson, *Behavior Therapy: Application and Outcome* (Prentice-Hall, 1975); A. J. Yates, *Theory and Practice in Behavior Therapy* (Wiley-Interscience, 1975); and G. Martin and J. Pear, *Behavior Modification: What It Is and How to Do It* (Prentice-Hall, 1978). It became apparent that there have been no major or significant developments in behavior therapy and that Kanfer and Phillips still provide the most comprehensive survey.

This edition recognizes two important developments in psychotherapy: (1) the increasing interest in the cognitive therapies and (2) the move toward eclecticism.

Books on behavior therapy now have chapters on cognitive methods, and book titles often include recognition of cognitive elements—for example, M. J. Mahoney, *Cognition and Behavior Modification* (Ballinger, 1974), and D. Meichenbaum, *Cognitive-Behavior Modification* (Plenum, 1977). The movement of behavior therapists into cognitive therapy—and into the use of other nonbehavioristic methods and techniques—raises the question as to whether behavior therapy, in any orthodox sense of a therapy based on behavioristic psychology, still exists.

The approach selected to represent cognitive-behavior therapy in the third edition (and retained here) was that of Meichenbaum, for a number of reasons.

1. It developed from Meichenbaum's training and experience in behavior therapy but is more than simply the addition of cognitive elements to behavior therapy.
2. Its theory, although incomplete and limited, is more systematic than are other cognitive-behavior approaches.
3. It derives from and is based on a program of research.

Its major limitation—and one that it shares with more purely cognitive approaches—is that it is essentially a teaching or training approach rather than a comprehensive psychotherapy. The chapter on cognitive-behavior therapy might have been included in Part One, but it was placed in Part Two because although it is not based on any standard learning theory, it is more clearly based on learning than are the cognitive therapies.

Interest in purely cognitive approaches to psychotherapy has increased. Two such approaches were considered for inclusion in the third edition: A. T. Beck, *Cognitive Therapy and the Emotional Disorders* (International Universities Press, 1976), and V. Raimy, *Misunderstandings of the Self: Cognitive Psychotherapy and the Misconception Hypothesis* (Jossey-Bass, 1977). These were again reviewed, and, as a result, both are included in this edition—Beck's because of its general popularity, and Raimy's because of its significance for the development of an eclectic psychotherapy. Raimy's approach deserves more attention than it has received. Although it could be contended that the approach has not been adopted by many practitioners (the same could be said about many of the theories, however), the methods and techniques considered by Raimy are used by many practitioners. He has provided a theoretical base for them.

A number of books published in the past few years purport to present an eclectic system of psychotherapy. They include L. E. Beutler, *Eclectic Psychotherapy: A Systematic Approach* (Pergamon Press, 1983); S. L. Garfield, *Psychotherapy: An Eclectic Approach* (Wiley-Interscience, 1980); J. T. Hart, *Modern Eclectic Therapy* (Plenum, 1983); and S. Palmer, *A Primer of Eclectic Psychotherapy* (Brooks/Cole, 1979). In addition, Lazarus's multimodal psychotherapy could be considered an eclectic approach (A. Lazarus, *Multimodal Therapy.* [McGraw-Hill, 1981]). None of them, however, offers a comprehensive, theoretically based systematic eclecticism. The approach developed by Hart was selected for inclusion in this edition because it most closely approaches such a system. Thorne was retained because his approach continues to be the most comprehensive, integrated eclecticism.

Two approaches were dropped in this edition—Williamson's and Bordin's. Both had been retained in earlier editions primarily because they included applications to vocational counseling. Summaries of both are now available in Crites's survey of theories of career choice (J. O. Crites, *Career Counseling: Models, Methods, and Materials.* [McGraw-Hill, 1981]). Williamson still is of historical interest and is accessible in library copies of earlier editions of this book.

The selection of a representative of psychoanalytic theory was particularly difficult. Analytic and neoanalytic theories (Freud, Adler, Jung, Rank, Horney, and Sullivan) were not included in earlier editions because summaries were available elsewhere. They still are available but are not so easily accessible. It seemed that some representative of the earlier psychoanalytic approaches should be included. Obviously, not all could be. It was reasonable that Freud should receive preference, since the others, as well as the practitioners of newer ego-analytic approaches, derive from him.

The task of condensing Freud's voluminous writings into one chapter would be tremendous. Fortunately, a basis for such a summary was present in the work of a colleague from my Fulbright year in England. The chapter on Freud's psychoanalysis is a major revision and extension of a chapter in Richard Nelson-Jones, *The Theory and Practice of Counselling Psychology* (London: Holt, Rinehart and Winston, 1982).

The discussion of Wolpe's behavior therapy has been revised on the basis of the third edition of *The Practice of Behavior Therapy.* The introductions to the various sections have been updated, and the final two chapters have been rewritten. Students might benefit from reading these chapters before, as well as after, reading the rest of the book. Instructors may not agree with all the positions taken by the author in these chapters, but they should serve as the stimulus for interesting class discussions.

Students should be cautioned that the summary chapters in this book are not a substitute for reading the original sources and certainly are not adequate as a basis for attempting to apply or practice any of the methods described.

Again, I must express my indebtedness to George Middendorf, my editor at Harper & Row for more than 20 years prior to his retirement, for the idea for this book.

C. H. Patterson

INTRODUCTION

Counseling and *psychotherapy* are both used in the title of this book because it appears to be impossible to make any clear distinction between them. If experts in counseling and psychotherapy were asked to list the theories that should be considered under each heading, there probably would be great overlapping in the lists. The difficulty in determining which are theories of counseling and which are theories of psychotherapy is taken as one evidence of the lack of clear or significant differences between them. The position taken by this writer is that there are no essential differences between counseling and psychotherapy.[1] Students in courses in which either *counseling* or *psychotherapy* appears in the title would be expected to be familiar with most of the theories included in this volume.

The difficulty in, or impossibility of, separating counseling and psychotherapy is apparent when one considers the definitions of each offered by various authors. The definitions of counseling would in most cases be acceptable as definitions of psychotherapy, and vice versa. There seems to be agreement that both counseling and psychotherapy are processes involving a special kind of relationship between a person who asks for help with a psychological problem (the client or the patient) and a person who is trained to provide that help (the counselor or the therapist). The nature of the relationship is essentially the same, if not identical, in both counseling and psychotherapy. The process that occurs also does not seem to differ from one to the other. Nor do there seem to be any distinct techniques or group of techniques that separate counseling and psychotherapy.

When objectives are considered, however, there may appear to be some differences. The objectives of counseling have been identified by the Committee on Definition, Division of Counseling Psychology of the American Psychological Association, as "to help individuals toward overcoming obstacles to their personal growth, wherever these may be encountered, and toward achieving optimum development of their personal resources."[2] Most psychotherapists would accept these as goals of psychotherapy also. Tyler, attempting to distinguish counseling from psychotherapy, states that it is *not* the job of counselors "to remove physical or mental handicaps or to get rid of limitations."[3] This is presumably the job of the therapist. This statement, however, appears to disagree with that of the Committee on Definition and, in my opinion, would not be acceptable to most counseling psychologists. Tyler goes on to note that the activity of the therapist "is aimed essentially at change in developmental structures rather than at fulfillment," while counseling does not attempt to "repair damage done to [the client] in the past, to stimulate inadequate [*sic*] development of some stunted aspect of his personality," but is the process of "helping a person attain a clear sense of personal identity," along with acceptance of limitations. Again, it would appear that many would reject these restrictions on counseling and would accept the goal of counseling as a goal of psychotherapy.

The distinction that it seems is being made by many, including Tyler, as well as Vance and Volsky, is that counseling applies to work with so-called normal individuals, whose problems are related to the development of their potential, while psychotherapy refers to work with individuals who are deficient in some respect.[4] This leads to an artificial distinction in terms of severity of disturbance on a continuum of adjustment–maladjustment. When a client has a serious psychological disturbance or is handicapped in functioning "normally" because of such disturbance, the process is called *psychotherapy* and is seen as a remedial process to bring the individual up to "normal." When a client is not seriously disturbed but has the problems of the so-called normal person, which interfere with the development of the individual's potential, the process is called *counseling.* It should be obvious, as Tyler recognizes, that no sharp line can be drawn between the two. So-called counselors practice psychotherapy, while psychotherapists practice counseling, for it is clear that a therapist cannot and does not make a determination that the client, after a period of psychotherapy, is now functioning at a minimal "normal" level and should therefore be transferred to a counselor for help beyond this point. In any case, the counselor or psychotherapist takes a client where he or she is and allows the individual to go as far as he or she can go or desires to go. Counselors are not limited to working with "normal" clients, nor do they limit their efforts with a client to what Tyler calls attempts to "bring about the best utilization of what the person already has,"[5] with acceptance of his or her limitations, without concern about, or even with avoidance of, personality weaknesses and personality change. Thus a distinction in terms of severity of disturbance or of the kinds of clients dealt with is an artificial one.

A second difference is also artificial or unessential. This is the distinction in terms of the setting in which services are provided. If the setting is a medical one, what is done is called psychotherapy, whereas if the setting is nonmedical, it is called counseling.

A further distinction is sometimes made in terms of the nature or content of the problem that the client brings to the counselor. So-called reality-oriented (or "conscious") problems, such as educational and vocational problems and choices, have been considered to be the province of counseling, while problems that are inherent in the personality of the individual ("unconscious" problems) are the province of psychotherapy. This line of thinking has led to the suggestion that cognitive, rational approaches are appropriate for dealing with reality, or conscious, problems, while problems involving the unconscious require a different approach. Again, however, no clear line can be drawn, and if there is concern with only the rational solution of so-called reality (nonego involved) problems, this is not counseling but teaching. Nor is the providing of information, which may be a part of counseling, itself counseling. This attempted distinction has led to an unwarranted extension of the term *counseling* to include functions that actually involve individual instruction or information giving. Counseling, in my opinion and in agreement with most definitions that have been offered, deals with or includes the conative or affective realm—attitudes, feelings, and emotions—and not simply with ideas. When there is little affect involved, the process is not counseling but is probably teaching, information giving, or an intellectual discussion.

It is concluded that there are no essential differences between counseling and psychotherapy in the nature of the relationship, in the process, in the methods or techniques, in goals or outcomes (broadly conceived), or even in the kinds of clients involved. For convenience, or for practical or political reasons, counseling often refers to work with less seriously disturbed clients or with clients who have rather specific problems with less accompanying general personality disturbance, usually in a non-medical setting; psychotherapy refers to work with more seriously disturbed clients, usually in a medical setting. This book, therefore, makes no distinction among theories on this basis and does not attempt to classify or dichotomize them into one category or the other.

THE NATURE OF THEORY

We have indicated that certain theories of counseling and psychotherapy will be presented, but what constitutes a theory of counseling or psychotherapy? How many theories are there?

A *theory* is more than an opinion, a speculation, a statement of position, or a point of view. It is more than a collection of principles, methods, or techniques. It is more than a summary of knowledge, principles, or methods derived from experience or research. A theory is an attempt to organize and integrate knowledge and to answer the question "Why?" A theory organizes, interprets, and states in the form of laws or principles the facts and knowledge in an area or a field. The organization or arrangement of what we know makes possible a systematic description from which explanations and predictions can be derived that then can be systematically tested. Theories are invented or constructed for these purposes; they do not exist by themselves somewhere waiting to be discovered. Practice may be based on empirical knowledge. An explanatory theory gives a sense of understanding, direction, and rationality to practice. It provides a guide to application, extension, extrapolation, and modification in new or different situations.

A formal theory has certain characteristics. First, it consists of a set of stated *postulates* or *assumptions*. (Assumptions are sometimes distinguished from postulates; the difference is in the degree of presumption of their being true. Postulates are more tentative.) These state the premises of the field with which the theory is concerned. They are the givens that are accepted and for which proof is not required. They must be internally consistent. Second, there is a set of *definitions* of the terms or concepts in the theory. These definitions relate the concepts to observational data or to operations and thus make possible the study of the concepts in research and experimentation. Third, the terms or concepts bear certain *relationships* to one another; these relationships derive from a set of rules, usually rules of logic. They include cause-and-effect relationships. Fourth, from these assumptions, definitions, and relationships, *hypotheses* are constructed or deduced. These are essentially predictions of what should be true if the assumptions, definitions, relationships, and the reasoning involved in the deductions are true, that is, if the theory is valid. Given certain assumptions, definitions, and relationships, certain things should follow or be true. Hypotheses state in a form that allows for testing what these things are. The testing of hypotheses leads to new knowledge. If hypotheses are not supported by adequate observation and experiment, the theory must be corrected or revised and new hypotheses must be deduced and tested. Theory thus directs research by providing hypotheses to be tested and by directing observation and experiment.

Theory not only predicts new facts and relations, but also organizes and integrates what is known in a meaningful framework. Whether this organization of existing knowledge comes with the formulation of the theory or follows its formulation is not always clear; some writers appear to think of organization as a late development or as a result of a theory. However, the assumptions or postulates of a theory do not arise out of thin air or apart from reality and experience. They are derived or developed from observation and experience or from empirical research; that is, existing facts and knowledge are the bases for the assumptions and definitions of a theory. The process of theory construction, testing, modification or reconstruction, and further testing is a continual process.

Theories cannot be evaluated as to their correctness or validity until they are tested. A theory may be good without being totally correct; in fact, few, if any, theories, even after considerable testing, can be accepted as valid in any complete or absolute sense. A good theory, however, is more likely to be true than a poor one. Certain formal criteria have been proposed for evaluating a theory.[6]

1. *Importance*   A theory should not be trivial but should be significant. It should be applicable to more than a limited, restricted situation, such as the behavior of rats in a T maze or the learning of nonsense syllables. It should have some relevance to life or to real behavior. Importance is very difficult to evaluate, however, since the criteria are vague or subjective. Acceptance by competent professionals or recognition and persistence in the professional literature may be indicative of importance. Also, if a theory meets other formal criteria, it is probably important.
2. *Preciseness and Clarity*   A theory should be understandable, internally consistent, and free from ambiguities. Clarity may be tested by the ease of relating the theory to data or to practice, or the ease of developing hypotheses or making predictions from it and specifying methods of testing them.
3. *Parsimony or Simplicity*   Parsimony has long been accepted as a characteristic of a good theory. This means that the theory contains a minimum of complexity and few assumptions. Maddi questions this criterion, however, and suggests that one cannot determine which of two theories is most parsimonious until everything is known about the area to which the theory applies. He also questions its value on the grounds that the most parsimonious theory on the basis of current data might not be the best theory: "It is distinctly possible that a theory which looks parsimonious in explaining today's facts may be actually such an oversimplification in terms of explaining all human functioning as to be wholly inadequate to cope with tomorrow's facts without major overhaul."[7] Nevertheless, it might be maintained that the phenomena of the world and of

nature are relatively simple in terms of basic principles. The law of parsimony appears to be the most widely violated in theory construction. This may be because of the stage of knowledge we have reached, where diversity and complexity are more apparent than are the underlying unity and consistency. Hall and Lindzey propose that parsimony is important only after the criteria of comprehensiveness and verifiability have been met. "This becomes an issue only under circumstances where two theories generate exactly the same consequences."[8]

4. *Comprehensiveness* A theory should be complete, covering the area of interest and including all known data in the field. The area of interest, however, can be restricted.

5. *Operationality* A theory should be capable of being reduced to procedures for testing its propositions or predictions. Its concepts must be precise enough to be measurable. A strict operationalism can be restrictive, however, as Maddi points out, when a concept is defined by a restricted or limited measurement operation.[9] A current lack of measurement to operationalize a concept should not rule out the use of a concept that is essential for a theory. The concept first should be defined and then a method of measurement, chosen or developed. Not all the concepts of a theory need to be operational; concepts may be used to indicate relationships and organization among concepts.

6. *Empirical Validity or Verifiability* The preceding criteria are rational in nature and do not directly relate to the correctness or validity of a theory. Eventually, however, a theory must be supported by experience and experiments that confirm it; that is, in addition to its consistency with or ability to account for what is already known, it must generate new knowledge. However, a theory that is disconfirmed by experiment may lead indirectly to new knowledge by stimulating the development of a better theory.

7. *Fruitfulness* The capacity of a theory to lead to predictions that can be tested, leading to the development of new knowledge, has often been referred to as its fruitfulness. A theory can be fruitful even if it is not capable of leading to specific predictions. It may provoke thinking and the development of new ideas or theories, sometimes because it leads to disbelief or resistance in others.

8. *Practicality* There is a final criterion of a good theory, which is seldom mentioned or recognized; that is, it should be useful to practitioners in organizing their thinking and practice by providing a conceptual framework for practice. A theory allows the practitioner to move beyond the empirical level of trial-and-error application of techniques to the rational application of principles. Practitioners too often think of theory as something that is irrelevant to what they do, unrelated to practice or to real life. Yet, as Lewin, the developer of topological psychology, is reputed to have said, "there is nothing as practical as a good theory."[10] Operating on the basis of a theory is the difference between being a technician and a professional.

If we looked for a theory of counseling or psychotherapy that met all these criteria, we probably would not find one. Nor would we find such a theory of personality or of learning. Existing theories are at a primitive stage, and the criteria constitute goals toward which theorists should strive. Most theories of counseling or psychotherapy are not cast in a formal form, although some are attempts at formulation in terms of a set of related postulates or assumptions, with their corollaries. In many instances, theoretical concepts are implicit rather than explicit. Explicit statements of points of view in counseling vary from specific statements concerned with only one aspect or element of the counseling process or relationship to very general expositions. Frank writes that

> some formulations [of psychotherapy] try to encompass all its aspects. Many of these have been immensely insightful and stimulating and have illuminated many fields of knowledge. To achieve all-inclusiveness, however, they have resorted to metaphor, have left major ambiguities unresolved, and have formulated their hypotheses in terms that cannot be subjected to experimental test.
>
> The opposite approach has been to try to conceptualize small segments of the field with sufficient precision to permit experimental tests of the hypotheses, but these formulations run the risk of achieving rigor at the expense of significance. The researcher is faced with the problem of delimiting an aspect of psychotherapy that is amenable to experimental study and at the same time includes the major determinants of the problem under consideration. He finds himself in the predicament of the Norse god Thor, who tried to drain a small goblet only to discover that it was connected with the sea. Under these circumstances there is an inevitable tendency to guide the choice of research problems more by the ease with which they can be investigated than by their importance. One is reminded of the familiar story of the drunkard who lost his keys in a dark alley but looked for them under the lamppost because the light was better there. This has led to a considerable amount of precise but trivial research.[11]

It appears that counselors and psychotherapists have been so engrossed in practice that little attention has been given to the development of formal theories. Nevertheless, although not formally stated, there are, in every practice or approach to counseling, implicit assumptions. They often are not clearly stated or perhaps not stated at all, but they are there. Theoretical discussions of counseling or psychotherapy frequently allude to assumptions and hypotheses, sometimes confusing the two. Many of these theoretical discussions are in a sense after-the-fact explanations or rationalizations and have not been developed formally for research. Thus they usually are not clearly or systematically stated. Nevertheless, they are embryo theories and should be capable of being explicitly formulated as formal theories.

It is not the purpose of this book to attempt to formulate such theories on the basis of the literature. Its purpose is rather to present existing theories in the forms in which they occur. Thus the word *theory* is used rather loosely, as it must be if the book is to have any content at all. The phrase *point of view* is probably more appropriate.

THE POINTS OF VIEW AND THEIR ORGANIZATION

Once the concession is made to include points of view or approaches to counseling rather than formalized theories, the candidates for inclusion become numerous. We might attempt either to reduce all theories or approaches to a few central ones or to deal with only the major theories. The Pepinskys, in 1954, classified theories into five major categories: (1) the trait-and-factor centered approach, (2) the communications approach, (3) self-theory, (4) the psychoanalytic approach, and (5) the neobehavioral approach.[12] It is perhaps possible to subsume most of the major approaches under these rubrics. The various learning theory approaches of Dollard and Miller, Salter, Shoben, and Wolpe, for example, might be included under the neobehavioral category, and the various neoanalytic theories might be included under the psychoanalytic approach.

To some extent, this is the procedure adopted here; that is, the various approaches have been grouped into categories that have some similarity to those of the Pepinskys, but the organization of the approaches, or their ordering, presents a problem. Is it possible to impose any organization on the various approaches, or are they too heterogeneous to order in any way? One possible manner of organization would be to arrange them on the commonly used continuum of directiveness, from highly directive to highly permissive approaches. There are other bases for organization. One such basis, probably not entirely independent of the directive–permissive continuum, is a continuum from highly rational to highly affective approaches, from theories that are highly cognitive to those that are highly conative in their emphases. Bordin suggested such a continuum, from an "emphasis on an intellectual process of reasoning out the problem" to "the emphasis upon stimulating the client to further and deeper expression of his attitudes through such methods as accepting and clarifying responses" as a dimension of the counseling process.[13] This continuum has been accepted as the basis for organizing the various points of view.

At the cognitive end of such a continuum are those theories or approaches to counseling that are rational, logical, or intellectual in nature. Perhaps the most extreme example of this would be the rational psychotherapy of Ellis. Farther along the continuum would fall the more psychological approaches, the learning theory and conditioned response theories of Dollard and Miller, Salter, and Wolpe. Still farther along would be the various analytic approaches. Toward the other extreme would be the self-theories or phenomenological approaches, with existentialism perhaps at the most extreme end of the continuum.

For convenience, this continuum has been divided into five parts, which make up five sections of this book. These are designated as (1) cognitive approaches to counseling, (2) learning theory approaches to counseling, (3) psychoanalytic approaches to counseling, (4) perceptual–phenomenological approaches to counseling, and (5) existential approaches to counseling. A sixth section has been included to accommodate the eclectic positions of Hart and Thorne. Within the sections, however, no attempt has been made to order the theories or approaches in terms of the underlying continuum; indeed, it probably would not be possible to do so in most instances. In some cases, the assignment of a theory to a particular section might be questioned. For example, some might place Dollard and Miller among the psychoanalytic approaches. Kelly's approach is in some respects quite cognitive or rational in its orientation. Any attempt to group or classify approaches to counseling or psychotherapy must result in arbitrary assignments in some cases. It might thus be questioned whether it is necessary or desirable to group the approaches at all. I confess to a need for some organization in their presentation and feel that some organization is better than none and that some basis for grouping and ordering groups is better than no basis. Students have felt that this organization was helpful.

A question arises as to how many points of view, or variants of a point of view, should be included. There are, of course, necessary limitations of space, but I have attempted to include, even though sometimes rather briefly, those positions that are dealt with in an extended manner (usually at book length) in the literature of the field. Thus students are introduced to most of the current writers in counseling or psychotherapy. Obviously, every book dealing with counseling or psychotherapy could not be represented here. The criterion for selection was whether the author presented either what might be considered a systematic point of view or a significant variant of a particular approach. Even so, it is obvious that I have neglected to include every possible point of view or variant, if for no other reason than that I am sure I have missed some through ignorance of their existence.

RELATION TO OTHER PSYCHOLOGICAL THEORIES

Theories of counseling or psychotherapy cannot be clearly separated from theories of learning, theories of personality, or general theories of behavior. Counselors deal with behavior. The fact that they work with clients who exhibit behavior that is more or less disturbed, abnormal, or unsatisfactory in some respects, to themselves or to society or to both, does not change the fact that it is behavior with which the counselor is concerned. Moreover, the aspect of behavior that is the primary focus of the counselor falls into the area of personality in its individual and social aspects. In addition, the goal of counseling is the changing of behavior or personality in some respect or to some extent. Different approaches to counseling vary in the specific nature and extent of behavior change toward which they are directed, but they all accept behavior change of some kind, including changes in attitudes, feelings, perceptions, values, or goals, as the objective of counseling. Since learning may be defined broadly as change in behavior, counseling is, of course, concerned with learning and thus with theories of learning.

In fact, it is difficult to distinguish among theories of learning, theories of personality, and theories of counseling or psychotherapy. All are concerned with behavior and are thus theories of behavior. Hall and Lindzey differentiate between theories that deal with any behavioral event of significance to the human organism (general theories of behavior) and those that are limited to certain aspects of human behavior (single-domain theories).[14] It is difficult, however, to make the separation clearly. Hall and Lindzey state that personality theories are general theories of behavior, and they admit that theories of learning may also be considered theories of behavior but so may theories of counseling or psychotherapy. Even theories of perception may be theories of behavior, since perception is central to all behavior. Behavior, in short, is all of one piece, and any theory dealing with a major aspect of behavior is or must become a general behavior theory. Theories concerned with the various aspects must be consistent among themselves and together must constitute a general theory of behavior. Eventually, a theory of learning, a theory of personality, a theory of perception, and a theory of counseling or psychotherapy must all be parts of a general theory of behavior.

The discussion of theories of counseling or psychotherapy, therefore, inevitably involves the areas of personality and learning. Every theory of counseling has, and must have, a theory of personality and of learning behind it. Usually, the related theories of personality and learning are implicit rather than explicit. When they are explicit, they usually have developed from the theory of counseling or psychotherapy, as in the case of client-centered counseling, although it may, of course, be the case that a theory of psychotherapy is consistent with an independently developed theory of personality. At any rate, theories of personality and theories of psychotherapy are interrelated, although there is not necessarily a theory of psychotherapy for every theory of personality that has been identified or developed.

Thus insofar as the authors of the various approaches presented deal with personality theory, it will be included as a part of the summary of the approach. There will be no attempt, however, on my part to provide a personality theory to accompany an approach that is lacking in an explicit theory. It is not the purpose of this book to go beyond what has been developed by those concerned with the various approaches to counseling or psychotherapy.

PHILOSOPHICAL IMPLICATIONS

Allport notes that "theories of learning (like much else in psychology) rest on the investigator's conception of the nature of man. In other words, every learning theorist is a philosopher, though he may not know it."[15] This applies perhaps even more forcefully to counseling theorists. It is, therefore, necessary to include in our discussions the philosophical bases that are implicit or explicit in the various counseling theories. Again, no elaborate philosophical formulation will be developed for each theory considered, but it does seem to be necessary to consider the assumptions regarding human nature underlying the various theories, as well as the goals or objectives of counseling or psychotherapy that are accepted or advocated by them. In many cases, of course, very little formal consideration was given in the original presentation of the approach, and this will be reflected in the summaries in this book.

NATURE OF THE PRESENTATIONS

It seems desirable that in the discussion of the various theories, some common method or outline should be followed. It is difficult, however, to develop a detailed outline that would be appropriate for all theories. The categories selected are, therefore, few, broad, and general.

The general procedure is to identify the theory in terms of its major proponents, giving some background or orientation to the approach. Then the major concepts, or the essential elements, of the approach are discussed. These include the philosophical background or implications and the related theories of personality and learning or of behavior and its change. Next, the goals of therapy and the therapy process are considered, followed by consideration of the techniques or the behavior of the therapist, who implements the concepts in the process. Then, when possible, one or more illustrative examples of the approach are presented. Finally, a summary and a general evaluation concludes the discussion.

The evaluations are not full-scale critiques of the theories but summaries of the major contributions of each approach and considerations of some of the major objections or criticisms that have been or might be raised against them.

The presentations are intended to be descriptive rather than polemic. The reader who is familiar with the author's point of view perhaps will be able to recognize areas where bias still may be present. I have, like Hilgard, "approached the task with the desire to be friendly to each of the positions represented, on the assumption that each of them has been proposed by an intelligent and sincere person or group of persons, and that there must be something which each of them can teach us."[16] The final section, of course, represents my own attempt at evaluating or drawing out differences and similarities among current approaches to counseling. The purpose of the book is not to present a critique or comparison of the various theories or to attempt to develop a single theory by integrating aspects of various approaches. The purpose is to present in a relatively brief, objective form various current points of view in counseling or psychotherapy. This is difficult to do without danger of misrepresentation because of brevity, misunderstanding, or biased perception. It is hoped that this danger has been minimized by having the presentations read in many cases by the representatives of the various approaches. I do, however, accept the responsibility for what appears in the following chapters.

Unlike the works of Hilgard and of Hall and Lindzey, this book does not attempt to review the research associated with the various theories presented. There are a number of reasons for this. First, to attempt to cover the research in counseling and psychotherapy would be prohibitive in terms of the space requirements. Second, although there has been considerable research in the field of counseling and psychotherapy, very little of it has been directly associated with a particular theory or point of view. There seems to have been, in general, a separation between theory and research, on the one hand, and practice and research, on the other, so that advocates or practitioners of a particular orientation, unlike those in the field of learning, have not engaged in research related to the theory espoused or practiced. The major exceptions are the research of Rogers and his associates on client-oriented counseling and the behavioral approaches. This may be related to the fact that, for the psychologist, there is not much one can do about a personality theory or a theory of learning except research; however, counseling and psychotherapy are applied fields, and practitioners seem to have little time, or perhaps inclination, for research.

References

1. Patterson, C. H. *Counseling and psychotherapy: Theory and practice.* New York: Harper & Row, 1959. Chap. 1; Patterson, C. H. Counseling and/or psychotherapy. *American Psychologist,* 1963, *18,* 667–669; Patterson, C. H. Distinctions and commonalities between counseling and psychotherapy. In G. F. Farwell, N. Gamsky, & P. M. Coughlan (Eds.), *The counselor's handbook.* Scranton, Pa.: International Textbook, 1974; Patterson, C. H. *Relationship counseling and psychotherapy.* New York: Harper & Row, 1974. Chap. 1.
2. American Psychological Association, Division of Counseling Psychology, Committee on Definition. Counseling psychology as a specialty. *American Psychologist,* 1956, *11,* 282–285.
3. Tyler, L. E. Theoretical principles underlying the counseling process. *Journal of Counseling Psychology,* 1958, *5,* 3–10.
4. Vance, F. L., & Volsky, T. C. Counseling and psychotherapy: Split personality or Siamese twins. *American Psychologist,* 1962, *17,* 565–570.

5. Tyler, L. E. Minimum change therapy. *Personnel and Guidance Journal,* 1960, *38,* 475–479.

6. Hall, C. S., & Lindzey, G. *Theories of personality* (2nd ed.). New York: Wiley, 1970; Maddi, S. R. *Personality theories: A comparative analysis.* Homewood, Ill.: Dorsey Press, 1968; Steffire, B., & Matheny, K. *The function of counseling theory.* Boston: Houghton Mifflin, 1968.

7. Maddi, *Personality theories,* p. 456.

8. Hall & Lindzey, *Theories of personality,* p. 13.

9. Maddi, *Personality theories,* p. 454.

10. Lewin, K. Science, power and education. In G. W. Lewin (Ed.), *Studies in topological and vector psychology.* 1944.

11. Frank, J. D. *Persuasion and healing.* Baltimore: Johns Hopkins University Press, 1961. Pp. 227–228.

12. Pepinsky, H. B., & Pepinsky, P. *Counseling: Theory and practice.* New York: Ronald Press, 1954.

13. Bordin, E. S. Dimensions of the counseling process. *Journal of Clinical Psychology,* 1948, *4,* 240–244.

14. Hall & Lindzey, *Theories of personality,* p. 17.

15. Allport, G. W. *Patterns of growth in personality.* New York: Holt, Rinehart and Winston, 1961. P. 84.

16. Hilgard, E. R. *Theories of learning* (1st ed.). Englewood Cliffs, N.J.: Prentice-Hall, 1948. P. v.

THEORIES OF COUNSELING
AND PSYCHOTHERAPY

one

COGNITIVE APPROACHES

Cognitive approaches to counseling or psychotherapy are those that tend to take a logical, intellectual approach to the process and/or the solution of the client's problems or difficulties. These approaches usually are relatively simple and eclectic; that is, a variety of techniques is likely to be accepted or adopted. Although this may be rationalized on the basis that different problems or different clients require different methods or techniques, the choice of techniques usually is made on the basis of common sense or empiricism. The empiricism does not rest on experiments as much as on experience. Methods and techniques are loosely tied to theory if, indeed, any real theoretical foundation exists. (See the introduction to Part Six for a critique of this kind of eclecticism.)

Earlier editions of this book opened with the so-called Minnesota point of view of Williamson. Williamson's model was a medical model that emphasized the necessity of diagnosis before commencing treatment, which presumably was dictated by the diagnosis. The medical model has been questioned and has not been closely followed by other theorists.

Williamson's approach was omitted from this edition to make room for other representatives of the rational approach to psychotherapy, or, to use the current term, the cognitive therapies. Ellis was the first to develop a purely rational psychotherapy. (Williamson differentiated between counseling and psychotherapy and emphasized that he was concerned with counseling and not with psychotherapy.) More than a decade passed before others, notably Beck and Raimy, developed their cognitive therapies. They all share a number of similarities, as the reader will recognize. They present the counselor or therapist as essentially a teacher who attempts to get the client to apply information, logic, or reasoning to correct the faulty interpretations and inferences and

1

the irrational thinking that are assumed to be the bases of emotional disorders. Emotions do not cause wrong thinking; wrong thinking causes disturbing emotions.

This view of the relation between cognition and emotion probably is an oversimplification. Participants at the 1984 World Congress on Behavior Therapy noted that contrary to the beliefs of some cognitive therapists, emotional disturbances can cause distortion in thinking, and cognition and emotion can occur simultaneously, neither apparently being the cause of the other.[1]

The nature of American culture would appear to be conducive to a logical approach to counseling and psychotherapy because of the emphasis on science. Frank points this out and in doing so also indicates the weakness of this approach in psychotherapy. The scientific ideal, he says,

> values objectivity and intellectual comprehension, and these features may not be entirely advantageous for psychotherapy. They tend to result in an overevaluation of the cognitive aspects. From the patient's standpoint "insight" in the sense of ability to verbalize self-understanding may be mistaken for genuine attitude change. From the therapist's standpoint, the scientific attitude may lead to undue stress on the niceties of interpretation and avoidance of frankly emotion-arousing techniques . . . even though there is universal agreement that in order to succeed, psychotherapy must involve the patient's emotions.[2]

REFERENCES

1. Cordes, C. Behavior therapists examine how emotion, cognition relate. *APA Monitor,* 1984, *15,* 18; Zajonc, R. B. On the primacy of affect. *American Psychologist,* 1984, *39,* 117–123; Lazarus, R. S. On the primacy of cognition. *American Psychologist,* 1984, *39,* 124–129.
2. Frank, J. D. *Persuasion and healing.* Baltimore: Johns Hopkins University Press, 1961. Pp. 219–220.

chapter 1

Rational-Emotive Psychotherapy: Ellis

Perhaps the most extreme of the attempts to introduce logic and reason into counseling or psychotherapy is the approach of Albert Ellis, first presented in several journal articles. Originally called *rational psychotherapy,* it became *rational-emotive psychotherapy* in 1962 and is now often referred to as RET.

Albert Ellis (b. 1913) earned a B.B.A. at the City College of New York in 1934 and obtained his M.A. in 1943 and Ph.D. in 1947, both at Columbia University. He began private practice in the field of marriage, family, and sex counseling in 1943. Ellis became interested in psychoanalysis, so he obtained training in this field and underwent a three-year personal analysis. He held positions briefly as clinical psychologist in a mental-hygiene clinic attached to a state hospital and in a state diagnostic center, as chief psychologist of the New Jersey Department of Institutions and Agencies, and as instructor at Rutgers University and New York University. The major part of his professional life, however, has been spent in private practice, although in the past several years, he has lectured extensively and conducted workshops in RET. In 1958, he established the Institute for Rational Living, and in 1968, the Institute for Advanced Study in Rational Psychotherapy, of which he is executive director. The institute operates the Living School, where normal children are taught the principles of rational-emotive psychology. Ellis is a Diplomate in Clinical Psychology of the American Board of Professional Psychology.

Ellis has been a prolific writer: he is the author of numerous popular books dealing with sex, as well as more scientific discussions of sex and homosexuality. He appears as one of three therapists in the film *Three Approaches to Psychotherapy,* produced by Everett L. Shostrom. He has extended the rational-emotive approach to group psychotherapy and encounter groups. He has published summaries of his approach in several edited books.

BACKGROUND AND DEVELOPMENT

In his early practice of marital counseling, Ellis was concerned essentially with giving authoritative information. However, he became aware that the problems brought to him involved more than the lack of valid information or knowledge; his clients also were psychologically or emotionally disturbed. He then turned to psychoanalysis for help and, after his training and personal analysis, began practicing orthodox psychoanalysis. Although he feels that he was as successful as other analysts (he claims that 50 percent of all his patients and 70 percent of the neurotics were significantly helped), he was dissatisfied with the results and, more important, with the theory and techniques of psychoanalysis. He felt that there was a lack of correspondence between the passivity and inactivity of the orthodox analysis and his own personality and temperament. "Why," he writes,

> when I seemed to know perfectly well what was troubling a patient, did I have to wait passively, perhaps for a few weeks, perhaps for months, until he, by his own interpretive initiative, showed that he was fully "ready" to accept my own insight? Why, when patients bitterly struggled to continue to associate freely, and ended up by saying only a few words in an entire session, was it improper for me to help them with several pointed questions or remarks?[1]

As a result of his dissatisfaction, Ellis changed to a neo-Freudian approach and then to psychoanalytically oriented psychotherapy, becoming more active and directive. Although he feels that his effectiveness increased (63 percent of all patients and 70 percent of neurotics showing significant improvement) and that results were achieved in less time and with fewer interviews, he was still dissatisfied. Even though his patients achieved insight into their behavior and its origins, they did not necessarily change their behavior or improve.

Ellis then became interested in learning theory (that is, conditioning) and attempted to apply it in deconditioning his patients by directing them to engage in pertinent activities. Again, he felt that this activity directed eclectic therapy was more effective, but he still was not satisfied.

His rational approach began to develop at this point (in 1954). He became convinced that irrational, neurotic early learnings persist rather than being extinguished, as they should be if they are not reinforced, because individuals persist in reinforcing them by reindoctrinating themselves and in resisting therapy and its insights. Ellis then turned to teaching his patients to change their thinking to agree with a rational approach to their problems. He feels that about 90 percent of those treated by this method for ten or more sessions showed distinct or considerable improvement.

This approach was developed in a series of articles, beginning in 1955[2–8] and culminating in the book *Reason and Emotion in Psychotherapy,* which incorporates the earlier statements.

PHILOSOPHY AND CONCEPTS

Ellis claims no originality for the concepts that make up his system. While he discovered many of them through his own experience, he recognizes that they were already formulated by many ancient and modern philosophers, psychologists, psychotherapists, and social thinkers.

Rational-emotive therapy makes certain assumptions about the nature of human beings and about the nature and genesis of their unhappiness or emotional disturbances, among which are the following:

1. Human beings are uniquely rational, as well as irrational. When they are thinking and behaving rationally, they are effective, happy, and competent.

2. Emotional or psychological disturbance—neurotic behavior—is a result of irrational and illogical thinking. Thought and emotion are not separate or different functions. Emotion accompanies thinking, and thinking is, in effect, usually biased, prejudiced, highly personalized, and irrational.

3. Human beings are biologically predisposed toward irrational thinking, and environmental conditions and experiences build upon this predisposition. Seriously disturbed individuals (psychotics) have stronger predispositions toward disturbed thinking.

4. Human beings are verbal animals, and thinking usually occurs through the use of symbols or language. Since thinking accompanies emotion and emotional disturbances, irrational thinking necessarily persists if the emotional disturbances persist. This is just what characterizes disturbed individuals: they perpetuate their disturbance and maintain illogical behavior by internal verbalization of their irrational ideas and thoughts. "For all practical purposes the phrases and sentences that we keep telling ourselves frequently *are* or *become* our thoughts and emotions."[9] This perpetual stimulation is the reason that disordered behavior and emotions are not extinguished and that simple understanding of the origins of the disturbance, obtained through psychoanalysis, is not sufficient to eliminate the disturbance.

5. Continuing states of emotional disturbance, which are a result of self-verbalizations, are thus determined, not by external circumstances or events, but by the perceptions and attitudes toward these events that are incorporated in the internalized sentences about them. Ellis finds the origin of this concept in Epictetus, who wrote: "Men are disturbed not by things, but by the views which they take of them." He also quotes a similar phrase from Hamlet: "There's nothing either good or bad but thinking makes it so."[10]

6. Negative and self-defeating thoughts and emotions thus must be attacked by a reorganization of perceptions and thinking so that thinking becomes logical and rational rather than illogical and irrational. The goals of the therapist in the counseling or psychotherapy process are to demonstrate to clients that their self-verbalizations have been the source of their emotional disturbance, to show that these self-verbalizations are illogical and irrational, and to straighten out their thinking so that their self-verbalizations become more logical and efficient and so are not associated with negative emotions and self-defeating behavior.

Ellis identified 11 ideas or values that are irrational, superstitious, or "senseless" and that are universally inculcated in Western society and "would seem inevitably to lead to widespread neurosis."[11]

1. *It is essential that a person be loved or approved by virtually everyone in the community.* This is irrational because it is an unobtainable goal, and if a

person strives for it, the person becomes less self-directing and more insecure and self-defeating. It is desirable to be loved; however, the rational person does not sacrifice his or her own interests and desires to this goal but expresses them, including the striving to be a loving, creative, and productive individual.

2. *A person must be perfectly competent, adequate, and achieving to be considered worthwhile.* This, again, is an impossibility, and to strive compulsively for it results in psychosomatic illness, a sense of inferiority, an inability to live one's own life, and a constant sense of fear of failure. The rational individual strives to do well for his or her own sake rather than to be better than others, to enjoy an activity rather than to engage in it solely for the results, and to learn rather than to try to be perfect.

3. *Some people are bad, wicked, or villainous and therefore should be blamed and punished.* This idea is irrational because there is no absolute standard of right or wrong and very little free will. "Wrong" or "immoral" acts are the result of stupidity, ignorance, or emotional disturbance. All people are fallible and make mistakes. Blame and punishment do not usually lead to improved behavior, since they do not result in less stupidity, more intelligence, or a better emotional state. In fact, they often lead to worse behavior and greater emotional disturbance. Rational individuals do not blame others or themselves. If other people blame them, they try to improve or correct their own behavior if they have been wrong; if they have not been wrong, they realize that blame from others is an indication of disturbance in them. If others make mistakes, they try to understand them and, if possible, to stop them from continuing their misdeeds; if this is not possible, they try not to let others' behavior seriously upset them. When they make mistakes, they admit and accept their own behavior but do not let it become a catastrophe or lead them to feel worthless.

4. *It is a terrible catastrophe when things are not as a person wants them to be.* This is irrational thinking because to be frustrated is normal, but to be severely and prolongedly upset is illogical, since (a) there is no reason that things should be different from what they are in reality, (b) getting upset only rarely changes the situation and usually makes it worse, (c) if it is impossible to do anything about the situation, the only rational thing to do is to accept it, and (d) frustration need not result in emotional disturbance if one does not define the situation in such a way as to make obtaining one's desires a necessity for satisfaction or happiness. The rational person avoids exaggerating unpleasant situations and works at improving them or at accepting them if they cannot be improved. Unpleasant situations may be disturbing, but they are not terrible or catastrophic unless a person defines them as such.

5. *Unhappiness is caused by outside circumstances, and a person has no control over it.* Actually, outside forces and events, while they can be physically assaulting, usually are psychological in nature and cannot be harmful unless the person allows himself or herself to be affected by his or her attitudes and reactions. A person disturbs himself or herself by telling himself or herself how horrible it is when someone is unkind, rejecting, annoying, and so on. If the person realizes that disturbances or emotions consist of his or her own perceptions, evaluations, and internalized verbalizations, the disturbances can be controlled or changed. A person who is intelligent realizes that unhappiness comes largely from within, and while the person may be irritated or

annoyed by external events, he or she will recognize that his or her reactions can be changed by his or her definitions and verbalizations of these events.

6. *Dangerous or fearsome things are cause for great concern, and their possibility must be continually dwelt on.* This is irrational because worry or anxiety (a) prevents an objective evaluation of the possibility of a dangerous event, (b) often interferes with dealing with a dangerous event effectively if it should occur, (c) may contribute to bringing about a dangerous event, (d) leads to exaggerating the possibility of a dangerous event's occurrence, (e) cannot possibly prevent inevitable events, and (f) makes many dreaded events appear worse than they are. A person who is rational recognizes that potential dangers are not as catastrophic as he or she fears and that anxiety does not prevent them but may increase them and may be more harmful itself than the feared events. The person also realizes that he or she should do those things that are feared in order to prove that they are not actually frightful.

7. *It is easier to avoid certain difficulties and self-responsibilities than to face them.* This is irrational because avoiding a task often is more difficult and more painful than performing it and leads to later problems and dissatisfactions, including loss of self-confidence. Also, an easy life is not necessarily a happy one. A person who is rational does without complaint what has to be done, although the person intelligently avoids unnecessary painful tasks. When the person finds himself or herself avoiding necessary responsibilities, the person analyzes the reasons and engages in self-discipline and then realizes that a challenging, responsible, problem-solving life is an enjoyable life.

8. *A person should be dependent on others and should have someone stronger on whom to rely.* While we all are dependent on others to some extent, there is no reason to maximize dependency, for it leads to loss of independence, individualism, and self-expression. Dependency causes greater dependency, failure to learn, and insecurity, since the person is at the mercy of those on whom he or she depends. The person who is rational strives for independence and responsibility but does not refuse to seek or accept help when necessary. The person recognizes that risks, while possibly resulting in failures, are worth taking and that failing itself is not a catastrophe.

9. *Past experiences and events are the determinants of present behavior; the influence of the past cannot be eradicated.* On the contrary, what was once necessary behavior in certain circumstances may not be necessary at present; past solutions to problems may not be relevant in the present. The presumed influence of the past may be used as an excuse for avoiding changing behavior. While it may be difficult to overcome past learnings, it is not impossible. The person who is rational recognizes that the past is important but also realizes that the present can be changed by analyzing past influences, questioning those acquired beliefs that are harmful, and forcing himself or herself to act differently in the present.

10. *A person should be quite upset over other people's problems and disturbances.* This is erroneous because other people's problems often have nothing to do with himself or herself and, therefore, should not seriously concern a person. Even when others' behavior does affect a person, it is the person's definition of its implication that is upsetting. Becoming distraught over the behavior of others, while it implies that the person has power to control them, actually lessens the ability to change them. In any event, the person suffers in the process and neglects his or her own problems. The person who is

rational determines whether the behavior of others warrants becoming disturbed and, if so, then attempts to do something that will help the other person to change. If nothing can be done, the person accepts it and makes the best of it.

11. *There is always a right or perfect solution to every problem, and it must be found or the results will be catastrophic.* This is irrational because (a) there is no such perfect solution, (b) the imagined results of failure to find such a solution are unreal, but the insistence on finding one leads to anxiety or panic, and (c) such perfectionism results in poorer solutions than are actually possible. The person who is rational attempts to find various possible solutions to a problem and accepts the best or most feasible one, recognizing that there is no perfect answer.

These fallacious ideas are almost universal in our society, and when they are accepted and reinforced by continual self-indoctrination, they lead to emotional disturbance or neurosis, since they cannot be lived up to. Disturbed individuals are unhappy because they are unable to achieve their unreasonable "shoulds," "oughts," and "musts."

> For once a human being believes the kind of nonsense included in these notions, he will inevitably tend to become inhibited, hostile, defensive, guilty, ineffective, inert, uncontrolled, unhappy. If, on the other hand, he could become thoroughly released from all these fundamental kinds of illogical thinking, it would be exceptionally difficult for him to become intensely emotionally upset, or at least to sustain his disturbance for any extended period.[12]

While the Freudians are right in pointing out the influences of early childhood on emotional disturbances, these influences are only secondary causes and could not continue to be influential if the individual did not acquire any of the basic illogical ideals listed above. It is not early experiences alone that cause the disturbance, but an individual's attitudes and thoughts about them that are engendered by the illogical ideas.

Ellis discusses the relationship of his position to certain philosophies and philosophical issues. His early designation of his approach as rational therapy was abandoned because it led to confusion with other "rational" therapies and with the classical rationalist philosophy, which he does not accept. He is, however, sympathetic to modern rationalism, or neorationalism, which applies reason and logic to science and to the search for truth and which is opposed to supernaturalism, mysticism, dogmatism, and so forth. He is also in sympathy with most of the modern existentialists' goals for living and accepts the following themes from Braaten: "(1) Man, you are free, define yourself; (2) Cultivate your own individuality; (3) Live in dialogue with your fellow man; (4) Your own experiencing is the highest authority; (5) Be fully present in the immediacy of the moment; (6) There is no truth except in action; (7) You can transcend yourself in spurts; (8) Live your potentialities creatively; (9) In choosing yourself, you choose man; and (10) You must learn to accept certain limits in life."[13]

Rational-emotive therapy recognizes that human events include external causal factors, but human beings are not completely determined. They can transcend their biological and social limitations, difficult though it may be, and act in ways that will change and control the future. This recognition of the individual's ability to determine, in good part, his or her own behavior and emotional experience is expressed in the A-B-C theory of behavior and personality disturbance. A is the Activating Event or Experience; B is the individual's Belief System; and C is the Consequence, the emotional disturbance, such as feelings of rejection, anxiety, worthlessness, depression, inadequacy, and so on. But A is not the direct cause of C; C is actually the result of B. Belief Systems may be rational or irrational. If the Belief System is rational, reasonable, or realistic (rB), the Consequence will be rational or reasonable (rC); but if the Belief System is irrational or inappropriate (iB), the Consequence will be irrational or inappropriate (iC). The behaviors and attitudes of others constitute Activating Events, to which the individual responds rationally or irrationally, the latter responses being unhappiness or other forms of emotional disturbance, depending on how the individual perceives or interprets A. The recognition of this relationship leads to the possibility of changing and controlling one's attitudes and behaviors in reaction to circumstances.

THE GOALS OF THERAPY

The goal of therapy is to eliminate or reduce the Irrational Consequences (iCs) or emotional disturbances in clients. Two specific objectives are the minimization of anxiety (or self-blame) and the minimization of hostility or anger (blaming others or circumstances). In addition, clients are provided with a method by which they can maintain a state of minimum anxiety and hostility through rational analysis of their disturbances.

Other positive goals of mental health are implicit, if not explicit, in rational-emotive psychotherapy. These include an enlightened self-interest that recognizes the rights of others; self-direction, independence, and responsibility; tolerance of human fallibility; acceptance of uncertainty; flexibility and openness to change; scientific thinking; commitment to something outside of oneself; risk taking or willingness to try new things; and self-acceptance. These goals are shared with many philosophers and other psychotherapists. They are derivatives of the two major goals.[14]

THE THERAPY PROCESS

In view of the above philosophy and concepts regarding the nature of emotional disturbance, it follows that the process of counseling, according to Ellis, is the curing of unreason by reason. While there are other ways of controlling emotions—by electrical or chemical means, by sensorimotor techniques, or by doing something out of love or respect for someone else—counseling or psychotherapy does so by using the cerebral processes. Humans, as rational beings, are able to avoid or eliminate most emotional disturbance or unhappiness by learning to think rationally. This is what occurs during the therapy process.

The task of the therapist is to help clients get rid of illogical, irrational ideas and attitudes and substitute logical, rational ideas and attitudes for them. The first step in this process is to show clients that they are illogical, to help them understand how and why they became so, and to demonstrate the relationship of their irrational ideas to their unhappiness and emotional disturbance. Ellis recognizes that most therapeutic approaches do this; but they do it passively and indirectly, and they stop there.

In the second step, rational-emotive therapy goes beyond this by showing clients that they maintain their disturbance by continuing to think illogically; that is, their present irrational thinking, not the continuing influence of early events, is responsible for their condition.

The third step is to get clients to change their thinking and to abandon irrational ideas. While some approaches depend on clients doing this themselves, rational-emotive therapy recognizes that illogical thinking is so ingrained that clients cannot change it by themselves.

The final step goes beyond dealing with the specific illogical ideas of clients and considers the main general irrational ideas, together with a more rational philosophy of living, so that clients can avoid falling victim to other irrational ideas and beliefs.

The result of this process is that clients acquire a rational philosophy of life; they substitute rational attitudes and beliefs for irrational ones. Once this is accomplished, the negative, disturbing emotions are eliminated, along with self-defeating behavior.

Rational-emotive therapy also deals with the problem of self-depreciation, or low self-esteem and feelings of worthlessness. The problem of personal worth arises when persons evaluate themselves on the basis of their acts, behavior, or performance, which reveal their inadequacies, mistakes, and failures. One approach to this problem—the usual one—is to help clients believe that they are worthwhile simply because they exist as persons, whatever their behaviors or opinions of others are. While this is effective if clients can accept this belief, it is more effective if they can be shown that they do not have to evaluate themselves at all. Without engaging in any self-evaluation, they can recognize that they are alive and that they can choose to remain alive and to enjoy life. Clients then do not ask such questions as "Who am I?" "What is my identity?" or "What is my worth?" Rather, they ask, "What are my traits?" "What sort of things do I enjoy and not enjoy doing?" "How can I improve some of my traits and find more things to experience, so that I will continue to live and to have a maximally satisfying existence?" They can rate their traits, but this does not require them to rate themselves as either good or bad.[15]

Ellis discusses the six necessary and sufficient conditions of constructive personality change proposed by Rogers[16] and points out exceptions to each.[17] He then asks, "Are there, then, any other conditions that are absolutely necessary for constructive personality change to take place?" Although he concludes that the answer is probably "No," he is inclined to feel that there is one

> and that is that somehow, through some professional or non-professional channel, and through some kind of experience with himself, with others, or with things and events, the afflicted individual must learn to recognize his irrational, inconsistent, and unrealistic perceptions and thoughts, and change these for more logical, more reasonable philosophies of life. Without this kind of fundamental change in his ideologies and philosophic assumptions, I am tempted to say, no deep-seated personality changes will occur.[18]

However, he recognizes that some people *seem* to change without meeting this condition, including those who change as a result of modification of environmental conditions. Ellis notes that it is largely tautological to say that individuals must change their thinking or value system to change their personality. Thus he admits that he is not talking about necessary conditions, which would deal with *how* such a change occurs. In this connection, he also admits that it probably is not necessary for counselors to go beyond the second step described above, although he feels that few clients or other people "seem to have significantly improved in spite of their not having a competent rational therapist to help them understand how they acquired, how they are currently sustaining, and how they can and should forthrightly attack and annihilate their basic irrational attitudes and assumptions."[19]

Thus Ellis concludes that there are no necessary conditions for personality change, but only desirable ones, and that it is an either/or situation. Nevertheless, he still feels that rational-emotive therapy is, in his experience at least, the most effective method for achieving basic personality change.

IMPLEMENTATION: TECHNIQUES OF THERAPY

Ellis refers to rational-emotive therapy as "a somewhat unusual technique of therapy."[20] His discussion of technique is not extensive, however. Perhaps it is because there is essentially only one technique, which is illustrated in his book by several excerpts. These excerpts are all apparently edited to bring out clearly the method of therapy.

Pointing out that "all effective psychotherapists, whether or not they realize what they are doing, teach or induce their patients to reperceive or rethink their life events and philosophies and thereby change their unrealistic and illogical thought, emotion, and behavior,"[21] Ellis feels that the techniques other therapists use to accomplish this are relatively indirect and inefficient. Techniques such as abreaction, catharsis, dream analysis, free association, interpretation of resistance, and transference analysis are often successful, at least in bringing clients to recognize their illogical thinking. However, Ellis believes that even when most successful, these "emotional" methods are wasteful. The relationship itself and expressive-emotive, supportive, and insight-interpretive methods, although used in rational-emotive therapy, are preliminary techniques to establish rapport, to enable the client to express himself or herself, and to show the client that he or she is respected.

> If, because the patient is exceptionally upset when he comes to therapy, he must first be approached in a cautious, supportive, permissive, and warm manner, and must sometimes be allowed to ventilate his feeling in free-association, abreaction, role playing, and other expressive techniques, that may be a necessary part of effective therapy. But the rational therapist does not delude himself that these relationship-building and expressive-emotive methods are likely to really get to the core of the patient's illogical thinking and induce him to cogitate more rationally.[22]

While occasionally this is sufficient, more often it is not.

The essential technique of rational-emotive therapy is active, directive teaching. After the initial stage, the counselor assumes an active teaching role to reeducate the client. The counselor demonstrates the illogical origin of the client's disturbance and the persistence of illogical self-verbalizations that continue the disturbance. Clients are shown that their internalized sentences are quite illogical and unrealistic in certain respects. . . . The effective therapist should continually keep unmasking his patient's past, and, especially, his present illogical thinking or self-defeating verbalizations by (a) bringing them forcefully to his attention or consciousness; (b) showing him how they are causing and maintaining his disturbance and unhappiness; (c) demonstrating exactly what the illogical links in his internalized sentences are; and (d) teaching him how to re-think, challenge, contradict, and reverbalize these (and other similar) sentences so that his internalized thoughts become more logical and efficient.[23]

Rational-emotive psychotherapy makes a concerted attack on the disturbed person's illogical positions in two main ways: (1) The therapist serves as a frank counter-propagandist who directly contradicts and denies the self-defeating propaganda and superstitions which the patient has originally learned and which he is now self-instilling. (2) The therapist encourages, persuades, cajoles, and occasionally even insists that the patient engage in some activity (such as doing something he is afraid of doing) which itself will serve as a forceful counterpropaganda agency against the nonsense he believes.[24]

The rational-emotive counselor thus uses logic and reason, instruction, suggestion, persuasion, confrontation, deindoctrination, indoctrination, and prescription of behavior to show the client what his or her irrational philosophies are, to demonstrate how these lead to emotionally disturbed behavior, and to change the client's thinking —and thus emotions—by replacing these irrational philosophies with rational, logical ones. In addition, as was indicated earlier, the counselor goes further to instruct the client, as a protective measure, in the major irrational ideas of our culture and to provide the client with more effective rational ones.

In effect, any method or technique that will induce clients to look at, question, and change their irrational assumptions or beliefs can be used. Clients may be literally forced "to look at the simple exclamatory sentences that they are telling themselves to create their emotions of anger and hostility." For example,

Whenever a client tells me, for example, "My wife accused me of being unfaithful to her, and that got me terribly angry, because it was so untrue and so unfair of her to accuse me of it," I stopped him immediately and ask: "What do you mean *that* got you angry? How could her false accusations do anything whatever to you? You mean, don't you, that your wife accused you unjustly and then *you* got yourself angry by idiotically telling yourself: (1) 'I don't like her false accusation,' and (2) 'Because I don't like it, she shouldn't make it.' Isn't *that* what got you upset, your own irrational premise, rather than her accusation?"[25]

The method is thus highly active and directive. Homework assignments are frequently given, requiring the client to engage in specified activities: asking for a date, applying for a job. "The therapist quite actively tries to persuade, cajole, and at times even command the client to undertake such assignments as an integral part of the therapeutic process."[26]

The rational-emotive therapist is verbally active:

I do a great deal of talking rather than passively listening to what the client has to say. I do not hesitate, even during the first session, directly to confront the client with evidences of his irrational thinking and behaving. I most actively interpret many of the things the client says and does, without being too concerned about possible resistance and defenses on his part. I consistently try to persuade and argue the person out of his firmly held irrational and inconsistent beliefs, and unhesitatingly *attack* his neurosis-creating ideas and attitudes after first demonstrating how and why they exist.[27]

The therapist not only deals with the specific irrational beliefs of the client, but also teaches the client the rational-emotive theory of emotional disturbances by assigning reading materials.

The relationship is thus one of teacher and student and is on a cognitive level.

I am deliberately not very warm or personal with most of my clients, even those who crave and ask for such warmth, since, as I quickly explain to them, their main problem is usually that they think they need to be loved, when they actually do not; and I am there to teach them that they can get along very well in this world *without* necessarily being approved or loved by others. I therefore refuse to cater to their sick love demands.[28]

The therapist provides either nonjudgmental acceptance or unconditional positive regard of the client as a person, demonstrating the worth of the individual regardless of his or her behavior.

Rational-emotive therapy is an insight-producing form of therapy. The insights are not of the usual kind—explaining the origins or historical causes of the client's behavior. There are three kinds of insight. The first consists of the client's recognition that his or her present dysfunctional behavior has antecedent causes, which include past experiences. More important is the second: understanding that the original causes continue to be disturbing because of the irrational beliefs about these experiences that the client continues to harbor and recall. The third insight is the acknowledgment that "there is no other way for him to overcome his emotional disturbance but by *his* continually observing, questioning, and challenging his own belief systems, and his working and practicing to change his own irrational philosophic assumptions by verbal and by motor counterpropagandizing activity."[29] The first two insights are of little value without the third.

Although rational-emotive therapy emphasizes cognition and reason, it also recognizes the importance of experiential-emotive and behavioristic factors. The expression of emotions is encouraged, even provoked, not simply to permit catharsis or to make the client feel better, but also to analyze and to change the emotions. Emphasis is on here-and-now feelings. In addition to homework assignments, other behavioristic techniques are used, including operant conditioning, reinforcing desirable verbalizations and behaviors, and deconditioning and desensitization. RET is thus, Ellis claims, a comprehensive approach.

Therapy essentially consists of attacking Irrational Beliefs (iBs) by Disputing them (D). The result is a Cognitive Effect (cE) and usually a Behavioral Effect (bE). The client's Irrational Beliefs (iBs) become Rational Beliefs (rBs), and the Irrational Consequences (iCs) become Rational Consequences (rCs).

Rational-emotive therapy may be either short-term or long-term. Individual and group therapy often are combined. The usual range is from 1 to 20 individual sessions with 20 to 80 group sessions. "Ideally, however, clients are to be seen for a total period of about two years, during which they will have about twenty individual and about seventy-five group sessions. . . ."[30]

LIMITATIONS

Ellis cautions about overexpectations from any method of counseling or psychotherapy.[31] He feels that many biological tendencies (which he enumerates) lead to the development and persistence of emotional disturbance and neurotic behavior. In addition, socioenvironmental factors have a strong influence on the impressionable child. Psychotherapy, therefore, requires hard work by the client during therapy and continuing hard work when therapy is ended to avoid reversion.

Although most clients have strong self-actualizing and regenerating capacities, some, such as the severely psychotic and the seriously mentally deficient, do not appear to have the capacity to help themselves much. Nevertheless, "all kinds of clients can be helped with the rational-emotive method, including disturbed individuals whose traits include fixed homosexuality, psychopathy, schizophrenic reactions, mental deficiency and other syndromes that are usually unresponsive to most therapeutic methods."[32]

It is less effective with "those who will not face their problems or who refuse to work at therapy, such as individuals with character disorders and overt psychotic reactions." It is "more effective with younger and brighter clients."[33]

Results depend on the characteristics of the therapist. "Usually, RET gets best results when employed by a vigorous, active-directive, outgoing therapist who is willing to take risks and to be little concerned about winning his clients' approval." However, it can be successfully used "by less outgoing therapists, as long as they are sufficiently active to keep challenging and questioning their clients' irrational ideas and as long as they persist at teaching these clients a more scientific method of looking at themselves and the world and of working against their own self-indoctrination."[34]

EXAMPLE[35]

The patient with whom the following recorded interview is held is a thirty-one-year-old free-lance copywriter who has been a fixed homosexual since the age of fourteen. He has had only a few heterosexual experiences, when girls have taken the initiative with him; and these did not turn out well, since he has shown himself to be too passive, effeminate, and "campy," and the girls therefore quickly sought other lovers. He has been very promiscuous homosexually; but even in this area has tended to be unaggressive and passive, and never to make the first overtures himself and thereby risk possibly being rejected.

The recorded interview [of which the first half is reproduced below] comprises the fifteenth session with the patient, who had been seen irregularly for individual psychotherapy over a period of seven months at the time it occurs. However, he has more regularly attended group psychotherapy for the past five months. He first came to therapy largely because he wanted to do creative writing but did not have the courage to try, even though he was competent as a copywriter. After a few months of therapy, he did actively try some creative writing, and has been steadily progressing at it ever since. He also considerably improved his general working habits. At first, however, he made no attempt to work on his homosexual problem; and only in the few weeks before the fifteenth session did he show any inclination to do so. Both the therapist and his therapy group had been encouraging him to try going with girls, and he now seemed ready to make a serious attempt to do so—though, as the contents of this interview show, he is resisting heterosexual participation in several subtle and obvious ways.

The recorded session that follows is a fairly typical interview, employing rational-emotive technique, except that the patient, probably because of the previous individual and group sessions he has had, is more accepting than many other patients are, and requires relatively little counterattacking and annihilating of his irrationally held positions. But he does give considerable lip service, as so many patients do, rather than true allegiance, to sane views and actions; and the therapist consequently keeps trying to induce him to question and challenge his lip service, and to think and act in a manner that will lead to truly rational convictions, and hence to thoroughgoing emotional and behavioral changes.

[The first few minutes of the session consist of joking about making the tape recording.]

THERAPIST: How are things?

PATIENT: Oh, pretty good. I'm uh, haven't been too well, I can't say I haven't been too disturbed. I've been keeping pretty busy, but I'm on that going to sleep routine again.

TH: Yeah?

PT: And I don't, you know, I don't, I don't think I really need the sleep but I just sleep.

TH: How much have you been sleeping?

PT: Uh, well, like last . . . I've been making it a point to get home at midnight and usually if I'll go to, you know, if I, if I go to sleep at midnight I feel that I should wake up around eight or nine, you know eight-thirty in the morning . . .

TH: Yeah?

PT: And it's to my advantage to wake up then 'cause I can get a day started. And I'm discovering that I'm waking up at nine-thirty and ten and eleven . . . (laughs while saying this)

TH: Yeah, yeah?

PT: And then in the afternoons, if I get tired . . . Like yesterday afternoon I went in and I thought, "Well I'll flop down." I was sort of, I'd been writing all day; my eyes were tired; and I thought, "I'll sleep for an hour because, um, then I'll go out to dinner." And this was at five and I woke up at eight-thirty. And this is just too much sleep, you know. I'm just wasting too much time sleeping . . . (laughs while saying this)

TH: Yeah?

PT: And I don't, uh . . . You know, if, if I were physically exhausted it might make sense, but I'm not.

TH: Are you sleeping past an alarm, or anything like that? Or are you not bothered with the alarm?

PT: Uh, no, I haven't. I haven't bothered with the alarm, except that I know for a fact last night I slept through a phone call; the phone rang and it didn't wake me up. And the messenger boy from the desk had a package and he came up about, he said about six, and said he knocked and knocked on the door and I didn't wake up. So evidently I'm really going out, you know. I'm not waking up to noises.

TH: Yeah, really sleeping right through them . . .

PT: Yeah, yeah. And you know, and it, like an unexpected noise. I would, I should think I would, wake up, you know, more rapidly. At least I used to be a very light sleeper. Anybody walked through the room, I'd wake up.

TH: Yeah?

PT: And if somebody . . . (last part of sentence inaudible because of TH's interruption)

TH: Well, uh, why don't you have an alarm on?

PT: Well, up until just recently . . . oh, the last year . . . I've always been able to flop down and say I'm going to sleep for an hour, and I'd sleep for an hour and wake up.

TH: Yeah.

PT: And now I'm getting, you know, like . . . I don't know, an attitude of "I can sleep." Or, or I don't, I don't respond to what I'm telling myself: that I'm gonna wake up.

TH: You don't have that internal alarm clock going . . .

PT: No, which I used to . . . could count on.

TH: Yeah.

PT: You know, if I'd say, "I'm gonna wake up at seven," I'd be up at, you know, five minutes till.

TH: But isn't the thing, then: if your internal alarm isn't working, to use the . . .

PT: Yeah.

TH: . . . external until it does work?

PT: But it's uh; it's just that I, you know . . . If, if I have to get up, I suppose I could, you know. I would use an alarm . . .

TH: Yeah?

PT: But just the. . . . What bothers me is the idea of, of why am I wanting to sleep so darn much (laughs while saying this), you know, when I know it's physically not necessary for me now, because I'm getting more sleep than I ever have . . .

TH: Yeah.

PT: Unless it's uh, you know, just a hiding kind of habit . . .

TH: And then you think it, it possibly might be that you're trying to evade work, or evade life, or something like that?

PT: I think that probably that's the only thing I can figure. But one thing: since I told you I was, you know, I was quitting with the boys . . .

TH: Yeah?

PT: I've, uh, you know, seen some of the, the, the boys that I've known . . .

TH: Yeah? (barely audible)

PT: They have come to dinner and things like that. But this is where I've made it a point to be home by twelve o'clock. And I haven't, I ain't had no sex at all for two or three weeks, 'cause I haven't made it with any of the girls I've met yet.

TH: Yeah.

PT: And, uh, you know, I have the feeling that maybe I'm sort of hiding behind sleeping, you know. I know, I know I'm not getting the sex I would like, so I go to sleep and sleep it off, you know. (laughs while saying this)

TH: Yeah.

PT: That's the only reason I can, think I can figure. Of course, I don't feel frustrated in any . . . particularly in any other area.

TH: But when you're awake, do you feel sexually frustrated?

PT: No. Now this is also the strange part. I was noticing this morning that since this, you know, since I said I was gonna try really working at getting girl friends and things, I haven't been at all, uh particularly desirous of sex. You know, I haven't, uh, just felt like gee, you know, I've gotta go out and, and, and find something or somebody.

TH: Yeah.

PT: Of course, for one thing, frankly, the times I have felt I want to have some, you know, have sexual relief, it's just too easy to masturbate, you know. I can always take care of myself that way (laughs while saying this), which isn't, you know, doesn't really solve the problem particularly except . . .

TH: Yeah.

PT: . . . it is a relief.

TH: Well, again: do you think that your lack of sex desire is an evasion for . . . ?

PT: Yeah, I do. I think that on one, on one hand, uh, I'm thinking, you know. . . . I say now, you know, I want this and logically this is what I want to do; and still I'm some, you know, more subconsciously then and, and sort of sneaky subconsciously (sort of laughs) I must be fighting it too, dodging it, ducking it, not, you know. . . . Taking the easy way out . . .

TH: All right now. Let's ask ourselves. . . . Let's assume for the moment that this is true, that you are "sneaky subconsciously," as you say, fighting it. Let's ask ourselves exactly what you would be saying to yourself, sneaking subconsciously, in order to fight it. What would you be afraid of with, let us say, the girls, that would induce you (a) to sleep more, which you are doing, and (b) when you're awake, not to have that much of a sex desire?

[Up to this point, the therapist has waited, somewhat more patiently than is often done in the highly active-directive method of rational-emotive psychotherapy, for the patient to bring out some material that would show that he is not yet acting on his resolve to go with girls instead of, as in his whole previous life, with boys; when this material is brought up, the therapist is then able to use it to illustrate to the patient exactly what he is telling himself—consciously or unconsciously—to create his inactivity and his indecision. He now tries to get the patient to see that his lack of sex desire and his greater demands for evasive sleeping do not exist in their own right, but *are* related to concrete, simple exclamatory sentences with which the patient is indoctrinating himself.]

PT: Now that's the . . . that's the hard one, frankly, 'cause I don't think I'm afraid, in the sense of being afraid of girls . . .

TH: Yeah?

PT: . . . I mean, uh, of a sex relationship. I think what I'm afraid of is probably just the going out and the, and the first. . . . I'm really afraid of the first contact, the how to get into it.

TH: Yeah, of the encounter, the meeting . . .

PT: Yeah, yeah.

TH: That you do have to go out first and get to meet and know the girl . . .

PT: Yeah. And, and that's, when I, you know, I get terribly shy and I get all, you know, messed up. And I think probably what I'm doing is, is, you know, well, if you oversleep, then you don't have to go out.

TH: Yes, that's true. And if you don't have the sex desire, you don't have to go out.

PT: Yeah, yeah!

[The therapist solidly nails down the circumlocuting patient, and gets him to admit that his sleepiness and his lack of sex desire are both excuses for his not wanting to go with girls because he is afraid of rejection, especially during the first contacts. But, not being satisfied with this admission or insight on the patient's part, he still tries to get him to see the exact self-sentences he is employing to create his fear so that he can then logically parse and attack these internalized sentences.]

TH: All right, now. Let's assume that, for the moment, that you're afraid of the contact. Now let's get the exact sentence which you're saying to yourself to make yourself afraid of this contact. What are you saying is *dreadful?*

PT: Well, it sounds too simple to say, "They won't like me," you know . . .

TH: In oth . . .

PT: . . . And I'm sure that's the bottom of it.

TH: Yeah. In other words, you're saying, "If I go . . ."

PT: But I'm inventing a lot of crap to say (sort of laughs) "I won't . . . They won't like me," I guess.

TH: Well, let's get that a little more specific. You're saying, "If I go out and meet the girls or a girl," let us say, "then there's a good possibility that she won't like me and that would be *dreadful . . ."*

PT: Yeah.

TH: ". . . if she didn't." Is that the sentence you think you're saying?

PT: I don't, I don't, I can't say that that's just it, though.

TH: Yeah?

PT: It's, it's like, uh, you know. I defeat myself before I go out, because pretty, half the time I just said, "well, I'm gonna go somewhere and I'm. . . ." You know, like, you know. I joined the Museum of Modern Art and I've gone a couple of times and I walk in and I look around and immediately I don't e . . . , I don't even see a girl I, that, that is appealing looking to me.

TH: Yeah.

PT: You know. So already before I, you know, I'm, I'm, I'm cutting myself short before I even start.

TH: Yeah, but again . . .

PT: And I don't know whether . . .

TH: . . . is that just another technique for the fear again? You, you've given two techniques so far: one, you say . . .

PT: (interrupting and answering TH's first question) It probably is, it probably is.

TH: . . . asleep; two, you lose the desire. And three is you're saying, "The girl isn't good-looking enough."

PT: Yeah.

TH: But we still get back to the proposition that if you did have the desire, if you did get up early, and if she were good-looking enough, and you did make some kind of a, an overture, that she then wouldn't like you?

PT: Yeah.

TH: And that would be terrible?

PT: Yeah, I guess. Yeah, uh, I, I, I'm, I mean, that, that's, that's right . . .

TH: Uh-huh. (barely audible)

PT: But I don't even think I've got to the stage of finishing it out and saying, "that would be terrible." (laughs while saying this)

TH: But you don't say it . . .

PT: (interrupting) I mean, I'm, I'm, you know, I'm not rationally saying, I mean, I'm not letting, openly saying it to myself . . .

TH: You're not consciously saying that. Right. But doesn't your behavior show *by inference* that you must be saying something like that? Because if you were saying just "If I went out and did these things, didn't sleep, had the sex desire, and liked the girl physically, she might reject me"—just that; if you were saying that, would you then start going into these evasive dives of yours? If you weren't saying that "It would be terrible if she did reject me," because if she rejected you, you'd still get the lovely *experience* of being rejected . . .

PT: Yeah, yeah.

TH: So on some level you must be saying that "It would be terrible, it would be awful! I couldn't take it; look what a crumb I would be if she rejected me!"

PT: Also involved in there is that, uh. . . . As we talk I'm realizing that I think I'm still very, I'm too much on my own terms. Like when I go out to the, to the Modern and I wanna meet a girl and I don't meet her in the first ten minutes . . .

TH: Yeah.

PT: Then, you know, it's a bad deal; and I walk out and go home. (laughs while saying this)

[Although the patient keeps talking in a slippery, somewhat overcavalierly accepting and yet evasive manner, the therapist keeps trying to pin him down; and insists that his behavior, if not his words, *shows* that he must be telling himself that it would be awful if he were rejected by a girl. Instead of becoming defensive about this persistence on the therapist's part—which according to many psychoanalytic and client-centered theories he is theoretically supposed to do—the patient is partly driven from his lair, and makes an even more incriminating admission: namely, that he not only goes to sleep and downs his own sex desires, but that even when he finally drives himself to the museum to look for girls, he doesn't really give them a chance, but rejects them during the first ten minutes and gives up the search. This often occurs during rational-emotive therapy: the therapist's active persistence brings out more confirming material from the patient, instead of leading to classic resistance.]

TH: Is there a little . . . ?

PT: You know, uh, I'm, I'm sort of making the effort but not really the effort, at least, uh . . .

TH: Yeah. Now is there a little grandiosity here? Really . . .

PT: Yes, unfortunately, I, I, you know, I'm looking for somebody good enough for me, not me good enough for them. (sort of laughs while saying this)

TH: Yes, and is this . . . ?

PT: And I think it is part of the problem . . .

TH: Is there another sentence?—that if John goes out and does these kinds of things . . .

PT: . . . they ought to come flocking and they don't! Yeah.

TH: That's right. "And they don't and this is terrible!"

PT: I think that's even more than the fear . . .

TH: Yeah.

PT: You know, more than the physical fear . . .

TH: The fact that it's so unfair that they're not flock . . .

PT: Yeah, yeah!

TH: And they should!

PT: Yeah. Because, you know, I get, it's, uh, it's a crooked thing. I get all this shit from everybody about, you know, "You're a good-looking guy and . . ." you know . . .

TH: Yeah.

PT: "You shouldn't have any problems about meeting people . . ."

TH: Yeah.

PT: And I do! (sort of laughs) You know, I just flat out do. And I go out with this great feeling of gee, you know, "I'm God's gift to women." And then nothing happens (laughs while saying this), you know . . .

[Again, the therapist, by his insistent, direct interpretation, has smoked out the patient a little more. Rather than wait for the patient to see that, in addition to being overly fearful, he is also grandiose—which he might or might not finally see—the therapist directly questions him about this, and he admits that there is a grandiose element mixed in with his fear. In fact, as the patient goes on to see, his feelings of grandiosity then lead to his becoming still more fearful; since, when he starts out with the idea that he's God's gift to women, and, largely because of his own quick withdrawal or lack of full participation, nothing happens to help him meet suitable girls, he then becomes *more* afraid to make overtures and thereby prove that he is not so great as he assumes he is.]

TH: Yes. But isn't that notion that you're a good-looking guy and you shouldn't have any trouble meeting people, isn't that rather unrealistic? Because, no matter how good-looking you are and how bright you are and how well educated, don't we *all* have trouble meeting people?

PT: Well, I don't know about the rest of the world; but *I* do! (laughs while saying this). No, really, you know, it's . . .

TH: But, but don't you think that most people have some degree of trouble—even though they have relatively less than others who are not good-looking, or are stupid and uneducated? Don't they always have some trouble? And don't they have to do some work to overcome that some degree of trouble?

[The therapist emphasizes here one of the main ideas of rational-emotive therapy: namely, that insight into one's disturbances is not enough, and that after gaining such insight, one must *work* to counteract one's self-defeating philosophies and to *do* what one is afraid to do.]

PT: Yeah, that's it. I think that really, you know, a lot of the problem is that I, I, it's, it, I finally made up my mind that I would work at it and . . . But I'm not performing.

TH: Yeah.

PT: You know, up here I'm, I said it once. . . . I'm gonna work at it, but then I'm ducking it by going . . .

TH: But, that is, what is it, you're, what is . . . ?

PT: . . . at, at, at meeting people: at, at pushing myself a little more into walking up and saying, you know, "What's your name?" (laughs) Just that simple . . .

TH: That's fine. But isn't that the *second* thing you have to work at? You do have to work at that. But don't you also have to work at that crap you're telling yourself?—"They should . . ."

PT: Yeah, yeah.

TH: ". . . they *should* do this for dear old John. And wouldn't it be *awful* if they didn't!"— and so on? Now isn't *that* where the work may *first* be required, before you can secondly get off your ass and go out and actually talk to girls . . .

PT: Yeah.

TH: . . . and meet them and so on? So you're seeing it, number two, as your . . .

PT: The goal, but I'm not seeing the, uh . . .

TH: Yeah. But are you seeing the *more important goal,* which has plagued you all your life in so many other respects, in your work and so on? The number one, that I must work on *me,* on John . . .

PT: Um-hm. (barely audible)

TH: . . . on what *I* tell myself. Now are you seeing *that* very clearly?

PT: Not really. That's where I get bogged down.

TH: Yeah.

[The therapist, again as an integral part of the rational-emotive therapeutic approach, wants to make sure that the patient just doesn't jump in, without any real understanding of the basic issue involved, to approach the girls he wants to meet. Instead, the therapist insists that he must first tackle problem number one—the basic philosophic nonsense that he is telling himself to create his fear of girls—and to create difficulties in his work and other aspects of his life. If he tackles this number-one problem and sees what irrational sentences he is telling himself to create his anxiety and his inertia, then he can more easily and logically tackle problem number two, the actual making of overtures to the girls.]

PT: And that, that was where the other day, I was, uh . . . , I no—, I . . . I noticed after I'd been talking to the whole group (that is, his therapy group) that I kept talking about things; and that in a sense is my thing.

TH: Yeah.

PT: Is, I mean. . . . The, the goal is, I'm substituting the goal as a thing rather than, than working on *me* as a thing . . . (sort of laughs while saying this)

TH: That's right, that's right; you got it with the others in the group . . .

PT: Yeah.

TH: You could see it with Betty the other time in the group—but are you really seeing it with *you?*

[In his previous group therapy session, the patient pointed out to some of the other members of the group that they were not really working on *themselves,* but on changing certain things about their external lives. He now begins to see that he is doing exactly this himself, trying to change his overt behavior with girls, but not trying to change his own basic catastrophizing philosophies, which create his fearful behavior.]

PT: I mean, now. . . . Like the first date is the thing I'm shooting for; and it really shouldn't be that important to me.

TH: Yes. Oh, it should be important . . .

PT: I mean, it should be important. But it shouldn't be the. . . . It's for *later.* (laughs) That it happened . . .

TH: The main, right. . . . The main thing is changing *John.*

PT: Yeah.

TH: What *he's* telling himself; *his* ideas, *his* philosophies. Which have kept you back, as we just said a minute ago, in lots of other respects, including and especially this one with the girls. Now shouldn't most, or a great deal, of the work, at least, be *there?* Then, finally, you still will have to do the work of . . .

PT: Yeah.

TH: . . . getting up, as I said, off your ass and going out and meeting the girls. But you never quite get to that when you're doing the counterwork, we might say, of falling asleep . . .

PT: Yeah, yeah. (barely audible)

TH: . . . so much; of not having sex desires; of seeing that the girls are ugly; and so on— which is John. That's *John.*

PT: Yeah, yeah. (barely audible)

TH: There: that's what you're telling yourself at what I call point *B* . . .

PT: At the, yeah. At the same time I must, I must, ah, ah, just out of sheer fairness to me and the discussion (sort of laughs) admit that I *have* been noticing pretty girls more lately . . .

TH: Yes?

PT: I mean, uh, occasionally on the subway, I haven't had, haven't had . . . have to get the nerve to walk over to a pretty girl I'll see on the subway . . .

TH: Yeah?

PT: . . . and say, you know, you know, "I'd like to call you or something . . ." (sort of laughs)

TH: But the defenses are going down somewhat . . . ?

PT: But I'm seeing a lot prettier girls than, than I have, and . . .

TH: Yeah?

PT: . . . and discovering that I'm no—, that the, the prettier girls I'm seeing are younger . . .

TH: Yeah?

PT: . . . than me. Which is, I never noticed people, girls that were younger than me . . .

TH: You didn't notice all . . . ?

PT: They were always my age, or a little older.

TH: Yeah. Because you edited out . . .

PT: Yeah, yeah.

TH: . . . the most eligible and best-looking ones . . .

PT: Yeah.

TH: . . . so you wouldn't have to do anything about it.

PT: I'm, I'm, I'm sure that's it. But I, I really am noticing that there is an awful lot of younger, prettier girls around . . .

TH: All right. So that, that, that fearful and that grandiose sentence at point *B* of "Wouldn't it be awful if I failed or they should do this to me!" seems to be going down a bit and giving you leeway.

PT: At least I can look now! (laughs)

TH: That's right. At least you can look. But it's still there . . .

PT: Yeah.

TH: . . . and it requires more work, apparently; you have done some on it, 'cause you have asked yourself, uh, *"Would* it be so awful?" And in your copywriting work and all, you are doing things now . . .

PT: Yeah.

TH: . . . which you've never done before in your life. Isn't that true?

PT: Um-hm. And I've even, I've even been active enough that I have made a couple of passes at people, and, you know, been refused. But at least I'm, I'm sort of trying even there.

TH: Yeah.

PT: Granted, I, the, that, one, one of the gals I made a pass at is as sick as I am, I think, and this is her problem, too. (laughs) But, uh, you know, at least I tried in some way to make known what I wanted to happen. (sort of laughs while saying this)

TH: And you weren't too afraid?

PT: No.

TH: So you're contemplating the fact that maybe it *isn't* so awful?

PT: No, actu—, and, and it was, uh, as I say. I, I, uh, uh, you know, it was. . . . It's a girl, I, I know, Jane Hall; and I know she's, she and I have known each other for a long time and sort of been, you know, just good friends for years. I, I find Jane very appealing.

TH: Yeah.

PT: And, uh. . . . But I don't think I'd ever get anywhere with Jane, 'cause ah, she's, she's just a little too, uh, too hip on being a big businesswoman and one of the editors of *Harper's* and *Vogue.* And her career's gonna come first and all that kind of stuff . . .

TH: Yeah.

PT: . . . so that she sort of builds the wall out, too.

TH: Yes.

PT: And we had dinner the other night and she invited me up for a drink after dinner. And I went, and uh, I made a pass and she said No and that was that. But at least I tried.

(laughs) Although granted I was, it was a pretty safe territory, 'cause I must, I, you know I, it was, I, I guess in a way, I felt that I probably would be refused anyway. It was like practice time. (laughs)

TH: I see. Yeah. So you were able to do it easier than with some girl that you wouldn't be sure of . . . ?

PT: Yeah, that I had no idea of.

TH: Yeah. But still it was an advance; and the practice is good, isn't it?

PT: Yeah, yeah, and I found, and I really did find, that I could make a pass without being embarrassed myself . . .

TH: Yeah.

PT: . . . at having, you know, made an improper approach or something.

TH: Sure.

PT: And I didn't get hit, so I guess I came out on top! (laughs while saying this)

TH: And you did get some experiences, too . . .

PT: Yeah, yeah. I mean, I came out more plus than minus, I guess. (still is sort of laughing)

TH: Right. How many girls have you made a pass at in your whole life?

PT: Four or five.

TH: So this was one of the four or five.

PT: Um-hm. I've been very reticent in that area, I will admit it. (laughs)

TH: Yeah.

PT: No. In fact, uh, even carry it further back. I don't think I've even made a pass with a guy, it was always, you know, they chased me . . .

TH: Yeah.

PT: And I'm sure that this has a lot of bearing on it. I want the women to chase me, too.

TH: Yes, that's right, too . . .

PT: You know, it's an old habit pattern as well as, yeah . . .

TH: Yeah, and isn't that one of the main reasons for homosexuality—that boys find that other boys will chase them, while women won't?

PT: Yeah.

TH: And it's much safer; and it wouldn't be so terrible, because they won't get rejected that often . . .

PT: Yeah. You can say Yes without being the villain of the piece.

TH: That's right.

[As usual, the therapist tries to go a bit beyond the immediate conversation and to make the educational point that the patient is much like many other homosexuals, that he has been afraid to be assertive with girls and to risk rejection thereby; so he has found it easier to be passive with males. Fear of rejection will naturally lead to nonassertive behavior, the therapist is saying; and only by tackling this fear and seeing that it is not terrible to be rejected will the patient become truly nonhomosexual and otherwise more assertive.]

PT: You know . . .

TH: You refuse them, but they're not going to refuse you . . .

PT: Yeah, that's, that's very true, because . . .

TH: Let's get back to changing John. *Would* it be so terrible if you got refused, even by a girl you didn't know that there was a good chance beforehand she was going to refuse you, and you didn't know at all what was going to be? Or *would* it be so terrible if you grandiosely *didn't* get exactly what you wanted without any effort and without their selecting you?

PT: No, it, it, uh, it wouldn't be bad. This I, you know, I, this I can, I can logically believe this.

TH: At *times.*

PT: Yeah, at times.

TH: But *most* of the time, more strongly, you still believe the other things . . .

PT: Yeah. And somehow, I, I don't catch myself saying it to myself.

TH: That's right.

PT: It's, it's an old habit pattern of . . . I, I mean, you know, I don't even really know when I say to myself, you know, "duck and dodge!"

TH: And yet isn't that the value of the symptom, such as the sleeping too much . . .

PT: Yeah.

TH: . . . and so on—that if you track 'em down, you'll find that you must be saying . . .

PT: Yeah.

TH: . . . these things to yourself if the symptom is still there?

[The therapist points out that even though at times the patient believes that it is not terrible if he gets refused by a girl, most of the time he still believes that it *is,* and he is concretely telling himself that it is. The patient agrees, but points out that he does not clearly see that he is saying catastrophizing sentences to himself. Persistently, however, as is common in this form of psychotherapy, the therapist shows him that his symptoms prove, behaviorally, that he *must* be telling himself something along these catastrophizing lines.]

PT: But the, what I'm saying is that I see it *after* the fact . . .

TH: Right.

PT: After I've gone to sleep (sort of laughs) and wake up, I think, "Oh, oh, it's eight o'clock! You've shot the whole evening, you know . . ."

TH: Yes, but if you . . .

PT: ". . . you goofed!" (laughs) But . . .

TH: All right. But if you clearly see it *after* the fact and keep admitting completely after the fact even, that, "Yes, I still do have this horrifying idea," won't you get it back to *before* the fact, in time?

PT: I guess I will.

TH: We must perceive that we have the negative notions—the fears and the hostilities and the grandiosities—before we can really get to work on them. And if you can perceive and perceive and perceive them through these symptoms—the lack of sex desire, the oversleeping, and so forth—then you can finally get back and clip them, contradict them, challenge them, kick them in the teeth.

SUMMARY AND EVALUATION

Rational-emotive therapy assumes that although there are powerful biological and social forces leading to irrationality, human beings have the potential for being rational. Emotional disturbance and neurosis *are,* in fact, irrational thinking and can be remedied by changing such thinking and, in consequence, emotions and behavior to logical, rational thinking. The process of counseling or psychotherapy is thus to teach the client to think rationally. While other commonly practiced techniques of therapy—such as reflection of feeling, abreaction, and reassurance—may be used at the beginning of the process, the rational-emotive therapist quickly moves into an active-directive didactic, or teaching, process, wherein the irrational ideas and beliefs of the client are pointed out, their relationship to the client's emotional disturbance or unhappiness is explicated, and the client's thinking is changed by logic and reasoning, suggestions, argument and persuasion, and prescription of activities.

The aims or goals of counseling stated by Ellis are similar to those of most other counselors or psychotherapists. He speaks not only of the elimination or minimization of anxiety, hostility, depression, feelings of inferiority and inadequacy, unhappiness, and other symptoms, but also of happiness, effective living, rational behavior, independence, responsibility, and even self-actualization. Because the methods of Ellis are quite different from those of many, if not most, other therapists who seek the same goals for their clients, it is necessary to determine if the results are the same. Other therapists, as Ellis recognizes, place most, if not all, of the responsibility for correction of irrational and illogical ideas and beliefs on the client. Ellis, perhaps because of the nature of his personality, although he claims to provide unconditional positive regard for his clients, clearly does not have confidence in their ability to change or correct their perceptions and beliefs. In fact, he gives them no opportunity to do so. He recognizes that clients have the potential for growth and health, but he believes that this potential is so overgrown with longstanding irrational attitudes, beliefs, and emotions that only an active, direct attack on the part of the therapist can uncover it. "Unless these current residuals of his old cognitive errors are vigorously and persistently attacked, there is little chance of his modifying them significantly."[36] It might be questioned how well such an approach would help clients learn to think for themselves; it would appear that it teaches them to be dependent on the therapist.

If the arguments of Ellis regarding the helplessness, dependence, and self-discouragement of clients were valid, it would seem that less directive methods would have little chance of success, although Ellis himself admits that they are sometimes, if not often, successful but unnecessarily time consuming. The less directive counselors would argue that time is necessary for clients to mobilize their growth potential and that it is better for them to do this themselves and to reach their own solutions than for the therapist to present them with ready solutions to their problems. These counselors would argue that the obsession of many therapists with efficiency, their emphasis on speeding up the counseling process, their desire to achieve results quickly, may have some disadvantages or possibly some undesirable results. In addition to depriving clients of the satisfaction of achieving their own solutions, it is possible that this active, efficiency oriented approach may lead to the clients' dependency and lack of confidence in themselves. Lasting changes in personality and behavior may be achieved better by the slower process in which individuals work through their problems in their own way and at their own pace.

This is, of course, a matter for research, and a not unimportant question should be "Better for what; in what way?" It may well be true, of course, that these clients would not, by themselves, reach the same end results as do those clients who are treated by Ellis's methods. This is likely because rational-emotive counseling includes indoctrination in a large number of rather specific concepts, ideas, and philosophies that average clients might not explore and develop by themselves. However, it is a question of how many disturbed people hold beliefs in the absolute or extreme form in which Ellis states them. No data on this are provided. Ellis appears to impose, project, or assume an extreme form of beliefs in his clients in order to attack them and argue against them. Arguing a client out of a belief in its extreme form will not necessarily solve all the client's problems with interpersonal relationships. Wolpe has made this same point: "In practice, . . . he often seems to project onto the patient the irrational beliefs he supposes the patient ought to have."[37] It does appear, however, that the irrational ideas that Ellis identifies as being at the basis of emotional disturbance characterize many, if not most, disturbed individuals.

The emphasis on the importance of perceptions of and attitudes toward events in influencing behavior and emotional disturbance suggests that Ellis's approach might be similar to that of those counselors who accept a perceptual or phenomenological theory of human behavior. Ellis does not talk about the self-concept or self-ideal, however, although these concepts are apparent in the individual's self-verbalizations and shoulds and musts as controlling ideas. He recognizes the importance of self-worth, self-esteem, and self-acceptance, and the difference between one's self-evaluation as a person and one's behaviors or performances. The A-B-C sequence clearly is phenomenological because it states that it is not events or experiences that are harmful or cause emotional disturbances, but a person's perceptions or interpretation (or misinterpretation) of them.

Ellis agrees that the essence of effective counseling or psychotherapy is the changing of attitudes. While many other therapists believe that since attitudes are emotion laden, a direct attack on them is ineffective, Ellis believes that since the attitudes of disturbed persons are irrational, a direct attack on their irrationality is best. He states that one of the main methods for changing attitudes is the didactic method and points to the effectiveness of propaganda as evidence for this approach. However, the evidence for the success of direct methods in changing attitudes probably is not as great as Ellis appears to believe. Goldfried and Davison comment on Ellis's reliance on argument and persuasion: "Rather than arguing with the client and trying to convince him how foolish he is for accepting any of these beliefs, it would be far more effective for the client *himself* to offer arguments to refute these expectations. The social-psychological literature suggests that this method is more effective in creating attitude change."[38]

Everyday experience and common sense also indicate that direct methods and argument are not effective ways to change attitudes and behavior, but lead to resistance. Ellis recognizes the existence of resistance. While some resistance may be created by poor technique on the part of the counselor, there is also the client's resistance to change; but this resistance, Ellis notes, is to be expected and should not prevent the counselor from persisting in attempts to overcome it. Ellis does not appear to be aware of or concerned about the possibility that direct attacks on a client's resistance constitute a threat to the client, which only increases this resistance and makes change more difficult, if not impossible. There seems to be sufficient evidence that threat results in impairment of learning and reasoning to warrant cautiousness on the counselor's part in the use of direct, active methods, which might constitute a threat. However, it must be remembered that these methods are used within a therapeutic relationship; it would appear that the relationship aspects of rational-emotive therapy are underemphasized.

The fact that these methods are incorporated into a counseling situation, which involves a special kind of relationship, may influence their success. Even the special kind of relationship established in so-called brainwashing may lead to changes in opinions, beliefs, and attitudes, particularly when the indoctrinator genuinely and sincerely believes in what he or she is indoctrinating the subject in and is concerned about the subject's accepting it. Ellis's approach, with its emphasis on persuasion, suggestion, and repetition, bears much resemblance to brainwashing. These and other aspects of the approach—the clear role of the therapist as an expert and authority— also maximize the placebo effect. Ellis recognizes these criticisms:

> Many therapists, of course, still vigorously oppose RET and insist that it is far too simple, and oververbalized, too intellectualized, authoritarian and brainwashing. Actually it is none of these, but is complexly philosophic, quickly gets at unconscious and unverbalized material, deals with the individual's basic emotions, and helps him to *act* as well as to *think* in order to change them. It is authoritative rather than authoritarian, and is aimed at inducing people to be less suggestible and more independent in their thinking.[39]

This leads to a comment on the imparting of values in counseling. There is, of course, no question that values are involved in counseling; that the values of the counselor must be considered; and that all counselors, since they determine the goals of counseling, are, to that extent at least, directive. Still, there are degrees of indoctrination of, or imposition of, values or philosophies on clients. It would appear that rational-emotive counseling is rather extreme in the extent and detail of the values it imposes on its clients. Ellis notes the danger that the counselor "may use his authority to induce his patient to acquire *his,* the therapist's, particular brand of beliefs,"[40] yet he does not seem to recognize that this is essentially what he does, although, to be sure, he uses reason and logic, together with authority.

There are clearly grounds for criticism of rational-emotive therapy as being too rational and as neglecting the emotions. The popularity of psychoanalysis and other in-depth psychologies has brought with it acceptance of the belief that disturbed behavior is due to mysterious repressed emotions. It has never been clear just how unexpressed emotions can exist and influence behavior. Nor has it been clear just how psychoanalysis or any other therapy deals with such unexpressed emotions directly. Making the so-called unconscious conscious is nothing more than putting into words unexpressed thoughts and ideas. Ellis has contributed to our understanding of the relation between emotion and thinking and has clarified what goes on in all counseling, since all counseling involves some verbalization.

Ellis also notes that cognition is gaining increasing recognition and attention in psychology, but just as the emphasis of psychoanalysis and depth psychology as a corrective against extreme rationalism has gone too far, it is possible that the emphasis on cognition may likewise overextend itself. There appears to be much in experience or experiencing that cannot be verbalized. Such experiencing is important, and sometimes the sharing of the experience with another understanding person can be clarifying and helpful.

Thus it may be contended that the role, importance, and effectiveness of logic and reason are overemphasized, while the importance of the relationship is neglected. Things can go on in counseling when there is no overt verbalization, and changes in the client can occur. Now, of course, it can be noted that there are subvocal verbalizations going on in the client, and no doubt this is so at least some of the time, but it is not necessarily so. When there is internal verbalization on the part of the client, it is the relationship with the counselor that makes this possible.

I would suspect that Ellis's results are more influenced by the relationship he has with his clients than he is willing to admit. His genuine interest in and concern for his clients are apparent and must be important factors. In fact, if there are any necessary and sufficient conditions for personality change resulting from a personal relationship, they are probably these characteristics of the relationship. Ellis himself cites a case in which a paranoid client insisted that Ellis did not understand her, yet she accepted and adopted some of his attitudes and values.[41] Ellis feels that it was the force of his logic that influenced her. It is also possible that it was the relationship itself. Of course, it might possibly have been Ellis's authority and prestige, as these undoubtedly enter into other of his cases, for regardless of how logical and persuasive Ellis is, it is unlikely that he succeeds by logic and persuasion alone.

It is also true, as Ellis emphasizes, that rational-emotive counseling is not a cold, rational analysis but does involve emotions. The client's self-verbalizations, which are related to his or her disturbance, are emotionally charged. Assuming that these thoughts are present—and there is no doubt that clients have many unexpressed and relevant emotionally charged thoughts—it would appear that rational-emotive counseling is essentially an interpretive method in which the counselor, on the basis of his or her theory of the nature and causation of emotional disturbance, interprets the client's unexpressed thoughts. While the apparent success of the method might be taken as evidence for the validity of the theory, it must be remembered that other interpretive methods, which use other theories (for example, psychoanalysis), claim success and apparently *are* successful. As in these other systems, the client's acceptance of the interpretation does not validate it. But if various interpretive methods are successful, it is possible, and indeed quite likely, that they all utilize the same (or some of the same) valid concepts, although they may use different language.

How effective is rational-emotive psychotherapy? Ellis claims 90 percent success, although by "success," he does not mean cure but improvement, and no adequate statistical evidence is presented. As is true of all therapists, however, there is a selective factor operating in the acceptance of clients for therapy; many are attracted by Ellis's writings and have favorable expectations, which support the placebo effect. It is questionable whether 90 percent of all those who are disturbed and seek counseling would benefit from this approach at the hands of other rational-emotive therapists. The criteria of success must also be considered. There are numerous favorable case reports in Ellis's writings and in a published casebook.[42]

Ellis claims that "the rational-emotive approach to psychotherapy is not only unusually effective clinically but is now backed by a considerable amount of experimental evidence which almost consistently supports phenomenological tenets and indicates that human emotions are enormously influenced by cognition. . . . There is clinical, experimental, and other support for rational-emotive therapy."[43] He also raises the question, "Is RET really more effective than other forms of psychotherapy?" and replies:

The evidence is not in that will answer this question. Clinical findings would seem to indicate that it benefits more people than do most other methods; that it can obtain beneficial results in surprisingly short order in many instances; and that the level of improvement or cure that is effected through its use is more permanent and deep-seated than that obtained through other methods. But this clinical evidence has been haphazardly collected and is now being substantiated through controlled studies of therapeutic outcomes.[44]

Findings is probably too strong a word to use to refer to clinical reports. The research studies mentioned by Ellis are not always evaluations of the effectiveness or outcomes of RET or even directly or clearly related to its theoretical basis. Since he includes among the methods of RET many of the techniques of behavior therapy, he cites research supporting these techniques as also supportive of RET. In a review published in 1977,[45] he includes research supportive of 32 clinical and personality hypotheses of RET and other modes of cognitive-behavior therapy. He concludes that "a vast amount of research data exists, most of which tends to confirm the major clinical and personality hypotheses of RET." He refers to the survey of Di Giuseppe, Miller, and Trexler[46] for further studies of the effectiveness and outcomes of RET.

Meichenbaum, in his comments on Ellis's review,[47] notes that the review is selective of research supporting Ellis's hypotheses, that it ignores the fact that many of the studies and their conclusions have been questioned, that some of the studies actually do not bear specifically on the hypotheses they purportedly support, and that the claims for support are possible because the theory is general and imprecise. Ellis has extended his theory to include most of the areas of psychology and other theories of therapy and behavior change—phenomenology, desensitization, biofeedback, expectancy, attribution theory, cognitive dissonance, the placebo effect, locus of control, information giving, teaching, skill training, modeling, self-control, and so forth—and, of course, finds some evidence for the validity of all these. However, this expansion of RET theory to include so much is accompanied by the loss of what integration and systematization was present in the earlier, simpler theory. As Mahoney notes,[48] these hypotheses are not "a model or theory at all. Instead, this is a collection of loosely related and poorly elucidated propositions." Ewart and Thoresen[49] are also critical of the vagueness and consequent untestability of the hypotheses, of their lack of specificity and their broad generality, of the ambiguity of the relationship between certain predictions and RET theory, of the inconsistencies among predictions, and of the lack of discriminative relationship of some hypotheses to RET; that is, they are parts of other theories, and thus support for them supports other theories as well. Finally, they note that those few instances of distinctive and specific predictions are supported by little or no research or that research is absent.

Support for theoretical concepts and hypotheses does not constitute support for the effectiveness of RET. Ellis refers to "about seventy-five" studies comparing RET with other therapies and control groups with "almost uniformly favorable results." The review by Di Giuseppe, Miller, and Trexler[50] includes only 21 studies (in some of which it is questionable whether RET was actually the method used). (Ellis claims that there are over 20 other confirmatory studies.[51]) Their evaluation is that the results, while they are generally positive, are "far from conclusive." Mahoney, in 1974, came to the following conclusion: "Experimental research evaluating the efficacy of (RET) has been sparse, methodologically poor, and summarily modest in its implications. . . . This, of course, means that the clinical efficacy of RET has yet to be adequately demonstrated."[52]

We may conclude that rational-emotive counseling is probably effective, at least with some clients. But a number of questions still must be raised.

1. Is it effective for the reasons Ellis believes?
2. In what ways is it effective; that is, does it achieve the same kinds of results as other approaches? Does it lead to independence and responsibility in the client, especially when compared with the results of other approaches that emphasize the activity and responsibility of the client during the counseling process?
3. Finally, does the improvement persist?

These, of course, are questions that must be asked of every approach to counseling.

REFERENCES

1. Ellis, A. *Reason and emotion in psychotherapy.* Secaucus, NJ: Citadel Press, 1962. p. 7.
2. Ellis, A. New approaches to psychotherapy techniques. *Journal of Clinical Psychology Monograph Supplement,* 1955 (No. 1).
3. Ellis, A. Psychotherapy techniques for use with psychotics. *American Journal of Psychotherapy,* 1955, *9,* 452–476.
4. Ellis, A. An operational reformulation of some of the basic principles of psychoanalysis. *Psychoanalytic Review,* 1956, *43,* 163–180.
5. Ellis, A. Rational psychotherapy and individual psychotherapy. *Journal of Individual Psychology,* 1957, *13,* 38–44.
6. Ellis, A. Outcome of employing three techniques of psychotherapy. *Journal of Clinical Psychology,* 1957, *13,* 344–350.
7. Ellis, A. Rational psychotherapy. *Journal of General Psychology,* 1958, *59,* 35–49.
8. Ellis, A. Rationalism and its therapeutic applications. In A. Ellis (Ed.), *The place of values in the practice of psychotherapy.* New York: American Academy of Psychotherapists, 1959.
9. Ellis, *Reason and emotion in psychotherapy,* Secaucus, NJ: Citadel Press, 1962, p. 50.
10. Ibid., p. 54.
11. Ibid., p. 61.
12. Ibid., p. 89.
13. Braaten, L. J. The main theories of existentialism from the viewpoint of the psychotherapist. *Mental Hygiene,* 1961, *45,* 10–17.
14. Ellis, A. Goals of psychotherapy. In A. R. Mahrer (Ed.), *The goals of psychotherapy.* Englewood Cliffs, N.J.: Prentice-Hall, 1967. Pp. 206–221. Also in Ellis, A. *Humanistic psychotherapy: The Rational-emotive approach.* New York: Julian Press, 1973. Pp. 147–162. (Paperback published by McGraw-Hill)
15. Ellis, *Humanistic psychotherapy,* chap. 2.
16. Rogers, C. R. The necessary and sufficient conditions of therapeutic personality change. *Journal of Consulting Psychology,* 1957, *21,* 95–103.
17. Ellis, *Reason and emotion in psychotherapy,* chap. 5.

18. Ibid., p. 117.
19. Ibid., pp. 118–119.
20. Ibid., p. 38.
21. Ibid., pp. 36–37.
22. Ibid., p. 95.
23. Ibid., pp. 58–59.
24. Ibid., pp. 94–95.
25. Ellis, *Humanistic psychotherapy,* pp. 153–154.
26. Ibid., p. 154.
27. Ibid.
28. Ibid., p. 155.
29. Ibid., p. 158.
30. Ibid., p. 43.
31. Ellis, *Reason and emotion in psychotherapy,* chap. 20.
32. Ellis, *Humanistic psychotherapy,* p. 35.
33. Ibid, p. 51.
34. Ibid.
35. From a typescript provided by Albert Ellis.
36. Ellis, *Humanistic psychotherapy,* p. 35.
37. Wolpe, J. Cognition and causation in human behavior and its therapy. *American Psychologist,* 1978, *33,* 437–446.
38. Goldfried, M. R., & Davison, G. C. *Clinical behavior therapy.* New York: Holt, Rinehart and Winston, 1976. P. 166.
39. Ellis, *Humanistic psychotherapy,* pp. 35–36.
40. Ellis, *Reason and emotion in psychotherapy,* 367.
41. Ibid., p. 116.
42. Ellis, A. *Growth through reason: Verbatim cases in rational-emotive therapy.* Palo Alto, Calif.: Science and Behavior Books, 1971. (Paperback published by Wilshire Books)
43. Ellis, *Humanistic psychotherapy,* p. 27.
44. Ibid., p. 65.
45. Ellis, A. Rational-emotive therapy: Research data that support the clinical and personality hypotheses of RET and other modes of cognitive-behavior therapy. *Counseling Psychologist,* 1977, *7* (1), 2–44. Also in Ellis, A., and Whiteley, J. M. (Eds.). *Theoretical and empirical foundations of rational-emotive therapy.* Monterey: Calif.: Brooks/Cole, 1979.
46. Di Giuseppe, R. A., Miller, N. J., & Trexler, L. D. A review of rational-emotive psychotherapy outcome studies. *Counseling Psychologist,* 1977, *7* (1), 64–72.
47. Meichenbaum, D. Dr. Ellis, please stand up. *Counseling Psychologist,* 1977, *7* (1), 43–44.
48. Mahoney, J. J. A critical analysis of rational-emotive theory and therapy. *Counseling Psychologist,* 1977, *7* (1), 43–46.
49. Ewart, C. K., & Thoresen, C. E. The rational-emotive manifesto. *Counseling Psychologist,* 1977, *7* (1), 52–56.
50. Di Giuseppe, Miller, & Trexler, A review of rational-emotive psychotherapy outcome studies.
51. Ellis, A. Rejoinder: Elegant and inelegant RET. *Counseling Psychologist,* 1977, *7* (1), 73–82.
52. Mahoney, M. J. *Cognitive and behavior modification.* Cambridge, Mass.: Ballinger, 1974. P. 182.

chapter 2

Cognitive Therapy: Beck

Aaron T. Beck (b. 1921) received his M.D. from the Yale University School of Medicine in 1946. From 1946 to 1948, he served an internship and residency in pathology at the Rhode Island Hospital; following that, a residency in neurology and psychiatry at the Cushing Veterans Administration Hospital in Framingham, Massachusetts. Beck has been on the faculty of the University of Pennsylvania Medical School since 1954 and is now professor of psychiatry and the director of the Center for Cognitive Therapy. He also has been a fellow in psychiatry at the Austen Riggs Center in Stockbridge, Massachusetts; a consultant to the Philadelphia Veterans Administration Hospital; a member of the board of directors of the West Philadelphia Mental Health Consortium; a trustee of the American Academy of Psychoanalysis; and the president of the Society of Psychotherapy Research.

Beck was certified in psychiatry by the American Board of Psychiatry and Neurology in 1953, and he graduated from the Philadelphia Psychoanalytic Institute in 1958. He is a recipient of the Foundations' Fund Award for Research in Psychiatry from the American Psychiatric Association.

Besides serving as associate editor of the journal *Cognitive Therapy and Research,* Beck is the author of numerous journal articles and the author or coauthor of *Depression: Clinical, Experimental, and Theoretical Aspects* (1967), republished as *Depression: Causes and Treatment* (1972); *The Diagnosis and Management of Depression* (1973); *Cognitive Therapy and the Emotional Disorders* (1976); and, with Rush, Shaw, and Emery, *Cognitive Therapy of Depression* (1979).

BACKGROUND AND DEVELOPMENT

Beck, like Ellis, was trained in and engaged in the practice of orthodox psychoanalysis. But he became dissatisfied with its complexity and abstractness, and his studies that attempted to validate psychoanalytic concepts failed to support the psychoanalytic hypotheses. Beck's encouragement of his patients to engage in cognitive analysis of their thoughts led him to reformulate concepts of depression, anxiety, phobias, and obsessive–compulsive neuroses in terms of cognitive distortions. He developed various maneuvers to correct the faulty thinking involved and thus relieve the neurosis.

Beck also was attracted to the newly developing field of behavior therapy, which he studied and practiced. He felt that behavioral techniques are effective, but not for the reasons given by behavior therapists. Rather, they are effective because they bring about attitudinal or cognitive changes in the patients. Behavior therapy is limited, however, because it ignores patients' thinking about themselves, about the therapist, and about the therapy itself. Its emphases on obtaining objective data from patients, on systematic planning of the treatment process, and on quantifying behavioral change appears to have been of value to Beck in developing cognitive therapy.

Beck felt that his cognitive model provides a much simpler, parsimonious explanation of patients' problems than does psychoanalytic theory or behavior therapy, which explains neither the common neuroses nor patients' improvement.

PHILOSOPHY AND CONCEPTS

A Commonsensical Approach

Cognitive therapy rejects the views of the three major therapeutic schools: psychoanalysis, which posits the unconscious as the source of emotional disturbance; behavior therapy, which regards only overt behavior as significant; and traditional neuropsychiatry, which considers physiological or chemical disorders to be the cause of emotional disturbances. Cognitive therapy is based on the commonsensical idea that what people think and say about themselves—their attitudes, ideas, and ideals—is relevant and important.

In the course of development, people acquire a vast store of information, concepts, and formulas for dealing with the psychological problems of living. This knowledge is applied through observing, developing and testing hypotheses, and making judgments—essentially acting as a practical scientist. From their cultural heritage and through education and experience, people learn to use the tools of common sense—forming and testing hunches, making discriminations, and reasoning—to resolve conflicts and judge whether they are reacting realistically to situations.

Common sense, however, fails to provide explanations for the emotional disorders. The thoughts and behaviors of depressed patients, for example, contradict the basic principles of human nature—that is, the survival instinct. Yet when one gets inside the conceptual system of such patients and sees the world through their eyes, their behavior begins to make sense. Through empathy, one can understand the meanings that they give to their experiences and offer explanations that are plausible from their frames of reference.

In relation to reality, however, the thinking of depressed patients is controlled by erroneous ideas about themselves and their world. "Crucial information . . . is lacking. However, *once the missing data are supplied,* we can apply common-sense tools to solve the puzzle."[1]

"The formulation of psychological problems in terms of incorrect premises and a proneness to distorted imaginal experiences represents a sharp deviation from generally accepted formulations of the psychological disorders."[2] Cognitive therapy does not require a concept of the unconscious. Psychological problems "may result from commonplace processes such as faulty learning, making incorrect inferences on the basis of inadequate or incorrect information, and not distinguishing adequately between imagination and reality. Moreover, thinking can be unrealistic because it is derived from erroneous premises; behavior can be self-defeating because it is based on unreasonable attitudes."[3]

Cognitive therapy helps patients to use the problem-solving methods that they employ during normal periods of their lives. "The formula for treatment may be stated in simple terms: The therapist helps the patient to identify his warped thinking and to learn more realistic ways to formulate his experiences."[4] This approach makes sense to patients because of their earlier application of their knowledge about correcting misconceptions and misinterpretations.

Internal Communications

Emotional reactions are not direct or automatic responses to external stimuli. Rather, stimuli are processed and interpreted by an internal cognitive system. A major discordance between the internal system and external stimuli may result in psychological disorders.

"The principle that there is a conscious thought between an external event and a particular emotional response is not generally accepted by the major schools of psychotherapy."[5] Although subjects or patients ordinarily are not aware of or ignore these thoughts and therefore do not report them, they can be taught to observe them introspectively before experiencing an emotion. "In fact, it is difficult to conceive of how a person can react emotionally to an event before he has appraised its nature."[6] By eliciting a person's cognitions, the therapist can arrive at an understanding of apparently unrealistic emotional reactions.

"Since these thoughts appeared to emerge automatically and extremely rapidly, I labelled them 'automatic thoughts.' "[7] These automatic thoughts are specific and discrete; occur in an abbreviated style; do not arise from deliberation or reasoning but are relatively autonomous and involuntary; and are regarded as reasonable by the patient, even when they appear to be implausible to others or are contradicted by objective evidence. These thoughts are close to the patient's problems, however, and thus are more useful in therapy than is ordinary free association, which, indeed, does not even uncover automatic thoughts.

"Internal signals in a linguistic or visual form play a significant role in behavior. The way a person instructs himself, praises and criticizes himself, interprets events, and makes predictions not only illuminates normal behavior, but sheds light on the inner workings of emotional disorders. . . . Self-monitoring of behavior may be involved in maladaptive reactions. Overmonitoring can lead to self-consciousness and over-regulation to excessive inhibition."[8] Underregulation leads to loss of inhibition—excesses in eating, drinking, or smoking. Overmobilization of self-instruction leads to excessive striving. Self-instruction may revolve around avoidance or inhibition of actions, as in anxious and depressed patients, and gives rise to self-punishments and self-rewards—

self-evaluations of badness or unworthiness, on the one hand, and of goodness or pride, on the other hand.

"The role of anticipations in influencing feelings and action is far more dominant than is generally recognized. The meaning of a person's experiences is very much determined by his expectations of their immediate and ultimate consequences."[9]

People's reactions to many situations are consistent, which suggests that these responses are guided by a set of rules. The rules form the basis for individuals' interpretations, expectations, and self-instructions and thus provide a framework for understanding life's experiences. Such guidelines include not only "equations, formulas, and premises that enable the person to order, classify, and synthesize his observations of reality so that he can come to meaningful conclusions,"[10] but also standards to guide actions and to evaluate the behaviors of the self and of others.

Rules are a part of the social heritage and thus are absorbed through personal experience and observation of others. The rules under which a patient operates help the therapist to understand illogical behavior and abnormal emotional responses. "When rules are discordant with reality or are applied excessively or arbitrarily, they are likely to produce psychological or interpersonal problems."[11]

Meaning and Emotions

People react to events in terms of the meanings that they give to the events. These personal interpretations of an event lead to various emotional responses to the same situation by different people or by one person at different times. "The thesis that the special meaning of an event determines the emotional response forms the core of the cognitive model of emotions and emotional disorders."[12]

Those objects to which people assign a special relevance constitute their personal domain, at the center of which is the self or self-concept. "The nature of a person's emotional response—or emotional disturbance—depends on whether he perceives events as adding to, subtracting from, endangering, or impinging upon his domain."[13] *Sadness* results from the perception that something of value has been lost, thus subtracting from the personal domain. The perception or expectation of a gain leads to *euphoria* or *excitation*. Threats to the physical or psychological self or of the loss of something important causes *anxiety*. *Anger* arises from a perceived direct attack, intentional or unintentional, or from the violation of laws, morals, or standards held by the person when it is interpreted as an attack on his or her personal domain. The person must take the attack seriously and focus on the wrongfulness of the offense rather than on any injury suffered.

The kind of ideation leading to sadness, euphoria, anxiety, or anger, if it involves a distortion of reality, results in depression, mania, anxiety reactions, or paranoid states.

The Emotional Disorders

Disorders of thinking are a characteristic not only of schizophrenia, but also, in less severe forms, of all the common psychiatric disorders. All patients show distortions of reality of varying degrees and "systematic departures from reality and logic, including arbitrary inferences, selective abstractions, and overgeneralizations . . . in ideation

. . . relevant to the patient's specific problem."[14] Distorted ideas have the characteristics of automatic thoughts; that is, they appear to arise reflexively, seem plausible to the patient but not to others, and are resistant to change by reason or evidence.

Three characteristics of thinking are common to all emotional disorders.

1. *Personalization*   Patients interpret all events as applying to themselves. Such egocentric views replace objective judgments.
2. *Polarized Thinking*   Patients think in extremes and in absolute terms. Related to making extreme judgments are selective abstraction, arbitrary inference, and overgeneralization.
3. *"Law of Rules"*   Patients respond consistently to situations, but the regularity of reaction goes beyond that of normal persons, becoming unconditional and absolute. Each kind of disorder has its own set of rules.

Acute Emotional Disturbance

The acute neurotic reaction has been labeled a "catastrophic reaction." The patient may be overwhelmed by intense anxiety, sadness, or rage and has to struggle to retain control of concentration and attention.

Cognitively, the reaction is characterized by intense self-consciousness, misinterpretation of harmless stimuli as representing great danger, and attention to irrelevant thoughts and feelings. "The misconstruing of situations constitutes cognitive distortion ranging from mild inaccuracy to gross misinterpretation."[15]

Depression

The development of depression begins with an experience connoting loss to the patient. The loss may be real or may be a hypothetical or a pseudo-loss. In either case, it is exaggerated and perceived as permanent and irreversible and is viewed as a reflection on oneself, one's attributes, or one's competence, leading to a negative self-concept—one is a "loser" or is unworthy. The patient "is likely to assign the cause of the adverse event to an heinous defect in himself"[16] and to appraise every subsequent experience, even if only slightly negative or ambiguous, in terms of self-deficiency. Comparisons with others further lower self-esteem. The ultimate result may be total self-rejection.

Negative views of the self lead to negative views of the future. Pessimism pervades the patient's outlook on life. Hopelessness results in loss of motivation. Since the outcome is expected to be negative, there is no point in making an effort. The ultimate end of such pessimism is suicidal thoughts, wishes, and attempts, which are rational on the basis of such a premise. A second premise for suicide is the belief that, given the patient's self-concept, others would be better off if he or she were dead. A negative self-concept, negative interpretation of events and experiences, and negative view of the future constitute the cognitive triad of depression.

Such manifestations of depression as inertia, fatigue, and agitation are outcomes of the negative cognitions, and "the vegetative signs of depression—loss of appetite, loss of libido, sleep disturbance—appear to be the physiological concomitants of the particular psychological disturbance in depression."[17]

Anxiety Neurosis

Anxiety is abnormal and constitutes a neurosis when its degree exceeds that evoked by an actual threat or when no threat is present. Anxiety is the emotion that arises with the activation of fear, which is the ideation representing the appraisal of potential harm. "Common among patients with anxiety neurosis is fear of loss of control leading to feelings of humiliation, embarrassment, sadness. Among these fears are: losing control of one's faculties as in fear of becoming insane; not being able to function; not attaining crucial objectives; harming others."[18]

These fears seem plausible to the patient, whose thinking is dominated by themes of danger, manifested in (1) repetitive thoughts about danger; (2) reduced ability to "reason" with the fearful thoughts, to evaluate them objectively; and (3) generalization of anxiety-evoking stimuli to the point that almost any stimulus or situation may be perceived as a threat. The patient's attention is stuck or bound on the concept of danger, with involuntary preoccupation with danger stimuli. "[B]ecause of the fixation of most of his attention on concepts or stimuli relevant to danger, the patient loses most of his ability to shift his voluntary awareness to other internal processes or external stimuli."[19] Danger is exaggerated, with a tendency to catastrophize, and hypothetical dangers are equated with actual dangers.

Phobias and Obsessions

A phobia is a "fear of a situation that, by social consensus and the person's own intellectual appraisal when away from the situation, is disproportionate to the probability and degree of harm in that situation."[20] Phobics are not afraid of the situation itself but of the *consequences* of being in the situation, which they thus avoid in order to prevent the excessive anxiety that it arouses. Each phobia is characterized by a specific central fear, which often is a composite of fears that varies with individuals. The agoraphobic fears befalling a calamity when away from home. The acrophobic fears falling from a high place and being injured or killed. The person afraid of elevators fears getting stuck and suffering some harm. The person afraid of tunnels fears being suffocated. The person with a social phobia fears the reactions of other people toward him or her. The fear of consequences is the cognitive element behind phobias and makes them understandable.

Obsessions are repetitive thoughts relating to actions that patients believe they should have taken but doubt that they have or to actions that they have taken but should not have. Obsessive doubt leads to compulsions, or repetitive actions to allay the doubts.

Psychosomatic Disorders and Hysteria

Psychosomatic disorders include "(1) physiological disturbances or structural abnormalities in which psychological and constitutional factors combine to produce the disorder. . . . (2) Primary physical disorders that are exacerbated by psychological processes. . . . (3) Aberration of sensation or movement, but with no demonstrable tissue pathology or disturbed physiology. This category includes a broad spectrum of conditions ranging from 'somatic imaging' and the hysterias to somatic delusions."[21] Whether a psychosomatic disorder results instead of or in addition to anxiety is determined by genetic factors.

Under stress, all people tend to overreact in a particular vulnerable physiological system. Thus patients who overreact to the extent of developing continuing or severe psychosomatic disorders are similar to anxiety-prone or anger-prone patients in general: they conceptualize innocuous life experiences as threatening and exaggerate minor threats into major calamities. Actual stressful situations are less important than is the way the patient perceives them.

Most patients with psychosmatic disorders are not under specific external stresses. But there are internal stresses; a major one is the demands people place on themselves. Hard-driving individuals manifest faulty cognitive appraisals concerning the importance and difficulty of the tasks they face, underestimate their capacity to deal with them, and exaggerate the consequences and probability of failure.

"Hysteria is the illustration *par excellence* of the phenomenon of cognitive distortion in psychiatric disorders."[22] It consists of physical dysfunctions with no demonstrable organic disease or physical abnormality.

As a result of an injury to himself or identification with a constellation of symptoms in others, the hysteric comes to believe that he has a physical disorder. As he thinks about having this disorder, he experiences physical sensations—somatic imaging. A circular mechanism is set up. The person "reads" his physical sensations as evidence that he has the disorder. His belief becomes consolidated, and the physical manifestations are proportionately intensified.[23]

PRINCIPLES OF COGNITIVE THERAPY

"In the broadest sense, cognitive therapy consists of all the approaches that alleviate psychological distress through the medium of correcting faulty conceptions and self-signals."[24]

Targets of Cognitive Therapy

Cognitive therapy is the application in treatment of the common methods of thinking that have been developed in normal living. It is most appropriate for those who have the capacity for introspection and reflection and who are able to think adequately in areas of their lives outside the problem area. It focuses on helping the patient overcome blind spots, blurred perceptions, self-deceptions, and incorrect judgments. Since the emotional reactions that bring the patient to therapy are the results of incorrect thinking, they are alleviated when the thinking is corrected.

Direct and Tangible Distortions of Reality

Direct distortions of reality are most obvious in paranoid patients but exist in other patients. They are relatively clear to the therapist or are easy to check.

Illogical Thinking

Reality may not be distorted, but thinking may be based on faulty premises, involve erroneous inferences or wrong conclusions from observations, or represent gross over-generalization.

The Therapeutic Collaboration

The patient and the therapist must agree on the problem to be dealt with, the goal of the therapy, the methods of achieving the goal, and the duration of therapy. Emphasis is on solving problems rather than on changing the patient's personal characteristics or defects. The therapist must be sensitive to the patient's need or desire to discuss certain topics at each session. As a collaborator in the therapy, the therapist should be accepting, warm, and empathic.

Establishing Credibility

Therapists must avoid authoritative methods that lead, on the one hand, to blind acceptance of interpretations and suggestions by some patients but, on the other hand, to resistance and rejection by others. "A more appropriate approach in establishing credibility is to convey a message such as: 'you have certain ideas that upset you. They may or may not be correct. Let us examine some of them.' "[25] A cautious, trial-and-error approach is then followed, especially in dealing with delusions, which should not be confronted prematurely or directly.

Reducing Problems

Problem reduction includes (1) "identifying problems with similar causes and grouping them together"; (2) "concentrating on the key components of the disorder"; and (3) identifying "the first link in a chain of symptoms"[26] and concentrating on that.

Learning to Learn

By actively participating in problem solving, the patient learns how to solve problems.

TECHNIQUES OF COGNITIVE THERAPY

"The therapist, directly or indirectly, conveys certain principles to the patient. First, a perception of reality is not the same as reality itself. . . . Second, his interpretations of his sensory input are dependent on inherently fallible cognitive processes. . . . [A]ppraisal of reality can be flawed by unrealistic patterns of thought."[27]

The therapist attempts to clarify the patient's distortion of reality, the self-injunctions and self-reproaches that lead to distress, and the rules that underlie the faulty self-signals. The therapist uses the problem-solving methods that patients have used in their successes in the past or with other problems: "defining the problem areas precisely, filling in the informational gaps, establishing relationships among the data, and forming generalizations."[28] Patients then are encouraged to use their own problem-solving abilities to change their ways of interpreting experiences and controlling actions. When patients become aware that their self-signals are maladaptive, they tend to correct them automatically.

Recognizing Maladaptive Ideation

"The term 'maladaptive thoughts' is applied to ideation that interferes with the ability to cope with life experiences, unnecessarily disrupts internal harmony, and produces inappropriate or excessive emotional reactions that are painful."[29] Patients may not be fully aware of these thoughts, but with instruction and training, they may become aware of them and then can focus on them.

Filling in the Blank

When patients report events and their emotional reactions to the events, there is usually a gap between the stimulus and the response. In Ellis's A-B-C theory, B is the blank. It is the task of therapy to fill in this blank. Again, this is accomplished by instructing the patient to focus on the thoughts that occur during experiencing the stimulus and the response.

Distancing and Centering

"The process of regarding thoughts objectively is labeled *distancing*."[30] It involves recognizing that automatic thoughts are not reality, are not reliable, and are maladaptive, and it includes depersonalizing events.

Authenticating Conclusions

Although patients may be able to distinguish between internal mental processes and external stimuli, they still have to learn the procedures for obtaining accurate knowledge. This includes recognizing that a hypothesis is not a fact and that an inference is not reality. The therapist helps patients to explore their conclusions and to test them against reality, applying the rules of evidence.

Changing the Rules

Maladjustment occurs when unrealistic and absolute rules are applied inappropriately and arbitrarily. Therapy attempts to substitute more realistic and adaptive rules. Rules seem to focus on *danger versus safety* and on *pain versus pleasure.* Patients overestimate dangers and the risk involved in common situations. Psychosocial dangers are the source of most problems. Fears of humiliation, criticism, rejection, and so on are challenged, and the serious consequences of their occurrence are questioned. Exaggerated estimates of the probabilities of physical harm or death are examined, leading to their reduction.

Beliefs and attitudes act as rules. Attitudes that predispose people to excessive sadness or depression include the following:

1. In order to be happy, I must be successful, accepted, popular, famous, wealthy, and so on.
2. If I make a mistake, I am incompetent.
3. I cannot live without love.
4. When people disagree with me, they do not like me.

These beliefs are framed as absolutes or extremes and cannot be satisfied. "A major technique of cognitive therapy consists of making the patient's attitudes explicit and helping him decide whether they are self-defeating. . . . The therapist's role should be to suggest alternative rules for the patent's consideration—not to 'brainwash' him."[31]

Rules often are related to "shoulds" that implement them. Some of the common shoulds are the following:

1. I should be generous, considerate, courageous, unselfish, and so on.
2. I should be able to endure hardship.
3. I should be able to solve any problem.
4. I should know and understand everything.
5. I should never tire or become sick.
6. I should always be at top efficiency.

COGNITIVE THERAPY OF DEPRESSION

Rationale of the Cognitive Approach

Depression includes "(a) the observable abnormal behavior or symptom, for example, easy fatigability, crying spells, suicidal threats; (b) the underlying motivational disturbances (if any), such as the wish to avoid activities or to escape from life; (c) underlying the motivation, a cluster of cognitions, such as the belief that striving toward a goal is futile, that there are no satisfactions ahead, and that he is defeated, deprived, and defective."[32] Intervention could be directed at any of these three areas, which constitute a cycle. Cognitive therapy attacks the underlying attitudes, although with the severely depressed patient, intervention may be directed first at a behavioral target.

Symptom, Technique, and Maladaptive Attitude

Although the therapeutic approach may begin at the behavioral level, the underlying attitude component must ultimately be changed. "Thus, the goal is *cognitive modification.* Engaging in activities leading to concrete successes (behavioral method) may help to counteract the attitude."[33] But a multiple approach, focusing on a variety of targets, must be used.

Mechanics of Cognitive Reorganization

The therapist helps the patient to identify the assumptions that underlie his or her depression. The assumptions then are challenged and subjected to argument through questioning them, eliciting the patient's reasons for accepting them, and "marshaling, as in a debate, the evidence in favor of or contradictory to this assumption."[34] Experiments may be set up to test the assumptions.

The following specialized techniques are used in the problem areas, or "targets," considered in the next section.

1. *Scheduled Activity*   Scheduling activities with patients actively structures time and enables the patients to observe their own potential effectiveness.
2. *Graded-Task Assignment*   Success in graded tasks changes patients' self-concepts.
3. *Mastery and Pleasure Therapy*   Patients keep records of all activities and designate each mastery experience with an *M* and each pleasure experience with a *P,* thus increasing their awareness of positive experiences.
4. *Cognitive Reappraisal*   Cognitive reappraisal involves the identification of maladaptive cognitions and attitudes.
5. *Alternative Therapy*   By considering alternative explanations for negative experiences, patients are helped to recognize their biases. By considering alternative ways of handling psychological and situational problems, patient's find solutions to problems previously considered insoluble.
6. *Cognitive Rehearsal*   By imagining that they are carrying out an activity, patients report obstacles and conflicts, which are then discussed.
7. *Homework Assignments*   Assignments are made at each session to counteract depressive symptoms. Patients keep records of negative cognitions in one column and of rational responses in another.

Targets of Cognitive Modification

Inertia, Avoidance, and Fatigue

An activity tailored to the patient is proposed. Reasons against the proposal are elicited from the patient, who is then asked to weigh their validity. The therapist points out why these reasons are self-defeating and invalid and stimulates the patient's interest in attempting the activity. The project is designed to test the validity of the patient's ideas; successful completion will refute the patient's assumption that he or she is incapable of doing it. Constructive attitudes earlier proposed by the therapist are reviewed so that they may be used by the patient to combat negative thoughts and attitudes. The patient is then trained to identify and challenge negative thoughts and to substitute reasonable answers.

Hopelessness and Suicidal Wishes

Skillful questioning reveals the assumptions behind hopelessness and suicidal tendencies. Alternative therapy then shows the patient that there are other interpretations of his or her present and future and other choices than the current behavior, which is leading down a blind alley.

Self-criticisms and Self-blame

Depressed patients blame themselves for all their difficulties. Cognitive therapy aims at making patients aware of their extreme self-criticisms and increasing patients' objectivity about the irrationality and self-destructiveness of their self-criticisms. By questioning and role playing the patient, who is coached to play a harsh critic, the therapist can demonstrate the patient's distortions and false inferences. Training in recognizing and challenging the validity of automatic self-deprecatory thoughts also is effective.

Painful Affect

Encouraging emotional release may reduce the intensity of unpleasant emotions. Patients may feel sympathy for themselves or may direct anger at others, both of which emotions are inconsistent with self-blame. By eliciting amusement through irony or by stimulating patients to engage in an interesting activity, the therapist raises the threshold for sadness. Encouraging the ignoring of unpleasant feelings may raise the threshold for psychic pain.

Mastery and pleasure therapy helps patients to recognize that they have more positive and pleasant experiences than they realize. By having patients record events and asking significant others to assist in recalling pleasant events, the therapist stimulates patients to increase their sense of satisfaction and their sense of competence. This leads to their attempting and succeeding in problem-solving activities, resulting in a more positive self-image. A program of graded-task assignments is useful here.

Imagery techniques are helpful in having patients recollect and recapture earlier pleasant events and successful experiences.

Exaggeration of External Demands

Depressed patients often feel overwhelmed by everyday problems to the point of contemplating suicide. "When the problems are discussed, however, it becomes apparent that the patient has greatly exaggerated their magnitude and importance. Through rational exploration, the patient may regain his perspective and then set about defining what has to be done and how to go about doing it. The therapist generally has to take the lead in helping the patient to list his responsibilities, set priorities, and formulate the appropriate course of action."[35] Cognitive rehearsal can be used to prevent the implementation of this new course of action from being blocked by self-defeating thoughts.

EXAMPLES[36]

The patient was a fifty-two-year-old man who had spent over a year in a hospital without moving away from his bed. He had had many trials of antidepressant medications without any improvement. I saw him for only one visit. At this time, the patient was sitting in a chair next to his bed. After preliminary introductions and general social interchanges, the interview proceeded thus:

Therapist: I understand that you haven't moved away from your bedside for a long time. Why is that?
Patient: I can't walk.
TH: Why is that . . . Are your legs paralyzed?
PT: [irritated] Of course not! I just don't have the energy.
TH: What would happen if you tried to walk?

PT: I'd fall on my face, I guess.
TH: What would you say if I told you that you were capable of walking any place in the hospital?
PT: I'd say you were crazy.
TH: How about testing that out?
PT: What's that?
TH: Whether I'm crazy.
PT: Please don't bother me.
TH: You said you didn't think you could walk. Many depressed people believe that, but when they try it they do better than they expected.
PT: I know I can't walk.
TH: Do you think you could walk a few steps?
PT: No, my legs would cave in.
TH: I'll bet you can walk from here to the door [about 5 yards].
PT: What happens if I can't do it?
TH: I'll catch you.
PT: I'm really too weak to do it.
TH: Suppose I hold your arm. [The patient then took a few steps supported by the therapist. He continued to walk beyond the prescribed 5 yards—without further assistance. He then walked back to his chair, unassisted.]
TH: You did better than you expected.
PT: I guess so.
TH: How about walking down to the end of the corridor [about 20 yards]?
PT: I know I don't have the strength to walk that far.
TH: How far do you think you can walk?
PT: Maybe, to the next room [about 10 yards].

The patient easily walked to the next room and then continued to the end of the corridor. The therapist continued to propose specific goals and to elicit the patient's responses to the goals. After successful completion of each task, a greater distance was proposed.

Within 45 minutes, the patient was able to walk freely around the ward. He was thereby able to "reward" himself for his increased activity by being able to obtain a soda from the vending machine. Later, when he extended the range of his activities, he was able to walk to different points in the hospital and gain satisfaction from various recreational activities. Within a few days, he was playing ping-pong and going to the hospital snack bar, and, in less than a week, he was able to walk around the hospital grounds and enjoy seeing the flowers, shrubs, and trees. Another automatic reward was the favorable response he received from members of the hospital staff and from the other patients. The patient began to speak about himself in positive terms and to make concrete plans for leaving the hospital permanently—a goal he reached in a month.

An example of how a patient may become aware of the logical inconsistencies in his belief system is presented in the following interchange with a woman who had made a recent suicide attempt and still wanted to commit suicide. She had nothing to look forward to since her husband was unfaithful. The therapeutic technique is illustrated below.

TH: Why do you want to end your life?
PT: Without Raymond, I am nothing . . . I can't be happy without Raymond . . . But I can't save our marriage.
TH: What has your marriage been like?

PT: It has been miserable from the very beginning . . . Raymond has always been unfaithful . . . I have hardly seen him in the past five years.

TH: You say that you can't be happy without Raymond . . . Have you found yourself happy when you are with Raymond?

PT: No, we fight all the time and I feel worse.

TH: You say you are nothing without Raymond. Before you met Raymond, did you feel you were nothing?

PT: No, I felt I was somebody.

TH: If you were somebody before you knew Raymond, why do you need him to be somebody now?

PT: [Puzzled] Hmmm . . .

TH: Did you have male friends before you knew Raymond?

PT: I was pretty popular then.

TH: Why do you think you will be unpopular without Raymond now?

PT: Because I will not be able to attract any other man.

TH: Have any men shown an interest in you since you have been married?

PT: A lot of men have made passes at me, but I ignore them.

TH: If you were free of the marriage, do you think that men might be interested in you—knowing that you were available?

PT: I guess that maybe they would be.

TH: Is it possible that you might find a man who would be more constant than Raymond?

PT: I don't know . . . I guess it's possible.

TH: You say that you can't stand the idea of losing the marriage. Is it correct that you have hardly seen your husband in the past five years?

PT: That's right. I only see him a couple of times a year.

TH: Is there any chance of your getting back together with him?

PT: No . . . He has another woman. He doesn't want me.

TH: Then what have you actually lost if you break up the marriage?

PT: I don't know.

TH: Is it possible that you'll get along better if you end the marriage?

PT: There is no guarantee of that.

TH: Do you have a real marriage?

PT: I guess not.

TH: If you don't have a real marriage, what do you actually lose if you decide to end the marriage?

PT: [Long pause] Nothing, I guess.

Following this interview, the patient was more cheerful and it appeared that she was over the suicide crisis. In a subsequent interview, she stated that the point that really struck home was: How could she be "nothing" without Raymond—when she had lived happily and was an adequate person before she ever knew him? She eventually was divorced and settled down to a more stable life.

SUMMARY AND EVALUATION

Cognitive therapy is based on the commonsensical idea that what people think and say can be taken at face value and is significant. Concurrent with thoughts at the level of awareness, however, is a stream of thoughts that usually is outside of awareness. Termed automatic thoughts, these consist, in part, of ideas that may be unreasonable to others but are plausible to the person having them and, in part, of rules and regulations used in self-monitoring and self-instruction. These rules may lead to maladaptive actions.

People respond to events on the basis of the meaning that they attribute to the events, which are interpreted according to their relevance to the self or the personal domain. Different emotions are evoked by the different interpretations. Interpretations that involve distortion of reality give rise to emotional disorders, which are actually disorders in thinking, including the personalization of events, the polarization of thought, and the application of rules in an unconditional, absolute manner.

Cognitive therapy attempts to alleviate emotional disorders by correcting faulty interpretations of reality and faulty reasoning. Therapist and patient establish a collaborative relationship, which emphasizes solving problems rather than changing personal defects.

It is not entirely clear from *Cognitive Therapy and the Emotional Disorders* just how the numerous methods and techniques of cognitive therapy are used. Beck's discussions of techniques are brief, are not systematic, and often repeat earlier comments on the nature of irrational thinking in the various emotional disorders. The use of cognitive therapy to treat depression, which is Beck's special interest, is laid out in more detail.[37] It appears that Beck employs a number of techniques that he has not discussed, such as persuasion, suggestion, admonition, and instruction. Reason alone probably is not the source of the claimed improvement rate of patients and success rate of the therapy. Beck as a therapist apparently exerts a strong personal influence on his patients through his interest, understanding, caring, and concern. The excerpts from therapy sessions may not convey all that goes on in Beck's interaction with patients. It is not clear whether the excerpts are verbatim transcripts or reconstructions from notes and memory. It is difficult to believe that the approach described by Beck could be effective with seriously disturbed patients. While supported by common sense, cognitive therapy is too simplistic to be considered an effective psychotherapy. Emotions are more powerful than are cognitions in everyday normal behavior. The powerlessness and limitations of reasoning and logic are clear when we realize that we cannot persuade another to love or to have any other feeling or emotion.

Mahoney, in his review of Beck's *Cognitive Therapy and the Emotional Disorders,* writes, "This is an important book, pragmatically, historically, and theoretically."[38] The present writer cannot agree. Beck's approach is not new, and it appears to be overrated at a time when cognition is receiving renewed attention. Meichenbaum's evaluation is more reasonable:

> It would appear that the relationship between cognition and emotional and behavioral dysfunctions may be more complex than Beck and his colleagues propose. . . . It is also important to recall that just because we can use cognitive techniques to alleviate some forms of depression, this does not imply that the cognitive events per se cause the emotional disturbance. It is one thing to have clients entertain the notion that their emotional disturbances are due to maladaptive thoughts, and another to demonstrate this empirically.[39]

REFERENCES

1. Beck, A. T. *Cognitive therapy and the emotional disorders.* New York: International Universities Press, 1976. P. 17.

2. Ibid., p. 19. (Italics in original)
3. Ibid., pp. 19–20.
4. Ibid., p. 20.
5. Ibid., p. 27.
6. Ibid., p. 28.
7. Ibid., p. 33.
8. Ibid., pp. 37–38.
9. Ibid., pp. 40–41.
10. Ibid., p. 43.
11. Ibid., p. 46.
12. Ibid., p. 52.
13. Ibid., p. 56.
14. Ibid., p. 90.
15. Ibid., p. 81.
16. Ibid., p. 112.
17. Ibid., p. 130.
18. Ibid., pp. 141–142.
19. Ibid., p. 153.
20. Ibid., p. 159.
21. Ibid., pp. 189–190.
22. Ibid., p. 207.
23. Ibid., p. 211.
24. Ibid., p. 214.
25. Ibid., p. 221.
26. Ibid., pp. 226, 227.
27. Ibid., pp. 233–234.
28. Ibid., p. 258.
29. Ibid., p. 235.
30. Ibid., p. 243.
31. Ibid., p. 257.
32. Ibid., p. 265.
33. Ibid., p. 268.
34. Ibid., p. 270.
35. Ibid., p. 300.
36. Ibid., pp. 284–286, 289–291.
37. For a greatly expanded discussion of the use of cognitive therapy in treating depression, see Beck, A. T., Rush, A. J., Shaw, B. F., & Emery, G. *Cognitive therapy of depression.* New York: Guilford Press, 1979.
38. Mahoney, M. J. Cognitive therapy—a revolutionary contender? (Review of *Cognitive therapy and the emotional disorders* by A. T. Beck). *Contemporary Psychology,* 1977, *22,* 104–105.
39. Meichenbaum, D. Treating depression. (Review of *Cognitive therapy of depression* by A. T. Beck, A. J. Rush, B. F. Shaw, & G. Emery). *Contemporary Psychology,* 1980, *25,* 879–880.

chapter 3

Cognitive Therapy and the Misconception Hypothesis: Raimy

Victor Charles Raimy (b. 1913) received his A.B. from Antioch College in 1935 and his Ph.D. from Ohio State University in 1943. He was an instructor at Ohio State University from 1941 to 1943, when he joined the navy. In 1946, he was assistant professor at the University of Pittsburgh; from 1946 to 1948, associate professor at Ohio State University, and from 1948 to 1978, professor at the University of Colorado, where he was chairman of the Psychology Department from 1954 to 1962. Since 1978, he has been in private practice in Honolulu.

At Ohio State University, Raimy was one of Rogers's first students. His doctoral dissertation, "The Self-Concept as a Factor in Counseling and Personality Organization," was published in 1971. The study of the self-concept has continued to be a focus of his interest. In 1983, Raimy was selected to deliver the Walter V. Clarke Memorial Lecture at the University of Rhode Island. His address was entitled "The Self-Concept: A Forty-year Review."

Raimy is a Diplomate in Clinical Psychology of the American Board of Professional Psychology and is a member of the Division of Clinical Psychology, the Division of Counseling Psychology, and the Division of Psychotherapy of the American Psychological Association, of which he has been a fellow since 1950.

Raimy was the editor of the Boulder Report (*Training in Clinical Psychology,* 1950), which established the scientist–professional training model and in which *psychotherapy* is defined as "an undefined technique applied to unspecified problems with unpredictable outcome. For this technique we recommend rigorous training." Raimy reports that the origin of this definition is unknown.[1]

BACKGROUND AND DEVELOPMENT

The misconception hypothesis developed from Raimy's long interest in the self-concept. He was searching for ways in which self-concept theory could be applied to psychotherapy. The self-concept "is composed of the more or less organized notions, beliefs, and convictions that constitute an individual's knowledge of himself and that influence his relationships with others."[2] Although beliefs about others that contain no self-reference are important in adjustment, they are not as central as are those beliefs that involve the self. Misunderstandings of the self are most important. Therapy based on this hypothesis "emphasizes the role of specific and concrete faulty beliefs in therapy rather than the incomplete and often confusing theories of the self."[3] This approach is not new; indeed, it probably is the oldest method of psychotherapy. It is the essence of the therapy of Adler, the perceptual theory of Combs and Snygg, and, of course, the rational-emotive psychotherapy of Ellis. (Raimy does not refer to Beck.) Elements are present in the approaches of Janet, Breuer, Sullivan, Kelly, Berne, and Freud and in behavior therapy.

PHILOSOPHY AND CONCEPTS

The misconception hypothesis proposes that psychological disturbances are the result of faulty beliefs or convictions—that is, misconceptions. The goal of therapy is the changing of the client's misconceptions, the correction or modification of which leads to improved adjustment. The approach neither specifies nor is limited to any particular methods but recognizes that the changing of misconceptions is one of the goals of most therapies, even those that do not regard cognitive change as the essential nature of psychotherapy. The misconception approach integrates these methods and provides a comprehensive rationale for them.

The misconception hypothesis states that *"if those ideas or conceptions of a client or patient which are relevant to his psychological problems can be changed in the direction of greater accuracy where his reality is concerned, his maladjustments are likely to be eliminated."*[4] The "reality" referred to is not an assumed objective reality, but reality as perceived by clients. Clients who ignore aspects of the reality that they know have misconceptions, or distortions of their own reality.

The self-concept organizes and guides behavior. "Misconceptions about the self may drastically and unrealistically limit the kinds of behavior an individual is willing to engage in, or they may relentlessly force him into unwise behavior which leads to perpetual defeat."[5]

The misconceptions of most individuals are corrected by experience. Those of abnormal or neurotic people are impervious to correction by training, experience, or reasoning by others—the so-called *neurotic paradox*. Many explanations have been proposed for the existence of the neurotic paradox, all of which may have some validity. A central or common core of these explanations is the isolation of misconceptions from conscious awareness. "When misconceptions are avoided, denied, or repressed, they are often kept inaccessible to correction by still other misconceptions, which can be termed 'defensive misconceptions.'"[6] The individual is thus protected by the defensive misconceptions from recognizing more threatening misconceptions.

The individual may appear to be acting on the basis of ignorance, but this is almost never the case. The therapist may carefully explain to the client his or her error, but the misconception remains uncorrected—the so-called teacher's fallacy. Misconceptions may be partially based on ignorance, but they are strong, persistent false beliefs and false convictions that are very difficult to eliminate.

The therapeutic strategy of detecting and changing convictions has a number of advantages.

1. Many common misconceptions are known to most therapists and have been noted in the writings of many therapists (Adler, Combs and Snygg, Rotter, Ellis).
2. Many therapies employ procedures for uncovering misconceptions: free association, nondirective interviewing, Gestalt techniques, dream interpretation, and standard history taking. Thus the therapist can be flexible in choosing ways to discover the client's misconceptions.
3. Misconceptions become a concrete, specific focus of treatment.
4. The procedures and reasoning behind the correction of misconceptions are understandable to the client from experience in other areas of life. No technical language or jargon need be used.
5. Both the therapist and the client have had experience in changing misconceptions. Nothing new or mysterious is required.
6. The therapist has a consistent orientation toward anything and everything that occurs in therapy.
7. Changes in core misconceptions can result in swift and radical changes, in contrast with the slowness of change through other approaches.
8. Past, present, and future are considered, with no focus on a particular time in the client's life.
9. The misconception hypothesis is pragmatic, focusing on observed products of learning, while not denying fundamental processes such as conditioning and other kinds of learning.

In addition to problems common to all psychological treatment, there are a number of specific hazards in locating and changing the client's misconceptions.

1. The client may not recognize or be willing to admit that the problem involves misconceptions. The therapist must infer the misconceptions from the client's presentation of problems.
2. The client may resist the approach as "too rational," insisting that the problem is emotional. The therapist also may resist the method for the same reason.
3. Misconceptions may be couched in an abstract, intellectualized form, leading to fruitless discussions.
4. The client may reject misconceptions identified by the therapist early in treatment but may consider them later, after his or her thinking has changed.
5. The therapist may focus on irrelevant rather than significant misconceptions.
6. The therapist may focus on particular kinds of misconceptions that seem to be important and fail to see others that are more important.
7. Misconceptions may be phrased in inappropriate language for the client, leading to resistance.

8. There are innumerable hazards in attempting to change perceptions. Those that have existed for a long time become convictions that are held tenaciously by the client and sometimes are almost impossible to change.

The number of misconceptions held by the client may be great, overwhelming the therapist. But not all misconceptions need be considered. Some misconceptions are not related to the client's maladjustment; they are "benign" rather than "malignant" or are of minor importance. The client tends to discuss those symptoms and problems of greatest concern. Misconceptions cluster in a hierarchy; when the central misconception is treated, the others are likely to change.

Clusters of Misconceptions

Misconceptions fall into clusters, or syndromes, which facilitates treatment. Five clusters of misconceptions constitute the major standard diagnostic categories, and two other major clusters are commonly seen in clients.

Major Diagnostic Clusters

Many of the symptoms of the common psychiatric disorders are or involve misconceptions. Individuals with *paranoid disorders* manifest delusions: failure of reality testing, disordered content of thought, delusions of persecution, and ideas of reference. Misconceptions are easily identifiable in *depressive neurotics* and include the following:

1. I am, have been, and always will be hopeless.
2. I am, have been, and always will be helpless.
3. I am, have been, and always will be worthless.
4. I never will recover.
5. I am unable to engage in normal activities.
6. I am so guilty and hopeless that suicide is the only solution.
7. I am losing my mind and may become "insane."
8. I alone am responsible for my condition.
9. I am rejected by others because I am worthless.

Obsessives show many of the following misconceptions:

1. I always must be punctual, orderly, conscientious, and reliable.
2. I cannot tolerate dirt and germs.
3. I must control everything and everyone, including myself.
4. I believe that details are important.
5. I must be efficient at all costs.
6. I should not really trust anyone.
7. Being right is more important than anything else.

Hysterical personalities, while suffering acute anxiety and depression, also manifest such misconceptions as the following:

1. I am effective when I am flirtatious, seductive, vivacious, and dramatic.
2. I cannot tolerate frustration and disappointment.
3. By acting helpless and dependent, I can achieve my goals.
4. I am a victim and am not responsible for my problems.
5. I deserve more attention and help from others.
6. I have little interest in sex.

Individuals with *phobic reactions* show three clustered misconceptions.

1. The feared object is dangerous.
2. I probably will collapse when the feared object is present.
3. I cannot eliminate my fear reaction to the object.

Other misconceptions are also present.

Other Major Clusters

Phrenophobia

Phrenophobia is "the false belief, and associated fear, that there is something wrong with one's mind which may result in 'insanity.' "[7] This belief, although widespread, is not widely recognized and often is denied by clients or concealed by misleading terms or euphemisms, such as "nervous breakdown." Phrenophobia is prevalent in all the psychoses and underlies much of the anxiety in sufferers of other conditions and the self-isolation of many patients.

Although there are individual variations in the misconceptions of phrenophobics, a cluster of five usually is present.

1. My pervasive feelings of anxiety and apprehension point to approaching insanity.
2. My memory failures and distortions are signs of mental breakdown.
3. My difficulties in concentration indicate imminent mental disorder.
4. My irritability signals severe mental disturbance.
5. If these symptoms do not lead to psychosis, my persistent insomnia will.

All are misinterpretations of anxiety symptoms arising from sustained tension and stress. In addition to holding these five misconceptions, phrenophobics usually believe that there is little to be gained from working on other problems in the face of impending insanity.

Special-person Misconception

"The psychological core of the special-person cluster of misconceptions is exaggerated self-importance, which has various names—superiority complex, arrogance, vanity, conceit, egotism, and many others."[8] The individual is constantly engaged in attempts to have others acknowledge his or her superiority, which, if threatened, is defended vigorously. If the defense is unsuccessful, serious psychological problems result.

Although the central misconceptions vary with the person, the following six false beliefs are manifested by most.

1. I must control others.
2. I am superior to others.
3. I should not compromise.
4. I suffer from more frustrations than do others.
5. I must strive to be perfect.
6. Others cannot be trusted.

These beliefs may be difficult to recognize early in therapy, since they are overshadowed by anxiety and depression.

The special person's "constant efforts to control, his attitudes of superiority, his refusal to compromise, his masked hostilities, and his empty perfectionism betray the highly competitive person who must have his own way and must be right at all costs. The failure to trust others is manifested by suspiciousness which may at times verge on the paranoid."[9] Such suspiciousness is not actually paranoid, since it is not delusional. Other characteristics of the special person are a highly critical attitude toward others, little empathy with others, lack of insight about the self, and self-righteousness.

Overindulgence in childhood probably is a major determinant of the special-person misconception, although other sources may include early identification with an illustrious parent or with fantasized heroes or heroines. Some persons are successful in maintaining their special self-conception and can be well-adjusted, although their self-centeredness may result in problems with their families and with intimates. Some have been recognized as leaders in various fields. Although a leader, Hitler clearly showed all the misconceptions characteristic of the special person misconception.

THE THERAPIST'S TASK: PRESENTING EVIDENCE

"Therapy based upon the misconception hypothesis provides the therapist with constant, specific goals throughout treatment: to find and change the misconceptions which control undesirable behavior."[10] After diagnosing the central problems of the client and determining the crucial clusters of misconceptions, the therapist turns to the task of changing these misconceptions. "One of the major contentions . . . is that misconceptions of the client or patient can be changed by evidence. When attempting to change misconceptions, the therapist must therefore find ways to present evidence or information which the client can utilize to correct his misconceptions."[11] The core misconceptions are protected by defensive beliefs that must be attacked in the same way. "The process of therapy is, therefore, a cognitive one which attempts to bring the patient closer to reality by rational methods, even though it deals much of the time with the irrationalities of the patient."[12] The term *cognition* is used in the broad sense, as defined by English and English: "A generic term for any process whereby an organism becomes aware or obtains knowledge of an object."[13] Accuracy of perception or correctness of knowledge is not part of the definition.

"The term *evidence* . . . refers to sudden untested insights (or the cognitive component of an emotional outburst, or of a 'feeling') as well as to carefully analyzed data."[14] Feelings, attitudes, and emotions have cognitive elements, either causes or consequences, of which individuals are aware and make use in attempting to understand themselves and to develop self-evaluations. Thinking and cognition are not limited to logic or the rules of evidence; evidence is weighed by emotion and feeling.

Therapists use four methods to present evidence to their clients: (1) self-examination, (2) explanation, (3) self-demonstration, and (4) vicariation. Each is not used in isolation, but all are used together and overlap in most treatment approaches.

Self-Examination

The therapist promotes self-examination by encouraging the client to talk and think about himself or herself—to engage in self-exploration. The client can "discover for himself the information necessary for locating and changing one or more misconceptions. . . . [S]elf-examination can be regarded as a procedure in which the therapist indirectly makes evidence available to the client or patient."[15] The purest form of self-examination is employed in client-centered therapy, which encourages reflection and clarification to facilitate the client's self-exploration.

The client's self-examination can lead to the elimination of defensive misconceptions, to the perception of new relationships, and to the discovery of previously undetected characteristics about the self and others.

Self-examination is limited if the client's misconceptions are based on technical information—for example, false beliefs about physical, physiological, or psychological conditions. It also can be inefficient, sometimes taking months for a client to discover some of his or her major misconceptions. Yet early intervention by the therapist can lead to the client's dependence on the therapist.

Explanation

Explanation includes a number of techniques, in addition to helping clients locate misconceptions and to leading them into self-examination, self-demonstration, and vicariation.

In *interpretation* and *confrontation,* the therapist gives the patient information that he or she does not have or does not regard as relevant. *Reflection of feeling* subtly emphasizes meanings that the client has expressed, including cognitions and emotions, and that convey information by focusing the client's attention on meanings that have not been recognized or emphasized. *Questions* can call the client's attention to unacknowledged or ignored evidence. *Suggestion and exhortation* present evidence directly, in a way that does not give the client the opportunity to question it, and depend on the therapist's authority as an expert. Finally (although this does not exhaust the kinds of explanation), by teaching the client specific *therapeutic frames of reference,* the therapist can lay the groundwork for correcting misconceptions. *Structuring* the client's role, correcting misconceptions about psychotherapy, is a form of this technique.

Explanations are not always effective. However, "if, as the misconception hypothesis proposes, the primary task of the therapist is to change misconceptions, then explanations aimed directly at relevant misconceptions can be one of the effective methods for changing them."[16]

Self-Demonstration

"Self-demonstration refers to any procedure whereby a therapist encourages a patient to participate in a situation in which he can observe his own misconceptions or obtain direct evidence from self-observation that he can change his misconceptions."[17] It includes both real and imagined situations. "The therapist maneuvers the patient into experiencing his false convictions or beliefs about himself, or about himself in relation to others"[18] Maneuvering differs from manipulating because the therapist openly and clearly explains the purpose of self-demonstration.

As people grow up, they engage in self-demonstration in everyday living. Self-demonstration also is used in several therapies: the structure of client-centered therapy makes it a continual self-demonstration procedure; it is part of analysis of the transference in psychoanalysis, a major element in the Gestalt therapy of Perls, and a technique of behavior therapy, encounter groups, and psychodrama.

Vicariation

Vicariation includes modeling, in which clients observe a model performing an activity and imagine themselves performing the same activity. In the process, they correct their misconceptions that the activity is dangerous or unpleasant, that the experience would lead to their being overwhelmed or collapsing, and that they are incapable of performing the activity.

THE PATIENT'S TASK: COGNITIVE REVIEW

Little is known about the process of cognitive review. The principle is simple: "For an individual to change a concept of any kind, he must ordinarily be afforded opportunities to examine and reexamine all available evidence that is relevant to the concept."[19] Complex misconceptions seldom are changed after only one examination of the evidence.

In working on the psychological problems of daily life, people engage in cognitive review. In therapy, it is not simply a cold intellectual process but includes cognitive aspects of affective responses. Communicating with another, as in therapy, facilitates cognitive review, not only because therapists can make a contribution, but also because clients must organize their thought and communication and can adopt a more objective attitude toward their problems. Most people resolve their problems through solitary cognitive review, however.

Cognitive review is not always successful, for a number of reasons.

1. Simple introspection may not uncover the central misconceptions.
2. It is more difficult to recognize one's own misconceptions than those of others.
3. "[E]motionally toned misconceptions, with much negative affect, produce avoidant reactions during introspection."[20]
4. Learned avoidance reactions may require more than cognitive review to dislodge them. The therapist should utilize such methods as extinction or counterconditioning in stubborn cases.
5. Patients may not verbalize their misconceptions clearly and may fail to modify their style of self-examination, falling into a vicious circle.

The client who engages in repeated cognitive review reaches a different and better solution. In addition to simple verbal review, the client can be led to engage in imagined repetition of interactions with objects or persons who are the source of misconceptions.

Cognitive review is employed in most major approaches to psychotherapy, including psychoanalysis, Gestalt therapy, Frankl's therapy of paradoxical intention, client-centered therapy, and behavior therapy.

AFFECT AND INSIGHT IN COGNITIVE THERAPY

Cognitive therapy cannot ignore feelings and emotions, since "inappropriate emotions and feelings are probably the best indicators of the presence of misconceptions."[21] That is, cognitions produce the emotional arousal, and changes in cognitions will reduce or eliminate the emotion.

Cognition and Affect

Theorists are faced with the dilemma of separating inappropriate affect from cognition. The cognitive viewpoint "has a major advantage for psychotherapists in that its referents—the conceptions and misconceptions of the patient—are more accessible to direct observation whereas 'expression' of affect and conditioning are not. In fact, the latter two usually must be inferred from the patient's reported cognitions unless the more laborious procedure of examining behavioral changes *in vivo* is adopted."[22]

Emotional experiences always include cognitive elements. Emotions that have different labels have the same physiological indicators; it is their cognitive aspects that distinguish them. Thus if "clients or patients can be induced to perceive differently those situations which produce disruptive feelings or emotions, their affect can be altered in a therapeutic fashion. In other words, the bonds between cognition and a given maladaptive emotion or feeling can be severed if the cognition is changed."[23]

Research supports the contention that cognitive factors enter into the *appraisal* (interpretation and evaluation) of situations, which determines how the situations are evaluated emotionally. "If cognition creates emotions and feelings, then therapists can use cognitions to modify or eliminate emotions and feelings—mainly by encouraging the client to repeatedly review the misconceptions embedded in a particularly affect-laden topic which interferes with his adjustment."[24]

Therapy is also influenced by *reflexive awareness* (memory of feelings and emotions), which is a factor in the client's perception of the self. Discussions of these memories and self-labels, which are cognitive, may result in additional affect, which leads to recognition of the cognitive factors that produced the inappropriate affect. Cognitive components of appraisal and reflexive awareness can be misinterpreted, resulting in misconceptions, which can be changed by cognitive review.

Insight

In psychotherapy, *insight* is defined as "the individual's recognition that he suffers from a specific misconception or a cluster of related misconceptions."[25] Recognition of misconceptions represents a changed perception, which makes it possible to discard the misconception. Thus therapy consists of a series of insights. Verbalization of insights can be very difficult; the therapist can help the client to phrase and clarify the misconceptions as they are recognized.

It is not necessary to distinguish between intellectual insight and emotional insight. The former may involve the client's simply verbalizing what the therapist has said, without any real recognition of the misconception. The insight may relate to an irrelevant misconception or may be only a partial understanding. Insight may not lead to change if the client does not have a good solution to the problem.

EXAMPLES

Employment of Cognitive Review[26]

The following brief case of Pete is presented only as an illustration of the procedure. This forty-eight-year-old truck driver was hospitalized at his own request for treatment of arm and shoulder pains which prevented him from working and led to his decision to sell his truck. Because he was also mildly depressed, had little self-confidence, and had suffered a blackout period while driving his truck, he was transferred to a psychiatric ward. No physical disabilities were discovered except for mild arthritis.

During several hours of history taking and general orientation for the therapist, it was discovered that Pete's primary problem seemed to reside in his complete avoidance of anyone but his immediate family. He feared that he had cracked up and was greatly ashamed about a feud which he had carried on with a government agency. His symptoms had persisted for about six weeks before I saw him. He complained of being reduced to watching television outside the hospital, since he had been a very sociable person who greatly enjoyed the company of other men; at one time he had owned a bar.

Since Pete had mentioned one of his former supervisors, Bill, with whom he had been friendly for several years but had not dared visit for six weeks, I asked him to close his eyes and imagine that he was paying a social call on Bill during his next weekend pass. At first he protested that it was impossible; that he had tried to visit Bill several times but had never reached his house. Finally he agreed to try, and closed his eyes while grimacing. As expected, Pete's first reaction was again an avoidance response: he described reaching Bill's house only to find a car parked in front of it; he returned home because he was certain that Bill had visitors. I then assured him that there were no visitors there. Pete started his second attempt by saying that he was taking his wife with him on the visit because her presence would take some of the "spotlight" away from him. This time he managed to ring the bell and entered the house with his wife. Bill greeted him in his usual fashion but "looked carefully at me to see how crazy I am." Pete was so uncomfortable that he left after only a few minutes, feeling very tense. On the third try, Pete again took his wife with him and managed to stay about half an hour; this time Bill did not seem very suspicious of his mental status. Since our time was up, the three scenes having taken about forty minutes, I suggested that he try visiting Bill over the weekend, but Pete shook his head doubtfully.

When I saw him again, on Tuesday of the following week, Pete talked about other things until, looking pleased, he said that he had visited Bill two days ago without his wife. He said that he was quite tense at first but that Bill had treated him as always and he had had a good time. He had not only talked the whole afternoon with Bill, but Bill's brother, whom Pete barely knew, was there for an hour during his visit. After having demonstrated to himself that he could engage in his usual social activities, Pete visited other friends the following day, attended to some business matters in downtown offices, and asked for his discharge before the week was out.

Exploration of Cognitive Content of Affective Reactions[27]

A client described a series of claustrophobic-like episodes which interfered with his normal social life and caused him considerable concern. Claustrophobic in itself implies that a misconception is at work, and the patient's report of his emotional reactions to confined places revealed the misconception. But why did he develop these fears at the age of thirty-four when he had not previously been claustrophobic? Further exploration revealed that he was engaged to a woman who was about to become his second wife. She lived in a small apartment and drove him about in her Volkswagen. Unknown to her, he had become seriously disillusioned and wanted to terminate the engagement. He was held back by his desire to keep from hurting her, his own fear that he was messing up his second marital relationship, and the fact that his fiancée was the niece of his employer. When each of these factors was worked through, his symptoms disappeared. The path to them had been marked, however, by his initial fear of small, enclosed places. The path to recovery also revealed his misconceptions about the consequences of terminating the engagement.

Development of Insight[28]

The following incident exemplifies the attainment of insight in a patient of high verbal ability who was able to put his changed perception of himself into words. Since this patient had shown a lack of confidence when seeking work, I asked him to picture and describe himself applying for a job. Instead of complying, he began to object strenuously on the grounds that "all that psychology is for the birds." Switching tactics, I quickly asked him to repeat exactly what he had said, and with the same intensity, but to listen to himself as he did so. Taken by surprise, he complied. At the end of the second repetition, he launched himself out of his chair and in a wonder-struck tone exclaimed, "My God, I'm really an arrogant bastard!" That self-description would have been accepted by many who knew him, but this was the first time I had heard him reveal such insight.

Prior to his recognition of his misconception about himself, he had described himself as a downtrodden, oppressed person who was trying by sheer will power to return to normal. My efforts at treatment had usually been derided as "all that psychotherapy nonsense." He had been told by others that he had a supercilious attitude, but he had always rationalized this as due to the hostility of others. When his attention was directed to his own repeated acting out of his angry rejection of the therapist's efforts, he was able for the first time to recognize his arrogance. His insight was lacking in historical elements, but he saw clearly that he had had a faulty conception of himself.

The following illustration shows that essentially similar insights can result from either a historical or a contemporaneous approach. A thirty-year-old school teacher regarded himself as a "sensitive" person who valued being a "nice guy." Having read widely in psychoanalysis, he invariably explored his past during treatment in an effort to understand his not infrequent current rejections. Although I had suggested to him that some of his behavior might produce rejection by others, he much preferred to believe that his greater sensitivity somehow elicited "envy" in others.

In the course of his historical explorations, he eventually remembered that during the first few years of school he had "been picked on by the other kids." Aloud, I wondered why. He tried to explain that even then he had been very sensitive, to the extent that his peers took advantage of him. At that point, he had another recollection that he had been in many fights during that period. He also remembered the rages which overcame him, so that he himself provoked some of the fights. This recollection made him question his assertion that he had always been a nice guy.

As he continued the exploration, he remembered that in junior high he had decided to imitate an older brother, and to act as though he liked everyone to avoid social conflicts. He added that at first he had felt hypocritical but that this feeling had disappeared. His underlying hostilities had not disappeared, but he felt that they were under control.

Armed with the knowledge that he was more hostile than he had surmised, he began to explore his current behavior with others. For the first time, he recognized that despite his own claim to being always a "nice guy," he would occasionally vent his hostilities toward someone who did not appreciate him sufficiently or who interfered with him "too much." Previously he had ascribed these displays of hostility to temporary feelings of fatigue or to the tendency of others to envy his sensitivity. Now he was able to recognize that there were understandable internal sources for his hostility, quite different from those he had assumed.

In the illustration, the client had started his self-examination in the past because of his own predilection for that orientation. He had, however, continued to examine the findings for their implications for the present. If he had started with his present relationships, he undoubtedly would have arrived at the same insight—that he was often hostile and that he was not always a nice guy.

SUMMARY AND EVALUATION

Raimy summarizes his approach in fourteen principles.

1. Effective therapy must modify or change learned misconceptions, which are faulty beliefs or mistaken ideas.
2. When clearly identified in therapy, misconceptions are specific and concrete.
3. Misconceptions often are kept from awareness by less threatening, defensive misconceptions. The existence of defensive misconceptions and the difficulty of clearly identifying misconceptions result in extensive therapy rather than simple reeducation.
4. The goals of therapy are to find and change the misconceptions that lead to undesirable behavior.
5. Among the many procedures for discovering relevant misconceptions are the interview, self-examination by the client, and the techniques used by therapists of other schools of thought.
6. Misconceptions usually fall into clusters, which facilitates the therapist's task.
7. The therapist must identify the crucial clusters, which may take considerable time.
8. Clusters of misconceptions are related to diagnostic categories, which can be more meaningful to the therapist than can the common psychiatric diagnoses.
9. Misconceptions can be attacked with many procedures and techniques, including self-examination, explanation, self-demonstration, and vicariation (modeling). These are used, to some extent at least, in all therapies.
10. Repeated cognitive review by the client leads to modification or elimination of misconceptions, which is an element in all therapies.

11. Emotions and feelings are controlled by cognitions; faulty perceptions, beliefs, and convictions lead to emotional disturbance.
12. Emotional reactions that are evoked during therapy point to underlying misconceptions that may require correction.
13. Insight is the client's recognition that he or she has one or more misconceptions.
14. The number and quality of a client's insights provides a measure of therapeutic progress.

These general principles can be implemented by many techniques. "Perhaps the most useful contribution of the hypothesis to the practicing therapist is that it frees him from the tyranny of technique."[29]

Raimy's approach to cognitive therapy appears to be the most adequate of the three included in this book.

1. It gives much attention to theoretical foundations.
2. It presents a systematic and integrated approach, with its concept of the clusters of misconceptions and its organization of treatment techniques.
3. It provides an excellent survey of the cognitive aspects of other major theories, resulting in an almost eclectic approach.
4. It deals with the problem of the relation between affect and cognition, although not in an entirely satisfactory way.

Raimy recognizes that feelings, attitudes, and emotions have cognitive consequences,[30] but he goes no further with this line of thought. Rather, he focuses, as do Ellis and Beck, on the cognitive *causes* of emotion. "Affect is largely controlled by cognitions which produce emotional arousal . . ."[31] and "Cognitions control emotions and feelings."[33] Raimy has said that he chooses to focus on cognitions because they are more easily observable than are affect or emotions—a poor reason for neglecting the latter—and has referred to research that shows the influence of cognition on perception and resultant emotions, but not to research that shows the influence of beliefs and attitudes on perception and cognition.[32]

While the recognition of a circular or a reciprocal relationship between cognition and emotions would allow for intervention at the cognitive level, it is possible that intervention at the emotional level would be more effective. It is clear that intervention at the cognitive level is very difficult and often futile. Raimy recognizes the frequent ineffectiveness of explanation, which includes suggestion and exhortation, in the face of strongly held beliefs and attitudes. Cognitive therapists apparently do not know how to deal with affect except by cognitive methods of explaining reasoning, persuading, and so on. The three cognitive approaches presented in this book are clear in showing the struggle and difficulty of trying to cure unreason by reason. There must be a better way. The concern of the therapist and the effort expended suggest that something more than reason is involved in any successes of cognitive therapy. Indeed, most, if not all, of the effects of the cognitive therapies may be due to the placebo.[33]

It is certainly true that affect must be recognized as a cause as well as a consequence of misconceptions[34] and dealt with directly by methods other than the limited ones of cognitive therapy.

Raimy does not claim to present a new form of therapy but to focus on the therapeutic elements of all therapies, which he considers to be cognitive. It may be argued that since few therapists have adopted or practice Raimy's approach, it does not warrant inclusion in this book. But many, if not most, therapists use one or several of the methods or techniques considered by Raimy, who has organized them and given them a theoretical rationale. The concept of misconception as the basis of emotional disturbance is the core. The discovery and treatment—or correction—of misconceptions can be and are achieved in different ways by means of different therapies. Raimy has made a significant contribution by showing how these methods can be integrated and in doing so, he has provided a partial basis for an eclectic psychotherapy.

REFERENCES

1. Raimy, V. Personal communication, March 28, 1984.
2. Raimy, V. *Misunderstandings of the self: Cognitive psychotherapy and the misconception hypothesis.* San Francisco: Jossey-Bass, 1975. P. xi.
3. Ibid., p. xii.
4. Ibid., p. 7. (Italics in original)
5. Ibid., p. 9.
6. Ibid., p. 14.
7. Ibid., p. 103.
8. Ibid., p. 109.
9. Ibid., pp. 111–112.
10. Ibid., p. 187.
11. Ibid., p. 42.
12. Ibid., pp. 42–43.
13. English, H. B., & English, A. *A comprehensive dictionary of psychological and psychoanalytical terms.* New York: Longmans, Green, 1958.
14. Raimy, *Misunderstandings of the self,* p. 43.
15. Ibid., p. 46.
16. Ibid., p. 52.
17. Ibid., p. 53.
18. Ibid.
19. Ibid., p. 61.
20. Ibid., p. 63.
21. Ibid., p. 80.
22. Ibid., p. 83.
23. Ibid., p. 84.
24. Ibid., p. 85.
25. Ibid., p. 92.
26. Ibid., pp. 77–78.
27. Ibid., pp. 87–88.
28. Ibid., pp. 93–95.
29. Ibid., p. 199.
30. Ibid., p. 43.
31. Ibid., p. 82.
32. Ibid., p. 195.
33. Bootzin, R. B., & Lick, J. R. Expectancies in therapy research: Interpretive artifact or

mediating mechanism? *Journal of Consulting and Clinical Psychology,* 1979, *47,* 852–855; Kazdin, A. E. Nonspecific treatment factors in psychotherapy outcome research. *Journal of Consulting and Clinical Psychology,* 1979, *47,* 846–851; Kirsch, I. The placebo effect and the cognitive-behavioral revolution. *Cognitive Therapy and Research,* 1978, *2,* 255–264.

34. Zajonc, R. B. On the primacy of affect. *American Psychologist,* 1984, *39,* 117–123; Lazarus, R. S. On the primacy of cognition. *American Psychologist,* 1984, *39,* 124–129.

two

LEARNING THEORY APPROACHES

Learning may be defined as changes in behavior that are not due to native response tendencies, maturation, or temporary states of the organism (for example, fatigue or drugs).[1] Counseling or psychotherapy is concerned with behavior change and must, therefore, involve learning and learning theory. Counseling or psychotherapy would thus be an application of principles of learning or learning theory.

While this reasoning is essentially acceptable to most psychologists and counselors, the actual situation is not as simple as such reasoning may suggest. Most approaches to counseling or psychotherapy have not developed from learning theory. Although it would appear that any approach must be consistent with or explainable by learning theory, most approaches have not been systematically evaluated from this point of view.

Two reasons apparently account for this lack of rapprochement. First, learning theory is still in a stage where it cannot be automatically applied widely to practical situations, particularly to situations involving abnormalities of behavior or deviation from normal behavior. While experimentation and research have recently burgeoned beyond the laboratory, they are limited for the most part to relatively simple behaviors in controlled situations.

Kimble, summarizing the situation regarding conditioning, writes:

It may, some day, be known whether the laws of conditioning do or do not explain (say) psychopathological behavior. But that day is still far in the future. For the time being all that is possible is to attempt the explanation of complex phenomena in simpler terms. It is to be expected that the resulting explanations will be incomplete and imperfect. Complex behavior, if it is explainable at all in these terms, certainly

63

involves the simultaneous operation of many principles of conditioning. Unfortunately, these principles are not exactly known, and we know even less about the way in which they combine and function together.[2]

This statement should be kept in mind when reading accounts of therapy based on learning theory and principles. These accounts usually state or imply that the methods are based on known and experimentally demonstrated principles of learning.

Second, it is not possible to speak of *a* learning theory or *a* theory of learning. There is no single theory, but many theories usually related, in the case of human beings, to limited areas of behavior, such as paired-associates learning of nonsense syllables or learning a simple psychomotor performance. Thus when the claim is made that a particular approach or method of psychotherapy or counseling is an application of, or is based on, learning theory or learning principles, one must ask, "What theory?" or "What principles?"

The two major sources in learning for the various methods and techniques of learning based approaches to counseling or psychotherapy are classical (or respondent) conditioning and operant (or instrumental) conditioning. Classical conditioning derives from the work of Pavlov. Although others before him had recognized and studied conditioning, he was the first to study it systematically and intensively. The paradigm for classical conditioning is the presence of an unconditioned stimulus that automatically evokes an unconditioned response and a conditioned stimulus that evokes a conditioned response—which is similar to, or a part of, the unconditioned response—when paired with (presented shortly before) the unconditioned stimulus. Three aspects of classical conditioning are overlooked or ignored by many of those who apply this model to complex behavior in counseling or psychotherapy. The first is that the conditioned response is not identical with the unconditioned response, sometimes being quite different and constituting an anticipatory response. The second is that (as Pavlov noted in his work with dogs) the specific response is not the only behavior evoked by the unconditioned or the conditioned stimulus; the total organism responds, so that there are what might be termed "side effects" in conditioning. The third is that in laboratory work on conditioning, the subject is in a situation from which it cannot escape by developing avoidance (or instrumental) responses.

In operant conditioning, voluntarily or spontaneously emitted (operant) behavior is strengthened by positive reinforcement (reward) or is discouraged by negative reinforcement, which is a stimulus whose removal increases the probability of the behavior it follows, by lack of reinforcement (failure to reward either positively or negatively), or by punishment. The terms *operant* and *instrumental* derive from the concept that the conditioned behavior operates on the environment or is instrumental in obtaining the reinforcement or the reward. In this sense, the behavior appears to be beyond the control of the experimenter. Behavior, it is emphasized, is controlled by its consequences. Yet, since the experimenter controls the consequences or the application of reinforcers or punishment, he or she does control the behavior of the subject. There is an implication of cognitive awareness and choice, yet awareness is not necessary for conditioning to occur; in fact, strict behaviorists reject the existence of choice.

Classical and operant conditioning are not distinctly separable. In classical conditioning, the unconditioned stimulus follows the conditioned stimulus. Thus the unconditioned stimulus may be seen, in operant conditioning terms, as reinforcing the associa-tion between the conditioned stimulus and the response. In operant conditioning, the reinforcement follows the response that it is desired to strengthen, and this response may be said to become associated with the action (or stimulus) that preceded it. In operant conditioning, the voluntary, spontaneously emitted behavior that is said to "produce" the reinforcement may be seen as the unconditioned stimulus. In classical conditioning, the unconditioned stimulus is independent of the subject's behavior, while in operant conditioning, it is dependent (contingent) on the subject's behavior. As Yates points out, if a classical conditioning experiment, in which a conditioned stimulus is associated with a shock leading to a dog's involuntarily lifting its paw when the conditioned stimulus is presented alone, is changed so that the animal is allowed to escape or avoid the shock by lifting its paw before the unconditioned stimulus has occurred, then classical aversive conditioning becomes instrumental, or operant, aversive conditioning.[3]

Attempts have been made to combine or integrate the two types of conditioning into one model. Pavlov tried to reduce instrumental conditioning to classical condition-ing. Hull's system sought to reduce classical conditioning to instrumental conditioning. Mowrer, who earlier proposed a two-factor theory of learning based on distinction between classical and instrumental conditioning,[4] later attempted to bring them to-gether under the classical position.[5]

Concern about the relationship between learning and counseling or psychother-apy dates back many years.[6–13] The early discussions were mainly concerned with reinforcement theory and were mainly limited to interpretation or translation of meth-ods of counseling or psychotherapy, such as psychoanalysis, into learning theory terms. The work of Dollard and Miller[14] is classical and is, therefore, included in this section. Rotter's social learning theory,[15] involving reinforcement, is an interesting variant and is also included. It is similar to the work of Dollard and Miller in that it is theory based, deductive in orientation, and related to clinical experience in counseling or psychother-apy. Two other systematic attempts are those of the Pepinskys[16] and of Pascal.[17] Phillips's interference theory approach is also a variant of reinforcement theory.[18]

In contrast to these essentially reinforcement theory approaches is Salter's appli-cation of classical conditioning.[19] Wolpe's method,[20] included here, is also based essen-tially on classical conditioning. The classical conditioning approach to modifying human behavior dates back to the work of Jones with Peter and the rabbit,[21] under the influence of Watson.[22]

Learning approaches to counseling or psychotherapy are not restricted to either the classical or the instrumental paradigm, however. Salter is probably closest to the classical approach. Wolpe is less restricted to classical conditioning, although his theoretical base derives essentially from this paradigm. Dollard and Miller, developing their work from Hull's theory, emphasize reinforcement and are thus closer to the operant paradigm.

The recent work in operant conditioning derives from Skinner.[23] Operant condi-tioning was first considered in relation to counseling or psychotherapy in terms of verbal conditioning in interviews.[24–32] This work has not been developed into an integrated systematic approach to counseling or psychotherapy, which is no doubt because of the atheoretical and operationalistic influence of Skinner.

The use of operant conditioning in modifying the behavior of hospitalized psychiatric patients was apparently first explored by Peters[33] and by Lindsley.[34] Its application in institutional settings, including the classroom, has burgeoned tremendously since then.

The term *behavior therapy* probably was first used by Lindsley.[35] (Lazarus[36] and Eysenck[37] later used the term independently of Lindsley and of each other.) It has come into common usage and refers to the application of a wide variety of techniques derived from or related to learning principles or theory in order to modify more or less specific abnormal behaviors, both in the counseling or therapy interview and outside. The term *behavior modification* is also widely used, often interchangeably with *behavior therapy,* particularly in this country, to refer to operant conditioning methods as distinguished from the behavior therapy of Wolpe or, more generally, to cover the application of learning principles in a wide variety of situations outside the therapy interview. Here we are limiting our concern to interview-mediated behavior change; programs or systems for changing behavior in institutions, such as token economies, are not considered.

Research and writing in this area proliferated rapidly in the 1960s, with new journals being established to accommodate briefer reports of research and case studies (for example, *Journal of the Experimental Analysis of Behavior, Behavior Research and Therapy, Journal of Applied Behavior Analysis*), edited books being published to provide surveys and reviews,[38–47] and case studies and books being written to include more extensive treatments of the field.[48–51] The extent of the activity and the implications for psychotherapy and behavior change have led to the application of the word *revolution* to the movement.[52–53] Levis suggests that behavior therapy constitutes the fourth revolution (following Pinel, Freud, and community mental health).[54]

Unlike earlier approaches to counseling or psychotherapy, and although the term *learning theory* is frequently used, behavior therapy or behavior modification is essentially atheoretical and even nonsystematic. It is empirical, experimental-analytic, and inductive rather than deductive. Ullmann and Krasner note that "while there are many techniques, there are few concepts or general principles involved in behavior therapy."[55] Books on behavior therapy thus are essentially compendiums of techniques and methods. They are not systematic in the sense that an author has adopted a theoretical point of view, developed its philosophy and assumptions, and presented techniques derived from, or consistent with, the assumptions and theory. Behavior therapy, Yates claims, is inductive rather than deductive, is based on experiments, and applies the experimental method to the treatment of the individual client. Thus Yates states that Dollard and Miller were not behavior therapists and that even Wolpe is not considered a behavior therapist in the British usage of the term.[56]

Yates defines behavior therapy as

> the attempt to utilize systematically that body of empirical and theoretical knowledge which has resulted from the application of the experimental method in psychology and its closely related disciplines (physiology and neurophysiology) in order to explain the genesis and maintenance of abnormal patterns of behavior; and to apply that knowledge to the treatment or prevention of those abnormalities by means of controlled experimental studies of the single case, both descriptive and remedial.[57]

Not all those who call themselves behavior therapists function in this manner or only in this manner, however. Nor is the atheoretical, empirical limitation accepted by all behavior therapists. Franks, for example, writes:

In the best of all possible worlds, it would seem highly desirable for the therapist to aspire to be a scientist even if this goal were difficult to realize. To function as a scientist, it is necessary to espouse some theoretical framework. . . . How the behavior therapist practices (including his choice of technique, his approach to the problems or general strategy, and his specific relationships with his patient) thus depends both upon his explicit theoretical orientation and upon his implicit philosophical and cultural milieu.[58]

There is evidence that behavior therapists are becoming more diverse and are moving toward so-called traditional counseling or psychotherapy, particularly in recognizing the importance of the counselor–client relationship. (The importance of the experimenter–subject relationship in verbal conditioning has been demonstrated by the research referred to earlier.) Many behavior therapists are acknowledging the importance of cognitive and affective variables, including awareness or consciousness.[59] There appears to be a movement away from the application of techniques taken from laboratory research to the recognition of the complexities of human *in situ* behavior, as compared with the behavior of animals in the laboratory. Franks, for example, asks:

Can it be assumed, on the basis of a concomitance that is sometimes observed between certain measures of acquisition and extinction in the laboratory, that there must inevitably be a high positive relationship between the rapidity and strength with which new responses are acquired during behavior therapy and the resistance to the therapeutic extinction of possibly quite different responses which are already in existence? Similar issues arise with respect to the generalization of conditional responses during therapy. If the basic parameters of laboratory conditioning are still in dispute, it is hardly surprising that the relationships between conditioning in the laboratory and conditioning in the clinical situation remain unclear. Unfortunately, many clinical investigators proceed as if the relationships were clear.[60]

With such diversity among those who call themselves behavior therapists, it may be questioned whether there is *a* behavior therapy or behavior *therapies.* Nevertheless, Franks argues for the term *behavior therapy,* even though he admits that "there is a bewildering conglomeration of techniques," on the basis that "all forms of behavior therapy are predicated upon the common, explicit, systematic, and a priori usage of learning principles to achieve well-defined and pre-determined goals."[61] He feels that the term *behavior therapies* "implies little more than a grab bag of behaviorally oriented therapeutic techniques." Yates takes the same position.[62] The Association for the Advancement of the Behavioral Therapies changed its name to the singular in 1968, and the singular is used by most writers, even though they include or refer to a variety of methods or approaches that are not integrated into any system.

Yet the observer may obtain the strong impression that behavior therapy is essentially little more than a grab bag of techniques, applied to specific problems with little theoretical justification or support. Certainly, no systematic, integrated, theoretically oriented presentation of behavior therapy has appeared. Perhaps this represents the state of the field at the present time, and it is too early to expect an integration of the proliferating techniques and methods into a systematic approach. Certainly, any such attempt would be exceedingly difficult. It is not the function of this book, nor is it within the capabilities of this author, to present a systematic position when none exists or has been attempted by proponents of the position.

Krasner notes that "as one plods through the vast literature on behavior therapy, one is reminded of the parable of the blind men who described the elephant solely on the basis of their feeling the animal." Each described a different part of the elephant. Krasner feels that "the elephant of behavior therapy does indeed exist and can be discriminated from other creatures of the jungle."[63] He proposes to do so in his review and lists 15 streams of development of behavior therapy, including social psychology and social learning, and reviews the literature of the latter 1960s to give a broad overview of behavior therapy, but he does not articulate the parts of the elephant into a whole.

Kanfer and Phillips call for "establishing a well integrated framework from which a practitioner can derive new techniques with clearly stated rationales with predictable effects and with well defined criteria and methods for examining their efficacy."[64] So far, there is no well-integrated framework. The earlier works of Dollard and Miller and of Wolpe, as well as others who are not included here, while they are not comprehensive or all-inclusive, are systematic. Apparently, no one is interested enough or feels able to attempt a current integration. No doubt this is in part a result of the current reaction against schools or systems. It is also perhaps rooted in the empirical foundations of behavior modification.

Wolpe's work, including his 1958 book and its supplementation in 1969, 1973, and 1982, offers a relatively systematic view of behavior therapy based mainly on classical conditioning theory and research. There appears to be no comparable presentation of therapy based on operant conditioning theory and research, nor is there a systematic attempt to integrate both these approaches under a broader, more comprehensive learning theory. However, there is a broadly based compendium of behavior therapy that includes both of these approaches, presenting them as separate models, and therapeutic procedures that partake of both models, presenting them as mixed models. This is the work of Kanfer and Phillips. This section includes a summary of this work, which probably presents the best statement of a comprehensive behavior therapy to date.

Space does not permit an adequate evaluation of behavior therapy here. A number of critiques (and rejoinders) have been published.[65] The most comprehensive review and evaluation currently available is probably the chapter by Murray and Jacobson in *Handbook of Psychotherapy and Behavior Change*.[66] Behavior therapists in general appear to be becoming less parochial, less narrow and rigid, and less simplistic. As experience and research accumulate, there is a recognition of the complexities of human behavior and behavior problems and a realization that behavior therapy is not a panacea. The book by Kanfer and Phillips is a case in point.

Lazarus, who has been identified as a behavior therapist and who was associated with Wolpe for several years, has presented a critical review of behavior therapy. He writes that "the methods of behavior therapy are extremely effective when applied to carefully selected cases by informed practitioners. But when procedures overstep the boundaries of their legitimate terrain, ridicule and disparagement are most likely to ensue. Far from being a panacea, the methods are then held to have no merit whatsoever, and the proverbial baby gets thrown out with the bath water."[67] He continues:

"The danger lies in a premature elevation of learning principles into unwarranted scientific truths and the ascription of the general term of 'modern learning theory' to what in reality are best described as 'modern learning theories'. . . . Thus, Eysenck's insistence that behavior therapy denotes 'methods of treatment which are derived from modern learning theory' amounts to little more than a beguiling slogan."[68] He regards Wolpe's 20 or so behavioral techniques as "a useful *starting point* for increased clinical effectiveness rather than a complete system which can put an end to 90 percent of the world's neurotic suffering."[69] He regards behavior therapy as an objective psychotherapeutic adjunct. He states that "several behavior therapists now acknowledge the fact that more varied and complex interactional processes other than reciprocal inhibition and operant conditioning permeate their interviews and contaminate or facilitate the application of their specific techniques."[70]

The more complex and varied processes, to use Lazarus's term, include not only processes associated with the relationship between the therapist and the client, but also cognitive processes. Cognitive elements have always been present in learning theory approaches to psychotherapy. Dollard and Miller explicitly consider higher mental processes in the development and treatment of emotional problems. Kanfer and Phillips also acknowledge cognitive aspects. Still, many, if not most, behavior therapists have not explicitly recognized or acknowledged such elements. In the past few years, however, this has changed. Most behaviorists now acknowledge cognitive elements and openly espouse purely cognitive methods and techniques. There are few pure behavior therapists left; most have become cognitive-behavior therapists. Textbooks on behavior therapy recognize this in their titles or in chapters or sections devoted to cognitive methods. [71–74]

Behavior therapists have not, however, systematically integrated cognitive methods or techniques with standard behavioristic techniques (which also include cognitive elements) on any theoretical basis, nor have they attempted to use any particular cognitive theory. Probably because behavior therapy has been essentially atheoretical or empirically oriented, cognitive methods have been included with its other techniques. This incorporation of cognitive techniques has been questioned by Wickramasekera: "It appears to me that it is highly unlikely that this approach by itself will advance our ability to reliably and powerfully control private events. This simplistic approach to forcing a marriage between operant conditioning and cognitive learning ignores the richness of investigative effort, which has collected around the construct, cognition."[75]

The question is whether the marriage between behaviorism and cognition is compatible or whether it is simply a pragmatic association to keep behaviorism respectable. There appear to be basic inconsistencies between a strict or orthodox behaviorism, which rejects mental events as causally important or significant, and cognitive psychology. Thus the efforts to combine the two do not represent a systematic approach, which would warrant separate treatment in a book such as this.

There is, however, an approach to cognitive-behavior modification that is both theoretically and research based. This is the approach developed by Meichenbaum,[76] which is included in this section. Both the theory and research support are admittedly incomplete and are related more to education and training than to the kinds of problems usually brought to a counselor or therapist, and although the approach grew out of the author's training and experience in behavioristic therapy, its relationship to behavior therapy is at best tenuous—it would better be called a cognitive approach than a cognitive-behavior approach. Its concern with change in overt behavior as its goal apparently is the author's justification for using the term. Concern with behavior, however, is not limited to behavior therapists and hardly justifies the use of the word for approaches that no longer adhere to behavioristic psychology. Meichenbaum's approach, therefore, might just as well have been placed in the first section as here.

REFERENCES

1. Hilgard, E. R., & Bower, G. H. *Theories of learning* (4th ed.). Englewood Cliffs, N.J.: Prentice-Hall, 1975. P. 17.
2. Kimble, G. A. (Ed.). *Foundations of conditioning and learning.* Englewood Cliffs, N.J.: Prentice-Hall, 1967. P. 436.
3. Yates, A. J. *Behavior therapy.* New York: Wiley, 1970. P. 34.
4. Mowrer, O. H. On the dual nature of learning: A reinterpretation of "conditioning" and "problem solving." *Harvard Educational Review,* 1947, *17,* 102–148.
5. Mowrer, O. H. *Learning theory and behavior.* New York: Wiley, 1960.
6. Shaw, F. J. A stimulus response analysis of repression and insight in psychotherapy. *Psychological Review* 1946, *53,* 36–42.
7. Shaffer, L. F. The problem of psychotherapy. *American Psychologist,* 1947, *2,* 459–467.
8. Shoben, E. J., Jr. A learning theory interpretation of psychotherapy. *Harvard Educational Review,* 1948, *18,* 129–145.
9. Shoben, E. J., Jr. Psychotherapy as a problem in learning theory. *Psychological Bulletin,* 1949, *46,* 366–392. Reprinted in H. J. Eysenck (Ed.), *Behavior theory and the neuroses.* New York: Pergamon Press, 1960.
10. Shoben, E. J., Jr. Some observations on psychotherapy and the learning process. In O. H. Mowrer (Ed.), *Psychotherapy: Theory and research.* New York: Ronald Press, 1953.
11. Magaret, A. Generalization in psychotherapy. *Journal of Consulting Psychology,* 1950, *14,* 64–70.
12. Kanfer, F. H. Comments on learning in psychotherapy. *Psychological Reports,* 1961, *9,* 681–699.
13. Bandura, A. Psychotherapy as a learning process. *Psychological Bulletin,* 1961, *58,* 143–159.
14. Dollard, J., & Miller, N. E. *Personality and psychotherapy: An analysis in terms of learning, thinking, and culture* New York: McGraw-Hill, 1950.
15. Rotter, J. B. *Social learning and clinical psychology.* Englewood Cliffs, N.J.: Prentice-Hall, 1954.
16. Pepinsky, H. B., & Pepinsky, P. *Counseling: Theory and practice.* New York: Ronald Press, 1954.
17. Pascal, G. R. *Behavioral change in the clinic—a systematic approach.* New York: Grune & Stratton, 1959.
18. Phillips E. L. *Psychotherapy: A modern theory and practice.* Englewood Cliffs, N.J.: Prentice-Hall, 1956.
19. Salter, A. *Conditioned reflex therapy.* New York: Creative Age Press, 1949. (Capricorn Books, 1961)
20. Wolpe, J. *Psychotherapy by reciprocal inhibition.* Stanford, Calif.: Stanford University Press, 1958.
21. Jones, M. C. A laboratory study of fear: The case of Peter. *Journal of Genetic Psychology,* 1924, *31,* 308–315.

22. Watson, J. B., & Rayner, R. Conditioned emotional reactions. *Journal of Experimental Psychology,* 1920, *3,* 1–14.

23. Skinner, B. F. *The behavior of organisms.* Englewood Cliffs, N.J.: Prentice-Hall, 1938; Skinner, B. F. *Science and human behavior.* New York: Macmillan, 1953.

24. Greenspoon, J. S. The effect of a verbal stimulus as a reinforcement. *Proceedings of the Iowa Academy of Science,* 1950, *59,* 287; Greenspoon, J. S. The reinforcing effect of two spoken sounds on the frequency of two responses. *American Journal of Psychology,* 1955, *68,* 409–416.

25. Hildum, D. C., & Brown, R. W. Verbal reinforcement and interviewer bias. *Journal of Abnormal & Social Psychology,* 1956, *53,* 108–111.

26. Krasner, L. Studies of the conditioning of verbal behavior. *Psychological Bulletin,* 1958, *55,* 148–170.

27. Salzinger, K. Experimental manipulation of verbal behavior: A review. *Journal of General Psychology,* 1959, *61,* 65–94.

28. Krasner, L. The therapist as a social reinforcement machine. In H. H. Strupp & L. Luborsky (Eds.), *Research in psychotherapy* (Vol. 2). Washington, D.C.: American Psychological Association, 1962, P. 62.

29. Krasner, L. Reinforcement, verbal behavior and psychotherapy. *American Journal of Orthopsychiatry,* 1963, *33,* 601–613.

30. Krasner, L. Verbal conditioning and psychotherapy. In L. Krasner & L. P. Ullmann (Eds.), *Research in behavior modification.* New York: Holt, Rinehart and Winston, 1965.

31. Kanfer, F. H. Implications of conditioning techniques for interview therapy. *Journal of Counseling Psychology,* 1966, *13,* 171–177.

32. Salzinger, K. The place of operant conditioning of verbal behavior in psychotherapy. In C. M. Franks (Ed.), *Behavior therapy: Appraisal and status.* New York: McGraw-Hill, 1969. Pp. 375–395.

33. Peters, H. N. An experimental evaluation of learning as therapy in schizophrenia. *American Psychologist,* 1952, *7,* 354 (abstract); Peters, H. N. Learning as a treatment method in chronic schizophrenia. *American Journal of Occupational Therapy,* 1955, *9,* 185–189; Peters, H. N., & Jenkins, R. L. Improvement of chronic schizophrenics with guided problem-solving, motivated by hunger. *Psychiatric Quarterly Supplement,* 1954, *28,* 84–101.

34. Lindsley, O. R., & Skinner, B. F. A method for experimental analysis of the behavior of psychotic patients. *American Psychologist,* 1954, *9,* 419–420; Lindsley, O. R. Operant conditioning methods applied to research in chronic schizophrenia. *Psychiatric Research Reports,* 1956, *5,* 118–139.

35. Lindsley, O. R., Skinner, B. F., & Solomon, H. C. *Studies in behavior therapy. Status Report I.* Waltham, Mass.: Metropolitan State Hospital, 1953.

36. Lazarus, A. A. New methods in psychotherapy: A case study. *South African Medical Journal,* 1958, *33,* 660–664.

37. Eysenck, H. J. Learning theory and behavior therapy. *Journal of Mental Science,* 1959, *195,* 61–75.

38. Eysenck (Ed.), *Behavior therapy and the neuroses.*

39. Eysenck, H. J. (Ed.). *Experiments in behavior therapy.* New York: Pergamon Press, 1964.

40. Franks, C. M. (Ed.). *Conditioning techniques in clinical practice and research.* New York: Springer, 1964.

41. Krasner & Ullmann (Eds.), *Research in behavior modification.*

42. Ullmann, L. P., & Krasner, L. (Eds.). *Case studies in behavior modification.* New York: Holt, Rinehart and Winston, 1965.

43. Rubin, R. D., & Franks, C. M. (Eds.). *Advances in behavior therapy: 1968.* New York: Academic Press, 1969.

44. Krumboltz, J. D., & Thoresen, C. E. (Eds.). *Behavioral counseling: Cases and techniques.* New York: Holt, Rinehart and Winston, 1969.

45. Franks, C. M. (Ed.). *Assessment and status of the behavioral therapies.* New York: McGraw-Hill, 1970.

46. Levis, D. J. (Ed.). *Learning approaches to therapeutic behavior change.* Chicago: Aldine, 1970.

47. Osipow, S. H., & Walsh, W. B. (Eds.). *Behavior change in counseling: Readings and cases.* Englewood Cliffs, N.J.: Prentice-Hall, 1970.

48. Eysenck, H. J., & Rachman, S. *The causes and cures of neurosis: An introduction to modern behavior therapy based on learning theory and principles of conditioning.* San Diego: Knapp, 1965.

49. Bandura, A. *Principles of behavior modification.* New York: Holt, Rinehart and Winston, 1969.

50. Kanfer, F. H., & Phillips, J. S. *Learning foundations of behavior therapy.* New York: Wiley, 1970.

51. Yates, *Behavior therapy.*

52. Krasner, L. Review of *The causes and cures of neurosis* by H. J. Eysenck and S. Rachman. *Contemporary Psychology,* 1966, *11,* 341–344.

53. Krumboltz, J. D. (Ed.). *Revolution in counseling.* Boston: Houghton Mifflin, 1966.

54. Levis, D. J. Behavioral therapy: The fourth therapeutic revolution? In Levis (Ed.), *Learning approaches to therapeutic behavior change.*

55. Ullmann, L. P., & Krasner, L. *A psychological approach to abnormal behavior.* Englewood Cliffs, N.J.: Prentice-Hall, 1969. P. 252.

56. Yates, *Behavior therapy,* pp. 15, 18.

57. Ibid., p. 18.

58. Franks, C. M. Introduction: Behavior therapy and its Pavlovian origins: Review and perspectives. In Franks (Ed.), *Behavior therapy,* p. 21.

59. See, for example, the discussions of Patterson, C. H. Some notes on behavior theory, behavior therapy and behavioral counseling. *Counseling Psychologist,* 1969, *1,* 44–56, and Murray, E. J., & Jacobson, L. I. The nature of learning in traditional and behavioral psychotherapy. In A. E. Bergin & S. L. Garfield (Eds.), *Handbook of psychotherapy and behavior change: An empirical analysis.* New York: Wiley, 1971. Pp. 709–747. See also Lazarus, A. A. In support of a technical eclecticism. *Psychological Reports,* 1967, *21,* 415–416, and Lazarus, A. A. *Behavior therapy and beyond.* New York: McGraw-Hill, 1971.

60. Franks, C. M. Introduction: Behavior therapy and its Pavlovian origins, p. 22.

61. Ibid., p. 2.

62. Yates, *Behavior therapy.*

63. Krasner, L. Behavior therapy. *Annual Review of Psychology,* 1971, *22,* 483–532.

64. Kanfer, F. H., & Phillips, J. S. A survey of current behavior therapies and a proposal for classification. In Franks (Ed.), *Behavior therapy,* p. 448.

65. Grossberg, J. M. Behavior therapy: A review. *Psychological Bulletin,* 1964, *62,* 73–88; Breger, L., & McGaugh, J. L. Critique and reformulation of "learning theory" approaches to psychotherapy and neuroses. *Psychological Bulletin,* 1964, *63,* 338–358; Rachman, S., & Eysenck, H. J. Reply to a "critique and reformulation" of behavior therapy. *Psychological Bulletin,* 1966, *65,* 165–169; Weitzman, B. Behavior therapy and psychotherapy. *Psychological Review,* 1967, *74,* 300–317; Wiest, W. M. Some recent criticisms of behaviorism and learning theory with special reference to Breger and McGaugh and Chomsky. *Psychological Bulletin,* 1967, *67,* 214–225; Breger, L., & McGaugh, J. L. Learning theory and behavior therapy: A reply to Rachman and Eysenck. *Psychological Bulletin,* 1968, *65,* 170–173; Patterson, Some notes on behavior theory, behavior therapy and behavioral counseling, pp. 44–56.

66. Murray & Jacobson, The nature of learning in traditional and behavioral psychotherapy.

67. Lazarus, *Behavior therapy and beyond,* p. 1.

68. Ibid., pp. 5, 6.

69. Ibid., pp. 6–7.

70. Ibid., p. 9.

71. Mahoney, M. J. *Cognition and behavior modification.* Cambridge, Mass.: Ballinger, 1974.

72. O'Leary, K. D., & Wilson, G. T. *Behavior therapy: Application and outcome.* Englewood Cliffs, N.J.: Prentice-Hall, 1975.

73. Goldfried, M. R., & Davison, G. C. *Clinical behavior therapy.* New York: Holt, Rinehart and Winston, 1976.

74. Martin, G., & Pear, J. *Behavior modification: What it is and how to do it.* Englewood Cliffs, N.J.: Prentice-Hall, 1978.

75. Wickramasekera, I. (Ed.). *Biofeedback, behavior therapy and hypnosis.* Chicago: Nelson-Hall, 1976. P. 2.

76. Meichenbaum, D. H. *Cognitive-behavior modification.* New York: Plenum, 1977.

chapter 4

Reinforcement Theory and Psychoanalytic Therapy: Dollard and Miller

The learning theory developed by Hull and his students and associates, including Neal Miller, has been applied to psychotherapy by John Dollard and Neal Miller in their *Personality and Psychotherapy: An Analysis in Terms of Learning, Thinking, and Culture.* [1] John Dollard (1900–1980), after taking his Ph.D. at the University of Chicago in 1931, went to the Institute of Human Relations at Yale University, where he became professor of psychology in 1952. He was the author of *Caste and Class in a Southern Town* (1937), among other books.

Neal E. Miller (b. 1909) earned his Ph.D. in 1935 at Yale and remained there until 1966, except for a postdoctoral year of training at the Psychoanalytic Institute in Vienna and during the Second World War, when he was associated with the Air Force selection and classification program. He was James Rowland Angell Professor of Psychology from 1952 to 1966, when he went to Rockefeller University as professor of psychology. In addition to being the author of numerous articles in the field of learning and learning theory, he is coauthor with Dollard of *Social Learning and Imitation* (1941) and with Dollard, Doob, Mowrer, and Sears of *Frustration and Aggression* (1939).

BACKGROUND AND DEVELOPMENT

Unlike the approaches that attempt to apply principles of conditioning to counseling, the approach of Dollard and Miller attempts to integrate learning theory—essentially Hullian behaviorism—with the insights of psychoanalysis about human behavior and personality and with the contributions of social science to the social conditions of learning. The result, Dollard and Miller hope, will be a general science of human

75

behavior. The nature and treatment of neurosis would be included as part of this science. Psychotherapy, particularly psychoanalysis, is seen as providing a window that allows one to look into the mental life in a way that cannot usually be done in the study and observation of the normal individual. The laws and theory of learning applied to psychotherapy should provide a rational foundation for psychotherapy.

PHILOSOPHY AND CONCEPTS

Neurosis is a product of experience rather than primarily of instinct or organic damage. Therefore, it must be learned, and learning is governed by laws, some of which are known and some of which, now unknown, may be discovered through the study of neuroses by means of psychotherapy. Thus learning theory and psychotherapy supplement each other. In their book, however, Dollard and Miller attempt "to give a systematic analysis of neurosis and psychotherapy in terms of the psychological principles and social conditions of learning."[2]

What Is a Neurosis?

The neurotic is miserable, is stupid in handling emotional problems, and suffers from a variety of symptoms. Neurotics are capable of normal activity but are unable to function normally or to enjoy life. The more common symptoms are sleeplessness, restlessness, irritability, sexual inhibitions, phobias, headaches, irrational fears, distaste for life, and lack of clear personal goals. This condition is the result of conflict produced by two or more strong drives leading to incompatible responses. The neurotic is unable to solve these conflicts because he or she is not clearly aware of them. The neurotic's conflicts are repressed—that is, unlabeled—and "he has no language to describe the conflicting forces within him."[3] Neurotics appear to be stupid because of an inability to use higher mental processes to deal with problems, since they do not know what the problems are.

Although the symptoms cause the neurotic to suffer, they actually reduce the conflict. "When a successful symptom occurs it is reinforced because it reduces neurotic misery. The symptom is thus learned as a habit."[4]

Basic Principles of Learning

The behavior of all human beings, which ranges from the child's very simple avoidance of a hot radiator to the scientist's construction of a theory, is learned. Four basic factors are important for all learning.

The first factor is *drive,* or motivation. Drives are strong stimuli that impel action. Certain classes of stimuli are primary, or innate, drives: pain, thirst, hunger, and so on. There are also secondary, or learned, drives, which "are acquired on the basis of primary drives, represent elaborations of them, and serve as a façade behind which the functions of the underlying innate drives are hidden."[5] Many of the most important drives are learned. Fear (or anxiety) is a major learned drive.

The second factor in learning is the *cue,* or stimulus. When a person is impelled by a drive, "cues determine when he will respond, where he will respond, and which response he will make."[6] Both external and internal stimuli may function as cues (as well as being drives) for specific responses. Changes in, differences among, and patterns of stimuli serve as cues. Fear has the properties of a strong external cue. "When fear is learned as a response to a new situation, it serves as a cue to elicit responses that have previously been learned in other frightening situations,"[7] such as verbal responses expressing fear, meek muteness, or withdrawal. Fear may also become a cue to avoid an act or a response that leads to punishment when it has become attached to cues produced by the thought of performing the prescribed act. After effective punishment for an act, the individual feels afraid when he or she thinks about or begins to perform the punished act and is thus led to stop or withdraw. The fear is reduced, and thus the stopping or withdrawing becomes reinforced.

Fear produces or is associated with certain innate responses, such as increase in stomach acidity, increase in and irregularity of heartbeat, muscular tension, trembling, being startled, freezing (with fear), perspiration, dryness of mouth and throat, feelings of unreality, mutism, and amnesia. Many of these reactions are the symptoms of neurosis or psychosis.

The third factor in learning is *response*. Cues lead to responses, which may be arranged in a hierarchy in terms of their probability of occurrence. A dominant response (one high in the hierarchy) has a strong connection with the stimulus. The nature of this causal connection is unknown. The changing of the strength of connections between stimuli and responses (or the changing of the position of responses in the hierarchy) is learning, but a response must occur before it can be connected with a stimulus. Such new responses may occur as the result of trial and error, of imitation, or of verbal direction. All these methods are ways of producing responses that can be rewarded. In conditioning, the response to the unconditioned stimulus is the dominant response. Fear is an innate response to certain stimuli.

The fourth factor is *reinforcement,* or reward. "Any specified event . . . that strengthens the tendency for a response to be repeated is called reinforcement."[8] The reduction or cessation of a painful or noxious stimulus acts as a reinforcement, as does the reduction in the strength of a strong drive or stimulus. There are learned, or secondary, reinforcements, for example, money, as well as innate reinforcements. Learned rewards function in the same way as unlearned rewards. While reinforcement may operate in a situation of awareness on the part of the subject, reinforcement may also operate directly, occurring without awareness.

In addition to these four factors or conditions of learning, there are several other aspects of the learning process that require definition. One of these is *extinction*. When a learned response is repeated without continued reinforcement, it tends to occur less and less often; that is, it is extinguished. If responses were not subject to extinction, they would persist indefinitely, even responses that were rewarded by chance. Responses are extinguished at different rates, with strong responses persisting longer than weak ones. The strength of the drive during learning, the magnitude of the previous reward, and the strength of the drive during extinction influence the rate of extinction. Although the extinction process may be prolonged, all learned habits that have been studied have been found to be extinguished eventually when they are no longer reinforced.[9]

When a response has been extinguished, it may recur after a period of time without having been rewarded in the meantime. This is known as *spontaneous recovery* and indicates that the response or habit has only been inhibited, not destroyed. After repeated extinctions, however, the response does disappear.[10]

The reinforcement accompanying a particular stimulus not only increases the tendency of that stimulus to elicit the response, but also spreads to similar stimuli, so that they tend to elicit the same response. The less similar the stimuli or cues, the less the tendency for the response to occur. This spread or transfer to other stimuli is termed *generalization,* and the variation in tendency for responses to occur is known as the *gradient of generalization.* No two stimuli or stimulus situations are exactly the same, and if there were no generalization, learning could not occur.

If the response occurred with any stimulus, though, learning would not occur either. Dissimilar stimuli are differentiated and not responded to. Or *discrimination* between responses may be established by not rewarding or by punishing responses to stimuli that differ in some way or degree from the rewarded stimulus.

Reinforcement is more effective the closer the response is to the reinforcement, so that delayed reinforcement is less effective than immediate reinforcement. There is thus a *gradient of reinforcement:* responses occurring before the final reinforced response are also reinforced but less so than is the final response.

The gradients of generalization and of reinforcement lead to the principle that "responses near the point of reinforcement tend, whenever physically possible, to occur before their original time in the response series, that is, to become anticipatory."[11] *Anticipatory responses* thus crowd out useless acts. Withdrawal from a painful stimulus will occur prior to touching the object that causes pain. The anticipatory tendency is involuntary and may lead to errors or nonadaptive responses as well as to adaptive elimination of useless acts. Use of reinforcement, such as punishing or not rewarding responses that are not preceded by desirable anticipatory responses, may prevent the elimination of these desirable responses.

The importance of fear in behavior becomes apparent when it is realized that fear is one of the most significant of the learned drives. Fear is easily learned and transferred to new stimuli and can develop into a powerful drive, thus becoming involved in the production of conflicts leading to neurotic behavior. When fear becomes attached to a new situation, it is accompanied by many of the reactions that are a part of the innate pattern of fear. It serves as a cue to elicit responses that have been learned in other fearful situations. When drive-reducing responses are punished, fear is learned and will then motivate responses that prevent reduction of those drives, leading to inhibitions that result in disturbance and neurotic symptoms. Fear seems to be a part of many socially learned drives, such as guilt, shame, pride, the need for social conformity, and the desire for money or power. Fear of the loss of love or status, of failure, and of poverty seem to be socially learned. The reduction of fear is reinforcing for the learning and performance of new responses such as avoidance responses. Fears are often highly resistant to extinction, and sometimes they appear not to be extinguished completely. Like other responses, fear can be inhibited by incompatible responses such as eating.

There are many other learned social motives, but some that are especially important for personality development and psychotherapy are gregariousness, sociability, dependence and independence, conformity and nonconformity, the need to receive and show affection, the desire for approval from others, pride, fairness, and honesty.

Learned drives and their reinforcements vary among cultures and among social classes within a culture. Therapists must be aware of this variability.

Normal Use of Higher Mental Processes in
Solving Emotional Problems

Little is known today about the solution of social and emotional problems, compared with the solution of problems posed by the physical environment. Psychotherapy itself, which is concerned with social and emotional problems, offers an opportunity to learn more about this area.

Behavior may be divided into two "levels": the first consists of immediate, automatic responses; the second includes behavior that follows or is mediated by a series of internal responses, images, or thoughts called *higher mental processes.* It is this latter kind of behavior with which we are concerned. In the former kind of behavior, responses are instrumental acts in that they influence the individual's relationship to the environment directly and immediately: they are instrumental in changing the environment. In the second kind of behavior, the intervening responses are called cue-producing responses. They may or may not be verbalized. Their main purpose is to produce a cue that functions as a part of the stimulus pattern for another response. Such cues, when verbalized, may serve as substitutes for instrumental responses, stimulating another person to perform the response—as, for example, in asking another person to do something for one. The important function here is that of serving as cues to the person making the responses. These cue-producing responses are usually in the form of words and sentences. It is assumed that language and other cue-producing responses, rather than thoughts that have not been articulated, are central to the higher mental processes. The laws that apply to responses to external cues are assumed to apply to such internal response-produced cues.

Attaching the same label (cue-producing response) to different objects gives them a certain "learned equivalence" resulting from verbally mediated generalization. Giving different labels to similar objects increases their distinctiveness and facilitates their discrimination. Labeling is important "because language contains those discriminations and equivalences that have been found useful by generations of trial and error in a given society."[12]

Labels or words can arouse drives; that is, learnable drives can be attached to words. Drives elicited by words are called *mediated learned drives.* Words, spoken or unspoken, can also provide reassurance, thus mediating rewards. Verbal and other cue-producing responses are important in helping people respond to future possibilities and thus in producing foresight. The association of motivational and instrumental responses with verbal cues makes possible great economy in verbal learning, so that much of human learning is in terms of verbal responses or hypotheses that may lead to sudden changes in many other responses (a process often called insight). Verbal learning is often described as logical learning, in contrast to rote learning; in this light, it is apparent why logical learning is superior to rote learning.

Verbal cue-producing responses make possible reasoning and planning. Reasoning involves, but is not restricted to, verbal or symbolic trial and error. Verbal cue-producing responses are not limited to a single sequence, as are instrumental responses, but "it is possible for certain cue producing responses that have been associated with the goal to move forward in the sequence and provide cues that have a selective effect on subsequent responses."[13] These are called *anticipatory goal responses*. It is also possible for a chain of cue-producing responses to begin at the goal and work backward to the correct response in the problem situation. Reasoning and planning require the inhibition of immediate instrumental responses, the occurrence of appropriate cue-producing responses, and the execution of appropriate instrumental responses in place of the direct responses that have been inhibited.

Society has developed solutions to many problems and passes these solutions on to its new members through education and training. Social training in language is important in leading to problem solving. Words and sentences copied from others can be used in reasoning and planning. Verbal responses are learned in social interaction, but the process is not clearly understood. Imitation plays a central role in the process of learning to talk.[14] Training that involves listening, following the suggestions of others, stopping to think, matching words correctly to the environment, making oneself understood, being logical, being oriented, and responding to verbal cues with appropriate action and emotion helps to make a person's behavior appropriate to the social situation. When such training is not too effective, the individual may appear to have a poor sense of reality or a weak ego. Cue-producing responses that are not socially evident, such as images of various kinds, are not subject to direct social training; they may be less inhibited but also less orderly and less useful in problem solving.

How Neurosis Is Learned

Neurotic behavior is based on an unconscious emotional conflict, usually originating in childhood. "Neurotic conflicts are taught by parents and learned by children."[15] The patterns of child training contain inconsistencies and, thus, inherent conflicts, and parents vary in their consistency, effectiveness, and goodness in conducting child training. The task is complex and difficult, and the appropriate rules and conditions are only partly known. There is also the problem of determining what kind of child it is desirable to produce. Although our knowledge is inadequate, we know that the period of childhood is important, and we must attempt to reconstruct childhood in order to understand adult life.

Children are helpless and thus are at the mercy of confusing patterns of training. "The young child is necessarily disoriented, confused, deluded, and hallucinated—in short, has just those symptoms that we recognize as psychosis in the adult. Infancy, indeed, may be viewed as a period of transitory psychosis."[16] Rather than being indulged, supported, and gradually trained during infancy, the child is pushed by incompatible and impossible demands and is expected to control impelling drives and to learn rapidly.

The child is faced with training demands in four critical situations. The ways in which this training is handled lead to the development of learned responses that persist throughout life. The *feeding situation* may be handled so as to lead to optimism or apathy, to security or apprehension, to sociability or lack of social feeling, to fear of being alone or later compulsive sociability. Premature or rigid *cleanliness training,* which must proceed without verbal aids, arouses strong emotions—anger, defiance, stubbornness, and fear. Anxiety, conforming behavior, feelings of unworthiness, and guilt may result. *Sex training* may lead to conflicts generated by taboos, sexual anxieties, and heterosexual fears and conflicts deriving from the Oedipus situation. Finally, *the treatment of anger responses* in the child may give rise to anger-anxiety conflicts as fear is attached to anger cues. Anger is inevitable because of the many frustrations produced in the child during training, of sibling rivalry, and of the helplessness and mental limitations of the child. Repression of anger may go beyond inhibition of aggression to inhibition of feelings of anger and thus lead to an overinhibited personality.

These early conflicts of the child occur before he or she can verbalize or at least do so adequately. They are therefore unlabeled and unconscious. They cannot be reported later in life. We cannot learn from the individual (except to some extent in psychotherapy) the nature of these conflicts. Much of what we know about these conditions has come from neurotics in psychotherapy. Normal people may not have as severe conflicts; some individuals may be less able to handle conflicts through higher mental processes or may be more predisposed than others to neurotic reactions.

How Symptoms Are Learned

Phobias are learned fears whose basic origins currently are not understood. The avoidance response reduces the fear and thus is strongly reinforced. Phobias tend to persist because the avoidance of the phobia situation reinforces them through reduction of fear and so prevents extinction. Like phobias, *compulsions* are acts that reduce anxiety of unknown origin. They persist because they reduce the anxiety temporarily. *Hysterical symptoms* are likewise learned responses that avoid or reduce fear. The factors that determine the specific hysterical response, such as an arm paralysis, are unclear, although the origin of the fear, such as active combat in war, may be clear. *Regression* is the occurrence of the next strongest response (usually one learned as a strong habit during childhood) when the dominant (adult) habit is blocked by conflict or extinguished through lack of reward. When the dominant response is replaced by another response that is strong because of generalization, rather than by an earlier response, the process is called *displacement*. *Rationalizations* occur when, as a result of social training, the individual feels the necessity for logical explanations for his or her behavior but cannot accept the true explanation because it would provoke anxiety or guilt. *Delusions* are only quantitatively different from rationalizations; socially acceptable explanations are more difficult to find, and delusions are resorted to—and persist—to reduce the strong anxiety or guilt. *Hallucinations* are a result of wide generalization of strongly motivated perceptual responses. When external cues become highly disturbing, the shifting of attention to internal images (hallucinations) may reduce the fear. *Projection* results from the many factors that lead people to think that others are motivated as they are. When individuals erroneously impute motivation in others, it is called projection. The individual often is incorrect in labeling his or her own motives as well as those of others. Projection is reinforced by the reduction of anxiety when blame is shifted to someone else. *Reaction formations* are thoughts, statements, or behaviors opposite to those that the individual is motivated toward but which the individual fears or disapproves of. *Alcoholism* results from the reinforcement of the use of alcohol to reduce fear.

Although in the long run, many symptoms are maladaptive, they delay the increase in misery, and the immediate results are favorable, thus reinforcing the symptoms. The strengthening effect of an immediate reinforcement may be much greater than the deterring effect of a much stronger but delayed punishment. When there appears to be an immediate increase in misery, the explanation of the persistence of the symptoms presents a problem, but the situation can be accounted for theoretically in various ways consistent with a drive-reduction interpretation of reinforcement theory.

While any strong drive can motivate symptoms and its reduction can reinforce them, certain drives appear to be more likely to do so in our society than others. Fear is perhaps the most common motivating drive. Sex, aggression, and the striving for social mobility are others. The repression of verbal responses to these drives increases the likelihood of the appearance of maladaptive behavior or symptoms. When it is physically possible to perform direct drive-reducing responses, such responses may be prevented by conflict, so that the drive must be reduced by symptomatic behavior. Two strong drives may have incompatible dominant responses, but some of the less dominant responses may be compatible and will tend to occur. Symptoms are often such compromise responses, which are strongly reinforced because they reduce both drives.

Symptoms are resistant to elimination, or extinction, apparently because they have been strengthened by long reinforcement, they continue to be reinforced, and their interruption makes the individual feel worse. "If the symptom is reinforced by drive reduction so that interrupting it causes the drive to mount, we would expect this increased drive to motivate the learning and performance of new symptoms. Thus treatment that is aimed only at eliminating specific symptoms by such means as hypnosis or physical punishment should tend to be followed by the appearance of new symptoms. As is well known, this is indeed the case."[17] Elimination or reduction of the drive that motivates a symptom leads to the disappearance of the symptom. If the drive reappears, the symptom reappears, particularly if the elimination of the drive did not involve the pitting of incompatible responses against it, as in interpretation.

How Repression Is Learned

In the individual's psyche, the repressed or the unconscious, as Freud pointed out, is the unverbalized. Drives, cues, and responses that never have been labeled are unconscious. Most of what is repressed originates in childhood before the acquisition of language, but even later in life, some aspects of life remain unverbalized or poorly labeled. Suppression is the conscious avoidance of unpleasant thoughts, but repression is automatic; since it is not under the control of verbal cues, repression cannot be revoked by the individual. Repression is reinforced by the reduction of the unpleasant drive. The removal of repression results in an increase of the drive. An innate response to the drive of fear may be to stop thinking. For example, children learn to fear saying certain words, and the fear generalizes to the thoughts represented by those words. Thoughts themselves may become attached directly to fears, as when the thoughts precede acts that are immediately punished. Even delayed punishment may result in attachment of fear to thoughts when the punishment is accompanied by an explanation of the reason for the punishment. Sometimes parents can tell what a child is going to do and warn or reprimand the child while he or she is only thinking about the act, thus attaching fear to the thought.

Repression may intervene in a drive sequence in three ways.

1. The drive may not be labeled, or it may not be recognized for what it is and be mislabeled.
2. The drive may be inhibited by stronger competing responses. For example, fear may lead to the inhibiting of the sexual drive. Hunger may even inhibit fear if the hunger is strong and the fear is weak to begin with, as in the experiment of Jones with Peter and the rabbit referred to in the introduction to this section.
3. In the case of mediated learned drives, the inhibition of the mediating responses, which produce the cues that elicit the drive-producing responses, will eliminate the drive. Thus, for example, if one stops thinking about another's comments as insults, this can reduce anger.

It is the first type of repression, in which the drive is present at full strength but unlabeled, that leads to symptomatic behavior.

Repression may be viewed as the result of an approach–avoidance conflict, that is, a conflict between trying to remember or think about something and trying to avoid the topic because of its fear-producing quality.

The superego, or conscience, is in part unconscious. This may be because the emotional components of the moral sanctions were learned before language developed or because the responses were so strongly learned that they have become direct responses to nonverbal cues, like strong habits that may function without thought.

The presence of repression generates deficits in the higher mental processes, which involve verbal cue-producing responses. The inability to use labels leads to primary stimulus generalization or inadequate discrimination and thus to displacement. Inability to attach the same label to similar situations results in a decrease in learned (secondary) generalization. Absence of verbal responses removes the capacity for responding to remote goals or stimuli or for dealing with the future with foresight. Reasoning and planning will be affected, as well as ability to communicate with others and to obtain their help. Behavior is more childish and thus abnormal compared with that of other adults. Since repression usually is limited to certain areas or topics, not all behavior is affected, of course, or else the individual would not be able to function at all. These expectations drawn from behavior theory are all supported by clinical data and fit Freud's description of the results of repression.

To summarize, the neurotic is one in whom there is a conflict between drives such as sex and aggression, and a strong fear. The satisfaction of these drives is prevented, resulting in a state of chronic high drive described as misery. The strong drives tend to evoke behavior that elicits fear. The neurotic responds by avoiding such behavior and thus not approaching the goal, which reduces the fear and thus reinforces these responses. The state of conflict also results in tension, and the fear, too, is accompanied by unpleasant physiological reactions. In addition, the fear leads to repression of verbal and other cue-producing responses, so that thinking and reasoning are prevented and stupidity results. Symptoms are produced by the strong drives and/or fear and are reinforced by reduction of these drives or fear.

THE THERAPY PROCESS

The neurotic who comes for counseling or psychotherapy has suffered long, and relatives, friends, and even a personal physician have given up attempts to help the individual. The neurotic is becoming hopeless and does not know what to do. He or she cannot explain himself or herself, is afraid to express himself or herself or attempt to satisfy his or her drives, and is confused and cannot think adequately. The neurotic has failed in many areas of life, senses that others know that he or she is a failure, and thus lacks self-esteem. The neurotic cannot solve his or her own problems and requires new conditions of therapeutic learning to achieve a better adjustment. Counseling or psychotherapy offers these new conditions of learning. The therapy process is essentially a situation in which neurotic responses are extinguished and better, normal responses are learned.

The Selection of Clients

Since psychotherapy is a learning process, it is desirable for the therapist to exercise selection of those who can learn under the conditions of psychotherapy. If these conditions and the principles of learning are known, such selection should be possible. The rules of selection based on these principles seem to agree quite well with those developed from clinical experience and psychoanalytic theory.

First, the disorder must be learned, not organic. To be unlearned, the condition must first be a product of learning. Second, there must be motivation for therapy, since motivation is important in learning. A person who is miserable and suffering is more motivated than is one who is self-satisfied. A person who seeks therapy on his or her own is better motivated than is one who is compelled or forced into therapy. The more disadvantageous the symptoms, the stronger the motivation for therapy. Third, the more strongly the symptoms are reinforced, the poorer the prognosis. Secondary gains, such as pensions or compensation, may reinforce symptoms and reduce motivation for therapy. Fourth, the greater the potential rewards for improvement, the better the prognosis. Good physical health, youth, beauty, intelligence, education, special skills, a satisfactory position, a good social-class status, wealth, and a supportive marital partner or prospects of one increase the possibility of reward. Fifth, a certain minimum achievement in social learning is necessary, since psychotherapy does not provide the basic training that should be received in the family. A minimum ability to use and respond to language is required; this is related to intelligence, of course. The potentiality for higher mental functioning, evidenced by previous high-level functioning or by the presence of such functioning in some areas, increases the favorability of the prognosis. If age-graded achievements, such as aspects of the conscience or superego, are lacking, psychotherapy will be difficult. Sixth, a history of neurosis going back into childhood is unfavorable. Finally, habits that interfere with psychotherapy—such as inability to listen or to talk reasonably, extreme suspiciousness, excessive passivity and dependence, or great independence and pride—are unfavorable signs.

The Elements of Therapeutic Learning

The therapeutic process consists of a number of aspects. The first is the *lifting of repression* through extinguishing or counterconditioning the fear or anxiety associated with repressed material. "In therapy a new type of social situation is created, the opposite of that responsible for learning repression."[18] That is, the client says the words that have been attached to fear, shame, and guilt in a permissive, warm, and accepting atmosphere, and this verbalization leads to the extinction of the fear and guilt. The extinction generalizes from words to thoughts and from painful but not repressed topics to more repressed topics. The drives that motivate repression become weakened, and cycles of extinction and generalization occur until "the repression is gradually unlearned under permissive social conditions that are the opposite to the punitive ones under which it was learned."[19] Thus the therapeutic situation is characterized by permissiveness, which leads to the lifting of repression.

The process is slow and difficult because fear and anxiety accompany the discussion of repressed ideas. Even though the therapist is permissive and neutral, the fact that the therapist is a human being means that anxiety is generalized to him or her, but the therapist is also seen as a specialist in whom the client can have trust and confidence and who thus provides reassurance. The client experiences fear and anxiety while talking, which is a necessary condition for extinction. At the same time, the client experiences the benign attention of the therapist. Punishment does not occur, and the fear attached to the forbidden sentences is not reinforced. In terms of the approach–avoidance conflict that characterizes repression, the avoidance gradient is reduced by the attitudes and activity of the therapist, so that the client, as a result of the approach drive, can begin to move toward the goal that will satisfy his or her drive.

In addition to the client's verbalizations about himself or herself and the past, the *transference relationship* is the second necessary part of therapy. It provides information that the client is not able to give directly. The client reacts to the therapist emotionally—with fear, hate, and love—without being aware of it. These emotional reactions are called transference, since they are not elicited by the therapist as the therapist actually is but are transferred to her or him as a representative of other figures, to whom they were originally directed.

Transference occurs in all areas of normal life, for emotional reactions are evoked by many situations that would not be considered adequate stimuli for them. In therapy, these transferred reactions are utilized to obtain information that is useful in helping the client. The therapist stimulates transference reactions by attempting to remain ambiguous, which allows the client to generalize more easily. The weakening of repression through permissiveness also facilitates transference—avoidance reactions to the therapist thus are not as strong as they are to others.

The generalization, or transfer, of many previously learned adaptive habits to the therapy situation makes therapy possible to begin with. These habits include being sensible, logical, and reasonable; being self-critical; speaking in an orderly, intelligent way; listening; being influenced by experts; expressing appropriate emotions; having hope, trust, and confidence in the therapist and in science; and wishing to please the therapist.

These generalizations, or transference reactions, facilitate therapy. Others interfere with therapy. Fear and dependence or helplessness may be immediately transferred to therapy. False hopes of quick or easy cure may transfer from experience with doctors. The client also brings more specific responses to therapy that obstruct the process. These reactions are the client's habitual ways of escaping from anxiety situations; they include stopping talking or being silent, obscuring or confusing issues by quibbling, focusing on minor or irrelevant matters, talking in circles, and being repetitious. Fear may be reacted to with anger directed toward the therapist, or anger may evoke fear responses. A common well-learned response to an anxiety-producing situation is to leave it, and the client may thus break off therapy. These reactions are considered transference reactions because they are not appropriate to the therapy situation. It is, of course, possible that at times the emotional reactions directed toward the therapist are appropriate, as when the therapist is hasty, stupid, or cruel (which are indications of incompetence) or when the therapist makes a mistake (in which case it is best for her or him honestly to admit it).

While transferred reactions in the client may be considered as resistance on the part of the client, it must be recognized that they are generalized automatically to the therapy situation and are not purposely produced by the client. The transference situation is not a duel but a real battle. Therapy is not simply a verbal intellectual discussion. The emotions involved in the neurosis must be brought out in therapy, at least to some extent.

The appearance of emotional responses in therapy entails responses that the client cannot talk about because they have never been labeled. They are, therefore, brought out where they can be discussed and labeled. Thus the third aspect of the counseling process is *learning to label,* or to think about new topics. The feelings that arise with the lifting of repression and those that are manifested in transference must be dealt with verbally. "The neurotic is a person who is in need of a stock of sentences that will match the events going on within and without him. The new sentences make possible an immense facilitation of higher mental processes. . . . By labeling a formerly unlabeled response he can represent this response in reasoning."[20] Labeling must not be misunderstood as mere intellectualization. Therapy involves a new emotional experience with the therapist, which leads to learning that may occur unconsciously, but "the learning is more transferable, and therefore more efficient, when adequate labeling occurs."[21] The client must have his or her own emotional experience and must correctly label it. It is not sufficient for the client to acquire a collection of sentences that are not related to emotional or instrumental responses.

The fourth aspect of therapy is the *learning of discriminations*. The neurotic "must clearly see that the conflicts and repressions from which he suffers are not justified by the current conditions of reward and punishment. He must further learn that the conditions in the past which produced these conflicts are sharply dissimilar from those of the present. . . ."[22] Only then can the neurotic have the courage to try new responses, which, when rewarded, can break the neurotic impasse.

Discrimination, by enabling the client to recognize that the situation is different now, is useful in reducing the anxiety that prevents the client from making a formerly punished and now inhibited response. Simply using the labels *past* to refer to the dangerous situation and *present* to denote the harmless situation may provide a discrimination that can quickly reduce anxiety. Labeling thus facilitates discrimination, and discrimination tends to generalize to similar situations.

The importance of recovering past conditions is in contrasting them with present conditions so that differentiation or discrimination can occur. Describing the past constitutes a kind of reliving of the past, with some of its emotions. The past can thus be brought to some extent into the present and compared with it, thereby facilitating discrimination. The realization of the contrast between the client's present habit of repression and inhibition and the positive opportunities for gratification that exist in the environment helps the client mobilize his or her drives to be sensible and realistic; with the therapist's help, such realization may inhibit anxiety and stimulate action.

Verbal responses are important in discrimination, making possible the recognition of dissimilar stimuli to which similar responses are made and of similar stimuli to which dissimilar responses are made. Verbal cues can prevent generalization of anxiety from the past to the present. When anxiety is reduced by discrimination, new responses become possible; and as these responses reduce neurotic drives, they can become the basis for new habits that permanently resolve the neurotic conflict.

Result: Restoration of the Higher Mental Processes

Therapeutic gains can occur without improved labeling or insight. The permissive attitude of the therapist probably reduces the client's fear, and this lessening of fear should generalize from the therapeutic situation, leading to general improvement. This is usually not sufficient for complete cure, however; the removal of repression, new labeling, and improvement in discrimination and in the higher mental processes must also occur. The higher mental processes require verbal and other cue-producing responses and thus depend on the removal of repression and on labeling. A number of changes in thinking result.

One of these changes is the ability to make *adaptive discriminations,* which leads to the reduction of primary stimulus generalization and of irrational fears. The second is the ability to make *adaptive generalizations,* which improves secondary stimulus generalization and leads to adaptive responses to culturally defined similarities. The third change or improvement is anticipating danger and *motivating foresightful behavior.* Verbal and other cue-producing responses can mediate hope, as well as enable the individual to reward himself or herself for subgoal achievement and to wait for delayed rewards. The fourth is improvement in *reasoning and planning* through becoming aware of the real problem and defining it accurately. The fifth is the better *utilization of the cultural storehouse of tested problem solutions* that are available. The sixth is the *avoidance of the waste of contradictory behavior* through logical thinking. Finally, the verbalization of previously repressed material does not result in uninhibited behavior but in *behavior that is under better social control.* Such verbal control of behavior requires that the words be attached to proper emotional and instrumental responses and not merely to other words.

Considerable practice or "working through" is needed before appropriate labeling, and thus discrimination and generalization, becomes a habit. Also, thoughts and plans must be translated into action, which is then rewarded, if behavior is to improve. All this takes time, so that therapy is a long process, and improvement may continue after therapy sessions have ended.

Real-World Aspects of Therapy

The therapy sessions are the "talking" phase of therapy. The second phase is the outside, or real-world, aspect. Real-life problems must be solved with new behavior outside of therapy. An aspect of this is the generalization of responses to the therapist to other persons. This is an important part of cure. These responses will be strengthened or extinguished depending on whether they are rewarded or punished.

The performing in the real world of responses learned in therapy is not sufficient, however. Responses never performed in therapy will be necessary. Therapy can prepare for these responses by reducing the anxiety associated with them, but the responses must be made to persons in the client's real world. The extinction of fear of talking about such actions must generalize to fear of performing them. Once this fear is reduced, the drives leading to these actions increase and overcome inhibitory drives or stimuli. As the goal becomes nearer, strong anxiety reactions may arise, but they are overcome by the drive to respond. The approach–avoidance conflict must be resolved. Therapy contributes to this by reducing the avoidance gradient. In the neurotic, the attempt to increase the approach gradient leads only to increase in conflict and misery, with possible breaking off of the therapy. Therapy may be a slow process of trying and failing or of trying and succeeding in part, until success is achieved. Risks must be taken, and failures sometimes results. Therapy is not complete until actions follow verbalization.

Freudian theory seemed to assume that responses outside of therapy would occur automatically, although some analysts do encourage or direct real-life trials. While there is a tendency for such responses to occur without direction, it is not innate. However, if therapy is to be successful, verbal cues must be connected to overt responses; the client must act. Some clients are apathetic about acting, in which case the therapist must "get some 'action' responses following upon the cues of plans, and this connection must be slowly rewarded and strengthened."[23] In the later stages of therapy, when fear (avoidance) has been reduced, increasing motivation (approach) may have a good effect.

Since the major sources of drive reduction are not in the therapeutic situation, the therapist cannot provide the rewards that the client needs. They must come in real life. The nature of the life conditions or environment of the client are thus important for the success of therapy, and the therapist has no control over these conditions. Therapists do attempt to select clients whose life conditions are favorable.

Therapy is limited in what it can do. It cannot give all that the client may wish —better speech, social advancement, an advantageous marriage, and so forth. It cannot remake the person, particularly the older person, nor can it remedy all the deficiencies of early development and training. Solutions must also be within the moral codes of society, otherwise the client exchanges an unconscious mental conflict for an open social conflict, which is likely to be still more maladaptive.

IMPLEMENTATION: TECHNIQUES OF THERAPY

The techniques of counseling are not completely separate, or discrete, but are blended or combined in infinite variety. Nevertheless, they can be identified and discussed separately.

Permissiveness

From the patient's standpoint, the novelty of the therapeutic situation lies in its permissiveness. He is allowed a good turn to talk. His statements are received by the therapist with an even, warm attention. The therapist is understanding and friendly. He is willing, so far as he can, to look at matters from the patient's side and make the best case for the patient's view of things. The therapist is not shocked by what he hears and does not criticize. The frightened patient learns that here is a person he can really talk to—perhaps the first such person in his life.[24]

In the accepting, permissive situation, fears attached to repressed topics are gradually extinguished. Without this therapy could not occur. Through permissiveness, lack of judgment, and lack of criticism the therapist sets himself or herself apart from those who are not accepting and permissive.

The permissiveness applies to thoughts but not to actions. Therapy attempts to remove repression of thoughts but not restraint of antisocial acts. There are also definite restrictions of actions during therapy: the client is asked not to take important steps, such as making changes in his or her marital status, job, or other significant areas. Such actions are to be suppressed until the client is in a position to take action that is free from neurotic influences. The client may also be asked to limit therapeutic conversation to the therapy hours.

Free Association

While permissiveness allows the client to speak, the rule of free association requires the client to speak without the inhibitions and censorship that influence ordinary conversation and without the consistencies and logic of such conversation. The client must report everything that comes to mind, immediately and without reservations. "The rule is a force which is applied against the force of neurotic fear. Without it, and unless he follows it, the patient will remain fixed in his neurotic habits and cannot recover the free use of his mind."[25] The client must talk; this is his or her responsibility. The therapist cannot obtain the relevant information by questioning, since he or she does not know the relevant questions. Furthermore, the client must volunteer information in the presence of fear, or extinction cannot occur. Thus free association is not free and easy.

The client begins with material that is less important and less anxiety producing; then, as the anxiety is extinguished by the therapist's responses and attitudes and as the effects generalize, the client proceeds to more important, significant, and relevant material. This cycle of fear, extinction, generalization, and fear again is repeated in a process that appears to be a testing of the therapist. The result of this process is a gradual lifting of repression—the remembering of forgotten experiences, events, repressed sentences, and emotions. The therapist listens to it all with no a priori hypotheses in order to obtain a complete and rational verbal account of the client's life. As the therapist attempts to make sense of it all, he or she will see gaps and inconsistencies and will develop hypotheses about them. The therapist's own thoughts may describe what remains repressed in the client's mental life. Blockings in the client's association serve as aids to the therapist, since they point to areas where repression exists. Failure to deal with common important areas, as well as dreams and slips of the tongue, also points to repressed material. The therapist deals with these gaps and indications of repression essentially by following to the letter the rule of free association, urging and encouraging the client to further exploration and pointing out certain omissions, attitudes, and so on ("permissive interpretation").[26]

Rewards for Talking

The client must be rewarded for talking while fearful and anxious in order to reinforce the talking and to enable the client to continue and to progress in uncovering repression. The therapist may reward such talking in various ways. One is by listening—giving full, free, and exclusive attention to what the client is saying. Another reward is the therapist's acceptance of what the client says and avoidance of judging and condemning. The client's talking without acceptance and forgiveness, or catharsis, is not effective. A third reward is the therapist's understanding and remembering what the client has said in the past. The therapist's calmness in the face of important revelations that the client is ashamed of or anxious about is a fourth reward. The therapist may even reward the client by expressions of sympathy or approval, but this is used sparingly. Finally, the therapist does not cross-question or make definite pronouncements but speaks tentatively and suggests possible implications or relationships. The therapist is patient and adapts to the pace of the client.

These rewards, instead of punishment, for forbidden sentences spoken with fear lead to the extinction of the fear. However, the fear of real dangers, of punishment for antisocial behavior, is not extinguished. "This discrimination must be made quite clearly by the therapist. The therapist can, so to say, promise nonpunishment for certain activities—those which were once punished but are now no longer forbidden—but the therapist cannot tamper with life's realities."[27]

Handling the Transference

The transference provides the therapist with indirect information about the client, in addition to what is obtained during free association. The therapist can label such data, while the client cannot.

The therapist is in many ways similar to teachers, parents, and age-graded superiors, which facilitates transference of responses learned in interaction with authoritative figures. The therapist encourages or produces such transference by remaining as ambiguous as possible. In addition, the extinction of anxiety related to speaking about forbidden matters under the permissiveness of the therapist generalizes to the fears that lead to avoidance and inhibition of emotional responses, so that these responses appear and are directed toward the therapist.

When the client impedes therapy because of transference-induced reactions, the therapist attempts to overcome the obstruction. If the client falls silent, the therapist may interpret this silence, assure the client that he or she cannot have a blank mind, or give a clue as to what thoughts the client might have. When obfuscation occurs, the therapist points out that it is an escape and urges the client to resume work.

> The therapist is under stress in accepting, identifying, and using transferred reactions for the ends of therapy. Though informative, transference emotions are often obstinate and difficult to deal with. . . . It is particularly important that the therapist should not imply that the patient is purposely producing these reactions, else he will confuse his patient and possibly give real cause for a feeling of injustice. The therapist's task is to identify these responses as transferred and find out how they arose.[28]

While the client feels that his or her reactions must be real, the therapist must prove to the client that they are not. The angry client may criticize obvious defects of the therapist (for example, a foreign accent), but the therapist must not respond with anger or irritation.

The therapist may have to identify the existence of the transferred response, show that it is not objectively justified as directed toward the therapist, and raise questions about its origin and the person from whom it is transferred. Since transferred responses are learned responses, they are a source of inference about early conditions in the client's life. When the inappropriateness of the transference response and its obstruction of therapy are pointed out, the acquired drives to be logical and to progress in therapy lead the client to resume work and free association. "If the therapist does not know how to recall the patient to his proper task, such responses may persist and may end therapeutic progress. Failure to understand transference manifestations is one of the commonest sources of failure for the amateur in psychotherapy. The therapist lost many patients in this way, and inexperienced therapists still do."[29]

Labeling

Free association and transference produce emotional responses that have never been labeled. The therapist must help the client label these responses. In order to do this, the therapist, on the basis of the material provided by free association and the transference, must develop an understanding of the client, so that he or she not only can empathize with the client (feel the client's feelings), but also can label the client's feelings. Labeling consists of producing new verbal responses by connecting words to the correct emotional or environmental cues. The client may acquire these new verbal responses in at least three ways.

1. The client may discover or create the new verbal units under the compulsion of free association. Anxiety associated with the responses is extinguished by the therapist's permissiveness. The production of the responses increases during therapy, both because anxiety is reduced and because there is increasingly more to build on. "The more of the essential work the patient can perform by himself during therapy, the more certain he is to be able to do what he needs afterward. The therapist should be careful not to deprive the patient of the pleasure of making his own discoveries."[30]

2. The therapist may selectively strengthen the clients responses that he or she thinks are important without contributing his or her own ideas. The therapist may reward the client in various ways, such as by saying "uh-huh," including the client's ideas in summaries, and repeating what the client has said. Questions that are asked for clarification of material already introduced by the client may also serve this purpose by focusing attention on the client's responses.

3. The client may rehearse responses provided by the therapist as interpretations. Strong anxiety or the failure of the label and the cues produced by the emotion to occur at the same time may prevent the client from being able to label his or her own responses. The therapist may provide the labels at the appropriate

time. The client's rehearsal may be in paraphrase, using the client's own words, or may take place in the client's thoughts rather than verbalizations. The client is rewarded by the reduction of anxiety, the increase of hope, and the feeling of progress. Sometimes anxiety is increased, however, and the client resists the interpretation. Resistance may be related to the client's strong desire to be independent and do it all alone, or it may occur when the therapist makes a stupid or an awkward interpretation.

An incorrect label may give some temporary relief by reducing anxiety, but because it is not correct, it will not continue to be rewarded and will not persist. Verbal responses may be attached to emotional cues, to environmental cues, to instrumental acts, and to other verbal cues. The last relationship may be termed clarification and often involves ordering responses, linking events in a temporal and causal order.

Interpretation, or "prompting," by the therapist is necessary if therapy is to be efficient and maximally successful, since the client usually cannot do it all alone, although this is to be preferred. The client who can do this makes rapid progress and is ready for dismissal when he or she can do it well alone. The second of the methods described above is necessary when the client makes a number of different and confusing or contradictory hypotheses or statements.

The third method, although sometimes necessary, has some disadvantages. The therapist cannot be certain that the client uses interpretation when the client rehearses the responses silently rather than saying them aloud. Silent responses are probably weaker and less effective than verbalizations. Weakening also occurs through generalization from the therapist's voice to the client. Finally, there is the resistance, or "interpretation shock."

The therapist should not intervene with interpretations until the client ceases to make progress by himself or herself, and then only to the extent that the therapist feels the client can bear. Moreover, "the skillful therapist . . . does not make interpretations on mere hunches. He waits until he has strong evidence for his hypothesis before he supplies a label, points out a transferred response, or teaches a discrimination. If the patient is to be convinced, the evidence must be convincing. The fewer ill-founded notions the therapist utters, the greater his authority when he does speak."[31]

Teaching Discrimination

Discrimination involves attaching different verbal cues to stimulus patterns that are actually different. The therapist uses various methods to teach the patient to discriminate. One technique is to call attention to a problem area in order to evoke new discriminations by failing to understand the client, which stimulates the client to reexamine the area. This is similar to the Socratic method of teaching. Applying a word or a label to which an elaborate series of responses is already attached transfers these responses to the new situation. The therapist may discourage certain responses by labeling them as false or doubtful. The therapist is thus "an operator in the field of language, exciting learned drives and administering learned rewards, eliciting adequate sentence chains to guide instrumental responses."[32] Generalizations to similar sets of stimuli can be facilitated if the therapist points out their similarity.

The therapist may also foster discrimination by pointing out the difference between the past and the present and assuring the client that the present environment is benign.

EXAMPLE

Dollard, Auld, and White have presented an analysis of a case of brief psychotherapy using techniques based on the theories of Dollard and Miller. The student would benefit from reading the complete presentation and analysis of this case, but only the verbatim transcript of the eleventh interview, which is given under the heading "Tactics: Examples of Therapeutic Techniques in This Case," is included here without comment.[33] It is perhaps well to note that the authors felt that the therapist was too active and, thus, that this interview does not illustrate free association well or not as well as other interviews in the case.

The Eleventh Hour of Therapy

PATIENT: . . . We've had a hectic day today. We've been working like slaves, my mother and I, all morning, since seven-thirty. For a big family dinner tonight. And I'm tired. But she's doing all the cooking . . . I haven't that to worry about, but the little things, you know. Do you know I've been thinking about the conversation that we had last week . . . and . . . my life is very boring and dull . . . but it really is my own fault. I really should go out and get a job and work, I think, so that during the day my mind is occupied— my time is taken up at night—I'll be very contented to sit home and do nothing. And . . . and I guess I shouldn't complain about it . . . being so dull. Because it really is my fault.

THERAPIST: How do you mean, it's your fault?

PT: Well, I mean I shouldn't . . . I should be so busy during the day that at night I won't mind staying in and being bored or leading a quiet life. But . . . I don't know what I . . . I'm not qualified to do anything really—I mean to get a job. I used to take those parts in our theater group plays but I could never go into show business professionally. I could only work in a gift shop or as a receptionist or a telephone-answering service, or something like that. I haven't taken any courses in . . . in any secretarial work or anything like that. But I suppose I could do it. Now I could take up bookkeeping or typing and shorthand.

TH: Yes, un huh.

PT: I could get . . . you know, take that course and six easy lessons, is that what they . . . (laugh) You see it advertised. It's a short course. I was thinking about doing that. But, it's funny, I don't know what's the matter with me, I . . . have two lovely children, I have a wonderful husband, I have a lovely home . . . but I'm not happy. That doesn't make sense.

TH: I don't understand, you say is life too easy . . .

PT: Well, I mean is it because I . . . I have things too easy that I'm . . . discontented . . . if I had it harder would I feel that I shouldn't complain about anything?

TH: How does that sound to you?

PT: It seems logical. It seems that my life is too easy for me. That . . . I have no complaints to make at all for . . . I mean as far as . . . having a wonderful husband and a wonderful daughter and son and a lovely home, and I entertain when I want to . . . and it seems as though I'm discontented. I'm not happy and I complain all the time.

TH: Well, there must be some reason, don't you think?

PT: Well, I don't know, that's what I can't understand; why should I feel this way? Why should I feel that I'm discontented, that I'm looking for something all the time? Why shouldn't I be contented to stay home and . . . and have the things I have? I can . . . I don't know. I still can't understand it. Why should I complain about my boring life or monotonous life? I have no right to, really.

TH: How's that?

PT: Well, people . . . many people are worse off than I am, that haven't got the things that I have. Why should I complain? Why should I be unhappy? Does it all have to do with what I went through as a child?

TH: Well, I don't see . . . of course other people have it more difficult and other people have greater problems . . .

PT: Yes.

TH: . . . but I don't think we should judge your problem on the basis of what other people's problems are but should try to understand your problems and see why you should have . . .

PT: What am I looking for? I don't know what I want in life. What am I . . . what's . . . what . . . I don't know what is my aim in life. Shouldn't I be contented—the way it is? But I'm not. I'm unhappy.

TH: Well, isn't that then our problem?

PT: Yes, but . . .

TH: Not the question whether you should or should not be contented, but the fact that you are not and that we want to find out why.

PT: But I'm ashamed to complain about it. Because I have so much. I mean I have a . . . a good husband and a nice house and a wonderful daughter and son. It really makes me ashamed. Am I making a mountain out of a molehill?

TH: Well, there's something in this picture which seems to be missing; I mean you mention all these things that are seemingly satisfying and yet you are not satisfied . . .

PT: But I'm not.

TH: . . . and there must be something that is wrong.

PT: I don't know why—I can't put my finger on it, really. Well, I don't know what I'm striving for. What do I want? What do I expect from life? Why should I get bored all the time? Why should life be so monotonous? Is it because I don't have enough to do? Is it because I have time on my hands? If I went out and worked I probably wouldn't feel this way. I kept asking myself that for the past two days. I don't know what I want out of life, what I'm striving for, but I expect what I want . . . my husband is good to me, my daughter is wonderful, and I have a fine boy. I entertain nicely. People have said that they feel very welcome in . . . and I'm a cordial hostess, and they were comfortable in my home. Doesn't everybody do that? Isn't that everybody's life?

TH: Well, if this were all so, then it would be very amazing that you shouldn't be satisfied. And I wonder whether these things really are so.

PT: But, they are all so, but still I'm unhappy, still I'm unhappy, still I want to run away . . . and . . . get away from my house. But I think it's lack of something to do, lack of interest, lack of . . . working maybe, that's what I need. Paul has gone away to school. Doris is growing up now, she doesn't need me for anything, really . . . except to get her meals and things like that, but that's nothing. And Paul is away at school all winter and at camp in the summer. My husband only needs me for the meals and things like that.

TH: What kind of things?

PT: Dinner, and washing, and cleaning, but outside of that I . . . my time is my own.

TH: Is that really the only thing that your husband needs you for?

PT: Well . . . he's very . . . he seems to be very contented with the life that he lives . . . leads. I don't interfere with his life. He seems to . . . like to come home, and stay home and relax, after putting in a tough day with those law cases of his. I certainly can't . . . interfere with that. It wouldn't do me any good if I tried. We are . . . a . . . two very different personalities completely. He's very placid and reserved and I'm the opposite. I'm happy-go-lu . . . I mean I used to be . . . happy-go-lucky and nothing bothered me too much. I like to have a good time. I like to have fun. I don't feel as though I'm old . . . too old to enjoy life. But he . . . he likes quiet things . . . the quiet life.

TH: But this difference in personality hasn't been bothering you—at least you haven't said so—all through the last sixteen yes or so.

PT: Oh, I thought about it . . . yes, I have. I've thought about it a long time . . . how we can be visiting and I'll have a good time and all of a sudden he'll say, "Come on, let's go home." So, quick like that I have to leave and go home . . . I mean it's been going on for years. It isn't anything new. And as I told you before, if we're invited out and he's tired, we don't go. I mean things like that. But I guess I can't be a playgirl all the time. But I don't feel old . . . really, I mean, where I have to stay home all the time. I feel as though I want to have fun and enjoy myself. Is that wrong?

TH: No. Of course, you are young; you are quite young enough to have an enjoyable life, and I think that you have a right to that kind of thing, but I'm just wondering . . .

PT: You mean it isn't wrong to still feel young in your heart and to want to get fun out of life.

TH: If one considers such a thing as "right" or "wrong," I'm quite sure that it is not wrong.

PT: Do I sound immature, do I sound like a child when I say things like that? Childish?

TH: Do you think you do?

PT: I'm afraid to say I do. I think it is childish just to want to have a good time and enjoy myself. I think now that my children are growing up and I'm getting older I should want to settle down and not do anything—and just lead a very quiet, simple life.

TH: Why do you think you should?

PT: We . . . I don't know, I just feel as though I . . . I can't go out and do the things I used to do, although I still feel as though I could . . . I mean, inside. But it doesn't look right; it isn't right to do it.

TH: With Doris getting older and more independent, do you feel that you are, well let us say, getting old, being an old woman now?

PT: No. It doesn't bother me. I never think of it that way. Is that wrong?

TH: No, what you say, that you feel that you should . . .

PT: Well, I do . . . I mean, I feel I should on account of the people around me, convention's sake, you know what I mean, having people talk about me. I still feel that I can . . . I ought to have fun . . . and . . . and enjoy myself, even though the children are growing up and don't need me as much now. I think I really could have a better time . . . but I'm afraid of what people will say. My friends, my husband.

TH: What do you think they might say?

PT: They'll say that she ought to grow up, she's not . . . she's got growing children, she should act like a mother. (embarrassed laugh) But Bob is very restrained . . . not restrained but placid; he's very quiet. We have been away—as a matter of fact I don't even enjoy going away with Bob, because he likes to go to a place where you can just eat, and sleep, and you know, relax, go to bed early. I do that every night. All the time. I don't even like to go away on vacations with him, or anyplace . . . but I go. He wants to relax all the time; I'm not tired, I don't feel that kind of tired that . . . I want fun, I want life, I want people around. Is that wrong?

TH: Just . . . how do you feel about this? You seem to feel . . .

PT: Well, I don't know . . . I can't understand . . . I mean, this . . . feeling that I've had about Bob being . . . placid. . . . I've always . . . held it in, I mean I've never said anything about it. I've never said, "Oh, I'd like to go someplace where it's fun." I've always kept my mouth shut and not said anything about it . . . because I knew it wouldn't do any good to say it. I mean it's always been in the back of my mind. We went on a vacation once for four days, and all I did was sit on the porch and read. I can do that at home. I . . . and people said, "Oh, you must have had a wonderful time on your vacation." I was bored to death! I hated every minute of it. Of course, I didn't say anything to him. I said it was very nice . . . but I hated it. And I won't go away with him anymore. And I can't go alone, so I'm stuck. (half-laugh) So I . . . so I guess for me the only way I can go . . . I mean get away . . . is to go with him and do what he wants to do. So you see how different we are? Exact—just like night and day. Maybe it's better. Maybe he holds me down. Maybe I need that sort of thing. But I feel that I've missed so much in my younger days. I wasn't allowed to do anything. But I thought being married, and . . . it would be different. But it hasn't changed a bit. I mean as far as . . . pleasure . . . and enjoyment. It sounds crazy, doesn't it? (pause) But he's so good that I can't. . . . I guess I can't be any different with him, I mean I can't . . . I can't go . . . a . . . I can't disagree with him, as far as things like that go. I can't say, "I'm going out to a nightclub tonight and you can stay home." I've never done it.

TH: At the time you were telling me about, when you used to be active in that amateur dramatic group and so on . . .

PT: The rehearsals were sometimes in the afternoon.

TH: Yes, but you were then also going out and having . . . fun. Did that have any relationship to this feeling?

PT: Sure. It made me feel that I could have fun one or two afternoons or evenings a week, and I could sit home the other evenings. At least I had some fun; I got that in. But he . . . I . . . listen . . . I . . . I feel he's entitled to living the kind of life he wants to live. I don't object to it, I mean, as far as he's concerned. He puts in a hard day; he's tired. He really—I'd never deprive him of going to bed at nine o'clock or ten o'clock; I would never say anything to make him feel that . . . that I was unhappy about it, I just don't say anything. Course I feel terrible, but I don't say anything about it. We . . . we refuse a million invitations on account of him. Is it wrong to feel that you still want to have fun in life?

TH: Well, there might be other compensations . . .

PT: Well . . .

TH: . . . for this, and I wonder whether you feel that there are or there are not . . . and, I mean, other compensations in your relationship.

PT: Well, he's . . . he's a . . . he's good.

TH: How do you mean?

PT: He's . . . reliable, he's honest, he's a hard worker . . . he's a homebody. (apologetic laugh) He likes to stay home. Maybe I haven't . . . maybe I'm not mature; maybe I'm still a child—I haven't matured enough, maybe I'm not grown-up enough, I don't know.

TH: Well now, the things you mentioned as . . . the good points of your husband. Are those really the only things you would expect from a husband?

PT: No. I think a husband should be . . . as excited to do something as the wife should. I feel that . . . Bob should feel like I feel, about having a good time, about going out and being with people. That he should be as congenial as I am. (pause) Even when we were younger—I mean even before we were married and . . . we were engaged, it was the same way, although I always figured, well, he has a hard day the next day and I wouldn't interfere. I would let him . . . he would . . . we . . . when we used to have dates he left me at ten-thirty or eleven o'clock, early. We never stayed up past midnight, ever. I never remember staying out till twelve or one o'clock. I sound silly, though, to make an issue of it, don't I?

TH: Well, this is a problem which is bothering you, and I don't see why you consider that silly.

PT: Yes, but how . . . I . . . I can't straighten it out. How can I do anything about it? There's no way of . . . of changing it. I certainly couldn't say to Bob, "I'm going out on a date tonight, good-by." (throaty laugh) Or, "I'm going out to have fun." I couldn't do that; I'm not built that way. As much as I would probably love to do it, I wouldn't do it. Is it . . . is it because I feel that I missed so much when I was younger that I feel that now I want to . . . do the things I didn't do before?

TH: Is that what you think it is?

PT: Yes, I do. I think I never really had a chance to . . . really go out and . . . well, I don't know, it sounds silly to even talk about. It's ridiculous. Can't do anything about it anyway. I sound like a child. Once the pattern is made you have to stick to it, I guess. Once you start your life the way you do you can't change. Especially your married life. I've never told Bob how I felt about this . . . because I knew it wouldn't do any good. I'm sure it wouldn't. Because he wouldn't understand, he wouldn't . . . he . . . he'd think I was acting like a baby. So, if I get myself something to do during the day, where I'd get busy and not think about it, maybe it'll be better to a . . . at night I'd be contented to stay home. It's like knocking your head against a stone wall, isn't it? Can you straighten out a problem like that? Is it possible?

TH: Well, I'm not sure whether we really have the whole problem in front of us.

PT: Well, what do you mean? I don't understand; I've told you how I felt about it.

TH: But you say yourself, again and again, it sounds childish and it doesn't make sense.

PT: But it's because there's no way of solving it. There's no way of solving that problem. How can I go to Bob and say, "I want to go out tonight. I want to have fun. I'm tired of staying home." If I did, he'd say, "I'm sorry, I'm tired." So what am I going to do? Go out by myself? Can I do that?

TH: Well, that's a question you'd have to ask yourself.

PT: Well, I can't, I've never done it, I wouldn't know where to—how to start. So I keep asking myself, well am I str—what do I want out of life? What am I striving for, what am I working for? Where am I getting? I have a nice home, a nice daughter and son, a nice husband, but that's all. It sounds stupid, doesn't it?

TH: No, it doesn't sound stupid; it sounds like an incomplete picture to me.

PT: Well, it isn't incomplete. That's exactly how I feel. I feel that I . . . do what I have to do, but I still want to get some pleasure out of life too. But why am I different from most people? Most people, I guess, don't feel the way I do. They don't complain about not going out. Well, what's wrong with me? Why should I feel like I want to enjoy myself and have fun?

TH: Well, of course, again we can't say what happens to most people, because we are dealing with—appraising—your problem rather than other people . . .

PT: Well, that's what I mean, there's no comparison, I mean I don't understand it. There are . . . there's a friend of mine who . . . who's in worse circumstances than I am, but she never complains. Maybe because she has three kids to take care of during the day and she's probably tickled to death when they go to bed so she can relax at night. Maybe it's because I don't have enough to do during the day. (pause) I don't know. But I've felt like this for a long time. I feel that I'm not getting everything out of life that I would like to.

TH: What would you like to get out of life? That you're not . . .

PT: I don't know. That's what I'd like to know. That's what I wonder. What do I want? What do I? That's where I can't put my finger on it. There's something that I . . . that I . . . I'm hoping for, but I don't know what.

TH: When you were engaged to your husband and this pattern had already been . . . you know, you say this pattern had already been established back then—was there something that you were hoping for that might compensate you for some of the socially unexciting times?

PT: There was nothing. Nothing. I was young, I didn't know, I was madly in love. I thought he was wonderful and I adored him. I thought he was a wonderful guy. I didn't look for anything else. He was sweet, he was . . . oh, I didn't need . . . I didn't want anything else. He was thoughtful and he was considerate. I used to work in a gift shop; I was substituting there one summer. He used to pick me up in the morning and drive me to work, pick me up at five-thirty in the afternoon. I thought he was just marvelous. And Bob is very secure. As far as I can see, he . . . he . . . nothing seems to bother him too much. And he's had a very tough life, too, because he worked his way through college . . . as a salesman . . . in the summertime. And his family were poor. He was really, he's really a terrific guy. Self-made. (pause) And I always felt that Bob was the "old reliable," I mean somebody you could depend on all the time. That was the feeling I had, he was always there when you wanted him, when you needed him. He still is, I mean that's the w . . . you know. That's what he is today.

TH: And yet, somehow you sound as if you were disappointed . . . I can't quite put my finger on it.

PT: Disappointed? (pause) No, I don't know. Maybe it's because I . . . that he's older that I'm disappointed. I mean, maybe if I had married somebody younger that . . . that wasn't so . . . set in their ways. Bob is a lot like I remember my father to be. He had a wonderful disposition, easygoing, reliable, I mean, those are the traits.

TH: Well, isn't there something that one expects from a husband that one doesn't expect from one's father?

PT: Love and companionship? Romance? (pause) That's when you're young. When you're older it doesn't mean anything anymore. Or when you're married a long time it changes completely, doesn't it?

TH: How do you mean, it changes completely?

PT: Well, I don't know, when you're young it's kid stuff I guess, but when you get older you don't . . . think about it, or . . . it doesn't mean anything. It's like . . . being married when you're older . . . it's like a habit. I mean it's like brushing your teeth. It's . . . it's . . . your husband is there and you're . . . and that's the way it is.

TH: I wonder whether that is the way it really has to be.

PT: Well, I don't know. I mean I can't answer that question. I don't know.

TH: Well, let me put it this way, could it be that you would rather that it were not that way?

PT: Well, I don't know that either, because I don't under—I don't know. I don't know any different. It's . . . it's . . . it's a different kind, it's . . . a deeper feeling you have than when you're younger, I think. It's a closer feeling when you get older. But in a different way. I don't know, I can't answer that either, I guess. It's more of a take-it-for-granted feeling. Doesn't that make sense? I mean, does that sound . . . you know he's there. That's all. You know that he's . . . that you have somebody, that you . . . that you feel close to. I can't . . . explain it. All I know is that it isn't the same as when you're young. But, it isn't supposed to be, I don't think. People are not . . . Bob is not a demonstrative person at all.

TH: How do you mean, "demonstrative"?

PT: Well, I mean, he . . . he . . . he doesn't call me pet names, like some husbands call their wives or he doesn't show any affection, like some husbands show their wives . . . from what I've seen. He's never been that way. I guess I'm the aggressive one. Oh, it's so silly to talk about this, because nothing can be done. It's so foolish. I can't go out and get a divorce tomorrow just because I have a husband that likes to stay home all the time. I can't do that.

TH: What made you think of divorce?

PT: Well . . . isn't that what people usually do when they're unhappy? Don't they usually . . . if they're not happy they . . . divorce? They . . . maybe . . . maybe I'm childish, thinking about it this way. Maybe I shouldn't even think about it. As my mother says, "You make your bed; you lie in it." I mean, not that I've even discussed this with her at all, but I mean it's just that she's passed that . . . she has said that about . . . you know.

TH: I wonder why you pick on this particular . . . saying.

PT: "You make your bed; you lie in it?"

TH: Yes.

PT: I don't know, I've heard my mother say it.

TH: Well, there are lots of other sayings. I wonder why you used this particular one.

PT: Well, it's . . . it's something that you do, and you just have to . . . take it. (sigh) There's no way of getting out of it. Oh, I don't know, some days I feel like I just . . . like to go away and . . . just see what the other side of the world looks like. But I'm not—do I sound like I'm complaining?

TH: Do you think you are?

PT: I don't know, is it a complaint? Or is it just unhappiness or is unhappiness a complaint too?

TH: I don't know. If you want to call it something, I think you sound disappointed.

PT: Disappointed. Maybe I am disappointed. I've been disappointed all my life. It's nothing new. (pause) But then I feel guilty about talking about it. . . . Because I feel that Bob is good to me . . . that I shouldn't complain, or I shouldn't say it. . . . It sounds crazy. Maybe it's that I'm not matured enough. Maybe I'm still a child. Maybe I . . . I haven't grown up. Maybe I expect too much. I don't know.

TH: What do you mean, expect too much?

PT: Maybe I expected more out of life.

TH: Such as what?

PT: Well, that's it, I don't know. I can't . . . I don't know. Everything isn't perfect. Sometimes I wonder if I had lived by myself, when I first got married, whether it would be any different.

TH: In which respect are you thinking of?

PT: I mean living by myself, alone, maybe our lives would be different?

TH: You say, how do you . . . I don't understand, you say by yourself, alone?

PT: Yes, I mean living in a room by ourselves, without living in . . . in the house with my mother.

TH: Is that "by myself alone" you mean "by ourselves"?

PT: No, I meant by ourselves alone. Maybe we would have lived differently, maybe we . . . I don't know.

TH: How would you have lived differently?

PT: Well, maybe it's because we were restrained when we were home. That we . . . that . . . maybe Bob felt that he didn't want to . . . do anything, I mean go out or anything on account of living at my mother's. I don't know, it's all . . . mixed up. But I keep thinking about that. Maybe our lives would have been different.

TH: In the very beginning, when we first met, you told me that in the years when you lived at your mother's house you felt . . . kind of restrained, or inhibited, about intercourse because you had the feeling that your mother might be coming into the room. If you had lived away, do you think that might have been different?

PT: It might have been. Maybe it would have. I don't know. So many years ago, it might have been different.

TH: Well, but then you moved out of your mother's house, and that restriction or restraint, inhibition, was removed. Did things change then?

PT: Yes and no.

TH: How do you mean?

PT: I don't know, I can't . . . I can't . . . I don't know. Maybe . . . Maybe, I don't know . . . I can under—I can't explain it. Maybe it . . . maybe that feeling stayed with us. (half-apologetic laugh) Is it possible?

TH: Well, you have to tell me whether it did or not.

PT: (laughing) Maybe it got to a point where it didn't matter. (cynical tone)

TH: That what didn't matter?

PT: Anything. That's not very clear, is it? (laughs)

TH: No.

PT: Well, maybe . . . maybe we felt that it wasn't important, because we had been restrained for so many years. Is that possible?

TH: Well, now, you say, "we felt," what did you feel?

PT: Well, both of us, I'm sure. I don't know, maybe it wasn't me, maybe my husband felt that way, I don't know. I've never asked him.

TH: Well, how did you feel about it?

PT: Well, I felt relaxed and relieved when I was in my own home . . . because I felt free. Nothing bothered me. (pause) I still feel free in my own home, as far as that goes. Maybe it isn't my fault. (half-laughing)

TH: What isn't your fault?

PT: What you said.

TH: What did I say?

PT: Maybe . . . maybe he's inhibited.

TH: You see, this whole picture you painted of your married life, and all the things you said about your husband, you said he's hard-working, he's conscientious, he's honest, and so forth. In all these things, there's always been something missing, and this was your sexual relationship and I always wondered why there was this hold, because after all, when one has been married for a number of years, one talks about one's relationship with one's husabnd. I mean there is the sexual relationship in addition to all the other things, and you have talked about all the other things and I wondered why you have always been leaving this out, and I wonder whether it's very difficult to talk about that and whether it may not be that this is one of the things that you have always been getting away from when we started talking . . . in this direction.

PT: Well, I don't like to talk about personal problems, things like that.

TH: But don't you know that, within the treatment, it's very important . . .

PT: I know . . . but I still think it's none of anybody's business (apologetic laugh)

TH: . . . not to leave anything out? Well, as long as you feel that some parts of your life are none of my business, we can't get very far in our treatment.

PT: I know. (pause) It's very difficult to talk about it because I never talked about it, with any—at all, ever.

TH: I know, and that's what I meant when I said repeatedly that you have to work real hard in order to say some of these unpleasant things that we don't ordinarily talk about, because only when we have all areas of your life clearly before us can we understand what some of your problems are.

PT: Um hum. I never liked to talk about things like that. I never have. I always thought it was something that belonged to me.

TH: But then you again have been holding out, haven't you?

PT: Um huh.

TH: And we can't possibly make any progress in the treatment . . .

PT: I know it.

TH: . . . as long as you have this private understanding . . .

PT: But I . . .

TH: . . . that you will hold out on certain aspects.

PT: To tell you the truth, I didn't think it would enter the picture. I always thought that those things were never talked about. I didn't know you discuss things like that too.

TH: Well, again, there shouldn't be anything that you think doesn't have any relationship, because whatever happens to come into your mind is what you want to say without any restrictions and . . .

PT: Embarrassing!

TH: Well, now, it is difficult to say and it's embarrassing and it's sometimes frightening to say, but nevertheless this is the hard work which is involved in the treatment, and you have to understand that there shouldn't be anything that you should keep to yourself, thinking that it has nothing to do with or has nothing . . . is none of my business.

PT: It's very embarrassing to talk about it. Because I always felt that those things, nobody was supposed to talk about. And I didn't know that I had to talk about them. I really didn't, honestly.

TH: Well, it's part of our general understanding . . .

PT: I know.

TH: . . . that you will say anything that comes to your mind, do you see?

PT: Yes, that's what you said. Well, I didn't realize that I had to . . .

TH: That includes everything.

PT: I didn't know I had to talk about those things too. (pause) The time is up. And I still didn't get anything. (sigh)

TH: Well, maybe this is one of the reasons why we haven't gotten very far, because you still . . .

PT: Because I've been holding out.

TH: . . . have some private understanding that there are certain things that are none of my business.

PT: I still don't understand why they're so important, I mean why things like that really . . . a . . . make a problem.

TH: Because it's part of the general picture and in order to understand it we have to get at all parts of it.

PT: Yes, that's what you said. See you on Monday.

SUMMARY AND EVALUATION

Neurosis is learned in early childhood. Although a single drive can be raised to traumatic heights and cause pain and suffering, neurosis is usually the product of the conflict of drives originating in the feeding situation, cleanliness training, sex training, and anger-anxiety situations. These conflicts are repressed; that is, they are unconscious. The unconscious is that which cannot be verbalized, that which is unlabeled. Fear is the most basic and the strongest drive involved in conflict; it inhibits the expression of other drives, thus preventing their satisfaction. Both fear and the conflicting drive produce symptoms that consist of responses—often compromise responses—that lead to some drive reduction. Thus they are rewarded or reinforced and persist. The neurotic is miserable because of his or her conflicts, which prevent the satisfaction of drives, and appears to be stupid because repression prevents the neurotic from knowing the nature of his or her problem.

The therapeutic situation provides the conditions for new learning. Free association leads to the uncovering of repression. The transference further reveals the nature of the conflicting drives. The client and the therapist engage in the process of labeling these drives, experiences, feelings, and conflicts. Such labeling makes possible both the discrimination of experiences and situations that are apparently similar but actually different and the appropriate generalization to situations that are actually similar. Labeling and the resultant insight enable the client to engage in the higher mental activities that are necessary for adaptive behavior.

Neurosis is essentially an approach–avoidance conflict, that is, a situation in which the individual has strong tendencies to approach and to avoid the same goal. The gradient of avoidance (the increase of the tendency for avoidance, or fear, with increasing proximity to the goal) is stronger than the gradient of approach (the increase of the tendency for approach with increasing proximity to the goal). The neurotic has strong avoidance tendencies. An attempt to increase the neurotic's motivation to approach the goal will increase only the person's fear and conflict. This is often what well-meaning relatives and friends try to do. If the therapist does the same, the client will tend to leave therapy. Therefore, rather than attempt to raise the approach gradient, the therapist attempts to reduce the avoidance gradient and, thus, the client's fears through acceptance, permissiveness, and understanding.

In one publication, Miller refers to the situation in which the client's fears are realistic and the achievement of the goal results in punishment. The client is then punished if the goal is reached or suffers strong fear or conflict if the punishment keeps the client just barely away from the goal. "In such cases, attempting to decrease fear and avoidance will indeed produce a negative therapeutic effect, while conversely, a positive therapeutic effect may be produced by increasing the strength of fear and avoidance to the point where the subject remains far enough away from the forbidden goal that he is no longer strongly punished or even tempted enough to be in conflict."[34] When punishment occurs some time after achieving the goal, strong fear (or guilt) is felt after the goal has been reached but only moderate fear, before it has been reached. Again, increasing the height of the avoidance gradient might produce therapeutic changes.

Dollard and Miller present a meticulous, systematic, and reasoned approach based on reinforcement learning theory. They have integrated learning theory with the clinical system of psychotherapy developed by psychoanalysis. They have shown essentially that psychoanalysis is consistent with, or can be rationalized to appear consistent with, reinforcement learning theory. The concept of reinforcement is substituted for Freud's pleasure principle. The concept of ego strength is translated into that of the higher mental processes and of culturally valued learned drives and skills. Repression becomes the inhibition of the cue-producing responses that mediate thinking and reasoning. Transference is a special case of generalization. Conflict is seen in terms of learning theory. Additional concepts and principles, such as inhibition and restraint, are added to extend some of those of psychoanalysis. The concept of reality is extended, or concretized, in terms of the physical and social conditions of learning. The need for responses to be made and reinforced outside of therapy, in real life, is emphasized.

Compared with the rather crude and narrow approaches of Wolpe and of Salter, that of Dollard and Miller is broad, comprehensive, and authoritative. Rather than reject psychological and social factors, such as the nature of the client–therapist relationship, it incorporates them and indicates their consistency with learning theory. There is a major point of disagreement with the techniques of Salter and of Wolpe. On the assumption, supported by empirical evidence, that the avoidance gradient is stronger than the approach gradient in an approach–avoidance conflict, Dollard and Miller base their techniques on the reduction of the avoidance gradient. (However, they do recognize the need to motivate some clients to go beyond talking and take action, although they do not specify how this is to be done.) In direct contrast to this, the techniques of Salter and of Wolpe appear to be directed toward the raising of the approach gradient. Since Dollard and Miller present empirical evidence and suggest clinical evidence for their position, how, then, can Wolpe and Salter achieve success with their techniques? Two possible explanations present themselves. First, as suggested in the discussion of Wolpe's approach, the clients (or many of them) are not clinically neurotic but possess isolated symptoms or limited disturbances that can be helped by these approaches; that is, they are individuals in whom the approach gradient, although somewhat weak, can easily be made stronger by techniques such as those used by Salter and Wolpe. Second, it is possible that their success is the result, not of the techniques to which they ascribe it, but of other aspects of the treatment, such as their earnest, sincere interest in, concern for, and efforts to help their clients.

The contrasting views of treatment in terms of the approach–avoidance gradient appear to be related to contrasting views of whether behavior changes first and feelings and attitudes change later or vice versa. Wolpe and Salter appear to accept the former position. Dollard and Miller appear to adhere to the latter. For them, fear is an attitude or a feeling, and their approach is to reduce fear through the therapeutic relationship before they expect behavior to change.

There is another related and somewhat contradictory aspect of this basic difference. Wolpe emphasizes that the client must be relaxed when engaging in desirable new behavior, such as sexual activity, so that behavior is reconditioned by being associated with a pleasant or nonanxious feeling. (Wolpe also describes it as the inhibition of fear by another incompatible response.) Dollard and Miller, on the contrary, advocate that the client make a sexual response while feeling afraid, so that when the behavior is not followed by punishment, extinction will occur.[35] It is, of course, likely that in the case of Wolpe's method, some anxiety or fear does exist, even though the client is somewhat relaxed, and that in the case of Dollard and Miller's technique, fear or anxiety has been reduced sufficiently to permit the client to act when he or she could not before. Wolpe emphasizes reconditioning, while Dollard and Miller emphasize extinction.

Dollard and Miller also disagree with Salter and Wolpe and behavior therapists in the latter's belief that symptoms are the neurosis and that removal of the symptoms is equivalent to a cure of the neurosis. Dollard and Miller state that since "a learned symptom produces a certain amount of reduction of the state of high drive motivating it . . . interfering with the symptom . . . will be expected to throw the patient back into a state of high drive and conflict. This will tend to motivate the learning of new responses. These new responses may be either more adaptive ones or new, and possibly worse, symptoms."[36] Dollard and Miller concede that "after the inhibitions blocking the more adaptive goal responses have been sufficiently reduced, however, we might expect different results."[37] Then the therapist might interfere with a symptom by means of an unfavorable interpretation, which might cause the goal response to become stronger than the weakened inhibition. This may be a factor in the apparent success of Wolpe's and Salter's methods. Dollard and Miller also rely more on discrimination than on automatic conditioning. Their approach is thus more verbal and more rational than are conditioning approaches. Although they recognize the affective and emotional aspects as essential, their emphasis on verbal labeling, discrimination, and generalization gives a more verbal-rational cast to their approach than traditional psychoanalysis has. It is interesting that at the close of the chapter on labeling, Dollard and Miller feel it necessary to note that they "are not advocating any mere intellectualization of the therapeutic process."[38] Yet, while there is concern with affective elements, there is emphasis on rational analysis. The therapist is seen as performing a teaching function to a great extent.

There are some gaps and inconsistencies in Dollard and Miller's approach. For example, what repression *is* receives attention, but the *process* of repression itself is given inadequate treatment. In discussing free association, they claim that speaking is easier or less anxiety producing than thinking, so that "the extinction effects which are first attached to talking out loud generalize swiftly to 'talking without voice' (thinking)."[39] Later, however, discussing client obstructiveness, they suggest that "even though the patient goes on thinking the sentences which produce anxiety, it may be that this anxiety is considerably less than when he makes the same responses out loud."[40] These are minor things, however. A more general criticism is that Dollard and Miller's approach is derived from a learning theory that has been developed mainly from experiments with animals and then extended to human behavior, often by analogy.[41] It suffers also from the limitations of reinforcement theory,[42] which does not appear to account adequately for all learning and behavior change, particularly the complex behavior of human beings. Dollard and Miller's approach is thus oversimplified and restricted to a view of the human being as a reaction system responding to situational stimuli that reduce its drives. Secondary, or learned, drives, which derive from the primary drives, are recognized, but their nature and their development, or derivation from the primary drives, remain rather vague.

Dollard and Miller present their ideas as hypotheses, not proven principles. They stress that their book is not complete or adequate for the practice of psychotherapy. They contemplated further books to fill in the gaps and deal with unsolved problems. It is a pity that this plan was not realized, but it is also a pity that the presentation in this book has not been given the attention it deserves by others interested in counseling or psychotherapy or in the education of counselors or psychotherapists. Dollard and Miller's is one of the few really systematic approaches to counseling. Their integration of so-called insight psychotherapy with learning theory anticipated current efforts by almost 20 years. It remains a classic well worth reading by all students of counseling or psychotherapy.

REFERENCES

1. Dollard, J., & Miller, N. E. *Personality and psychotherapy: An analysis in terms of learning, thinking, and culture.* New York: McGraw-Hill, 1950.
2. Ibid., p. 9.
3. Ibid., p. 15.
4. Ibid.
5. Ibid., pp. 31–32. In subsequent publications [Miller, N. E. Liberalization of basic S–R concepts: Extensions to conflict behavior, motivation, and social learning. In S. Koch (Ed.), *Psychology: A study of science. Study I: Conceptual and systematic.* Vol. 2. *General systematic formulations, learning, and special processes.* New York: McGraw-Hill, 1959. Pp. 196–292; Miller, N. E. Some implications of modern behavior theory for personality change and psychotherapy. In D. Byrne & P. Worchel (Eds.), *Personality change.* New York: Wiley, 1964. Pp. 149–179], Miller has modified his views to include the channeling by learning of certain presumably innate drives such as curiosity.
6. Dollard & Miller, *Personality and psychotherapy,* p. 32.
7. Ibid., p. 77.
8. Ibid., p. 39.
9. "This statement is no longer accurate. At present it is not known whether all learned responses would extinguish if given enough unreinforced trials." Miller, N. E. Personal communication, July 8, 1964.
10. Same comment as above applies to this statement.
11. Dollard & Miller, *Personality and psychotherapy,* p. 57.
12. Ibid., p. 103.
13. Ibid., p. 111.
14. Dollard, J., & Miller, N. E., *Social learning and imitation.* New Haven, Conn.: Yale University Press, 1941.
15. Dollard & Miller, *Personality and psychotherapy,* p. 127.
16. Ibid., p. 130.
17. Ibid., p. 196.
18. Ibid., p. 240.
19. Ibid.
20. Ibid., p. 281.
21. Ibid., p. 303.
22. Ibid., p. 305.
23. Ibid., p. 338.
24. Ibid., pp. 243–244.
25. Ibid., pp. 241–242.
26. Ibid., p. 259.
27. Ibid., p. 250.
28. Ibid., p. 274.
29. Ibid., p. 278.
30. Ibid., p. 287.
31. Ibid., p. 284.
32. Ibid., p. 312.
33. Reprinted with permission of The Macmillan Company from *Steps in psychotherapy* by J.

Dollard, F. Auld, Jr., and A. M. White. Copyright 1953 by The Macmillan Company, pp. 128–143.

34. Miller, Some implications of modern behavior theory for personality change and psychotherapy, p. 154.

35. Dollard & Miller, *Personality and psychotherapy,* p. 307.

36. Ibid., p. 385.

37. Ibid., p. 386.

38. Ibid., p. 303.

39. Ibid., p. 250.

40. Ibid., pp. 270–271.

41. Miller, J. G., & Butler, J. M. Review of *Personality and psychotherapy* by J. Dollard and N. E. Miller. *Psychological Bulletin,* 1952, *49,* 183–185.

42. Raimy, V. C. Clinical methods: Psychotherapy. *Annual Review of Psychology,* 1952, *3,* 321–350.

chapter 5

Behavior Therapy: Wolpe

Joseph Wolpe (b. 1915) was educated in South Africa and received his M.B. and B.Ch. in 1939 and his M.D. in 1948 from the University of Witwatersrand, Johannesburg. While engaged in the private practice of psychiatry, he was lecturer in psychiatry at Witwatersrand from 1949 to 1959, except for the year 1956 to 1957, when he was a fellow at the Center for Advanced Study in the Behavioral Sciences at Stanford University. From 1960 to 1965, Wolpe was research and clinical professor of psychiatry at the University of Virginia Medical School in Charlottesville, Virginia. In 1965, he became professor of psychiatry in the Department of Behavioral Sciences of the School of Medicine at Temple University and the Eastern Pennsylvania Psychiatric Institute in Philadelphia, Pennsylvania, where he has remained. In 1979, he received a Distinguished Scientific Award for the Application of Psychology from the American Psychological Association. The announcement of the award in the *American Psychologist* (1980, *35,* 44–51) includes a biography and a bibliography of his publications through 1979.

Wolpe's M.D. thesis was entitled "An Approach to the Problem of Neurosis Based on the Conditioned Response." Publication of journal articles in 1952, 1954, and 1956 preceded publication of his book *Psychotherapy by Reciprocal Inhibition* (1958). With Lazarus, he wrote *Behavior Therapy Techniques: A Guide to the Treatment of Neuroses* (1966). Wolpe also is the author of *The Practice of Behavior Therapy* (1969; 2nd ed., 1973; 3rd ed., 1982) and, *Theme and Variations: A Behavior Therapy Casebook* (1976).

BACKGROUND AND DEVELOPMENT

Wolpe dates the beginning of his method of psychotherapy to 1944, when his reading, while he was serving as a medical military officer, led him to a questioning of psychoanalysis. He learned that psychoanalysis was not accepted in the Soviet Union, and when he looked into the reason for this, he was led to Pavlov, thence to Hull and to studies of experimental neuroses in animals. This resulted in his conducting experiments with cats in which neurotic reactions first were induced by administering an electric shock and then were removed by getting the animal to eat in the presence of small, and then incrasingly larger, doses of anxiety-evoking stimuli. Thus there occurred a conditional inhibition of the anxiety responses.[1]

These results led to the idea that human neurotic anxieties might be dealt with —as in Jones's experiments with Peter—by counterconditioning them with eating. Wolpe never actually attempted this, but he used other anxiety-inhibiting responses.

All behavior conforms to causal laws. There are three classes of processes that lead to lasting changes in an organism's behavior: growth, lesions, and learning, "Learning may be said to have occurred if a response has been evoked in temporal contiguity with a given sensory stimulus and it is subsequently found that the stimulus can evoke the response although it could not have done so before. If the stimulus could have evoked the response before but subsequently evokes it more strongly, then, too, learning may be said to have occurred."[2] The strengthening of the connection between the new stimulus and the response is called reinforcement, and the events that lead to strengthening are reinforcements. A number of factors are related to reinforcement. The new, or conditioned, stimulus must precede the unconditioned stimulus at an optimal interval. The shorter the interval between the response and the reduction of a strong drive (by reward), the greater the reinforcement. The greater the number of reinforcements, the greater the strength of the connection; spaced reinforcements are more effective than massed reinforcements. In general, the greater the reinforcement, the greater the reduction in drive, although there appear to be instances when increase in drive is reinforcing.

When a conditioned stimulus occurs repeatedly without the unconditioned stimulus or without reinforcement, the response ceases to occur or is extinguished, although there is partial recovery if the stimulus is not applied for some time and then is reapplied. The disappearance of the response is the result of negative conditioning and of reactive inhibition due to fatigue, which dissipates with time, allowing for recovery.

Reciprocal inhibition is the inhibition, elimination, or weakening of old responses by new ones. "When a response is inhibited by an incompatible response and if a major drive reduction follows, a significant amount of conditioned inhibition of the response will be developed."[3]

Wolpe performed a series of experiments in which neurotic reactions (anxiety and fear, with their behavioral and physiological concomitants) were induced in cats by electric shock. These symptoms were generalized, occurring outside the experimental cage. They were intensified by an auditory stimulus that had been presented with the shock. The magnitude of the symptoms varied directly with the similarity of the environment to the room in which the neuroses had been induced.

The neurotic reactions were produced in a feeding situation, which provided the possibility of removing them by reciprocal inhibition. Two methods were used. The first was the addition to the stimulus situation in the experimental cage of a factor to favor or strengthen or induce the feeding response. Since in their living cages, the cats were fed by hand, it was expected that the hand had become a conditioned stimulus that evoked approach responses to food. Food was therefore presented on a spatula held in the experimenter's hand. Four of the nine cats so treated were induced to eat in this manner and gradually were led to eat from the food box. Three cats were forcibly led to eat from the food box. Over several days, the neurotic reactions decreased and finally were eliminated.

A second method consisted of feeding the animals under conditions in which the anxiety-producing stimuli were less potent. The five (out of nine) cats who did not respond to the hand-feeding method were offered food outside the experimental cage in surroundings that aroused decreasing symptoms of anxiety, until they were able to eat the food. When all were able to eat in some situation, they were offered food in situations that had evoked increasing symptoms of anxiety. Eventually, all apparently were brought to the point where they could eat from the food box inside the experimental cage, and symptoms of anxiety disappeared.

When the conditioned auditory stimulus was presented, however, anxiety recurred. Two cats were induced to eat at gradually decreasing distances from the auditory stimulus, until they were able to eat in the cage with no anxiety. The remaining seven cats were given food in the experimental cage, followed by a brief presentation of the auditory stimulus, followed by more food, and so forth, with the result that the cats' delay in eating the food decreased. Then the duration of the stimulus was increased until the cats were able to eat with no anxiety in the presence of the auditory stimulus. Eventually, the stimulus became a conditioned stimulus for food-seeking movements. To determine whether the neurotic reactions were still present but dormant, the food-seeking response to the auditory stimulus was extinguished by not following the response with food. Then food was offered, and when the cat approached it, the auditory signal was presented continuously, with no effect either in anxiety or in inhibition of eating.

Prior to the removal of the anxiety-evoking effects of the auditory stimulus, two cats were offered food, and then the stimulus was presented as they moved toward it. Neurotic anxiety developed, and eating was inhibited in the situations in which the stimulus was presented.

Are the experimental neuroses in animals and the clinical neuroses in humans the same? The criteria of a clinical neurosis are anxiety, nonadaptive behavior, persistence, and acquisition through learning. These criteria appear to have been met by the cats in these experiments. The responses of the cats in the experimental environment without the shock were the same responses made in the presence of shock, thus conforming with the definition of learning given above. Learning under shock occurs very rapidly because of the great reduction in drive on cessation of the shock and because of the secondary reinforcement of stimuli from the experimental environment that become anxiety inducing, so that removal from the experimental environment reduces anxiety and at the same time reinforces the anxiety responses to the stimuli of this environment.

The question arises as to the persistence of neurotic habits that are not reinforced, that is, their resistance to extinction. Since neurotic responses are nonadaptive, they are unrewarded. However, they have an antecedent drive that is reduced when the neurotic is removed from the action of the anxiety-producing stimulus. Thus responses associated with such removal are reinforced. Responses such as autonomic reactions, which are continuously evoked and inevitably present at the time of such drive reductions, are therefore highly persistent, whereas more variable or intermittent motor responses may be extinguished.

The removal or cure of the experimental neurosis is the result of making possible the feeding response in the presence of stimuli conditioned to anxiety responses that otherwise inhibit feeding. "When stimuli to incompatible responses are present simultaneously, the occurrence of the response that is dominant in the circumstances involves the reciprocal inhibition of the other. As the number of feedings increased, the anxiety responses gradually became weaker, so that to stimuli to which there was initially a response of the anxiety pattern there was finally a feeding response with inhibition of anxiety."[4] It seems that there are a number of aspects to this process.

1. Neurotic (anxiety) responses are inhibited.
2. There is a positive conditioning of the feeding response by reduction of the hunger drive.
3. There is a reduction of the drive antecedent to the anxiety responses by the reciprocal inhibition.

"With repetition more and more conditioned inhibition was built up, so that the anxiety-evoking potential of the stimuli progressively diminished—eventually to zero."[5] The general principle formulated on the basis of the experiments is as follows: "If a response antagonistic to anxiety can be made to occur in the presence of anxiety-evoking stimuli so that it is accompanied by a complete or partial suppression of the anxiety responses, the bond between these stimuli and the anxiety responses will be weakened."[6]

PHILOSOPHY AND CONCEPTS

Learned Versus Physiopathological Psychiatric Syndromes

There are two kinds of nonadaptive habitual behavior: organically based and learned. The latter includes (1) neuroses, (2) other "pure" nonadaptive habits (not accompanied by anxiety), (3) psychopathic personality (antisocial personality disorder), (4) drug addictions, and (5) nonadaptive behavior of schizophrenics. Psychotherapy, including behavior therapy, is feasible only with those psychiatric syndromes that involve learning. Only the neuroses are dealt with by Wolpe.

The Manifestation of Neuroses

A *neurosis* is *"a persistent unadaptive habit that has been acquired by learning in an anxiety-generating situation (or a succession of such situations) and in which anxiety is usually the central component"*[7] [Italics in original]. Fears, particularly social fears but also phobias, are most common. Free-floating anxiety may be present. Anxiety often has secondary effects that cause suffering—shyness, stuttering, sexual inadequacy, kleptomania, exhibitionism, fetishism, obsessions, compulsions, and neurotic depression.

The Cause of Neuroses

Definition of Anxiety

Anxiety is *"the individual's characteristic pattern of autonomic responses to noxious stimulation."*[8] Fear is synonymous with anxiety.

How Fear Is Learned

This definition of anxiety refers to an unconditioned response. "But fear can be learned when "neutral" stimuli are conditioned to evoke the fear response. Further fear responses may develop not only through second-order classical conditioning of conditioned fear responses, but also on the basis of information, by which fears are associated with ideas of "danger" through language.

The Etiology of Neurotic Fears

Neurotic fears develop just as do normal fears—on the basis of classical conditioning or of information or misinformation (cognitive learning). Neurotic fears, though, are a reaction to a stimulus situation that is not objectively a source or a sign of danger. Predisposing factors include emotional sensitivity, preexisting mild anxiety, lack of information, and misinformation.

Experimental and Clinical Neuroses

Experimentally induced neuroses in animals and neuroses in humans are similar.

1. The neurotic behavior resembles that evoked in the precipitating situation.
2. The neurotic responses are under the control of the same or similar (generalized) stimuli as were present in the precipitating situation.
3. The neurotic responses are most intense when the stimuli are most like those to which the behavior was originally conditioned.
4. The neurotic responses are resistant to extinction.
5. The neurotic responses are subject to second-order conditioning.

"The main *difference* between experimental and clinical neuroses is that, whereas in the former the original fear aroused is by an unconditioned stimulus such as electric shocks, in clinical neuroses it is a conditioned stimulus such as the comprehension of a grave danger. Clinical neuroses originate in second-order conditioning."[9]

THE THERAPY PROCESS

Behavior therapy is "the use of experimentally established principles and paradigms of learning to overcome unadaptive habits."[10] The therapist views the patient as the product of his or her genetic endowment and the learning that has taken place through exposure to stimuli in the environment, resulting in nonadaptive attitudes, thoughts, verbal behavior, and emotional behavior. Thus the therapist never blames or disparages the patient, but offers sympathy, empathy, sensitivity, and objectivity.

Behavior Analysis

Therapy is preceded by behavior analysis. "Behavior analysis is the process of gathering and sifting information to be used in the conduct of behavior therapy. The therapist's central focus is on the distress and disablement that have brought the patient to seek treatment."[11] Psychotic illness and organically based conditions must be ruled out.

Establishing Stimulus Antecedents of Reactions

The therapist explores the patient's fears and other complaints to obtain information about their determinants and their later extensions through second-order conditioning. Current stimulus–response relationships are scrutinized, since they usually will be the focus of therapy. Complaints other than anxiety—stuttering, compulsions, "psychosomatic" illnesses—complicate a stimulus–response analysis. The therapist must determine whether a fear is based on classical conditioning or on misinformation.

Gathering Background History

Following the exploration of the presenting reactions, the patient's life history is obtained, focusing on family relationships, education, employment, sexual development, and social relationships. The patient is then given the Willoughby Personality Schedule, the Fear Survey Schedule developed by Wolpe and Lang, and sometimes the Bernreuter Self-Sufficiency Scale. A medical examination is obtained if there is any suggestion of organic disease. Anxiety attacks with no constant stimulus antecedents may be caused by hypoglycemia, hyperthyroidism, or, less commonly, other neurological or physiological disturbances.

Therapeutic goals and strategies are discussed with the patient, although the therapist decides, on the basis of the degree to which a neurotic habit is handicapping the patient, which areas should be given priority. Therapy is an individual matter, but there are some general rules.

1. The emotional climate is a blend of objectivity and permissiveness with regard to acts and attitudes that the patient may deplore.
2. The patient must be assured that reactions, having been learned, can be unlearned.
3. Misconceptions about symptoms must be corrected as soon as possible.
4. Unless there are extreme phobia reactions against it, assertive behavior should be instigated early in the treatment.

Preparing for Behavior Therapy

Although most patients are aware that fear (anxiety) is involved in their neurosis, the central role of fear must be emphasized, in statements such as the following:

You know that your trouble is having too much fear. It is an emotion that is normal in everybody's life whenever a real threat arises—for example, walking alone and unarmed at night in an unsafe neighborhood, learning that one's firm is about to retrench its staff, or being confronted by a poisonous snake. It is a different matter when fear is aroused by situations that contain no real threat—such as seeing somebody receive an injection, entering a crowded room, or riding in a car—to take examples other than your own. To be fearful in such situations is obviously inappropriate, and this is what we call neurotic fear. It is the task of therapy to detach this from the stimuli or situations that provoke it.

Let us consider how neurotic fears originate. The process is really what common sense would lead you to expect. A severe fear reaction that is aroused in the presence of a particular sight or sound becomes "attached" to it. As a result, the later occurrence of the sight or sound under any circumstances automatically triggers the fear reaction. For example, an American lieutenant "went through hell" in the bursting of high explosive in a pass in Vietnam. A few weeks after he returned to the United States, when he and his wife were walking to a wedding in New York City, a truck backfired near them. He reacted with instant panic, "rolled up next to a parked car, cringing in the gutter."

Your own fears were likewise acquired in the course of unpleasant experiences, which we touched upon in your history. The unpleasant emotions you then had became conditioned, or connected, to aspects of the situation that made an imprint on you at the time. This means that subsequent similar experiences led to the arousal of these same unpleasant feelings. Now, just because this happened as a result of a process of learning it is possible to eliminate the reactions by the application of principles of learning. If, as in the case of the Vietnam lieutenant, your fears are automatic emotional habits, we will have to use other emotions to break down those habits. If any of your fears are due to misinformation, we will provide corrective information.[12]

IMPLEMENTATION: TECHNIQUES OF THERAPY

Cognitive Procedures

Cognitive elements are present in all psychotherapies. Besides the cognitive activity that is part of all human interaction, and contrary to allegations of some cognitive therapists (such as Beck), "cognitive *procedures* have always been part of the stock-in-trade of behavior therapy as a matter of common sense."[13] In addition to the gathering of information for behavioral analysis and the preparing of the patient for therapy, there are a number of other cognitive procedures.

Combating Cognitively Based Fears

Cognitively based fears are the result of misinformation about the dangerousness of a situation rather than a conditioned reaction to a situation. Corrective information similar to the following is provided and sometimes is amplified with detailed instructions, demonstrations, and arguments: "Your fears are based on faulty thinking. In the instances where this is a matter of incorrect information, I will point this out and provide correct information, in as much detail as necessary. To the extent that, even with correct information, you are in the habit of making self-defeating, fear-arousing statements to yourself, I will attempt to reveal this, and will help you break the habit."[14]

Thought Stopping

Thought stopping is used to eliminate unrealistic, unproductive, anxiety-arousing, persistent, or obsessive thoughts. The patient is asked to close his or her eyes and recite the thought sequence; the therapist shouts "Stop!" and points out to the patient that the thoughts did stop. This procedure is repeated a number of times, and the patient is told to practice stopping thoughts by saying "Stop" to himself or herself. The method may be modified by accompanying the stop signal with an uncomfortable shock or by having the patient press a buzzer when a useless thought occurs, at which signal the therapist shouts "Stop!"

Contrary to the assertions of cognitive therapists, cognitive errors, distortions, or misconceptions are not the only cause of neuroses. "For the cognitivists, emotional conditioning, and specifically, learned automatic triggering of fear responses do not exist. I reject the view that the psychotherapeutic task is a matter of nothing but cognitive correction, both because it is contrary to established facts about autonomic responses, and because it is substantially contradicted by clinical data."[15]

Assertiveness Training

"*Assertive behavior* is defined as the proper expression of any emotion other than anxiety toward another person."[16] While this includes affectionate and positive behaviors, it more often involves negative or oppositional statements or behaviors. Normal assertive behavior is inhibited because of fear. Suppression of feeling resulting from inhibitory actions about which one feels strongly causes inner turmoil and psychosomatic reactions. Therapy is directed toward eliciting the inhibited responses, which leads to reciprocal inhibition of anxiety and weakening of the anxiety response. Thus counterconditioning and operant conditioning both occur, facilitating each other.

Patients may question the morality of assertive behavior. Three possible approaches to interpersonal relations may be pointed out to them. The first is to consider oneself only, attempting to get what one wants regardless of the effects on others. The second is submission, unselfishly putting others before oneself. Both of these approaches lead to difficulty. The third is the golden mean, in which onself is placed first but others are considered.

The patient's need for assertiveness training may emerge naturally from his or her complaints, from the Willoughby Personality Schedule, or from questions by the therapist, such as "What do you do if somebody pushes in front of you in a line?" Patients must recognize and accept the need for assertiveness as reasonable and desirable and not in conflict with their religious or ethical beliefs.

Simple instruction often is sufficient to get patients to try assertive behavior. If the patient finds assertive behavior very difficult, more vigorous efforts are necessary; the therapist may even refuse to see a patient until some actions are taken. When assertive actions are taken, the patient reports his or her experiences and is commended for successes, and mistakes are corrected. It usually is desirable to give the patient graded-task assignments, as in systematic desensitization, particularly when there are "phobic" reactions to assertiveness or fear of aggression from others. A basic rule is *"never instigate an assertive act that is likely to have punishing consequences."*[17]

Behavior rehearsal, in which the therapist takes the role of a person toward whom the patient is unadaptively anxious and inhibited, may be used when the patient seems to be unable to become assertive in real life. It gives the patient the opportunity to practice assertive statements and to be coached in improving them.

For situations in which direct assertion may be inappropriate (as in dealing with one's boss), indirect ways of controlling the situation, such as those in Potter's *life-manship* (or one-upmanship) approach, may be encouraged.

The case of Mrs. Schmidt, presented later in this chapter, illustrates assertiveness training. Although used less than the method of systematic desensitization, it is frequently used early in therapy, since it is simple and effective and involves the patient in the therapy.

Systematic Desensitization

Systematic desensitization is the step-by-step breaking down of habits of neurotic anxiety response. A state that is physiologically inhibitory to anxiety, usually relaxation, is induced, after which the patient is exposed to a weak anxiety-arousing stimulus. Progressively stronger stimuli are introduced as the weaker ones are tolerated, until the strongest stimulus is reacted to with the degree of anxiety that the mildest stimulus evoked, which is then reduced to zero. The method parallels closely the technique of feeding cats in the presence of increasing amounts of anxiety-evoking stimuli. Systematic desensitization is useful in the treatment of noninterpersonal neuroses for which training in assertive behavior is not useful, such as phobias, or of patients in whom the mere presence of another person evokes fear.

Desensitization requires the training of the patient in relaxation, following Jacobson,[18] for about six or seven lessons, interspersed with the patient's practicing at home for two quarter-hour periods a day. Relaxation of the arm muscles is first, followed by those of the head and face (second and third session), the neck and shoulders, the back, the abdomen and thorax, and, finally, the lower limbs.

At the same time that training in relaxation is progressing, anxiety hierarchies are constructed, but not while the patient is under relaxation. "An anxiety hierarchy is a list of thematically related anxiety-evoking stimuli, according to the amount of anxiety they evoke."[19] Hierarchies are constructed from the patient's history, from responses to the Willoughby Personality Schedule and to the Fear Survey Schedule, and from probings, including the patient's listing, as homework, all situations, thoughts, or feelings that are fearful or disturbing in any way. The various fears are grouped into themes. Stimuli or situations need not have been experienced to be included but can be imaginary. Basically objective fears are not included and are not, of course, treated by desensitization.

These items are general and must be developed into specific situations that can be placed in a hierarchy. There may be multiple dimensions, such as room size and duration of confinement in claustrophobia. The hierarchy may be constructed by having the patient rate the items according to the amount of anxiety they would evoke, using a scale of 0 to 100. An example of a hierarchy of external stimuli is the following:

1. the sight of a physical deformity (90)
2. someone in pain (the greater the evidence of pain, the more disturbing) (50–80)
3. the sight of bleeding (70)
4. the sight of someone seriously ill (for example, heart attack) (60)
5. automobile accidents (50)

      6. nurses in uniform (40)
      7. wheelchairs (30)
      8. hospitals (20)
      9. ambulances (10)[20]

If the patient cannot achieve adequate relaxation, drugs (diazepam or codeine), carbon dioxide–oxygen mixtures, hypnotism (in about 10 percent of cases), or the imagining of relaxing scenes may be used. When the patient is adequately relaxed, the therapist presents a neutral scene and asks the patient to imagine it. Then the procedure itself begins: the patient is asked to imagine the least anxiety-arousing stimulus in the hierarchy and to raise a finger when he or she sees it clearly; the therapist allows the scene to remain for a few seconds (5 to 7), terminating it by saying "Stop the scene" and then asking the patient to rate the degree of induced anxiety felt (using the scale of 0 to 100). Relaxation is then induced again for 10 to 30 seconds. This procedure continues for as long as is necessary to reduce the anxiety accompanying each scene to 0 (with repetition for overlearning in some cases), going through all the stimuli in the hierarchy. Sessions are usually 15 to 30 minutes in length, with the number of scenes presented varying with the patient. Sessions are usually once or twice a week.

Systematic desensitization involves the imagining of anxiety-evoking scenes, not the actual experiencing of them. Yet progress is reflected in improvement in reaction to real situations. Difficulties or failures usually reflect difficulties in relaxing, misleading or irrelevant hierarchies, or inadequate imagery.

In the cases of 39 patients randomly selected from the files, systematic desensitization was judged effective in 35 patients, or 90 percent, with the median number of sessions per patient being 10.

Variations of Systematic Desensitization

Technical Variations of Standard Desensitization Procedure

Two ways have been used to reduce the amount of time the therapist has to spend with patients.

Mechanical aids to systematic desensitization   A specially modified tape recorder has been used to enable patients to desensitize themselves. Relaxation instructions are taped, and a pause switch enables patients to stop the tape while relaxing according to the specific instruction. Before the presentation of the first scene, brief general relaxation directions are given, followed by an instruction to pause. Then instructions to visualize the first scene are given, followed by the direction to pause until visualization is clear and then to continue. After ten seconds of silence comes the instruction to stop visualizing and, if anxiety is felt, to press the repeat button, which winds the tape to the beginning of the general relaxation instructions, where a metal foil stops it. The process of visualization can then be repeated. If the repeat button is not pressed, the tape continues to the next relaxation instructions (also preceded by a metal foil), followed by the second scene and so on. The tape is recorded by the patients themselves, following instructions. A simpler tape recording has also been developed.

Group desensitization   Patients with the same phobia have been treated successfully in groups, not only by Wolpe, but also by others.

Alternative Counteranxiety Responses for Use with Imaginal Stimuli

Responses evoked by therapy   The therapy situation itself evokes positive emotions—hopeful expectation, confidence in the expert, and so forth—that inhibit weak anxiety responses. Patients who are unable to learn to relax may be presented with hierarchical scenes in the hope that the therapist evoked positive emotions will inhibit the anxiety associated with the scenes.

Relaxation substitutes   A number of procedures result in the calmness and autonomic effects produced by relaxation. *Autogenic training* uses suggestions of heaviness and warmth to produce muscle relaxation. *Transcendental meditation* encourages the physiological changes that accompany muscle relaxation. *Yoga* exercises also lead to control of autonomic responses. *Electromyographic biofeedback* can reduce tension levels, leading to muscle relaxation.

Responses triggered by electrical stimulation   In the first technique, desensitization based on inhibition of anxiety by a conditioned motor response, the patient is asked to imagine a mildly anxiety-arousing scene in the usual way. When the patient signals that the scene is clear, he or she receives a mild electric shock in the forearm, at which time the patient flexes the arm, as the therapist instructed. The muscle activity and the weak electrical stimulation itself weaken anxiety. In the second technique, external inhibition, two mild to moderate electric half-second shocks are administered when the patient imagines a scene; the shocks are repeated 5 to 20 times until the scene is no longer anxiety arousing, the anxiety having been inhibited by the shocks.

Responses evoked by verbally induced imagery   Three methods are included in this category. In the emotive-imagery technique, the hierarchical stimuli are presented to the patient while he or she is in a suggested imaginary situation that includes emotional states counteractive to anxiety. The anxiety-arousing scenes are then introduced into this setting. The induced situation, with its emotional state, is a substitute for relaxation. In the second technique of induced anger, anger-arousing imagery is paired with fear-arousing imagined scenes, suppressing the fear or anxiety. Hostility or aggression does not replace the fear. In the third technique, direct suggestion, various responses, including relaxation, are induced, which act as counteranxiety responses.

Responses encouraged by physical activity   Numerous physical activities may be a source of reciprocal inhibition of anxiety when engaged in during the imagining of fear or anxiety-arousing scenes. These include oriental defense exercises—such as karate, kung fu, and aikido—yoga, and transcendental meditation.

Responses produced by relief from distress   In the aversion-relief technique, the patient is presented with a phobic- or an anxiety-arousing stimulus on the termination of a period of unpleasant electrical stimulation. Another technique is to present the phobic- or anxiety-arousing stimulus at the moment of respiratory relief after the patient holds in his or her breath for as long as possible.

Pharmacological inhibition of anxiety by carbon dioxide–oxygen inhalation Anxiety stimuli can be desensitized when they are presented while the patient inhales the gas.

Desensitization to Exteroceptive Stimuli to Anxiety

Either the actual feared objects or pictorial representations of them are used in these procedures.

Desensitization in vivo Having patients expose themselves to the actual stimulus situation up to the level in the hierarchy to which they have been desensitized in imagination has been used to consolidate progress and to get feedback. It also can be the prime method in those 10 to 15 percent of patients who cannot imagine hierarchical scenes or do not respond to them emotionally. Natural stimuli can be used, with graded exposure and the therapist present, as a guide and anxiety inhibitor.

Anxiety-relief conditioning is another method used *in vivo.* It consists of the direct conditioning of an anxiety-inhibiting response to a neutral stimulus word, such as *calm,* by administering an uncomfortable shock that can be stopped when the patient says the word aloud. The relief, in people who experience not only pain, but also emotional disturbance in response to shock, may be strong; on repetition, the patient often becomes conditioned to the word, which can be used subsequently to reduce anxiety in disturbing situations.

Modeling Bandura and his associates have demonstrated that observation of filmed or live models engaging in fear-provoking interactions is effective in eliminating or reducing fears or phobias.

The Treatment of Inhibited Sexual Responses

Anxiety responses may become conditioned to stimuli associated with sexual responding. Since they are incompatible with sexual responding, they inhibit it. Shame and disgust may also cause inhibition, but "reciprocally, sexual responses may be used for overcoming the anxiety habits that inhibit them. As always, such utilization depends upon arranging for the sexual response to be strong enough to dominate the anxiety response so that, by inhibiting it, it will diminish the anxiety-response habit."[21] Sexual emotions can also be used to overcome nonsexual anxieties or neuroses.

Male sexual inadequacy Biological bases for impotence must be ruled out. Since the treatment of impaired sexual performance (including premature ejaculation) requires the removal of anxiety from the sexual encounter, the cooperation of the wife must be obtained, so that she will avoid making her husband tense or anxious. The process is slow and gradual.

If the husband cannot obtain the cooperation of his wife, the therapist should see her. If the wife will not cooperate, "it is usually appropriate to encourage the husband to seek out another woman who may be more responsive to him."[22] The restoration of potency may improve the marriage, but even if it does not, the man is better off.

In 18 cases of male sexual inadequacy, 14 (78 percent) achieved entirely satisfactory sexual performance, and another 3 (17 percent) attained a level acceptable to their partners. The mean time was 11.3 weeks; the median was 8.0 weeks.

Female sexual inadequacy   Frigidity is a matter of degree and is either general or situational (limited to a particular male, usually the husband). General frigidity may have an organic basis, but it is usually the result of conditioned inhibition.

Reeducation and the correction of misconceptions is often a first step in treatment. Treatment of the remaining negative emotional attitude and anxiety is done generally by systematic desensitization. If the frigidity is a by-product of a long, simmering resentment toward the husband, assertiveness training is useful. If the wife no longer cares for her husband, nothing can be done. However, efforts can be made to change the husband's behavior, the wife's behavior, or both to achieve a more satisfactory relationship.

The Use of Chemical Agents in the Deconditioning of Anxiety

Conventional drugs   To reduce anxiety, many people resort to alcohol and other nonprescription sedatives, as well as to numerous prescription drugs (Valium, Librium, Stelazine, Mellaril, Atarax, Parnate, Nordil). Conditions that presumably are secondary to anxiety (enuresis, encopresis, premature ejaculation) can be controlled by drugs. Amelioration of premenstrual reactions may be obtained by the administration of female-sex-hormone preparations.

Carbon dioxide–oxygen to reduce pervasive anxiety   Drugs can be used to facilitate relaxation in systematic desensitization, as noted earlier. In cases of pervasive free-floating anxiety, the most satisfactory measure is one to four single, full-capacity inhalations of a mixture of 65 percent carbon dioxide and 35 percent oxygen. The mechanism of anxiety reduction is not known. It is not simply pharmacological and may be based on reciprocal inhibition of anxiety by the responses produced by the gas, the postinhalation state of relaxation, or both. The effect may last from hours to weeks or months.

Drugs for specific deconditioning   Chlorpromazine meprobamate, codeine, and alcohol have been prescribed for patients to take before exposure to disturbing situations. It has been found that after use for several weeks, or months, the drug is no longer necessary. Classroom anxiety and phobias have responded to such treatment. Chlordiazepoxide (Librium) and related drugs (Valium and Serax) have been used effectively.

"It is reasonable to think that reciprocal inhibition was the mechanism of the observed relearning"[23] associated with the use of drugs. Avoidance responses apparently are inhibited by other responses to other stimuli in the environment. The effectiveness of programs of in vivo systematic desensitization that use tranquilizing drugs "almost certainly depends upon insuring that *high-anxiety evocation never occurs,* for whenever it does, it may be expected to recondition a substantial degree of anxiety and lose hardwon ground. . . . the hazard of addiction is small when the duration of drug treatment is thus limited."[24]

Intravenous anxiety inhibitors   Methahexitone sodium (Brietal or Brevital) acts as a primary anxiety-inhibiting agent and can be used with or instead of relaxation instructions in systematic desensitization.

Procedures Involving Strong Anxiety Evocation

Abreaction   Abreaction is not a strictly behavioral technique; its occurrence and outcome are not controllable or predictable by the therapist. It is not always therapeutic, but its dramatic success in some cases warrants attempts to elucidate its mechanisms; it may work through the same processes as flooding.

Abreaction is "the re-evocation with strong emotional accompaniment of a fearful past experience." It is most useful with those patients whose nonadaptive emotional responses were conditioned to intricate stimulus compounds that are not present in current or contrived stimulus situations; recalled images can thus be introduced into therapy. The effectiveness of abreaction is related to the protective psychotherapeutic relationship and may be "a special case of nonspecific effects."[26] Abreaction may occur during the application of other methods: history taking, desensitization, and so on.

Flooding   The first successful case of flooding appears to have been reported by Crafts and colleagues,[27] who do not name the physician involved. The therapist ordered the patient, a young woman who was afraid to ride in an automobile on strange roads, especially over bridges and through tunnels, to be driven the 50 miles from her home to his office, over bridges and through the Holland Tunnel. During the ride, the patient was panicked, but her terror diminished as she neared the physician's house. On the return trip and later trips, there were no problems.

Flooding thus presents the patient with maximum stimulation, or the highest anxiety-producing scene in a hierarchy. Stampfl's implosive therapy[28] is an example of flooding, using the patient's imagination.

Flooding techniques apparently are based on the paradigm of experimental extinction, but "so far, nobody has cured an experimental neurosis simply by exposing the animal for long periods (hours or days) to the stimuli to which anxiety has been maximally conditioned . . . it seems most unlikely that [flooding] leads to change on the same basis as extinction."[29] There are two other possibilities: (1) that "the anxiety is inhibited by the patient's response to the therapist" or (2) "that if the stimulation is not so strong as to cause the subject to withdraw or to 'switch off' entirely, the continuing strong stimulation may lead, after a varying time, to transmarginal inhibition of the response."[30]

Flooding is an important addition to behavior therapy, but because of its unpleasant nature, it should not be the first choice for use except when it can be shown to be more effective than desensitization. One such case is the obsessive–compulsive neurotic with fear and avoidance of contamination.

Paradoxical intention   Paradoxical intention, developed by Frankl, resembles flooding in that it brings about high respose levels by having the patient expose himself or herself to feared situations and deliberately try to precipitate feared symptoms. While "it is a resource worth considering when the usual behavior therapy techniques are unsuccessful . . . its effectiveness is a matter of trial and error."[31]

Operant Conditioning Methods

"There is only one *kind* of learning process. The distinction between respondent and operant conditioning is not in the nature of the conditioning, but in the fact that in the former nonvoluntary, especially autonomic, behavior is predominantly involved, whereas in the latter the behavior is predominantly motor."[32] Operant procedures, thus, are not prominent in the treatment of neuroses, which are primarily autonomic habits. Nevertheless, autonomic responses can be brought under the control of reward contingencies.

Operant conditioning is involved in assertiveness training and is central in the treatment of many other nonadaptive habits that have no particular relation to conditioned anxiety—for example, nail biting, enuresis, encopresis, and chronic tardiness. Although there are other operant techniques (differential reinforcement, punishment, and response shaping), Wolpe considers three.

Positive reinforcement Establishing a habit by arranging for a reward or reinforcement to follow each or many of its performances is a powerful means of changing behavior. Its therapeutic potentials have been demonstrated mainly with schizophrenics, in whom it effects changes in behavior but does not "cure" the psychosis, which probably is an organic illness. Anorexia nervosa is one of the few neurotic conditions for which positive reinforcement has been used successfully as the main method of treatment. Operant procedures also may be used in treating the phobias in whose maintenance physical avoidance is a major factor, such as school phobias. They are also increasingly being used with problem behaviors in children and delinquent behavior.

Negative reinforcement Negative reinforcement, which increases the rate or strength of a response by removing an unpleasant stimulus, often requires the therapist to introduce the aversive stimulus in the first place.

Extinction When a response is made repeatedly without reinforcement, it is extinguished. Extinction may be slow in clinical cases because the responses have been sustained by long periods of intermittent reinforcement. Dunlap's method of "negative practice," which is now mainly used in the treatment of tics, depends on extinction through massed responses without reinforcement. The undesirable response must be performed to the point of exhaustion in order to produce strong reactive inhibition.

Aversion Therapy

Aversion therapy is a special application of the principle of reciprocal inhibition in which an aversive stimulus is administered coincident with an unwanted response (thus differing from punishment, which follows the response), inhibiting the response. Although not usually the treatment of first choice, it is useful in the treatment of obsessions, compulsions, fetishes, and attraction to inappropriate objects (for example, persons of the same sex). Aversive therapy is feasible for the treatment of homosexuality only when homosexual preference is a result of positive erotic conditioning to the same sex. If the maladaptive habit has a basis in neurotic anxiety, the anxiety should be deconditioned first, in which case the undesirable behavior may disappear. Even after successful aversion therapy, anxiety may remain and need to be deconditioned.

When a strong aversion stimulus, such as an electric shock, is administered in the presence of the stimulus for the undesired response, "besides eliciting an avoidance response, the shock will inhibit the undesired emotional response,"[33] establishing a conditioned inhibition of the response.

Electric stimulation is advantageous because the strength and timing of administration can be precisely controlled and can be tailored to the individual patient. It can be used in relation to actual objects or situations or with imagery. Drugs have been used extensively in the aversion treatment of alcoholism. The procedure is difficult and not highly successful; if successful, it does not allow social drinking. Other unpleasant stimuli have been used in aversive treatment of smoking, obesity, and other conditions.

Evaluation of Behavior Therapy

Behavior therapy is applicable to clinical states resulting from learning. These are mainly neuroses. Evaluation is therefore concentrated on the neuroses.

The nonspecific effects of the therapeutic relationship are common to all therapies and presumably account for the fact that about 40 percent of neurotic patients are reported to be markedly improved by treatment. Because there are factual grounds for believing that behavior therapy does exceed the common average in both percentage and speed of recoveries, its techniques are confidently offered in this volume.

In an uncontrolled statistical study of cases treated by Wolpe in private practice, which was reported in 1958, 89 percent of patients apparently recovered or showed at least 80 percent improvement; the mean number of sessions was 30. The criteria were those proposed by Robert P. Knight for evaluating psychoanalytic therapy: (1) symptomatic improvement; (2) increased productivity at work; (3) improved adjustment and pleasure in sex; (4) improved interpersonal relationships; and (5) enhanced ability to handle ordinary psychological conflicts and reasonable reality stresses. No selection of patients was present except for a diagnosis of neurosis. A follow-up of 45 patients 2 to 7 years later found that all but 1 had maintained their gains.

Wolpe writes that "on the strength of recent reexaminations of misleading analyses of comparative studies, there is good reason to hope that the time is approaching when behavior therapy will at last begin to displace the dominating psychoanalytically oriented approaches and their progeny of muddled eclecticisms."[34] Although a comparison by Sloane and colleagues[35] of behavior therapy with psychoanalytically oriented therapy found no difference between the two, and comparisons by Luborsky, Singer, and Luborsky[36] and by Smith, Glass, and Miller[37] of behavior therapy with other methods found no differences among them, Wolpe criticizes these studies on the basis of evaluations by Andrews and Harvey[38] and by Giles.[39] He concludes, "In sum, the outcome evidence is impressively on the side of behavior

therapy, making it currently the therapy of choice and easily the most cost-effec-
tive."[40] This is in spite of the fact that, he admits, most practitioners of behavior
therapy are inadequately trained.

EXAMPLE

The following material consists of excerpts from two interviews held with a client before
a seminar audience, to demonstrate the behavioristic approach. The comments between
the two interviews are Wolpe's.[41]

First Interview

THERAPIST: Good morning, Mrs. Schmidt. What's your trouble?
CLIENT: I get very upset sometimes.
TH: What upsets you?
CL: Lately the children.
TH: What, what is there about the children that upsets you?
CL: Uh, before I moved where I am now, I used to . . . they used to listen to me and all
    that. It disturbs me also that my husband is to—not enough home with them. He is,
    doesn't spend enough time with the children and I feel like I am raising them by myself.
TH: What does your husband do?
CL: He works as a barber now.
TH: What prevents him from being home enough?
CL: He has long hours.
TH: What are his hours?
CL: He leaves at seven, and he comes home half past eight.
TH: Certainly very long. Well, that's a practical problem. Is there anything else that upsets
    you?
CL: Yes, many things.
TH: Well, for example?
CL: The things that I read in the paper.
TH: Like what?
CL: Oh, like, uh, I have seen plenty killings in the war and now I feel the same like over
    here. When I first came here I . . . I just thought there is no place like this, I . . . I thought
    that you could live in peace and there would never be any trouble. You, you couldn't,
    you wouldn't hear of anything and now, I . . . I hear more and more things and I get
    very upset about it.
TH: What year did you come here?
CL: In '47.
TH: In '47. How old were you then?
CL: 21.
TH: Now let me get one thing clear. If you had gone on feeling the way you felt during those
    few years, then you would not be here?
CL: I would not have to come here.
TH: Right. Can you say what happened to make you unhappy again after that?
CL: I don't know. It might be . . . you see, uhm, when I was born my mother died in childbirth
    and she never wanted to even look at me, my grandmother used to tell me . . . she
    didn't even want to hold me once and as she was dying she was sorry that she was
    leaving the house behind. She had a feeling for home but she never said that she was

leaving the child behind and my grandmother used to always talk about that, which she shouldn't have. And so hard things, I have so many things to talk about and uh . . .

TH: Was your grandmother with you here?

CL: No, my grandmother got killed.

TH: Oh, well. . . . But, can you say more or less what year you began to feel that you were not so happy anymore?

CL: You see, I was disappointed in the family life. I was always looking for somebody like a mother, you know. A somebody. And they would tell me that they would be like a mother to me. And then I found out different—many things and ever since then and —like if I would find somebody and I would get, I can't get too close to them. When I get too close I am afraid that I get hurt and then I run.

TH: Does that mean that at first when you came here you were trusting people and you . . . you felt you could easily form close relationships with them and then . . . and then at some stage you found that these people were disappointing you?

CL: Uh, uh, I had a few but one I remember is my aunt. She told me that she wanted to be like a mother to me when I came here and I thought that she would and—well, many things happened but if I remember very closely I was expecting my first one. When I was in the hospital waiting, uh, to give birth, I had the baby at 11:55 and my hus . . . 10:55 and my husband called her to say . . . to tell her the news so she said, "You woke us up and we couldn't go back to sleep." She said, "Couldn't it wait till the morning?" And he shouldn't have even told me that—I was very sad. But there were many, many things I knew happened but this I remember.

TH: Are the other things that happened of this kind? Were they always things that some-body who should have been friendly to you was in some way uh . . .

CL: I don't get that close. I don't wait to find out.

TH: Yes, well, but in that case you did get close.

CL: Yes.

TH: You mentioned that your children don't obey you properly and you mentioned that your husband works too much; therefore, he doesn't help you with the children. Now, both of these things are things that any person could be expected to be upset by and, well, maybe solutions could be worked out. But, if you come for psychiatric treatment it means that you feel that there is some kind of situation where you're not reacting as you should . . . where you are perhaps more upset than you ought to be.

CL: There were many times, days that I just didn't feel like going on living. If I had the courage I would have just killed myself many times and I still feel like that. I used to feel like that when I was a child. If I, uh, where I lived with my grandparents, my uncle and my aunt lived there and they just didn't want me. They used to call me all kinds of names and my grandmother used to tell me it would be good if I run away because they didn't want me and that's the time I started feeling that, I just felt like I didn't want to go on living.

TH: Uh-huh. I want to ask you how you react in certain rather common situations. Suppose that you're standing in a line and somebody gets in front of you. What do you do?

CL: Sometimes I let—if I, if I feel that there is a reason for it I let them go. But if I, if I have to make time, I just don't like it.

TH: What do you do?

CL: I don't do nothing. I get upset. (laughs)

TH: If you go into a shop and you buy, say, a woolen pullover like that and when you come home you inspect it and you see there is a little moth hole in the sleeve, what do you do?

CL: I take it back. I show it to them.

TH: You don't mind taking it back?

CL: I don't know.

TH: I mean, can you do it quite easily or is it difficult to take it back?

CL: I, I don't like to bother people too much. I don't like to—for that reason I don't like to take it back. I—if something goes wrong in the house—they don't fix things right or they don't make them right, my husband has to force me to talk and he, he tells it often that I can't do it. He says that's why people take advantage of me, because I don't have the courage to speak up.

TH: Well, that is very much a matter of habit. Now, it's a thing that one can learn to change.

CL: So far I haven't succeeded.

TH: Well, but, I . . . I want to tell you how you can succeed. Look, let's let's take this, uh, little example that we used first where somebody gets in front of you in the line. Suppose you're in a hurry and somebody does that. You get cross. You are annoyed. But when you, when you have any thought of doing anything about it, you're kept back at the same time by feeling you don't want to hurt his feelings, you don't want to distress him, maybe it will make a scene, things like that. Now, what I want you to do in the future in this little situation is express these feelings. Now, of course it's difficult, but if you will express this feeling that you have and say, "Will you kindly get to the back of the line?" then, in the act of doing it, you will sort of push back the fear feelings. You will push them down to some extent. And if you do that, the next time it will be a little easier.

CL: I will try.

TH: Well, the more you try, the easier it will become, and of course there are many situations like this. But it requires action.

CL: But if somebody asks me for a favor and I know I can't do it, I just can't tell them *no.* I go out of my way and I do it. There has to be a *no* which I am trying to learn.

TH: That's right. You can only learn to make the *no* a part of action if you say the *no* and it's usually easier if you start saying *no* in a small situation.

CL: Maybe at home to the children?

TH: Yes, that kind of thing. Now, oddly enough, last month I had a patient who has exactly this problem but probably much worse than you—this is a man who works in a university and the situation has been that if his secretary says to him, "Will you go to the post . . . to the post office and register this letter?" he can't say *no.* He has to do it for his secretary. And you see how ridiculous this is. The first—I, I said to him, "Will you please crawl across the room for me?" (patient laughs) And it was very hard for him to say *no,* but he said *no* and after a little while it became easy. So, anyway, there are many many things of this kind where it is reasonable and right for you to express your feelings, to do according to your feelings and you must learn to be able to—of course that does not mean that you are becoming rude or nasty. There is one general thing I want to tell you that if you get into the habit of saying *no* correctly at the right time, then you don't have to become violent about it. But if you, if you don't exert your authority immediately, and the other person goes on doing what you don't want, then you become more and more annoyed and eventually you can't control yourself and it comes out in violence. I would like to consider for a moment some of these situations where you feel, that people are rejecting you.

CL: I don't try to get that close to them to find out. I don't want to find it out.

TH: Yes, but there are other kinds of rejection and, which are a smaller kind, and I would also like to know about those. For example, suppose you walk in the street and there is an acquaintance, a person you don't know well, and you expect that person to greet you and she just walks past. Does that worry you?

CL: Yeah, I don't like it. Because I say hello to everybody that I know.

practice in the anxiety-evoking situation of responses that are antagonistic to anxiety, which results in the suppression of the anxiety responses. Therapy involves motivating and enabling the client to perform responses antagonistic to anxiety. Techniques of motivating the client include explanation and instruction concerning the nature and origin of his or her condition, the prescription of specific activities, reasoning and assurance that the prescribed activities will remedy the situation, and encouragement, support, and pressure to engage in the activities.

The claim of success (90 percent apparently cured or much improved) must be viewed with some skepticism. As Wolpe recognizes, in order for his figures to be comparable with data from other methods, which usually report much lower rates of success, two assumptions must be made. The first is that the clients are similar and that they are not selected in any way that would bias the results. While this assumption cannot be disproved, neither is there any evidence to support it. Wolpe does limit his clients to those diagnosed as neurotic. The case examples that he uses indicate that some were severe cases; but many, if not most, appear to present rather minor or limited problems. The behaviors treated are certainly specific, and while sometimes they are seriously disabling, they are not usually part of a complex disturbance. They certainly do not appear to be similar to the run of cases treated by practitioners of other methods of psychotherapy. According to Wolpe, the common rate of improvement in other methods of psychotherapy is 40 percent markedly improved. Some improvement occurs in about 66 percent of those treated, according to other estimates. Wolpe attributes this common rate of improvement from diverse methods to "nonspecific" factors common to all methods, or relationship factors. This could be interpreted as indicating that about 66 percent of the patients accepted for therapy by other practitioners have problems for which relationship therapy is effective. Such therapists (except for those practicing orthodox psychoanalysis) are less discriminating in their selection of patients. Thus the remainder, who do not improve, probably have other kinds of problems —many of them, perhaps, problems suitable for various techniques of behavior therapy. That behavior therapists have a higher rate of success could be because of their selection of patients or of problems appropriate to their methods. Behavior therapy, therefore, could not be claimed to be more effective for all the kinds of patients or problems seen by therapists who utilize other methods.

As with other behavior therapy approaches, Wolpe's greater rate of success may be explained in terms of the selection of clients who present only rather isolated, even if severe, symptoms. Since these symptoms are not necessarily part of a deeper and/or general personality disturbance, their removal is not followed by the development of other symptoms. The value of symptom removal as a goal of therapy may be questioned. It may not be sufficient or adequate in comparison with other goals, and it may have some undesirable accompaniments or consequences. As London says, "The relief from symptomatic pain in Action therapy may encourage its parties to disregard the cost or consequences of that relief."[43] Mowrer suggests that the method may remove symptoms at the expense of character.[44]

The second assumption is that the criteria for success are similar to those applied by others. There is no evidence for this assumption. The evaluations were made by Wolpe only. Some of his clients were not included in his tabulations; clients were included "only if they have had an 'adequate' amount of therapy. Therapy is naturally regarded as adequate in every patient who is either apparently cured or much improved. In those who have benefitted less, it is regarded as adequate if a reasonable trial has been given to each of the reciprocal inhibition techniques that seem applicable to the case."[45] Such selection of clients must be considered in any evaluation, in terms of both the kinds of problems for which an approach is applicable and the results with clients who are accepted. Stevenson notes that if we were to take the entire series of 295 cases that Wolpe reports having seen for at least an intake interview, the success rate would drop to 65 percent.[46] This, however, would appear to be an unduly rigid criterion for inclusion, since no treatment was attempted on the basis of inapplicability of the techniques in at least some of these cases. However, it is not clear how many of these patients had more than one interview and were actually treated. Wolpe does not specify what he considers an adequate amount of treatment.

The main criterion for success is symptom improvement. Wolpe appears to agree with Eysenck that "there is no neurosis underlying the symptom, but merely the symptom itself. Get rid of the symptom and you have eliminated the neurosis."[47] It does seem that many of the clients treated by Wolpe presented rather circumscribed symptoms. But more general changes occurred than only the disappearance of symptoms, including general improvement in functioning, increased confidence, and development of a more favorable self-concept.

It probably cannot be denied that results are achieved by Wolpe's method, even if they may be more limited in extent than his claims suggest. The question arises as to how and why they occur and if they occur in the way and for the reasons that Wolpe indicates. A number of points may be raised.

The first has to do with the nature and origin of neuroses, or nonadaptive behavior. The analogy between experimental neuroses in animals and clinical neuroses in humans is only an analogy and, indeed, one whose validity has been questioned. Wolpe's arguments are not highly convincing. He agrees that noxious stimuli usually do not operate in the production of human neuroses. Nor are the conflicts that give rise to anxieties in humans the same kinds of ambivalent stimuli that result in animal neuroses. Conflicts of needs, desires, and so on are equated with discriminatory ambivalence, although they do not appear to be the same. Wolpe seems to recognize a weakness in the analogy when he writes: "*Apparently,* simultaneous, strong, conflicting action tendencies *somehow* generate high degrees of anxiety within the nervous system."[48] This kind of reasoning and evidence is characteristic of the application of the animal analogy to human neuroses.

Wolpe seems to imply that second-order conditioning is involved in human neuroses.[49] Since second-order conditioning is not as stable or as persistent as first-order conditioning, the problems of the persistence of nonadaptive neurotic anxiety and other behavior must be faced. As Mowrer points out, in ordinary life, as in the laboratory, fears that are not reinforced spontaneously are extinguished, contrary to the assumptions of behavior theory and of psychoanalysis.[50] Here again, Wolpe's arguments are not impressive, even in terms of the animal neuroses that are the bases for his argument.[51]

As for the concept of reciprocal inhibition, taken from Sherrington, who used it in reference to reflex behavior, it may be questioned whether what Wolpe includes under this term is anything more than what already is covered by the concepts of extinction or counterconditioning. Extinction consists of the disappearance of anxiety and nonadaptive behavior and is made possible by the inhibition of the neurotic (or anxiety) responses by any means. Essentially, the stimulus for anxiety is allowed to occur in a situation where it is not reinforced. If the neurotic responses are inhibited, the activity causing them to be inhibited becomes (positively) conditioned to the former anxiety-arousing stimulus. Thus in addition to experimental extinction, Wolpe instigates other behavior in the presence of the anxiety-evoking stimulus. It would appear that an aspect of his approach and a reason for his success is the inducement of such behavior. He does this by encouragement, support, suggestion, command, and, in the interview, suggestion and hypnosis. His method can thus be viewed as reconditioning.

In the therapy situation, the client faces anxiety-evoking situations in his or her imagination and learns that they are not to be feared. Outside of the therapy session, the client is led or forced to face such situations and finds that they are not to be feared. In effect, the client is put into the anxiety-producing situation and learns that there is no reason to fear it; that is, the unconditioned stimulus receives no reinforcement. The methods and techniques for inducing or forcing the client to enter and stay in the anxiety-producing situation are devices to create a situation in which extinction can take place. The client cannot do it alone because of this fear. An alternative approach, the one used by most counselors and therapists, is to work on reducing the fear, so that the client will voluntarily approach and face the anxiety-producing situation. In effect, Wolpe's approach consists of changing attitudes or feelings by first changing behavior. As London says, "In effect, by his own admission then, a large part of reciprocal inhibition therapy consists simply of getting people to do the very things they fear."[52]

Wolpe agrees that the relationship between therapist and patient is probably the most important factor in conventional therapy, but he claims that behavior therapy has effects additional to these relational effects that are common to all forms of psychotherapy. A reading of transcripts of Wolpe's interviews demonstrates clearly that a great deal besides the behavior therapy techniques enter into his therapy. Included are cognitive restructuring, correction of misconceptions, teaching, acceptance, expressions of concern and of interest, reassurance, suggestions, persuasion, and a desire to help. Wolpe says that "no basis exists for the idea that others have more compassion than the behavioristic psychotherapist."[53] Thus there are strong relationship variables, including those contributing to a powerful placebo effect.

Klein, Dittman, Parloff, and Gill, after closely observing Wolpe and Lazarus, wrote: "Perhaps the most striking impression we came away with was of how much use behavior therapists make of suggestion and of how much the patient's expectations and attitudes are manipulated."[54] Lazarus, who was at that time associated with Wolpe, commented on this statement: "Both Wolpe and I have explicitly stated that relationship variables are often extremely important in behavior therapy. Factors such as warmth, empathy, and authenticity are considered necessary but often insufficient." Later he wrote: "If suggestion enables the person to attempt new responses, these may have positive effects. One thus endeavors quite deliberately to maximize the 'placebo' effect." He agrees that "even the results of a specific technique like systematic desensitization cannot be accounted for solely in terms of graded hierarchies and muscle relaxation."[55] Wolpe probably would not go as far as Lazarus, but it would appear that in the absence of any evidence to the contrary, Wolpe's success could be the outcome of relationship variables, including the placebo effect, which would result in desensitization, counterconditioning, and extinction. Indeed, the argument could be made that Wolpe has reversed the true situation: what he regards as the placebo effect is the psychotherapy, and what he labels the specific effect is the placebo.

Brown[56] analyzed Wolpe's therapy and concluded that Wolpe's personality as well as cognitive factors were important elements; his therapy is far from being a pure behavior therapy but is an amalgam of his personality, verbal and cognitive activities, and specific behavior techniques. The cognitive elements are clear and pervasive from a reading of Wolpe's presentation of his methods and cases.

That Wolpe's procedures are not behavioristic has been argued by Locke, who points out that they require the patient to introspect about the content and intensity of his or her negative emotional states and to think, reason, remember, judge, discriminate, and imagine, none of which are behavioristic.[57] Wilkins questions the theoretical formulations that Wolpe puts forward for the effectiveness of systematic desensitization. He points out that "neither hierarchy construction nor training in muscle relaxation, but only instructed imagination of fear-relevant scenes, is a necessary element of Wolpe's procedure." He suggests that its effectiveness is due to cognitive and social factors involved in the patient–therapist relationship, including the therapist's social-reinforcing qualities, information feedback of success, training in the control of attention, and the client's expectation of improvement.[58] Wilkins supported his evaluation against criticism by Davison and Wilson.[59] His position was also supported by an extensive review by Kazdin and Wilcoxson, who concluded that the apparent greater effectiveness of desensitization over other methods was due to the presence of expectation of improvement in the experimental groups but not in the control groups. "A review of the research that has controlled for expectancies for improvement does not support the proposition that desensitization has a specific therapeutic ingredient . . . nonspecific treatment effects, at least at present, cannot be ruled out in accounting for the effects of desensitization."[60]

Wolpe has attempted to answer some of these criticisms. While admitting that nonspecific factors contribute to the results of behavior therapy, he insists that desensitization involves more than expectation and includes specific factors. To the charge that relaxation does not contribute to the efficacy of systematic desensitization, he argues that many of the studies cited by Yates and by Kazdin and Wilcoxson were analogue studies that included subjects who had weak fears and that sometimes used inadequate relaxation. Wolpe also denies that relaxation is indispensable to desensitization, a position that he says has been attributed erroneously to him, noting that "*numerous* responses can compete with anxiety, including the emotional response that the patient makes to the therapist."[61]

Wolpe's therapy, as well as behavior therapy in general, may well be effective, not for the reasons claimed, but for the same reasons that other methods probably are effective: the relationship provided by the therapist and the patient's expectations. This relationship engenders, among other things, an environment in which the patient can experience anxieties without their being reinforced, which allows them to be extinguished. Although Wolpe contends that fear or avoidance is not susceptible to extinction in animals or humans, Wilson and Davison show that this contention is inconsistent with experimental findings.[62]

Behavior therapy may be more limited than is now apparent, since it does not seem to be applicable to problems of meanings or goals and the fears and aspirations related to them. Not all the problems for which people seek help are symptoms or limitations of function; many involve systems of meaning. The behavior therapist must, as London notes, "drastically curtail the range of persons and problems he attacks. Courting specificity, the Actionist risks wedding triviality."[63] If the therapist widens the concept of symptoms, as many do, until it includes meaning, his or her position becomes scientifically tenuous, according to London. One might ask the behavior therapist how he or she would decondition the pain or suffering of the client who realizes that he or she is not functioning up to full potential or up to his or her aspiration level, who has a concept of himself or herself as a failure, or who experiences a lack of meaning in life. Then the therapist's method of treatment or the effective ingredient may be the relationship rather than the specific techniques of behavior therapy. As London suggests,

> there must be men who, freed of all their symptomatic woes, discover then a truer misery, until now buried underneath a lot of petty ills. Preoccupied no more with pedantries, with headaches, phobias, or vile thoughts, a nauseating emptiness appears to them ahead, a nameless terror of a nameless end. Can this still be a symptom, and if so, still violable by some concrete act, by formulation of a habit or association with some pleasantness-arousing stimulus pulled from a bag of therapeutic tricks?[64]

Lazarus, who, as indicated earlier, was associated with Wolpe for several years, has voiced several criticisms of Wolpe's approach. Responding to Wolpe's definition of behavior therapy as "the use of experimentally established principles and paradigms of learning to overcome unadaptive behavior,"[65] he asks, "Just what are these so-called 'experimentally established principles of learning'? Do they apply to human beings as well as to animals? . . . Some established principles of learning may exist in animal laboratories, but insofar as their relevance for human behavior is concerned, there are, to say the least, many debatable points of issue."[66] Again, Lazarus points out that although there is considerable evidence that neurotic behavior is learned, it is still a hypothesis, while Wolpe treats it as an established fact. Finally, he criticizes the narrowness of Wolpe's approach, which treats human beings as animals without a cerebral cortex, a "hypothalamic, subcortical creature dominated by a primitive autonomic nervous system" whose neuroses are in all essential respects like those experimentally induced in animals. But, Lazarus continues, "when confronted by people intent on self-destruction, torn asunder by conflicting loyalties, crippled by too high a level of aspiration, unhappily married because of false romantic ideals, or beset by feelings of guilt and inferiority on the basis of complex theological beliefs, I fail to appreciate the clinical significance of Wolpe's neurotic cats and sometimes wish that life were really as simple as he would have us believe."[67]

Rotter, in his review of Wolpe's 1958 book, makes some comments that may serve to summarize this evaluation:

> The description of how human beings learn or what they learn that Wolpe presents seems . . . inadequate and highly oversimplified. It does not explain satisfactorily how

human beings learn in more simple situations and it is far from explaining the therapeutic changes which Wolpe himself obtains with his methods. It appears . . . that all of Wolpe's theorizing regarding the neural locus of learning, the nature of the autonomic responses and of the conditioning process are not only controversial at best but are also more or less superfluous to what he actually does. One could say, after a careful reading of the wide variety of methods and the great variety of behaviors which he attempts to substitute for the patient, that he has one basic principle: when the patient presents certain unadaptive behaviors or symptoms, then other behavior, which the therapist considers to be more adaptive and possible to substitute in specific situations, should be taught directly to the patient by whatever method is possible. Apparently, what has frequently been referred to in the past as prestige-suggestion is the method he relies on most heavily. The patient is led to expect that his problems will be solved if he will do as the therapist suggests, and at least in many cases the patient is willing to try out these behaviors, finds them successful and so maintains them.[68]

REFERENCES

1. Wolpe, J. *Psychotherapy by reciprocal inhibition.* Stanford, Calif.: Stanford University Press, 1958. Pp. ix–xi.
2. Ibid., p. 19.
3. Ibid., p. 30.
4. Ibid., p. 67.
5. Ibid., p. 71.
6. Ibid.
7. Wolpe, J. *The practice of behavior therapy* (3rd ed.). New York: Pergamon Press, 1982. Pp. 9–10.
8. Ibid., p. 23.
9. Ibid., p. 41.
10. Ibid., p. 1.
11. Ibid., p. 57.
12. Ibid., p. 87.
13. Ibid., p. 86.
14. Ibid., p. 89.
15. Ibid., pp. 114–115
16. Ibid., p. 118. (Note that assertive behavior is not aggressive behavior. Assertion involves expressing one's rights; aggression involves imposing on the rights of others.
17. Ibid., p. 128.
18. Jacobson, E. *Progressive relaxation.* Chicago: University of Chicago Press, 1938.
19. Wolpe, *The practice of behavior therapy,* p. 145.
20. Ibid., p. 154.
21. Ibid., p. 204.
22. Ibid., p. 213.
23. Ibid., p. 230.
24. Ibid., p. 233.
25. Ibid., p. 236.
26. Ibid., p. 237.
27. Crafts, L. W., Schneirla, T. C., Robinson, E. E. et al. *Recent experiments in psychology.* New York: McGraw-Hill, 1938.
28. Stampfl, T. G., & Levis, D. J. Essentials of implosive therapy: A learning based psychodynamic behavioral therapy. *Journal of Abnormal Psychology,* 1967, *72,* 496.

29. Wolpe, *The practice of behavior therapy,* pp. 241, 245.

30. Ibid., p. 246.

31. Ibid., p. 247.

32. Ibid., p. 249.

33. Ibid., p. 258.

34. Ibid., pp. 326–327.

35. Sloane, R. B., Staples, F. R., Cristol, A. H., Yorkston, N. J., & Whipple, K. *Psychotherapy versus behavior therapy.* Cambridge, Mass.: Harvard University Press, 1975.

36. Luborsky, L., Singer, B., & Luborsky, L. Comparative studies of psychotherapy: Is it true that "Everyone has won and all must have prizes"? *Archives of General Psychiatry,* 1975, *32,* 995–1008.

37. Smith, M. L., Glass, G. V., & Miller, T. I. *The benefits of psychotherapy.* Baltimore: Johns Hopkins University Press, 1980.

38. Andrews, G., & Harvey, R. Does psychotherapy benefit neurotic patients? *Archives of General Psychiatry,* 1981, *38,* 1203.

39. Giles, T. R. *Bias against behavior therapy in outcome reviews: Those who have won have not received prizes.* Unpublished paper; Giles, T. R. *Behavior therapy vs. psychotherapy: A review of Sloane et al. study and of the behavioral outcome literature.* Unpublished paper.

40. Wolpe, *The practice of behavior therapy,* p. 333.

41. Wolpe, J. *The case of Mrs. Schmidt.* Typescript and record published by Counselor Recordings and Tests, Box 6184, Acklen Station, Nashville, Tenn. Typescript reproduced by permission.

42. "It is important at this point to recognize the condensed nature of the passages dealing with relaxation. In the total interview the patient's attention was drawn to a number of muscle systems, and she was instructed in the relaxation of these systems. The passages must thus be regarded only as illustrative of the total relaxation method." (Wolpe's note)

43. London, P. *The modes and morals of psychotherapy.* New York: Holt, Rinehart and Winston, 1964. P. 119.

44. Mowrer, O. H. Freudianism, behavior therapy and "self-disclosure." In O. H. Mowrer (Ed.) *The new group psychotherapy.* New York: Van Nostrand Reinhold, 1964. P. 221.

45. Wolpe, *Psychotherapy by reciprocal inhibition,* p. 205.

46. Stevenson, I. Discussion. In J. Wolpe, A. Salter, & L. J. Reyna (Eds.), *The conditioning therapies.* New York: Holt, Rinehart and Winston, 1964. P. 17.

47. Eysenck, H. J. Learning theory and behavior therapy. In H. J. Eysenck (Ed.), *Behavior therapy and the neuroses.* New York: Pergamon Press, 1960. P. 9.

48. Wolpe, *Psychotherapy by reciprocal inhibition,* p. 79. (Italics added)

49. Ibid., pp. 78–79.

50. Mowrer, Freudianism, behavior therapy and "self-disclosure," p. 217.

51. Wolpe, *Psychotherapy by reciprocal inhibition,* p. 66.

52. London, *The modes and morals of psychotherapy,* p. 91.

53. Wolpe, *The practice of behavior therapy,* p. xix. (Reprinted preface of first edition).

54. Klein, M., Dittman, A. J., Parloff, M. B., & Gill, M. M. Behavior therapy: Observations and reflections. *Journal of Consulting & Clinical Psychology,* 1969, *33,* 259–266.

55. Ibid.

56. Brown, B. M. Cognitive aspects of Wolpe's behavior therapy. *American Journal of Psychiatry,* 1967, *124,* 162–167.

57. Locke, E. A. Is "behavior therapy" behavioristic? (An analysis of Wolpe's psychotherapeutic methods). *Psychological Bulletin,* 1971, *76,* 318–327.

58. Wilkins, W. Desensitization: Social and cognitive factors underlying the effectiveness of Wolpe's procedure. *Psychological Bulletin,* 1971, *76,* 311–316; Wilkins, W. Desensitization:

Getting it together with Davison and Wilson. *Psychological Bulletin,* 1972, *78,* 32–36. Wolpe has acknowledged the presence and importance of cognitive elements in his practice: Wolpe, J. Cognition and causation in human behavior and its therapy. *American Psychologist,* 1978, *33,* 437–446.

59. Davison, G. C., & Wilson, G. T. Critique of "Desensitization: Social and cognitive factors underlying the effectiveness of Wolpe's procedure." *Psychological Bulletin,* 1972, *78,* 28–31.

60. Kazdin, A., & Wilcoxson, L. Systematic desensitization and non-specific treatment effects: A methodological evaluation. *Psychological Bulletin,* 1976, *83,* 729–758. A comment by Yates is of interest and relevance here: "If relaxation is unnecessary, if hierarchies can be worked equally well through from top to bottom as the reverse, if only the most feared items need to be presented, if the rate of progressing through the hierarchies is unimportant, if the process can be massed or spaced with equivalent results, if the process can be completely automated, can we then continue to accept that we are dealing with a form of therapy that can meaningfully be called systematic desensitization, as Wolpe originally used the term? Can we meaningfully refer to the Cheshire cat when only its smile is left?" (A. J. Yates. *Theory and practice in behavior therapy.* New York: Wiley, 1975. P. 163)

61. Wolpe, *The practice of behavior therapy,* p. 178.

62. Wilson, G. T., & Davison, G. C. Processes of fear reduction in systematic desensitization: Animal studies. *Psychological Bulletin,* 1971, *76,* 1–14.

63. London, *The modes and morals of psychotherapy,* p. 122.

64. Ibid., p. 38.

65. Wolpe, *The practice of behavior therapy,* p. 1.

66. Lazarus, A. A. *Behavior therapy and beyond.* New York: McGraw-Hill, 1971. Pp. 3–4.

67. Ibid., p. 6.

68. Rotter, J. B. Substituting good behavior for bad. (Review of *Psychotherapy by reciprocal inhibition* by J. Wolpe). *Contemporary Psychology,* 1959, *4,* 176–178.

chapter 6

Learning Foundations of Behavior Therapy: Kanfer and Phillips

Frederick H. Kanfer (b. 1925) obtained his B.S. in 1948 from Long Island University and his M.A. in 1952 and Ph.D. in 1953 from Indiana University. From 1953 to 1957, he was assistant professor of psychology at Washington University; from 1957 to 1962, associate professor of psychology at Purdue University; and from 1962 to 1969, professor of medical psychology and psychiatry at the University of Oregon Medical School (Portland). Between 1969 and 1973, he was professor of psychology at the University of Cincinnati. Since 1973, Kanfer has been professor of psychology at the University of Illinois at Urbana-Champaign. He is a Diplomate in Clinical Psychology of the American Board of Professional Psychology. Since 1954, Kanfer has been writing extensively in professional journals on learning and psychotherapy.

Jeanne S. Phillips (b. 1929) received her B.A. in 1951 and her Ph.D. in 1957 from Washington University, where she was an assistant in 1951 to 1952, a teaching assistant in 1952 to 1953, and a fellow in medical psychology in the medical school from 1953 to 1955. Between 1955 and 1957, she was a research fellow at Massachusetts General Hospital. In 1957, she went to the University of Oregon Medical School (Portland), where she was instructor of medical psychology from 1957 to 1959, assistant professor of medical psychology from 1959 to 1965, and associate professor from 1965 to 1969, when she became professor of psychology at the University of Massachusetts. Since 1971, Phillips has been professor of psychology at the University of Denver. She is a Diplomate in Clinical Psychology of the American Board of Professional Psychology.

BACKGROUND AND DEVELOPMENT

Kanfer and Phillips developed their interest in presenting their integration of behaviorally oriented therapeutic practices from their experiences with graduate students in clinical psychology, interns, residents, and experienced clinicians in the Department of Psychiatry at the University of Oregon Medical School. They "became aware of the clinician's great need for a storehouse of behavioral psychological principles" as a basis for clinical practice. They felt that the student needed more than an understanding of the technology of the specific behavioral techniques that were attracting attention in the early 1960s. Armed with these principles,

> any professional should be able to judge for himself the appropriateness of a given technique for his own cases or research. He should be able to construct idiosyncratic treatment programs to suit the circumstances of a particular clinical situation. He should be able to adapt to the changes and innovations that are inevitable and necessary in a new and often unproven field. By his grasp of the ties between theory, laboratory investigation, and application, the professional should understand the utility and limitations of various techniques.[1]

PHILOSOPHY AND CONCEPTS

Kanfer and Phillips refer to their work as "an integrated storehouse" of behavioral psychological principles and methods or a "cohesive framework" for a general understanding of these methods.[2] It is not "a manual for clinicians, however. Its main purpose is to present the research and theory underlying the current application of learning principles and techniques to therapeutic change, as well as to point out the problems involved in practical usage."[3] It is thus research based, rather than clinically based. Basic behavior theory is covered "as it applies to the treatment of behavioral problems, rather than dwelling on the causes of human maladjustment or the significance of the person's behavioral adjustment in his own life," although these are recognized as important.[4] Similarly, biological and cultural variables, although significant, are only mentioned briefly.

Profiting from the advancement of other fields of psychology, the learning principles approach to clinical behavior change provides a broader, more flexible frame of reference than do other approaches and thus places clinical psychology in the position of an applied science that can contribute both to human welfare and to the understanding of human behavior. This approach rejects the medical-disease concept and the current psychiatric diagnostic system. The locus of psychological problems is not in people's mental apparatus but in the integration of people with their social environment.

The behavioral learning model based on neobehaviorist methodology and experimental earning data, with the methods of behavior modification derived from it, is primarily a content-free model. Its methodology focuses on the systematic analysis of behavior in order to specify functional relationships between independent variables and response classes. No theory can encompass all the details of human behavior, but this is not necessary for effective therapeutic intervention. The clinician must exercise skill and judgment in applying the general principles of psychology to the individual case. Although incomplete, the learning model—which includes perceptual, motivational, and biological phenomena—integrates the results of research on behavior change and has led to the development of the clinical techniques comprising behavior therapy.

The theoretical orientation adopted tends toward Skinner's point of view but includes elements from social learning, cognition, and other pertinent areas. The theory attempts to utilize all the findings of experimental psychology, not those of learning and conditioning alone. Thus it draws on research in perception, cognition, emotion, and social psychology and interpersonal relations, going far beyond the stimulus–response model. "A simple conditioning model may be a basic beginning for a learning approach to behavior change, but it does not reflect the limitations of this approach in taking advantage of man's manifold potentialities."[5] The scientific methodology and a few basic principles are the foundations for the clinical researcher to build on or to use in developing progressively better approximations to a model of human behavior.

The Behavioral Learning Model

The behavioral learning model of psychopathology and therapy has only recently received widespread attention in comparison with the psychodynamic model. The psychodynamic model developed from clinical experience, philosophical considerations of the nature of humanity, and conceptualizations concentrating on subjective experiences. Learning models evolved from laboratory studies, with emphasis on observation and manipulation of objective events and reduction of complex variables into simpler components.

No single learning theory exists today, nor is there any theory, as yet, capable of handling social, perceptual, verbal, and intrapersonal processes, although progress is being made. Skinner's approach, particularly, has stimulated research in the analysis of complex behaviors. This approach serves as a basis for organizing the methodological characteristics and assumptions about human behavior that are common to most learning approaches.

Common Assumptions of Behavioral Learning Models

1. The learning based model focuses on *behavior*. A person's activity is described in objective terms without resort to theoretical constructs or concepts. The person's verbalizations and self-descriptions are behaviors.
2. In the learning model, an attempt is made to change deviant behavior or symptoms directly, not to modify traits, impulses, or other hypothesized personality structures. A symptom is "any target response selected for change" and "does not imply a surface indicant of underlying causes or a disease state. Recognition that the environment plays a crucial role in determining behavior implies that the appearance of symptoms may be restricted to an identifiable range of situations and is not invariantly characteristic of the person's behavior."[6]
3. All behaviors, including social-response patterns, responses to emotional stimuli, and the learning of skills, result from the operation of the same principles of learning that (together with biological and social conditions) shape any class of behavior.
4. The common methods of inquiry of all other sciences are accepted in the learning model.
5. "Although training is necessary to enable any observer to recognize and reliably report the incidence of a specified behavior, no greater skill or theoreti-

cal knowledge is needed for learning approaches than for observation of any behavior—in man or animal, in naturalistic settings or in the laboratory. . . . Precise definition of the observed (or treated) behavior, and the underlying requirement for dealing only with publicly observable responses, therefore permit use of observers with limited knowledge of psychological theory."[7] Additional training and talent is required, however, for the formulation of a behavioral analysis and a treatment program and its evaluation.

6. While the importance of past events in the *formation* of learned behaviors is recognized, programs for behavior modification deal with *current* behaviors, which constitute the problem.

In contrast to the psychodynamic approaches to assessment and treatment, the behavior modification approach emphasizes empirical data and experimental techniques.

The Behavioral Equation as a Unit of Analysis

Behavior is continuous, but for purposes of study, it must be partitioned into segments. The formula for the behavioral equation may be written as:

$$\longleftarrow \text{Antecedent} \longleftarrow \text{Consequent}$$
$$\text{S O R K C}$$

where

S = prior stimulation

O = biological state of the organism

R = response repertoire

K = contingency relationship

C = consequence

The behavioral equation summarizes *all* the relevant conditions acting at the time of the response, thus indicating that all behavior is considered to be a function of specific and limited determinants, which are fully represented by the elements in the equation.

The response, R   Responses have been classified as *respondents* when they are elicited by a specific stimulus without training and as *operants* or *instrumental responses* when the eliciting stimuli are not known and the responses are conditioned by their consequences. The value of the distinction has been questioned. The most significant difference is that respondents are modified by variations in prior stimulus conditions, while operants are modified by changes in subsequent reinforcing consequences. Simple operants are rare; most responses are under the control of a signal, cue, or discriminative stimulus and, therefore, can be brought under stimulus as well as reinforcement controls.

Emotional behaviors, involving autonomic activity, are considered to be respondents and are controlled by stimulus control. Behaviors involving the skeletal system, motor movements, and verbal responses are operants and are controlled by the manipulation of consequences. Clinical behavior modification deals mainly with operants. Most specific behavior patterns are learned and can be modified. Human beings are highly pliable.

Responses are not limited to body movements but include social and verbal responses. The latter are responses and are not to be taken as substitutes for mental events, internal states, or other inferred processes. Covert processes—thinking, perceiving, controlling oneself, or deciding—can be dealt with "only when they can be directly measured, observed, or defined in such a way that there need be no recourse to hypothetical intervening events that are not demonstrable. Whether the behaviors examined are ordinarily overt or covert, responses are defined by the experimental operations performed to measure or manipulate them."[8] It is often difficult in clinical work to achieve clarity of response specification. Most target responses, such as enuresis, phobia, and depression, are very general classes without operations for precise identification and measurement.

Responses usually are treated as dependent variables and their "causes", sought; in behavior therapy, they are also treated as independent variables, in terms of their consequences for others as well as for the person.

External and internal environments, S   While the unconditioned stimulus in respondent behavior is inherently related to the response that it elicits, control is built up in operant conditioning by discrimination through differential reinforcement. Although free operant behavior does not involve the S of the behavioral equation, operants encountered in the clinic are not randomly emitted; they are emitted and reinforced only in the presence of an environmental signal, or discriminative stimulus (SD). Thus the stimulus is a *discriminated operant.* Discriminative stimuli include stimuli produced by the person as well as by others. Behavior is composed of series, or chains, of responses in which one response becomes a discriminative stimulus for the next response, each response being affected by the terminal consequences.

The stimulus components must be defined from the viewpoint of the behaving organism, not from the viewpoint of the observer.

Social influences are mediated by discriminative stimuli provided by persons in the environment. Such influences vary with different social and cultural environments.

The organism, O   There is disagreement about the influence of biological or genetic factors in behavioral disturbances. Whatever the degree of influence, biological characteristics, both permanent and temporary, must always be included in the behavioral equation. Since attitudes toward biologically deficient conditions differ, the social milieu must be taken into account in the definition of biological adequacy.

The consequence, C   Thorndike's *law of effect,* Hull's *drive reduction* principle, and Skinner's *reinforcement* are recognitions that the consequences of a response influence the subsequent probability of the occurrence of the response.

The effectiveness of a reinforcing stimulus for a given response varies as a function of all the components in the behavioral equation. . . . Even a reinforcing stimulus that appears to have a fairly constant physical relationship to an organism's activity may of the problem, as well as changes in treatment. Also, the direction of change is predicted; it is not simply an effect. Clinicians cannot eliminate or control extraneous variables; they may use them therapeutically, however, since clinicians are not mainly concerned with understanding but with control. Favorable outcome supports their assessment of the problem and choice of procedures, as accurate prediction supports the hypothesis of experimenters. Clinicians discontinue the process when favorable effects are produced, even though they are not clear about how these effects were achieved. Since extraneous circumstances affect outcomes, outcome alone is not validation—or lack of validation—of hypotheses. "Behavior change, not understanding, is the clinician's main goal."[12] It is limited to the specific problem presented rather than to change in the total life pattern of the patient.

Clinicians deal with individual cases. Objective, reliable behavior records, comparable to the scientist's laboratory data, are the goal of behaviorists. However, their observations are limited for practical reasons, although they often go beyond the office interview and subject report to direct observation. Even here, however, clinicians cannot, as can researchers, control situational variables.

The individual-case approach can be subjected to research analysis. Skinner and other operant conditioning researchers utilize the single case for a functional analysis of behavior. General statements of relationships are derived from replication with other individual cases. The procedure for such research involves (1) a baseline, or free-operant, measure of the dependent variable (A); (2) introduction of a treatment condition, with a second measure of the variable or response (B); and (3) removal or cessation of the treatment condition, or a return to the baseline condition, with a third measure of the dependent variable (A). The therapist, of course, does not or cannot leave the patient in this condition but reinstates the treatment. The fact that the condition is reversible with cessation of treatment constitutes a problem, of course, since the patient may revert following treatment. The ideal clinical method would change behavior from A to B so that it is not easily reversible.

Clinicians are participant observers, which introduces bias in a number of ways, including their expectations of their patients. While some of these factors, such as the "demand characteristics" of the situation, are present in the laboratory as well as in the clinic, they are more prominent in the clinic.

Even though they recognize that their main responsibility is improving the patient's behavior, behavior therapists are aware of their potential for contributing to general psychological knowledge. Research, however, is limited by the restrictions of the clinical setting. Nevertheless, more than other therapists, behavior therapists apply the scientific method to their actual therapeutic practice.

Behavior Therapy and Other Approaches

Behavior therapists tend to select specific symptoms or behaviors as targets for change, to employ concrete, planned interventions to manipulate these behaviors, and to monitor progress continuously and quantitatively. A patient's early life history is largely ignored, except as it may provide clues about such factors as currently active events which maintain symptoms, or hierarchies of reinforcers. Behavior thera-

produce opposing effects under changing conditions. . . . In fact, in application of operant learning methods to behavior modification it must constantly be remembered that a particular event selected as a potential reinforcing stimulus can be so defined with certainty only *after* it succeeds in changing the probability of the preceding response.[9]

Conjugate reinforcement requires continuous behavior to maintain the reinforcing event. *Episodic reinforcement* requires a long sequence of events before reinforcement occurs. Much complex social behavior represents conjugate or episodic reinforcement.

The response-consequence–contingency relationship, K There are many different relationships between behavior and its consequences. Many behaviors have inevitable relationships between behavior and its consequences. Social behaviors have few such inevitable consequences because of the nature of our physical world. Social behaviors have few such inevitable consequences. Contingencies may be deliberately withheld and presented on schedules.

In schedules of reinforcement, the *proportion (ratio)* of reinforced responses or the time *interval* after which reinforcement is given may vary. Ratios or intervals may be *fixed* or *variable. Multiple,* or combination, schedules often characterize human behavior.

The speed with which a response is acquired, its strength, and its decay, or extinction, are determined not only by its consequences, but also by the schedule of reinforcement. Intermittent schedules (with less than 100 percent reinforcement) predominate. (Intermittent reinforcement is ineffective in learning, but when it is used following continual reinforcement, it leads to resistance to extinction.)

In *shaping,* the experimenter at first reinforces behavior that is only similar to the behavior that is ultimately desired but does not yet exist. Responses that are more similar to the desired ones are gradually reinforced, and those that are less similar are not reinforced, which leads eventually to the performance of the desired behavior.

Implications of the Behavioral Equation in Clinical Use

The behavioral equation is related to the assumptions of the behavior therapies.

Stress on current influences Knowledge of the original controlling variables, which may be obtained from the patient's history, seldom indicates how the current behavior can be controlled. Current behavior is controlled by variables acting in the present. The clinician must locate these variables, whether they are S (stimulus), O (organism), or K (contingency) variables.

Symptoms are learned If problem behavior is learned, either it may be unlearned or the environment may be modified to eliminate the antecedent conditions that control it.

Subjective experiences Clinical complaints often involve subjective reactions and feelings, which cannot be dealt with directly, since they cannot be brought under the therapist's control. However, "subjective experiences are assumed to have their origin in some earlier social experience and can be influenced through therapeutic operations."[10] Analysis of the patient's verbal reports of such behaviors can bring some of the patient's self-reactions under control by altering the behaviors leading to them.

Continuity of behavior across species   The behavioral model is derived from laboratory research with animals. Although the behavior of higher species is more complex than that of laboratory animals, "the basic principles of learning are expected to remain unchanged for all living organisms and no special psychological principles are required for the understanding of human behavior. It is necessary to supplement the more general principles with special relationships due to the unique features of human life."[11] But the same methodological approach is appropriate for the analysis of these relationships.

The Clinician as Researcher

Behavior modifiers function as therapists and as researchers. Clinicians are bound by certain practical considerations.

1. The clinician's task is to observe and to treat the single individual, whose behavior is subject to simultaneous influences from many uncontrolled variables.
2. The patient's condition requires immediate action, even though scientifically validated methods may not exist. Therefore, the clinician acts on objective data and "educated guesses."
3. Scientific knowledge is blended with personal experience and information.
4. Since the clinician's decisions may have immediate and far-reaching impact on several people, the clinician must constantly evaluate goals and methods for effectiveness and social consequences.

These practical considerations limit the solutions available to therapists, leading to compromise solutions.

Scientific laboratory research requires systematic, empirical study involving control of all variables. The researcher must (1) focus on a preselected class of events (dependent variables), defined objectively so as to be publicly observable and measurable, (2) systematically manipulate one or more similarly defined other classes of events (independent variables) to assess their effects on the dependent variables, (3) avoid other sources of influence, and (4) attend to sampling of subjects, events, definitions, measures, and manipulations to allow for generalization.

The clinical and research models differ, yet they are similar and overlap. The behavioral clinician's plan of conduct should follow the steps followed by the experimental psychologist: (1) formulation of the problem, (2) design of operational procedures to test hypotheses derived from the problem, (3) execution of the treatment (independent variables), (4) analysis of the data (dependent variables), and (5) evaluation of the implication of the results for the problem. In clinical procedures, the steps are not as discrete, and there is more shifting back to the formulation or reformulation

pists tend to concentrate on an analysis of particular symptoms. They devote far less attention than other clinicians to subjective experiences, attitudes, insights and dreams.[13]

They are more concerned with evidence from observations of behavior than from empathy. A planned, carefully outlined procedure is carried out with the monitoring of its effects.

The following behavioral assumptions underlie differences between the procedures of traditional therapy and those of behavior therapy.

1. Psychological problems are not regarded as diseases rooted in early faulty personality development.
2. The behavior to be changed is not a symptom of an underlying disease process but is itself the problem. It is a learned response that is detrimental to the patient.
3. Treatment is directed toward changing the problem behavior.
4. Treatment methods are tailored to the individual's specific problems, not to a diagnostic label attached to the patient or to his or her condition.

Relationship Variables

Behavior therapy is "only one area of application of knowledge from the broader field of behavior influence and interpersonal communication."[14] The variables of interpersonal influence are not technique specific, and they are involved in any personal contact with a clinician, including behavior therapy. The quality of the interpersonal relationship influences the process and outcome of therapy, whatever the theory of behavior change or the techniques used. Thus in behavior therapy, the effectiveness of behavioral techniques may be enhanced or hindered by the therapist's personal and interactional characteristics. These characteristics may be used for deliberate enhancement of the therapeutic effect. However, the number and nature of specific variables, their interrelationships and the basic factors involved, and the mechanisms responsible for their effects are not well enough known for effective use of these variables. Two broad factors under which interactional variables may be classified appear to be positive social reinforcement and expectancy congruence between the therapist and the client.

The diverse variables, functional relationships and variables in laboratory and clinical studies of effective models, and social reinforcers must be clarified and integrated before they can be useful. Beyond this, the results must be translated into stimulus–response language and given demonstrable behavioral referents.

Relationship variables, such as "mutuality of role expectations," are complex and involve cognitions and expectancies that often are excluded from behavior therapy models, but a learning theory approach is not incompatible with such constructs if the behavioral events to which they refer are clearly defined, operational, and repeatable. Expectancies, attitudes, and "meanings" can be put into behavioral terms and incorporated into behavioral or learning methods of therapy.

Although relationship variables are viewed by some as the major effective variables in behavior change, they are viewed in behavior therapy as nonspecific effects.

The Issue of Humanism

The humanists' criticism of behavior therapy is that "the emphasis on behavior may run the risk of disregarding the value and dignity of human life itself." This criticism questions the adequacy of the scientific method for the study of human beings. The objectivity and detachment of the method seem to involve the danger of reducing the person to "nothing but" a set of relationships, leaving out the richness of feelings, ambitions, dreams, and agonies. "The implicit assumption appears to be that knowledge of laws that govern behavior is incompatible with sensitivity to the variations in the expression of these lawful relationships. This assumption is parallel to the assumption that a knowledge of chemistry or natural processes reduces the aesthetic and utilitarian values of products, such as stained glass windows, or natural processes, such as the bloom of flowers."[15] The high degree of control involved, with deprivation and restrictions to enhance the utility of incentives and the use of aversive stimuli, have led to fears of dehumanization or the reduction of human beings to the status of laboratory animals.

The success of behavior modification, however, even on a simplistic level, as in work with psychotic patients, increases the human dignity of the patients as they regain an ability for independent living.

Behavior modification is a technology that can be used for whatever purposes society wants to accomplish. It is nonhumanistic rather than antihumanistic and is nonethical in that it does not set standards of values, as do some other psychotherapeutic schools. It is pragmatic and can be applied to achieve humanistic values and goals. These values originate in society and its institutions, not in the therapist. In modifying behavior, the therapist acts as an instrument representing the goals of others, either the patient or a social agency. However, as a citizen and a humanist, the psychologist, with his or her knowledge of human behavior, is in a position to participate in the shaping or changing of value systems, particularly in providing methods of studying the consequences of different value systems.

The Issue of Control

"Each therapist must ask himself questions such as: To what extent do techniques of behavior control violate the individual's freedoms? Does *failing* to apply a potential technology for behavior change represent ultimate loss of freedom for the individual and society and an unjustified waste, or a necessary caution against manipulation?" Behavior therapy may be viewed as threatening humanistic values and respect for human dignity and choice. "Social prescription of behavior may ignore experiential and emotional needs, which are perhaps more basic to human fulfillment."[16] The therapeutic community of a mental hospital ward differs little from authoritarian thought reform, both having the same assumption of social control "for your own good" and depending on the same procedures. "Whatever the setting, the danger is that a therapist may assume the right to decide how the patient and environment *should* act, using his own criteria of desired social effectiveness instead of the criteria offered by the therapeutic influence or society."[17]

The problem of social control applies to traditional psychotherapies, to the extent that they are effective, as well as to behavior therapy. Scientific progress leads inevitably to the ability to control behavior. The issue becomes that of "who controls whom, by what methods, in respect to which behaviors, and according to whose set of values."[18]

The picture of the client as an automaton who is controlled by the behavior therapist is inconsistent with the knowledge of the importance of warmth, spontaneity, and genuineness in therapeutic effectiveness. The specific goals achieved by planned and subtle methods are compared unfavorably with the more fluid process of self-actualization as a goal, a goal also selected or prescribed by the therapist and achieved by subtle, covert operations of the therapist. The goals of the abstract therapeutic processes reduce to the goals of the behavior therapies when they are operationalized.

Some critics object to the use of positive reinforcement as a method of control, since it is not easily detectable by the recipient or is characterized as a bribe. It is regarded as more dangerous, more potentially threatening, and of lesser moral value than control by aversive stimuli; yet punishment is questionable as a method of control, both psychologically and ethically.

The behavior therapist is in a difficult position because he or she does not view the patient as sick. Therapy is sanctioned by society for sick people and as punishment for illegal acts, but society is not so clear about other behaviors.

> Despite conflicting social values, the behavior therapist must decide which behaviors require change and which can be overlooked. By the nature of his work, the behavior therapist not only has to accept the onus of behavior control. Often he must also assume the burden of siding as an accomplice either on the side of the patient or on the side of society in determining what behaviors should be controlled. This issue is not easily resolved.

The problem of the individual's rights and civil liberties is also present. However, it must be recognized that the patient is actually being controlled by his or her social environment, and the ethical problem is not simply one of control or no control. To leave the patient under the control of an unfavorable environment is an ethical decision.

While control in the acquisition of motor skills is valued, control of interpersonal skills and of complex functions is resisted. Some deny that behavior methods can control such complex functions as creativity, self-control, empathy, or value formation. Yet such control is sought in traditional therapy and by other means.

Behavior therapists are concerned about the ethics of control. They openly state their goals and operations, which may be rejected by the client or society. Behavior therapy "is doing in a planned and efficient way what other procedures strive for but approach with less efficiency or clarity; and the therapeutic goals are defined by society, its agents, or the patient and not by the theory underlying the modification process itself."[20] The problem of which social agency should establish acceptable goals for manipulation is an unsolved social issue for discussion.

BEHAVIOR THERAPY

Behavioral Diagnosis and Assessment

The process of assessment or diagnosis has been given inadequate attention by behavior therapists, although models and techniques for behavioral diagnosis are beginning to be suggested. Thus rather than being based on laboratory or clinical research, assessment must deal with trends, tentative directions, and future potentials.

The goal of behavior therapy is the development of a complete set of psychological principles to apply to an individual patient from the initial presentation of the patient's complaint to his or her discharge. This requires systematic methods of collecting information to appraise the patient's difficulties and to reach decisions about a treatment program. The behavioristic framework requires that the therapist (1) locate the problem and (2) translate the initial complaint into a language and a set of questions appropriate for available behavioral technology.

Behavioral Models of Pathology

"The behavioral model of abnormal psychology has no place at all for traditional diagnostic labels in the formulation of treatment strategies."[21] Such nonspecific and unreliable labels are appropriate only for a therapy whose goals are vague and subjective.

The medical model of psychopathology is rejected, as noted above. Two other, related learning theory models have been proposed. One, which has been accepted by the stimulus-control therapies (the Pavlovian, classical conditioning therapies represented by Eysenck and Rachman), accepts the classification of neurosis, psychosis, and sociopathic and homosexual behaviors. Neurotic behaviors are viewed as classically conditioned respondents (anxiety) and behaviors reinforced by a reduction of the anxiety drive and are "cured" by Pavlovian procedures. Psychotic behaviors are endogenous; operant conditioning of psychotic symptoms is referred to as "rehabilitation." Sociopathic behaviors represent a failure of conditioning or an appetitive conditioning that leads to unlawful behaviors.

The other model, that of operant conditioning, tends to view all deviant behaviors as the result of untoward reinforcement processes, past and present; the behavior is deviant because it is discrepant from the behavior desired by the society or culture. Since behavior is a result of a multitude of interactions, it is difficult to obtain evidence of the reinforcement history of problematic behavior. Animal research and longitudinal studies may establish that various behaviors can be produced by various reinforcement patterns, but it may not be possible to specify this for the individual patient.

The traditional psychological tests of the clinical psychologist, including projective tests and questionnaires, are of little use to the behavior therapist. "Behavioral assessment is aimed neither at personality description nor patient assignment to particular personality types. . . . Behavioral diagnosis attempts to provide information that permits the clinician to define targets for change, to identify conditions maintaining the undesirable behavior, and to select the most practical means for producing the desired changes."[22] Such a diagnosis requires a wide range of data, including historical, social, cognitive, and biological factors, as well as directly observable behavior. These data may be organized under the following components: (1) analysis of the problem situation, (2) clarification of the problem situation, (3) motivational analysis, (4) developmental analysis, (5) analysis of self-control, (6) analysis of social relationships, and (7) analysis of the sociocultural and physical environment. The specificity of the data may be seen by the description of the first component: "The patient's major complaints are categorized into classes of behavioral excesses and deficits. For each excess or deficit the dimensions of frequency, intensity, duration, appropriateness of form, and stimulus conditions are described. In content, the response classes represent the major targets of the therapeutic intervention. As an additional indispensable feature, the behavioral assets of the patient are listed for utilization in a therapy program."[23] Data included are often direct samples of behavior, reports of past behavior, and patient self-ratings. Assessment is a continuing part of behavior therapy, with quantitative evaluation of change in target behavior and in therapeutic tactics on the basis of continued monitoring.

The assessment of factors that maintain problem behaviors and of effective or potent reinforcers is particularly difficult at present and is based on little more than hunches. The construction of behavioral assessment procedures is a difficult but feasible task, and it utilizes extensions of laboratory analogue and response-sampling techniques. Until such procedures are developed, the behavior therapist must operate on the basis of clinical lore and judgment in evaluating patients and deciding where to intervene.

> As yet the decision making processes of the behavioral clinician are poorly understood. There is little scientific basis for the selection of the best course of treatment for particular patient-target-environment combinations. The clinician tries to sort and match variables on the basis of a functional analysis to achieve the optimal solutions of the problems presented by an individual patient, with only the crudest rules to guide him. Many of the factors that influence the chosen treatment approach are not specific to the behavior therapies, although they are described in behavior terms.[24]

Behavior Modification by Control of Stimulus–Response Arrangements

The classical conditioning paradigm controls an undesirable response by controlling the stimuli that elicit it. Emphasis is on the S, O, and R, rather than on the C, of the behavior equation. Aversion therapy parallels the classical conditioning model most closely. (Counterconditioning under Wolpe's reciprocal-inhibition principle, using a positive new stimulus, includes elements besides classical conditioning and is an example of a mixed model, to be discussed later.)

In *aversive therapy,* a noxious unconditioned stimulus (UCS) (producing an unpleasant event) is paired with a stimulus associated with the undesirable behavior (CS). "It is assumed that the stimulus function of the CS becomes predominantly one of signaling the onset of an unpleasant, fear arousing event." The CS now evokes an unpleasant response that is incompatible with the original pleasurable consequence. "Its effects may serve to interrupt the objectionable behavior sequence. New and more appropriate responses can then be developed."[25]

Aversion therapy has been used extensively with sexual deviations, alcoholism, and enuresis. Its use in the treatment of alcoholism may be taken as illustrative. The cues that are associated with alcohol and elicit drinking, including the sight, smell, taste, and thought of alcohol, are the conditioned stimuli; they are paired with unconditioned stimuli for pain or unpleasant reactions until they take on a similar stimulus function.

In early studies in the 1920s, drugs were used as the unconditioned stimulus, and these studies were not very successful because of factors related to this (for example, impairment of conditioning because of sedation) and other factors. Thus the method of treatment was abandoned for about 20 years. Antibuse, a drug that operates not through conditioning but by causing nausea and vomiting when followed by ingestion of alcohol, came into use. Emetic drugs (for example, emetine) have been used as unconditioned stimuli. Following injected and/or oral emetine, patients are given alcohol to smell or taste just before the expected onset of nausea and vomiting. In an early study of 4,000 patients, 60 percent remained abstinent for at least 1 year; 51 percent, for at least 2 years; and 38 percent, for at least 5 years. Electric shock has been used more recently as the unconditioned stimulus.

Alcoholism is difficult to treat because of the wide variability of the external and internal stimuli and their surroundings. In addition, it is difficult to find a competing alternative response. "Neither classically conditioned cues nor universal operant reinforcers present appropriate alternatives for the response of drinking alcohol. Hence, arriving at a substitute for drinking is difficult or impossible until one can state for *which* aspect of the chain of behaviors and consequences in alcohol consumption the substitution is made."[26] The same problem is present in treating overeating, use of narcotics, or cigarette smoking by conditioning. A punishment model may be more effective than aversion therapy. Therapy should include behavioral treatment of anxiety symptoms, development of social and vocational skills, and provision of necessary environmental reinforcers as well as aversion conditioning.

Imagined aversive events, instead of drugs or shock, have been employed as the unconditional stimulus. The terms *covert sensitization* or *aversive imagery* have been used to designate this technique. The conditioned stimulus may also be imagined.

When the symptom itself is used as the conditioned stimulus, the assumption that classical conditioning is the basic mechanism is doubtful. When such behaviors are followed by aversive stimuli, the aversive stimuli serve as punishing consequences for the symptom. In other cases, such as the treatment of alcoholism by aversive conditioning of the smell and taste of alcohol, the unconditioned stimulus has aversive reinforcing characteristics for other behaviors occurring immediately prior to its onset, such as raising the glass, taking a sip, and tasting. Thus operant conditioning of these instrumental acts takes place.

The operant conditioning paradigm is likewise not pure. A reinforcing stimulus can become associated through classical conditioning with other cues in the situation that function as conditioned stimuli.

> In our alcoholism example, if only the sight or smell of alcohol is used as the CS, and if preceding approach responses are ignored, then shock (UCS) is controlled by the experimenter and is delivered in a noncontingent fashion. If the subject's response of raising the glass and sipping from it is the critical response for shock delivery, and if spitting out the alcohol is immediately followed by termination of the shock, then the reinforcing stimulus is contingent and controlled by the subject's own behavior. He can avoid the UCS by not engaging in the target response.[27]

Effective treatment, as does the everyday behavior of alcohol consumption, may depend on both conditioning processes, "thereby changing the discriminative (or eliciting) and secondary reinforcing values of the CS (by classical conditioning) and suppressing the target response (R) while reinforcing an alternative responsive (by operant conditioning)."[28]

It is apparent that learning situations cannot be classified as either classical or operant conditioning, even in the laboratory. Aversive stimulation in therapy includes three practices: (1) punishment or use of an aversive stimulus to suppress undesirable behavior, (2) escape and avoidance learning, in which the aversive stimulus serves to establish new responses that prevent or terminate the noxious stimulation, and (3) classical conditioning, in which the aversive stimulus leads to unpleasant results that become associated with and thus inhibit the undesirable behavior. The distinction between aversive conditioning and punishment often depends on whether the therapist identifies with classical or operant learning theory.

Combinations of classical and operant conditioning thus occur in most behavior therapy, with or without the intention of the therapist. Some therapists deliberately combine the procedures, particularly in the treatment of homosexuality.

Mixed Models of Stimulus–Response Control

The combination of classical and operant methods is particularly applicable to complex situations in which emotional responses surround the target instrumental response and covert and overt verbal responses serve as controlling stimuli for behavior. The latter are cognitive-mediating responses.

The major emotional response present in behavior disorders is anxiety. Since there are various and unrelated measures of anxiety, the selection of the therapeutic target presents a problem. The unconditioning of physiological-emotional responses may or may not result in changes in other behaviors. Many symptomatic responses are considered as adjustive reactions that avoid or terminate anxiety. When such actions successfully avoid the anxiety, there is the puzzling question of why they are continued and are so resistant to extinction; since anxiety is not experienced, the avoidance reactions are not reinforced by its relief or cessation. The problem has not been adequately resolved. The avoidance responses, rather than the anxiety responses themselves, often constitute the target for modification.

Awareness and instructions, operating through verbal structuring, influence the acquisition and extinction of responses in humans. Many behavior therapy techniques are based almost entirely on manipulation of verbal responses believed to affect other behaviors. Although people cannot stop being anxious by simply telling themselves not to be, labeling emotional states can affect behavior. Thus cognitive factors are important in individuals regulation of their own behavior, and cognitive set (expectations) can influence anxiety and the effects of aversive stimuli.

Wolpe's method of reciprocal inhibition is widely used in the treatment of neurotic anxiety. The subject is exposed to a weaker form of the conditioned stimulus presumed to have been originally conditioned to anxiety through association with some potent unconditional stimulus (desensitization), followed by the introduction of a response that is antagonistic to the anxiety response (reciprocal inhibition), which conditions a more probable competing response to the conditioned stimulus (counterconditioning). (See Chapter 5 for more detail.)

Wolpe's method usually has been categorized as classical conditioning, but it demands that an antagonistic response, toned with positive affect, be elicited and maintained, and such responses are usually operants. Thus the method is a mixed model. Assertive responses are such operants and are usually rewarding when made by the patient. Relaxation, sexual behaviors, eating, and so on are also operant responses maintained by reinforcement.

Research involving controlled experiments on systematic desensitization support its effectiveness, but they are not clear regarding the bases for its effectiveness. Relaxation alone and the relationship alone are not effective; apparently, desensitization alone usually is not effective; but desensitization with relaxation is effective. These results suggest that inhibition is more effective than extinction. Extinction is, however, effective or more effective than counterconditioning in elementary avoidance responses.

Flooding rather than gradual desensitization appears to be effective in many situations. Stampfl's *implosion therapy* utilizes flooding without the counterconditioning or relaxation. The method is successful, and its *modus operandi* is assumed to be extinction. However, investigators other than Stampfl and his co-workers have not had as much success (Chapter 5), suggesting that other factors in the situation are important.

The influence of the reinforcing effects of the therapist's words and actions must not be overlooked in the classical or the mixed model of behavior therapy. In the latter, as well as in operant conditioning, the fact that response-contingent reinforcement may serve as information may lead to behavior change through cognitive verbal control. The patient's evaluation of his or her own behavior may affect subsequent behavior through a new set of controlling verbal stimuli that arises during the treatment process. Suggestion and verbal operant conditioning would also appear to function in desensitization therapy. It is apparent, then, that behavior therapy is not a simple matter of conditioning.

Once the desensitization procedure is modified to suit the particular problems encountered with other behavior disorders [besides emotional arousal and phobic avoidance behavior], the very elegance and clarity of the systematic desensitization operations are lost. The restricted applicability of the desensitization paradigm to particular problems and the success obtained when this technique is fitted into the patient's total therapeutic program remind us once again to guard against the false hope that all the richness and complexity of human behavior may be encompassed by one single model. We must also keep in mind that it is naive to expect a single standardized procedure to be effective for all instances of a particular class of problems or to believe that only one therapeutic procedure may be applicable to each class of behavior problems.[29]

Moreover, the effectiveness of a therapeutic method does not necessarily substantiate the theoretical explanation of why it works. Although the mixed models discussed above have been demonstrated to be effective, the specific effective variables and necessary elements of the methods have not been clearly established, even though considerable research has been done. The models have been adopted widely, however, on pragmatic grounds.

Social Learning and Behavior Rehearsal

Social learning, through observation, imitation, or modeling, broadens behavioral learning principles by extending them to the characteristically human aspects of persons and their environments. The recent interest in principles of social learning reflects dissatisfaction with the conditioning models and is an attempt to deal with more complex social phenomena and human capacities within the learning theory model. The acquisition of most adult behaviors is not easily explained in learning terms, particularly S–R learning.

Living organisms are not passive but engage in exploratory behavior that changes their environment. Many species (including rats, monkeys, and humans) engage in behavior that results in the imitation of the behavior of peer models. They learn vicariously by observation. The higher the level of the necessary behavioral repertoire for survival, the greater the role of observational learning. Language, or the ability to verbalize observations, enhances such learning. Such learning can be used to change behavior in psychotherapy.

Five classes of observational learning can be differentiated.

1. *Matched-Dependent Learning (or Learning to Imitate)*   The subject learns to follow the example of a leader, and there is a reward for success.
2. *Identification*   The subject acquires noninstrumental (nonessential) idiosyncratic behaviors (style) of a model by observation and is not rewarded for specific instrumental responses but for imitation of the style.
3. *No-Trial Learning*   Following observation of a model, the subject is given the opportunity to perform the same task without apparent practice or contingent reinforcement for performance.
4. *Colearning*   The model and the observer engage in the same learning task, with alternate opportunities for watching and doing.
5. *Vicarious Classical Conditioning*   The subject witnesses the administration of an unconditioned stimulus for an emotional response or the response itself, and its impact on the subject's observation, learning, and performance is measured. The arousal of emotional responses by observation of another person occurs frequently in the dramatic arts. The observer's vicariously elicited response becomes connected, through temporal contiguity, to formerly neutral stimuli.

Although there has been considerable research on observational learning, the theoretical aspects are vague and incomplete. Several theories have been proposed, including Dollard and Miller's and Skinner's theories of matched-dependent behavior, Mowrer's and Bandura's theories of imitation, Gewirtz's model of conditioned discrimination learning, and Berger's hypothesis of vicarious instigation. This lack of a clear conceptualization of the process may be related to the fact that therapists make little use of the methods.

Social learning, or modeling, has been utilized in behavior modification mainly in three forms. In the *modeling treatment of phobias,* subjects are exposed to live models or to films depicting models who engage in activities related to the phobic object, for example, children playing with dogs or adolescents and adults handling snakes. Live demonstrations appear to be more effective than films, unless films depict a broader range of models and aversive stimuli. Modeling has been shown to be more effective than desensitization in the treatment of snake phobias in research done by Bandura and his associates.[30] Live modeling plus guided experience was the most effective procedure. Subjects who had failed to lose their phobias under symbolic modeling, desensitization, and control conditions lost their snake-phobic behavior in a few sessions of live modeling with guided experience. Modeling of approach responses, according to Bandura, reduces the arousal potential of the aversive stimulus to a level that does not activate avoidance responses; this allows the observer to make approach responses, which do not result in aversive consequences.

Modeling approaches to interview behavior include exposing clients prior to the counseling process to interviews (in live, taped, or typescript form) in which desirable client behaviors are modeled. Such behaviors can include problem statements and self-exploration. Discussion following the pretherapy exposure to modeling can reinforce the desirable behaviors. Whether such modeling is superior to simple instructions is not known.

In interview therapy, the therapist serves as a model for the client. "In fact, the skillful therapist has often been described as a person who is able to model, by his comments and his actions, the way in which a patient ought to view himself, consider his problems, and arrive at an effective plan for action."[31]

Replication techniques do not clearly involve vicarious learning but include the therapist's use of information input as stimulus control for therapeutic ends. These techniques replicate, or simulate, relevant parts of the environment of the patient, who can then evaluate his or her problem behaviors and try out new behaviors in a protected environment. Such situations thus reduce anxiety and foster the elimination of problem behaviors by rehearsal or observational learning. Audiotapes or videotapes of the patient's behavior enable the patient to discover improved behaviors. Role enactment, with reinforcement for new behaviors, can be used. Role playing, including psychodrama, provides feedback and practice in new behaviors. Kelly's fixed-role therapy enables the patient to practice new behaviors in an "as if" situation, which facilitates the acquisition of new perceptions and feedback. Behavior rehearsal is used as an adjunct to desensitization.

Neither the underlying process involved in vicarious learning nor the effectiveness of role-rehearsal techniques has been established. The procedures usually are inadvertently or loosely used in therapy, rather than being deliberately applied.

Behavior Modification by Manipulation of Consequences

While classical conditioning focuses on the S and O of the behavioral equation and their relationships to the following responses, operant conditioning concentrates on the relationship of the response (R) to the subsequent elements, K and C. "Therapeutic interventions based on the operant model primarily rearrange contingent behavioral consequences, including rewards and punishments, in order to alter undesired behaviors or to remedy behavioral deficiencies. The operant paradigm, since it does not require specification of antecedent conditions, is more convenient for conceptualizing and manipulating a wide range of responses in natural settings that do not permit clear identification of eliciting stimuli."[32] The relation or interaction between the behaving organism and the environment is the focus of attention.

Characteristics of the Operant Paradigm

There are four aspects of the operant approach that are particularly relevant to therapeutic behavior change.

1. It is empirical, and there is no need for internal variables or mediational constructs. The existence of inner states or variables is not denied, but they are not considered necessary or relevant.
2. It is a practical engineering approach. While atheoretical, it is capable of testing hypotheses through variation of consequences. It focuses on observable and easily measured behaviors, such as frequency of specific responses. Interest is in experimental control of behavior, and discovery of the independent variables that provide such control is sufficient without further conceptual explanations.
3. Analysis of the single case is emphasized. The single individual is studied, and the effects of the consequences (C) or schedules (K) on the individual, rather than statistical analysis of group data, are of concern. Replication of effects on different individuals provides a basis for generalization.
4. The emphasis on present determinants does not deny the importance of historical variables. Problematic behaviors may have originated and have been maintained by determinants that no longer function. It is important to know the determinants for cases where they may be operating in the establishment of problem behavior, but when dealing with a current problem situation, it is sufficient if the present disturbing behavior can be modified by dealing with its current reinforcers without regard to its original determinants.

The response that is of concern in therapeutic behavior change may consist of a large response class such as "disruptive behavior." Positive reinforcement, negative reinforcement (removal of aversive stimuli), punishment, extinction, response differentiation (shaping), and discrimination are operations involved in treatment. The choice of procedures used in modifying a particular response class depends on (1) the availability of controlling stimuli, (2) the limits of the individual's repertoire for acquiring new patterns of simpler response components, and (3) the availability of reinforcing stimuli for therapeutic purposes.

Reinforcement operations   "Reinforcement basically involves an environmental event or stimulus consequence (C) that is contingent upon the particular response (R) and whose occurrence increases the probability that the response will occur again."[33] It is not necessary to be concerned with how reinforcements work (through expectancy mechanisms, positive-feedback mechanisms, contiguity mechanisms?) or what they have in common that determines their reinforcing power (reduction of drive, change in hedonic state, production of central arousal?). It is sufficient that they work.

Reinforcement operations are of four kinds: positive stimuli can be presented (positive reinforcement) or removed (response cost) contingently, or negative stimuli can be presented (punishment) or removed (negative reinforcement) contingently. In addition, positive stimuli can be withheld after a period of presentation (extinction), and negative stimuli can be similarly withheld (avoidance). Complexity is introduced, since stimuli may be manipulated noncontingently as well as contingently. Further complications are present: reinforcers cannot be defined in advance because they are dependent on the individual and the circumstances. Thus "in any experimental design or clinical application, the effectiveness of a particular stimulus or reinforcer must first be demonstrated for the given situation and a given subject. In the clinical situation, in which conditioning may proceed over a long period of time, it is even necessary to reevaluate the effectiveness of a reinforcing stimulus a few days or weeks after its general introduction."[34] In addition, the effectiveness of a stimulus varies with the reinforcement schedule (K).

Reinforcement and motivation   Motivational constructs are unnecessary in operant conditioning. Differing probabilities of response can be accounted for by variables such as degree of deprivation or satiation. Some stimuli, called primary reinforcers, are reinforcing to most members of a species regardless of prior conditioning history. These include food, water, stimuli that reduce pain or discomfort, and sexual stimuli.

Conditioned reinforcement and social reinforcers   Most reinforcers have acquired their potency from repeated association with other reinforcing events and are thus *conditioned reinforcers*. They are resistant to extinction, presumably because they have been acquired on an intermittent schedule of reinforcement. Conditioned reinforcers that have been conditioned to many different primary and secondary reinforcers are called *generalized reinforcers*. Money, tokens, and attention are examples.

Social reinforcement   The verbal and nonverbal actions of other people constitute powerful reinforcers for human behavior. Many patients' complaints relate to interpersonal interactions and social evaluations. Social reinforcement is probably significant in conformity, imitation, social evaluation, and self-evaluation.

Chaining of responses   Complex response chains can be built up, in which component responses become discriminative stimuli for the following response. The final chain may be seen as a single operant in which all the components are related to the final reinforcing event. Analysis of the chain is often necessary in therapeutic situations, in which "the behavior modifier's task is often that of slowly building up appropriate response chains through positive reinforcement." Chains involving alternative reinforced elements, or "branching," appear to represent much of normal behavior. "With few other procedures are we as strongly reminded of the applied technological nature of therapeutic operant behavior modification; success in building repertoires of response chains in behavior-deficient patients is mainly a matter of careful engineering."[35]

Schedules of reinforcement, K   Reinforcement may be given not only continually (following each response), but also intermittently on various schedules in terms of *time intervals* that must elapse before reinforcement or in terms of the number of responses per reinforcer, or *ratio schedules.* Time intervals or ratio schedules may be fixed or variable. Behavior established by intermittent schedules is more resistant to extinction. Programs of behavior modification begin with continual reinforcement, which is gradually thinned out on a schedule. Too rapid thinning out and changing of schedules can disrupt behavior.

Therapeutic Use of Reinforcement Operations

Positive reinforcement is most useful in treating behavior deficits, that is, in dealing with responses that fail to occur with sufficient frequency or intensity in appropriate form or under appropriate conditions. Thus it builds new responses, rather than removes pathological responses, although the latter may be eliminated by extinction when they are replaced by desirable responses or desirable competing responses.

Strengthening incompatible responses When there is an undesirable response, treatment may consist of strengthening a different, desirable response. "If the two response classes are competitive and cannot occur at the same time, strengthening the more desirable class should reduce the probability of the symptomatic one. This tactic, often termed 'counter-conditioning,' is a parallel within instrumental conditioning of Wolpe's substitution of relaxation for anxiety as classically conditioned responses to particular stimuli."[36] This method has the advantage over punishment or extinction of filling the gap and thus avoiding symptom return or substitution. It can be used when the reinforcers of the undesirable response are unknown or cannot be controlled.

The withholding of positive reinforcement, or extinction, is useful when behavioral excesses are the target. It may be a necessary preliminary to positive reinforcement of weak but desired behaviors. Extinction involves several problems. Removing all reinforcers of the behavior, including self-reinforcement, may be difficult. Complete control of the environment is required. The rate and intensity of response rise briefly immediately following nonreinforcement, and subsequent reduction is not smooth but is highly variable, which may lead environmental reinforcers (such as teachers or parents) to abandon the procedure. Less-than-perfect withholding of reinforcement constitutes intermittent reinforcement and increases the response. Resistance to extinction may be great for a response that has developed under intermittent reinforcement. Extinction has aversive characteristics, thus producing undesirable side effects.

Response differentiation, or shaping When new and complex responses are desired, shaping, or the use of successive approximation, may be used. This method combines reinforcement and extinction into a technology "which reorganizes elements of available behaviors into what appear to be new responses, either by molding complex new behaviors from simple elements or by building complex chains of simpler responses."[37] Shaping is important in remedying behavior deficits, since the rewarding of small steps ensures adequate reinforcement throughout the treatment. Waiting for the complex behavior to occur before reinforcement would be impossible. Even so, the shaping process may be a long and slow one. Shaping enters into therapies that involve vicarious- and imitation-learning paradigms, as well as into replication techniques, such as role playing and psychodrama.

Discrimination and stimulus control   The function of the discriminative stimulus is to set the stage for responding by indicating when a particular response is appropriate. Most behavior involves discriminated operants; thus stimulus control plays a vital role in behavior modification, and therapy may be described as being primarily a matter of discrimination training.

A problem in therapy arises when stimulus control is limited to the therapy situation, without generalization outside.

Environmental Engineering

Operant technology is particularly applicable to natural environments and to use by persons without extensive training in psychology or therapy. Technicians can be trained easily to use the methods. Instrumentation of procedures by mechanical devices extends their applications. Patients can be trained in self-regulatory behaviors.

Behavioral engineering can be applied in families, classrooms, and institutions for the mentally retarded, delinquent, and emotionally disturbed. Tokens, which become general reinforcers, can be used systematically and on a large scale; such systems are often called token economies. The operant model is well suited to the construction of special therapeutic-educational, or "prosthetic," environments in hospitals, schools, prisons, and other institutions.

Behavior Control by Aversive Consequences

Aversive stimuli in the operant model, where they are contingent on the behavior of the subject, differ from their use in the classical model, where they are not consequences of the behavior of the subject. Much everyday behavior is controlled by aversive consequences, and society relies heavily on punishment or threats of punishment. "Discipline" usually consists of punishment rather than positive reinforcement. Yet many psychologists see the origin of personality disorders in aversive social control.

Paradigms for aversive control of behavior   The presentation of an aversive stimulus that cannot be avoided or escaped following an act is *punishment*. The contingent removal of an aversive stimulus following a response is *negative reinforcement* (in the language of instrumental conditioning, it fits the escape paradigm). It is often termed *aversion relief*.

Positive stimuli can be manipulated aversively. Forced consumption of excessive stimuli, or *satiation,* can be aversive. *Extinction,* involving the omission of reward, can be considered aversive. *Time-out,* or removal from all positive reinforcement, is similar. *Response cost,* or the removal of positive reinforcers by imposing fines, for example, or by increasing the requirements for reward, is also aversive. Finally, neutral stimuli that are associated with removal of positive reinforcement (by classical conditioning) may become secondary aversive stimuli.

Noncontingent delivery of aversive stimuli usually leads to *arousal.* The stimuli may become adventitiously connected to a preceding response, resulting in *superstitious* conditioning, or they may be noncontingently removed, producing *superstitious negative reinforcement. Punishment* is the contingent delivery of an aversive stimulus. Acts that are successful in leading to *escape* or *avoidance* of an aversive stimulus are reinforced. When aversive stimuli are removed in the presence of a neutral stimulus, the latter may come to function as a positive reinforcer (a "relief" stimulus) through classical conditioning.

A difficulty arising in work with aversive stimuli is the lack of a universal definition of the term *aversive.*

Respondent and operant elements in aversive control   As was indicated earlier in the discussion of mixed models, the separation of classical and operant models that use aversive stimuli is arbitrary.

At the level of theoretical description, the distinction between the stimulus-building function of classical conditioning and the response-contingency function of the operant conditioning model seems clear. In actual practice, however, the two models cannot be made mutually exclusive. Observed effects can usually be ascribed to either model only by arbitrary decision, or by attending only to certain elements in the behavioral equation.[38]

Inescapable aversive stimulation   Sudden, intense aversive stimulation is the unconditioned stimulus for emotional reactions, including anxiety. Noncontingent aversive stimulation has been used therapeutically to arouse anxiety that may lead to learning. However, aversive stimuli, whether contingent or not, can produce unexpected effects because of the (unknown) past history of the individual with such stimuli.

Escape and avoidance training   In escape learning, onset of the aversive stimulus becomes a discriminative cue for the response (escape) that terminates it, and the termination acts as a positive reinforcer. In avoidance, however, since the occurrence of the aversive stimulus is prevented, there is a dilemma in explaining what is reinforcing. Yet avoidance behaviors are extremely resistant to extinction.

Many behavioral deviations represent avoidance or defensive reactions, but escape-avoidance training has therapeutic uses. Examples of aversion therapy include many examples of escape and avoidance training. Autistic children have been rapidly taught to approach the experimenter when such approach behavior resulted in the avoidance of shock.

Generalization in aversion therapy is more difficult to obtain, since the patient's everyday environment cannot be relied on to support the treatment. Also, the necessary special equipment and procedures separate the situation from everyday life. The influencing of the patient's verbal and thought processes through interviews is used as an ancillary procedure to bridge this gap. The use of multiple-paradigm procedures also helps.

Punishment   "While avoidance teaches the individual 'what to do,' punishment teaches him 'what not to do.' In both cases the training goal is achieved when aversive stimulation is no longer suffered. The practical difference is that passive 'not responding' is sufficient for evasion of punishment. No new behaviors are substituted unless they are positively reinforced."[39]

Punishment is often the procedure chosen in situations where the reinforcement history and the reinforcers for the current maintenance of the undesired behavior are unknown. If the latter were known, extinction could be used. The use of punishment can be complicated by the patient's previous experience with the punishing stimulus, including adaptation to it or its association with positive reinforcement when it becomes a signal of a reward. The availability of alternative responses leading to positive reinforcement without punishment enhances the effects of punishment. On the contrary, the effectiveness of punishment is weakened when there is opportunity for escape or avoidance responses.

Removing the subject from positive reinforcers, or time-out, is aversive. It is useful when punishment is impractical, when extinction may not be possible, and when the interaction—as of teacher and pupil or parent and child—can escalate to explosive levels. To be effective, the situation from which the subject is banished must be relatively rewarding, and the time-out period or situation must not offer the opportunity for escape or avoidance responses. Physical isolation as time-out may be aversive in itself, in addition to removing positive reinforcement.

Punishment has long been unpopular because of presumed undesirable or harmful consequences and of the apparent greater effectiveness of positive reinforcement. Recent research and clinical experience have reduced the fears of harmful consequences. The effectiveness of punishment is limited by the difficulty of achieving generalization, since subjects discriminate so highly that therapeutic goals may be thwarted. "Application of the aversive event in a range of naturalistic settings, by a variety of persons, for a variety of examples of the target response class, and rapid and complete suppression of the naturally occurring behaviors are suggested as safeguards."[40] Other problems may arise, including the patient's modeling of the therapist's punishing or aggressive behaviors, the development of substitute responses, or other side effects. Side effects may be positive. "By breaking up an old behavior pattern, punishment can provide the occasion for the positive reinforcement of new operants that are of greater value to the person. The combination of positive reinforcement with punishment appears most effective."[41]

The influence of punishment on the punisher is an important factor from a social point of view. Punishment of a child's obnoxious behavior, for example, terminates this behavior, thus giving the parent relief. There is thus a danger that punishment may be used, by therapists as well as by parents, more extensively than might be desirable, because of the satisfaction received by the person administering it.

Verbal Mediation and Self-Regulation

Verbal Behavior and the Interview

The complete control of the individual's environment is impossible, in part because human beings can create their own subjective environment, enabling them to become to some extent independent of their physical environment. In many cases, verbal and thought processes, interposed between stimulus and action, constitute the problematic behavioral process.

learning processes and the mutual influence of interviewers and interviewees seem to be useful mainly as a conceptual guide for the clinician rather than to offer a set of rules for interview conduct."[45]

A learning view of interview therapy differs from the traditional approach. It stresses reportable or observable behavior rather than hypothetical states or dynamics. The interview is not

> employed primarily to permit the patient to develop his own insights and understanding of his unconscious motivation, of his feelings, and of the events in his past history that have resulted in his maladaptive behavior. However, the importance of the therapeutic relationship in interview therapy is not denied. The relationship between therapist and patient can serve to promote behavioral change through the therapist's efforts to establish himself as a potential source of reinforcement during each interview. Therapeutic tactics in later interviews consist in selectively reinforcing verbal behaviors that promise to serve as controlling stimuli for more effective action on the part of the patient.[46]

Behavior modification techniques have been developed for cases in which interview therapy is neither feasible nor efficient. Behavior modification can be obtained by direct control of the environment. Conditioning is not to be substituted for all interviewing therapy; rather, both are to be used so as to be most effective for the particular patient. The use of conditioning methods, however,

> is not merely a minor revision of interview methods but a drastic change in the relative importance of interviews as therapeutic instruments. Improvement in conditioning techniques may eventually relegate interview therapy to the status of an *adjunct* for behavior modification techniques. . . . When the focal symptoms consist of public behaviors, understanding the patient's thinking becomes less important and treatment requires fewer interviews and a less intimate personal relationship if direct modification techniques can be applied.[47]

The close personal relationship, however, is "an ideal vehicle for modifying directly those problems that consist of a patient's difficulties in relating to another person and in using appropriate interactional behaviors," though it is not necessarily always *the ideal* method.[48] Interview therapy is also useful for patients who require information, attitude changes, or the development of verbal behaviors for efficient assessment of life situations, evaluation of feelings, or decision making. The principles of behavior modification can be applied in the interview by the therapist. "This view differs from the assumptions that change is due to spontaneous growth for which the therapist serves only as a catalyst, or that *internal* processes are simply directed or set free by the therapist."[49]

Self-Regulation and Its Clinical Application

Procedures that bring about behavior changes by environmental control and reinforcement require the presence of the therapist (or of other behavior modifiers) and give little responsibility for change to the patient. Self-regulation and patient regulation of the environment go beyond this. The interpersonal relationship through which this is accomplished consists essentially of a training or tutoring relationship to help the patient learn skills that enlarge his or her repertoire in the control and regulation of his or her own behavior. The term *instigation therapy* may be applied to this approach, since the relationship is used for joint planning and for instigating actions by encouraging and supporting the patient. The patient's active role and self-perception as the major agent of change increases a predisposition toward further change and personal development.

The self-construct   The self is not a process entity or a mental structure but the system of attitudes and responses toward the self. These self-reactions are learned, as responses to external objects and events are learned. Since the social environment provides inadequate feedback regarding the individual's effects on it, self-knowledge is often incorrect, yet self-knowledge is an important motivational factor in behavior.

Self-control   Instigation therapy requires that the patient have the capacity to put behavior under his or her own control. Self-control involves the same components (S, R, K, and C) as does external control, but all are in the person (O). Self-control requires the subject's manipulation of controlling responses that make the undesirable response less probable or impossible. Application of a time lock to a refrigerator or cigarette case is an example. Self-reinforcement and self-punishment can be used, but the conceptualization of these processes is not clear. The role of reinforcement in self-control is not yet well defined, since no data are available on how critical it is or on whether it is, indeed, required. The response to be controlled always has conflicting consequences; either the response has immediate positive and long-range aversive consequences or immediate aversive but long-range positive effects. "Generalized social reinforcement and self-descriptive statements with reinforcing properties can be made contingent on the execution of self-control. Thereby some behaviors may be strengthened that, at first look, appear detrimental to the organism."[50] Self-control involves the abandonment of immediate or close reinforcers for later and more important ones or the delay of gratification. Training in delayed gratification is affected by the organism's experience with postponed rewards. The internalization of social norms, or socialization, is an example of the inculcation of self-control by various learning mechanisms, especially aversive methods creating guilt. Modeling and positive reinforcement are also equally important in the genesis of conscience.

Clinical use of self-control procedures   Patients can be trained through instruction to bring their behavior under control by *setting up behaviors that change the environment or by rearranging behavioral sequences.*

In the method of *covert sensitization,* patients are taught to relax, then to visualize the undesirable behavior, and to follow this by imagining aversive stimuli. Following successful avoidance or escape, patients are told to imagine a positive reinforcement, such as a feeling of relief. The technique is used increasingly by patients on their own in daily life. It has been successful in the treatment of obesity and homosexuality.

Contingency management teaches patients covert verbal responses (coverants) that serve as controlling cues for desirable behaviors. Patients may be helped to relax and then taught to associate this state with the word *relax.* They may be taught to make positive coverant statements such as "I am master of my own fate" prior to engaging in desirable behaviors.

In *contract management,* the therapist and the patient agree on specific behaviors that the patient will engage in, which will be followed by a predetermined reinforcement by the therapist.

Patients can be taught to apply either positive reinforcement or an aversive stimulus according to a planned treatment program. Patients can also be given behavioral analysis training, which enables them to recognize functional relationships between their actions and antecedent and subsequent environmental events. "Use of this technique is limited to persons with sufficient educational background, strong motivation, and interest to undertake a program that at first seems to have only distant relevancy to his current behavioral problems."[51]

With the introduction of self-regulatory techniques, the behavior therapies have moved beyond techniques using only external or environmental control into the area of "mental" events, which were earlier excluded from behaviorist systems. However, numerous problems are involved that stem from limited knowledge of behaviors in which the person is both subject and object.

EXAMPLES

Kanfer and Phillips present no clinical examples of the methods that they consider. This is consistent with their purpose, which was not to write a manual for clinicians or to present a series of illustrative case studies but to "present the research and theory underlying the current application of learning principles and techniques to therapeutic change, as well as to point out the problems involved in practical usage."[52] Clinical examples are given in the research summaries.

SUMMARY AND EVALUATION

Kanfer and Phillips have presented the most comprehensive survey of the methods and techniques of the behaviorists currently available. They have covered the usual techniques developed from the classical model of conditioning, which have been available to some extent in other sources, including Wolpe, and the methods derived from the operant conditioning paradigm, which have not heretofore been collected. In addition, they consider the mixed model of methods and techniques that are complex and overlap both the classical conditioning and the operant conditioning models. Finally, they go beyond other behavior therapists in discussing the self-regulation of behavior from the point of view of behavioral models. They were among the first to recognize and explicitly discuss cognitive aspects of behavior therapy.

Their presentation is not clinically oriented but research based. For the practitioner, this is a weakness as well as a strength. It was not the intention of the authors, however, to provide a textbook of clinical practice. They succeed in presenting the learning foundations of behavior therapy.

Kanfer and Phillips have not presented a systematic theory or approach to behavior therapy. Instead, they have presented a storehouse of behavioral psychological principles, as was indicated at the beginning of this chapter. Their failure to present a systematic approach lies not in themselves but in the nature of the material that they set out to integrate. There appears to be no single systematic behavior therapy. The authors at least implicitly recognize this in their preference for the term *behavior therapies* rather than *behavior therapy.*

Because no (over) simplified system is presented, the book is very difficult to read, as is no doubt its condensation here. Indeed, it is impossible to do it justice in a condensation because of the comprehensive detail it contains. It is, in effect, a (selective) review of the experimental and research literature on the major methods or techniques of the behavior therapies. It is difficult to digest and summarize because the results of the research are contradictory and confusing, so that few conclusions or generalizations can be made. The major conclusion that forces itself on the reader is that the methods and techniques of the behavior therapies are much more complex and involve more variables and factors than most practitioners realize or are aware of; certainly behavior therapy is not as simple as the writings of Wolpe and some others imply.

The fact that the results of research are not clear or always in agreement surely means that the field is not in a state in which the results of laboratory research can be directly applied in practice. Kanfer and Phillips, in introducing their discussion of those techniques styled as Pavlovian, note that this

> will serve to plunge us into some of the complexities involved when theoretical models, or even controlled laboratory procedures, are used to provide, describe, or explain procedures for modifying naturally occurring symptom behaviors. It can raise questions not only about the extent and manner in which therapies have actually been deduced from learning principles, but also about the interaction of incomplete principles and impure techniques to produce the uncertainty still remaining as to which techniques are more effective and why.[53]

The same statement could be made about methods and techniques supposedly based on models other than the Pavlovian.

The reading of Kanfer and Phillips certainly does not support the repeated claim that behavior therapy is based on the results of laboratory experiments. The repetition of this claim without supporting evidence by so many behavior therapists suggests that its very repetition is being used as a method of conditioning the reader (and perhaps the writer as well) to accept behavior therapy as more scientific than other methods. Such phrases as "scientific research," "laboratory-based," "experimentally derived," "modern learning theory," and "experimentally established" appear to be used for their prestige value by many behavior therapists. As a matter of fact, it seems clear that the methods and techniques are more clearly empirical than based on experimental (or nonexperimental) research results. Many behavior therapists seem to be unaware that (1) other methods are supported by research; (2) the procedures used by behaviorists are not always founded on prior research that demonstrates their effectiveness (not that this should necessarily be the case) but are often developed on the basis of clinical experience; (3) the research evidence for the validity of their method is far from conclusive, and, indeed, as more research data have accumulated, the more complex the apparently simple methods appear to be; and (4) the methods are not necessarily explainable only by so-called modern learning theory (whatever that is) but can be rationalized in other ways.

Behavior therapists do operate from a more experimental approach than do other therapists. Their model is inductive, developing from a context of discovery, rather than deductive, developing from assumptions or hypotheses. Thus they operate with a different image of the person—an image derived from empirical investigation rather than from theory or philosophy.

Contrary to the impression often given that the methods are simple and clear-cut and that the modes of operation are clearly understood, it is becoming evident that they are highly complex and not clearly understood, as some behaviorists are willing to admit. Moreover, there is no integrating theory to tie together the many techniques. "While there are many techniques, there are few concepts or general principles involved in behavior therapy."[54] Weitzman suggests that behavior therapy is actually "a nontheoretical amalgam of pragmatic principles."[55] The behaviorists make a virtue out of necessity in expressing their willingness to try anything that seems to work or that might work. Behaviorists will try anything, and, of course, sometimes with some clients, anything will work. Thus specific techniques are being tried, recommended, and accepted on a superstitious basis until they are extinguished after enough failures.

Kanfer and Phillips, however, are not extremists. They make no unsupported claims. They are laboratory and research oriented, and perhaps it is just because of this that they are cautious in their statements. This lack of conclusiveness can be frustrating to the practitioner, but it is a good and necessary antidote to the oversimplified conclusiveness of writers such as Wolpe.

One might ask if Kanfer and Phillips provide us with a picture of the elephant of behavior therapy referred to by Krasner. As presented by Kanfer and Phillips, the outline is certainly blurred, since there is no clear distinction between the behavior therapy elephant and the cognitive therapy rhinoceros. (Kanfer believes that "liberalized behavioral approaches, even when using mediational constructs, can be differentiated from cognitive theory on two broad bases: (1) they presume the same processes to operate in overt and covert events; and (2) they attempt to organize models inductively, with minimal use of constructs that are not anchored in data."[56]) Within the skin of the elephant, there is some question about how the bones of classical and operant conditioning articulate; perhaps they mesh in an amorphous soft structure rather than in a bony skeleton. The question can be raised: Can all the methods and techniques be brought together under a general systematic learning or behavior theory? If they can —and it is assumed that eventually they will be—the resulting theory will be a behavior theory in a much broader sense than the term is currently being used.

Further evaluation of behavior therapy will be provided in Chapter 18.

REFERENCES

1. Kanfer, F. H., & Phillips, J. S. *Learning foundations of behavior therapy.* New York: Wiley, 1970. P. vii.
2. Ibid., pp. viii, 2.
3. Ibid., p. 1.

4. Ibid., p. 2.
5. Ibid., p. 20.
6. Ibid., p. 52.
7. Ibid., p. 53.
8. Ibid., p. 60.
9. Ibid., p. 70.
10. Ibid., p. 75.
11. Ibid., p. 76.
12. Ibid., p. 29.
13. Ibid., p. 17.
14. Ibid., p. 460.
15. Ibid., p. 21.
16. Ibid., p. 532.
17. Ibid., p. 533.
18. Ibid., p. 535.
19. Ibid., p. 35.
20. Ibid., p. 538.
21. Ibid., p. 520.
22. Ibid., pp. 504–505.
23. Ibid., p. 508.
24. Ibid., p. 461.
25. Ibid., p. 109.
26. Ibid., p. 122.
27. Ibid., pp. 97–98.
28. Ibid., p. 99.
29. Ibid., p. 183.
30. Reported in Bandura, A. *Principles of behavior modification.* New York: Holt, Rinehart and Winston, 1969.
31. Kanfer & Phillips *Learning foundations of behavior therapy,* p. 231.
32. Ibid., p. 241.
33. Ibid., p. 250.
34. Ibid., p. 254.
35. Ibid., pp. 266, 267.
36. Ibid., pp. 279–280.
37. Ibid., p. 287.
38. Ibid., p. 331.
39. Ibid., p. 351.
40. Ibid., p. 365.
41. Ibid., p. 359.
42. Ibid., p. 373.
43. Ibid., p. 384.
44. Ibid., p. 391.
45. Ibid., p. 399.
46. Ibid., p. 401.
47. Ibid., p. 402.
48. Ibid.
49. Ibid., p. 403.
50. Ibid., p. 416.
51. Ibid., pp. 439–440.
52. Ibid., p. 1.

53. Ibid., p. 95.
54. Ullmann, L. P., & Krasner, L. *A psychological approach to abnormal behavior.* Englewood Cliffs, N.J.: Prentice-Hall, 1969. P. 252.
55. Weitzman, B. Behavior therapy and psychotherapy. *Psychological Review,* 1967, *74,* 300–317.
56. Kanfer, F. H. Personal communication. Letter dated February 11, 1972.

chapter 7

Social Learning Approach: Rotter

A theory of personality and behavior and of its application to counseling or psychotherapy that has been derived from behavior theory is presented by Julian B. Rotter in *Social Learning and Clinical Psychology.*[1] Rotter (b. 1916) took his Ph.D. in 1941 at Indiana University. After a brief period working in a state mental hospital, he spent four years in the armed forces as a personnel consultant and aviation psychologist. In 1946, he became professor of psychology and director of the psychological clinic at Ohio State University. In 1963, he moved to the University of Connecticut, where he is professor of psychology. Rotter is a Diplomate in Clinical Psychology of the American Board of Professional Psychology. Rotter has been president of the Divisions of Personality and Social Psychology and of Clinical Psychology of the American Psychological Association. He is the author of *Clinical Psychology* (1964; 2nd ed., 1971), (with Chance and Phares), *Applications of a Social Learning Theory of Personality* (1972) and *The Development and Application of Social Learning Theory: Selected Papers* (1982).

BACKGROUND AND DEVELOPMENT

Rotter describes his approach as "an attempt to apply a learning theory to complex social behavior of human beings. It is, consequently, a more molar theory than other learning theories. . . ."[2] He refers to it as an expectancy-reinforcement theory. Rotter treats expectancy in a Hullian manner, but his reinforcement principle is empirical, rather than a drive-reduction principle. His theory is presented as tentative—an unfinished system. Its objective is not to present the true nature of reality but to develop a system of constructs that will provide maximum prediction and control of behavior.

PHILOSOPHY AND CONCEPTS

General Principles

Personality is a construct that refers to the stable, characteristic modes of behaving or of interpreting the world of a unified, complexly organized person. *Behavior* (or experience) is an event in which a living organism is one of the referents. A *construct* is a term that represents an attempt to abstract the nature of an event or events. *Mode of description* refers to a set of constructs that describes events from a consistent orientation.

Postulate 1

The unit of investigation for the study of personality is the interaction of the individual and the individual's meaningful environment.

Corollary 1 Personality study is the study of learned behavior, or of behavior that is modifiable, changing with experience.

Corollary 2 Personality study is the historical investigation of experience, or sequences of events.

Postulate 2

Personality constructs, while consistent with constructs in fields such as physiology, biology, or neurology, are not dependent on these other constructs for explanation.

Postulate 3

Behavior as described by personality constructs occurs in space and time and is one way of describing events.

Corollary 1 Any conception of behavior in which "physiological behavior" is conceived as causing "psychological behavior," or vice versa, is rejected as dualistic.

Postulate 4

Only behavior at a particular level or stage of complexity may be usefully described by personality constructs.

Corollary 1 Physiological or other constructs may be used to describe some of the conditions present at the time of the acquisition of personality characteristics.

Corollary 2 Such constructs may be used by psychologists for practical purposes.

Corollary 3 Learned meanings (or symbols) describing physiological states may be used by the human organism in reacting with itself.

Postulate 5

A person's experiences influence one another, so that the personality has unity.

Corollary 1   Behavior as described by personality constructs can be spoken of only in terms of the conditions necessary for its occurrence, not in terms of causality.

Postulate 6

Behavior has a directional aspect; that is, it is goal directed (motivated). This is inferred from the effect of reinforcing conditions. Reinforcement is broader than drive reduction, which is inadequate to explain all motivated behavior. It is "any action, condition, or state that affects movement toward a goal."[3]

Corollary 1   Needs or goals are learned or acquired, early needs arising from association with physiological homeostatic conditions and later ones arising as means of satisfying earlier learned goals. We speak of needs when our attention is on the individual and of goals when we are looking at the environmental conditions.

Corollary 2   Early acquired goals are the result of satisfactions and frustrations controlled by other people; this is the basis for a social learning theory.

Corollary 3   To occur regularly in a given situation or situations, a particular mode of behavior must have been made available to an individual by having led to reinforcement during previous learning experience.

Corollary 4   Behaviors, needs, and goals are related in systems in ways determined by previous experience.

Postulate 7

Behavior is determined not only by the nature or importance of goals or reinforcement, but also by anticipation or expectancy, based on previous experience that these reinforcements will occur. In human beings, at least, "it seems extremely difficult even to attempt an explanation of human learning in complex social situations without some construct that deals with the effect on behavior of the anticipation of future reinforcements."[4]

Basic Concepts

There are three basic constructs utilized in the measurement and prediction of behavior.

1. *Behavior potential* is the probability of the occurrence of specific behavior in any given situation (or situations) as measured (relatively) in relation to a single reinforcement or a set of reinforcements. Implicit behavior is recognized and accepted; that is, "behavior that is not readily observed directly" but "must frequently be determined by the presence of the behavior with which

[it is] associated either invariably or with high frequency."[5] Examples would be the clenching of a fist when frustrated or the looking for alternative solutions, which may be measured by the time taken by subjects for the solution of problems.

2. *Expectancy* is the probability assumed by the individual that a particular reinforcement will occur following specific behavior in a specific situation or situations. In a given situation, expectancy may be formulated as a function of probability of occurrence as based on past experience in situations perceived as the same and on the generalization of expectancies for the same or similar reinforcements to occur in other situations for the same or functionally related behaviors (that is, behaviors leading to the accomplishment of the same or similar reinforcements or goals). Objective probability is only one of several factors entering into internal probability.

3. *Reinforcement value* is the degree of preference for any one of several reinforcements to occur when the possibilities of occurrence are equal. Such preferences are independent of expectancy.

The relationships among these three concepts are expressed in several formulas, which may be translated as follows:

1. The potential for a particular behavior to occur in a particular situation in relation to a particular reinforcement is a function of the expectancy of the occurrence of the reinforcement following the behavior in the situation and the value of the reinforcement.

2. The potential for a particular behavior to occur in a particular situation in relation to all potential reinforcements for which the individual has expectancies is a function of the expectancies of the occurrence of all these reinforcements in the situation and the values of these reinforcements.

3. The potential for a particular behavior to occur in relation to all potential reinforcements in all situations is a function of the expectancies of the occurrence of these reinforcements in these situations and the values of these reinforcements.

4. The potential for a group of functionally related behaviors to occur in all situations is a function of the expectancies of these behaviors leading to particular reinforcements in these situations and the values of these reinforcements.

5. From these formulations, the constructs of need potential, freedom of movement, and need value (to be defined later) may be derived and may be used to reduce formulation 4 to a more general prediction: the potentiality of occurrence of a functionally related set of behaviors that leads to the satisfaction of some need (need potential) is a function of the expectancies that these behaviors will lead to these reinforcements (freedom of movement) and the strength or value of these reinforcements (need value); or, need potential is a function of freedom of movement and need value.

The Nature of Reinforcement

When the occurrence of an observable event changes the potentiality of occurrence of a behavior that has preceded that event with regularity, such an event is by definition a reinforcement. This definition avoids the difficulties of postulating drives to be reduced and makes possible a measurable criterion of reinforcement. Internal reinforcement is the subject's experience of an event that has value for her or him. External reinforcement is the occurrence of an event known to be reinforcing for a group to which the subject belongs. The two are not necessarily related in a one-to-one manner, although when it is known that an occurrence has resulted in internal reinforcement for a particular person, it may also be considered an external reinforcement for that person.

The value of any reinforcement is a function of the reinforcements it has been paired with, has led to, or is perceived as leading to. Stated in terms of expectancy and reinforcement value, this may be formulated as follows: the value of a particular reinforcement in a particular situation is a function of the expectancies that this reinforcement will lead to other reinforcements in the same situation and of the values of these other reinforcements in the situation.

Psychological Directionality

Need refers to the potentiality of occurrence of a set of functionally related behaviors directed toward a group of functionally related reinforcements. Psychological needs arise through learning, although their source is the drives described in physiological terms. They are activated more by the correct cues or stimuli than by a cyclical internal condition on a physiological level. Psychological goals need not be explained in terms of their satisfaction or reduction of a physiological drive. "Behavior directed toward the attainment of a learned goal or external reinforcement may be predicted through knowledge of the situation the organism is in and from a knowledge of his past experience."[6] In other words, psychological needs can become independent of their origin in physiological drives, and their strength is determined by learned or acquired goals or satisfactions.

Relationships Among External Reinforcements

Values of various reinforcements may be predicted on the basis of functional relationships among them, which may be described by concepts of generalization. Primary stimulus generalization occurs on the basis of original functional similarity among external reinforcements or goals. Mediated stimulus generalization gives rise to functional equivalence of behaviors that lead to (are mediated by) the same reinforcement. Generalization of expectancy changes is a function of the similarity of reinforcements; the occurrence (or nonoccurrence) of a given reinforcement changes the expectancy for the occurrence of other reinforcements, following a gradient.

Reinforcements may be grouped as similar, and the classification may be broadened until an overall concept of directionality or need is reached. This single need may be called security or psychological homeostasis. The broader the classification, the greater the variety of behaviors about which predictions can be made, but the lesser the accuracy in any particular case. The development of a classification system for categorizing needs has not been accomplished but is necessary. It is an endless task, however, since new problems will require new abstractions. Six broad categories of needs are suggested: (1) recognition and status, (2) protection and dependency, (3) dominance, (4) independence, (5) love and affection, and (6) physical comfort.

Broader Conceptions

The preceding concepts are more relevant for the testing of theoretical principles than for clinical use. The four descriptive concepts that follow are more useful in the clinical situation.

1. *Need potential* is the mean potentiality of a group of functionally related behaviors occurring in any segment of an individual's lifetime. The classification of behaviors into need groups was considered above. A practical estimate of need potential may be arrived at by sampling behaviors in a variety of situations. Individual deviations from the cultural definitions of the nature of external reinforcements must be considered. To estimate a person's need potential, one should have a thorough knowledge of the individual's prior learning background, the person's own description of his or her needs and the significance of his or her behavior, and a broad general knowledge of all aspects of the person's behavior. Need potential must be separated from expectancy.

2. *Need value* is the mean preference for a set of functionally related reinforcements. It involves the selection of one set of reinforcements over another, with expectancy held constant, and it is determined, as is need potential, by preferences for alternatives. Here also, individual differences from cultural values must be considered. Need values may be classified as goals by using the same system that is used to classify need potential.

3. *Freedom of movement* is the mean expectancy of obtaining positive satisfactions as a result of a set of related behaviors directed toward the attainment of a group of functionally related reinforcements. High freedom of movement consists of expectancies of success for many behaviors, while low freedom of movement implies expectancies of failure or punishment. Freedom of movement is perhaps related to concepts such as anxiety and feelings of inadequacy. Behaviors known as defense mechanisms or escape mechanisms may be an indirect measure of freedom of movement or of the absence of it.

4. *The psychological situation* refers to the fact that behavior is related to the situation as perceived by the person who is performing the behavior. Although this has been recognized, little attention has been paid to the categorizing of psychological situations. It is proposed that situations be categorized in terms of their characteristic reinforcements, that is, in a manner parallel to the categorizing of psychological needs. An individual's classification of situations may differ from the cultural classification. Expectancies are dependent on the characterization of the situation. The values of reinforcements also vary with the situation. Social roles consist of learned behaviors appropriate to (or reinforced in) particular situations. The same situation may with experience (or new reinforcements) be categorized differently, thus resulting in changes in behavior (or expectation for future reinforcements) in the same situation. Categorization of people or events on the basis of a common objective characteristic of the stimulus or situation constitutes a social attitude.

Minimum-Goal Levels

Potential outcomes may be placed on a continuum—for example, from failure to success—in terms of preference. The minimum-goal level is the lowest goal or outcome perceived as a satisfaction. Levels vary widely among individuals. Maladjustment or dissatisfaction occurs when the minimum-goal level is consistently above the reinforcements that follow behavior. Minimum goals may change with experience, although this usually occurs as a result of the changing standards of others—actual or anticipated —rather than as a direct or an automatic result of success or failure. Some minimum goals are set by the culture and represent relatively inflexible standards.

Language in Social Learning

Verbalization appears to speed up both learning and extinction of behavior, including conditioned responses. Language as a stimulus may represent objects and events of both the past and the future through a process of symbolizing or abstracting. Words are thus cues, or they direct attention to specific cues in a complex situation, applying previous experience to a current situation, so that it can be dealt with on the basis of past learning rather than as a new situation to be handled by trial-and-error behavior. Language thus serves to enhance generalization. Words are also reinforcers, and even though their values are acquired, they are frequently more powerful as satisfiers than are the original nonverbal stimuli.

Implicit language is difficult to define, but it seems to be a very important factor in changing behavior through changing expectancies by recategorization of situations. Language can be used to change other person's expectancies and thus their behavior. The fostering of generalization may also be stimulated in others, with resultant behavior changes.

Social Learning Theory and Maladjustive Behavior

In social learning theory, many of the concepts used in other systems to describe behavior are avoided. These include such terms as *maladjusted, anxious, neurotic, conflicted, abnormal, repressed,* and *unconscious,* all of which refer to behavior that is felt to be in need of change through counseling or psychotherapy. From the point of view of social learning theory, individuals who are candidates for therapy are those whose behavior is not satisfying and/or does not contribute to the welfare or satisfaction of others. In terms of this theory, such persons have either low expectancies for gratification or low freedom of movement with high need values. They have minimum goals that are too high to allow for reinforcement or satisfaction.

Thus anticipating punishment, they avoid situations either physically or by repression. They may attempt instead to reach goals by rationalization, fantasy, or symbolic means. Such behaviors are unreal. Other implicit behaviors—including awareness of disturbed body states, fixation on punishment, narrowing the field of attention, and preoccupation with obsessive thoughts—may be present and may interfere with constructive problem-solving behavior.

Social reinforcement theory "attempts only to describe *how* social behavior is developed and changed—which behavior, if any, the clinical psychologist should accept as his responsibility to change, he must decide on some basis that goes beyond a systematic psychological theory."[7]

THE THERAPY PROCESS[8]

Psychotherapy is a learning process. The changes that take place both inside and outside the therapy room follow the same laws and principles. "The therapist himself has no special characteristic."[9] While the therapist may have some advantages over relatives in attempting to change behavior, he or she also has some disadvantages. For example, a change of attitude on the part of a child's parents may be more effective than hours of play therapy.

Social learning theory, like any other theory applied to psychotherapy, may be used in different ways or lead to different methods, depending on the goals of the therapist, which are not a part of the theory or derivable from it. The goals of therapy accepted by Rotter are "helping the patient to lead a more constructive life, to contribute to society, to maximize his potential for achievement, to maximize his feeling of affection or contribution to others," and "to help the patient reach a state of greater happiness or comfort or pleasure."[10] The following value commitments are made:

1. The therapist expects his or her behavior, as well as goals and ethical judgments, to influence the client's behavior and accepts some responsibility for these changes.
2. The therapist seeks to direct the client's behavior to goals that the client values or that will provide the client with satisfaction.
3. However, the therapist avoids or seeks to eliminate goals that he or she feels are clearly detrimental to others in society.
4. The therapist believes that the client should make some contribution to society in return for the satisfaction received.

In an expectancy-reinforcement theory of social learning, such as this one, the therapist's function is to increase freedom of movement and to reduce need value. This is accomplished by changing expectancies and reinforcement values, which result in changes in unrealistic minimum goal levels.

Changing Expectancies

In agreement with Mowrer[11] and with Dollard and Miller,[12] the maladjusted person is seen as an individual who does not learn adjustive behavior automatically because he or she engages in persistent avoidance behavior and thus keeps away from situations in which more adjustive behavior could be learned. Although in the long run such behavior is not satisfying and is eventually punished, it is immediately satisfying and thus persists. Punishment not only is delayed, but also may not be as great as the anticipated punishment that is being avoided. In addition, maladjustive behavior may bring attention, sympathy, protection, or other desirable reactions.

Thus the individual's high expectancy of punishment or failure leads to continued avoidance of situations and consequent failure to learn that his or her fears are no longer realistic. Or the individual may have an expectancy that avoidance behavior will lead to greater satisfaction (or less punishment) than would behavior seen by others as more desirable or adjustive. A major problem of therapy is thus "lowering the expectancy that a particular behavior or behaviors will lead to gratifications or increasing the expectancy that alternate or new behaviors would lead to greater gratification in the same situation or situations. In general learning terms we might say we have the choice of either weakening the inadequate response, strengthening the correct or adequate response, or doing both."[13] Research indicates that reward for the correct response is more effective than punishment for the incorrect response. Most approaches to therapy operate on the assumption that elimination of the bad response is more effective, and little attention is given to acquisition of adjustive responses, but it is difficult to eliminate maladaptive responses when the client has nothing better to substitute. Therapy, then, consists primarily of increasing the expectancy for gratification for alternative or new behaviors, and secondarily of reducing the potential for maladaptive behavior.

Changing Reinforcement Values

Changing the value of external reinforcements or goals requires changing the expectancy that immediate reinforcement will lead to specific subsequent reinforcements. The problem is essentially the same as that of changing expectancies for the occurrence of reinforcement but with added practical difficulties.

The values of goals may be maintained over a long period of time with relatively stable expectancies for subsequent rewards if the relationships have not been verbalized and the individual is unaware of them. Thus a delayed negative reinforcement may follow an earlier reward, but the individual may fail to see the relationship and may persist in seeking the goal. The values of goals can therefore be changed sometimes by the therapist and client analyzing earlier rewards, which may no longer be operating, and by recognizing present and future consequences that have not been associated with the goals. Insight into the acquisition of particular goals and into the delayed consequences of present behaviors and goals may lead to the changing of the values of goals.

Goals are usually firmly established and are often still being reinforced; thus they are difficult to change. In some cases, it may not be the goal but the way of reaching it that is unacceptable, inadequate, or ineffective. "It seems a great deal easier to change the behavior that a person uses to reach a goal than to change the importance of the goal for him."[14] This may be regarded as a pedagogical problem; the client may be taught to search for alternative ways of reaching goals as a general method of dealing with problems and of finding ways of achieving more satisfaction in life. "The assumption that once the patient is free from some kind of internal disorganization, conflict, repression, etc., he will automatically be able to find adequate ways to reach his goals, does not appear useful to this writer. It is often precisely because the patient does not have alternate pathways that he frequently holds on to his less effective behavior in spite of insight into his situation."[15]

Low freedom of movement may be a result of using inappropriate behaviors, as well as a result of using ineffective behaviors. Inappropriate behaviors indicate a failure to make discriminations among social situations. Analysis, with the therapist, of the nature of different situations may help the client make these discriminations. Insight into others, including their thoughts, feelings, and expectations, is as necessary as insight into oneself.

The therapist's behavior varies, depending on the nature of the problem, of the resources available outside of therapy, and of the client. Social learning theory implies that the therapist must show great flexibility in adjusting to the specific needs of the client. Since therapists are inherently limited in flexibility, perhaps there should be more concern with matching clients to therapists or with changing therapists early in therapy when this is indicated.

IMPLEMENTATION: TECHNIQUES OF COUNSELING

Structuring

Structuring is discussion concerned with the purpose and goals of therapy, the plans of the therapist, the respective roles of the therapist and the client, and the attitudes of each. It continues throughout therapy. It is minimal in therapy that consists of direct reinforcement but of great importance in therapy that involves rational techniques, verbal communications, and insight. The purpose of structuring in therapy is to get the client to attend to, react to, or be concerned with appropriate things in a situation, instead of leaving a situation ambiguous or leaving what the client learns almost to chance.

In structuring, the therapist makes it clear to the client that while therapy includes understanding one's attitudes and reactions and discovering alternatives to them, this is not sufficient for "cure": the client must be motivated to change and be willing to try out new behaviors. The practice of requiring the client to avoid important decisions is not acceptable, since it places the client in a passive role; it should be made clear that the therapist is not going to make decisions or prescribe actions for the client.

The therapist should also make clear the limitations of therapy. "The objective is not to produce a perfectly adjusted person who has acquired some power to avoid frustration, but for the patient to learn to handle problems as they arise, to enjoy many aspects of his life more, and to deal with frustrations without allowing them to lead to self-defeating and socially unconstructive defenses."[16] The client's conceptions should be discussed, and any misconceptions should be corrected.

Structuring should be continued as necessary during therapy to explain what is occurring when improvement is followed by losses, when progress is not as rapid as the client expects, or when encouragement that therapy will be helpful is needed. "In other words, the patient's behavior of seeking help and coming for therapy must be reinforced so that the expectancy that it will lead to satisfaction is maintained at a high enough level to insure continuation of his efforts."[17]

Continued structuring is necessary to keep the client aware of why he or she is doing what he or she is doing and what the ultimate purpose of therapy is. Fixation on means—such as uncovering unconscious repressions, dreaming more interesting dreams, and achieving a less inhibited form of expression—must be avoided.

Relationships and Transference

The client must feel that the therapist is concerned for, is interested in, likes, and wants to help her or him; others who have attempted to change the client may not have shown these attributes. But the therapist must avoid the kind of personal involvement that others have with the client and that frequently interferes with attempts to change behavior. The counseling relationship, as a result of its atmosphere of acceptance and reassurance, leads to the client's developing expectations for direct reinforcement from the therapist.

While the psychoanalytic conception of transference may be supported to some extent by the concept of generalization, it is actually contrary to the evidence regarding generalization. The therapist is quite different from other figures in the client's life. He or she is not a plastic medium onto which the client's attitude toward parents or others can be projected; rather, the client sees the therapist as an individual. Transference also relates to the degree of involvement the client has with the therapist. From a social learning point of view, it is a direct function of the amount of reinforcement the client receives or expects to receive from the therapist. The client becomes dependent on the therapist for future satisfactions, and the relationship may involve affectional goals. This dependence on the therapist for acceptance, warmth, and liking is not to be confused with dependence on the therapist to solve the client's problems. While the therapist does not foster dependence, he or she must be able to accept the dependency needs of those clients who bring them to therapy.

The therapist's *acceptance* of the client as a person without judgments of moral inadequacy is apparently necessary for successful therapy. "If the therapist is able to accept the patient's problems as real, as problems that do not call for scorn or criticism but require understanding and help, the patient not only finds a comfort and satisfaction in the therapy situation but tends to generalize his expectations that the therapist will not react with criticism or punishment for his other behaviors."[18] Thus the client is able to speak openly and frankly about his or her attitudes and past experiences. The therapist must avoid any indication of sympathy or approval, which would reinforce existing attitudes such as projection of blame.

Certain kinds of *reassurance* seem to be required or are beneficial in therapy. These include reassurance that the client's problems are real and that seeking therapy is justified and not an indication of weakness. A second kind of reassurance involves fostering the expectation that therapy can be successful and can lead to satisfying alternatives in behavior. Of course, no guarantee of cure can be given by the therapist. A third kind involves giving direct reassurance that the client is capable of achieving specific goals in order to increase his or her expectancy of success. Caution must be used, so that the client does not interpret this reassurance to mean that therapy is not needed or that reassurance can be a substitute for actual accomplishments. From the social learning point of view, reassurance is a direct reinforcement, the occurrence of which increases the expectancy for future reinforcement for some behavior.

The therapist must limit the kind and frequency of direct reinforcement, as well as the direct satisfactions the client obtains from the therapist, by interpretation of their relationship and of the client's defenses in order to avoid the development of an extreme relationship in which the therapist becomes more satisfying as a person than anyone in the client's environment. The therapist also uses this reinforcement value to develop independent behavior in the client, even encouraging the client to conclude therapy and try to become independent.

The therapist may obtain reinforcement from the client, becoming attached to him or her in a countertransference relationship. Such a relationship is not detrimental but natural and helpful, as long as the therapist is aware of it and its influence.

Catharsis

Catharsis as the recalling and reliving of earlier painful (and now repressed) experiences without the original punishment, resulting in extinction, only weakens an inadequate response pattern; it does not provide new responses. It is thus useful only in *some* cases and only as a part of therapy.

Catharsis as ventilation of feelings to a warm, sympathetic, accepting therapist reinforces the client's defenses, even though the client may feel better as a result and become attached to the therapist. Catharsis as encouragement of the release of pent-up feelings in play therapy or through expressive arts may result in some extinction, but generalization may be limited. Catharsis through physical exercise and activities is similarly limited. Catharsis as discussion of past history and experiences without dramatic recall or emotional reliving may result in insight, but this is more the result of the therapist's direction and help than of the so-called cathartic process.

Thus catharsis may be either harmful or useful, depending on its nature and the activities of the therapist. Positive effects are the result of guided new learnings and the direct reinforcement provided by the therapist.

Insight

Insight is defined in many ways, and a distinction often is made between intellectual and emotional insights, the former usually being verbalization of understandings without any influence on behavior. Intellectual insight may not affect behavior because the client is only repeating what the therapist has said or what he or she thinks the therapist will approve of. There may be stronger competing responses, strengthened over the years, that prevent the development of new responses, or motivation to change may be low.

Verbalizing or understanding the underlying bases for behavior may lead to the development of new expectancies through the recategorization of previous experiences. In general, however, it has only the effect of reducing the expectancy for satisfaction from present maladaptive behavior and thus of reducing the behavior potential of such behavior.

New understanding and new learning may occur without the therapist's assistance or interpretation. "However, the patient's unguided discussions of past or present are usually not enough to effect substantial changes, nor are they efficient in any sense."[19]

Interpretation

The therapist may aid the client by guiding the client through interpretation in the process of verbalizing experiences, that is, by focusing the client's attention on particular aspects of those experiences or by directly suggesting explanations of relationships.

Almost all the verbal responses of the therapist may be considered as interpretations of some kind. Thus the question of how much the therapist should interpret is essentially the question of how active the therapist should be. The social learning therapist would be fairly active in order to provide new experiences, ideas, and relationships. He or she would first have to develop an understanding of the client, although since many interpretations are in the form of questions, the therapist would not have to have a complete knowledge of the client. As the client progresses, there is less need for the therapist's interpretations. Thus the therapist is relatively inactive in the early part of therapy, becomes more active as therapy progresses, and then becomes less active again toward the end.

Interpretations may be ordered on a continuum in terms of the degree to which they may be threatening or provocative of defensive behavior. The least threatening kind of interpretation is perhaps the directing of the client's attention to a particular aspect of his or her experience or statements. This might be termed reflection of content. Reflection of feeling would be a little farther along the continuum. The leading question would represent a second stage of interpretation. The next stage might be the interpretative question: "Have you ever thought . . . ?" Direct statements are at the farthest end of the continuum and may vary considerably in their conditionality, from "Sometimes this means . . ." or "I wonder if . . ." to "It seems to me . . ." or "I think . . ." Stronger statements could, but probably should not, be made in therapy. It is desirable that the client achieve new meanings and relationships alone to as great an extent as possible, but it is often inefficient to wait for the client to do so. The therapist faces the dilemma of wanting therapy to be as brief and efficient as possible and yet not wanting to push or hurry the process too much.

So-called deep interpretations may be dangerous in that they may result in new defense or avoidance behaviors that are more serious than the old ones. Some resistance to interpretation must be expected, however, and sometimes progress cannot be made without the occurrence of resistance and its subsequent interpretation. Deep interpretation of unacceptable motivations may result in changes in expectancies or reinforcement values and thus in behavior, but the importance of such interpretations may be overemphasized in comparison with the development of alternative new behaviors.

Interpretations need not be correct or "true" to be effective but only plausible and acceptable to the client. Interpretations are more easily accepted when they are phrased in commonsensical language than when they use theoretical concepts or complex terms from psychoanalytical jargon.

Premature interpretation may lead to the client's leaving therapy, but progress may be delayed if interpretations are avoided because they meet with resistance. "In fact, the interpretation that is readily accepted is probably not necessary. *The interpretation that is in itself helpful and provides something new for the patient may have to be presented many times in many different forms before the patient accepts it, and it needs to be supported by different evidences or experiences of the patient himself.*"[20]

Threatening interpretations should be avoided when the relationship is not strong or if the patient is likely to react with increased maladjustment. Interpretations implying that the therapist has a good understanding of the client should not be made early in therapy, since the client may justifiably question the competence of the therapist.

The content of interpretation is not limited to a particular area, such as underlying motivation and childhood influences, but includes all areas. If there is any place of emphasis, it would be on the relationships between the behavior of the client and the behavior of other people in the client's present situation.

This discussion has dealt with the utilization of common techniques in therapy within a social learning framework. It might be well to summarize or integrate them in terms of how they are used to achieve the changes in expectancies and in reinforcement values to which therapy is directed.

Techniques for Changing Expectancies

Five ways are suggested to increase the expectancy for gratification for new behaviors.

1. Direct reinforcement is the most straightforward and simple way. Adjustive behaviors are used in some situations by maladjusted persons. The therapist can teach parents to reinforce these behaviors when they occur in children. With adults, this is more difficult to do; therapists do not leave their therapy rooms to work with relatives, associates, and bosses of their clients. The therapist can and does reinforce adjustive behavior—chiefly verbal behavior —in therapy.
2. The therapist can place the client in or help the client find and enter situations where he or she may observe alternative behaviors and their consequences in others or in group therapy, where the client can try to understand the behavior of others retrospectively.
3. The therapist may deal with the client's history of alternative behaviors, reducing his or her expectancy that the behaviors will now result in negative reinforcements, as they did in the past, and verbally increasing the client's expectancy that these alternative behaviors will now lead to gratification.
4. The therapist may discuss new possible alternatives, showing how the behaviors are carried out and creating an expectancy that they may lead to gratification.
5. The therapist can create and reinforce an expectancy that the client may solve problems more effectively by looking for and trying out alternative solutions or behaviors.

In lowering expectancies for reinforcement, the therapist may also use direct reinforcement or a verbal technique. By failing to react with concern, sympathy, protection, or attention, the therapist may reduce the potentiality of previously rewarded behavior. The therapist's failure to reinforce such behavior may place a strain on the relationship with the client, and such a technique should be balanced by positive rewards for desired behavior. Verbal methods may contrast the client's past situation with the present to point out the carry-over of inappropriate expectations. In the discussion, the client may discover that the punishments or failures he or she has been avoiding are not likely to occur now. Reduced expectancy for punishment will lead to reduced expectancy that he or she is achieving any goal by avoidance. Alone or through the therapist's interpretation, the client may also discover that punishment is not avoided in this way but only delayed.

Techniques for Changing Reinforcement Values

Direct reinforcement often is not effective in changing expectancies for subsequent reinforcements, since these are further removed from behavior directed toward the initial reinforcement and the client may not associate them with the problem behavior. Verbal interpretation seems necessary and desirable in attempts to change goal or need values. Such verbal interpretations may be used with children. Reinforcement of goal values may also be changed by verbal analysis of past, present, and future experiences. Such analysis frequently concerns the relationships between goals and past, present, and future dissatisfactions.

The reduction of minimum goal levels may be achieved by reinforcing lesser accomplishments with praise instead of punishment, criticism, or exhortations to do better. Direct reinforcement by the therapist, through acceptance and understanding rather than criticism and condemnation of transgressions, errors, and inadequacies, is effective here. Discussion of the inadequate bases on which or inappropriate manner in which high standards or minimum goal levels were established is possible.

Therapy must be flexible rather than technique centered. Different people learn most effectively under different conditions. One may need little interpretation, while another may benefit from relatively threatening interpretations. One may change more quickly through verbal analysis of the origins of his or her behavior, while another may respond more to the therapist's direct reactions to his or her behavior. In every case, however, the therapist is guided by the same set of logical principles based on social learning theory.

Reinforcement is a principal method in therapy. The warmth, understanding, and acceptance expressed by the therapist make her or him an important source of reinforcement to the client. At the beginning of therapy, reinforcement leads to the development of a relationship in which the client learns to desire and expect reinforcement.

The experience of success early in therapy provides reinforcement of the client's interest in continuing therapy and reduces resistance to change. Such success can be ensured if the therapist deals first with problems that are of minor significance or of recent origin and thus are most amenable to change.

Generalization of changes in behavior from the therapist in the therapeutic situation to other people in situations outside of therapy does not occur simply or automatically. The therapy situation and the therapist's behavior are quite different from what the client experiences elsewhere. It is necessary for the therapist to deal with these other situations, at least on a verbal level, in therapy.

The effectiveness of reinforcement appears to be related to "the degree to which an individual feels that what happens to him is a function of his own characteristics, skills, behavior, etc., or, instead, depends on events external to himself over which he has no control."[21] Those who have a high degree of belief in external control and who see reinforcements as being lucky or the results of others' actions appear, on the basis of research studies, to be less susceptible to the influence of positive reinforcement and to persist in behavior that is not reinforced. With such clients, an analysis of this attitude may be required before change can take place.

The implications of social learning theory for therapeutic practice may be summarized as follows:

1. Psychotherapy is a learning situation in which the function of the therapist is to assist clients to achieve planned changes in behavior and thinking. Since clients have different motives, values, goals, expectancies, and skills, condi-

tions of optimal learning will vary, so that the therapist must be flexible and willing to experiment. Thus no one technique is applicable to all clients.

2. Clients' difficulties are frequently seen as problems that can be solved through the application of problem-solving skills, such as searching for alternative approaches to goals, seeing differences or making discriminations, and recognizing the needs and attitudes of others.

3. The therapist generally sees his or her role as partly one of guiding a learning process and thus actively engages in interpretation, suggestion, and direct reinforcement. "The therapist, however, does not consider himself merely a mechanical verbal conditioner, but rather a person whose special reinforcement value for the particular patient can be used to help the patient try out new behaviors and ways of thinking. The patient ultimately determines for himself the value of new conceptualizations and alternate ways of behaving in his experiences outside of therapy."[22]

4. While an understanding of the origins of behaviors and expectancies is important and is an aspect of insight, of greater importance is insight into the future consequences of behaviors and the influence of expectancies on present behavior.

5. In social learning, emphasis is placed on clients' understanding of others. "It is usually believed that what the patient lacks most is insight into himself, but it is likely that in general what characterizes patients even more consistently is lack of insight into the reactions and motivations of others."[23]

6. Important insights and new experiences occur in the life situation, not in the therapy room. Thus there must be discussion in therapy of clients' current experiences, and, when possible, the clients' environment must be controlled and manipulated.

7. Psychotherapy is a social interaction in which the laws and principles that apply in other interpersonal situations apply. The therapist is an active partner in the process, applying learning principles to help clients achieve better ways of dealing with the problems of life.

SUMMARY AND EVALUATION

Rotter outlines an expectancy-reinforcement theory of social learning and presents seven postulates and their corollaries, which define the theory in terms of underlying assumptions. Personality is the interaction of the individual and his or her meaningful environment. The area for study is psychological behavior, which is not dependent on any other field such as physiology or neurology; these are different ways of describing the same events. Experiences interact in a unified personality. Behavior has a directional aspect—it is goal-directed. Behavior is determined not only by goals or reinforcements, but also by the anticipation, or expectancy, that these goals will be achieved.

Three basic constructs are proposed to describe and predict behavior. *Behavior potential* is a function of *expectancy* and *reinforcement value;* or, in broader terms, *need potential* is a function of *freedom of movement* and *need value.* Maladjustive behavior is behavior that is unsatisfying. Maladjusted individuals have low freedom of movement with high need value; that is, they have low expectancies for gratification and high goals. They often are individuals who have minimum goal values that are too high to allow for satisfaction or reinforcement.

Counseling or therapy is directed toward changing expectancies and reinforcement values to allow for satisfaction and reinforcement. Inadequate responses must be weakened, and adequate responses must be strengthened. Social learning theory emphasizes the acquisition of new, adjustive responses, rather than, as do most other approaches, the elimination of bad responses. Therapy is concerned not merely with assisting clients to obtain a better understanding of themselves, but also with changing their behavior. The therapist is active, using both direct and verbal reinforcement, including interpretation. Therapy is concerned both with what happens in the interview situation and with the changes resulting from new experiences that occur as the result of trying out new and alternative behaviors.

Rotter's theory not only utilizes the reinforcement theory of Hull and the expectancy concept of Tolman, but also includes aspects of the theories of Lewin, Adler, and others. Phenomenology is implicit in Rotter's concept that the individual interacts, not with any real or objective world, but with a meaningful world, or the world as perceived (or organized or constructed) by the individual. It is thus a comprehensive theory, and as a social learning theory, it goes beyond learning theories that are simply transplanted from animals to human beings. Its empirical concept of reinforcement is not subject to the criticisms made of a drive-reduction theory of reinforcement. The addition of expectancy to reinforcement gives the theory an advantage over a single-variable drive or need theory. It goes beyond orthodox behaviorism in recognizing and accepting implicit or internal behavior. The theory is supported by a number of research studies that were derived from the theory and conducted to test deductions from it.

Comprehensiveness is associated with complexity—a characteristic recognized by Rotter—but his theory also tends to be abstract and contains relatively little content. Its concepts (accompanied by symbols and formulas) are sometimes difficult to comprehend, and the argument is difficult to follow, partly as a result of the use of a terminology that must be learned. Although the basic concepts are few, they represent complexes or classes of variables, which tend to be confusing at times and difficult to keep in mind. Rotter feels that a complex theory is necessary in view of the infinite complexity of human behavior. This may be true, but even a complex theory must and can be organized and presented clearly, systematically, and simply. Rotter is fairly successful in doing this, although not as successful as Dollard and Miller. The theory is difficult to understand in terms of or to transfer to clinical and everyday behavior, whereas Dollard and Miller have successfully done this for the reader. Concepts are not always phrased in the simplest form for communicating understanding, and there are instances of poor grammatical construction that impede understanding.

In spite of its comprehensiveness and complexity, the theory is probably oversimplified or incomplete, as Rotter would no doubt be ready to admit. While incorporating many of the concepts in general use in other personality and behavior theories, Rotter excludes others—such as maladjustment, neurotic behavior, the unconscious, psychosomatic illness, anxiety, the self, and conflict—and discusses his reasons for doing so. In some cases, however, it would appear that the rejected concepts are, to some extent at least, included in his system. The self and anxiety are two such concepts. The psychological unit of the person is similar to the self, and Rotter notes that the expectancies that people have regarding the outcome of their behavior might be considered as the self-concept. Anxiety is felt to be an ambiguous concept with varying connotations and definitions, and behaviors commonly included under it are felt to be accounted for in other ways. However, as Rotter recognizes, anxiety may be an expectancy—the expectancy of punishment. It would appear that concepts that have such general acceptance and apparent usefulness should be included in the system, refined, if necessary, or redefined in terms of the variables of the system.

Rotter's approach to counseling or therapy is not greatly different from many, if not most, other approaches. It shares with the other conditioning and learning theory approaches the concern for behavior outside of the therapy situation. It utilizes most of the techniques that other approaches commonly use and in much the same way. It tends to be an active approach. Yet it recognizes the importance of the relationship between the counselor and the client and the importance of the participation of the client in learning, including the desirability of the discovery method of problem solving, in which the client achieves his or her own solutions. But it also is concerned with efficiency and is not always able to wait for the client to reach his or her own solutions, lacking confidence that all clients can do so, at least within acceptable time limits. Although not emphasized or specifically identified as such, one reason that clients cannot be expected to achieve solutions without active interpretation by the therapist is discussed. This is the concept of secondary gain, which suggests that clients are not likely to give up easily or without resistance—without some pressure, coercion, or support from the therapist—behaviors that may be providing them with considerable satisfaction.

The theory as a whole is coherent, consistently developed, and consistently applied to counseling, although not as rigorously developed as Hull's theory. Undefined terms are used at times, along with implicit assumptions. Causality is denied, yet there appears to be at least implicit acceptance of causality in the relationship between reinforcement and expectancy and behavior potential. Details, particularly in techniques of application, are lacking. There are no verbatim illustrations of the counseling process. Nevertheless, the theory stands as one of the better attempts at a systematic approach to behavior and its change through counseling or psychotherapy.

The emphasis on learning leads to an emphasis on a rational, problem-solving approach to counseling, with neglect of feelings and emotions. However, Rotter's approach is an advance over traditional learning theory approaches in at least two respects. One is the concept of expectancies, which makes this a theory that looks toward the future rather than the past. The other is the concern with the social aspects of learning and behavior. These two concepts generate a counseling situation concerned with present behavior and with its future consequences, as well as with expectations of the future and with the current experiences of clients in their social interactions with others.

REFERENCES

1. Rotter, J. B. *Social learning and clinical psychology.* Englewood Cliffs, N.J.: Prentice-Hall, 1954.
2. Ibid., p. 80.
3. Ibid., p. 98.
4. Ibid., p. 103.

5. Ibid., p. 136.

6. Ibid., p. 116.

7. Ibid., p. 226.

8. This and the following section, "Implementation: techniques of counseling," incorporate material from Rotter, J. B. Some implications of a social learning theory for the practice of psychotherapy. In D. J. Levis (Ed.), *Learning approaches to therapeutic behavior change.* Chicago: Aldine, 1970. Pp. 200–241.

9. Rotter, *Social learning and clinical psychology,* p. 335.

10. Rotter, Some implications of a social learning theory for the practice of psychotherapy.

11. Mowrer, O. H. Learning theory and the neurotic paradox. *American Journal of Orthopsychiatry,* 1948, *18,* 571–610. (Reprinted in O. H. Mowrer (Ed.), *Learning theory and personality dynamics.* New York: Ronald Press, 1950. Pp. 483–530.)

12. Dollard, J., & Miller, N. E. *Personality and psychotherapy: An analysis in terms of learning, thinking, and culture.* New York: McGraw-Hill, 1950.

13. Rotter, *Social learning and clinical psychology,* p. 338.

14. Ibid., p. 346.

15. Rotter, Some implications of a social learning theory for the practice of psychotherapy.

16. Rotter, *Social learning and clinical psychology,* p. 354.

17. Ibid., p. 356.

18. Ibid., p. 361.

19. Ibid., p. 380.

20. Ibid., p. 391.

21. Rotter, J. B. Unpublished paper, 1962.

22. Rotter, Some implications of a social learning theory for the practice of psychotherapy.

23. Ibid.

chapter 8

Cognitive-Behavior Modification: Meichenbaum

Donald Herbert Meichenbaum (b. 1940) was born and obtained his early education in New York City. He received his B.A. from City College in 1962. He entered the University of Illinois at Urbana-Champaign in 1963 and received his M.A. in 1965 and Ph.D. in clinical psychology in 1966. During 1965 to 1966, he was a U.S. Public Health Service fellow. In 1966, he was appointed assistant professor of psychology at the University of Waterloo in Ontario, Canada, where he became associate professor in 1970 and is now professor. Meichenbaum is a member of the American Psychological Association, the Canadian Psychological Association, and the Society for Research in Child Development. He is the author of *Cognitive-Behavior Modification,* [1] *Stress Inoculation Training,* [2] and *Cognitive-Behavior Modification: An Integrative Approach,* [3] on which this summary is based.

BACKGROUND AND DEVELOPMENT

Meichenbaum relates an experience during his doctoral studies at the University of Illinois that was the beginning of the research and theory development leading to his cognitive-behavioral approach to behavior modification and psychotherapy. His research involved training hospitalized schizophrenic patients to emit "healthy talk" by operant conditioning procedures. He observed that some of the patients, while they were being given a follow-up interview as part of the evaluation of the effectiveness of the treatment, repeated aloud to themselves the experimental instruction "Give healthy talk; be coherent and relevant," thus engaging in spontaneous self-instruction.

It might be noted that the use of such experimental instructions constituted a departure from strict operant conditioning, thereby introducing a cognitive element into the treatment. An incident reported by William Gilbert, director of the Counseling Center at the University of Illinois, occurred at about the same time that Meichenbaum was engaged in his research. A psychology student working in a mental hospital decided to attempt to eliminate an antagonizing behavior in a patient, which consisted of sticking his tongue out at members of the hospital staff, by the method of aversive conditioning. After several interviews, the patient caught on to the psychology student's objective and said, "Say, Doc, if you're trying to get me to stop sticking my tongue out, just tell me and I'll be glad to."[4] Whether Meichenbaum was aware of and influenced by this incident is not known, but it points to the influence of cognitive factors in behavior change.

Meichenbaum's experience led him to wonder if schizophrenic patients and other patients or clients could be explicitly trained to talk to themselves in a way that would lead to changes in their behavior. He entered on a program of research to study the role of cognitive factors in behavior modification. He focused on inner speech, or inner dialogue, seeking to alter it, and on images, hoping to learn if such changes would lead to changes in thinking, feeling, and behavior. He also began to develop a theoretical explanation for the operation of such factors in behavior change. His results are presented as a progress report, not as a finished or proven theory and practice.

Building on the research that shows that overt and covert private speech influence the behavior of children, Meichenbaum explored the use of self-instructional training with hyperactive, impulsive children. He found that impulsive children manifested less verbal control of nonverbal behavior than did reflective children in laboratory studies and that impulsive children used private speech differently in natural play situations. In the latter situation, impulsive children were deficient in outer-directed and self-regulatory speech. Impulsive children "do not habitually and spontaneously analyze their experience in cognitively mediated terms (i.e., both verbal and imaginal) and . . . they do not formulate and internalize rules that might guide them in new learning situations."[5] Meichenbaum then developed a program to train hyperactive, impulsive children to talk to themselves differently so that they could better comprehend problem tasks, spontaneously produce verbal mediators and strategies, and use these mediators to guide, monitor, and control their behavior.

Meichenbaum and others have succeeded in changing the behaviors of impulsive, hyperactive and aggressive children through a training program in which the experimenter models the self-instructions as well as the behaviors and in which the child rehearses the self-instructions. The addition of operant procedures, that is, reinforcement, led to greater improvement. Conversely, the addition of self-instructional training to operant procedures enhanced the results over those obtained from operant procedures alone. However, extrinsic reinforcements were not effective with children who attributed results to luck or chance rather than to their own efforts. Self-instructional training was effective in helping children change their attributions from luck or lack of ability to effort. Meichenbaum concluded that self-instructional training can be effective in altering children's attributional and cognitive styles but cautioned that its effectiveness has not yet been fully demonstrated.

Meichenbaum also developed a program of training in self-instruction for patients diagnosed as schizophrenic. He began with structured sensorimotor tasks, rather than with social interactions, since there is evidence that interpersonal-relationship pressures increase symptomatology such as bizarre verbalizations. The initial tasks included a digit-symbol test and the Porteus Maze Test. The patients were trained to develop and use self-controlling self-statements. As the patients developed proficiency, tasks such as a proverbs test and an interview were added. When a patient used symptomatology to control the situation, the patient was made aware of this as a cue to use self-instructional controls learned earlier in the simpler tasks. "Each subject was individually trained to first monitor and evaluate his own performance by means of self-questioning. Then, if he judged his performance to be inferior, he learned to self-instruct in a task-relevant fashion in order to produce a more desirable response."[5] The experimenter modeled verbalizations as he or she performed the task, and subjects overtly and then covertly used the same verbalizations as they in turn performed the task. Verbalization included (1) a restatement of the task requirements, (2) instructions to perform the task slowly and to think before acting, (3) a cognitive strategy using imagery in seeking a solution, (4) self-rewarding statements, (5) an example of a poor or an erroneous response, followed by the reason it was inappropriate, and (6) a statement describing how to cope with failure and come up with an adequate response. Early training sessions were simple, and later sessions gradually added more elements. In final sessions, the patient was asked to observe and report the reactions—verbal and nonverbal—of staff and other patients to inappropriate behavior. Discussion then led to suggesting self-statements the patient could use in such situations, such as "Be relevant, be coherent, make myself understood." Other self-statements, such as "I'm not making myself understood, let me try again," were used to maintain task relevance.

Compared with control subjects who were trained by operant social reinforcement, the experimental subjects showed significantly greater improvement on all criterion tests except one (digit recall without distraction).

Self-instructional training is not effective unless the necessary concepts and skills are present. For example, self-instructional training will not improve performance in arithmetic if the basic skills are lacking. "Teaching children to respond to such self-directed verbal commands as 'stop and think' will not result in incremental improvement of performance in specific tasks unless the prerequisite performance skills are already in the repertoire."[7] Also, actions may not follow self-verbalizations if there is no incentive to perform the actions. Reinforcement of the sequence of verbal and nonverbal behavior increases the frequency of action following verbalization. Language alone may not change behavior; thought is also necessary. Thinking can occur without language, but language can significantly increase thinking and thus change behavior. "That is the promise of the self-instructional cognitive-behavior treatment approach."[8]

ASSUMPTIONS AND CONCEPTS

Self-instructional training is based on the assumption that "the things people say to themselves determine the rest of the things they do."[9] Behavior is affected or influenced by various aspects of a person's activities, which are designated by various constructs: physiological responses, affective reactions, cognitions, and interpersonal interactions. Inner speech, or internal dialogue, is one of these activities or constructs.

"The goal of a cognitive-functional assessment is to describe, in probabilistic terms, the functional significance of engaging in self-statements of a particular sort [being] followed by an individual's particular behavior or emotional state (e.g., mood), or his physiological reactions or his attentional processes, etc. How does the internal dialogue influence, and, in turn, is it influenced by other events or behavioral processes?"[10] There is little research on conscious thought or internal dialogue, as a variable affecting other behaviors. Studies in three areas, however (interpersonal instructions, cognitive factors in stress, and the effects of instructional sets on physiological reactions), have dealt with the consequences of self-statements and are a source for suggestions regarding the functional value of inner speech.

Functions of Internal Dialogue

Interpersonal Instructions

Descriptions of the function of interpersonal instructions (by Gagné, for example)[11] are very similar to the descriptions of self-instructions (by McKinney, for example).[12] Both provide procedures and a rule or a principle for mediating behavior. Thus it can be hypothesized that self-instructions operate in a similar fashion to interpersonal instructions. Self-instructions are derived from adults' instructions that children internalize or incorporate and use to control their behavior, as the Russian psychologists Vygotsky and Luria theorized.

Cognitive Factors in Stress

Although the psychosocial literature on coping with stress does not deal with self-statements, it does suggest that "how one responds to stress in large part is influenced by how one appraises the stressor, or to what he attributes the arousal he feels, and how he assesses his ability to cope."[13] A person's self-statements about the stress situation and ability to handle it influence that person's behavior in the situation. Anxiety level is related to such self-appraisals in relation to the situation. High anxiety is associated with a person's focusing on the self and his or her inadequacy and self-deprecating thoughts. Low anxiety is associated with a person's focusing on the external situation, with a resulting higher level of coping. "[O]ne function of internal dialogue in changing affect, thought, and behavior is to *influence the client's attentional and appraisal processes.*"[14]

Instructional Sets and Physiological Effects

There is considerable evidence that cognition influences physiology and emotions. Studies have shown that there is a relationship between self-statements and mood. Clients' thoughts and cognitive sets are related to psychosomatic disorders; hypnotized subjects who have been instructed to feel the attitudes reported by psychosomatic patients have suffered the symptoms of the patients. Cognitive activity has been postulated as a mediational factor in operant autonomic conditioning. Meichenbaum found that following cognitive-behavior-modification treatment, subjects labeled their physiological reactions as facilitative rather than inhibitive. "Sweaty palms, increased heart and respiratory rates, muscular tension, now became 'allies,' cues to use the coping techniques for which they had been trained. . . . This shift in cognitions in itself may

Thus the effective change process involves new behavioral skills, new internal dialogues, and new cognitive structures. Different therapies emphasize one or another of these. The cognitive-behavior approach involves all three. There is the question of where to begin, which requires research to answer. Different types of clients may require the focus or emphasis on one or another of the three basic processes, but the others are also involved.

IMPLEMENTATION: METHODS AND TECHNIQUES

Cognitive-Behavioral Assessment

Since psychiatric patients suffer from disorders of affect, cognition, and volition, assessment should deal with these areas of functioning. Traditional assessment strategies in the study of psychological deficits have been inadequate for such assessment. Two research approaches have been used. The first is the *comparative-groups approach*. Clinical groups are given a series of tests, and the results are compared with those of a matched normal control group. The clinical population is found to differ from or do more poorly than the control groups. Such results are of little assistance in revealing the nature of the deficit, what underlies or causes it, or what can change it. Deficient performance can arise from different reasons.

The second approach is the *specific-deficits approach,* in which tests are used to detect the client's deficient performance, the nature of which has been hypothesized. A normative control group is used, but the focus is on specific tests rather than on a global "shot-gun" comparison. This approach may result in a new label for the deficiency, but it does not explain or define the problem. Speculation may result in hypothetical explanations derived from either of these approaches, but there is no basis for choosing among the various explanations or conceptualizations. A cognitive-functional approach to deficit analysis appears more promising.

A Cognitive-Functional Approach

A *functional analysis of behavior* involves a detailed examination of environmental antecedents and consequences in relation to a response repertoire. It requires a careful definition of the response class, a knowledge of the responses' frequency in various situations, and the manipulation of environmental events to demonstrate causal relationships. A *functional-cognitive analysis* includes and focuses on the role of cognitions in the behavioral repertoire,

> "in order to determine which cognitions (or failure to produce which key cognitions), under which circumstances, are contributing to or interfering with adequate performance. . . . The cognitive-functional approach analyzes *sequential psychological processes . . .* required for adequate performance. . . . [A] failure in the internal dialogue of the client, what he says or fails to say to himself prior to, accompanying, and following his performance on a task, becomes the concern of the analysis.[23]

The clinician may engage in the task in order to speculate about the factors that lead to the client's poor performance.

[being] followed by an individual's particular behavior or emotional state (e.g., mood), or his physiological reactions or his attentional processes, etc. How does the internal dialogue influence, and, in turn, is it influenced by other events or behavioral processes?"[10] There is little research on conscious thought or internal dialogue, as a variable affecting other behaviors. Studies in three areas, however (interpersonal instructions, cognitive factors in stress, and the effects of instructional sets on physiological reactions), have dealt with the consequences of self-statements and are a source for suggestions regarding the functional value of inner speech.

Functions of Internal Dialogue

Interpersonal Instructions

Descriptions of the function of interpersonal instructions (by Gagné, for example)[11] are very similar to the descriptions of self-instructions (by McKinney, for example).[12] Both provide procedures and a rule or a principle for mediating behavior. Thus it can be hypothesized that self-instructions operate in a similar fashion to interpersonal instructions. Self-instructions are derived from adults' instructions that children internalize or incorporate and use to control their behavior, as the Russian psychologists Vygotsky and Luria theorized.

Cognitive Factors in Stress

Although the psychosocial literature on coping with stress does not deal with self-statements, it does suggest that "how one responds to stress in large part is influenced by how one appraises the stressor, or to what he attributes the arousal he feels, and how he assesses his ability to cope."[13] A person's self-statements about the stress situation and ability to handle it influence that person's behavior in the situation. Anxiety level is related to such self-appraisals in relation to the situation. High anxiety is associated with a person's focusing on the self and his or her inadequacy and self-deprecating thoughts. Low anxiety is associated with a person's focusing on the external situation, with a resulting higher level of coping. "[O]ne function of internal dialogue in changing affect, thought, and behavior is to *influence the client's attentional and appraisal processes.*"[14]

Instructional Sets and Physiological Effects

There is considerable evidence that cognition influences physiology and emotions. Studies have shown that there is a relationship between self-statements and mood. Clients' thoughts and cognitive sets are related to psychosomatic disorders; hypnotized subjects who have been instructed to feel the attitudes reported by psychosomatic patients have suffered the symptoms of the patients. Cognitive activity has been postulated as a mediational factor in operant autonomic conditioning. Meichenbaum found that following cognitive-behavior-modification treatment, subjects labeled their physiological reactions as facilitative rather than inhibitive. "Sweaty palms, increased heart and respiratory rates, muscular tension, now became 'allies,' cues to use the coping techniques for which they had been trained. . . . This shift in cognitions in itself may mediate a shift in autonomic functioning. The present theory postulates that it is not the physiological arousal *per se* that is debilitating but rather what the client says to himself about that arousal that determines his eventual reaction."[15]

Thus there is considerable evidence that thought influences behavior. Yet it must be recognized that much of our behavior is automatic or the result of habit. We do not always think before we act (habits are useful for quick, efficient actions), but *"if we are going to change behavior then we must think before we act.* Such thinking (i.e., the production of inner speech) 'deautomatizes' the maladaptive behavior act and provides the basis for providing the new adaptive behavior."[16]

Structure of Internal Dialogue

A second important function of inner speech is to influence and change cognitive structures. A construct such as cognitive structure is necessary to account for the nature of self-statements. Cognitive structure provides the system of meanings or concepts that gives rise to a particular set of self-statements. "By *cognitive structure* I mean to point to that organizing aspect of thinking that seems to monitor and direct the strategy, route and choice of thoughts. I mean to imply a kind of 'executive processor' which 'holds the blueprints of thinking' and which determines when to interrupt, change, or continue thought."[17] Learning or change occurs without a change in cognitive structure, but learning a new skill requires a change in cognitive structure. Structural changes occur by *absorption,* in which new structures incorporate old structures; by *displacement,* in which old structures continue along with the new; and by *integration,* in which parts of the old structure continue to exist in a more comprehensive new structure (from Neisser, following Piaget's concepts of assimilation and accommodation).[18] Cognitive structures determine the nature of inner speech, but inner dialogue changes cognitive structures, in what Meichenbaum calls a "virtuous cycle."

THE CHANGE/THERAPY PROCESS

There are certain underlying mechanisms of change common to all procedures (therapy systems) and contexts (in therapy and in nonprofessional contacts) in which change occurs. These mechanisms involve the individual's cognitive processes. First, the client must recognize or become aware of his or her inadequate behaviors. Second, this awareness is a cue that produces a certain internal dialogue. The nature of this dialogue is guided by the theoretical orientation of the therapist, to which the client adapts. Third, there is a change in the nature of the internal dialogue from that which the client engaged in prior to therapy. There is a "translation" process fostered by the therapist's reflections, explanations, interpretations, information giving, and cognitive modeling. In addition, the client engages outside of therapy in coping behaviors that are discussed and rehearsed in therapy, resulting in an internal dialogue that influences the client's cognitive structures as well as behaviors. "Some clients require explicit teaching of such copying responses, and this is where the technology of behavior therapy is of particular value."[19] The three phases are elaborated as follows.

Phase 1: Self-Observation

Prior to therapy, the client's internal dialogue consists of negative self-statements and images. In therapy, the client, through heightened awareness and attention, focuses on his or her thoughts, feelings, physiological reactions, and interpersonal behaviors. The translation process leads to new cognitive structures that allow the client to view his or her symptoms or problems differently and to produce thought and behaviors that are incompatible with the maladaptive ones. This reconceptualization process leads to a redefinition of problems in ways that give the client both a sense of understanding and a feeling of control and hope that are required for acts of change. Reconceptualization gives new or different meanings to thoughts, feelings, and behaviors. These meanings vary with different schools of therapy, and different conceptualizations may be effective in facilitating change. However, "one of the more essential variables that determines therapy outcome is the degree to which a given conceptualization leads to specific behavioral changes that can be transferred to the real-life situation."[20]

Therapists vary in the directiveness and force with which they attempt to change their clients' conceptualizations. Therapists must be concerned with their clients' self-statements, descriptions, definitions, and attributions of their problems and their conceptions of the therapy process and dependence on the therapist, but therapists do not simply uncritically accept clients' views. The reconceptualization is a joint process, and clients' acceptance of it is an implicit result of the interaction between therapist and client.

Phase 2: Incompatible Thoughts and Behavior

In the second phase, the client's self-observation triggers an internal dialogue. "[I]f the client's behavior is to change, then what he says to himself and/or imagines, must initiate a new behavioral chain, one that is incompatible with his maladaptive behaviors."[21] This new internal dialogue involves all the functional properties of inner speech indicated above (affecting attentional and appraisal systems and physiological responses, and instigating new behaviors). This inner speech, guided by the translation involved in the therapy, influences the client's cognitive structures, enabling the client to organize his or her experiences around the new conceptualization in a way that leads to more effective coping.

Phase 3: Cognitions Concerning Change

The third phase has to do with the client's performing coping behaviors on a day-to-day basis and self-talk about the outcomes of these "personal experiments." It is not enough for the client to focus only on skills training, as behavior therapy does.

> For what the client says to himself about his newly acquired behaviors and their resultant consequences will influence whether the behavioral change process will be maintained and will generalize. . . . To the extent that the client changes both his behavior and his internal dialogues, to that extent therapy becomes a success. In other words, a person is how he behaves, as well as what he says to himself (including his attributions), which says much more than that a person is only how he behaves.[22]

Thus the effective change process involves new behavioral skills, new internal dialogues, and new cognitive structures. Different therapies emphasize one or another of these. The cognitive-behavior approach involves all three. There is the question of where to begin, which requires research to answer. Different types of clients may require the focus or emphasis on one or another of the three basic processes, but the others are also involved.

IMPLEMENTATION: METHODS AND TECHNIQUES

Cognitive-Behavioral Assessment

Since psychiatric patients suffer from disorders of affect, cognition, and volition, assessment should deal with these areas of functioning. Traditional assessment strategies in the study of psychological deficits have been inadequate for such assessment. Two research approaches have been used. The first is the *comparative-groups approach.* Clinical groups are given a series of tests, and the results are compared with those of a matched normal control group. The clinical population is found to differ from or do more poorly than the control groups. Such results are of little assistance in revealing the nature of the deficit, what underlies or causes it, or what can change it. Deficient performance can arise from different reasons.

The second approach is the *specific-deficits approach,* in which tests are used to detect the client's deficient performance, the nature of which has been hypothesized. A normative control group is used, but the focus is on specific tests rather than on a global "shot-gun" comparison. This approach may result in a new label for the deficiency, but it does not explain or define the problem. Speculation may result in hypothetical explanations derived from either of these approaches, but there is no basis for choosing among the various explanations or conceptualizations. A cognitive-functional approach to deficit analysis appears more promising.

A Cognitive-Functional Approach

A *functional analysis of behavior* involves a detailed examination of environmental antecedents and consequences in relation to a response repertoire. It requires a careful definition of the response class, a knowledge of the responses' frequency in various situations, and the manipulation of environmental events to demonstrate causal relationships. A *functional-cognitive analysis* includes and focuses on the role of cognitions in the behavioral repertoire,

> "in order to determine which cognitions (or failure to produce which key cognitions), under which circumstances, are contributing to or interfering with adequate performance. . . . The cognitive-functional approach analyzes *sequential psychological processes . . .* required for adequate performance. . . . [A] failure in the internal dialogue of the client, what he says or fails to say to himself prior to, accompanying, and following his performance on a task, becomes the concern of the analysis.[23]

The clinician may engage in the task in order to speculate about the factors that lead to the client's poor performance.

Task analysis involves breaking down the task into its components or into the cognitive strategies required for its performance, beginning with comprehension of the nature of the task or the instructions. Then various manipulations are performed, and the changes that result are noted. There are three types of manipulation. The first is the *modification of the task* in a variety of ways, permitting assessment of the client's capabilities and deficits under different conditions. The second type of manipulation is the *alteration of nontask environmental variables,* such as presence or absence of distortions and interpersonal factors. This permits observation of aspects of the situation that facilitate or disrupt performance. The client is also a source of such information. "Soliciting from the client his perception of the task, his description of his strategy, his appraisal of his performance, and his assessment of his own situation are key elements of a cognitive-functional analysis. . . . [O]ur clients have something to tell us if we would only ask and then listen."[24] The third type of manipulation consists of *providing the client with supports* in the form of various aids and suggestions and observing changes in performance. Thus cognitive-functional assessment involves the client as the subject of an experimental investigation.

Such an experimental analysis leads directly into treatment suggestions. Assessment and treatment merge or overlap. "Assessment of deficiencies and capabilities go [*sic*] hand-in-hand with remediation."[25]

Clinical Application of the Approach

In the individual assessment process two questions are asked: "First, what is the client failing to say to himself, which, if present, would help lead to adequate performance and adaptive behavior? Second, what is the content of the cognitions that interfere with adaptive behavior?"[26] A number of procedures are used to answer these questions.

The clinical interview   The initial interview begins with an exploration of the extent and the duration of the client's problem as the client presents it and of the client's expectations of therapy, following the outline provided by Peterson,[27] which involves a situational analysis of the client's behavior. Beyond this, the cognitive-behavior therapist asks the client to imagine incidents involving personal problem(s) and to report his or her thoughts, images, and behaviors before, during, and after these incidents. Then the therapist explores the presence of similar thoughts and feelings in other situations and/or at earlier periods in the client's life and may ask the client to look for them during the next week.

The cognitive-functional assessment leads the client to recognize that part of the problem derives from self-statements and that a person can control and change his or her thoughts if the person chooses to do so. The client may be unaware of what he or she has been saying to himself or herself, since because of "the habitual nature of one's expectations and beliefs, it is likely that such thinking processes and images become automatic and seemingly involuntary, like most overlearned acts."[28]

Behavioral tests   In a behavioral test, the client engages in the behaviors involving his or her problem, either in a laboratory situation or in real life. This is followed by an exploration of thoughts and feelings during the experience. In the laboratory situation, the client can be videotaped, and the videotape can be viewed and discussed with the therapist, or the client can be asked to think aloud during the behavior test. Although such reconstruction and verbalization while engaging in the task are subject to inaccuracy or distortion, they can reveal the client's thinking style.

A TAT-like approach   Pictures similar to those in the Thematic Apperception Test (TAT) but related to the client's problem behavior may be used to elicit thoughts and feelings related to the behaviors.

Other psychometric tests   Tests of cognitive processes, such as creativity and problem-solving tests, may be administered, followed by the client reporting on his or her thinking while the test was taken.

Assessment may be conducted on a group basis, particularly if the clients have the same problem. Exploration of thoughts and feelings in a group can help clients appreciate the role of cognitive factors in behavior and lead to self-disclosure and self-examination.

Cognitive Factors in Behavior Therapy Techniques

Behavior therapy techniques have overemphasized the importance of environmental events (antecedents and consequences) at the same time that they have overlooked or underemphasized the cognitive factors in these techniques. "Our research on cognitive factors in behavior therapy techniques has highlighted the fact that environmental events *per se,* although important, are not of *primary* importance; rather what the client says to himself about those events influences his behavior."[29] However, behavior modification techniques can be used to modify the client's internal dialogue as well as behaviors, but when standard behavior therapy procedures are supplemented by self-instructional techniques, they are more effective, generalization is greater, and effects are more persistent. This raises questions about the learning theory basis of the standard techniques, which is a simple contiguity model. Research on cognitive factors in behavior therapy, testing the effectiveness of changing cognitions through behavior therapy techniques, suggests a new and different conceptualization.

Anxiety-Relief Conditioning

In the behavioristic anxiety-relief procedure, the cessation of an aversive stimulus is paired with the emitting of a word such as *calm.* Anxiety can then be reduced by the client instructing himself or herself to be "calm." Meichenbaum, on the basis of an experiment in which subjects reported using coping verbalizations other than the words *calm* or *relax,* conducted a study incorporating such self-instructions. He also made the onset of shock punishing for some subjects. Thus subjects said the name of the phobic object (for example, "snake"), followed by fear-engendering thought (for example, "It's ugly; I won't look at it") that elicited the shock. Then the subjects said the coping self-statements (for example, "Relax, I can touch it"), which led to cessation of the shock, and the clients then relaxed. A control group of subjects were *shocked contingent on the coping self-statements,* and the shock was terminated by the *emission of fear-engendering* self-statements. The expanded anxiety-relief treatment was, as expected, effective in reducing fears, but, surprisingly, the inverted or reversed treatment was also effective. Both treatments were more effective than the standard procedure. The results of the inverted treatment are inconsistent with the "learning theory" model; these subjects should have done poorly.

Other studies have confirmed these results, both with aversive conditioning and with other behavior therapy techniques. Flooding techniques, for example, are difficult to explain by learning theory. Similar studies using covert conditioning have yielded similar results. The conditioning paradigm is inadequate in explaining such behavioral changes, questioning the so-called basic laws of learning.

In questioning the subjects in this study, Meichenbaum found that they emitted coping statements to prepare for the forthcoming shock and perceived the fear-engendering self-statements as signals to the experimenter to turn off the shock. "What seemed to be happening was that the subjects were learning a set of coping skills that could be employed *across* situations, including confronting the phobic object."[30] The results also might be explained by psychosocial theories, such as social learning theory, dissonance theory, attribution theory, and self-perception theory. Essentially, what a client learns in behavior therapy are cognitive and behavioral skills, including changes in maladaptive beliefs as a result of nonconfirming experiences in therapy; changes in the self-concept and beliefs about others through information learning; and the development of new problem-solving and interpersonal skills (as in Murray and Jacobson, 1971)[31]

Systematic Desensitization

Systematic desensitization, according to Wolpe, eliminates fear because fear is incompatible with relaxation. This counterconditioning explanation has been questioned by a number of writers. Observation of Wolpe's therapy sessions have shown the presence of cognitive factors, which were confirmed by reports of his clients.

Systematic desensitization can be modified to utilize the clients' cognitions explicitly. The relaxation component of desensitization can be simplified and shortened by having clients adopt a mental set of relaxation through self-instruction. The imaginal component can be improved by having clients see themselves as coping with the anxiety induced by visualizing the scene, breathing slowly and deeply, relaxing, and engaging in self-instructions. The anxiety-producing experience then becomes a cue to cope and to function in spite of the anxiety. Anxiety is thus seen by the client as facilitating rather than debilitating—it is a signal for coping behavior, as shown in experiments by Meichenbaum and others. "The proposed changes in the desensitization procedures are consistent with (a) observations that desensitization should be viewed as an active means of learning coping and self-control skills and (b) notions of the therapeutic value of the 'work of worrying' " (anticipatory problem-solving and cognitive rehearsal).[32]

Modeling

Bandura[33] has emphasized that in the modeling technique, the observer converts the information obtained from the model to covert perceptual-cognitive images and covert verbal, mediatory rehearsal responses that are used later as cues to overt behavior. Such responses are essentially self-instructions. Explicit modeling of such responses should facilitate behavior change. Models can think aloud as they perform, including the demonstration not only of the mastery behavior, but also of coping behaviors, such as facing and dealing with self-doubts and frustrations, and ending with self-reinforcing statements following success. Research by Meichenbaum and others have shown this method to be more effective than the usual modeling technique.

Aversive Conditioning

In aversive conditioning, an undesirable response is paired with an aversive condition such as shock, which is terminated by cessation of the response. In the cognitive-behavioral approach, the undesirable response is expanded to include cognitions in the form of self-statements and images. In treating smoking, for example, shock is terminated by having the client put out the cigarette *and* emit personally selected self-statements about smoking behavior, such as not wanting a "cancer weed." This approach was more effective than the usual approach in a study by Meichenbaum. The explanation of the facilitating effect of mental rehearsal is not yet clear, but it may be related to "a better representation of the implicit stimuli that contributed to the maladaptive behavior," to the involvement of "many more different situational cues in the training," and to "greater emotional involvement."[34] The acquisition of motor skills can be enhanced by mental practice involving similar processes, as well as imagery.

A number of behavior therapists have recognized the cognitive factors in behavior therapy and have made "comments that converge to suggest that the alteration of the client's self-statement may represent a common mediation of the behavioral change brought about by many of these behavior therapy techniques. . . . If the hypothesis that the client's self-instructions mediate behavior change is valid, one would expect that explicit self-instructional training would enhance treatment effectiveness."[35] Research has confirmed this hypothesis.

Cognitive-behavior modification includes two other major methods, in addition to behavior therapy techniques.

Stress-Inoculation Training

Stress-inoculation training follows the biological model of immunization. It builds up resistance to stress through a program of teaching the client how to cope with graded stress situations. It incorporates suggestions from research on coping with stress. The training procedure is multifaceted in order to provide flexibility because of the complexity of coping devices, the variability of stress situations, and the differences among individuals and cultural factors.

Procedures of Stress Inoculation

Stress-inoculation training consists of three phases.

1. Educational phase   In the educational phase, the client is provided with a conceptual framework for understanding the nature of his or her reactions to stress. This is in lay terms, and it should be plausible to the client and lead naturally to the practice of specific cognitive and behavioral techniques. Thus "the scientific validity of a particular conceptualization is less crucial than its face validity or air of plausibility for the client."[36] The purpose of the framework is to help the client view a problem rationally and accept and collaborate in the appropriate therapy.

In a study of multiphobic clients, following an assessment interview, the client's anxiety was presented as involving two major elements: (1) heightened physiological arousal (increased heart rate, rapid breathing, sweaty palms, or other symptoms stated by the client) and (2) a set of anxiety-evoking avoidance thoughts indicated by the client (disgust, sense of helplessness, thoughts of panic, desire to flee, embarrassment, and so on). The client was then told that the self-statement during arousal led to emotional avoidance behavior and that treatment would be directed toward (1) helping the client control his or her physiological arousal and (2) changing the self-statements that were made under stress conditions. The client was then encouraged to view the phobic or stress reactions as consisting of four stages rather than being one undifferentiated reaction: (1) preparing for the stressor, (2) confronting or handling the stressor, (3) possibly being overwhelmed by the stressor, and (4) reinforcing himself or herself for having coped.

2. Rehearsal phase   In the rehearsal phase, the client was provided with coping techniques, including both direct actions and cognitive coping modes, to use in each of the four stages of the phobic reaction. Direct action included obtaining information about the phobic objects, arranging for escape routes, and learning physical relaxation exercises. Cognitive coping consisted of helping the client become aware of negative, self-defeating statements and using these as cues or signals for producing incompatible, coping self-statements. Examples for each of the four stages are: (1) "You can develop a plan to deal with it"; (2) "Relax, you're in control. Take a slow, deep breath"; (3) "When fear comes, just pause"; (4) "It worked; you did it."

3. Application training   When the client became proficient in the coping techniques, he or she was exposed in the laboratory to a series of graded ego-threatening and pain-threatening stressors, including unpredictable electric shocks. The therapist modeled the use of the coping skills.

The training was thus multifaceted because it involved a variety of therapeutic techniques, including didactic training, discussion, modeling, self-instructional and behavioral rehearsal, and reinforcement. Research is necessary to determine which are the necessary and sufficient conditions for achieving change. The total procedure was more effective than systematic desensitization, more effective than the use of phase 1 and 2 techniques without phase 3, and more effective than no treatments (as shown by an untreated control group). Self-instructional rehearsal is thus a necessary but not a sufficient condition for the elimination of fears; application or practice training also is necessary. Both the total procedure and the treatment involving the first two phases only were more effective than desensitization in terms of generalization. Stress-inoculation training provided a way of altering the client's cognitive self from one of "learned helplessness" to one of "learned resourcefulness." "It was quite common for clients in the stress-inoculation group to report spontaneously that they had successfully applied their new coping skills in other stressful situations, including final exams and dental visits. . . . The change in attitude seemed to encourage clients to initiate confrontations with real-life problems."[37]

Stress-inoculation training has been successfully used to teach personal competence in managing provocations and regulating anger in individuals who have problems in controlling anger and in experiments on pain tolerance. There are reports of success in other clinical situations. Meichenbaum is cautious in his claims for its effectiveness, however: "[T]he evidence for the efficacy of stress-inoculation is encouraging but not proven. The data on the full usefulness of the procedure have yet to be obtained. The stress-inoculation procedure is not offered as a panacea nor a replacement for other treatment approaches."[38] It offers promise as a preventive measure with high-risk populations.

> An explicit training program that would teach coping skills and then provide application training in handling a variety of stressors is in marked contrast to the haphazard and chance manner in which people now learn to cope with stress. The research on stress seems to indicate the necessary skills required to cope, and the method of cognitive-behavior modification seems to provide a promising means for teaching such skills.[39]

Cognitive-Restructuring Techniques

There are a variety of therapeutic methods subsumed under the names cognitive-restructuring therapy or semantic therapy. They focus on modifying the client's thinking and reasoning—the premises, assumptions (beliefs), and attitudes underlying his or her cognitions. Mental illness is viewed as a disorder of thinking that involves distorted thought processes leading to distorted views of the world, unpleasant emotions, and behavioral difficulties. These methods constitute what is often called "insight-oriented therapy." Actually, the diversity of methods is so great that they do not constitute a single therapy but, rather, differing therapies. Although they are concerned with clients' cognitions, different therapists conceptualize their clients' cognitions differently, leading to different treatment techniques.

Cognitions as Instances of Irrational Belief Systems

Ellis's rational-emotive therapy falls under the category of restructuring therapy. The basic irrational belief is that a person's self-worth is determined by others. The semantic therapist attempts to get clients to realize that their maladaptive behaviors and emotional disturbances are possibly related to or determined by what they say to themselves, although they may not be aware of what they are saying. Once clients accept this conceptualization (of the therapist), they are ready for any of a number of therapeutic approaches of a cognitive-restructuring nature. Ellis forcefully attempts to change the clients' beliefs.

Although leading clients to view their behavior from Ellis's conceptualization may result in change, the existence of self-negating beliefs is not necessarily the difference between clients and nonclients. Many, if not most, normal people may hold the same beliefs. Rather, it may be that they differ in what they say to themselves about the irrational beliefs or in what mechanisms they employ in order to cope. Normal people "may be more capable of 'compartmentalizing' such events and be more able to use coping techniques such as humor, rationality, or what I have come to call 'creative repression.'"[40] Thus other treatment techniques, such as self-instructional methods, may be useful, particularly since there are little, if any, experimental data supporting Ellis's method.

Cognitions as Instances of Faulty Thinking Styles

A second cognitive-restructuring approach is that of Beck,[41] whose focus is on clients' distorted thought patterns. Distortions include faulty inferences not supported by evidence; exaggeration of the significance of an event; cognitive deficiency, or disregard for an important element in a situation; dichotomous reasoning, or seeing things as either black or white (good or bad, right or wrong, with no in-betweens); and overgeneralization from a single incident. Clients are taught to identify these distortions through semantic and behavioral techniques. The therapist then challenges the "silent assumptions" underlying clients' attitudes and conceptions by demonstrating the clients' unrealistic interpretations of their experiences. The clients then collaborate with the therapist in observing and analyzing their own experiences.

Cognitions as Instances of Problem-Solving Ability and Coping Skills

An alternative cognitive-structuring approach is that of D'Zurilla and Goldfried, among others.[42] The focus is on identifying the *absence* of specific adaptive, cognitive skills and responses and on teaching clients problem-solving skills—how to identify problems, generate possible solutions, tentatively select one solution, and then test and verify its efficacy. Other therapists, including Meichenbaum, focus on coping skills. In problem solving, clients are taught how to face and solve future problem situations. Coping skills are taught in the actual crisis or problem situations.

These cognitive-restructuring methods differ in a number of ways, including the emphasis on formal logical analysis, the prescriptiveness of the treatment, and the relative use of adjunctive behavior therapy procedures. The cognitive-behavior therapist faces a dilemma in choosing among them and numerous other cognitive techniques. The result could be a technical eclecticism or a trial-and-error clinical approach and a preoccupation with "engineering" questions, such as which treatment, by whom, is most effective with what clients, with what specific problems, in what situations. More important are the questions of how and why change comes about. The answers to these questions require a theory of behavior change. Meichenbaum's theory attempts to provide a beginning toward such a theory.

SUMMARY AND EVALUATION

Meichenbaum's cognitive-behavior modification is not simply behavior therapy with the addition of some cognitive techniques, as are the methods of a number of behavior therapists who have recognized the usefulness of cognitive techniques (for example, Goldfried and Davison, and O'Leary and Wilson).[43] It is much more cognitive than behavioristic. Behavior therapy techniques include many cognitive elements. The "learning theory" on which behavior therapy is based is not adequate to account for the cognitive aspect of behavior therapy.

Meichenbaum has attempted to develop a theory- and research-based cognitive therapy. It recognizes the importance of what people say to themselves in determining their behavior. Thus the focus of therapy is on changing the things clients say to themselves, implicitly if not explicitly, which lead to ineffective behavior and emotional disturbance. Therapy becomes training in modifying clients' self-instructions so that clients can cope with the problem situations they face. In addition to their independent use, these training methods can be incorporated into the standard behavior therapy techniques to increase the effectiveness of these techniques. They can also be incorporated into cognitive-restructuring techniques.

Both the theory and practice are incomplete, as Meichenbaum recognizes. Nevertheless, it is a promising beginning. His claim that the theory applies to all behavior change in any therapeutic procedure[44] may be true, in the sense that self-instruction is *part* of what goes on in all successful therapy. Other theories emphasize the importance of the client's self-exploration, which includes or involves an internal dialogue. The question arises as to the best way to facilitate this process in the client. Is it necessary or more efficient to teach the client directly? Is didactic instruction necessary for or the most effective way to achieve client learning? Is the client's failure to think logically or rationally always because of a lack of understanding of the nature of reasoning, logic, or problem solving? Is the most effective way to change the client's self-statements through teaching? Teaching does not always lead to learning, and learning occurs without teaching. Learning by means of self-exploration and self-discovery may be more effective and more persistent than learning as a result of being taught, although it may not always be as rapid. If the client lacks necessary information or skills, certainly the client should acquire them; if this is all that is lacking, perhaps the client does not need therapy, and if this is not all that is lacking, perhaps the client can acquire them from persons other than the therapist.

The issue is, then, is therapy teaching, even though it involves learning? Even if cognitive therapy is defined as teaching, is teaching a purely cognitive process?

Meichenbaum does not explore the nature and conditions of learning. He does appear to recognize that not all clients require explicit teaching of coping responses,[45] but his theory and practice appear to assume that all clients do. Affective factors are not dealt with adequately; his only explicit reference to affect is when he notes that in the process of giving himself or herself new self-instructions, the client must engage in meaningful and not simply mechanical self-instructions; nor does he consider the relationship between client and therapist in other than its cognitive, teaching aspect. Ellis, in his review, takes Meichenbaum to task for not having adequately indicated "how cognitive, emotive, and behavioral approaches to psychotherapy significantly interact and have profound reciprocal effects on each other."[46] It might be noted, however, that it was not Meichenbaum's purpose to attempt this kind of integration.

Nevertheless, Meichenbaum has made a contribution. He has given theoretical and research support for the importance of internal dialogue in behavior and behavior change. He has gone beyond behavior therapy, not simply by adding a few cognitive techniques to behavior therapy but by providing a broader theory that can encompass behavior therapy and make it possible for those who have clung to a narrow behavior therapy because of its "learning theory" and research base to abandon it for a broader theory that also has a research base.

REFERENCES

1. Meichenbaum, D. *Cognitive-behavior modification.* Morristown, N.J.: General Learning Press, 1974. (A unit in University Programs Modular Studies series.)
2. Meichenbaum, D. *Stress inoculation training.* Elmsford, N.Y.: Pergamon, 1985.
3. Meichenbaum, D. *Cognitive-behavior modification: An integrative approach.* New York: Plenum, 1977.
4. Gilbert, W. M. Discussion. In J. W. Whiteley (Ed.), *Research in counseling.* Columbus, Ohio: Merrill, 1968. Pp. 30–35.
5. Meichenbaum, *Cognitive-behavior modification: An integrative approach,* p. 30.
6. Ibid., p. 71.
7. Ibid., p. 80.
8. Ibid., p. 82.
9. Farber, I. E. The things people say to themselves. *American Psychologist,* 1963, *18,* 185–197.
10. Meichenbaum, *Cognitive-behavior modification: An integrative approach,* 202.
11. Gagné, R. Problem solving. In A. Melton (Ed.), *Categories of human learning.* New York: Academic Press, 1964.
12. McKinney, J. A. developmental study of the effects of hypothesis verbalizations and memory load on concept attainment. Unpublished manuscript, University of North Carolina, Chapel Hill, 1973.
13. Meichenbaum, *Cognitive-behavior modification: An integrative approach,* 202.
14. Ibid., pp. 206–207.
15. Ibid., pp. 207–208.
16. Ibid., pp. 210–211.
17. Ibid., pp. 212–213.
18. Neisser, U. Cultural and cognitive discontinuity. In J. E. Gladwin & W. Sturtevant (Eds.), *Anthropology and human behavior.* Washington, D.C.: Anthropological Society of Washington, 1962.
19. Meichenbaum, *Cognitive-behavior modification: An integrative approach,* pp. 218–219.
20. Ibid., p. 222.
21. Ibid., p. 224.
22. Ibid., p. 225.
23. Ibid., pp. 236, 237.
24. Ibid., p. 242.
25. Ibid., p. 246.
26. Ibid., p. 249.
27. Peterson, D. *The clinical study of social behavior.* Englewood Cliffs, N.J.: Prentice-Hall, 1968.
28. Meichenbaum, *Cognitive-behavior modification: An integrative approach,* p. 252.
29. Ibid., p. 108.
30. Ibid., p. 117.
31. Murray, E. J., & Jacobson, L. I. The nature of learning in traditional and behavioral psychotherapy. In A. E. Bergin & S. L. Garfield (Eds.), *Handbook of psychotherapy and behavior change: An empirical analysis.* New York: Wiley, 1971. Pp. 709–747.
32. Meichenbaum, *Cognitive-behavior modification: An integrative approach,* p. 124.

33. Bandura, A. *Principles of behavior modification.* New York: Holt, Rinehart and Winston, 1969.

34. Meichenbaum, *Cognitive-behavior modification: An integrative approach,* pp. 137–138.

35. Ibid., p. 141.

36. Ibid., p. 151.

37. Ibid., p. 159.

38. Ibid., p. 181.

39. Ibid., p. 182.

40. Ibid., p. 191.

41. Beck, A. T. *Cognitive therapy and the emotional disorders.* New York: International Universities Press, 1976.

42. D'Zurilla, T., & Goldfried, M. R. Problem solving and behavior modification. *Journal of Abnormal Psychology,* 1971, *78,* 107–126; Goldfried, M. R., & Davison, G. C. *Clinical behavior therapy.* New York: Holt, Rinehart and Winston, 1976.

43. O'Leary, K. D., & Wilson, G. T. *Behavior therapy: Application and outcome.* Englewood Cliffs, N.J.: Prentice-Hall, 1975. Ellis, however, in his review of Meichenbaum's book, contends that the position "originates more from a behavioristic than from a cognitive-philosophic framework." Ellis, A. Review of *Cognitive-behavior modification: An integrative approach* by D. Meichenbaum. *Contemporary Psychology,* 1978, *23,* 736–737.

44. Meichenbaum, *Cognitive-behavior modification: An integrative approach,* p. 261.

45. Ibid., p. 219.

46. Ellis, Review of *Cognitive-behavior modification: An integrative approach.*

three

PSYCHOANALYTIC APPROACHES

Psychoanalysis and its offshoots, the various psychoanalytic and neoanalytic theories, have long been considered *the* psychodynamic or depth psychotherapies. With the advent of client-centered therapy in the 1940s and 1950s and of behavior therapy in the 1960s, the psychoanalytic therapies declined. A recent review of a book on psychoanalysis was entitled "Is Psychoanalysis Moribund?"[1]

But psychoanalytic therapy, if not orthodox psychoanalysis (that is, strict adherence to Freud and the use of the couch in daily sessions) is far from dead. Indeed, during the past decade, there has been a great revival of interest, with the publication of a flood of books on psychoanalysis as well as the foundation, in 1982, of a publishing house specifically for books and journals in this areas (The Analytic Press), and the establishment, in 1983, of a journal to review material on psychoanalysis (*Review of Psychoanalytic Books,* International Universities Press). The Division of Psychoanalysis became the thirty-ninth division of the American Psychological Association in 1980.

Psychoanalytic psychotherapy is not a single, unified approach. There were early dissenters from Freud's theories (summarized by Freud in his later publications[2]): Adler,[3] Fromm,[4] Horney,[5] Jung,[6] Rank,[7] and Sullivan.[8] More recently, psychoanalytically trained and oriented writers— Hartmann,[9] Erikson,[10] Rapaport,[11] and Kohut[12]— have recognized the importance of the ego, or the self, in human development and its disorders.

To include all these theorists is manifestly impossible without extending this work to two volumes. There can be no question that students should be familiar with Freudian psychoanalysis and its major variants. Earlier editions of this book included none of them, since synopses were available.[13] They are still available, although not easily accessible. The thumbnail sketches in many textbooks are inadequate. Rather than providing a chapter of such thumbnail sketches, it was decided to select one approach to present in detail. It seemed clear that if only one could be included, it should be Freud's original contribution, since all the others derive from and depend on it. The task of summarizing Freud's voluminous writings, with changes over time, is formidable. Fortunately, much of the work already had been done by a colleague in England, Dr. Richard Nelson-Jones, in a chapter in his book *The Theory and Practice of Counselling Psychology* (London: Holt, Rinehart and Winston, 1982). This summary is an extensive expansion and revision of Nelson-Jones's chapter, with permission of the publisher.

Psychoanalysis and standard psychoanalytic therapy is long-term therapy. During the 1940s, psychoanalysts at the Chicago Institute for Psychoanalysis questioned whether therapy based on psychoanalytic principles had to be conducted on a daily basis for months or years. They adapted the practice of psychoanalysis to a more active, controlled approach that required less time and thus, presumably, was more efficient than traditional psychoanalysis. It is interesting that it was in the United States, with its emphasis on speed and efficiency, that brief psychoanalytic therapy, as well as other forms of brief psychotherapy, developed.

As a method of therapy, psychoanalysis and, even more so, some of its variants —particularly psychoanalytically oriented therapy—have become quite rational in their approach. This is paradoxical because it was with psychoanalysis that the study of the role of feelings and emotions in psychological experience originated as a reaction against the rationalism and intellectual emphasis of nineteenth-century psychology and psychiatry. Thompson notes that one of the dissatisfactions of Rank and Ferenczi with psychoanalysis in the 1920s was that it had become too much of an intellectual process.[14] Although Rank and others moved away from this rationality, it has persisted. Hobbs, reviewing Sullivan's *The Psychiatric Interview,* notes that while psychoanalysis "helped the world see the forces of unreason operating in all of us . . . it is in the psychoanalytic prescription for this state of affairs that the great paradox occurs: the cure for unreason is reason; the antidote for hurtful experience is rationality."[15] Hobbs sees Sullivan as stressing a person's unreason, with the therapist unraveling the truth against the opposition of the client. Then the therapist presents his or her findings to the client and prescribes a reasonable course of action. Alexander's psychoanalytic therapy, although rational in its general approach, emphasizes "corrective emotional experience" rather than intellectual insight.

It should be noted that what is at issue is not rational behavior as the goal of counseling or psychotherapy, but the use of reason as the method for meeting and resolving emotional situations and problems. In using reason, psychoanalysis and psychoanalytically oriented approaches differ relatively little from other approaches, except perhaps in the greater complexity of the reasoning, or interpretation, that is utilized.

Students who are interested in more extensive accounts of the various psychoanalytic approaches may begin with the books and articles cited in the references.

REFERENCES

1. Meltzer, J. D. Is psychoanalysis moribund? (Review of *An introduction to contemporary psychoanalysis* by A. E. Bernstein & G. M. Warner). *Contemporary Psychology,* 1982, *27,* 991–992.

2. Freud, S. *Introductory lectures on psychoanalysis.* London: Allen & Unwin, 1929; Freud, S. *New introductory lectures on psychoanalysis.* New York: Norton, 1933; Freud, S. *A general introduction to psychoanalysis.* New York: Liveright, 1935.

3. Adler, A. *The neurotic constitution.* New York: Moffatt, 1917; Adler, A. *The practice and theory of individual psychology.* New York: Harcourt Brace Jovanovich, 1927; Adler, A. *Understanding human nature.* New York: Greenberg, 1927; Ansbacher, H. L., & Ansbacher, R. R. *The individual psychology of Alfred Adler.* New York: Basic Books, 1956; Dreikurs, R. *Fundamentals of Adlerian psychology.* New York: Greenberg, 1950; Dreikurs, R. *Adlerian family counseling: A method for counseling centers.* Eugene: University of Oregon Press, 1959.

4. Fromm, E. *Escape from freedom.* New York: Holt, Rinehart and Winston, 1941; Fromm, E. *Man for himself.* New York: Holt, Rinehart and Winston, 1947; Fromm, E. *The sane society.* New York: Holt, Rinehart and Winston, 1955.

5. Horney, K. *The neurotic personality of our time.* New York: Norton, 1937; Horney, K. *New ways in psychoanalysis.* New York: Norton, 1939; Horney, K. *Our inner conflicts.* New York: Norton, 1945; Horney, K. *Neurosis and human growth.* New York: Norton, 1950.

6. Jung, C. G. *Collected works.* Vol. 16: *The practice of psychotherapy.* New York: Pantheon Books, 1954; Dry, A. M. *The psychology of Jung: A critical interpretation.* New York: Wiley, 1961.

7. Rank, O. *Will therapy and truth and reality.* New York: Knopf, 1947.

8. Sullivan, H. S. *Conceptions of modern psychiatry.* Washington, D.C., William Alanson White Psychiatric Foundation, 1947; Sullivan, H. S. *The interpersonal theory of psychiatry.* New York: Norton, 1953; Sullivan, H. S. *The psychiatric interview.* New York: Norton, 1954.

9. Hartmann, K. *Ego psychology and the problem of adaptation.* New York: International Universities Press, 1958. (Originally published, 1939.)

10. Erikson, E. H. *Childhood and society.* New York: Norton, 1950.

11. Rapaport, D. A historical survey of psychoanalytic ego psychology. *Psychological Issues.* New York: International Universities Press, 1959. (Monograph No. 1)

12. Kohut, H. *The analysis of the self.* New York: International Universities Press, 1971.

13. Ford, D. H., & Urban, H. B. *Systems of psychotherapy.* New York: Wiley, 1963; Harper, R. A. *Psychoanalysis and psychotherapy: 36 systems.* Englewood Cliffs, N.J.: Prentice-Hall, 1959; Munroe, R. *Schools of psychoanalytic thought.* New York: Holt, Rinehart and Winston, 1955; Stein, M. I. (Ed.). *Contemporary psychotherapies.* New York: Free Press, 1961; Thompson, C. *Psychoanalysis: Evolution and development.* New York: Hermitage, 1950. (Paperback published by Grove Press, 1957)

14. Thompson, *Psychoanalysis,* p. 14.

15. Hobbs, N. Curing unreason by reason. (Review of *The psychiatric interview* by H. S. Sullivan). *Contemporary Psychology,* 1956, *1,* 44–45.

chapter 9

Psychoanalysis: Freud

Sigmund Freud (1856–1939) was born in Freiberg, Moravia, a small town in what is now Czechoslovakia. He was the eldest of eight children (five girls, three boys) of his father's second wife. His father, a wool merchant, moved his family to Vienna when Freud was 4. At age 9, he entered Sperl Gymnasium (high school) where he was at the top of his class, graduating with distinction at 17.

His interests were not then in medicine, but he wrote that "it was hearing Goethe's beautiful essay on nature read aloud by Professor Carl Brühl just before I left school that decided me to become a medical student."[1] He enrolled in medicine at the University of Vienna in 1873. From 1876 to 1882, he worked in Ernst Brücke's physiological laboratory, focusing on the histology of nerve cells. In 1881, he passed the final examinations with a grade of "excellent" and received his M.D. degree.

In 1882, Freud began the practice of medicine. But his research interests led him to enter the General Hospital of Vienna, where he engaged in research at the Institute of Cerebral Anatomy. He wanted to study nervous diseases, but found that he had to become his own teacher. In October 1885, he went to Paris on a traveling fellowship and stayed until February 1886, studying at the Sâlpetrière (a hospital for nervous diseases) under Charcot. It was here that he became interested in hysteria, which Charcot was investigating.

On his return to Vienna, Freud married Martha Bernays and set up a private practice as a specialist in nervous diseases. The youngest of his six children was Anna, who followed her father's calling, becoming a well-known child analyst. His "therapeutic arsenal contained only two weapons, electrotherapy and hypnotism."[2] He soon dropped electrotherapy (not to be confused with electroshock) and began to realize the limitations of hypnosis.

In the early 1880s, Freud had developed a close relationship with Josef Breuer, a prominent Viennese physician who, between 1880 and 1882, had successfully treated a young girl with hysterical symptoms by hypnotizing her deeply and encouraging her to verbalize her memories of early emotional situations. Freud began using the method with his patients in the late 1880s, being aware "of the possibility that there could be powerful mental processes which nevertheless remain hidden from the consciousness of man."[3] In 1893, Freud and Breuer wrote a paper on the cathartic method (unrestrained and undirected emotional outpouring), and two years later, they published *Studies on Hysteria* (1895).[4]

During the 1890s, Freud suffered from neurotic symptoms, including depression, apathy, and anxiety attacks. Cocaine appeared to calm the agitation and ease the depression; Freud did research on cocaine. Yet it was during this period that he did his most original work. He developed a close friendship with Wilhelm Fliess, a nose and throat specialist, who regarded sexual problems as central in his own work and was the only physician who encouraged Freud in his exposition of his theories of psychosexual development.

Freud abandoned both hypnosis and the technique of placing his hands on the patient's head and exerting pressure, which he sometimes used with hypnosis, but continued the practice of sitting behind the patient, who lay on a sofa. (It appears that this position was not chosen for theoretical or empirical reasons, but because Freud was uncomfortable under the gaze of his patients, whose appointments often totaled up to 12 hours a day.) Freud undertook his self-analysis, which provided material for *The Interpretation of Dreams* (1900),[5] his first major book, and revealed his love for his mother and jealousy of his father, representing a condition that he considered universal and that he termed the Oedipus complex. Another major work, *Three Contributions to the Theory of Sex* (1905),[6] traces the development of sexuality from its earliest childhood beginnings.

Neuroses developed by soldiers who had fought in the First World War raised questions about Freud's theories of the relation of psychosexual development and neurosis. He began to develop a theory of the total personality, including the idea that aggression as well as sex could be an important repressed impulse. In the 1920s, he turned to an attempt to understand society, but from a biological basis that neglected cultural influences. "He became increasingly pessimistic, and his final paper on therapy, "Analysis Terminable and Interminable" (published in 1937[7]), brought his biological thinking to its logical dead end."[8]

Three months after the Nazis overran Austria in 1938, Freud, a Jew, left Vienna and went to London. Freud habitually smoked 20 cigars a day and, in 1923, he had learned that he had cancer of the jaw. For the rest of his life, he lived in pain, having 33 operations on his jaw. He died in London on September 23, 1939.

Toward the end of his life, Freud evaluated his work: "Looking back, then, over the patchwork of my life's labours, I can say that I have made many beginnings and thrown out many suggestions. Something will come of them in the future, though I cannot myself tell whether it will be much or little. I can, however express a hope that I have opened up a pathway for an important advance in our knowledge."[9]

BACKGROUND AND DEVELOPMENT

Freud spent more than 40 years developing his theory of personality. His writings are voluminous, and it is not possible to summarize all the various and changing aspects of his theory.

Thompson divides the years from 1895 to 1939 into four periods.[10] The first period, from about 1895 to 1900, were the years of Freud's collaboration with Breuer. It saw the beginnings of his theories of unconscious motivation, repression, resistance, transference, anxiety, and the etiology of the neuroses, which derived from his work with patients using hypnosis and free association or catharsis. These methods formed the basis of psychoanalysis. Thompson notes, "In my opinion, this was the period of Freud's greatest creativeness. No theories he later developed can compare with the brilliance of the early discoveries."[11]

The second period, from 1900 to about 1910, saw the development of Freud's sexual theory from the idea that neurosis is caused by sexual traumas, to the concept that sexual development is all important in etiology—the first instinct theory, or libido theory. Sex (procreation or preservation of the species) and self-preservation are the two great drives. Breuer broke with Freud at the beginning of the period.

The third period, from 1910 to the early 1920s, began with Adler's attack on Freud's sexual theory and with Jung's defection in 1913. The recognition of the importance of aggression as a drive laid the foundation for a second theory of instincts, which finally was presented in the early 1920s. Aggression and the drive toward repetition are related to Thanatos, the death instinct, while the libido and self-preservation are parts of Eros, the life instinct. This period also saw the emergence of a theory about the total personality (the id, ego, and superego). Little change in the method of therapy occurred.

The fourth period, from the mid-1920s to 1939, were the years of Freud's focusing on methods of therapy and extending the therapy. No new methods were developed; however. Freud's interests turned from therapy to society, and in his writings, he expounded his theories rather than developing new theories. Changes in the methods of therapy were introduced, however, by Freud's followers: Rank, Ferenczi, Reich, Sullivan, Horney, and Fromm, the last three of whom incorporated social and cultural elements into the theory and practice of psychoanalysis.

PHILOSOPHY AND CONCEPTS

Freud's orientation was biological, a natural result of his medical training and of the period in which he began his work. His theories of the instincts reflect this biological focus.

The Instincts

Psychic energy is no different from physical energy. Each may be transformed into the other. Instincts constitute psychic energy, representing the transformation of physical energy into psychic energy. The binding of the energy in an action or image to satisfy an instinct constitutes an *object-cathexis.* Instincts drive and direct behavior, the goal of which is the satisfaction of needs derived from the instincts. Needs create tension, and behavior is directed toward reduction of the tension. Tension is unpleasant; its reduction is pleasurable. This concept of needs is the *pleasure principle,* the attempt to keep excitation or tension as low as possible.

> In the theory of psychoanalysis we have no hesitation in assuming that the course taken by mental events is automatically regulated by the pleasure principle. We believe, that is to say, that the course of those events is invariably set in motion by an unpleasurable tension, and that it takes a direction such that its final outcome coincides with a lowering of that tension—that is with an avoidance of unpleasure or a production of pleasure.[12]

The dominance of the pleasure principle is qualified, since other forces oppose it, and the final outcome does not always fulfill the tendency toward pleasure.

There are many instincts, but they are grouped into two basic ones: *Eros* and *Thanatos.* Eros is the life instinct—the preservation of the self and of the species, ego love and object love. Its energy is called *libido.* The erotic instincts "seek to combine more and more living substance into even greater unities," while the death instincts "oppose this effort and lead what is living back to an inorganic state."[13] Thanatos is the death and destructive instinct; it includes aggression and the *repetition compulsion,* which is the automatic repetition of earlier situations in order to master or control them and which may be stronger than the pleasure principle. The death instinct is the compulsion to repeat the earlier inorganic state before living things originated. "The goal of all life is death."[14] Aggression is primarily directed toward the self; it is turned outward toward others in self-preservation.

Instincts, the source of energy in behavior, constitute the dynamics of personality. The basic instincts may either work together or oppose each other. The evolution of civilization represents the struggle between Eros and Thanatos in the human species. The question is whether Eros will assert itself. "But who can foresee with what success and what results?"[15]

The Unconscious and Consciousness

Part of a person's life goes on outside awareness. The unconscious influences experience and behavior and includes some material or experiences that are inadmissible to consciousness and some that can relatively easily become conscious. The inadmissible material has been dissociated from conscious thinking, either by never having been admitted to consciousness or by having been repressed from consciousness. The admissible material is in a part of the unconscious called the *preconscious.* Material may remain in the preconscious without causing problems and usually becomes conscious without therapy. The preconscious may be viewed as a screen between the conscious and the unconscious. Unconscious material may be modified and appear in consciousness in a distorted form, as in dreams.

Consciousness has the function of a sense organ for the perception of psychic qualities. Unlike the two kinds of the unconscious, consciousness has no memory, and a state of consciousness is very transitory. Material becomes conscious, or flows into the consciousness sense organ, from two directions: the external world and inner excitations. Speech enables such internal events as sequences of ideas and intellectual processes to become conscious.[16]

The unconscious is a figure of speech and cannot be located in any bodily area. Yet "the word *unconscious* has more and more been made to mean a mental province rather than a quality which mental things have."[17]

The Structure of the Personality

The personality consists of three major systems: the id, the ego, and the superego. Although each has its own functions, operating principles, dynamisms, and mechanisms, the three interact closely. Behavior is usually the result of an interaction among the systems.

The Id

The *id* is the original system, from which the ego and the superego become differentiated. It consists of everything that is inherited and constitutional, including the instincts, which provide the energy for the operation of the other two systems. It strives to bring about the satisfaction of instinctual needs on the basis of the pleasure principle. The id is the "true psychic reality," since it represents the inner world of experience and has no knowledge of objective reality. Its psychic processes are *primary processes* —undirected attempts at immediate satisfaction—which provide the individual with mental images of the objects required for the satisfactions of needs or for *wish fulfillment.* The hallucinations and visions of the psychotic are examples of primary processes. The id is "a chaos, a cauldron full of seething excitement," which "knows no values, no good and evil, no morality."[18] It is not governed by logic; it contains contradictory yet coexistent impulses. It is the individual's primary subjective reality at the unconscious level. The id is the seat of the unconscious.

The Ego

The *ego* is a portion of the id that has undergone a modification through the influence of the external world. It develops from the id because of the organism's need to cope with reality for the satisfaction of its instinctual requirements. Although it seeks pleasure and the avoidance of unpleasure, the ego is under the influence of the *reality principle,* which is the delay of immediate gratification in recognition of social requirements. It operates by means of *secondary processes*—perception, problem solving, and repression—that is, realistic, logical thinking and *reality testing.*

The ego is the executive of the personality, mediating and reconciling the demands of the id, the superego, and the outside world. With the aid of the superego, the ego transforms strong id demands into weaker ones that are acceptable to the ego by forming sublimations and reaction formations from them. The ego, however, derives its power from the id, cannot exist apart from or independent of the id, and functions to serve the id, not to frustrate it.

Most of the ego is unconscious most of the time; much of it is preconscious, so that it easily can be brought into consciousness.

The Superego

The *superego* is a portion of the ego that has incorporated standards from society, mainly through the influence of the parents in early childhood. The superego also includes later, nonparental influences and the person's own ideals. *Conscience* is one subsystem of the superego; the person's *ego ideal* is the other. The incorporation of parental and social standards is called *introjection.* "The superego is the representative for us of every moral restriction, the advocate of a striving for perfection—it is, in short, as much as we have been able to grasp psychologically of what is described as the higher side of human life."[19]

The superego works to inhibit the id's impulses, especially those that are sexual or aggressive; to persuade the ego to substitute moralistic for realistic goals; and to strive for perfection. It opposes both the id and the ego. It is nonrational, however, attempting to block rather than simply to control the instincts. The primary struggle of human beings is with their instincts. Much of the superego is unconscious.

The Development of Personality

The child progresses through a series of stages of development, which are sexual. The term *sexual* refers to a broad range of behaviors, including both affectionate impulses, often called love, and pleasure from the erogenous zones of the body. The sexual impulse is the sexual aspect of the libido. The term *genital* refers to sexual behavior whose aim is reproduction. Sexual life starts soon after birth; sexual behavior does not suddenly emerge at puberty. There are four stages of sexual or personality development. The first three are pregenital, and the fourth is genital. Between the pregenital and genital stages is the latency period.

Persons of each sex have elements of the opposite sex, so that all individuals are bisexual; a degree of homosexuality thus is congenital, with the final determination of sexual behavior being the result of the intensity of constitutional predisposition and of life experiences and restrictions in one or the other direction. Both the female and the male develop out of a child with a bisexual inclination.

The Oral Stage

The infant's first source of pleasure is oral, deriving from the mouth. The oral stage begins with the incorporation of food by sucking. Fixation at the sucking phase results in such traits as passivity, trust, optimism, and interest in the acquisition of knowledge or possessions—the oral-receptive character. The biting and chewing phase later develops. Fixation at the biting phase leads to such traits as aggressiveness, exploitative behavior, argumentativeness, and sarcasm—the oral-sadistic character.

The Anal Stage

During the second year, cathexes (instinctual energies seeking discharge) and counter-cathexes (energies blocking such discharge) develop around the eliminative functions, which lead to the child's first experiences with external regulation of an instinctual impulse, involving the postponement of the pleasure from relieving anal tensions. Strict toilet training may lead to the development of such traits as obstinacy and stinginess —the retentive character. Or the child may vent rage by inappropriate expulsion, which may lead to such traits as cruelty, hostility, and destructiveness. If expulsion is praised and given high importance by the mother, the ground may be laid for productivity and creativity in later life.

The Phallic Stage

During the phallic stage develop the sexual and aggressive feelings related to the genital organs, including masturbation. The *Oedipus complex* or *Electra complex* appears: the boy develops an object cathexis for his mother and jealousy and hostility toward his father, while the opposite occurs in the girl. The boy develops a fear of castration by his father, and the girl believes that she has been castrated and blames her mother. The boy represses his desire for his mother and hostility toward his father, with whom he identifies; the superego reaches its final development. The girl transfers her early love for her mother to her father although her love is tinged with envy because he has what she lacks. Her Electra complex is not repressed but is modified by reality and weakens with time.

The Oedipus situation is often more complex because of the child's bisexual inclination. The child's feelings for the parent of the same sex may be ambivalent. "In both sexes the relative strength of the masculine and feminine sexual dispositions is what determines whether the outcome of the Oedipus situation shall be an identification with the father or with the mother."[20]

It is in the phallic stage that the sexuality of early childhood reaches its greatest intensity and that male and female development become differentiated.

The Latency Period

During the latency period, from about age five or six to puberty, sexual impulses are repressed, and sexual inhibitions develop. Sublimation of sexual impulses occurs.

The Genital Stage

Puberty reactivates pregenital impulses; if these impulses are displaced and sublimated by the ego, the person passes into the mature genital stage. The genital zones are primary. The narcissm of the pregenital stages becomes channeled into object choices. The adolescent begins to love others altruistically. Sexual attraction, socialization, group activities, vocational planning, and preparation for marriage and a family develop. The person changes from a narcissistic pleasure-seeking child into a reality-oriented socialized adult.

There are no sharp divisions between one stage and the next, and the final outcome includes contributions from the earlier stages.

Personality Dynamics: Vicissitudes of the Instincts

Normal development involves a continuous clash between instinctual impulses, which seek immediate gratification, and the restraining forces of a moralistic society and the realities of a physical world.

There are four sources of tension: physiological growth processes, frustrations, conflicts, and threats. The individual is forced to learn new methods of reducing tension and responds in various ways, some normal and some abnormal. The processes by which instinctual tensions are handled include identification, displacement, sublimation, and anxiety and its defenses, involving defense mechanisms.

Identification

Identification involves incorporating features of another person into the self, including modeling one's behavior after that of another. It is the method by which energy from the id is diverted into processes of the ego. The id does not distinguish between subjective imagery and reality, but since imagery cannot satisfy a need, the individual must learn to recognize the difference between an image and perception of a real object and to match them by means of the secondary processes.

The child first identifies with the parents and, in so doing, introjects their morals and ideals. Their ideals become the child's ego ideals, and the energy for the superego is provided. Identification also may be a regressive substitute for a libidinous object tie, by means of introjection, so that the ego assumes the characteristics of the object.

Displacement

Displacement is the transfer of psychic energy, or cathexis, from an original but inaccessible object choice of an instinct to another but similar object choice. If this second choice is blocked, displacement to another choice occurs—and so on until an object is found that can reduce the tension. For example, anger toward a person as an object may displaced to a door, a wall, or a cat, which is struck instead of the person. A series of displacements constitutes much of personality development. The source and aim of the instinct remain stable, while its object varies. Substitute objects are not as satisfying or as tension reducing as is the original object; each successive object is less satisfying. As a result, over a sequence of displacements there accumulates a pool of undischarged tension, which becomes a permanent motivation for behavior. New and better ways of reducing tension are sought, leading to variability and diversity in behavior. The complex personality is made possible by displacement.

Sublimation

Sublimation is a form of displacement in which instinctual sexual impulses are diverted to socially more acceptable and creative channels. Thus Leonardo da Vinci's drive to paint Madonnas was a sublimation of his wish for intimacy with his mother, from whom he had been separated at an early age.[21] Sublimation does not result in complete satisfaction but leaves some residual tension—a nervousness or restlessness that is the price paid by human beings for civilization.[22]

Anxiety

Anxiety is a specific state of unpleasure that is accompanied by motor discharge along definite pathways. Anxiety is the universal reaction to danger; the ego is the sole seat of anxiety. Danger may be actual or may be anticipated or perceived as impending. There are three kinds of anxiety.

1. *Realistic anxiety* results from real dangers in the external world.
2. *Moral anxiety* is fear of the conscience and results from conflict with the superego.
3. *Neurotic anxiety* is the fear that the id's instinctual impulses will get out of control. It involves fear of the punishment that will ensue.

Anxiety is a warning of danger, informing the ego that something must be done. If anxiety cannot be avoided or dealt with effectively, it is traumatic. When the ego cannot deal with anxiety by rational methods, it resorts to unrealistic methods—the defense mechanisms. Repression, for example, is a result of anxiety, not the reverse (as Freud early thought).

Defense Mechanisms

When the ego observes that an emerging instinctual demand may place it in danger, it utilizes defense mechanisms to cope with the sources of anxiety, selecting some among the several available, which then become fixated in the ego. The development of defense mechanisms begins with the child's struggle against its sexuality during the first five years of life. Defense mechanisms deny, falsify, or distort reality. They operate unconsciously and may impede realistic behavior long after they have outlived their usefulness. There are numerous defense mechanisms, including repression, regression, reaction formation, projection, introjection, isolation, undoing, turning against the self, reversal, denial, rationalization, compromise, and sublimation. Only the more common and most important ones are considered here.

Repression

There are two kinds of repression. The first consists of making an experience unconscious; that is, material in the preconscious that is inadmissible to consciousness is pushed back into the unconscious. The second consists of forbidding material to enter the preconscious; that is, it remains in the unconscious. Painful memories are thus shut off from consciousness. Sometimes only part of an experience may be repressed; memory of it may remain in consciousness, but feelings are not attached to it. Repressed experiences seek expression in dreams and slips of the tongue. Repressions occur before the age of six. Once formed, they are difficult to overcome.

> The process of repression is not to be regarded as something which takes place once and for all, the results of which are permanent, as when one living thing has been killed and from that time on is dead; on the contrary, repression demands a constant expenditure of energy, and if this were discontinued the success of the repression would be jeopardized, so that a fresh act of repression would be necessary.[23]

Fixation

Fixations arise when for traumatic or constitutional reasons, one phase in the course of development is emphasized, with a strong binding of libido to that phase and with some libido remaining at that phase. Later, when the forward movement of the libido meets a certain degree of frustration, it reverts to the point of fixation. Fixation at the oral or the anal stages leads to the development of the oral character or the anal character. Fixation may involve arrested development, in which the individual is fixated at an immature level, or it may involve manifestation of habits related to a particular defense mechanism, which may be represented in the character—for example, the oral character or the anal character.

Regression

Regression is the movement back to the point of fixation. The individual does not necessarily revert completely to the earlier phase; rather, the personality develops infantilisms and manifests childish conduct when frustrated. When a behavior is blocked or frustrated, the individual substitutes another behavior, one that was strongly established at an earlier phase of development.

Reaction Formation

Reaction formation is the defense against an anxiety-producing impulse by replacing it with its opposite. Compared with a natural expression of behavior, it is showy, compulsive, and extreme. Reaction formation is an example—some overzealous reformers may actually be warding off the anxiety resulting from an attraction to the behavior against which they are crusading. Reaction formation and sublimation are sources of various types of character (anal, oral, and their variants).

Projection

In projection, the ego deals with the threat of an unacceptable instinctual impulse by externalizing it. Thus the individual, instead of being aware of libidinous and aggressive impulses, may be sensitive to and aware of such characteristics in others and even attribute them incorrectly to others. Anxiety is reduced by substituting a lesser, external danger for the inner one, and impulses can be expressed under the cover of defending oneself against others.

Defense mechanisms are utilized by normal persons when faced with threats and frustrations. They do not in themselves necessarily constitute abnormal behavior or neurosis.

The Neuroses

Biological, phylogenetic, and psychological factors contribute to neurosis. The human animal is born biologically unfinished and undergoes a long period of helplessness and dependence. This helplessness creates the initial situation of danger and the consequent fear of object loss, which in turn creates the human's need to be loved, which never disappears.

The phylogenetic factor arises from the interruption in human sexual development by the latency period, whereas sexual maturation in related animals proceeds uninterrupted. According to Freud, following the Lamarckian view of evolution, this must be the result of a momentous occurrence in the history of the human species; its pathogenic importance is evident in the fact that most of the demands of infantile sexuality are regarded by the ego as dangers to be guarded against. There is also the danger that the sexual impulses of puberty will follow their infantile prototypes into repression.

The psychological factor involves three elements, which comprise the pathogenic neurotic conflict. The first is the frustration of libidinous impulses by the ego, resulting in the damming up of the sexual instinct. Repressions occur in infancy and in early childhood, when the ego is still underdeveloped and relatively weak in relation to the sexual impulses. "We recognize the essential precondition of the neuroses in this lagging of ego development behind libidinal development."[24] Repression takes place in reaction to anxiety; the ego anticipates that satisfaction of the emerging sexual drive will lead to danger and represses the dangerous impulse. By the act of repression, however, the ego renounces a part of its organization, and the repressed impulse remains inaccessible to its influence.

The second psychological element in the neurotic conflict is the possible transformation of the frustrated, although not quiescent, sexual impulses into neurotic symptoms, which are the substitute satisfactions for the frustrated sexual instincts. Repression does not always result in symptom formation, however. In the successful resolution of the Oedipus complex, the repressed impulses may be destroyed, with their libidious energy being transferred to other uses.

The third psychological element is the potential inadequacy of repression with the reawakening and intensification of the sexual instincts at menarche and puberty, following its effectiveness during childhood and the latency period. The individual then experiences an intense neurotic conflict. Without assistance in undoing the repression, the ego will have little or no influence over the transformed instincts of the repressed id. There may also be an alliance of the id with the superego against the ego.

A comparison of normal and neurotic development is given in the story of the caretaker's and the landlord's daughters.[25] When they were young, the two girls played games with sexual elements, including stimulating each other's genitals. These experiences awakened sexual impulses that later found expression in masturbation. The caretaker's daughter regarded this sexual activity as natural and harmless, and, unscarred by it, she eventually took a lover and became a mother. The landlord's daughter, however, while still young and as a result of education, became an intelligent, high-minded young woman who renounced her sexuality and whose subsequent neurosis precluded her from marrying. While consciously unaware of her sexual impulses, she was unconsciously still fixated on her early experiences. Because of the higher moral and intellectual development of her ego, she came into conflict with the demands of her sexuality.

Neuroses originate in childhood (up to the age of six), although the symptoms may not appear until much later, when precipitated by mainly or particularly sexual stress or crisis. The stressful situation corresponds to an early repressed disturbance or its effect, which is reactivated and, attempting to return to consciousness, produces symptoms. "The child is father of the man."[26] The neurosis is perpetuated because the repression is unconscious, and the ego does not have access to the repressed material to resolve the conflict. As long as the repression continues, the conditions for the formation of neurotic symptoms exist through the rechanneling of frustrated libidinous impulses. Actual sexual experiences are not necessarily involved, only a disturbance in the sexual processes, "of those organic processes which determine the development and form of expression of the sexual craving."[27] Patients' reports of childhood seduction or assault are often fantasies, defenses against memories of their sexual activities when children.

In a broad sense, perpetuation of neuroses results from the unsatisfactory way in which society regulates sexual matters. Morality, or the group superego, requires a bigger sacrifice of libidinous impulses than is necessary or desirable.

Major Neuroses

Hysteria   In hysteria, repression involves pushing out of the mind experiences and their memory, rather than forbidding the rise into consciousness of material that had never been in consciousness. The repressed memory remains permanently outside of awareness unless a special event or life situation succeeds in disturbing it. Then it erupts in the form of a hysterical symptom, which represents the point or organ at which the early blocked sexual energy became bound. The intolerable ideas connected with sexual experiences are made innocuous by the transmutation into a physical form of the excitation attached to them, a process of *conversion.* The symptom expresses in a symbolic way the forgotten and repressed memory. A person may develop a hysterical paralysis while remaining otherwise "normal." Regression in hysteria is to the phallic stage of development.

Obsessive neurosis   As with all the neuroses, the origin of obsessive neuroses is in a disturbance of the early sexual life, with the immediate cause being disturbance in the "nervous economy." In obsessions, only part of the sexual experience is repressed; the memory remains in consciousness, but with no feelings attached to it. The intolerable ideas become associated with other, neutral or innocuous ideas; the obsession acts as a surrogate for the unbearable sexual ideas, taking their place in consciousness. "The detachment of the sexual idea from its affect, and the connection of the latter with another idea, are processes which occur outside consciousness—they may be presumed, but they cannot be proved by any clinical analysis."[28]

Regression in obsessive neurosis is to the anal stage of development.

Minor Neuroses

Phobias   Phobias are similar to obsessions. The internal danger of sexual impulses is projected onto an external object.

Neurasthenia   The source of neurasthenia is similar to that of hysteria, obsessive neurosis, and anxiety neuroses; it involves the present sexual life. Instead of being manifested by specific symptoms, neurasthenia consists of vague symptoms, mainly chronic fatigue and weakness.

Traumatic neuroses   Traumatic neuroses are precipitated by a traumatic situation, such as war. Repetitive dreams of the traumatic situation represent attempts to master the emotions aroused by the experience.

Perversions

Repression of perverse sexual interests results in neuroses. In the perversions, infantile sexual interests remain conscious and are gratified. Thus libido is discharged; energy is not dammed; and repression does not occur. Since there is no neurosis, there is nothing to be analyzed; homosexuality is not a neurosis and thus cannot be treated by analysis.

PSYCHOANALYSIS: THE THERAPY

Objectives

The aim of life is to be able to love and to work. The neurotic is handicapped in or prevented from a life of enjoyment and efficiency in love or work. If an individual is to live efficiently, the ego must have the energy of the libido at its disposal rather than wasting energy in warding off libidinous impulses through repression. The individual's superego must allow the expression of the libido and the efficient use of the ego. Thus the objectives of psychoanalysis are (1) the freeing of healthy impulses; (2) the strengthening of reality-based ego functioning, including widening the perceptions of the ego, so that it approves more of the id; and (3) the altering of the contents of the superego, so that it represents humane rather than punitive moral standards.

Psychoanalysis involves the process of reeducating the ego. Repressions were instituted when the ego was weak; now it is stronger and has an ally in the therapist. The pathogenic conflicts of neurotics are different from normal mental conflicts because of the weakness of the ego relative to the id and the superego. Psychoanalysis attempts to remove the cause of the neuroses rather than simply removing symptoms.

Psychoanalysis is appropriate for the treatment of the major neuroses, in which the ego has a minimum of coherence and reality orientation. This is not to be expected in the psychoses, for which psychoanalysis is not indicated.[29]

In psychoanalysis, the patient lies on a couch, with the analyst behind the head of the couch, out of the line of vision of the patient. The patient is seen six times a week for one hour a day, in order to focus the patient on his or her problems; the analysis thus essentially involves the patient's whole life. (Freud sometimes saw patients for fewer than six hours a week, and most psychoanalysts now see patients for three to five hours a week.)

Implementation

Freud never presented a systematic statement of the practice of psychoanalysis but discussed techniques in many of his writings. There are five major elements in the process of psychoanalysis.

Free Association

The basic rule of psychoanalysis is that the patient engage in free association—that is, let the mind wander and report everything that comes to mind, agreeable or disagreeable, meaningful or meaningless, logical or illogical. Censorship and self-criticism must not intervene. Although the patient's productions may appear to have no relation to one another, each association is related in a meaningful way to the preceding one, in a continuous chain of associations. There may be digressions and blockings, but the chain will reveal the patient's mental history and the present organization of the mind.

Dream Analysis

Patients spontaneously relate their dreams in the process of free association and give free associations to them. During sleep, the ego reduces its repression, and unconscious material thus becomes conscious in the form of dreams. Dreams represent wish fulfillments, being disguised fulfillment of repressed wishes. Even in sleep, the ego retains some censorship, and the latent dream thoughts are distorted in order to make the manifest dream content less threatening. Dreams represent compromises between the repressed impulses of the id and the defensive operations of the ego. The interpretation of a dream involves understanding the latent dream thoughts, which are disguised in the process of dreamwork. Elements of dreamwork involve condensing the latent thoughts into much smaller dream content, displacing the psychic intensity among the elements, and using symbolism. "The interpretation of dreams is the royal road to a knowledge of the unconscious activities of the mind."[30]

Transference

Transference is an aspect of the repetition compulsion. In therapy, it is the repetition of earlier life situations in relation to the therapist; that is, attitudes toward the parents during the Oedipus stage are transferred to the therapist. Female patients try to win the love of a male analyst, while male patients become hostile to and competitive with the analyst. The patient reacts as though he or she were a small child and the analyst were an authority figure, reliving a situation at the time of the original repression.

Therapy begins with the patient having friendly feelings, even love and affection, for the therapist—the positive transference. But as therapy proceeds, negative, hostile feelings develop—the negative transference. The transference thus represents the childhood ambivalence toward the parents, now being relived with the therapist as the parent substitute. The patient's neurosis manifests itself in the therapy situation, constituting the "transference neurosis." Therapy becomes an analysis of the transference in order to show the patient that his or her feelings are not pertinent in the relationship with the analyst but are related to an earlier time, involving a reliving of the original situation with its affect. The analysis of the transference constitutes a major part of the psychoanalysis and is an important source of insight when the patient is able to see its significance in his or her life.

The analyst does nothing either to foster or to prevent the transference; it occurs naturally. However, the analytic situation, in which the analyst is hardly a real person (being out of sight of the patient and impersonal), contributes to the attribution or projection by the patient of an authority figure to the analyst.

In *countertransference,* the analyst transfers elements from his or her past (or present) unconscious or unresolved emotional conflicts or needs to the analytic situation. It is avoided by the analyst refusing to become personally involved with the patient and by becoming aware of sources of countertransference by means of his or her own analysis.

Interpretation

Interpretation attempts to provide the patient with the meaning of material revealed in free association, reports of dreams, slips of the tongue, symptoms, and transference. It is the means of relating present behavior to its origins in childhood; repressed and unconscious material enters the preconscious and consciousness. Interpretation helps the patient gain insight into the defense mechanisms and resistances that the ego uses to cope with repressed material and to thwart the therapy process. Part of the work of interpretation is to fill in memory gaps. The analyst reveals and interprets the impulses that have become subject to repression and the objects to which they have become attached, in order to help the patient replace the repression with judgments appropriate to the present situation rather than to the childhood situation. The analyst allies with the patient's ego, thus encouraging it to take control of the hitherto repressed libidinous energy. Unconscious impulses are exposed to criticism by being traced back to their origin.

The timing of interpretations is important. Premature interpretations meet with resistance. The material preferably should be in the preconscious, and the patient should be close to the moment of insight, for interpretation to be effective.

Resistance

Resistance includes a number of behaviors on the part of the patient: omitting thoughts in free association because of shame or distress; claiming that the associations lack importance; having no thoughts to express; arriving late for appointments; forgetting appointments; losing interest in exploring problems and in the therapy; trying to win the love of the analyst; and engaging in a battle with the analyst. Acting out problems or difficulties in life rather than dealing with them in therapy also constitutes resistance, which may also involve withholding material because of distrust of the analyst, the desire to make a good impression or to gain the analyst's approval, or fear of rejection by the analyst.

The threat of anxiety represented by the analysis and by the analyst's interpretations arouses the defense system of the ego, which attempts to maintain the repression through resistance. Resistance is a conservative force that seeks to maintain the status quo. Secondary gains, or the advantages of symptoms in the patient's life, are also a source of resistance. The unconscious sense of guilt or the need for punishment emanating from the superego is also a powerful source of resistance to recovery. The struggle to overcome resistance is a major part of analysis and requires time.

EXAMPLES

There are, of course, no typescripts of Freud's work. Thus it is not clear just how he practiced therapy. He did publish a number of case histories, one of which, the Shreber case,[31] was not that of a patient of Freud. Another, Little Hans,[32] was treated by the boy's father under Freud's guidance. Four of the cases were treated by Freud: "Dora,"[33] the "Rat Man,"[34] the "Wolf Man,"[35] and a case of female homosexuality.[36] The notes in these cases were made after interviews, since Freud felt that note taking during the interview would interfere with therapy and that the therapist would remember important material and forget the trivial.

The following brief report of a patient suffering from obsessions gives the flavor of Freud's case studies.[37]

A young woman who in five years of married life had only one child complained to me of an obsessive impulse to throw herself from the window or balcony, and also the fear of stabbing her child which seized her at the sight of a sharp knife. She confessed that marital relations seldom occurred, and only with precautions against conception; but she added that this was no privation to her as she was not of a sensual nature. I ventured to tell her that at the sight of a man she had erotic ideas and that she had therefore lost confidence in herself and regarded herself as a depraved person, capable of anything. The re-translation of the obsession into the sexual was successful; in tears she confessed at once to her long-concealed misery in her marriage and later on related in addition some painful thoughts of an unchanged sexual nature, such as the often-recurring sensation of something forcing itself under her skirts.

An excerpt from the case of Dora involves the interpretation of a dream. Dora was an 18-year-old girl brought to Freud by her father. She was

in the first bloom of youth—a girl of intelligent and engaging looks. But she was a source of heavy trials for her parents. Low spirits and an alteration in her character had now become the main features of her illness. She was clearly satisfied neither with herself nor with her family; her attitude towards her father was unfriendly, and she was on very bad terms with her mother . . . [When] one day, after a short passage of words between [the father] and his daughter, she had her first attack of loss of consciousness—an event which was subsequently covered by amnesia—it was determined, in spite of her reluctance, that she should come to me for treatment.[38]

Freud had met the father and daughter about two years earlier and had recommended treatment for the girl, but her father had declined the suggestion.

The analysis lasted from October 1900, on a six-day-a-week basis, to December 31, 1900, when Dora broke off the analysis, being unable, according to Freud, to accept the truth of his insights. The case is not a sequential account of the therapy, but a reconstruction of Dora's problems based on Freud's analysis and interpretations. The treatment appears to have been quite forceful, with Freud pressing insight and interpretations on her. About two years later, she returned to Freud for treatment, but he refused to accept her because he felt that she was not sincere in her desire to change.

The Herr K. referred to was a friend of the family; his wife was the mistress of Dora's father, and on two occasions in the past, he had made sexual advances to Dora, the first time at L——.

Here is the dream as related by Dora, with Freud's analysis.[39]

"A house was on fire.* My father was standing beside my bed and woke me up. I dressed myself quickly. Mother wanted to stop and save her jewel-case; but father said: 'I refuse to let myself and my two children be burnt for the sake of your jewel-case.' We hurried downstairs, and as soon as I was outside I woke up."

*In answer to an inquiry Dora told me that there had never been a fire at their house.

As the dream was a recurrent one, I naturally asked her when she had first dreamt it. She told me she did not know. But she remembered having had the dream three nights in succession at L—— (the place on the lake where the scene with Her K. had taken place), and it had now come back again a few nights earlier, here in Vienna.† My expectations from the clearing up of the dream naturally heightened when I heard of its connection with the events at L——. But I wanted to discover first what had been the exciting cause of its recent occurrence, and I therefore asked Dora to take the dream bit by bit and tell me what occurred to her in connection with it. She had already had some training in dream interpretation from having previously analysed a few minor specimens.

"Something occurs to me," she said, "but it cannot belong to the dream, for it is quite recent, whereas I have certainly had the dream before."

"That makes no difference," I replied. "Start away! It will simply turn out to be the most recent thing that fits in with the dream."

"Very well, then. Father has been having a dispute with mother in the last few days, because she locks the dining-room door at night. My brother's room, you see, has no separate entrance, but can only be reached through the dining-room. Father does not want my brother to be locked in like that at night. He says it will not do: something might happen in the night so that it might be necessary to leave the room."

"And that made you think of the risk of fire?"

"Yes."

"Now, I should like you to pay close attention to the exact words you used. We may have to make use of them. You said that *'something might happen in the night so that it might be necessary to leave the room.'* "‡

But Dora now discovered the connecting link between the recent exciting cause of the dream and the original one, for she continued:

"When we arrived at L—— that time, father and I, he openly said he was afraid of fire. We arrived in a violent thunderstorm, and saw the small wooden house without any lightning-conductor. So his anxiety was quite natural."

What I now had to do was to establish the relation between the events at L—— and the recurrent dreams she had had there. I therefore said: "Did you have the dream during your first nights at L—— or during your last ones? In other words, before or after the scene in the wood by the lake of which we have heard so much?" (I must explain that I knew the scene had not occurred the very first day, and that she had remained at L—— for a few days after it without giving any hint of the incident.)

Her first reply was that she did not know, but after a while she added: "Yes, I think it was after the scene."

So now I knew that the dream was a reaction to that experience. But why had it occurred there three times? I continued my questions: "How long did you stop on at L—— after the scene?"

"Four days more. On the fifth day I went away with father."

"Now I am certain that the dream was an immediate effect of your experience

---

†The content of the dream makes it possible to establish that in fact it occurred *for the first time* at L——.

‡I laid stress on these words because they took me aback. They seemed to have an ambiguous ring about them. Are not certain physical exigencies referred to in the same words? Now, in a line of associations ambiguous words (or, as we may call them, "switch words") act like points at a junction. If the points are switched across from the position in which they appear to lie in the dream, then we find ourselves upon another set of rails; and along this second track run the thoughts which we are in search of and which still lie concealed behind the dream.

with Herr K. It was at L—— that you dreamed it the first time, and not before. You have only introduced this uncertainty in your memory so as to obliterate the connection in your mind. But the figures do not quite fit in to my satisfaction yet. If you stayed at L —— for four nights longer, the dream might have occurred four times over. Perhaps this was so?'' She no longer disputed my contention; but instead of answering my question she proceeded:§ ''In the afternoon after our trip on the lake, from which we (Herr K. and I) returned at midday, I had gone to lie down as usual on the sofa in the bedroom to have a short sleep. I suddenly awoke and saw Herr K. standing beside me . . .''

''In fact, just as you saw your father standing beside your bed in the dream?''

''Yes. I asked him sharply what it was he wanted there. By way of reply he said he was not going to be prevented from coming into his own bedroom when he wanted; besides, there was something he wanted to fetch. This episode put me on my guard, and I asked Frau K. whether there was not a key to the bedroom door. The next morning (on the second day) I locked myself in while I was dressing. In the afternoon, when I wanted to lock myself in so as to lie down on the sofa, the key was gone. I am convinced that Herr K. had removed it.''

''Then here we have the theme of locking or not locking a room which appeared in the first association to the dream and also happened to occur in the exciting cause of the recent recurrence of the dream.** I wonder whether the phrase *I dressed myself quickly* may not also belong in this context?''

''It was then that I made up my mind not to stay with Herr K. without father. On the subsequent mornings I could not help feeling afraid Herr K. would surprise me while I was dressing: *so I always dressed myself very quickly.* You see, Father lived at the hotel, and Frau K. used always to go out early so as to go on expeditions with him. But Herr K. did not annoy me again.''

''I understand. On the afternoon of the second day after the scene in the woods you resolved to escape from his persecution, and during the second, third and fourth nights you had time to repeat that resolution in your sleep. (You already knew on the second afternoon—before the dream, therefore—that you would not have the key on the following—the third—morning to lock yourself in with while you were dressing; and you could then form the design of dressing as quickly as possible.) But your dream recurred each night, for the very reason that it corresponded to a resolution. A resolution remains in existence until it is carried out. You said to yourself, as it were: 'I shall have no rest and I can get no quiet sleep until I am out of this house.' In your account of the dream you turned it the other way and said: *'as soon as I was outside I woke up.'* ''

SUMMARY AND EVALUATION

Freud divided human instincts into two broad categories: Eros, the erotic or life instincts; and Thanatos, the death or destruction instincts. The energy of the life instincts is the libido. Mental life includes conscious, preconscious, and unconscious

§This was because a fresh piece of material had to emerge from her memory before the question I had put could be answered.

**I suspected, though I did not as yet say so to Dora, that she had seized upon this element on account of a symbolic meaning it possessed. "Zimmer" [*room*] in dreams stands very frequently for "Frauenzimmer" [a slightly derogatory word for *women;* literally, *women's apartments*]. The question whether a woman is "open" or "shut" can naturally not be a matter of indifference. It is well known, too, what sort of "key" effects the opening in such a case.

levels. The mental apparatus consists of three agencies: the id, which is constantly striving for instinctual satisfaction; the ego, which aims to meet the instinctual demands of the id in conformity with the reality principle; and the superego, which represents parental and moral influences. The ego has three taskmasters—the external world, the id, and the superego—each of which may cause it anxiety. Psychic energy is distributed among the three mental agencies, which may be in harmony or in conflict with one another.

Individuals are sexual from infancy, although they tend to be subject to amnesia about sexual feelings and experiences. There are four stages of sexual development: the oral, the anal, the phallic (grouped as pregenital)–followed by the latency period—and the genital. The normal development of personality may be seen as three interrelated strands. One involves the individual's libidinal development, which starts with a combination of constitutional and infantile predispositions that mature into genital sexuality in successive but overlapping stages. The second strand involves the development of both the ego, as it gains in ability to mediate between the demands of the instincts and the reality of the external world, and the superego, based on identification with parental influences. The third strand is the establishment by the ego of favored defense mechanisms to ward off the anxiety caused by the strength and persistence of the libidinal impulses of the id. Thus normal development consists of passing through successive stages of sexual maturation without major fixations and regressions; developing an ego that can cope reasonably effectively with the external world; developing a superego based on identifications that are constructive and are not punitively moralistic; and evolving defense mechanisms that drain off some of the energies of the id without serious restriction of the ego's functioning. The failure to achieve this balance provides the basis for the neuroses.

Excessive repression results in an ego weakened by having to maintain the repression and in susceptibility to stress. The repressed impulses become transformed into neurotic symptoms. Psychoanalysis aims to strengthen the ego by lifting the childhood amnesia and repression, thus allowing the ego to act from strength rather than from weakness. Free association, dream analysis, interpretation, and analysis of transference are the major methods of psychoanalysis.

It must be remembered that this chapter presents Freud's theories and practice only. Freud's contributions were complete by the mid-1920s. But beginning about 1910, other theorists had begun to modify and add to his contributions. The early modifiers include Adler, Rank, Ferenczi, Abraham, Reich, Jung, Sullivan, Horney, and Fromm; more recent adapters include the ego-analysts, such as Hartmann and Erikson, and the object-relations theorists, such as Klein, Kernberg, and Fairbairn.

These and many other writers have provided numerous critiques of Freud's views.[40] An adequate evaluation would require much more space than is available here. It will have to suffice to list the major contributions and criticisms of Freud's psychoanalysis.

Freud's major contributions include the following (not necessarily in order of importance):

1. Probably the most important contribution of Freud is his discovery that early childhood experiences are significant for later personality development and

that the effects of these experiences continue to influence the adult without his or her awareness of their operation.

2. Related to this contribution is Freud's recognition of the sexual aspects of childhood.
3. Freud developed the first comprehensive theory of personality, including the origins of personality characteristics in childhood experiences.
4. The discovery of unconscious processes, the activities going on in mental life without the individual's awareness, is a significant contribution to psychology.
5. The recognition of unconscious determinants of or influences on behavior contributed to the theory of motivation.
6. Freud's development of the method of free association was a major contribution to the field of psychotherapy. Ernest Jones, Freud's major biographer, rated this as one of the two great achievements of Freud.[41] (The other was his self-analysis.)
7. The discovery of transference was also a major contribution to the psychotherapy process.
8. Freud provided a major example of the study of single cases in psychotherapy as a source of insights about psychological development.

The criticisms of Freud have been numerous and varied. Only a few of the major ones can be listed here.

1. Freud overemphasized the biological factors—hereditary, constitutional, and maturational—in human development. The almost exclusive emphasis on sexual development is a basic part of this biological focus.
2. Freud's view of human behavior is deterministic and therefore pessimistic. All behavior, including even the simplest—such as slips of the tongue—are, he held, determined by past experiences, especially those of the earliest years, which are no longer conscious. These experiences, in turn, are determined by innate biological strivings, most of which are also unconscious. These internal forces are sexual and aggressive energies that are basically antisocial or destructive and must be controlled. This negativistic determinism would appear to pose a problem in explaining how psychotherapy can change behavior.
3. The focus on organic, constitutional, and sexual aspects of development is accompanied by an almost complete neglect of social aspects of development as positive rather than as purely restrictive. Interpersonal relationships—with the parents early in life and with others later (except for sexual aspects)—were ignored by Freud.
4. Freud failed to recognize that much of what he saw in his patients was related to a particular time and place in human history. As a result, he overgeneralized from nineteenth-century Vienna to all humanity, failing to recognize cultural differences in human development.
5. Critics among the psychoanalysts note that Freud failed to recognize adequately the autonomy of the ego as against the dominance of the id and to realize that the ego has its own sources of energy, interests, motives, and objectives independent of those of the id.
6. Freud recognized that his ideas and theories influenced his patients' "free" associations. His theories, biases, and predilections (expectations) also entered into his observations and interpretations of the data he observed. Thus the

reliability of his methods of investigation has been questioned, as has the representativeness of the sample of cases he studied.

7. Related to Freud's influence on his patients is his apparent use of interpretation as a method of indoctrination. This is particularly clear in his report of the case of Dora.

In spite of these and many other criticisms and of the many changes in and additions to Freud's theories by other psychoanalysts, Freud's niche in history remains secure. "Freud's genius has won him a permanent place in the history of psychology and in the intellectual history of the world."[42]

Hall and Lindzey summarize Freud's contributions.

But a fine literary style and an exciting subject matter are not the main reasons for the great esteem in which Freud is held. Rather it is because his ideas are challenging, because his conception of man is both broad and deep, and because his theory has relevance for our times. Freud may not have been a rigorous scientist nor a first-rate theoretician, but he was a patient, meticulous, penetrating observer and a tenacious, disciplined, courageous original thinker. . . . For many people [his] picture of man has an essential validity.[43]

REFERENCES

1. Freud, S. *An autobiographical study*. London: Hogarth Press, 1935. P. 14.
2. Ibid., p. 26.
3. Ibid., p. 29.
4. Freud, S., & Breuer, J. *Studies on hysteria*. London: Hogarth Press, 1956. (Originally published, 1895.)
5. Freud, S. *The interpretation of dreams*. New York: Macmillan, 1913. (Originally published, 1900.)
6. Freud, S. *Three contributions to the theory of sex*. New York: Dutton, 1962. (Originally published, 1905.)
7. Freud, S. Analysis terminable and interminable. *International Journal of Psychoanalysis*, 1937, *18*, 373–405.
8. Thompson, C. *Psychoanalysis: Evolution and development*. New York: Grove Press, 1957. P. 14.
9. Freud, *An autobiographical study*, pp. 129–130.
10. Thompson, *Psychoanalysis*.
11. Ibid., p. 5.
12. Freud, S. *Beyond the pleasure principle*. New York: Liveright, 1950. p. 1. (Originally published, 1920.)
13. Freud, S. *New introductory lectures on psychoanalysis*. New York: Norton, 1933. P. 140.
14. Freud, *Beyond the pleasure principle*, p. 38.
15. Freud, S. *Civilization and its discontents*. New York: Norton, 1962. P. 92. (Originally published, 1930.)
16. Freud, *The interpretation of dreams*, Freud, S. *An outline of psychoanalysis*. New York: Norton, 1949; Freud, S. *The ego and the id*. London: Hogarth Press, 1962. (Originally published, 1923.)
17. Freud, *New introductory lectures on psychoanalysis*, pp. 104–105.
18. Ibid., pp. 106–107.

19. Ibid., p. 98.
20. Freud, *The ego and the id,* p. 23.
21. Freud, S. *Leonardo Da Vinci: A study in psychosexuality.* New York: Random House, 1947. (Originally published, 1910.)
22. Freud, S. "Civilized" sexual morality and modern nervousness. In *Collected papers* (Vol. II). London: Hogarth Press, 1924. Pp. 76–99. (Originally published, 1908.)
23. Freud, S. Repression. In *Collected papers* (Vol. IV). London: Hogarth Press, 1925, pp. 84–97. (Originally published, 1915.)
24. Freud, *An outline of psychoanalysis,* p. 113.
25. Freud, *New introductory lectures on psychoanalysis.*
26. Freud, *An outline of psychoanalysis,* pp. 83–87.
27. Freud, S. *Collected papers* (Vol. I). London: Hogarth Press, 1924, p. 282.
28. Ibid., p. 67.
29. Freud, *An outline of psychoanalysis,* pp. 72–79.
30. Freud, *The interpretation of dreams,* p. 769.
31. Freud, S. Psychoanalytic notes upon an autobiographical account of a case of paranoia (dementia paranoides). In *Collected papers* (Vol. III). London: Hogarth Press, 1933, pp. 390–472. (Originally published, 1911.)
32. Freud, S. Analysis of a phobia in a five-year-old boy. In *Collected papers,* (Vol. III). London: Hogarth Press, 1933, pp. 296–389. (Originally published, 1909.)
33. Freud, S. Fragments of an analysis of a case of hysteria. In *Collected papers* (Vol. VII). London: Hogarth Press, 1933. pp. 13–148. (Originally published, 1905.)
34. Freud, S. Notes upon a case of obsessional neurosis. In *Collected papers* (Vol. III), pp. 296–389. (Originally published, 1909.)
35. Freud, S. From the history of an infantile neurosis. In *Collected papers* (Vol. III), pp. 473–605. (Originally published, 1918.)
36. Freud, S. The psychogenesis of a case of homosexuality in a woman. In *Collected papers* (Vol. II). London: Hogarth Press, 1933, pp. 202–231. (Originally published in 1920.)
37. Freud, S. *Collected Papers* (Vol. I). London: Hogarth Press, Press, 1924, p. 71.
38. Freud, S. Fragments of an analysis of a case of hysteria. *The Standard Edition of the Complete Psychological Works of Sigmund Freud* (Vol. VII). London: Hogarth Press, 1953, p. 23 In *Collected Papers* (Vol. IV). New York: Collier Books, 1963, p. 38.
39. *Ibid.,* pp. 64–67.
40. Grünbaum, A. *The foundations of psychoanalysis: a philosophical critique.* Berkeley: Calif.: University of California Press, 1984.
41. Jones, E. *The life and work of Sigmund Freud* (Vol. II). New York: Basic Books, 1955.
42. Hilgard, E. R., & Bower, G. H. *Theories of learning* (4th ed.). Englewood Cliffs, N.J.: Prentice-Hall, 1975, p. 373.
43. Hall, C. S., and Lindzay, G. *Theories of personality.* New York: Wiley, 1957, p. 72.

chapter 10

Psychoanalytic Therapy: Alexander

Franz Alexander (1891–1963) was born in Budapest, Hungary, and received his M.D. degree in 1913 from the University of Budapest. After several years of research in medicine (bacteriology), he did graduate work in psychiatry at the University of Berlin in 1920 to 1921. He was the first student to matriculate (1921) at the first psychoanalytic institute, the Berlin Psychoanalytic Institute, founded in 1920; a few years later, he was appointed to its staff and continued as a lecturer until 1930. In 1930, he came to the United States. After a year at the University of Chicago as visiting professor of psychoanalysis and a year at the Judge Baker Foundation in Boston as research associate in criminology, Alexander became the first director of the Chicago Institute for Psychoanalysis, where he remained until 1955. During 1955 and 1956, he was a Ford Foundation Fellow at the Center for Advanced Study in the Behavioral Sciences at Stanford. In 1956, he became chief of staff of the Psychiatric Department and director of the Psychiatric and Psychosomatic Research Institute at Mount Sinai Hospital in Los Angeles. He was continually engaged in private practice and held appointments at various universities; at his death, he was associated with the University of Southern California. Alexander was the author of numerous articles in psychoanalytic journals and of a number of books, some of which are *The Psychoanalysis of the Total Personality* (1929), *Mental Hygiene and Criminology* (1930), *The Medical Value of Psychoanalysis* (1936), *Our Age of Unreason* (1942), *Psychoanalytic Therapy* (with French and others, 1946), *Fundamentals of Psychoanalysis* (1948; rev. ed., 1963), and *Psychoanalysis and Psychotherapy* (1956).

BACKGROUND AND DEVELOPMENT

In the 1930s, Alexander and other staff members of the Chicago Institute for Psychoanalysis began questioning some of the traditional psychoanalytic beliefs. Among these were the beliefs that (1) the depth of therapy is necessarily proportionate to the duration of treatment and the frequency of interviews, (2) results achieved in a small number of interviews are necessarily superficial and temporary, (3) prolongation of an analysis is justified on the basis that the client's resistance will eventually be overcome and success achieved. As a result of this questioning, an attempt was begun to define principles and to develop methods and techniques that would make possible a shorter and more efficient psychotherapy.

When little was known about the genesis and pathology of neurosis and when each case was the subject of research, the extensive and standard form of treatment was necessary and desirable. "With the advance of knowledge in this field, however, we can now use generalizations and principles tested by our extended experience to develop a more flexible and economical procedure adjusted to the individual nature of the great variety of neurotic patients."[1] This approach is not to be considered a shortcut to therapy. While at first a sharp differentiation was made between the more flexible methods and "standard" psychoanalysis, it was later recognized that there is no essential difference between the two sets of procedures but only a difference in the extent to which various procedures are used. The same theories, as well as techniques, are involved. The inducing of emotional discharge to facilitate insight and the exposing of the ego to the unresolved emotional constellations that it must master are present in both methods. The approach was therefore designated as psychoanalytic psychotherapy, as distinguished from psychoanalysis.

> Perhaps the most significant development in psychiatry consists in the emergence of what is commonly called "psychoanalytically-oriented psychotherapy." Psychoanalytically-oriented psychotherapy consists in the flexible application of the fundamental principles of psychodynamics. . . . It applies these principles in various technical procedures which are precisely adjusted to the individual nature of each case. The routine application of the same standardized procedure (the standard psychoanalysis) gradually is becoming enriched by more individualized and more economical treatment.[2]

The standard approach is applicable to a limited and relatively small number of psychiatric patients, few of whom require strict adherence to the standard technique during the entire treatment. This approach is not as suitable for severely disturbed individuals, whose basic deficiency in ego functions makes them unable to face their conflicts, as for those with milder acute incipient disturbances. It is with the second group that the modified procedures of psychoanalytic therapy can be useful. Early skillful treatment of these cases can prevent the development of chronic conditions, which often resist the most intensive therapy.

The modifications characterizing psychoanalytic therapy are not new; it is the clarification of their usefulness and their systematic use that constitute the contribution of Alexander's approach. The application of the approach to the milder chronic and acute neuroses is an important social contribution because of their prevalence. The postulation of the etiology of neurosis in childhood, based on the observation of this etiology in those cases selected as suitable for psychoanalysis, is not valid for acute neurotic breakdown or mild chronic cases. Latent neurotic tendencies, present in everyone, may develop into acute neurotic states under stress or exposure to difficulties beyond the individual's power of adaptation.

The utilization of psychoanalytic psychotherapy rather than psychoanalysis does not imply that any different or lesser qualifications or training are required. Not only those practicing psychoanalytic therapy but all psychotherapists should be trained in psychoanalytic theory and should undergo a personal analysis.[3]

PHILOSOPHY AND CONCEPTS

The basic principles of psychoanalytic theory underlying psychoanalytic therapy are presented in *Fundamentals of Psychoanalysis.*[4]

Principles of Psychodynamics

Fundamental Postulates

There are two underlying assumptions of psychology as a science. The first assumption is that minds can study minds. The second assumption is that the process of life can be studied by two approaches, the somatic and the psychological. The functions of the mind are biological and eventually will be described in terms of physics and chemistry. At present, however, the psychological approach, in which human beings describe their sensations to others, affords insight into the complex biological functions.

The Principle of Stability

Life is a dynamic equilibrium. Disturbances are manifested as needs and wishes that motivate behavior. The organism seeks to keep these tensions at a constant level; this is the principle of stability, which Freud borrowed from Fechner and whose physiological aspect, first recognized by Claude Bernard, was labeled homeostasis by Cannon. The function of the ego is to implement this principle through the recognition of internal needs and external conditions and to integrate these needs and conditions in such a way as to gratify the needs as much as possible. The principle of stability is a more precise and useful formulation of the instinct of self-preservation.

The Principle of Economy, or Inertia

In addition to innate, automatic functions, there are functions that the organism must learn through trial and error and repetition. The principle of stability requires that the organism find ways of reducing internal tensions. The economy principle, or the principle of inertia, refers to the tendency of the organism to perform the functions necessary for the maintenance of equilibrium with a minimum expenditure of energy. It overlaps partly with the so-called repetition compulsion. The principle of inertia interferes with new learning, leading to *fixation* on behavior that was satisfactory in the past but is not adequate under changed conditions. Under new, difficult, or threatening conditions, the individual reverts, or *regresses,* to earlier patterns of behavior. Changing conditions require flexible behavior, but the organism clings to old patterns, thus causing a continuous struggle.

The Principle of Surplus Energy

Growth and propagation require a principle in addition to those of stability and inertia. Growth is biologically predetermined. Activity is spontaneous and pleasurable. Playful activity belongs to the "erotic" category. Erotic phenomena expend rather than conserve energy; they are creative and progressive. The energy expended is surplus energy.

The Vector Analysis of the Life Process

Life is a relationship among three vectors: the intake of energy (food, air), the partial retention of energy for use in growth, and the expenditure of energy to maintain existence—its loss in waste, in heat, and in erotic playful activity. Surplus energy is the source of all playful erotic activity in the child and of sexual activity and sublimated creative activity in the adult.

The Different Forms of Erotic Behavior

Oral eroticism   The oral phase of growth and development includes the pleasure sensation in the oral zone from both sucking and thumbsucking as a form of oral play; these can be exercised for their own sake without self-preservative aspects but constitute the expenditure of surplus excitement. Security, dependence, and passive, receptive, and demanding attitudes toward the mother become linked with the relieving of hunger and the receiving of oral pleasure. This complex of emotions is referred to as oral-receptive or oral-incorporative. When the flow of milk is inadequate, the child bites; this represents an oral-aggressive attitude and is linked with envy and possessiveness.

Anal eroticism   Anal retention is pleasurable, interfering with training, and is related to stubbornness, independence, and possessiveness. Expulsion is also pleasurable and is associated with pride. Toilet training, following weaning, is the second serious interference with the child's basic biological functions and results in frustration, leading to sadistic aggression. Sadism is aggression or hurting for its own sake or for the sake of the pleasure achieved and is thus like all erotic phenomena.

Other early types of eroticism   A great many functions of the body, including the use of the limbs and eyes, may be sources of erotic pleasure.

Phallic eroticism   Phallic eroticism includes urination and masturbation, and their emotional complements are competitiveness, assertiveness, pleasure in achievement, and ambition. This stage usually reaches its peak in the fifth or sixth year. The Oedipus complex is the typical emotional constellation of this age. It is a "mixture of love, jealousy, inferiority, and guilt occasioned by the child's possessive sexual attraction to the parent of the opposite sex."[5] Like the earlier periods, this period is later obscured by infantile amnesia due to repression. The child's conflicts are the result of the uneven development of instinct, intellect, and genitality, which makes childhood the most vulnerable period of human development. Traumatic experiences increase the conflict, leading to pathogenic influences in later life. The repression of the conflicts of the Oedipus period begins the period of latency, which lasts to puberty.

Genital impulses   In puberty, endocrinological changes lead to a more adult form of sexual impulses. Sexual maturity is reached, and the adolescent struggles to adjust to his or her new biological status. Competitiveness, showing off, and other forms of defensive behavior are ways of overcoming inferiority and achieving security. With maturity and security, genital sexuality is possible; that is, "love assumes for the first time a generous, giving quality, the evidence of strength and energy which the mature organism no longer requires for its own maintenance."[6] Pregenital love is based on identification with its objects; it is narcissistic. In adult love, the impulse to give of oneself is added.

The Concept of Sexuality

Early Freudian Views

Freud first accepted the distinction between self-preservation and race preservation, or the sexual instinct, but with the recognition of sexual libido in infancy, sexuality was extended beyond the concept of race preservation. All early pleasurable excitations that do not aid self-preservation were labeled sexual. Although Freud persisted in his dualism, this distinction between self-preservation and sexuality could not be maintained, since early eroticism is related to self-preservative functions.

The Theory of Life and Death Instincts

To overcome the difficulties of the dualism of self-preservation and sexuality, Freud proposed another in the theory of life and death instincts. According to this dualism, the erotic drive is constructive, or anabolic, while the death instinct is destructive, or catabolic. This distinction is basic.

The description of life as a process of anabolic construction and catabolic destruction is supported by biology, but there is a difficulty with the philosophical concept of the disintegrating factor as a death instinct. Death is an inevitable result of the disruptive tendency but not necessarily its aim. Contrary to Freud's theory, the death instinct is not necessary to explain social disintegration. In both the individual and the social situation, the disintegrating factor is the individualistic tendency of each biological unit. The death instinct has been assumed to be a component of every neurosis, but the analysis of masochistic manifestations indicates that they are aimed at eliminating guilt and gaining love.

Thus there are two dynamic opposing vectors in life, one constructive and one destructive, but they are not manifestations of opposing instincts. Biological units organize to survive under pressure of external danger, but when the need for cooperation diminishes, the individualistic tendencies of the units result in disintegration. In the multicellular organism, the units cannot exist alone, so that disintegration leads to the death of the cells. The integration of functions in the organism is adaptive and promotes survival. The so-called death instinct is the disintegration of mature behavior, leading to regression, in situations beyond the organism's adaptive capacity. "What Freud called the death instinct is a tendency not toward death, but toward old and worn patterns of life."[7]

A Psychosomatic View of Sexuality

The erotic pleasures of the infant are varied, involving many functions and many parts of the body, but they are sexual. The sexual impulse is not specific; any emotion can become sexualized. Sexuality represents the discharge of any surplus excitation, in both infants and adults. In the course of maturation, the genitourinary tract assumes the function of draining surplus excitation. The persistence of other ways of discharge leads to the adult perversions. "Propagation results from surplus energy generated by growth. The psychological equivalent of propagation is love."[8]

The Functions of the Ego and Its Failures

The Structural Theory of the Mental Apparatus

Freud divided the mind into three structurally different parts: (1) the id, or reservoir of chaotic instinctual impulses; (2) the ego, or integrating part, which coordinates the id impulses with external reality; and (3) the superego, which embodies the code of society. It is difficult to maintain this structural division. Although it is justifiable to distinguish different functions, the boundaries are fluid. The unconscious superego cannot be sharply separated from the ego, and the latter merges with the id developmentally. For various reasons, including the emphasis in psychoanalysis on irrational behavior, we know relatively little about the integrative functions of the ego. We do know that it has two perceptive surfaces, one directed inward toward the instinctive impulses and the other directed outward toward external reality through sense perception, and that its integrative function is to harmonize the conflicting demands of these two sorts of perceptions. It also has an executive function in controlling voluntary motor behavior, adaptively maintaining homeostasis within the organism. The ego is the most flexible part of the mind, engaged in a continuous reconciliation between the demands of external conditions and desires incompatible with such demands. Under strong or continued stress, the adaptive functioning of the ego may break down, resulting in neurosis or psychosis. Behavior then reverts to the use of defense mechanisms that had been utilized earlier to cope with impulses that the child could not equilibrate.

Development of the Ego Functions

The ego is the agent of the stability principle, concerned with maintaining constant conditions. It must ward off or reduce external and internal stimuli. Before these functions have developed, the child's impulses seek gratification without regard to the needs of the total organism; the child is dominated by what Freud calls the pleasure principle. He or she learns to coordinate his or her impulses and to relate them to the environment according to the reality principle. In addition to learning from trial and error, the ego can learn from experiences with others, such as parents, through identification.

The early stages of ego development are not well known, since they not only have not been observed, but also cannot be communicated during the prespeech period of childhood. An early phase is the gradual differentiation between the internal and external worlds, the ego and nonego. Fantasy gratification, probably present at the beginning, is given up and replaced by real satisfaction, which is learned when uncoordinated activity deriving from tension leads to behavior that results in relief from tension. Impulses are controlled primarily by repression until better methods of control are gradually developed.

Defense Mechanisms of the Ego

Repression   Repression is the ego's fundamental defense measure. It consists of excluding impulses and their ideational representations from consciousness and occurs when the impulse would cause unbearable conflict and anxiety if it were to become conscious. It is an unconscious inhibition that thus "presupposes an unconscious inner perception which leads to automatic reflex inhibition."[9] The censorship, or unconscious judgment, is unable to make subtle differentiations and thus may repress impulses that might be acceptable later. Thus all sexual impulses may be repressed along with early incestuous impulses. This broad and oversevere repression is one of the causes of psychoneuroses. Impulses that cannot be integrated within the (weak) ego by sublimation or other means are excluded in order to maintain the ego's integrity. Conscious manifestations in the form of countercathexis (for example, pity against tendencies toward cruelty) and anxiety appear. The repressed psychological forces continue to exist, requiring the ego to drain its resources in defensive measures, so that it loses the surplus energy that is the source of sexual and socially creative activities.

Anxiety   Anxiety is internalized fear. Fear is aroused by the memory of painful past experiences, that is, experiences associated with punishment for the gratification of an impulse, and thus becomes connected with the impulse. Anxiety, then, is aroused by a dangerous impulse, and it serves as a signal to the ego of the breaking through of the impulse. As an unconscious reaction to repressed tendencies, it is rationalized, or it may appear as free-floating anxiety. In male neurotics, the unconscious anxiety is the fear of castration; this fear appears openly in children, compulsive–obsessive neurotics, and schizophrenics. The Oedipus complex leads to the castration wish (to replace the father) and thence to fear of retaliation, or castration fear. Freud regarded this fear as the primary factor in the resolution of the Oedipus complex, in which the boy relinquishes his sexual attachment to the mother and develops identification with the father. This process is not smooth even in normal individuals and may involve complications leading to neuroses. The process in girls is different, but there is little agreement on it.

Overcompensation (reaction formation)   The development of attitudes or character traits exactly opposite to those that have been repressed is the most common defensive measure against repressed tendencies. Persistent overcompensatory measures that become character traits are reaction formations. The principle of polarity, or opposites, was one of Freud's fundamental principles in personality. Philosophical assumptions about opposing forces are not necessary to explain this apparent polarity, however. As the child becomes a member of various groups, the surplus energy is expressed in libidinous, or erotic, attachments to others. The only genuine polarity is that between love of self and love of others. What Bleuler described as ambivalence—

love and hatred directed toward the same person at the same time—is a universal polar phenomenon and is a result of the fact that human beings are both individuals and members of society. The antithesis of love of self and love of others arises because the more one loves another, the more love one takes away from oneself, so that all love objects are enemies of the narcissistic core of personality and thus objects of hate under certain conditions. One of these attitudes normally is buried, but in abnormal conditions, both parts may be conscious.

Rationalization   All human acts are overdetermined, that is, impelled by a number of conflicting motives. Rationalization consists of selecting the most favorable motives to explain behavior. Other, unacceptable motives are repressed.

Substitution and displacement   Displacement consists of the replacement of the object of an emotional attitude by another, with the attitude remaining the same. Substitution, often used synonymously with displacement, is the changing of the act but not the object, as when anger toward a person is replaced by destructive, but energy-consuming and useful acts, such as chopping wood. Displacement and substitution may result from frustration as well as from repression, and if they are successful as a compromise, they may make repression unnecessary.

Sublimation   The modification of unacceptable urges so that they become socially acceptable is sublimation. It is a form of substitution. Aggressive sports are sublimations of destructive, hostile impulses. Creative activities are sublimations of sexuality.

Provocative behavior   The provocation of hostility toward oneself justifies the release of one's hostility in retaliation.

Projection   Projection is the attributing of characteristics in oneself to others. It occurs when the ego can no longer repress objectionable tendencies that are unacceptable to the individual, who must deny them by projecting them onto the external world. The differentiation between the ego and the external world is thus obliterated.

Turning feelings toward oneself   When repression fails, alien impulses may be directed toward the self instead of projected onto others. Hostility toward others is unacceptable and so becomes hostility toward the self. Directing hostility toward the self releases it and relieves guilt feelings.

Identification as a defense   In traumatic situations, the ego may compensate for an unbearable loss by identifying with the lost love. This introjection incorporates the ambivalent attitudes toward the love object, which may lead to hostile and destructive attitudes toward the self. Identification with a threatening person may be a means of allaying anxiety.

Guilt feelings and masochistic defense   The sense of guilt is the fear of one's conscience, which demands punishment to relieve anxiety and remorse. Thus the individual must punish himself or herself or induce others to punish her or him. Suffering relieves guilt or is atonement for misbehavior. Expressed allegorically, "the ego bribes the superego through suffering to lessen its dependence upon the latter."[10] Masochism results when the need for punishment is eroticized and its discharge leads to erotic gratification. Suffering becomes an erotic aim rather than serving merely to relieve guilt.

Defenses against inferiority feelings and their relationship to guilt feelings In inferiority feelings, self-condemnation is the result of feelings of weakness or inadequacy, rather than the result of recognition of wrongdoing, as in guilt. Inferiority feelings stimulate competition and aggression; showing superiority in competition eradicates the inferiority feelings. Guilt feelings lead to the opposite—self-debasement and punishment. The coexistence of guilt and inferiority feelings thus results in a conflict that characterizes many neuroses. Inferiority feelings represent a deeper conflict than do guilt feelings, stemming from earlier childhood conflicts between the wish to grow up and become an adult and the regressive desire for dependence. The regressive wish is reacted to by the ego, which identifies itself with the progressive attitude, with the resultant development of a sense of inferiority.

Conversion In conversion, the unacceptable impulses are converted into innervations or inhibitions of the voluntary neuromuscular and sensory systems, resulting in such symptoms as hysterical paralysis, contracture, anesthesia, blindness, deafness, and so on.

Regression Regression is a tendency of the individual to reestablish an earlier situation and thus is essentially Freud's repetition compulsion. It has been referred to earlier as a common manifestation of the inertia principle. Under stress, more recently acquired adaptive mechanisms may break down, and the individual may revert to more automatic behavior patterns. Regression is present in all psychopathological manifestations, although it is one of the most ineffective defenses of the ego against demands that cannot be met on a mature, acceptable level.

Psychopathology

Definition of Neurosis

Neurosis is a disease rooted in disturbances in the functioning of the organism, centered in the ego and resulting in discomfort and suffering. It is characterized by the failure of the ego in its coordinating or integrating function, with the development instead of defense mechanisms, mainly repression, and regression, to deal with the rebellious impulses. It originates in excessive repression of impulses in childhood, with repression becoming the method of dealing with impulses, so that they remain in the unconscious to cause trouble later, rather than being allowed into consciousness to be dealt with by the ego and to contribute to its healthy development. Early traumatic experiences of an overwhelming, intimidating nature favor repression. Parental attitudes are the most important sources of such experiences. Children, of course, vary in their susceptibility to traumatic experiences. While these early experiences are basic, they result essentially in vulnerability to strain later in life, so that neuroses then develop. The relative contributions of childhood experiences and later environmental stress vary. Thus heredity, childhood experiences, and current difficulties all contribute in varying degrees in different cases. Neurosis is a breakdown of the ego in a given situation.

There are two types of regression: (1) regression to fixation points that represent earlier successful adaptations, and (2) regression to unresolved traumatic situations. The first represents a seeking for gratification in the face of a situation that the ego cannot master, and the second represents a return to a traumatic event in an attempt to master it. Both types of regression occur in the transference situation, probably equally frequently, and they usually are combined or occur together. The first type of regression is a form of resistance; it is both an evasion of a conflict centered in a later stage of development and an attraction to a fixation point. The second type is an ally of the therapeutic aims. The estimation of the balance between the two is difficult or impossible to assess.

Psychoneurotic and Psychotic Symptoms

The nature of a neurosis and a psychosis is to a large extent determined by the kinds of defenses adopted by the ego for its protection against emancipated impulses. There are also certain general characteristics or symptoms.

Psychoneurotic symptoms   Neurotic symptoms appear to be irrational, both to the neurotic and to observers. They are dissociated from the conscious psychic life and are regressive.

Dynamic Structure and Development of a Psychoneurosis

The failure to satisfy emotional needs in human relations, occupational activities, or sexual life, accompanied by internal conflict, leads to neurosis. After a struggle, recourse is taken to regressive neurotic gratifications. This revives earlier anxieties and frustrations, which have been repressed. Neurotic behavior is the ego's defense against these early emotions; anxiety keeps the regressive tendencies repressed. Different methods of defense result in different forms of neurosis. Substitute gratifications, for example, are of various types: conversion symptoms, phobias, obsessive–compulsive states, depressions and delusions of grandeur, paranoid projections, hallucinations and delusions, the impulsive behavior of character neuroses (psychopathic personalities), and the manic phase of manic–depressive psychosis. The defenses are also varied, including those listed earlier. Symbolic gratification by means of symptoms is a form of defense, but it is not sufficient to allay anxiety, so that specific defenses are aimed at relieving the sense of guilt.

The development of a neurosis consists, then, of (1) precipitating factors, with (2) failure in the solution of actual problems, leading to (3) regression, which (4) revives primary conflicts, followed by a futile struggle to resolve them with (5) substitute gratifications and self-punishment expressed in symptoms, resulting in (6) secondary conflict and the impoverishment of the ego. Symptoms absorb energies, which impairs effectiveness in dealing with actual life situations, resulting in a vicious circle.

Secondary Gain

In addition to the primary suffering, illness has secondary consequences that are advantages. Financial compensation, avoidance of unpleasant duties and responsibilities, sympathy, and attention are some of these secondary gains. Dependent longings may lead to exploration of the illness. The existence of the infantile trait of dependence is, however, a significant factor in the neurosis. The point to note is that secondary gains prolong the illness and therefore should be reduced wherever possible.

Review of Psychopathological Phenomena

Anxiety neurosis   Anxiety neurosis is characterized by free-floating anxiety. Failure in important social or sexual relations is the precipitating factor, which results in regression to hostile and destructive impulses that threaten to become conscious. Anxiety, the fear of conscience, appears in consciousness. The ego develops defenses against the anxiety, which subsides but may recur. Other forms of neurosis or psychosis develop, depending on the defenses employed.

Phobias   Phobias are fears of specific situations; they replace early anxiety-laden situations. The situations avoided have an unconscious symbolic meaning, which is often sexual. Failure and regression lead to dependence; the phobia localizes anxiety and conceals the real problem from the ego.

Obsessive–compulsive states   Obsessive–compulsive states consist of obsessive (asocial) ideas and compulsive rituals. Character traits of rigidity, doubt, indecisiveness, and dependence are typical. Obsessions are breaches in the repressive defenses that are separated from normal thinking in order to disown them as one's own thoughts. Compulsions represent overdoing the good to allay anxiety. There is a struggle to maintain a balance. These states exhibit the "magic of ideas" or the "omnipotence of thought" of the child, in which need is gratified in fantasy, but anxiety results.

Depressions   Depressions are marked by symptoms of melancholy, hopelessness, retardation of psychic processes, self-criticism, and sometimes suicidal impulses. Hostile impulses are directed inward, arousing guilt. The depressive individual is dependent in love relations, and the loss of a love object is a common precipitating cause of depression. The hostility that is part of the ambivalent relationship to the love object is turned against the self; this is aided by introjection of the love object.

The manic–depressive reactions   It is improbable that manic–depressive psychosis is a metabolic or an endocrine disturbance, if only because it responds to psychotherapy. The depressive phase of the psychosis is similar to a reactive depression. The manic phase includes elation, self-confidence, flight of ideas, aggression, irritability, and unrestrained sexuality. The change in behavior corresponds to a change in the ego's handling of rejected impulses, from guilt and punishment to uninhibited expression. Each form of behavior is a reaction to the other. In the depressive phase, the individual pays —or overpays—for the guilt incurred in the manic phase and is then able to recoup this overpayment in a return to the manic phase. The first phase, which may be either manic or depressive, is precipitated by an event that disturbs the equilibrium between the repressed and the repressing forces in the personality.

The hypochondriac syndrome   Hypochondria is not one disease, but a syndrome that appears in different conditions, such as depressions and schizophrenia. It consists of an anxious preoccupation with the body or a part of the body, which is believed to be diseased. It represents a narcissistic withdrawal of interest from objects and a focusing of interest on the self, which is caused by the frustration of the wish to be loved, the need for punishment because of guilt feelings resulting from hostile impulses, and the displacement of anxiety to another organ as a defense against castration fears.

Neurotic character (psychopathic personality)   Psychopathic individuals act out their neurotic impulses. They were long considered to be asocial, lacking in conscience or constitutionally defective and untreatable. Actually, they are more like normal persons than are neurotics; they require realistic activity, not fantasy, to satisfy their needs. Their adjustment to the social environment is based on faulty principles, established by early parent–child relations. Such individuals include psychopathic criminals and eccentrics. They are characterized by the irrationality and stereotyped behavior patterns arising from the dominance of unconscious factors and by self-destructiveness arising from unconscious guilt. The guilt, stemming from repressed conflicts (usually from the Oedipus situation), is displaced to criminal behavior, which is less objectionable than the forbidden desire in the unconscious. The punishment for the former relieves the guilt for the latter. Psychopathic personalities thus unconsciously seek apprehension. "After severe punishment for a relatively minor offense the conscience is relieved and the neurotic offender is emotionally ready for recidivism. The psychiatric superstition that these patients are incurable stems from this psychodynamic phenomenon. They remain incurable as long as society conforms to their neurosis by punishing them."[11]

Alcoholism and drug addiction   Alcohol and drug abuse are usually secondary to depression and character neuroses. Alcohol is an escape from depression, a means of overcoming inhibitions, and its adverse consequences replace other forms of self-punishment.

Traumatic neurosis   Traumatic neurosis cannot be separated psychodynamically from other neuroses. Emotional experiences are more traumatic than physical experiences. Trauma is present to some degree in all neuroses; in the so-called traumatic neurosis, it is more dramatic. The varied symptoms manifest regressive responses to extreme stress and anxiety.

Conversion symptoms   Repressed wishes can be expressed and rejected at the same time. Freud used the term *conversion* to indicate the replacement of an emotionally charged idea by a physical symptom. There is no mysterious conversion or transformation of a psychological to a physical quality; the process is no different physiologically from the normal expression of emotions in expressive movements such as laughter or weeping. In neurosis, the conversion is motivated by unconscious, repressed impulses, which are expressed without passing through the ego. The inactive symptom is an inadequate expression of the impulse, which requires action for adequate release, so the symptom becomes chronic; but because the symptoms provide emotional release, the individual appears impassive and unemotional *(la belle différence).*

The schizophrenias   The psychoneuroses involve a conflict among the different structural parts of the mental apparatus rather than, as in the psychoses, a disturbance of the personality in its relation to the outside world. The psychotic, however, relinquishes contact with reality or alters it in order to mold reality to his or her subjective demands. The psychoses present two kinds of conflict. In one, the conflict between the world as it is and as the psychotic desires it to be is solved by developing a world of fantasy. The other, identical with neurotic conflicts, arises from unacceptable hostile and sexual impulses. But whereas the neurotic represses these impulses and develops symptoms, the psychotic projects them. The paranoid, however, represses impulses (usually of a homosexual nature), transforming them into hostile attitudes, and projects these attitudes onto others. The paranoid schizophrenias are thus different from those that are not characterized by paranoid hallucinations and delusions. They are more like the neuroses but with a less deteriorated ego structure. Yet they resemble the other schizophrenias in their abandonment of contact with reality. In psychotics, the first step in development has never been firmly established (the differentiation between the ego and the external world), while in neurotics, the later social adjustments have been disturbed.

The precipitating causes in psychoses and neuroses are the same, emerging in adolescence or adult life. The psychotic regresses farther, however. Because the foundations are laid in infancy, inherited constitutions play a more important role, although the constitutional theory is not established. The contribution of psychoanalysis to the schizophrenias is more explanatory than therapeutic.

Psychological factors in organic brain disease   "The contribution of psychoanalysis to the organic psychoses consists mainly in the dynamic understanding of the psychological content of the symptoms. It has little to contribute to their etiology and therapy. . . . The symptoms can be understood as reactions of the personality to these organic changes. The best known example is the explanation of the grandiose ideas of general paretics as compensatory defenses of the ego against the perception of waning mental faculties."[12]

Perversions   Perversions are of two kinds: (1) those in which the quality of sexual strivings is distorted—sadism, masochism, exhibitionism, voyeurism, transvestism— and (2) those in which the object of the sexual striving is abnormal—homosexuality, pedophilia, zoophilia. In fetishism, both kinds are involved. Perversions are the result of interrupted sexual development, which prevents the integration of the pregenital components of sexuality into a mature form. Fixation on the early immature forms of sexuality occurs. The interruption of sexual development is related to emotional involvements in the family arising from the Oedipus situation. The various forms of perversion are related to the components of the complex that are disturbed.

THE THERAPY PROCESS

The goal of psychoanalytic therapy is to restore mental health. There are two aspects of mental health: (1) adaptation to the external environment, and (2) adaptation to the internal environment. The environment includes "the possible environments which the patient can choose to enhance his satisfaction and efficiency as a human being. . . . Psychoanalytic treatment may enhance to a very great extent the adaptability and the flexibility of a person and by eliminating inhibitions may free the way to fuller utilization of the patient's talents and abilities."[13] In terms of the view of neurosis as the failure of the ego to harmonize impulses with one another and with internal standards and external demands, psychoanalytic therapy enables the individual to extend the integrative capacity of the ego over impulses that have been repressed.

Therapy reverses the process of repression. This is possible in the emotional atmosphere of the therapeutic situation. The therapist reacts differently from the way the patient's parents did—the therapist does not evaluate or judge. The patient learns that the therapist does not condemn her or him and becomes able to express thoughts and desires freely. The unconscious thus becomes conscious. "Helping unconscious material to become conscious is an indispensable part of the therapy."[14]

The repressed attitudes of the patient are directed toward the therapist in the transference neurosis; that is, attitudes originally directed toward the parents are transferred to the therapist. This emotional experience is an important aspect of the curative process. The patient's ego has an opportunity to face situations that it could not handle in childhood (when the ego was weak) in a new setting, with a person who does not react as did the parents. The patient recognizes that his or her reactions are no longer suited to the present. Along with an increasing freedom to react to the therapist, there is a similar change in behavior in everyday life.

The patient's recognition of the inappropriateness of his or her behavior is not only an intellectual insight, but also a "corrective emotional experience." This experience is the central therapeutic agent in the process of change, which consists of a series of corrective emotional experiences. These must take place under the special conditions of psychoanalytic treatment.

The three factors of emotional abreaction, intellectual insight, and appearance of repressed memories are interrelated and interdependent, although different writers emphasize one or another. Without emotional abreaction, intellectual insight is ineffective. Recollection of repressed events is a part of insight. "The recovery of memories is a sign of improvement rather than its cause."[15] Treatment is not complete after the analysis of the transference neurosis. The "lifting of the infantile amnesia" is a necessary part of treatment. The "working through" of the transference manifestations in terms of former experiences and the actual life situation also must be accomplished. Although there have been developments that have overemphasized either the emotional or the intellectual factors, it has generally been recognized that the two are indivisible. The therapeutic process consists of the insight that accompanies emotional experience.

The emphasis on ego analysis is an emphasis on the process of working through. In the course of treatment, there is a breaking down of the primitive emotional patterns of the unconscious material and a building up of new and more complex relationships. Freud long considered the emergence of preconscious material into consciousness as the establishing of a new connection. The ego performs a synthesizing function in the establishment of new connections. The new synthesis makes possible more flexible behavior in place of the rigid, automatic behavior produced by the unconscious synthetic patterns. "According to this concept, the process by which an unconscious content becomes conscious corresponds to a recapitulation of ego development, which also consists in a gradual building up of more and more complex and flexible systems of connections between different instinctual needs and sense perceptions. In this light the therapeutic process appears as the continuation of the learning process, which has been interrupted by repressions."[16]

As a result of interpretation, the neurotic patient learns to differentiate; therapy is thus a type of discriminatory learning. Interpretation serves the function of breaking down primitive connections and establishing new, more differentiated ones. Emotional experience and insight are synchronized in *the integrative principle of interpretation.*

Every new synthesis increases the ability of the ego to face new unconscious material and thus facilitates the appearance of such material. "In analytic therapy our main allies are the *striving of the unconscious forces for expression and the integrating tendency of the conscious ego.* Even if we do nothing else but not interfere with these two dynamic forces, we will be able to help many patients."[17]

To understand the process of therapy, we must consider the emotional involvement of the therapist as well as that of the patient. In 1910, Freud introduced the term *countertransference* to refer to this involvement. It was not until 30 years later that the analyst's reactions and their significance for the treatment were explored. There are differences of opinion as to the nature of this phenomenon. Most writers refer to countertransference as those reactions of the therapist that are inappropriate to the patient–therapist relationship, being determined by the therapist's own characteristic, preformed reaction pattern. All interpersonal attitudes, however, are a composite of realistic and unrealistic reactions to the relationship.

While the patient's transference is a complication in therapy, it is necessary and is the most important aspect of therapy. The countertransference, though, is a disturbing factor, an unavoidable impurity. The therapist must be aware of and control his or her own emotional reactions; one of the major objectives of the training analysis is to make this possible. The minimizing of the therapist's personality reactions in the therapy makes it possible for the therapist to approach the ideal of being the blank screen on which the patient can reflect reaction patterns; that is, it encourages the transference situation. The therapist cannot be entirely neutral, however, and remains a real person; after the transference relationship is established, the therapist's own spontaneous responses are important in therapy.

Still, the therapist does have emotional reactions that are not appropriate, that cannot be concealed, and that do enter into the therapy and interfere with progress. The therapist must recognize and control these reactions. Control usually means not expressing these reactions or behaving differently from the way he or she would if he or she did not know or understand these reactions. This will lead to an impersonal attitude, which, while best in the opening phase of treatment, is not necessarily best in later phases. The modification of this approach in psychoanalytically oriented psychotherapy will be considered below.

IMPLEMENTATION: TECHNIQUES OF THERAPY

"Psychoanalytic principles lend themselves to different therapeutic procedures which vary according to the nature of the case and may be variably applied during the treatment of the same patient."[18] The traditional method of psychoanalysis, with daily interviews continued for months or years, is only one technique, and not necessarily the most efficient and effective method in every case. It is best suited to severe chronic psychoneuroses and character disturbances, but even in these cases, therapy is more effective if the procedure is modified to meet the varying needs of the individual patient and the phases of treatment.

Psychoanalytic therapy emphasizes the value of developing *"a plan of treatment,* based on a dynamic-diagnostic appraisal of the patient's personality and the actual problems he has to solve in his given life conditions. In devising such a plan of therapy, the analyst must decide in each case whether a primarily supportive or uncovering type of treatment is indicated, or whether the therapeutic task is mainly a question of changing the external conditions of the patient's life."[19]

Whereas the traditional method has been passively to let the treatment take its own course, in psychoanalytic therapy, the analyst is more active, and systematic planning becomes necessary. "In addition to the original decision as to the particular sort of strategy to be employed in the treatment of any case, we recommend the *conscious use of various techniques in a flexible manner,* shifting tactics to fit the particular needs of the moment."[20] It is not possible to decide in advance just what course a treatment will take. The goal is to develop a more economical procedure in terms of time and effort by adapting the technique to the individual case.

Universal Factors in Psychotherapy

In all forms of psychotherapy, the therapist, by the mere fact of offering help, gives emotional support. This opportunity for the patient to gratify some of the regressive need for dependence may be therapeutic by reducing the need for gratification through symptoms. In addition to emotional support, the therapist provides intellectual support by giving the patient the opportunity to discuss problems objectively, which allows the patient to use his or her own intellectual capacities to handle practical problems. All forms of psychotherapy provide an opportunity for the patient to express emotions, which relieves tension and prepares the way for insight. These supportive measures grow out of the therapeutic situation and require only the techniques of instilling confidence and listening to the patient with benevolent understanding. These measures are based on common sense, although they have been recognized and improved by psychiatry.

Such measures, in some cases with the additional support of the ego's defenses and manipulation of the life situation, constitute supportive treatment and may be sufficient as treatment of individuals in whom the functional impairment of the ego is of a temporary nature, resulting from acute emotional stress. The use of these techniques, however, should be based on an understanding of the underlying psychopathology. If improperly applied, they may lead to aggravation rather than relief. Moreover, it is not possible at the beginning to determine the amount and type of therapy that a patient needs and thus to determine that supportive treatment rather than uncovering treatment is all that will be necessary. "All forms of psychotherapy must, therefore, be based on a knowledge of personality development and psychodynamics."[21] All therapists, then, should know psychoanalytic theory.

The Techniques of Psychoanalysis

Free Association

The rule of free association requires the patient to tell whatever comes to mind without conscious selection or the application of logic to any train of thought. Freud developed this method of reaching unconscious material after the failure of hypnosis and waking suggestion. Fantasies and dreams, as well as feelings and thoughts, are sources of unconscious material and thus are subjects of free association. Free association is a method of recalling the past and of discharging the emotions connected with the traumatic events of the past. As a technique to obtain self-evaluation on the part of the patient, it is facilitated by the objective, understanding attitude of the therapist. The rule of free association eliminates conscious suppression as a factor in keeping material in the unconscious, leaving only repression as a factor, and repression is not strong enough by itself to prevent some material from entering consciousness. Over a period of time, more and more of the repressed materials of the past, as well as impulses, are revealed. Until repressed tendencies become conscious, they cannot undergo modification and sublimation under the control of the ego.

The Transference

The transference consists, as was indicated earlier, of the emotional reaction of the patient to the therapist in which the patient directs impulses and attitudes toward the therapist. The word is used here in the strict sense, in which it is identical with the transference neurosis except that it includes transient neurotic reactions. It is thus "an irrational repetition of stereotyped reaction patterns which have not been adjusted to conform to the present situation."[22] In the transference, the patient reenacts his or her pathogenetic past, which therefore becomes accessible to the therapist. Psychoanalysis, in fact, consists essentially of the development of the transference neurosis and its resolution.

The patient naturally develops a transference to the therapist, who, in turn, does not discourage but encourages its development by his or her attitudes and techniques. The core of the transference is a dependent attitude, which is inherent in the manner in which the patient comes to the therapist for help.

The resolution of the transference neurosis is a major part of the therapy. The fact that it is only in the mind of the patient that the therapist becomes the parent or another important early figure provides the opportunity for the patient to become aware of his or her reactions. The patient can discriminate between the old conflicts and the transference conflicts, which, without adequate reason, have been directed toward the therapist. The therapist facilitates the differentiation by reacting differently from those early figures in the patient's life. The therapist does not retaliate, intimidate, or threaten. It is because the therapist does not react like the father that the transference reaction is unrealistic and so can be contrasted with the original situation.

Interpretation

The patient experiences the fact that the transference situation is not the same as the original situation, but the therapist also points out or interprets the fact that the patient's attitude is rooted in childhood and is not an adequate reaction to the therapist. This leads to insight, or "intellectual cognition." Interpretation thus aids differentiation. "The analyst's interpretations help the patient to replace the older automatic superego functions with conscious judgment, or, in other words, superego functions are replaced by ego functions."[23]

Although some analysts (for example, Reich) have distinguished between the interpretation of resistance and the interpretation of content, the two cannot be separated. There is no free-floating resistance; it is always directed against something. Therefore, "every resistance should preferably be interpreted in connection with what it is directed against, provided of course that the content interpretation is timely."[24] It is true, of course, that in the interpretation of content, the therapist can go only slightly beyond what the patient is able to understand alone at any given moment.

Interpretation facilitates therapy. "The longer the patient is exposed to material which puzzles him, which seems strange, and appears to him as a foreign body, the longer the analysis will be retarded and the appearance of new unconscious material blocked."[25] Interpretations connect unconscious material to what is already understood by the patient, so they should refer to previous insights. Interpretations point out connections formed by the mind in infancy, so that the patient can see the faulty identifications and generalizations. "It is perhaps too much to expect that the patient will be able without help to recognize the infantile generalizations as something self-evident. I do not doubt, however, that after the old primitive connections are broken up, the patient, because of the integrating power of his ego, would in time establish the new synthesis alone."[26] The therapist can accelerate this integrating process by interpretation and thus become an active participant in the process. "Through our interpretation we do help the synthetic functions of the ego. How much such active help each patient needs is one of the most timely issues."[27] A general principle of interpretation is that it should always start from the surface and go only as deep as the patient is able to go while experiencing the situation emotionally.

Interpretations that connect actual life situations with past experiences and with the transference situation are *total interpretations*. They best fulfill the double purpose of interpretation—the acceleration of the assimilation of new material by the ego and the mobilization of further unconscious material.

Modifications in Psychoanalytic Therapy

Indications for Therapy

Both internal and external factors must be considered in estimating treatability. The individual's adaptability may be estimated by a study of the life history, considering the severity and frequency of breakdowns, the amount of provocation, and the degree of mental health during intermissions. External factors such as physical defects, intelligence, age, and the life situation may facilitate or impede treatment. Sometimes a neurosis may be the only solution to the patient's problems. Responses to trial interpretations are helpful in gauging treatability.

Although both approaches are used in most therapy, a choice must be made between two general types of therapy. Supportive therapy, in which no attempt is made to effect permanent ego changes, is indicated in cases of acute neurotic disturbances in previously well-adjusted persons and with severe chronic patients with whom there is little hope of achieving permanent change. With the former, support is all that is necessary for recovery; with the latter, it is all that is possible. Uncovering therapy, which is aimed at achieving permanent change through insight and emotional experiences, is applicable in a wide variety of cases, both acute and chronic.

Planning Psychotherapy

Persistence and good intentions are no substitutes for consciously directed effort. Treatment can be more pertinent, efficient, and economical when it is planned. Goals and the general approach, anticipated problems, and solutions enter into the plan. The ground strategy may remain the same, but the tactics should be considered "subject to change." A comprehensive plan is a *sine qua non* for any properly handled psychotherapy.

Adequate dynamic formulations should be arrived at early. A clear perspective can be gained in the first few hours before the patient has become deeply involved emotionally. The preliminary investigative period varies with the emotional attitude of the patient. The history may be easy or difficult to obtain. It is important to determine the motive for treatment. This avoids later problems, such as those caused by the patient who does not consider his or her problem psychological but who expects medical treatment for a physical illness. Physical complaints must be investigated. A comprehensive therapeutic plan can then be mapped out. With this plan in mind, the therapist is less likely to be taken by surprise and become discouraged by disturbing complications.

Exploring psychosomatic complaints and external difficulties constitutes a first psychotherapeutic attack on the patient's problem and enables the therapist to observe how the patient approaches the problem. It also provides an evaluation of the patient's ego strength, which is important especially when uncovering therapy is being used with infrequent interviews. How the patient feels about things is more important for tentative formulations than is a large amount of merely factual data. The therapist also draws on experiences with similar cases in formulating a plan.

Since emotional readjustment, not insight, is the goal of therapy, the first question in the formulation of a therapeutic plan is what emotional readjustments are necessary to relieve the patient. These are the goals of therapy, and insight is only one method for achieving them. Some patients cannot tolerate insights into their conflicts. In many cases, emotional readjustment is necessary before insight is possible. The forcing of insight may lead to disturbing complications.

The Principle of Flexibility

In psychoanalytic therapy, techniques are selected and varied to suit the patient, rather than the patient being selected to fit the procedure, as in psychoanalysis. "As we now practice psychoanalytic therapy, we seldom use one and the same method of approach from the first day to the last day of treatment."[28] Either reclining on a couch or sitting face to face may be used, with free association or direct conversations; the full-fledged transference neurosis may be developed, or it may be avoided. Drugs and environmental manipulation may be used. An approach of this sort may be called psychoanalytic because it is based on psychodynamic principles. The so-called standard approach also varies in its techniques.

Choice of technique is determined by many factors, including the psychodynamics of the case, the actual circumstances of the patient's life, and the therapist's experience and skills. Therapists emphasize or specialize in certain techniques. Nevertheless, the therapist selects the techniques that seem most appropriate in the light of the total situation. The ability to choose appropriately is the result of training and long experience.

Frequency of Interview

Daily interviews tend to gratify the patient's dependency needs more than is desirable. The expectation of daily interviews for an indefinite period of time fosters regression and procrastination. The amount and remoteness in time of the regressive material is not a measure of the depth of the analysis but may represent neurotic withdrawal, resistance, and escape. Long, deep regressions can and should be avoided. Daily interviews often reduce the patient's emotional participation because they become routine. Lessening the frequency of interviews allows the intensity of impulses to be built up to the point at which the patient can become aware of them. The optimum level of emotional intensity varies from case to case; the analysis should maintain as high a level as the patient's ego can stand without losing its capacity for insight. After the relationship has become well established, therefore, the frequency of interviews can be varied to maintain this level and to prevent the treatment from becoming a withdrawal from participation in life. The same results as those obtained with the standard procedure may be achieved with fewer interviews and in less time by changing the frequency of interviews according to the needs of the patient. Psychotherapy is thus more economical.

Interruptions and Termination of Treatment

Patients may continue treatment indefinitely because of inertia as long as there are no excessive inconveniences associated with it. The number of interviews may be reduced in order to lead up to an interruption to test the patient's capacity to function without therapy. The patient has the assurance that he or she can return to therapy. Interruptions pave the way for termination. Length of treatment cannot be predicted, and the patient's capacity to function without treatment must be tested by blocking neurotic retreat to fantasy and pressing the patient toward the difficulties of his or her life situation.

The transference neurosis offers gratification of dependent needs and is not as unpleasant as either the original conflicts or those that the patient faced on entering therapy. Therefore, the patient may settle comfortably into the transference and tend to continue indefinitely. Interruption may test whether the patient is dependent on the transference relationship, in which case the patient will regress.

Extratherapeutic Experiences

The neurotic has given up efforts to deal with problems. Therapy is only a preparation for facing and dealing with these difficulties. The therapist must thus influence experiences in real life. This is in contradiction to the accepted attitude that the therapist should not interfere with the patient's life and that no important changes should be made in the patient's life during therapy. Changes may be necessary for progress in therapy. The rule should be: no changes unless both therapist and patient agree. Successes and accomplishments in life are more reassuring than any emotional discharge, recollection, or insight in therapy. The transference relationship is a rehearsal, which must be followed by an actual performance. The fostering of favorable life experiences at the right time shortens therapy. The therapist should encourage and even require the patient to experiment in life activities. "As a scientifically trained therapist, the physician feels he should center his whole attention on the interviews; as a man of common sense he knows he must guide the patient's daily activities to some degree. The common failure lies in not making this guidance an integral part of the whole treatment."[29]

Manipulation of the Transference Relation

In standard psychoanalysis, the transference neurosis is considered to be unavoidable and the *sine qua non* of psychoanalytic therapy. The analysis of the transference neurosis accounts for the length of psychoanalysis. It is "handled," not controlled. Gradually, as they have learned more about the "types" of transference relationships associated with various conflicts, psychoanalysts have made efforts to control the transference neurosis. It has become recognized that a transference neurosis is not always necessary or desirable and that it sometimes is impossible for it to develop, since not all neurotic conflicts can be transferred to a therapist, who may not be a suitable object.

In psychoanalytic therapy, the emphasis is on the transference relationship rather than on the transference neurosis, which may not be allowed to develop. The intensity and content of the transference relationship are controlled. The initial positive transference relationship is utilized, and a negative transference, or hostile attitude toward the therapist, which often complicates and prolongs therapy, may not be allowed to develop. In cases in which the transference relationship is controlled and directed and in which the therapist has become involved in extratherapeutic situations, progress tends to be more rapid, and fewer interviews are required.

The use of interpretations (through choice, timing, and manner of presentation) is the most powerful means of regulating the transference relationship and thus of controlling the intensity of treatment. Interpretation of the infantile neurosis encourages a dependent transference relationship, while restricting interpretations to the present situation avoids this relationship. The variations in conducting treatment, such as use of the couch and whether the therapist sits behind a desk, in a lounge chair, or on the couch beside the patient, all influence the transference relationship. The therapist's attitudes toward the patient also have a great deal of influence.

The technique of free association, which prescribes that the therapist follow the trend chosen by the patient, allows the patient to take the line of least resistance and avoid facing the major conflict by regressing to a relatively conflict-free period of adjustment. The regressive material is of significance and should not be disregarded, but the later conflicts that are being evaded should not be ignored. Interpretation is one method of making the patient aware that this regression is a form of resistance and an evasion.

Some patients may utilize the therapist in a rational manner without developing any transference relationship. Improvement in such patients may be permanent and cannot be denied by labeling it a "transference cure." Such a rational use of therapy may be blocked by the development of a transference neurosis in supportive therapy. In supportive therapy, when the patient reacts with guilt or shame, he or she may be unable to benefit from the permissive and supportive situation. The therapist may have to interpret the motives of guilt underlying the transference neurosis. By decreasing the patient's sense of dependency—by allowing the patient to perform a service for the therapist, for example—the guilt feelings may be relieved, and the transference neurosis may be blocked or diminished; or the therapist may encourage the development of healthy outside interests to lessen the patient's absorption in the therapeutic relationship.

Resistances to disturbing interpretations are not necessarily transference reaction but may be frank opposition to unwelcome interpretations as a normal reaction in defense of the neurosis; such resistances are irrational only in the sense that the neurosis itself is irrational. They may lead to a transference neurosis, however. Interpretations that are too disturbing are resisted by distorting the understanding of the nature of the therapeutic relationship, that is, by a transference reaction. Resistance of this sort is a sign that the patient is unable to assimilate the interpretation and is to be expected as a result of important interpretations. The experienced therapist will follow up such interpretations.

In insight therapy, too strong a transference relationship may impair the patient's judgment and interfere with an understanding of the motives for his or her irrational impulses and of the differences between the earlier situations in which the impulses arose and the present situation. The transference neurosis impairs reality testing, and it may be necessary to damp down the tendency to develop a transference neurosis in order to facilitate the process of reality testing.

Thus the ideal of impersonal behavior on the part of the therapist must be modified. The therapist should not aim to be a blank screen but should behave in the way patients would expect of one to whom they have come for help. "We also tentatively treat the patient as a normal and rational human being and we continue to do so except when the patient himself proves the contrary."[30] The patient can then behave as a normal human being, and any irrational tendencies are thrown into sharper contrast. The transference neurosis is allowed to develop and is encouraged only when and to the extent deemed desirable by the therapist. Concentration on the infantile neurosis encourages more than is necessary the tendency of the patient to interpret present situations as though they were identical with traumatic situations in the past. "Accordingly, insofar as it is our purpose to strengthen the reality testing function of the ego, our policy should be just the opposite; we should center the patient's attention rather on his real problems and should turn his attention to disturbing events in the past only for the purpose of throwing light upon the motives for irrational reactions in the present."[31] Similarly, the patient's attention should be focused on problems in the external world rather than on his or her reactions to the therapist. The focusing of attention on present problems follows Freud's concept of therapy as a process of reeducation, a resumption of an interrupted learning process. The primary concern in therapy is not the recovery of the past but the discovery of solutions for present problems.

Controlling the Countertransference

The standard approach emphasizes that the countertransference reactions of the therapist must be understood and controlled. However, it has been recognized that spontaneous countertransference reactions occasionally may by chance be helpful. If the countertransference attitude happens to be the same as the original parental attitude, the original conflict will easily repeat itself in the transference situation, but it will be difficult for the patient to modify it. However, if the therapist has, and unwittingly expresses, a different attitude, a novel situation is created that may contribute to the therapy. It is suggested that the therapist "should attempt to replace his spontaneous countertransference reactions with attitudes which are consciously planned and adopted according to the dynamic exigencies of the therapeutic situation."[32] Knowledge of the early interpersonal attitudes that contributed to the patient's neurosis can help the therapist assume an attitude that will provoke the kind of emotional experience that will be conducive to the undoing of the pathogenic effect of the original attitude. The therapist must be aware of his or her countertransference attitudes, must be able to control them, and must substitute the appropriate attitudes. While the intuitive therapist often functions in this way, it is desirable to replace intuition with conscious understanding. Thus it is possible that as transference first was considered to be an impurity and later became the axis of therapy, so the impurity of countertransference may become an important instrument of therapy.

The creation of a suitable interpersonal atmosphere through the expression of appropriate attitudes does not mean that the therapist plays a role or assumes the role of a significant person in the patient's past; neither does it mean that the therapist's personality does not enter into the relationship, nor does it deny the importance of the therapist's objective interest and permissiveness in the therapeutic process.

Dream Interpretation

Dreams express in a disguised form the alien impulses and desires of the patient. They are distorted by the resistance aroused by the impulses. The manifest (open) content of the dream is a compression or condensation of the latent (repressed) elements. Details often express hidden personal allusions. Causality is replaced by temporal sequences. Many things are represented by their opposites. The dream is the result of a compromise between two opposing forces: the wish to express a desire or relieve tension, and the tendency to reject the desire. Painful dreams, from which the dreamer awakes in terror, represent the failure of the dream work to disguise the objectionable content sufficiently or are the result of a guilty conscience.

Dreams are analyzed by having the patient engage in free association with regard to the manifest content. With the assistance of the therapist, the latent elements are discovered. The free association and the therapeutic situation lessen the patient's unconscious censorship, so that the pressure of the repressed wish breaks through. Certain dream elements are common symbols of universal human experience.

Resistance to the therapist's interpretation of a dream may lead to another dream rejecting the interpretation. The second dream may yield clues as to the nature of the resistance. Dreams provide an excellent estimate of the psychodynamic situation as the treatment progresses. Dream sequences reveal progressive integrative accomplishments of the ego.

The Principle of Corrective Emotional Experience

In all psychotherapy, the patient must undergo a corrective emotional experience to repair the traumatic influence of previous experiences. This experience may occur during treatment in the transference relationship or in the patient's daily life. Narcosynthesis is the simplest example of a situation in which an experience is relived, and with the help of the narcotic and the presence of the therapist to reduce anxiety, the outcome is different from that which originally occurred. The mastery of an unresolved conflict becomes possible in the transference relationship because it is experienced less intensely than it was originally and because the therapist's attitude differs from that of the parent in the original situation.

Intellectual insight is not sufficient for such resolution of conflict; the patient must *feel* the irrationality of his or her emotional reactions, which will lead to dealing differently with them. The difference between the old conflict situation and the therapeutic situation constitutes the value of the latter. The resulting relationship between the patient and the therapist is thus different, which leads to a new experience for the patient. The therapist must understand the genetic development of the patient's conflicts, so that the therapist can revive them in order to enable the patient to reexperience them. The control of the countertransference in the ways discussed above facilitates the development of corrective emotional experiences.

Manipulation of the Environment

In addition to supportive therapy and uncovering therapy, which attempts to modify the patient's personality structure in order to harmonize it with environmental requirements, therapy includes making the patient's situation easier by adapting the environment to the patient's needs. In actual therapy with a particular individual, these methods are used in various combinations.

Supportive therapy itself may be considered environmental treatment, since the therapist is part of the patient's environment and the patient's control of his or her own behavior constitutes manipulation of the environment. "Transference cures," in which the patient obtains great relief on beginning treatment without the development of any insight, may be considered environmental treatment.

Putting the patient in a different environment and changing the behavior and attitudes of people in the patient's environment are the main methods in what is usually considered manipulation of the environment.

Conclusion

In order to be relieved of his neurotic ways of feeling and acting, the patient must undergo new emotional experiences suited to undo the morbid effects of the emotional experiences of his earlier life. Other therapeutic factors—such as intellectual insight, abreaction, recollection of the past, etc.—are all subordinated to this central therapeutic principle. Re-experiencing the old, unsettled conflict *but with a new ending* is the secret of every penetrating therapeutic result. . . . In the patient–physician relationship, the therapist has a unique opportunity to provide the patient with precisely that type of corrective experience which he needs for recovery. It is a secondary question what technique is employed to bring it about. The *standard* psychoanalytic technique is only one—and not in every case the most suitable one—of the many possible applications of fundamental psychodynamic principles that can be utilized for this kind of emotional training.[33]

There are disadvantages in any routine procedure. Treatment must be flexible, allowing for the use of those techniques best suited to the nature of the case.

EXAMPLE

Alexander's writings do not include typescripts of interviews. The 1946 publication by Alexander and French contains many presentations and discussions of cases, however. Any single case may be atypical, and any one is limited in presenting a point of view as comprehensive as psychoanalytically oriented psychotherapy. Space does not allow the inclusion of several cases or even one long case. A brief case is presented here.[34] The interested reader may refer to *Psychoanalytic Therapy* for others.

Reactive Depression

A physician, a German refugee 45 years old, came for psychotherapy because of an intense depression resulting from extreme irritation with his son. He was seen for a single consultation with excellent results. The therapist (a man) was also a recent immigrant.

The patient had had no serious neurotic difficulties before. He had been in this country for ten months, and his wife and only child, a nine-year-old boy, had only recently joined him. His chief complaint was that he felt extremely irritated by his son, that he could not concentrate on his work in the boy's presence, that he was annoyed by his demanding attitude and his constant need for attention. He was now so discouraged over his inability to adjust himself to the child that he had become exceedingly depressed and decided to consult a psychiatrist.

In the course of the discussion, the patient's attention was distracted from his complaints about his son with a few questions about the way he had lived before his family joined him. He then talked freely about the circumstances of his immigration and about his first attempts to reconstruct his life in the new environment. Although he had had a hard time in the beginning, he had been fairly successful in getting established in his profession.

As he talked it became clear to him that his son and wife had joined him "too soon," that they had come before he was ready to offer them the security they needed. With considerable emotion—at first hesitantly, then with conviction—he said he realized that life would be easier now if his son and wife were not with him. He saw that the demands of his son were really not exaggerated but seemed so because he himself felt insecure—not only within himself but also in his economic adjustment. He felt guilty and responsible, and even saw some justification for his son's behavior, since his own difficulties in the new environment did not allow him to be the ideal father his standards demanded. As he talked the whole situation over, he gained more and more insight into these feelings (which were not far under the surface) and with this insight he experienced marked relief.

But insight alone was not enough. It was necessary also to help this patient make some practical arrangement whereby he could adjust his way of working to the American style of life—chiefly through having an office outside the home. This made it possible for him to divide his energies; he could be a hardworking doctor part of the time, and an attentive father and husband the rest of the time.

When he was seen by the therapist two years later, the patient referred to himself as a "week-end father." He expressed his gratitude for the insight he had gained in this one interview, and added that not only his relationship to his son but his relationship to other aspects of his family life and to the American scene in general had greatly improved.

Comments

It might be argued that a confidential talk with a friend would have helped this patient as much as the psychiatric interview. The evidence, however, is against this assumption, since the patient had often talked over his difficulties with his refugee friends, many of whom had had difficulty in adjusting themselves to new ways and conditions.

The therapeutic success in this case consisted mainly in bringing into consciousness conflicting emotions which were preconscious but still suppressed. This man had become rebellious against too much responsibility in a trying situation and was depressed as a result. Insight into his unconscious reaction to immigration in general, and to his family situation in particular, facilitated his emotional readjustment. He had a strong, efficient ego and its powers of integration were readily mobilized and set to work.

The fact that the patient was seen in only one interview precludes any analysis of the transference situation. We surmise, however, that the patient saw in this analyst who, he knew, had also gone through the trying experience of immigration a few years before, a good object for identification. This in itself speeded the rapport necessary for any successful therapy and served as a support of the patient's ego, which had begun to fail under the heavy load of responsibility.

Another reason for this therapist's being especially suitable for this patient was the fact that he had already learned the ways of American doctors and could give the patient concrete advice and help in establishing himself in the medical profession.

SUMMARY AND EVALUATION

Psychoanalytically oriented psychotherapy is psychotherapy that utilizes psychoanalytic principles and methods but is modified or adapted to the needs of the individual case. Modifications include varying the frequency of interviews, encouraging the patient to take actions with regard to his or her life situation, interrupting therapy on a trial basis, and manipulating the patient's environment. Therapy may vary from a supportive type—involving only listening, acceptance, and catharsis or confession—to deep uncovering therapy. The transference may not exist, may not be allowed to develop, or may be developed in a full-fledged transference neurosis. Its development is controlled through the frequency of interviews and the nature of the interpretations given. Emphasis is placed on the "corrective emotional experience" of the patient rather than on intellectual insight. Insight is not necessary for change in behavior and often follows rather than precedes such change.

The therapist is active in controlling the therapeutic process in the ways just indicated and in using countertransference attitudes. Rather than merely understanding and controlling countertransference feelings and attitudes, the therapist may express certain attitudes that seem desirable in order to provide a situation that varies from that in which the patient's conflicts developed.

Such an approach to therapy involves planning in advance. Early in therapy, the therapist develops a psychodynamic formulation, forms a general plan for the treatment, and attempts to anticipate problems or difficulties that might arise, as well as methods of meeting them. Details of tactics may change, as has been indicated, during the process of therapy. Such therapy differs from orthodox psychoanalysis, which French characterizes as "drifting" into therapeutic relationships. It requires more skill than does the orthodox method. When therapy is not on a daily basis, "an even greater alertness and an even greater agility are required of the therapist."[35]

Psychoanalytic therapy, it is claimed, is more widely applicable than psychoanalysis and is more efficient and economical. It adapts the method to the needs of the patient, rather than selecting patients to fit the method. Results are obtained in a shorter period of time. In their 1946 publication, Alexander and French report that their brief psychotherapy required from 1 to a total of 65 interviews over a period of 17 months in the cases on which it had been used (approximately 600 patients).

> Following the principle of adapting psychodynamic therapy to the structure of the individual case, we find that we can, in a relatively brief period, produce therapeutic changes previously considered possible only when the time-consuming technique of standard psychoanalysis was used. . . . It is not claimed that this abbreviated form of psychoanalysis is possible in all cases. Certain patients need prolonged treatment with frequent interviews. But, as this book shows, there are many instances in which more intensive but less frequent interviews—or even a less intensive treatment—than would have been prescribed in the past, will produce the desired therapeutic changes in an equally dependable but accelerated fashion.[36]

Psychoanalytic therapy, while incorporating modifications in methods and techniques, essentially accepts the orthodox psychoanalytic theory of psychodynamics. The modifications in psychodynamics are small compared with those made by Adler, Rank, or neoanalysts such as Horney and Sullivan. However, Alexander does not accept the association of various kinds of neuroses and psychoses with the psychoanalytic levels of sexual development. He writes that "the attempt to explain the inclination for certain types of symptoms formation from fixations to definite phases of development needs further investigation. This theory seems most applicable to schizophrenics and compulsion neuroses."[37] In addition, Alexander's approach does not limit itself to assuming a sexual etiology for all conflicts. Recognition is given to the role of other impulses, particularly hostility, in etiology.

The modifications in techniques have raised disputes as to whether Alexander's approach should be considered psychoanalytic. There are those who maintain that the presence of a full-fledged transference neurosis is essential for psychoanalysis or any treatment bearing the title psychoanalytic. Others feel that the other modifications, such as holding interviews on less than a daily basis, changing the frequency of the interviews, and minimizing insight, are basic deviations from the theory of psychoanalytic treatment.

Alexander, however, defends the use of the term *psychoanalytic* on the basis that he accepts and utilizes the psychodynamic principles of psychoanalysis and that he uses the techniques of standard analysis, introducing only conscious and planned application of them on a quantitative basis. No fundamentally new techniques are proposed, just the flexible application of accepted methods. "Moreover, every therapy which increases the integrative functions of the ego (through reexposing the patient under more favorable conditions to those conflicts which have before met with neurotic defense mechanisms) should be called psychoanalytic, no matter whether its duration is for one or two interviews, for several weeks or months, or for several years."[38]

Psychoanalytically oriented psychotherapy is certainly less rigid and more flexible than is standard psychoanalysis. In the controversy concerning insight and emotional experiencing, which has been going on outside psychoanalytic circles as well as within them, psychoanalytically oriented psychotherapists place the emphasis on the latter. French, in his contributions to the 1946 publication, appears to favor insight more than does Alexander. In some respects, the approach fosters less dependence of the patient on the therapist, as is evident in the control and manipulation of the transference relationship. In other respects, however, as in guiding and advising the patient, in encouraging the patient's extratherapy behavior, and in manipulating the environment, it appears to foster greater dependence. This approach is apparently more manipulative of the therapy relationship and of the patient's total behavior than is orthodox psychoanalysis.

It is claimed that psychoanalytically oriented psychotherapy is a "rational dynamic psychotherapy."[39] This claim presumably is based on its adaptation to the individual, following the development of a plan based on a diagnostic study of the patient, and its flexibility in adapting to the changing situation as therapy progresses. This departure from the standard method of utilizing the same techniques or procedures with every patient introduces the problem of choice of techniques for the individual case, which requires the identification of the patient's needs, on the one hand, and of appropriate techniques to meet these needs, on the other. Alexander and French make some attempt to do this, but it is hardly adequate. The discrimination of different needs or classes of needs or of diagnostic formulations is not systematically presented, and there is no evidence of the reliability of the diagnostic formulations that are necessary as a basis for planning the treatment. It is generally recognized that agreement of psychiatrists or psychologists on such formulations is not high. On the treatment side, also, the consideration of techniques, with the indications for their differential use, is not systematically approached. It appears that this whole area is to be the province of the clinical judgment of the individual therapist, based on training and experience—factors that are stressed by Alexander. He writes:

> Because of the variables involved in every treatment, techniques are best demonstrated on the material itself. We shall make no attempt, therefore, to consider the indications for each specific technique but shall try to show in the case presentations of later chapters how interlocked are the psychodynamics and circumstances with the method of procedure necessary for each case, and how we have learned from experience to choose, modify, and combine techniques as the therapeutic process demands.[40]

Alexander recognizes that although there are indications pointing to the desirability of interruption of treatment on a trial basis and of termination, there are no quantifiable criteria. The patient's own intimation is not acceptable.

While the analyses of the cases presented in *Psychoanalytic Therapy* may be impressive, there is no evidence for their reliability or validity. Many of the methods and techniques and their justifications appear reasonable and would be accepted by many psychotherapists. They are essentially not new departures or innovations, as Alexander clearly notes, but methods that have been used by psychoanalysts, as well as by other therapists, for many years.

In some respects, these methods, or their flexible use, are an improvement on the rigid insistence of orthodox psychoanalysis on an inflexible, standard procedure. In other respects, however, flexibility creates problems. These include problems of the bases for choosing among techniques and for changing them. Problems relating to the reactions of the patients are also unsolved, although they are not recognized by Alexander. While the avoidance of the full-fledged transference neurosis reduces one kind of dependence and may shorten therapy, the use of active guidance and direct influence on the patient through suggestion, advice, encouragement, and so on, while also apparently speeding up therapy, may lead to another kind of dependence. Finally, the possibility that changing techniques may appear as inconsistent to the patient, confusing the patient and thus slowing up therapy, must be considered.

Before his death, Alexander moved still farther from orthodox psychoanalysis, apparently as a result of the findings from a long-term study supported by the Ford Foundation and conducted at Mount Sinai Hospital in Los Angeles. This study involved the observation and tape recording of psychoanalytic therapy sessions. His concept of psychotherapy moved toward learning theory; some of the intimations of this move can be seen in the summary in this chapter. He wrote that the most important conclusion from his research is the fact that the traditional descriptions of the therapeutic process do not adequately reflect the immensely complex interaction between therapist and patient. The patient's reactions cannot be described fully as transference reactions. The patient reacts to the therapist as to a concrete person and not only as a representative of parental figures. The therapist's reactions also far exceed what is usually called countertransference. They include in addition to this, interventions based on conscious deliberations and also his spontaneous idiosyncratic attitudes. Moreover, his own values are conveyed to the patient even if he consistently tries to protect his incognito.[41]

Alexander's revised learning theory view appears to be closely related to that of Dollard and Miller.

REFERENCES

1. Franz Alexander and Thomas Morton French, *Psychoanalytic therapy.* Copyright 1946. Ronald Press, New York. P. vii. Reprinted by permission of John Wiley & Sons, Inc.
2. Alexander, F. M. *Fundamentals of psychoanalysis.* New York: Norton, 1963. P. 3.
3. Alexander, F. M. *Psychoanalysis and psychotherapy.* New York: Norton, 1956. P. 172.
4. Alexander, *Fundamentals of psychoanalysis.*
5. Ibid., p. 53.
6. Ibid., p. 55.
7. Ibid., p. 75.
8. Ibid., p. 76.
9. Ibid., p. 96.
10. Ibid., p. 119.
11. Ibid., p. 239.
12. Ferenczi-Hollos, quoted in ibid., p. 259.
13. Alexander, *Psychoanalysis and psychotherapy,* p. 11.
14. Ibid., p. 39.
15. Ibid., p. 55.
16. Ibid., p. 67.
17. Ibid., p. 69.
18. Alexander, *Fundamentals of psychoanalysis,* p. 273.
19. Alexander & French, *Psychoanalytic therapy,* p. 5.
20. Ibid., p. 6.
21. Alexander, *Fundamentals of psychoanalysis,* p. 157.
22. Alexander & French, *Psychoanalytic therapy,* p. 72.
23. Alexander, *Psychoanalysis and psychotherapy,* p. 45.
24. Ibid., p. 57.
25. Ibid., p. 67.
26. Ibid., p. 68.
27. Ibid., p. 70.
28. Alexander & French, *Psychoanalytic therapy,* p. 25.
29. Ibid., p. 19.
30. Ibid., p. 87.
31. Ibid., p. 88.
32. Alexander, *Psychoanalysis and psychotherapy,* p. 93.
33. Alexander & French, *Psychoanalytic therapy,* p. 338.

34. Franz Alexander and Thomas Morton French, *Psychoanalytic therapy*. Copyright 1946. The Ronald Press Company, New York. Pp. 155–157. Reprinted with permission of John Wiley & Sons, Inc.
35. Ibid., p. 140.
36. Ibid., p. 207.
37. Alexander, *Fundamentals of psychoanalysis*, p. 250.
38. Alexander & French, *Psychoanalytic therapy*, pp. 338–339.
39. Ibid., p. 341.
40. Ibid., p. 106.
41. Alexander, F. M. The dynamics of psychotherapy in the light of learning theory. *American Journal of Psychiatry*, 1963, *120*, 440–448.

four

PERCEPTUAL-PHENOMENOLOGICAL APPROACHES

A number of approaches to counseling or psychotherapy, although differing in many significant respects, have in common a major concern with the perceptions or perceptual field of the individual client. These approaches assume, explicitly or implicitly, that since behavior is determined by the individual's perceptual field, a change in the perceptual field is necessary before behavior will change. Differences occur in the methods employed to achieve such change.

George Kelly's psychology of personal constructs[1] is a perceptual-phenomenological theory. Personal constructs are perceptions, and changing personal constructs thus involves changing perceptions. Kelly's methods are highly rational or cognitive, which is probably the reason he did not identify himself as a phenomenologist.

Client-centered therapy is perhaps the first major approach to psychotherapy that is explicitly based on phenomenological psychology and explicitly concerned with the most effective or appropriate methods for changing the perceptions of clients. One of the sources for misconceptions of client-centered therapy is the lack of an adequate understanding of its phenomenological foundations. While Rogers[2] does deal with this, he does not elaborate on it. The student should be familiar with phenomenological psychology as a basis for understanding client-centered therapy. A systematic treatment will be found in Combs, Richards, and Richards.[3] Although a number of writers have presented the client-centered approach, Rogers was its originator and has been its chief exponent. Some of the newer developments of the approach have been included in Chapter 14 in this edition.

One perceptual approach in psychology is labeled "transactional" by those associated with its evolution.[4] The term *transaction* was taken from Dewey and Bentley.[5] It applies to the treatment of events as processes in time and environment. A segment of time in this process is labeled a transaction and includes in the case of human beings the individual organism and his or her environment. Activities of human beings cannot be treated as theirs alone or even as primarily theirs but must be seen as processes of the interaction of the organism and its environment; that is, neither one exists or can be understood without the other. *Transaction* is defined by English and English as "a psychological event in which all the parts or aspects of the concrete event derive their existence and nature from active participation in the event."[6] In this respect, the transactional view differs from the concept of interaction, with which it is sometimes confused.[7] The concept of interaction implies two separate or independently existing objects that interact with each other without being changed by the interaction. In a transaction, both are changed by the process. It appears that the transactional point of view has been adapted and utilized, at least to some extent, by many who do not use the term itself. These include George H. Mead, Kurt Goldstein, Gordon and Floyd Allport, Gardner Murphy, Prescott Lecky, and C. R. Rogers. Thus there is perhaps some point to Levitt's comment that "transactionalism is a somewhat fancy label applied to a viewpoint which is far from new."[8] It is a point of view that is implicit in much of the research and writing on perception as well as on phenomenological psychology.

Two approaches in counseling or psychotherapy have adopted the term *transactional.* One is presented in *Psychiatric Social Work: A Transactional Case Book,* by Grinker and his co-workers.[9] This approach was included in the first two editions of the book. It does not seem to be generally or widely accepted or applied and has been omitted from this edition.

In the same year that *Psychiatric Social Work* was published, Berne's first book-length publication on transactional analysis appeared.[10] It was followed by other publications, including two that were published after his death in 1970, and an edited book of selections from his writings. Berne's work was independent of that of Grinker and his associates, and both were apparently independent of the development of transactional psychology. In the foreword to his book on group treatment, Berne notes the differing origins and nature of the approaches.[11] Berne's transactional analysis developed out of and has been applied mainly in group situations, which was the main reason his approach was not included in the earlier editions of this book. It has relevance for individual psychotherapy, however, and has a wide popularity. It is included here to provide a summary of Berne's work in order to supplement—or even counteract—the popularized versions.

Another popular perceptual or phenomenological approach to psychotherapy is Gestalt therapy. Its development is associated with Frederick (Fritz) Perls, whose 1947 book[12] (republished in 1969) was followed by a book in collaboration with Ralph Hefferline and Paul Goodman in 1951[13] (republished in 1965) and by other books, including two published after his death in 1970. As has been the case with transactional analysis, numerous publications dealing with Gestalt therapy have appeared since Perls's death. However, the presentation here is based on Perls's writings, since little, if anything, of significance has been contributed by other writers.

It might be noted that Ellis's rational-emotive approach is basically phenomenological. However, its rational elements dominate, even in the phenomenological view of behavior as determined by (irrational) beliefs.

Finally, all the perceptual approaches have existential elements, as their proponents recognize. However, these elements are subordinate and not systematically developed, so the perceptual approaches cannot be classified as existential therapies.

REFERENCES

1. Kelly, G. A. *The psychology of personal constructs.* Vol. 1: *A theory of personality.* Vol. 2: *Clinical diagnosis and psychotherapy.* New York: Norton, 1955.
2. Rogers, C. R. *Client-centered therapy.* Boston: Houghton Mifflin, 1951.
3. Combs, A. W., Richards, A. C., & Richards, F. *Perceptual psychology: A humanistic approach to the study of persons.* New York: Harper & Row, 1975.
4. Cantril, H., Ames, A., Jr., Hastorf, A. H., & Ittelson, W. H. Psychology and scientific research. *Science,* 1949, *110,* 461–464; Ittelson, W. H. *The Ames demonstrations in perception.* Princeton, N.J.: Princeton University Press, 1952; Kilpatrick, F. P. (Ed.). *Human behavior from the transactional point of view.* Hanover, N.H.: Institute for Associated Research, 1952; Kilpatrick, F. P. *Explorations in transactional psychology.* New York: New York University Press, 1961.
5. Dewey, J., & Bentley, A. *Knowing and the known.* Boston: Beacon Press, 1949.
6. English, H. B., & English, A. C. *A comprehensive dictionary of psychological and psychoanalytic terms.* New York: McKay, 1958. P. 561.
7. Kanfer, F. H. Review of *Psychiatric social work: A transactional casebook* by R. R. Grinker, Sr., H. MacGregor, K. Selan, A. Klein, and J. Korman. *Contemporary Psychology,* 1962, *7,* 295–296.
8. Levitt, E. L. Review of *Perceptual changes in psychopathology* edited by W. H. Ittelson and S. B. Kutash. *Contemporary Psychology,* 1962, *7,* 255–256.
9. Grinker, R. R., Sr., MacGregor, H., Selan, K., Klein, A., & Korman, J. *Psychiatric social work: A transactional casebook.* New York: Basic Books, 1961.
10. Berne, E. *Transactional analysis in psychotherapy.* New York: Grove Press, 1961.
11. Berne, E. *Principles of group treatment.* New York: Oxford University Press, 1964. P. x.
12. Perls, F. S. *Ego, hunger and aggression.* New York: Random House, 1947, 1969.
13. Perls, F. S., Hefferline, R. F., & Goodman, P. *Gestalt therapy.* New York: Julian Press, 1951. (Paperback published by Dell, 1965)

chapter *11*

Psychology of Personal Constructs and Counseling: Kelly

One of the most systematic approaches to counseling or psychotherapy is that developed by George A. Kelly on the basis of his psychology of personal constructs. Kelly (1905–1967) received his B.A. in 1926 at Park College, his M.A. at the University of Kansas in 1928, his B.Ed. in 1930 from the University of Edinburgh, and his Ph.D. from the State University of Iowa in 1931. Although his Ph.D. was in psychology, his earlier work included study in education, sociology, economics, labor relations, speech pathology, biometrics, and cultural anthropology. In 1931, he became an instructor at Fort Hays State College in Kansas and was an associate professor when he entered the navy for two years in 1943. He was an associate professor at the University of Maryland during 1945 to 1946. In 1946, he became professor of psychology at Ohio State University and served as director of the psychological clinic from 1946 to 1951 and in 1963, while continuing as professor of psychology until 1965. He then became professor of psychology at Brandeis University, where he remained until his death in 1967. Kelly was a Diplomate in Clinical Psychology of the American Board of Professional Psychology. In 1969, Maher published a collection of Kelly's papers under the title *Clinical Psychology and Personality.* One of the papers in this book, "The Autobiography of a Theory," is a personal account of the development of the theory of personal constructs, beginning with Kelly's repudiation of stimulus–response determinism, through a Freudian period, to the present- and future-oriented view of constructive alternativism.

BACKGROUND AND DEVELOPMENT

The Psychology of Personal Constructs[1] began, Kelly reports, as a handbook of clinical procedures compiled 20 years before its publication as a two-volume work. The "how-to" approach was not satisfying, however, and he began to explore the "why." Kelly then discovered that the result he obtained was far different from traditional psychology. Many implicit assumptions were recognized, and this led to a third approach, that of system building, which required the development of explicit assumptions and the expression of convictions that had been taken for granted in clinical practice. The first task, then, was the construction of a theory of personality, followed by the development of its implications for psychological practice.

The resulting system differs from the familiar psychological systems. Far from occupying the central place, as it does in most contemporary systems, the term *learning* hardly appears. Concepts such as ego, emotion, motivation, reinforcement, drive, need, and unconscious do not appear. Instead, such concepts as foci of convenience, preemption, propositionality, fixed-role therapy, creativity cycle, transitive diagnosis, and the credulous approach are encountered. Other common concepts, such as anxiety, guilt, and hostility, carry new definitions. The result is an unorthodox theory of personality and of therapy.

PHILOSOPHY AND CONCEPTS

The Philosophy of Constructive Alternativism

Points of Departure

Two simple notions underlie Kelly's theory of personality. One is that human beings are better understood when they are viewed in the perspective of centuries; the other is "that each man contemplates in his own personal way the stream of events upon which he finds himself so swiftly borne."[2] Within these notions, there is the possibility of discovering ways in which individuals can restructure their lives. The long-range view focuses attention on humanity's progress and on *scientists,* seeking to predict and control the causes of events in which they are involved. Thus human motivation is seen in a new light, instead of in terms of appetites, needs, and impulses.

Humanity exists in a real universe, which it is gradually coming to understand. Thoughts also really exist, but the correspondence between what people think exists and what really exists is imperfect, although it is in a constant state of change. The universe is integral, with all its parts having exact relationships to one another, but it is constantly changing, so that there is a dimension of time that must be considered. While some aspects of the universe make sense without the time dimension, life makes sense only when it is viewed in the perspective of time.

Life has the capacity to represent other forms of reality or to represent its environment and can place alternative constructions on the environment; thus it does more than respond to its environment. The individual may misrepresent the real phenomenon, but the misrepresentation will itself be real; "what he perceives may not exist, but his perception does."[3] Human beings look at the world through patterns, which are ways of construing the world, or *constructs.* Although people seek to improve their constructs by increasing their repertory, in order to provide a better fit between perceptions and the real environment, the larger system of which their constructs are a part may resist change because of their personal investment in or dependence on it.

Construction systems that can be communicated can be shared, and progress in such communication has been great. Systems may be designed to fit special fields or realms—for example, those of psychology and physiology—but realms may overlap or may give rise to alternative systems or ways of representing or viewing the same facts, as is the case with psychology and physiology. There is no universal system of constructs. All our systems are miniature systems with limited ranges. The system of personal constructs is limited to human personality and problems of interpersonal relationships. Systems have centers or points where they work best. The theory of personal constructs tends to focus on the area of human readjustment to stress and thus proves to be most useful to the psychotherapist.

Constructs are used to predict events. They are thus tested in terms of their predictive efficiency. A construct may appear to be validated by events that are misrepresented because of the need to validate it. Constructs are more susceptible to revision when they are immediately tested on an experimental basis. The continuing course of events reveals constructs either as usefully valid or as misleading and thus provides the basis for revision of constructs and construction systems. Some people are afraid to express and test their constructs; this is a problem in psychotherapy.

The Philosophical Position

The world may be construed in various ways. Interpretations constitute successive approximations of an absolute construction. Constructive alternativism assumes "that all of our present interpretations of the universe are subject to revision or replacement. . . . We take the stand that there are always some alternative constructions available to choose among in dealing with the world. No one needs to paint himself into a corner; no one needs to be completely hemmed in by circumstances, no one needs to be the victim of his biography."[4] Some alternatives are better than others; some lead to difficulty. The criterion is the specific predictive efficiency of each and of the system of which it could become a part.

Constructs are not necessarily symbolized by words, nor are they capable of being verbalized; the concept as such may seem to be psychological rather than philosophical. Constructive alternativism is a philosophical point of view rather than a philosophical system. It bears some relation to various philosophical systems, however, falling within the area of epistemology called *gnoseology*. It also relies on *empiricism* and *pragmatic* logic, although it is in a measure *rationalistic* and stands apart from traditional realism, which makes human beings victims of circumstances. Ontologically, it is a *monistic* position.

The notion of an integral universe implies determinism. However, since there is no repetition and each sequence of events is unique, "there is not much point in singling it out and saying that it was determined. It was a consequent—but only once!"[5] The sort of determinism that is important here is the control exercised by a superordinate construct over its elements. The elements do not determine the construct, which is thus free from or independent of them. "Determinism and freedom are then inseparable, for that which determines another is, by the same token, free of the other. Determinism and freedom are opposite sides of the same coin—two aspects of the same relationship."[6] Thus the individual,

"to the extent that he is able to construe his circumstances, can find for himself freedom from their domination. . . . Theories are the thinking of men who seek freedom amid swirling events. The theories comprise prior assumptions about certain realms of these events. To the extent that the events may, from these prior assumptions, be construed, predicted, and their relative courses charted, men may exercise control, and gain freedom for themselves in the process.[7]

For those individuals whose constructs limit and restrict them, the theory of personal constructs is concerned with finding ways to help them reconstrue their lives in order to keep themselves from being victims of their past.

Basic Theory

Fundamental Postulate

A person's processes are psychologically channeled by the ways in which the person anticipates events. As a postulate, this assumption is not subject to question. It is accepted as a presupposition. The term *processes* indicates that the person is a behaving organism, so that it is not necessary to account for or establish the existence of some sort of mental energy. *Channeled* refers to a network of pathways, flexible but structured, that both facilitates and restricts a person's range of action. *Anticipates* indicates the predictive and motivational features, which point toward the future. "Anticipation is both the push and pull of personal constructs."[8] The psychology of personal constructs develops from this postulate through corollaries that in part follow from and in part elaborate it.

Construction Corollary

A person anticipates events by construing their replications. This means that events are predicted by placing an interpretation on or structuring the recurring aspects of events. Construing is not identical with verbal formulation; it may not necessarily be symbolized.

Individuality Corollary

Persons differ from one another in their construction of events. This is because no two persons participate in the same event in the same way.

Organization Corollary

Each person characteristically evolves, for convenience in anticipating events, a construction system that embraces ordinal relationships among constructs. A system of constructs minimizes incompatibilities and inconsistencies and involves a hierarchy of constructs, with some being superordinal and others, subordinal. An individual's system sometimes needs revision, but the individual may choose to conserve its integrity. While this appears to be similar to Lecky's concept of the need for self-consistency, it is not for consistency itself that the individual is seeking to preserve the system, but because the system is essential for an anticipation of events.

Dichotomy Corollary

A person's construction system is composed of a finite number of dichotomous constructs. Similarities and contrasts, which constitute replication, are in terms of the same aspect; that is, if we select an aspect in which A and B are similar but are different from C, this same aspect is the basis of the construct. "In its minimum context a construct is a way in which at least two elements are similar and contrast with a third."[9] Concepts are meaningless except in relation to or in comparison with their contrasts, opposites, or complements; for example, *good* has no meaning except in comparison with *bad*.

Choice Corollary

A person chooses the alternative in a dichotomized construct through which he or she anticipates the greater possibility for extension and definition of a system. Choice consists of placing relative values on the alternatives of the dichotomies. Extension and definition include both elaboration, or comprehensiveness, and explicitness, or clarity. While the choices might be said to constitute "a seeking of self-protection" or "acting in defense of the self" or "the preservation of one's integrity . . . from our point of view a person's construction system is for the anticipation of events. If it were for something else, it would probably shape up into something quite different."[10] The individual does not seek pleasure, satisfactions, or rewards to satisfy needs or reduce tensions but seeks to anticipate events; "there is a continuing movement toward the anticipation of events, rather than a series of barters for temporal satisfactions, and this movement is the essence of human life itself."[11]

Range Corollary

A construct is convenient for the anticipation of a finite range of events only. Constructs are limited and are applicable only within a restricted range of the perceptual field. Some persons use a construct more comprehensively than do others.

Experience Corollary

A person's construction system varies as he or she successively construes the replication of events. Events subject a person's construct system to a validation process, which leads to revision of the system or to a reconstruing of events and a reconstruction of life through experience. Learning is inherent in this corollary and is thus a part of the assumptive structure of the theory; it is not a special class of psychological processes but synonymous with any and all processes.

Modulation Corollary

The variation in a person's construction system is limited by the permeability of the constructs within whose range of convenience the variants lie. Permeability is the admitting of new, as yet unconstrued, elements. Variants are the old and the new constructs. Change thus occurs within a system in which superordinate constructs admit new constructs to its context.

Fragmentation Corollary

A person may successively employ a variety of construction subsystems that are inferentially incompatible with one another. Successive inconsistency between subsystems may be tolerated within a larger system. Successive formulations may not be derivable from each other; new constructs are not necessarily direct derivatives of old constructs but are derivatives of the larger system.

Commonality Corollary

To the extent that one person employs a construction of experience that is similar to that employed by another, his or her psychological processes are similar to those of the other person. It is not the experiencing of the same events or stimuli but the placing of the same construction on events (which may be phenomenally dissimilar) that results in similar psychological processes. Identity of construction or processes is impossible, phenomenologically speaking.

Sociality Corollary

To the extent that one person construes the construction process of another, the person may play a role in a social process involving the other person. This is more than seeing things as another does; it is also seeing the other's way of seeing, or outlook, for some measure of acceptance of that person, and his or her way of seeing things is a basis for playing a constructive role in relation to her or him. Construing what others are thinking enables us to predict what they will do. While commonality may make the understanding of another's construction system more likely, it is not essential.

The Nature of Personal Constructs

Personal Usage of Constructs

"A construct is a way in which some things are construed as being alike and yet different from others."[12] The contrast is included in the construct rather than considered irrelevant or as another concept, as it is in conventional logic. It differs in this respect from a concept. It includes not only the abstraction element of a concept, but also percepts. The dichotomy represents an aspect of all human thinking.

The individual is unable to express the whole of his or her construction system and may misconstrue what the construction of a situation will be in the future. The individual may not be able to express certain constructs in a way in which others can understand them or subsume them under their own systems without predicting the individual's behavior incorrectly. The individual may express constructs incompletely, omitting the contrast, by saying, for example, "Mary is gentle." To say that Mary is gentle implies that at least one other person is gentle and one other is not gentle or that at least two other persons are not gentle, since the minimum context for a construct is three things. Any other statement is illogical and unpsychological. To say that everyone is gentle, for example, has no meaning. Since constructs are primarily personal, they may not be easily understood by others. Thus there are a number of conditions that may make it appear that a person does not mean what he or she says.

Constructs abstract repeated properties of events and imply that the replicated properties may reappear in another event. Prediction is therefore implicit in construing. It is not a specific event that is predicted but its properties intersecting in a prescribed way. The prediction is validated only when an event occurs that can be construed like the intersect.

Constructs provide the means of binding or grouping events so that they become predictable, manageable, and controllable. A person controls his own destiny "to the extent that he can develop a construction system with which he identifies himself and which is sufficiently comprehensive to subsume the world around him. . . . According to this view, mankind is slowly learning to control his destiny, although it is a long and tedious process."[13]

The individual has a choice between the two ends or dichotomies of the constructs but is controlled by the network of the construction system. However, new constructs can be developed to expand his or her system. A construct, in effect, represents rival hypotheses on either of which the person can act.

The self is a construct. The use of the self as a datum in forming constructs leads to constructs that operate as rigorous controls on behavior, particularly behavior in relation to or in comparison with other people. These comparisons as the individual construes them control his or her social life. "As one construes other people, he formulates the construction system which governs his own behavior"[14]—that is, he defines his own role. A person's construct system is revealed when the person talks about others.

Formal Aspects of Constructs

Symbolism allows one of the elements of a construct to represent the construct itself. Communication is, then, the reproduction of the symbolic element to elicit a parallel construct in another person. Words are useful as symbols but are not always effective. Figures, such as the mother or father, may symbolize constructs. This sort of symbolization is characteristic of children. Such figures give clarity and stability or rigidity to the construct.

Dimensions against which the constructs of others can be evaluated may be set up. A commonly used dimension is abstract versus concrete, but this does not seem to be particularly useful; permeability versus impermeability, already referred to, is a more useful dimension. A *preemptive construct* is one that preempts its elements exclusively for its own realm—a ball can be nothing but a ball. It is a pigeonholing, or nothing-but, approach. A *constellatory construct* permits its elements to belong to other specified realms concurrently. A *propositional construct* leaves its elements open to construction and does not specify all the other realms to which it may belong. It is at the other end of the continuum from preemptive and constellatory constructs. There are also other dimensions, such as *anxiety, hostility, transference,* and *dependence,* which will be mentioned later.

Changing Construction

Validation is the payoff of an anticipation or prediction. Validation is not reinforcement; it is much broader, for it may include such things as the breaking of one's leg after it has been anticipated. Failure of validation leads not only to changes of prediction, but also to a turning to another construct on which to base a prediction or to a revising of the construct system. The formation of new constructs is favored by certain conditions, which include approaching the constructs in contexts that do not involve the self or family members and providing a fresh set of elements as a context. This is what therapy does. Other conditions are an atmosphere of experimentation, in which propositional constructs are "tried on for size," and the availability of validating data —knowledge of the results. Results must be seen from the subject's, not the experimenter's, point of view, however.

The most important condition unfavorable for the formation of new constructs is threat. "A construct is threatening when it is itself an element in a next-higher-order construct which is, in turn, incompatible with other higher-order constructs upon which the person is dependent for his living."[15] Such elements have been excluded from the person's construct system because they are incompatible and are seen as threats when they are presented as elements of a new construct and thus cannot be utilized easily.

"The effect of threat is to compel the client to claw frantically for his basic construct. Threat arouses the necessity for mobilizing one's resources. It should be borne in mind that the resources which are mobilized may not always be mature and effective. Therefore a threatened person may often behave in childish ways. Another effect of introducing threatening elements, and frequently an undesirable one, is the tendency for the traumatic experience to act as further subjective documentation or proof of the client's own maladaptive conceptual framework.[16]

A second unfavorable condition for the formation of new constructs is preoccupation with old material or old impermeable constructs or old habit. A third condition is the lack of a laboratory in which to try out new constructs in a relatively controlled or protected situation.

The Meaning of Experience

Our experience is the portion of the world's happenings that happens to us. However, things happen to us personally only when we behave in relation to them, when we construe them—not when we just react to them. People do not learn *from* experience; learning constitutes experience. Successive construing or reconstruing of happenings increases experience.

The psychology of personal constructs accepts the individual's experience as phenomenological but attempts "to lift our data from the individual at a relatively high level of abstraction. This is a little like saying that we deal concretely with a person's abstractions rather than abstractly with his concretisms. Behaviorism, for example, did it the other way, it created elaborate public abstractions out of minute personal concretisms."[17] The personal-construct psychologist observes the client's constructs or abstractions of behavior and takes what is seen and heard at face value, including what is seen and heard about the subject's constructs. This is commonly called acceptance; it is the *credulous attitude.* The abstractions in the subject's system are the concrete elements awaiting construction in the psychologist's system. "All of this means that we cannot consider the psychology of personal constructs a phenomenological theory, if that means ignoring the personal construction of the psychologist who does the observing."[18]

Personal-construct theory, like perceptual theories, takes an ahistorical approach, which is the view that since a person's activity at a given moment is determined by that person's outlook at that moment, the past influences behavior only through current perceptions. The basis of perception includes "nonconscious" as well as conscious processes. The historical method of study may be used to help reveal the successive patterning of the elements entering into a person's personal constructs.

Other people are important in the validation of a person's constructs. Their opinions may be validators of constructs about nonhuman events. In the case of constructs involving other people as elements, when another person fails to perform according to expectations, that person becomes threatening. The individual is affected in turn, and even though the individual may reject the expectancies of others, he or she construes himself or herelf in relation to those expectancies. Another aspect of validation by group expectancies involves the construction of a role. The term *role* applies to a course of activity played out in the light of a person's construction of one or more other persons' construct systems. Thus in playing a role, the individual acts according to what he or she believes others think, so that the construction of a role must be validated in terms of the expectancies of these others. This last situation illustrates the characteristic approach of the personal-construct psychologist, who seeks to establish a role in relation to other people. Personal-construct theory is essentially "role theory."

The culture influences the personal constructs of the individual, resulting in similarities among its members. The psychologist or therapist must understand these cultural influences and must see the group constructs as elements on which the individual builds personal constructs. Thus both the similarities and the differences among persons in a culture must be recognized.

Diagnostic Constructs

The purpose of diagnostic constructs is to give the clinician a set of professional constructs under which the personal constructs of his or her client can be subsumed, so that the clinician can assume a professionally useful role relation with them. These constructs are not disease entities, types of people, or traits; rather, they consist of a set of universal coordinate axes with respect to which it is possible to plot any person's behavior and the changes occurring in the person's psychological processes. They are not used to pigeonhole clients but to represent different lines of movement open to them. The tentative structuring of the client's experience record by the clinician is termed *structuralization*. *Construction* refers to the better organized formulation that arranges the client's behavior under his or her inferred personal constructs and then arranges them or subsumes them under the clinician's own system. The phenomenologist's approach is used to arrive at the individual's personal constructs, and then the normative approach is used to put these together with what is known about other persons, thus bringing each client's systems into the public domain.

A good diagnotic construct should have the characteristics of other good constructs, which include propositionality (relative independence), dichotomy, permeability, definability (operational), temporality, futurity (prognostic), sociality, and the ability to generate hypotheses, particularly treatment hypotheses.

General Diagnostic Constructs

Preverbal constructs   A preverbal construct is one that the client continues to use even though it has no consistent word symbol. Words facilitate the utilization and modification of constructs, while other symbols are more cumbersome, since they impede communication and discussion. Preverbal constructs usually originate in infancy and often relate to the client's dependence. They may represent a kind of core of the construction system and may be overlaid by misleading verbalized constructs. Signs of preverbal constructs are confusion in verbalization, greater ability to illustrate the construct than to verbalize it, the appearance of the construct in dreams that are not remembered clearly, and the remembering of events that the client is not sure actually happened. Preverbal constructs cover in part the concept of the unconscious. Other aspects of this concept are included in the constructs described below. The failure of the client to construe things in the same way as the clinician should not be interpreted to mean that the client really does construe things in this way but is unaware of it. The client's later ability to construe things as the clinician does constitutes a new construction for her or him, not a revelation of the unconscious.

Submergence   Submergence refers to the omission or avoidance of one of the ends of the dichotomous construct, usually the contrast end. Constructs that have one end submerged cannot be tested.

Suspension   As constructs are revised, some elements drop out and others become more prominent. "When a structure is rejected, because at the moment it is incompatible with the over-all system which the person is using, we may say that it has undergone *suspension*."[19] This is similar to forgetting, dissociation, and repression. What is unstructured is "forgotten" or "repressed."

Level of cognitive awareness   The preceding three constructs involve low levels of cognitive awareness. A high-level construct is one that is readily expressible in socially effective symbols, has alternatives that are both readily accessible, falls well within the range of convenience of the client's major constructions, and is not suspended by its superordinating constructs.

Dilation and constriction   Dilation is the broadening of the perceptual field to organize it more comprehensively, following a series of alternating uses of incompatible systems. Constriction occurs when the individual narrows the perceptual field to minimize apparent incompatibilities in the system.

Comprehensive constructs and incidental constructs   Comprehensive constructs subsume a wide variety of events; they are not necessarily superordinate constructs, however. Incidental constructs subsume a small variety of events.

Superordinate constructs and subordinate constructs   A superordinate construct utilizes another construct as its contextual element; the construct so utilized is a subordinate construct.

Regnancy   A superordinate construct that assigns each of its elements to a category on an all-or-none basis is a regnant construct. For example, if we were to say that all spades are implements, then implement would be a regnant superordinate construct. This is an example of classical logic and simplifies one's personal-construct system.

Core constructs and peripheral constructs   Core constructs are those that the individual uses to maintain identity and existence. In the healthy person, they are comprehensive and permeable. Peripheral constructs may be altered without serious modification of the core structure. Their reformulation is a much less complicated affair than is the reformulation of a core construct.

Tight constructs and loose constructs   Tight constructs lead to unvarying predictions, while loose constructs lead to varying predictions. Loose constructs are like preliminary sketches of a design.

Transitional Constructs

Constructs provide a stable element in experience. Yet constructs change, and the transitions present problems. Transitional constructs concern this process of change and include the following.

Threat   "Threat is the awareness of imminent comprehensive change in one's core structures."[20] The therapist, who expects the client to change, is thus threatening, especially when the client is on the verge of a major change.

Fear   Fear is the awareness of an imminent change in an incidental core construct rather than in a comprehensive construct.

Anxiety   Anxiety is the recognition on the part of the individual that the events confronting her or him lie outside the range of convenience of his or her construct system. Since the individual's constructs do not apply, an inability to construe the events meaningfully, or an ambiguity, results. Loosening the superordinate constructs may increase tolerance for ambiguity and may be sufficient to reduce anxiety; if loosening proceeds too far, however, it may lead to schizophrenia. Redefinition and increase in the permeability of the superordinate system is also effective against anxiety. Tightening is another defense against anxiety.

Guilt   Within the individual's core structure is the core role, which involves that part of the role structure by which the self as an integral being is maintained. Guilt is the experience resulting from the person's perception of an apparent loss of his or her core role structure. The core role is not a superficial role but "a part one plays as if his life depended upon it. Indeed, his life actually does depend upon it."[21] When the individual discovers that he or she has not been acting in accordance with this role, the individual feels guilt. Punishment is not the result of guilt, but vice versa. We punish those who threaten us in order to protect ourselves from the threat of being like them and to make them feel guilty.

Aggressiveness   Aggressiveness is the active elaboration of one's perceptual field. The aggressive individual has a greater than average tendency to set up choice points, precipitating himself or herself into situations that require decision and action. Areas of anxiety tend to be areas of aggressiveness. The aggressive person is seen as threatening.

Hostility   Hostility is the effort to force another person to validate a prediction that is invalid. "The other person is the victim, not so much of the hostile person's fiendishly destructive impulses, as of his frantic and unrealistic efforts to collect on a wager he has already lost."[22] Recurring evidence that he or she is wrong leads the hostile person to feel guilty.

Sequential Changes in Constructs

There are typical sequences of changes in constructs that people employ in order to function in everyday situations. Two of them are the C-P-C cycle and the creativity cycle.

The C-P-C cycle   The C-P-C cycle is a sequence of construction from circumspection to preemption to control, resulting in a choice involving the self. Circumspect construction employs a series of propositional constructs. Thus there is a process that goes from looking at elements in a multidimensional manner to focusing on one element and that results in a choice, or the control of the construct through superordination. To understand choice, we must understand the alternatives facing a person, from his or her point of view. *Impulsivity* is a form of control in which the period of circumspection preceding the choice or decision is shortened. It is an attempt at a quick solution.

The creativity cycle   The creativity cycle begins with loosened construction, involving exploration and experiment, followed by tightened and validated construction.
The diagnostic constructs are chosen as consistent with personal-construct theory and as useful to the clinical psychologist. They represent, primarily, lines along which persons may change in reconstruing their lives and, secondarily, ways in which individuals vary within themselves, as well as from one another, at different times. They are not categories for classifying people.

The Types of Psychological Disorders

To illustrate the use of the dimensions of diagnosis or the diagnostic constructs, the constructs are included in a multidimensional system that illustrates representative types of psychological disorders. The diagnostic constructs themselves do not necessarily refer to disorders, but they are designed to be relevant to various personal-construct systems. A disorder usually involves more than one dimension. Disorders are not nosologic categories or disease entities.

A disorder is any personal construction that is used repeatedly in spite of consistent invalidation. There may be other bases of explanation for psychological disorders, such as past events; but the past cannot be changed, and treatment on this basis is a tedious cancelling out of each old experience with a new one or a turning back of the clock. One can do something, however, about a person's personal-construct system. Repentance is substituted for atonement; reconstruction for compensation; and the future, for the past.

There are two major groupings of disorders: disorders of construction and disorders of transition.

Disorders of construction   There are three disorders of construction. The first of these are *disorders of dilation,* which occur when the individual has no superordinate constructs to order his or her dilated field. The individual may have lost or abandoned governing constructs and then reverted to inappropriate preverbal constructs of dependence, which are comprehensive and permeable. Dilation may occur with loose construction, which is an effort to span or embrace the dilated field. The so-called manic client is usually dilated. In the depressive phase, the client makes an effort to constrict the field. Dilation is also seen in cases diagnosed as paranoid.

The second of these are disorders involving tightening and loosening of constructs. The individual with tight constructions makes precise, exact predictions, but his or her other superordinate structure lacks permeability. The individual's anticipations fail to materialize, and constructs must be discarded. The individual becomes anxious and must resort to constriction or preverbal comprehensive structures. Suicide or psychosis may be the result. The person with loose constructs is variable, adapts to experiences by stretching constructions, and seldom misses in his or her other predictions because they are so broad. Extreme looseness of construing is difficult to follow and may lead to avoidance on the part of others and thus to social withdrawal. Such persons are often labeled schizophrenic. With the loss of a social role, guilt may develop if the individual is aware of the loss and does not deny it by constriction.

The third of these are disorders involving core constructs. Physical complaints often involve core constructs and also imply that dependence is involved. "Psychosomatic symptoms" are required, just as sustenance and safety are required. In conversion reactions, the client is thinking dualistically and translates a psychological into a physiological problem. In this preemptive construction, the problem is wholly physical.

Disorders of transition   *Aggression* and *hostility* are disorders of transition. Aggression is often a solution for hostility, giving rise to activities that relieve the hostility. Hostility requires solution by reconstruing, not draining by catharsis. Aggression may lead to ignoring one's role or failing to elaborate one's role, dealing with others as objects to be manipulated rather than as people to be understood. Coping with others as people rather than as objects requires time, which the impatient, aggressive person often is not willing to spend. The aggressive person has "authority problems" for this reason. Aggression may lead to guilt in various ways when the individual feels that his or her other role is jeopardized. Hostility is unrealistic, yet it may achieve results if it obliges others—in order to placate the hostile person or to indulge his or her whims —to provide the outcomes that the hostile person wants.

Disorders of anxiety, constriction, and guilt   The anxious person has a construction system that fails and has no better or new system available. In a sense, all disorders of construction involve anxiety. Anxiety cannot be observed, but it can be inferred from the measures undertaken to control or avoid it, such as weeping, impulsiveness, dilation, or constriction. All behavior may be seen as directed toward the avoidance of anxiety or of the perception of anxiety, but this would lead to nirvana. People usually seek to master rather than avoid anxiety.

Constriction may be viewed as an avoidance of anxiety. It is a way of shrinking one's world until it becomes manageable. Constriction and preemption often go together. The individual becomes narrow, limited, and restricted. Issues accumulate, which leads to insurmountable anxiety. Involutional melancholia is an example of what results.

Life is difficult in the face of extreme guilt, which involves the person's core role. Guilt may lead to hostility or to physical illness, if not to death. Paranoid homosexuality represents a disorder of guilt.

Disorders involving undispersed dependence   Dependence is not considered a principal axis of the diagnostic construct system, but it does constitute the basis for disorders. Everyone is dependent on others. The normal person dispenses his or her dependences widely and in a discriminative fashion; the disordered person is indiscriminate in dependences and seeks someone on whom all dependence can be unloaded at once. Hostility frequently results when the person's search does not turn out well.

"Psychosomatic" and "organic" problems   Somatic symptoms in a person with a psychological conflict are difficult to reach because they are perceived as physical in the client's dualistic way of thinking. Many psychological disorders involve "psychosomatic" symptoms, but the term has no precise meaning in the system of personal constructs.

The characteristics of the organically deteriorated person stem from an attempt to reconstrue the self in a constricted world. Deteriorated constructs or constructs that have become relatively impermeable may be used. The "organic" picture may also be found in a person with a deep-seated feeling of inadequacy who finds himself or herself beyond his or her depth.

Disorders involving control   Disorders of control reflect faulty superordinate construction systems. The superordinate construct may be such that it subsumes or controls all new experiences, with no change in itself. Disorders involving impulsiveness represent difficulties with the phases of the circumspection–preemption–control cycle, resulting in foreshortening of the cycle.

Not all disorders are disorders of the *form* of personal constructs, although these forms constitute the elements of the diagnostic dimensions. Some difficulties arise from the *content* of the constructs. In addition, some therapy can take place without concern for diagnostic constructs. Not all the important learning takes place on the couch.

THE THERAPY PROCESS

Counseling or psychotherapy is a psychological process that changes a person's outlook on some aspect of life. It involves reconstruing, usually of the client's life role or the role that the client envisions for himself or herself. Psychological disorders can be traced to the characteristics of a person's construction system. They manifest themselves in complaints—complaints of the person about himself or herself and others and complaints of others about the person. At the phenomenal level, then, the goal of psychotherapy is to alleviate complaints.

The Client's Conceptions and Expectations

The client's widely varying conceptions of psychotherapy must be accepted by the therapist at the outset. The therapist must be able to subsume the client's construction of psychotherapy in order to utilize it within a more comprehensive perspective. As therapy progresses, the client's concept changes. His or her view becomes more comprehensive. The client discovers that the outcome of psychotherapy is not a fixed state of affairs but a vantage point for viewing a life plan and the opening phase of a continuing process.

The client also conceptualizes the therapist and the therapist's role in relation to his or her (the client's) conceptualization of psychotherapy. The client's perceptions may be stretched to construe the therapist as one who will meet his or her expectations. The client may construe the therapist in various ways—as a parent, a protector, an absolver of guilt, an authority figure, a prestige figure, a possession, a stabilizer against change, a temporary respite from stress, a threat, an ideal person or companion, a stooge or foil, or a representative of reality. The last is best suited to achieve therapeutic goals, since it leads to a relationship in which the client tests out constructs in an experimental, or laboratory, situation. The therapist is expected to play the parts of many figures, to be articulate, and to serve as a validator. Any but the most inept therapist can help a client who construes him or her in such a way. Yet some fail, usually because they insist on an authoritarian rather than a cooperative relationship or because they are afraid of the outcome of such an experimental relationship.

The Therapist's Conceptualization of His or Her Role

Clinicians assist in the reconstruction or continual shifting of the client's construct system—a process that should continue throughout the client's lifetime. All change or movement, great or small, takes place as a function of change in constructs.

The role of the clinician is broad. It includes producing superficial change by creating an atmosphere of threat or anxiety, by consistently invalidating the client's devices, by precipitating the client into a situation in which he or she perceives a contrasting role that is expected of her or him, and by exhorting the client. Less superficial approaches include controlled elaboration or helping the client "work through" a construct system to bring certain minor constructs in line with the system.

The major or most fundamental role of the therapist is to help the client revise constructs. The therapist begins, however, by accepting the client's construction system as it is. Such acceptance does not mean approval, but readiness to use the client's system and to attempt to anticipate events the way the client anticipates them. Acceptance alone is not sufficient for therapeutic progress, except in simple cases. The therapist, while putting himself or herself in the client's place, maintains a professional overview of the client's problems. The therapist subsumes the client's construction system under a comprehensive frame that he or she provides.

Basic Approaches to the Revision of Constructs

The therapist helps the client develop new constructs or make major revisions of constructs in several ways.

1. The therapist selectively adds new conceptual elements. These experiential elements must not fit too neatly into the client's present system, or they will not challenge it and will lead only to superficial movement. But if the new element leads the client to attempt a sweeping revision of constructs, there is a danger that the client will become deeply disturbed. The therapist must be keenly aware of how the client is handling the new elements. The role of the therapist "includes the skillful introduction of new conceptual elements which challenge the client's construction system but which are carefully chosen so as not to precipitate a catastrophic revolution in it."[23]

2. The therapist accelerates the tempo of the client's experience. Life experience accelerates during therapy, both within and outside the interviews, with the therapist confronting the client with problems intended to pull the client through the normal succession of life experiences at an accelerated pace.

3. The therapist imposes recent structures on old elements. Although the emphasis of the approach is on the present, the way in which the adult sees the past influences the way the adult sees the present. Thus if the past is seen through the eyes of childhood, new events that are similar to those of the past may be dealt with in a childish way. The therapist helps the client apply his or her adult constructs in dealing with childhood recollections. The client then is better prepared to handle present and future events that may appear to be repetitions of the past.

4. The therapist helps the client reduce certain obsolete constructs to a state of impermeability. When it is not possible to get the client to reconstrue certain events or figures of the past, the therapist "may get the client to define the limits of the construct, to tie it firmly to past events and figures which are so unusual that there is little likelihood that their counterparts need be perceived in the future, and finally to wrap the construct up tightly with a word symbol by means of which it can be kept under control."[24]

5. The therapist helps design and implement experiments. Therapy is a laboratory for testing ideas, and the therapist helps the client survey new data and develop hypotheses for testing that do not involve too much risk at one time. The therapist may also participate in the experiment by enacting required parts.

6. The therapist serves as validator. By his or her reactions to the client's constructs. The therapist should be a sample of the social world and a reasonably faithful example of the natural human reactions that the client will meet outside therapy.

The therapist does not try to pass on personal constructs to the client. If the therapist should do so, the client will try to translate them into his or her own construct system. Thus a client who is told to be self-confident may respond with behavior that the therapist feels is conceited. Nevertheless, the therapist does shape the client's system by the elements he introduces, by the constructs he validates or invalidates, and by the hypotheses of the client that he selects for experimentation. "His very choice of points at which to clear his throat, nod his head, or murmur acceptance reflects his bias as to what is inconsequential, what is transitional, or what is understandable."[25]

Psychotherapy according to the psychology of personal constructs is an experimental process, since the system is built on the model of science. Constructs are hypotheses, with prediction the goal. The therapist helps the client to define hypotheses and to design and implement experiments, using the psychotherapy room as a laboratory. The therapist participates in the experiment, serving as a part of the validating evidence. "Psychotherapeutic movement may mean (1) that the client has reconstrued himself and certain other features of the world within his original system, (2) that he has organized his old system more precisely, or (3) that he has replaced some of the constructs in his old system with new ones."[26] The last is the most significant type of movement.

IMPLEMENTATION: PROCEDURES AND TECHNIQUES

The Appraisal of Experiences

The case history is elicited by the use of schedules and outlines. The material is structured in the light of the client's deep-seated personal outlook. The case history is important, not in terms of what happened in the past, nor even just in terms of what the client thinks now, but in terms of what it reveals about the client's outlook. The chronicle of events is also important in providing validational evidence and checkpoints against which the client's constructs may be understood.

Culture and Experience

The clinician must be aware of cultural variations, since the culture provides the client with evidence of what is "true" and with much of the data used in a personal-construct system. Culture controls in that it limits the data and evidence at the client's disposal, but there is a tremendous variety in the ways in which clients handle the data within their construct systems.

The client's culture must be seen critically through his or her eyes. Cultural-group memberships throw light on the client's constructs. These include or are expressed in socioeconomic class, racial and national extraction, family migration history, retirement plans, complaints, and church membership. Although the client cannot describe his or her own culture as a culture, the clinician can assess cultural-experiental determinants by inquiry along appropriate lines.

Personal Experience

The assessment of cultural influence can be made indirectly through the study of the client's community experiences. Information is first sought at a popular level of abstraction, with the psychological and sociological levels attempted after the data have been obtained. The inquiry regarding the community, and the neighborhood as well, covers descriptions of the population, community economics, transitions through which the community is going, religious organizations and mores, schools and educational patterns, and recreational resources.

An appraisal of the school will help in dealing with children from the school. Such an appraisal would include observation of the building, the playground, the classrooms, and classroom behavior, as well as interviews with teachers and the principal. In the interviews, the constructs of the teachers and principal indicate the directions along which the children can move. The teachers' attitudes toward tests and records are revealing of constructs.

The individual's community interrelationships should be studied through the eyes of the person. Groups, organizations, and individuals in the person's life reveal the influences on the person. Educational experiences are analyzed. In the case of a child, the teachers are interviewed to determine what they consider to be the problem or how they construe the situation. The person's home relationships constitute important social expectancies and should therefore be explored. Although people are not slaves of their biographies, the family history is important as seen through the client's eyes.

The Appraisal of Activities

Spontaneous Activity

All activity is spontaneous yet controlled in the sense that it is lawful and predictable. Interests direct activities along particular lines. Areas of spontaneous activity indicate areas of permeable constructs and thus areas in which optimal conditions for evolution exist. Inactivity, or "laziness," is the result of impermeable thinking. The analysis of the client's spontaneous activities is thus a basic task of the clinician. The discovery of permeable constructs provides leads to the client's capacity for psychotherapeutic change.

Spontaneous activities may be studied through verbal inquiry or by time-sampling observation. The way in which the individual interprets experiences is important, however. Activities include not only physical movements, but also conversation and reading. The observation of a child in a group is difficult but profitable. Observation of the child in the family is also revealing.

Vocational choice exercises a selective effect on experience. The vocation is usually an area of permeable constructs and thus gives an indication of the kinds of changes the individual may be prepared to make. A vocation or a course of study often represents the seeking of a compromise between what is challenging and what is safe. The vocation provides the system of validating evidence to which the individual's daily expectations are subject. It is also one of the principal means by which the individual's life role is given clarity and meaning.

Structural Interpretation of Experience

The biographical record is appraised by viewing it in five ways. The client must make sense from this. It reveals something of the person's past construction system and thus suggests behavior to which the client may have recourse if present constructs fail and become invalidated. It indicates the kinds of validators against which the client has to check his or her construct system. It throws light on the present construct system. Finally, it will have to be rationalized by the client in any therapeutic reformulation of a role. It is in these ways that birth, maturation, and physical care are evaluated, as well as behavior problems, interpersonal relations, education, and occupation.

The health of the client is a concern of the psychologist, since it has a bearing on psychological evaluation. The individual's physical being constitutes both part of the facts against which constructs must be validated and the implements with which his or her world must be explored. Illness and disability limit activity and interests and require psychological adjustment. Old dependence patterns are reactivated; there may be regression to earlier modes of conceptualization.

The clinician must interpret the client's structuralizations. In this way, the clinician subsumes the client's structure and establishes a role relationship with the client. The clinician is then in a position to anticipate the client's perceptions and behavior. The clinician's construction of a case develops by successive approximations. Structuralization, then, refers to the preliminary formulations, while construction is the final organization of the record into a well-subsumed system. The former is descriptive, limited to the past and present; the latter is dynamic, related to the future.

The structuralization of a case, utilizing the client's experience record, may make use of the terms that follow. These are not constructs but collecting terms. They represent section headings that may be used in case presentations and case records. Since they refer to the kinds of events the client has had to anticipate, they are validators.

1. *Figure Matrix*   This includes information regarding the kinds of people the client has known intimately. The individuals are *figure constructs,* which are assembled into the figure matrix.
2. *Cooperative Relationships*   This section would consist of information regarding the client's participation in socially constructive processes.
3. *Characterizations of the Client*   This heading includes the ways in which the client is described by people with whom he or she must live.
4. *Externally Imposed Group Identifications*   This topic refers to how the client is seen by others in terms of the client's group memberships.
5. *Areas in Which the Client Is Incorporated or Alienated*   Incorporation refers to the willingness to see others as like oneself; alienation is unwillingness to do this. This heading includes the groups who see the client as like themselves, and the ways in which they see the client like this.
6. *External Patterns of Conflict and Solution*   This area is concerned with the social issues and conflicts in the client's milieu that he or she must experience and construe.
7. *Thematic Repertory*   Thema are the themes and patterns of the social world surrounding the client, against which the client plays a part.
8. *Symbolic System*   The symbolic system includes the language, religious, nationalistic, institutional, proverbial, epigrammatic, and so on, background of the client.
9. *Climate of Opinion Out of Which Complaints Arise*   What are the conventionalized complaints in the client's social setting?

10. *Versatility* This includes the range or breadth of the client's activities or thinking, which indicate a freedom to experiment.
11. *Biographical Turning Points* Are there points of change in the experience record? The presence and nature of such changes suggest the client's capacity for change and the manner in which future changes may be expected to take place.
12. *Physical Resources* These include not only personal resources of property, but also the resources of the community.
13. *Dependences* Are there resources on which the client has become so dependent that their loss would interrupt his or her whole pattern of life?
14. *Supportive Status* This section consists of items indicating how and in what manner the client is seen as necessary to other people.

The clinical constructs used to bring together or structuralize the client's experience are of intermediate rather than salient significance from the point of view of the psychology of personal constructs.

Steps in Diagnosis

Diagnosis is the planning stage of client management. Client mangement is broader than therapy or treatment: it includes all actions directed toward the client's welfare.

There are many ways in which the same facts may be construed. Since the psychologist is interested in helping clients, clinical diagnosis construes the facts in terms of their relevance to a solution of the client's problem, or client reconstruction. The phrase "transitive diagnosis" is used to indicate the concern with transitions in the client's life, or bridges between the client's present and future. "Moreover, we expect to take an active part in helping the client select or build the bridges to be used and in helping him cross them safely. . . . If the psychologist expects to help him he must get up off his chair and start moving along with him."[27]

The diagnostic constructs or dimensions presented earlier represent avenues of movement as seen by the therapist, and they are the bases of transitive diagnosis. The psychology of personal constructs is directed against the tendency to impose preemptive constructs on human behavior, a tendency in which "diagnosis is all too frequently an attempt to cram a whole live struggling client into a nosological category."[28] The question in transitive diagnosis is not, "In what category should this client be classified?" but, "What is to become of this client?" A temporary preemptive construction is necessary for deciding the immediate disposition of the client, including whether to accept the client for treatment.

There are six practical issues that arise in the making of a transitive diagnosis. In outline form they are as follows:

I. Normative formulations of the client's problem
   1. Description of the manifest deviant behavior patterns (symptoms)
      a. The clinician's behavior norms
      b. Deviation from the ways of the primary group
      c. Incompatibility with own norms
      d. Inconsistency with common interpretations or expectations
      e. Frequent abandonment of adjustment patterns

      f. Distinction between deviations and transparency

      g. Deviation in the manner of complaining

      h. Data for description of the manifest deviant behavior

      i. Elicitation and description of the complaint

      j. Temporal patterns in the deviant behavior

  2. Description of the correlates of the manifest deviant behavior patterns

      a. The cultural context

      b. The personal-social context

      c. Threat or stress concomitants

      d. The occupational pattern

      e. The domestic pattern

  3. Descriptions of the gains and losses accruing to the client through symptoms (description of validational experience)

II. Psychological description of the client's personal constructions

  1. The client's construction of what he or she believes to be the problem area

  2. The client's construction of life roles

III. Psychological evaluation of the client's construction system

  1. Location of the client's areas of anxiety, aggressiveness (or spontaneous elaboration), and constriction

  2. Sampling the types of construction the client uses in different areas

  3. Sampling the modes of approach

  4. Determination of the client's accessibility and levels of communication

IV. Analyses of the milieu in which adjustment is to be sought

  1. Analyses of the expectancy system within which the client must make the life role function

  2. Assessment of the socioeconomic assets in the case

  3. Preparation of information to be utilized as contextual material in helping the client reconstrue life

V. Determination of immediate procedural steps

  1. Physiological construction of the available data

  2. Other professional constructions of the available data

  3. Evaluation of the urgency of the case

VI. Planning management and treatment

  1. Selection of the central psychotherapeutic approach

      a. Size of the client's investment

      b. Accessibility and level of communication

      c. Type of transference

      d. Threat implications

      e. Fear implications

      f. Anxiety

      g. Guilt

      h. Loosening

      i. Elaboration of the complaint

      j. Finding validation of new constructs

      k. Areas to be opened to elaboration

      l. Dealing with submerged ends of constructs

  2. Designation of the principally responsible clinician

  3. Selection of adjunctive resources to be utilized

      a. Dealing with other minor problems (for example, medical)

      b. Occupational therapy

      c. Recreation
      d. Dilation
      e. Community participation
      f. Resources for the nonhospitalized client
4. Designation of the responsible clinician's advisory staff
5. Determination of the ad interim status of the client
6. Setting of dates or conditions under which progress will be reviewed by the advisory staff

The issues at the beginning of the outline are essentially descriptive; those in the middle require more scientific sophistication in this handling; and those at the end require therapeutic training for their resolution.

"Effective diagnosis is a matter of making some reasonable predictions as to what a client will do under different circumstances and then proposing to create a set of circumstances which will lead to the client's doing what we think he generally ought to do."[29]

Psychological Testing in Diagnosis and Psychotherapy

One direct approach to the client's personal constructs is by means of psychological tests, which involve a formal assigned task. So-called objective tests are considered *dimensional measures* of personal constructs, for example, cultural commonality, rather than direct revelations of the constructs themselves. Other tests elicit the constructs themselves; these are the tests under consideration here. There are five functions of a test in a clinical setting: (1) to define the client's problem in usable terms; (2) to reveal the pathways or channels along which the client is free to move; (3) to provide clinical hypotheses that may subsequently be checked and put to use; (4) to reveal those resources of the client that might otherwise be overlooked by the therapist; and (5) to reveal those problems of the client that might otherwise be overlooked by the therapist.

The clinical utility of a test from the standpoint of the psychology of personal constructs can be appraised by considering the following questions:

1. Whose yardstick does the test represent? "Objective" tests utilize the clinician's axes, not the client's. Projective tests recognize the client's yardsticks. Clinicians cannot use their clients' yardsticks, however; they must use their own, but they should use them to attempt to measure their clients' yardsticks.
2. Does the test elicit permeable constructs? Can it embrace the future as well as pigeonhole the past? Does it measure constructs that are likely to be used again and that are not of only historical interest?
3. Are the test elements representative of life's events? Can the clinician infer from the client's reactions to the test elements how he or she will react to other elements, such as people? "It might be easier to predict what a subject would do on a Rorschach Test, for example, from a knowledge of how he deals with people in his world than it would be to predict what he would do with the people in his world from a knowledge of how he deals with ink blots."[30]
4. Does the test elicit role constructs; that is, does it relate to how the client manages life in a social setting?

     f. Distinction between deviations and transparency
     g. Deviation in the manner of complaining
     h. Data for description of the manifest deviant behavior
     i. Elicitation and description of the complaint
     j. Temporal patterns in the deviant behavior
  2. Description of the correlates of the manifest deviant behavior patterns
     a. The cultural context
     b. The personal-social context
     c. Threat or stress concomitants
     d. The occupational pattern
     e. The domestic pattern
  3. Descriptions of the gains and losses accruing to the client through symptoms (description of validational experience)

II. Psychological description of the client's personal constructions
  1. The client's construction of what he or she believes to be the problem area
  2. The client's construction of life roles

III. Psychological evaluation of the client's construction system
  1. Location of the client's areas of anxiety, aggressiveness (or spontaneous elaboration), and constriction
  2. Sampling the types of construction the client uses in different areas
  3. Sampling the modes of approach
  4. Determination of the client's accessibility and levels of communication

IV. Analyses of the milieu in which adjustment is to be sought
  1. Analyses of the expectancy system within which the client must make the life role function
  2. Assessment of the socioeconomic assets in the case
  3. Preparation of information to be utilized as contextual material in helping the client reconstrue life

V. Determination of immediate procedural steps
  1. Physiological construction of the available data
  2. Other professional constructions of the available data
  3. Evaluation of the urgency of the case

VI. Planning management and treatment
  1. Selection of the central psychotherapeutic approach
     a. Size of the client's investment
     b. Accessibility and level of communication
     c. Type of transference
     d. Threat implications
     e. Fear implications
     f. Anxiety
     g. Guilt
     h. Loosening
     i. Elaboration of the complaint
     j. Finding validation of new constructs
     k. Areas to be opened to elaboration
     l. Dealing with submerged ends of constructs
  2. Designation of the principally responsible clinician
  3. Selection of adjunctive resources to be utilized
     a. Dealing with other minor problems (for example, medical)
     b. Occupational therapy

     c. Recreation

     d. Dilation

     e. Community participation

     f. Resources for the nonhospitalized client

4. Designation of the responsible clinician's advisory staff

5. Determination of the ad interim status of the client

6. Setting of dates or conditions under which progress will be reviewed by the advisory staff

The issues at the beginning of the outline are essentially descriptive; those in the middle require more scientific sophistication in this handling; and those at the end require therapeutic training for their resolution.

"Effective diagnosis is a matter of making some reasonable predictions as to what a client will do under different circumstances and then proposing to create a set of circumstances which will lead to the client's doing what we think he generally ought to do."[29]

Psychological Testing in Diagnosis and Psychotherapy

One direct approach to the client's personal constructs is by means of psychological tests, which involve a formal assigned task. So-called objective tests are considered *dimensional measures* of personal constructs, for example, cultural commonality, rather than direct revelations of the constructs themselves. Other tests elicit the constructs themselves; these are the tests under consideration here. There are five functions of a test in a clinical setting: (1) to define the client's problem in usable terms; (2) to reveal the pathways or channels along which the client is free to move; (3) to provide clinical hypotheses that may subsequently be checked and put to use; (4) to reveal those resources of the client that might otherwise be overlooked by the therapist; and (5) to reveal those problems of the client that might otherwise be overlooked by the therapist.

The clinical utility of a test from the standpoint of the psychology of personal constructs can be appraised by considering the following questions:

1. Whose yardstick does the test represent? "Objective" tests utilize the clinician's axes, not the client's. Projective tests recognize the client's yardsticks. Clinicians cannot use their clients' yardsticks, however; they must use their own, but they should use them to attempt to measure their clients' yardsticks.

2. Does the test elicit permeable constructs? Can it embrace the future as well as pigeonhole the past? Does it measure constructs that are likely to be used again and that are not of only historical interest?

3. Are the test elements representative of life's events? Can the clinician infer from the client's reactions to the test elements how he or she will react to other elements, such as people? "It might be easier to predict what a subject would do on a Rorschach Test, for example, from a knowledge of how he deals with people in his world than it would be to predict what he would do with the people in his world from a knowledge of how he deals with ink blots."[30]

4. Does the test elicit role constructs; that is, does it relate to how the client manages life in a social setting?

5. What is the balance between stability and sensitivity? A test not only should show consistency on a day-by-day basis, but also should reflect changes over longer periods of time. Moreover, the test should measure constructs that continue in operation over long periods of time but that are expected to change or be revised during psychotherapy.
6. Will the test reveal constructs that are communicable to other clinicians?
7. Will the test serve its basic functions?

A good clinical test should fulfill the functions listed above. A diagnostic instrument that attempts to fulfill these functions and meets the above requirements has been developed to elicit personal constructs. It is the Role Construct Repertory Test (Rep Test), which is aimed at eliciting role constructs and is thus concerned with those persons with whom the subject has had to deal in daily life. The subject is given a Role Title List and asked to designate persons in his or her own realm of experience who fit the role titles. Then groups of three of the persons named are selected, and the subject is asked to tell in what important way two of them are alike but different from the third. There are various forms of the test, including tests for both group and individual administration.

The test has been developed on the basis of personal-construct theory. There are six assumptions in interpreting the results:

1. The constructs elicited are permeable.
2. Preexisting constructs are elicited by the test.
3. The figures are representative of the people to whom the subject must relate his or her self-construed role.
4. Constructs will be elicited that subsume, in part, the construction systems of the element figures.
5. The constructs elicited are regnant over the subject's own role.
6. The constructs elicited are adequate to communicate to the examiner some understanding of how the client organizes the elements in the test.

The test can be subjected to both formal and clinical analyses. Clinical analysis considers the number and overlap and the permeability or impermeability of the constructs elicited, fields of permeability, contrasting constructs, unique figures, linkage of constructs through contrasts and figures, preemptive constructs, superficial constructs, dependency constructs, and so forth. The test contributes to diagnosis in the area of the client's construction of a life role.

During therapy, tests may contribute to the understanding of the client's personal-construct system, thus broadening the therapist's perspective. They may also dispel some of the bias of the therapist or point to content related to one of the therapist's "blind spots."

Tests also affect the outlook of the client, bringing him or her face to face with issues that might otherwise be ignored or rejected as being the therapist's incorrect perceptions. Test material may be used as "entry material" or as a point of departure for beginning a therapy hour, although such material is probably not as useful as other entries devised by the therapist.

Tests may pose a threat to the psychotherapeutic relationship, more so later on in the relationship than at the start. Threat may be reduced by reassuring the client that there is no passing or failing involved and by structuring the use of the test as a help to the therapist in understanding the client better. Projective tests, particularly sentence-completion tests, are likely to be less damaging than objective tests. The word-association test seems to be most damaging.

The Psychotherapeutic Approach

Basic Techniques

Setting up the relationship   The therapist does not allow himself or herself to become an intimately known and sharply delineated personality for the client; instead, the therapist maintains a personal ambiguity. This makes it more likely that the client will develop a secondary rather than a primary transference and allows the therapist to play the versatile roles required. This ambiguity enables the client to cast the therapist in the parts necessary in reconstructive experiments. The therapist, therefore, avoids social relationships with the client, as well as contacts with members of the client's family. Nor should the therapist treat two members of the same family.

The client's relationships to others   There is no prohibition on the client's relationships with others. The purpose of therapy is to foster good relationships between the client and others, and this cannot be done if the client is limited to a relationship with the therapist. Therapy may even include helping others through the client.

Multiple approach   Several individuals sometimes may act as therapists with one client in *multiple therapy.* However, a versatile and flexible therapist should be able to provide a variety of relationships for the client without the confusion introduced by several therapists. Total-push therapy in an institution is another form of multiple approach.

Physical arrangements   Privacy or the sense of privacy is essential. Recording of interviews is done with the client's knowledge and consent but inconspicuously. Both the room and the therapist's desk should be uncluttered, and the room should be as quiet as possible. The interviews are conducted with a desk or table between the participants; this tends to focus the attention of each on the face of the other, where it should be. Chairs should be comfortable and should be placed 6 to 8 feet apart and both at right angles to the line between the therapist and the client in order to permit the client either to face or to turn away from the therapist. Group therapy and play therapy require special rooms and equipment.

Controlling interviews   Because of the different ways a client may have of construing the world, the therapist must maintain a flexible relationship with a client. Each interview, nevertheless, requires some planning, although the plan can be altered as necessary within prescribed limits. As therapy proceeds, the therapist becomes aware of danger areas to be avoided and develops the ability to predict what the client will say. Special activities of the client may call for special interviewing plans. Interviews may be spaced to meet the client's needs for contact. For most purposes, a 45-minute interview is adequate. Notes or summaries of interviews should be kept to assist the therapist's memory from interview to interview. They should include predictions of what the client will do before the next interview. This is an important point because "if the therapist is able to 'call the shots' on his client, he can be reassured that he is developing a fairly adequate construction of the case."[31]

Since he or she has prepared a plan, the therapist initiates the interview with that plan in mind. Interviews should be terminated on time and not continue out the door in "threshold therapy." The tempo of the interview is controlled by the therapist as necessary to broaden or narrow the scope of the client's immediate perceptual field and for other purposes. The therapist should avoid a guilt-laden dependence on the part of the client by not listening to outpourings of wrongdoings, unless the therapist is prepared to assume continuing responsibility for the client's welfare.

The psychotherapist's manner   Communication is not limited to words. The therapist should appear to be physically relaxed and mentally receptive during interviews. Gestures should be of the accepting type. The therapist's voice should be responsive, and speech should be clear yet colorful and adapted to the client's vocabulary. While the therapist should appear to be "shockproof," he or she should not be so impassive that the client cannot observe the results of experiments.

Teaching the client how to be a "patient"   The client should be taught how to respond in the therapeutic relationship. In long-term relationships, this may take months. Such structuring may include formal verbal structuring as well as intermittent instructions and orientation.

Palliative Techniques

Reassurance   Reassurance is never more than a temporary expedient to give the client the impression that his or her behavior and ideas are consistent, acceptable, and organized. It helps to hold together the client's construction system until it can be rebuilt. Reassurance can backfire if things turn out badly after the therapist has assured the client they would not. It tends to support existing maladjustive mechanisms. Too much reassurance leads to dependence.

Some ways of providing reassurance are less likely to produce unfavorable results than are others. Predictions made as reassurance should not be sweeping. Acceptance of anxiety-laden material as not unexpected is reassuring. Both the process of structuring and the therapist's manner can be reassuring. But value labels used as reassurance can be hazardous because they prevent the client from changing any evaluations. Comfort as reassurance may create "resistance" in a client who is ambivalent about complaints. It may lead the client to feel that there is no solution, that the therapist feels this way also, and that all he or she can do is "grin and bear it."

Since reassurance slows therapeutic movement, it should be used only when retardation is desired. For example, it may be used as a temporary preventive of fragmentation of constructs. It may be used to encourage loosening of conceptualization, with less danger of fragmentation. Reassurance controls anxiety. It may also be used to keep an important chain of associations temporarily from being broken. It should always be used in minimal and calculated amounts.

Support   Support is provided by acceptance without agreement or by understanding the client's communication without telling the client he or she is right before the client has had a chance to experiment. It is a response that allows the client to experiment widely and successfully. Support recognizes and accepts the client's dependence patterns of behavior; it thus may be threatening to the client and may arouse guilt feelings.

The therapist shows support by being on time for appointments, by remembering what the client has said in the past, and by construing things as the client does. This last is one of the therapist's main functions and is sometimes enough. Support includes adapting to changes in the client's thinking, helping the client to verbalize a new rationale, and doing things for the client outside the interview situation.

Support may be used in certain anxiety cases, as an approach to help a client understand his or her striving for dependence, or to stabilize a situation temporarily. Support, like reassurance, should be used sparingly and should be limited to situations in which the client cannot take everything in stride.

Transference   Transference is a construct. In its broad sense, transference is the lifting of a construct from one's repertory and transferring it, or applying it, to a particular situation. When facing a therapist, the client takes a construct from his or her repertory and uses it in looking at and dealing with the therapist. In psychotherapy, transference is concerned with role constructs and refers to the way in which a person attempts to subsume the constructs of others. In reference to the client, it represents the effort of the client to construe the therapist by transferring role constructs onto the therapist. The therapist is constantly extricating himself or herself from the client's constructions, both those that are useful and those that are not useful. The client tends to cast the therapist into the form of a highly elaborated prejudicial stereotype, such as the father or father figure, which becomes fixed.

Transference dependency   Transference sometimes involves dependency constructs, which may be immature and may not lend themselves to verbalization. The client responds to the therapist as if life depended on the therapist. Therapists sometimes invite dependency transferences by the attitude that they know what is best for the client.

Counterdependency transference   If the therapist cannot adequately construe the client within a set of professional constructs, the therapist runs the risk of transferring his or her dependencies to the client. Prevention of such counterdependency transference requires an organized and meaningful set of diagnostic constructs acquired through thorough professional training and the use of the client's own personal constructs within the subsuming system. The therapist who is overly concerned with and preoccupied by the client's relationships to himself or herself and others, in almost a jealous manner, should be alert to the possibility that he or she has developed counterdependency transference.

Primary and secondary transference   The application of a varying sequence of constructs from a variety of figures of the past is secondary transference. The therapist can utilize this transference to reorient the client's constructions of other persons by playing various parts. When the client construes the therapist preemptively, as a unique person, a type, and develops a personal identification with the therapist, a primary transference exists. This kind of relationship limits the experiments that the client can perform with the therapist. The client focuses on the therapist as a unique figure and is unable to generalize the lessons learned in the therapy situation to other persons outside therapy.

Control of transference   Transference should be allowed only to the extent that it appears to be safe and useful. Transference seems to go in cycles. The therapist must determine at the end of each whether to begin another or to terminate therapy. A transference cycle can be shortened by abandoning concept-loosening techniques, shifting to current material, dealing with lower levels of abstraction, and, in general, engaging in a more structured, superficial form of therapy. Primary transference, once it occurs, should be resolved immediately. Two methods may be used. In one, the therapist assumes a rigid, persevering, repetitive, and stereotyped role. In the other, less drastic, the therapist uses free roles, forcing the client to play opposite various other persons, whose parts the therapist enacts.

Elaborating the Complaint

Uncontrolled elaboration   Most therapeutic elaboration starts with an elaboration of the complaint. The elaboration may be uncontrolled, with the therapist being "nondirective." There are contraindications for this undirected elaboration. One is if the therapist is going to make a referral. Another is if there are excessive guilt feelings. A third is excessive repetition by the client. A fourth is in case of loose construction.

Controlled elaboration   Controlled elaboration avoids the hazards of undirected elaboration but not the serious hazard that the therapist may not be able to know precisely how the client managed to be incapacitated and thus may not be able to make contact with the client's personal-construct system in order to establish a meaningful role in relation to the client.

Questions should be used to get the client to place problems, if possible, on a time line; to see them as fluid and transient; and to interpret them as being responsive to treatment, the passage of time, and varying conditions. These procedures lead to construing the problems in ways in which they can be solved. Pressuring the client to explain why he or she has certain difficulties may be profitable but may lead to verbal rationalization. Questions about other people who have or have had the same problems put the complaint into a social framework. Sometimes it is advisable to confront the client with complaints or aspects of problems that have not been mentioned. This may clarify the diagnostic picture as well as the therapeutic relationship. Most frequently, such confrontation is used to broaden the client's field as new constructs are being formulated. Reflection of key terms or ideas may lead to elaboration by the client. Selected elements may be reflected to force the client to elaborate a theme. Review of previous sessions is a form of reflection and may be used to assure the client that the therapist was listening and to integrate or organize details on a higher level of superordination. It can also be used to draw contrasts between the past and the present. Review may threaten the client, however; it may block development by going back to the old material, or it may betray the therapist's prejudices. "The more the therapist talks or tries to place verbal structure on what the client has produced, the greater is the likelihood that the sensitive ear of the client will detect harsh notes of criticism and inflexibility."[32]

Elaborating the Personal System

The basic task of the therapist is to elaborate the construct system in which the client's difficulties are anchored.

Approach to the construct system   The turning from the complaint as a reference point to the client's system as a system broadens the picture, raises the issues to a higher level of abstraction, and places the emphasis on seeing alternatives.

Tests, as already mentioned, are one approach to an elaboration of the client's construct system. Another is self-description through the self-characterization sketch used in fixed-role therapy, which will be mentioned later. Broad, general questions rather than an outline should be used to help the client produce a self-characterization. The client may be asked to elaborate life-role structure, including earlier plans and goals, as well as a projection into the future—what the client wants to be like after therapy. Progressive confrontation with alternatives through use of the C-P-C cycle is another way to maintain the process of elaboration. Elaboration may take place in activities outside the therapy room, such as prescribed occupational, recreational, and social activities. The sorts of play and creative production in which the therapist can participate may also be used to encourage elaboration.

Elaboration of the construct system must be done systematically and cautiously. Limits are ordinarily set on the areas to be elaborated in any one phase of the therapy. Elaboration may lead to loosening of the system and thus must be controlled to prevent too much or too general loosening.

Elaboration of material arising during the course of therapy   The concern here is with the elaboration of bits of material to see where they fit into the total construct system and to determine their relationship to the sequence of developments in therapy.

Since not all clues can be followed up, material must be selected for elaboration. What is selected is determined only partly by its suspected significance; the readiness of the client to deal with it must also be considered. Some of the kinds of material that should be chosen for elaboration are the following: strange or unexpected material, material possibly indicative of an expected therapeutic movement or revision of the construct system, material apparently related to an area under intensive study, material lending itself to psychotherapeutic experimentation, material useful in validation of new constructs, material related to a construct taking shape, and material representing an extended range of convenience of an existing construct.

Recapitulation by the therapist or the client may point up the need for, and lead to, elaboration. Procedures used in recapitulation include the client's diaries and written summaries, playback of recordings, and discussions by the client in a therapy group of experiences in individual therapy.

Probing is a method of controlling the client's participation in the interview. It can be misused if it becomes an inquisition. Probing is used to get the client to explore an area. It may be immediate and done as soon as a cue has been given; but it is preferable to delay probing, so that it may represent a well-thought-out procedure for helping the client elaborate meaningful constructs. Probing can be used to elicit details about an important incident that may tie in with other incidents. Asking for the antecedents or consequents of an incident is also a means of elaboration. The therapist may ask the client to think of similar or contrasting incidents or experiences, which may lead to elaboration of the construct, or the therapist may try to relate experiences, which also may lead to elaboration of the construct. In addition, the therapist may relate experiences by asking the client how two are alike and different from a third.

Enactment, in which the therapist plays a role in an incident described by the client, may be an effective way of helping the client to elaborate. Four principles are important in the use of enactment. First, there should be no long preliminary discussions or preparation. Second, the enactment should be brief. Third, there should be exchange of parts, with the therapist taking various parts, including that of the client. Thus the client may be led to think, "This therapist is both sympathetic and versatile; with him, the therapy room can become a well-equipped laboratory for experimenting with life's perplexing social relations, provided, of course, that I dare to experiment." The client, in taking the part of another, begins to know a little of how another person might be construing the situation and can begin to adapt to what the construction is. Fourth, portrayal of a caricature of the client must be avoided. Enactment should be introduced with a relatively innocuous incident.

Loosening and Tightening

Loosening   The axis of loosened versus tightened construction is an important one and one with which the therapist deals early in therapy. Loosening is characteristic of those constructs that lead to varying predictions—those whose elements may vary in their classification from one pole to the other. Dreaming is an illustration of loose thinking. It allows for resilience, inconsistencies, and a shifty defense. It is a necessary phase of creative thinking. It frees facts, so that they can be seen in new aspects. Loosening prepares the ground for the changing development of constructs and the developing of new constructs. It is produced in psychotherapy in four principal ways:

1. *Relaxation*   The couch or chair, the surroundings, the relaxed manner of the therapist, and the therapist's systematic methods of eliciting physical relaxation induce relaxation in the client.
2. *Chain Association*   Chain association is the free association of psychoanalysis. The client sometimes has to be helped by being given a starting point, being allowed to think without speaking, and being instructed to let his or her mind wander without being concerned about the importance of the content.
3. *Reporting Dreams*   Dreams are so loose that it is difficult to report them. It is not the content of the dream, however, but the use of loosened construction in reporting it that is useful, even if the client can remember and verbalize little about the dream itself. In loosening, verbalization is slow. The manic flight of ideas is not loosening; the schizoid's thinking is. Interpretation of dreams tightens construction; therefore, the interpretation should not follow immedi-

ately on the reporting of dreams but should take place when the therapist wants to move in the direction of tightening. Dreams are often preverbal and thus throw light on preverbal constructs. They often also involve submerged contrasting poles of constructs. This accounts for the fact that dream elements often appear to represent their opposites.

4. *Uncritical Acceptance* Acceptance is the attempt by the therapist to employ the client's construct system. It is uncritical when the client's thinking is not questioned by the therapist. "Essentially the technique of uncritical acceptance provides the client with a passive validation for his loosened construing which is elastic and nonexperimental."[33]

There are difficulties involved in producing loosened constructions. The client has a tendency to move toward tightening of constructs; he or she has difficulty finding symbols or words to deal with ideas. Premature interpretation tightens up the client's construing. Distractions and interference from similar but tightly construed elements interfere with loosening.

Resistance to loosening may be dealt with not only by continuing to use the techniques to produce loosening, which have been mentioned, but also by using other special techniques. Enactment, or role playing, is one. The use of a context in which loosening is possible, followed by a gradual shifting to the desired area or context, is another. Reducing threat or increasing acceptance is a third technique.

Loosening has some hazards. Since it reduces anxiety, it may become like an addiction or an escape. Tight constructions may be a defense, and the loss of this defense may precipitate a severe anxiety state. The skillful use of loosening requires comprehensiveness and flexibility in the therapist's viewpoint.

Tightening   The functions of tightening are to define what is predicted, to stabilize construction, to facilitate organization of the construct system, to reduce certain constructs to a state of impermeability, and to facilitate experimentation. Tightening is a form of elaboration, and techniques of elaboration apply to it also. Other techniques include the following:

1. *Judging or Superordinating*   In judging or superordinating, the client is urged to cease free-associating, to judge rather than to experience, and to put a superordinate construction on a group of constructs that have been expressed unsystematically.

2. *Summarization*   In summarization, the client is asked to summarize what he or she has been saying. This leads to systematization, which involves the tightening of subordinated constructs. Written summaries between interviews may be assigned to the client.

3. *Historical Explanation*   of thoughts by the client.

4. *Relating the Client's Thinking*   to that of others.

5. *Direct Approach*   In the direct approach, the client is asked to be explicit—to explain or to clarify.

6. *Challenging the Construction*   The therapist may ask the client to repeat what he or she has said, express confusion, misinterpret, question, or even label what the client is saying as nonsense.

7. *Enactment*   The demands of extemporaneous role playing may at times lead to the tightening up of certain minor constructions.

8. *Concept Formation*   In concept formation, the client is asked to tell how two things are alike but different from a third.
9. *Asking for Validating Evidence*
10. *Word Binding*   The client is asked to name each construct and to stick with the name.
11. *Time Binding*   The client is asked to date constructs, restricting them in time.

Difficulties occur in getting the client to tighten up certain constructions. The client may use a symbol consistently, but the construct itself may be vague and inconsistently applied. Tightness may be achieved at the expense of permeability, comprehensiveness, or superordination. Impulsive clients, who can hold themselves together only with a loose construction of themselves, may cause difficulty. Clients who want to limit their world to the therapy room and the therapy relationship and clients who are unwilling to test constructs can also cause difficulty. Loose constructs that are preverbal are difficult to tighten.

There are hazards involved in tightening, too. One is the danger of premature tightening, which may bring clients face to face with the implications of their construing and force them to test hypotheses before they have any appropriate alternative constructions. Hostility may result if constructs are invalidated, and since the therapist is also involved in the experiment, the therapist also may become hostile at the failure. A second principal hazard in tightening is the possible loss of comprehensiveness, permeability, and propositionality.

Therapy involves the weaving back and forth between tightening and loosening, essentially in the repetition of the creativity cycle. Therapy proceeds by successive approximations. In the process, clients learn a way of developing better modes of adjustment.

Producing Psychotherapeutic Movement

The techniques considered below are those employed in the stages of therapy in which the therapist urges clients to experiment with new ideas and behaviors.

Interpretation, movement, and rapport   The client's constructs are personal, and the therapist must deal with them on an individual basis rather than in terms of general meanings. There is one basic principle in interpretation: "*All interpretations understood by the client are perceived in terms of his own system.* Another way of expressing the same thing is to say that it is always the client who interprets, not the therapist."[34] Again, the therapist's job "is to help the client make discoveries of his own; it is not to shower him with blessed insights."[35] The basic interpretive formats are those that invite the client to conceptualize in some new or generalized way what he or she has been discussing. In addition to interpretation, extending the range of convenience of the client's constructs and the use of elaboration are methods of increasing the permeability of the client's constructs.

Movement in psychotherapy is indicated by the client in various ways. One is the surprise of the client when things seem to fall into place; this is the "Aha!" experience. Another is the client's spontaneous documentation of the usefulness of a new construct. A third is the evidence of permeability when the client incorporates current experiences into a construct. A fourth is a positive change in mood or feeling. The perception of contrast between present and past behavior is a fifth indication. A sixth is the dropping of certain complaints or even the substitution of new ones for old ones. The client's summaries of previous interviews also indicate changes. Finally, the change in content, with the introduction of new content into the therapy, indicates movement.

There are also cues that indicate inadequate new construction. These include loose construction or erratic verbalization of a new construct, bizarre documentation, oversimplification, contrast behavior or "flight into health," and legalistic application of the new "insight."

How does the therapist know when the client's role relationship to her or him will support a certain type of inquiry into forbidden areas? There are several useful criteria, including relaxation, spontaneity, the ability to control loosening, and the dropping of guards. A fifth criterion is the contrasting of the client's present outlook with his or her outlook in the immediate past, and a sixth is the contrasting of the present with the future outlook. Optimism, flexibility, and the dropping of defensiveness constitute additional criteria. The ability to enact an aggressive role with the therapist is also a criterion. Another is the ability to construe the task of the therapist. Related to this is the individual's ability to relate attitudes and constructs to his or her role as a patient or client. Finally, lack of impulsiveness and of obliqueness in approaching a topic are useful criteria of readiness for new ventures.

Control of anxiety and guilt   Anxiety and guilt are not necessarily all bad. "The task of the therapist is to assess them, take account of their functioning in his client, and deal with them in the light of the welfare of the particular personality."[36] Anxiety is detected in various ways. The criteria for the client's readiness for movement listed above are related to anxiety. Knowledge of common anxieties and of the experiences of the client, observation of the client's behavior, and the client's communications are other sources for detecting client anxiety. Restriction of discussion, use of self-reassuring devices, and weeping may indicate anxiety.

One of the outcomes of therapy is to diminish or increase anxiety, as necessary. There are, however, temporary devices to keep anxiety under control. Support and reassurance techniques may be used to reduce anxiety as well as guilt. Acceptance, leading the interview into structured areas, allowing sufficient time for reconstruction before proceeding into another problem area, the use of binding, differentiating, introspection, anticipating hurdles, encouraging dependence, structuring the interview, and controlling the tempo of the interview are additional methods of controlling anxiety.

Guilt may be controlled by similar techniques. In addition, reconstruction of the core role—the awareness of the loss of this role being the cause of guilt—is an important method. Alternate roles may be sought with the client. Interpretation of the persons whom the client uses to delineate his or her role is useful. Broadening the base of the role relation to the therapist also temporarily replaces the lost role.

Psychotherapeutic experimentation   Psychotherapy and scientific research are similar. The client uses the scientific method in working out problems. The client first elaborates problems and then, in loosening, becomes creative in developing new ideas. Third, by tightening, the client formulates testable hypotheses. Finally, the client engages in experiments to test, or validate, his or her hypotheses.

Psychotherapeutic experimentation serves several functions. First, it provides a framework in which the client can anticipate alternative outcomes. Second, it places the client in touch with reality and tests the client's construct system. It also serves as a check on the therapist's construction of the case. In addition, experimentation opens up new vistas of experience. Finally, it puts the client in touch with other people and enables the client to see how others view their worlds, so that he or she may play a role in relation to them.

The therapist encourages experimentation, both inside and outside the interviewing room, by various techniques. Enactment, discussed earlier, is one of the most useful of these. Permissiveness, responsiveness, projecting the client into a novel situation, and seeing that the client has the necessary tools are methods that encourage and set the stage for actual experimentation. The therapist also gets the client to develop hypotheses or make specific predictions. The therapist asks the client to make interpretations of others' outlooks, to portray how another person views himself or herself, and to portray how another person views the client. Negative predictions may be encouraged. Or the client may be encouraged to elaborate the biographical conditions under which the client thinks his or her behavior would be different; this often leads to behaving differently. The therapist may directly encourage the client to take certain actions. Finally, the client may be placed in a social situation where others are enthusiastically attempting what the client could do well if he or she wanted to.

Obstacles to experimentation include the client's hostility, anxiety, guilt, or dependence; the threat of outcomes; and the nonelaborative choice, that is, the client's belief that no matter what the outcome, he or she is trapped. Some of these difficulties also constitute hazards in experimentation. Other hazards are present: the client may constrict as a result of being "burned"; excessive loosening may result; or the therapist may urge the client to experiment in an inappropriate setting, with disastrous results.

Fixed-Role Therapy

Fixed-role therapy is a type of psychotherapy that is specifically derived from the psychology of personal constructs and is based on observations of the effects of dramatic experience.

Fixed-role therapy begins by the therapist requesting the client to write a sketch of himself or herself. The client does so in the third person with no detailed outline but with only the following instructions:

"I want you to write a character sketch of Harry Brown, just as if he were the principal character in a play. Write it as it might be written by a friend who knows him very *intimately* and very *sympathetically,* perhaps better than anyone even really could know him. Be sure to write it in the third person. For example, start out by saying, Harry Brown is. . . ."[37]

The self-characterization is the basis for writing the fixed-role sketch. The sketch is designed to invite the client to explore certain sharply contrasting behaviors. It develops a major theme rather than correcting minor faults. It is intended to set the stage for the resumption of growth and movement rather than to attempt a major psychotherapeutic relocation. It sets up hypotheses that can be tested quickly. There is emphasis on role perceptions and role relationships with other people. It is desirable that the sketch be developed by a group of experienced clinicians if possible.

The procedure involved in fixed-role therapy is introduced to the client following the diagnostic phase of therapy, as preparatory to going into the client's problems. The character sketch is presented with another name than the client's. Following the reading of the sketch, the *acceptance check* determines whether the client understands and accepts the sketch as representing someone he or she would like to know, not someone he or she would like to be. If the sketch is accepted as plausible and not threatening, the rehearsal sequence begins. This is initiated with the request that the client for the next two weeks act as if he or she were the person in the sketch with the therapist's help in interviews scheduled every other day. The client keeps the copy of the sketch, reads it at least three times a day, and tries to act, think, talk, and be like the person in the sketch.

Clients are skeptical and report failure during the greater part of the two weeks; if the process were easy, it would be ineffective. The client is given help in enacting the role in work situations, social relationships, family situations, and situations involving life orientation and plan. Rehearsal takes place through role playing. The therapist treats the client as though the client were the person in the sketch. As interviews continue, the client contributes more and begins to feel like the person whose role he or she is playing. In the final interview, the role is withdrawn. The client is more active, while the therapist listens. The therapist does not resort to urging the client to adopt the new role. If the client has found it effective, the client will accept it. The therapist decides whether therapy should be continued by another method, or the therapist may, if the client requests it, continue the rehearsals for another predetermined period.

The experience is kept realistic by creating a role that has many day-to-day implications and by keeping the interviews geared to practical situations. Although it is not generally helpful to schizoid individuals, it has helped put some in contact with reality. The hazard of unreality is thus not a great one. A greater hazard is that by pressuring the client to act, the therapist will force the client to act within his or her present construct system and push the client to the opposite extreme of his or her dichotomous constructs.

The client's insistence that although the role is working out, he or she is only acting is not undesirable. It indicates that the client has not been threatened. If this attitude persists to the end, however, and the role is too easily accepted, the sketch may not be adequate to lead the client to face crucial issues. The development of spontaneous behavior in which the client forgets that he or she is acting is a good sign as long as the client does not look back on it with embarrassment. The reactions of other people to the client as being different indicate progress in fixed-role therapy and lead to further progress by reducing threat. The best evidence of progress is when the client says, "I feel as if this were the *real* me." This is always accompanied by a marked shift in the client's formulation of problems.

While difficulty with the role and criticism of it are not bad signs, the failure of the client to accept the method or to see the role and its implications in contrast to old constructs indicates that the method cannot be used as a vehicle for readjustment. Indications for fixed-role therapy include limited time for treatment, desirability of avoiding strong dependent transference, unavoidable client–therapist relationships outside of therapy, inexperienced clinicians, the presence of obvious social and situational components in the case, need for termination of another type of therapy sequence, need for establishment of contact with everyday reality, uncertainty of the client's readiness for change, and defensiveness on the part of the client with respect to therapy. The method is relatively safe, even though it substitutes a new, prefabricated construction system rather than reworking parts of the old one, because the new system is enacted or playacted with an artificial identity alongside the old structure, and there are no implications at the outset that the new structure may eventually replace the old one.

SUMMARY AND EVALUATION

The psychology of personal constructs is based on the philosophical position of constructive alternativism, which is the position that there are many workable ways for a person to construe the world. The system is developed on the basis of 1 postulate and its elaboration by means of 11 corollaries. The basic assumption is that "a person's processes are psychologically channelized by the ways in which he anticipates events."[38] The individual's system of personal constructs determines the way the world is construed. Constructs are dichotomous, and the individual chooses the alternative through which he or she anticipates the greater possibility for extension and definition of the system. Constructs have certain formal characteristics and are organized into a hierarchy of subsystems. The characteristics of constructs form the basis for setting up a system of diagnostic constructs, which are used by the clinician to analyze, understand, and subsume the client's construct system. Changes in behavior involve changes in the personal-construct system.

Therapy is thus directed toward the reconstruction of the client's system of personal constructs. In therapy based on the psychology of personal constructs, the therapist is active, responding to the client in a great variety of ways. Enactment, or role playing, plays a large part in therapy, and in one specific approach to therapy— fixed-role therapy—the playing of an assigned role by the client constitutes the major aspect of the therapy.

The process of therapy is conceived as being similar to the process of scientific experimentation. The task of the therapist is to help the client develop hypotheses and test them experimentally, both within and outside the interview situation. Science is thus the model that clients use in reconstructing their lives. The therapist participates in the process as a helper and collaborator, using a wide variety of methods and techniques.

Kelly's approach to counseling and psychotherapy is one of the most systematic, if not the most systematic, that has appeared. It is developed elaborately and in considerable detail, which makes it perhaps the most difficult approach to summarize of any of those included in this volume. Its detail makes it both fascinating and frustrating to read. Although the basic postulate and its corollaries are amazingly simple, their elaboration is amazingly complex. There are probably almost as many concepts as there are in psychoanalysis. Many common concepts or terms are used in somewhat different ways than is common in psychology or psychoanalysis. These include *anxiety, guilt, threat, hostility, aggressiveness,* and *fear.* There are also many new terms, such as *preemptive constructs, constellatory constructs, propositional con-*

structs, submergence, suspension, and *permeability.* It becomes difficult to keep all these in mind when reading about the development and application of the theory in therapy. The reader needs to have a system of constructs that is comprehensive, propositional, and permeable to be able to absorb the material.

The attraction of this approach could be limited by the formidability of the new concepts and the detail. Apparently, few have become attracted to it since its publication. To master it to the point of being able to practice it would require extensive study, training, and experience. In spite of its detail, the published material is not sufficient, as Kelly notes, for the application of the approach in therapy. While there is considerable discussion of method and technique, there are no actual therapy protocols to illustrate application.

Nevertheless, for the counselor or therapist who may not want to master this particular approach, there are an amazing number of details relating to problems and techniques in therapy—discussions of what the therapist should do when. For example, ten kinds of weeping are distinguished. There is a detailed discussion of what to look for in a classroom in appraising the school environment. The reader will also benefit from many other discussions, apart from the particular theoretical approach. There is a fresh, new way of looking at things, divorced from the usual clinical terminology or jargon. The approach is not diagnostically or externally oriented.

This lack of diagnostic orientation leads to a consideration of the phenomenological nature of the approach. One of its basic concepts is that "each man contemplates in his own personal way the stream of events upon which he finds himself so swiftly borne."[39] Kelly feels, however, that the phenomenological approach leaves the individual's personal constructs locked up in privacy,[40] whereas they must be brought out for public view. At least the psychologist or psychotherapist must be able to construe the personal constructs of the client, and this, according to Kelly, goes beyond phenomenology. It is difficult not to see this as an expression of the basic impossibility of avoiding a phenomenological approach, since the constructions of the psychologist, while external, public, or objective from the client's viewpoint, are nonetheless phenomenological from the psychologist's viewpoint. Here is one place where Kelly apparently is inconsistent in applying the basic concept noted above. The same difficulty appears later when he says, "We attempt to use the phenomenologist's approach to arrive at personalized constructs which have a wide range of meaning for the given individual; then we attempt to piece together this high-level type of data with what we know about other persons."[41] How do we obtain this knowledge of other people, except phenomenologically? In most instances, however, Kelly is consistently phenomenological in his approach, although he does not feel that his system is neophenomenological.[42] His basic conception of a role relationship is that the therapist, for example, subsumes the construct system of the client by an acceptance (defined as willingness to see the world through the client's eyes) and thus is able to construe things as the client does, which enables the therapist to predict or anticipate the client's behavior. This is exactly the approach taken by Combs and Snygg in their phenomenological system.[43]

It is interesting to consider Kelly's approach as an alternative to client-centered therapy, since both have a common phenomenological base. Nothing in phenomenology leads only to the client-centered approach to counseling or psychotherapy. Perceptions or the personal constructs related to perceptions may be changed in various ways. Whereas in the client-centered approach, the therapist operates in one way to facilitate change, in therapy based on the psychology of personal constructs, the therapist functions in another way. In the latter approach, the therapist appears to be a highly active, manipulative individual, constantly prodding, pushing, and stimulating the client.

It is this continually active nature of therapy that creates the need for the therapist to be constantly engaged in evaluation and judgment of the client and of his or her needs in order to make decisions about what to do next. This places a tremendous responsibility on the therapist. After reading Kelly's books, one may be left with the feeling that there are few therapists who would want to accept this responsibility. One is led again to the conclusion that it is not so much what is done as the way in which it is done that is important in therapy; the danger of damage is apparently minimized when the therapist is obviously interested and concerned. The client responds to the relationship rather than to the methods. The personal-construct counselor—or at least in Kelly's writings—gives the client the impression that the therapist is in control, knows just what he or she is doing, and knows what he or she is going to do. While it appears to be close to the "doctor-knows-best" approach, Kelly recognizes the dangers of this method and disavows it. He mentions several cases in which suicide attempts were precipitated and points out the errors of the therapists in terms of this theory. However, it may be that the errors were not so much due to a failure to apply the theory as to a failure to understand the client, together with excessive activity and manipulation, apparently in an effort to play the active, pushing role demanded by the approach. Kelly warns against the therapist playing God, but a therapist using this approach almost has to be God.

The fixed-role therapy is a method of instigating client activity that has some similarities to the prescriptions of client activity in other approaches, such as those of Salter and of Wolpe. It is a much more systematic and individually adapted approach, however, than those of Salter and of Wolpe; the prescription is not a blanket one but varies with the client. It also appears to differ in that through the fixed-role sketch, the client's attitudes and perceptions are changed prior to the change in activity, rather than the client's being forced into actions that, it is presumed, will generate changes in attitudes and feelings following reinforcement.

In addition to its active, manipulative aspects, Kelly's approach is also apparently highly rational and intellectual. "Psychotherapy is the intelligent manipulation of various psychological processes."[44] Psychotherapy is likened to a scientific experiment. Rogers, in his review of Kelly, emphasizes this aspect, noting, "He is continually thinking about the client, and about his own procedures, in ways so complex that there seems no room for entering into an emotional relationship with the client."[45] Nevertheless, it may be that Kelly's description of the way he practiced psychotherapy is not quite the way he actually practiced it. While he no doubt was highly active, manipulative, and cognitively oriented, there is evidence that he was sensitive to the various possible meanings that a client's behavior (such as weeping) or statements may have had.

The approach is highly provocative and stimulating. The theory of behavior and personality is probably more significant than is the application of the approach in psychotherapy; the theory can be useful in connection with other methods, since there seems to be nothing inherent in it that would lead to these particular methods of therapy. Many of the methods are those commonly used in other approaches to psychotherapy, including psychoanalysis. The unique approach developed in fixed-role therapy is limited, since, as Rogers points out,[46] it is useful only with clients who are not familiar with the method. Many of the concepts or constructs are similar to those of other theorists, but there are unique aspects that are more than the coining of new words for old concepts. The forward-looking aspect manifested in the basic postulate, involving anticipation, is unique; it is similar to the concepts of Rotter and of Phillips, although Kelly develops it much more extensively. There is also some similarity between the concept of self-actualization and the concept of elaborative choice (that persons choose for themselves the alternative in a dichotomized construct through which they anticipate the greater possibility for extension and definition of their systems).

Perhaps one of the major unique concepts is the notion of the dichotomous nature of constructs. The notion of contrast is, of course, nothing new, but it is one that has never been given the place it appears to deserve in psychological theory. It is easily recognized that satisfaction exists only in contrast to or in relation to lack of satisfaction or dissatisfaction. This relativity relationship has been elevated by Garan into the basic psychological causal law.[47] While perhaps it does not warrant such elevation, it does deserve more attention than it has received, and Kelly has made a real contribution here, which does not seem to have been recognized as yet. The relativity relationship contributes, for example, to the dilemma of determinism versus free will, which Kelly considers.

Finally, Kelly's handling of motivation is provocative. There is no concept of motivation or any need for such a concept, since he begins by postulating a process rather than an inert substance that must be put into movement. There is thus no consideration of the aspects of motivation, which are central to so-called dynamic psychology.

Kelly's basic postulate has a motivational aspect, however, including a goal or direction of all behavior. This postulate is not too different from the motivational theory of the phenomenology of Combs and Snygg that a person's basic motivation is the maintenance and enhancement of the phenomenal self.[48] Similarly, there is no place for the concepts of reward or reinforcement in Kelly's theory. Events are validated by perception of correct anticipation. The scientist is not controlled by reward. "The scientist who attempts only to accumulate a backlog of reinforcements is likely to become rigid, timid, opinionated, and generally inert. The scientist who is inventive, curious, receptive, and progressive is the one who is as happy over negative results and the enlightenment they offer as he is about the positive ones."[49] One might quibble over definitions of reward, but the general point is clear. The concept of validation is much broader and thus more useful than the concept of reinforcement.

The psychology of personal constructs presents a view of human behavior that is significant. Bruner has called it "the single greatest contribution of the past decade to the theory of personality functioning."[50] In a review of *Clinical Psychology and Personality: The Selected Papers of George Kelly,* Appelbaum,[51] while recognizing that Kelly "has been a significant figure in recent psychology," contends that he has given us little that is new, but simply reiterates the phenomenological and humanistic point of view. "His eminence [was] an accident of his time. . . . His point of view will fade away into the limbo of [the history of ideas], and even now its main interest lies more in what it tells us about our professional culture than in its substance." Kelly has not yet faded away. His personal-construct system is alive and well, at least in England, where work is being done with his Role Construct Repertory Test. Furthermore, the 1976 Nebraska Symposium on Motivation was devoted to personal-construct psychology, and contributions were made by several non-American scholars.[52] There is a sizable group of psychologists engaged in theoretical and research work in the field of personal-construct psychology. It may be true that Kelly has contributed little beyond what other phenomenologists and humanists have given us, but he has integrated it and systematized it. Perhaps his particular integration and his concepts and terminology will not persist, but the basic substance—the point of view—undoubtedly will, since it appears to be necessary for an adequate understanding of, and therapy with, human beings. In addition, Kelly has stimulated a reexamination of some traditional and current views of human behavior and therapy. He has succeeded in a wish stated in 1963: "If I had to end my life on some final note, I think I would like it to be a question, preferably a basic one, well posed and challenging, and beckoning me to where only others after me may go, rather than a terminal conclusion—no matter how well documented."[53]

REFERENCES

1. Kelly, G. A. *The psychology of personal constructs.* Vol. 1: *A theory of personality.* Vol. 2: *Clinical diagnosis and psychotherapy.* New York: Norton, 1955.
2. Ibid., Vol. 1, p. 3.
3. Ibid., p. 8.
4. Ibid., p. 15.
5. Ibid., p. 21.
6. Ibid.
7. Ibid., pp. 21–22.
8. Ibid., p. 49.
9. Ibid., p. 61.
10. Ibid., p. 67.
11. Ibid., p. 69.
12. Ibid., p. 105.
13. Ibid., p. 127.
14. Ibid., p. 133.
15. Ibid., p. 166.
16. Ibid., pp. 167–168.
17. Ibid., p. 173.
18. Ibid., p. 174.
19. Ibid., p. 472.
20. Ibid., p. 489.
21. Ibid., p. 503.
22. Ibid., p. 511.
23. Ibid., Vol. 2, p. 590.
24. Ibid., p. 592.
25. Ibid., p. 594.

26. Ibid., p. 941.
27. Ibid., p. 775.
28. Ibid.
29. Ibid., p. 829.
30. Ibid., Vol. 1, p. 209.
31. Ibid., Vol. 2, p. 635.
32. Ibid., p. 975.
33. Ibid., p. 1049.
34. Ibid., p. 1090.
35. Ibid., p. 1053.
36. Ibid., p. 1111.
37. Ibid., Vol. 1, p. 323.
38. Ibid., p. 46.
39. Ibid., p. 3.
40. Ibid., p. 173.
41. Ibid., p. 455.
42. Ibid., p. 517.
43. Combs, A. W., & Snygg, D. *Individual behavior: A perceptual approach to human behavior.* (Rev. ed.). New York: Harper & Row, 1959. P. 35.
44. Kelly, *The psychology of personal constructs,* Vol. 2, p. 1071.
45. Rogers, C. R. Intellectualized psychotherapy. (Review of *The psychology of personal constructs* by G. A. Kelly). *Contemporary Psychology,* 1956, *1,* 357–358.
46. Ibid.
47. Garan, D. G. *The paradox of pleasure and relativity: The psychological causal law.* New York: Philosophical Library, 1963; Patterson, C. H. Review of *The paradox of pleasure and relativity* by D. G. Garan. *Personnel Guidance Journal,* 1964, *43,* 82–84.
48. Combs & Snygg, *Individual behavior,* pp. 44–46.
49. Kelly, Vol. 2, p. 1166.
50. Bruner, J. Review of *The psychology of personal constructs* by G. A. Kelly. *Contemporary Psychology,* 1956, *1,* 355–357.
51. Appelbaum, S. A. The accidental eminence of George Kelly. (Review of *Clinical psychology and personality: The selected papers of George Kelly,* edited by B. Maher). *Psychiatry and Social Science Review,* 1970, *3,* No. 12, 20–25.
52. Cole, J. K., & Landfield, A. W. (Eds.). *Nebraska symposium on motivation: 1976.* Lincoln: University of Nebraska Press, 1976. See also Addams-Webber, J. R. *Personal construct theory: Concepts and applications.* New York: Wiley-Interscience, 1979; Landfield, A. W. and Leitner, L. M. (Eds.). *Personal construct psychology: psychotherapy and personality.* New York: Wiley, 1980; Bonarius, H., Holland, R., and Rosenberg (Eds.) *Personal construct psychology: recent advances in theory and practice.* London: Macmillan, 1981; Mancuso, J. C. and Addams-Webber, J. R. (Eds.). *The construing person.* New York: Praeger, 1982; Addams-Webber, J. R. and Mancuso, J. C. (Eds.). *Applications of personal construct theory.* New York: Academic Press, 1983; Epting, F. R. *Personal construct counseling and psychotherapy.* New York: Wiley, 1984.
53. Kelly, G. A. The autobiography of a theory. In B. Maher (Ed.), *Clinical psychology and personality: The selected papers of George Kelly.* New York: Wiley, 1969. Pp. 46–65.

chapter *12*

Transactional Analysis: Berne

Eric Lennard Berne (1910–1970) was born in Montreal, Canada. He was awarded his M.D. from McGill University in 1935 and served his residency in psychiatry at Yale University from 1936 to 1941. After two years as clinical assistant in psychiatry at Mount Zion Hospital, in New York, he entered the armed forces. As did a number of other psychiatrists and psychologists who joined the military, he discovered group therapy and began to develop his own approach. After leaving the service in 1946, he settled in Carmel, California, and returned to the study of psychoanalysis with Erik Erikson at the San Francisco Psychoanalytic Institute. He had begun the study of psychoanalysis at the New York Psychoanalytic Institute, with Paul Federn as his analyst, in 1941. His other teachers included Eugen Kahn and Wilder Penfield. He acknowledges being influenced also by Nathan Ackerman, Martin Grotjahn, and Benjamin Weininger.

In the early 1950s, Berne's ideas diverged from psychoanalysis, and he was denied membership in the San Francisco Psychoanalytic Institute when he applied in 1956. His ideas on transactional analysis, which he developed and put into practice during this period, were first publicized in an address at the meeting of the western region of the American Group Psychotherapy Association in 1957. Entitled "Transactional Analysis: A New and Effective Method of Group Treatment," the paper was published in the *American Journal of Psychotherapy* in 1958. In the 1957 volume of the same journal, he had published an article entitled "Ego States in Psychotherapy."

Berne's first book, *The Mind in Action* (1947), was republished under the title *A Layman's Guide to Psychiatry and Psychoanalysis* (1968).[1] *Transactional Analysis in Psychotherapy* (1961)[2] was followed by *The Structure and Dynamics of Organizations and Groups* (1963)[3] and *Principles of Group Treatment* (1966).[4] However, it was his book *Games People Play: The Psychology of Human Relationships* (1964)[5] that some time after publication and to Berne's surprise became a best seller and launched transactional analysis on its road to popularity. At the time of his death, two manuscripts were ready for publication: *Sex in Human Loving* (1970)[6] and *What Do You Say After You Say Hello?* (1972).[7] A compilation of selections from his books and articles was assembled by Claude Steiner and Carmen Kerr and published under the title *Beyond Games and Scripts* (1976).[8]

In addition to his private practice, Berne held numerous appointments, including consultant in psychiatry to the Surgeon General, United States Army; attending psychiatrist at the Veterans Administration Mental Hygiene Clinic in San Francisco; lecturer in group therapy at the Langley Porter Neuropsychiatric Institute; visiting lecturer in group therapy at the Stanford–Palo Alto Psychiatric Clinic; and adjunct psychiatrist at the Mount Zion Hospital.

In 1961, Berne founded and edited the *Transactional Analysis Bulletin,* which became the *Transactional Analysis Journal* in 1971, published by the International Transactional Analysis Association (ITAA). The association was founded in 1964 and grew out of the San Francisco Social Psychiatry Seminars that Berne began in 1958. It became a society of the ITAA under the name San Francisco Transactional Analysis Seminar.

BACKGROUND AND DEVELOPMENT

As noted above, Berne's training was in psychoanalysis. He apparently became dissatisfied with the passivity and length of psychoanalytic treatment: he writes in 1963 of his "ten years of experience with passive interpretive 'psychoanalytic group therapy,' followed by two years of existential group therapy" and then notes that this was followed by eight years of "active transactional group treatment."[9] However, he did not reject psychoanalysis but felt that "in many cases, it is clear that the most appropriate treatment is formal orthodox psychoanalysis" or modified psychoanalytic psychotherapy; such treatment is not adapted to the group situation, however.[10] Transactional analysis as a broad general approach can be preparation for psychoanalysis or other specific approaches.

Berne's ideas were formulated and tried out in a seminar at Carmel (the Carmel Seminar) during the early 1950s. He reports that he first began to use the ideas "with some regularity" in the autumn of 1954 and that by 1956, "the need for and the principles of transactional and game analysis had emerged with sufficient clarity to indicate a more systematic, ongoing therapeutic program."[11]

Most of Berne's writing, as well as his experience, related to group therapy, or group treatment, as he preferred to call it. This was the major reason for not including Berne's transactional analysis in the first edition of this book. The dilution and oversimplification because of its popularization was an additional reason for its absence in the second edition. It is included in this edition in an attempt to present an accurate summary drawn from Berne's own writings for serious students. Berne did work with individual clients, and his basic 1961 book, subtitled *A Systematic Individual and Social Psychiatry,* applies to individual therapy as well as to group therapy. Individual therapy may be useful in preparing an individual for group treatment, or it may be useful or necessary along with or following group treatment.

Although Berne's *Games People Play* became a popular book, Thomas Harris, a psychiatrist, popularized transactional analysis further with his book *I'm OK— You're OK*.[12] Two years later, a less successful attempt to popularize transactional analysis was published by Muriel James and Dorothy Jongeward (*Born to Win: Transactional Analysis with Gestalt Experiments*).[13]

PHILOSOPHY AND CONCEPTS

"The transactional theory of personality is also a theory of life." Every individual is born "with the capacity to develop his potentialities to the best advantage of himself and society, to enjoy himself and to be able to work productively and creatively, and to be free of psychological disabilities."[14] However, beginning with the first few days of life, the infant may run into difficulties. These and later obstacles may prevent many individuals from developing their full capacities.

Personality Development

The human organism is characterized by the need for various forms of contact and response from others in an interactional process. This need is designated by the term *stimulus hunger.*

The first form that this need takes in the infant is *tactile hunger,* or the need for physical closeness and intimacy. The lack of adequate physical contact may lead to susceptibility to disease and resulting death, a condition called *hospitalism* by René Spitz, who first recognized it in institutionalized infants.

The need for intimate physical contact continues throughout life, and the individual engages in a perpetual striving for attainment of physical intimacy with others. However, individuals learn early that they cannot have everything they want, so they begin to compromise, accepting other forms of contact. Tactile hunger becomes converted into *recognition hunger,* which includes the simple acknowledgment of existence by others, or "verbal touching." Such evidences of recognition are called *strokes* by analogy with the literal physical strokes or caresses given to infants. The stroke is a basic unit of social interaction; an exchange of strokes constitutes a *transaction.*

A third form of stimulus hunger is *structure hunger,* or the need to organize and fill time in order to avoid boredom. "The question is, what next? In everyday terms, what can people do after they have exchanged greetings . . .?"[15] Or, as it is put in the title of one of Berne's books, "What do you say after you say hello?" "The eternal problem of the human being is how to structure his waking hours. In this existential sense, the function of all social living is to lend mutual assistance for this project."[16] The ways in which people fill time will be considered later under the topic of social intercourse. *Excitement hunger* is the desire or the preference for structuring time in interesting and exciting ways. A derivative of structure hunger is *leadership hunger.* Leaders provide activities and programs through which people can fill and structure their time.

Personality Structure

Personality structure consists of a tripartite ego system. The three ego states are Parent, Adult, and Child. (Capitalization is used to designate an ego state as distinguished from actual persons.) "The term 'ego state' is intended merely to denote states of mind and their related patterns of behavior as they occur in nature. . . ."[17] Every individual incorporates all three ego states, which manifest themselves in different—and often inconsistent—sets of behavior patterns. These sets of behavior patterns are referred to as Parent, Adult, and Child.

The Parent Ego State

The Parent ego state derives from the *exteropsyche,* which involves identification activities. All adult individuals have had either actual parents or parent substitutes, who through exteropsychic functioning influence their behavior. Such behaviors are labeled Parent behaviors, indicating that the individuals are in the state of mind exhibited by one of their parents or parent substitutes in the past and are responding in the same way, for example, in postures, gestures, verbalizations, feelings, and so forth. In the transactional-analysis colloquialism, "Everyone carries his parents around inside of him."

The Parent is not Freud's superego, although the superego is one aspect of the Parent as the parental influence. The parental influence is not abstract; it is a result of direct, actual transactions with the parents. The parental influence includes not only prohibitions, but also permission, encouragement, nurturing, and commands. The parental influence leads individuals to respond as their parents would want them to respond; as the direct Parent, it responds as their parents actually responded.

The Parent functions as the actual parent of children. It also functions by performing many things automatically and thus freeing the Adult of minor decisions.

The Adult Ego State

"Every human being with sufficient functioning brain tissue is potentially capable of adequate reality testing."[18] The Adult ego state represents *neopsychic* functioning. The Adult ego state is focused on data processing and probability estimating. Colloquially, "Everyone has an Adult." The Adult is necessary for survival in the world. It also regulates the activities of the Parent and the Child, mediating between them.

The Child Ego State

Every adult was once a child, and the relics of childhood exist in later life as the Child ego state, or *archeopsychic* ego state. The Child is under the inhibitory, permissive, or provocative influence of the Parent. It is separate from the Parent, a distinct personality, inconsistent with but not necessarily opposed to the Parent. Colloquially, "Everyone carries a little boy or a little girl around inside of him."

The Child is not Freud's id, although it is influenced by the id. In particular, it is not the chaotic or disorganized state of Freud's id but is well organized.

The behavior of the Child is not immature or childish but is *childlike*. The child has three forms: the *natural* Child possesses charm and intuition and is spontaneous and creative; the *adapted* Child's behavior is modified or inhibited by parental influence; the *rebellious* Child resists parental control.

These three ego states are diagrammed as three nonoverlapping but touching circles arranged vertically to indicate their differentiation and usual inconsistency with one another. The Parent, at the top, is the ethical guide; the Adult is concerned with reality; and the Child is a purgatory or sometimes a hell for archaic tendencies. The three form a moral hierarchy. The Parent is the weakest, and the Child is the strongest. This order is shown when a person comes under the influence of alcohol: the Parent is decommissioned first, and soon the Child takes over and is the last to pass out. The same order prevails in falling asleep: the Parent gives way in the hypnogogic state, and the Child takes over during sleep in dreams. They are not, however, topographical parts of the individual, as the superego, id, and ego are often conceived, nor are they concepts, as these Freudian terms are; they are simpler, more scientifically economical and are "experiential and behavioral realities."[19]

Parent, Adult, and Child are entitled to equal respect, and each has a place in normal life. It is only when a healthy balance is disturbed that analysis and reorganization are necessary.

Personality Function

The three systems of personality react differently to stimuli. The Parent (exteropsyche) judgmentally attempts to enforce external ("borrowed") standards. The Adult (neopsyche) is concerned with processing and storing information derived from stimuli. The Child (archeopsyche) reacts more impulsively on poorly differentiated perceptions. Each perceives stimuli differently and responds in terms of its perception. The three systems interact with one another, but the Parent and the Child reenact the individual's relationship with the parents.

Psychic energy, or *cathexis,* flows from one to another ego state; the state that is cathected at a particular time has *executive power;* that is, it determines the individual's behavior. The active state is said to be cathected with *unbound energy;* the inactive state is said to be cathected with *bound energy.* There is also a *free cathexis,* which moves from one ego state to another; the feeling of Self resides in the state that is charged with free cathexis. The executive command, or active state, is usually the state that has unbound plus free cathexis.

Each ego state has boundaries that separate it from the other ego states, as indicated by their representation as nonoverlapping circles. Changes in ego state depend on the permeability of the boundaries between the states, the cathectic capacity of each state, and the forces acting on each state. Therapy must recognize these factors in working to induce changes in ego states.

The Four Life Positions

The child is faced, as noted earlier, with the necessity of compromising in satisfying needs, or stimulus hunger. Between the ages of four and seven, the child establishes compromises that affect later relationships. The child makes certain decisions—very specific decisions that can be located and dated—and on the basis of these decisions adopts a position toward the self and others and maintains this position against influences that question or threaten it. The life position is a major determinant of the life script (see below). (In fact, it would appear that they both derive from the same early experiences rather than that one determines the other.)

The four positions involve two polarities: "I–Others" and "OK–not OK." The resulting positions are:

1. I am OK; you are OK.
2. I am OK; you are not OK.
3. I am not OK; you are OK.
4. I am not OK; you are not OK.

"I" may extend to a group—"we." "You" may extend to "they" or may specify groups, such as men or women. "OK" may stand for any specific good, and "not OK" may stand for any specific evil.

Position 1 is the good or healthy success position. Position 2 is the arrogant position, the characteristic of which is dedication to betterment—for example, missionaries, district attorneys, and other "do gooders." This alternative is called colloquially "getting rid of people." In less healthy individuals, it may lead to homicide and paranoid states. Position 3, the depression position, leads to the individual cutting himself or herself off from other people in some way, such as becoming institutionalized or committing suicide. Colloquially, it is "resigning from the human race." The fourth position is the futility and schizoid position. It leads ultimately to the spiteful or aesthetic suicide. Berne believes that such suicides result from lack of stroking in infancy, leading to depression and despair. Colloquially, this is referred to as "knocking yourself off," and justifications that are presented by patients are called "trading stamps" (see below).

Social Intercourse

Social intercourse provides the opportunity for the satisfaction of structure hunger, or structuring time, as well as of stimulus hunger, or obtaining recognition or strokes from other persons. The unit of social intercourse is the transaction. It involves a *transactional stimulus* from the person who initiates the transaction by acknowledging the other in some way and the *transactional response.* Transactions are analyzed in terms of the sources of the stimuli and responses, that is, their origination in the Parent, Adult, or Child of the participants. The simplest transactions are Adult–Adult, that is, from the Adult of one to the Adult of the other and from this Adult in return. The next simplest is the Child–Parent transaction, usually a request.

Transactions may be *complementary* or *crossed.* Complementary transactions follow the natural order of healthy relationships. They are of various types: Adult–Adult, Parent–Parent, and Child–Child transactions are complementary; so also are Parent–Child and Child–Parent. Complementary transactions lead to smoothly continuing communication.

Crossed transactions result in the breaking down of communication. The most common and the most disruptive one is an Adult stimulus directed to the Adult of the other, who responds, however, from his or her Child to the Parent of the initiator. A response from the Parent to the Child of the other is a second type of crossed transaction. In the first type, the reply to the question, "Do you know where my cuff links are?" would be, "You always blame me for everything." The response to the second type would be, "Why don't you keep track of your own things? You're not a child any more." There are 72 varieties of crossed transactions and only 9 types of complementary transactions. Transactions may be further classified as simple or ulterior (involving two ego states and both social and psychological aspects), the latter of which may be either angular (36 types) or duplex (6480 types). Detailed discussion is not possible here. Only about 15 types of transactions occur in ordinary social intercourse.

Transactions occur in series. They may involve *material programming, social programming,* and *individual programming.* Material programming structures time through *activities* or *procedures* and deals with the material external reality. Procedures are simple complementary Adult transactions. These are of interest only insofar as they provide opportunities for recognition and more complex forms of social intercourse. Social programming involves *rituals* and *pastimes.* Activities, rituals, and pastimes are three of the four major ways of structuring time. The fourth is *games.* There are two other limiting cases of social behavior: *withdrawal* at one extreme and *intimacy* at the other.

Rituals

Rituals are socially prescribed forms for behavior in standard social situations. They are complementary Parent transactions. They meet the need for recognition and strokes. Perhaps the most common ritual is the "Hello–Goodbye" sequence. The withholding of symbols of recognition constitutes rudeness. There are various degrees and types of recognition. Fan letters are a depersonalized form; live applause or the presentation of a bouquet of flowers after a performance is more personal. Verbally, recognition proceeds form a simple "Hello" to "How are you?" The progression is from simple acknowledgment that someone is there, through recognition of feelings, sensations, and personality, to expression of a personal interest. "Mere recognition, however, is not enough, since after the rituals have been exhausted, tension mounts and anxiety begins to appear. The real problem of social intercourse is what happens after the rituals."[20]

Pastimes

Procedures and rituals are stereotyped and thus predictable. Pastimes are less restricted. They involve more time than rituals and may begin and end with rituals. They often fill in time while a person is waiting for a meeting or an activity to begin, or during a cocktail party. Pastimes may facilitate the social-selection process, since they bring together persons who have similar interests or interest in one another, often leading to more complex relationships (games) or friendships. Pastimes are highly varied and are given names such as "PTA," "Man Talk," "Lady Talk," "Do You know," and so on. They may be classified in various ways. Pastimes are complementary transactions. In addition to having other advantages, such as noted above, pastimes may confirm a person's role and stabilize his or her position (see the four positions above). Pastimes may be enjoyable in themselves or, for neurotics especially, simply a way of passing time. They are not particularly exciting, however.

Games

Pastimes and games are both *engagements;* they fall between *activities* and *rituals,* on the one hand, and *intimacy,* on the other. Whereas pastimes are straightforward transactions, games are dissimulations. Transactions in games are complementary but are ulterior and involve a payoff. "Procedures may be successful, rituals effective, and pastimes profitable, but all of them are by definition candid; they may involve contest but not conflict, and the ending may be sensational, but it is not dramatic. Every game, on the other hand, is basically dishonest, and the outcome has a dramatic, as distinct from a merely exciting, quality."[21] Games are not "fun and games"; they are deadly or grimly serious, as gambling may be. Selling involves games and is often referred to as such: the "insurance game," the "real-estate game," and so on, up to the "con game"; war is also a game.

Games are given names: 100 are named and described in *Games People Play,* from *A* ("Addict") to *Y* ("You've Got to Listen"). Numerous others have been identified since. The most common game between spouses is called "If It Weren't for You," with its social-pastime derivative, "If It Weren't for Him." Several kinds of gains can be obtained by a wife from such a game, including getting out of doing something that she is afraid to or cannot do, manipulating the husband, and providing a pastime to structure and fill social relationships with other women.

The most common game in social gatherings is "Why Don't You—Yes, But," which can be played by any number. The player who is "it" presents a problem. Others suggest solutions: "Why don't you . . .?" The one who is "it" objects with "Yes, but. . . ." "A good player can stand off the rest of the group indefinitely, until they all give up, whereupon 'it' wins."[22] The game is not played for the ostensible purpose of getting help or information but for the ulterior purpose of reasuring and gratifying the Child, who frustrates the Parents.

Games serve a number of functions; they fill up or occupy most of social life. In order to move from the boredom of pastimes without being exposed to the dangers of intimacy, people resort to games for excitement and social reinforcement or stroking. As with pastimes, those who play the same games associate with one another.

Games are also duplex transactions, involving two levels—the social and the psychological—the latter of which is covert. The payoff is at the psychological level, in the form of feelings, which may be good or bad. Repetition of the games leads to the collection of particular feelings or of *"trading stamps,"* which becomes a *"racket."* For some people, certain games are necessary for the maintenance of mental health. "Their dynamic function is to preserve psychic equilibrium, and their frustration leads either to rage or to a state which in transactional analysis is called *despair,"*[23] which is similar to existential despair rather than depression.

The payoffs of certain games are feelings of guilt, inadequacy, hurt, fear, resentment, and anger, which constitute trading stamps. Self-indulgence in these feelings is the racket. The games manipulate others so the player is entitled to display these feelings and to take major actions related to his or her life script without feeling guilty.

Games, like procedures, rituals, and pastimes, are taught in the family. While the last three are taught by parents directly, games are usually learned indirectly, or by imitation. They are passed on for generations.

Intimacy

"Pastimes and games are substitutes for the real living of real intimacy."[24] Intimacy involves highly individual programming at an intense level, which breaks through the restrictions of social patterning and ulterior restrictions. "Society frowns upon candidness, except in privacy";[25] intimacy is a private matter. Intimacy involves the natural Child. It is free of games. "Fortunately the rewards of games free intimacy, which is or should be the most perfect form of human living, are so great that even precariously balanced personalities can safely and joyfully relinquish their games if an appropriate partner can be found for the better relationship."[26]

To be able to rise above games and enter into intimacy, a person must have awareness and enough spontaneity to be liberated from the compulsion to play games and thus be free to choose and express feelings from the Parent, Adult, or Child. To free the self from games requires an autonomy from the influences of family and parents, from whom games were learned.

Scripts

Games are organized into scripts. "Operationally, a script is a complex set of transactions, by nature recurrent, but not necessarily recurring, since a complete performance may require a whole lifetime."[27] It is the unconscious life plan, originating in a decision made in early childhood. The earliest experience in script formation is called the *protocol* and derives from experiences with and the influence of parents; later it is influenced by the myths and fairy tales to which the child is exposed. It is repressed in later years but reappears in the preconscious as the *script proper.* The script proper is modified as a compromise with reality and becomes the *adaptation,* which is played out in life and in group treatment. All three forms are included in the term *script.* Other refinements include the *operative script,* which is derived from the adaptation, and then a *secondarily adjusted script,* which becomes the *shooting script* of the life production. There is also usually an *antiscript* or *counterscript,* which can be a safer or more constructive plan than the exciting but often *destructive script* and which alternates with the script. The counterscript also may dominate the style of life, while the script determines the ultimate destiny, which may come as a surprise to observers.

Although a script as a life plan requires a lifetime for its performance, it may be reenacted in lesser versions on a yearly or weekly basis, or even in a single group session or a few seconds. Scripts may be constructive or tragic. A common tragic script derives from the childhood belief that there is a kind of Santa Claus who will at some time magically bring success and happiness. When the individual reaches a stage of despair about this coming true, he or she may seek therapy. Scripts are related to the four positions, and the Santa Claus script is related to the "I am not OK; you are OK" position and may lead to the results noted above in the discussion of the four positions.

Scripts are the dominant influences in social intercourse, which is thus influenced by the early experiences that determined the script. Games are selected to fit the script, and transactions are selected to fit the games. Associates are selected on the basis of their participation in transactions: for more stable relationships, they are selected on the basis of willingness to participate in the games; for more intimate relationships, they are selected on the basis of ability to fill the roles in the script. There is an element of fate in a person's life script. A person is the captive of his or her script unless somehow he or she is able to transcend it. Thus a childhood decision determines a person's life and the way the person faces death.

Psychopathology

The general pathology of psychiatric disorders includes structural and functional pathology. *Structural pathology* involves anomalies of the psychic structure of Parent, Adult, and Child. There are two common types—exclusion and contamination.

In *exclusion,* one of the ego states defensively excludes the others and dominates behavior. In "compensated" schizophrenics, the Parent excludes the archaeopsyche, or the Child. In the cold scientist, the Adult is the excluding ego state. In narcissistic, impulsive personalities, the Child excludes the Parent and the Adult. The two ego states that are excluded are said to be *decommissioned.*

In *contamination,* one of the adjacent ego states intrudes on the Adult. The contamination of the Adult by the Parent leads to certain kinds of prejudice. The intrusion of the Child on the Adult is present in delusions. Double contamination involves the intrusion of both the Parent and the Child on the Adult.

The second type of psychopathology is *functional.* In functional pathology, the ego boundaries are permeable, which leads to lability (fluctuation) of cathexis from one ego state to another. Lability of cathexis can occur without defect in ego boundaries, however. Sluggish cathexis exists when shifts of cathexis are slow to occur. Ego boundaries can be rigid or highly impermeable; this is necessary for exclusion to take place.

The genesis of psychopathology is in the occurrence of traumatic ego states in childhood; the earlier the trauma, the more serious the consequences.

"Symptoms are each exhibitions of a single definite ego state, active or excluded, although they may *result from* conflicts, concerts, or contaminations between different ego states. The first symptomatic task in structural analysis, therefore, is to decide which ego state is actually exhibiting the symptom."[28] Hallucinations generally derive from the Parent. Delusions generally derive from the Child and arise from the area of contamination between the Adult and the Child; they are thus ego-syntonic, or experienced as from the Adult. After decontamination, they still may be experienced, but the person recognizes that they do not really exist; they become ego-dystonic. "Boundary symptoms" (feelings of unreality, estrangement, depersonalization, déjà vu, and so on) arise from "lesions of the boundary between the Adult and the Child."[29] All these symptoms are schizoid in nature.

"In hypomania there is an exclusion of the Parent by the Child with the cooperation of a contaminated Adult, so that neopsychic (Adult) judgment, impaired though it is, is influential. If mania supervenes, then the Adult as well as the Parent is overpowered by the hypercathected Child, who then has a clear field for his own frantic activity."[30]

The symptom in conversion hysteria derives from the Child, which is excluded by the Adult through repression. In general with the neurosis, however, the Parent is the enemy. Character disorders and psychopathies are also exhibitions of the Child with the cooperation of the Adult; impulse neuroses likewise erupt from the Child but without the cooperation of either the Adult or the Parent.

The functional psychoses include all the conditions usually diagnosed as manic–depressive and schizophrenic, but rather than being placed in the usual nosological classifications in terms of structural states, they are classified as *active* or *latent.* "An active psychosis exists when the Child has the executive power and is also experienced as the 'real self,' while the Adult is decommissioned."[31] In other conditions such as mild depression, hypomania, character disorders, and paranoia, the Adult is contaminated by the Child and cooperates with the Child but is not decommissioned. These may become active psychoses. In the latent psychoses, which include compensated psychoses, ambulatory psychoses, psychoses in remission, and prepsychotic or borderline conditions, the Adult is the executive and is experienced as the "real self," although it is contaminated and/or temporarily decommissioned.

Diagnosis consists of determining the ego state from which behaviors originate. "Ego states manifest themselves clinically in two forms: either as completely cathected coherent states of mind experienced as 'real self'; or as intrusions, usually covert or unconscious, into the activity of the current 'real self.' "[32] Diagnosis requires acute observation plus intuitive sensitivity to involuntary as well as voluntary and social behavior. Demeanor, for example, "the sternly paternal uprightness" or "the gracious mothering flexion of the neck," betrays the ego attitude, in these instances the Parent. Gestures also, as well as voice and vocabulary, indicate the ego state that is operative.

All ego states have four properties: (1) executive power; (2) adaptability; (3) biological fluidity; and (4) mentality. A complete diagnosis requires that all four be considered and correlated. The *behavioral* diagnosis is based on demeanors, voices, vocabularies, and other characteristics. It is corroborated by the *social* or *operational* diagnosis, which involves the appropriate ego-state behaviors in response to social stimuli. The *historical* diagnosis offers further corroboration; it involves the recall and statement by the individual of the specific origins or prototypes of the behaviors in his or her past.

Diagnosis in terms of the standard classification is therapeutically irrelevant. Therapy is based on the structural diagnosis.

THE GOALS OF THERAPY

Although made in the context of group treatment, the following statement would appear to apply to individual treatment as well: "Taking as the most general statement that psychiatric patients are confused, the goal of psychotherapy then becomes to resolve that confusion in a well-planned way by a series of analytic and synthetic operations. Again in the most general form, these operations will consist of decontamination, recathexis, clarification, and reorientation."[33] Transactional analysis is not satisfied with improvement or progress—in making patients more comfortable frogs—but aims for cure and for transformation of schizophrenics into nonschizophrenics, or frogs into princes.[34] In structural terms, therapy attempts to stabilize and decontaminate the

Adult; with the primacy of the Adult, the early decision of the Adult that led to a psychopathological position can be reconsidered, and the Parent can be brought to terms. The position of "I'm OK; You're OK" can then be assumed.

However, Berne seems to accept symptomatic control, symptomatic relief, and social control as goals in the therapy of the neuroses,[35] but "the ultimate aim of transactional analysis is structural readjustment and reintegration."[36]

THE THERAPY PROCESS

The aim of the therapy process requires, first, restructuring and, second, reorganizing. Restructuring "consists of clarification and definition of ego boundaries by such processes as diagnostic refinement and decontamination." Reorganization is concerned with "redistribution of cathexis through selective planned activation of specific ego states in specific ways with the goal of establishing hegemony of the Adult through social control. Reorganization generally features reclamation of the Child, with emendation or replacement of the Parent. Following this dynamic phase of reorganization, there is a secondary analytic phase which is an attempt to deconfuse the Child."[37] There appear to be a series of steps or stages in psychotherapy, and therapy may end with the success of any one of them. Transactional analysis is the name applied to the total process, although it also designates one of the stages.

1. *Structural Analysis* Structural analysis consists of the descriptive study of ego states, along the lines discussed above under psychopathology, to decontaminate the Adult, define ego boundaries, and stabilize Adult control. "The goal of this procedure is to reestablish the predominance of reality-testing ego states [the Adult] and free them from contamination by archaic and foreign elements [of the Child and Parent]."[38] Treatment may not need to continue beyond structural analysis. The patient who is treated as though he or she has a perfectly good ego or an Adult ego is likely to respond by activating the Adult ego state and to become more rational and objective, both toward himself or herself and toward the world. The result is stabilization, in which the Adult is the executive, and the Parent and Child states can be called on when this is desirable.

2. *Transactional Analysis Proper* Following structural analysis, therapy may terminate, the patient may go into psychoanalysis, or transactional analysis may begin. The aim of transactional analysis is social control; "that is, control of the individual's own tendency to manipulate others in destructive and wasteful ways, and of his tendency to respond without insight or option to the manipulations of others."[39] The group is the natural medium for transactional analysis. Transactions are analyzed in terms of whether they are complementary or crossed and the implications for the participants. Therapy may terminate here.

3. *Analysis of Pastimes and Games* The analysis of extended transactions is done in terms of pastimes, which constitute the initial phases of group therapy, and games. The individual's games are evaluated in terms of primary gains (external and internal), secondary gains, social gains, and biological gains (the removal of isolation by stimulation). The objective of game analysis is freedom from games in intimate relationships or, more practically in society, the free-

dom to choose what games to play, how far to go, with whom to play, and when not to play. Transactional group treatment focuses on the analysis of games.

4. *Analysis of Scripts*   Scripts are acted out in the group. The object of script analysis is "to close the show and put a better one on the road," or to free the patient from compulsive reliving of the original catastrophe on which the script is based. "Since scripts are so complex and full of idiosyncrasy, however, it is not possible to do adequate script analysis in group therapy alone. . . . "[40] Scripts may not become apparent except in an advanced group or through dreams. In patients who come for psychotherapy, life scripts are usually tragic rather than constructive. The object of therapy is for the patient to be able to transcend the script through the control of his or her life by the Adult. This does not mean that the Adult functions in exclusion of appropriate Parent and Child states. It is a stabilized state in which the individual is able to cathect the appropriate ego state at will. The breaking away from the script allows the real person to live in the real world. The most elegant way in which the therapist can get the patient out of his or her script is through the one single intervention that provides the most effective script antitheses. Further work is necessary, however, to achieve a permanent script cure. The intervention is in the form of a permission for the Child to disobey Parental injunctions and provocations.

5. *Analysis of Relationships*   Analysis of relationships is mainly in marital relationships and liaisons or impending liaisons. It is used sparingly, since it may be seen by the patient as unwarranted influencing of his or her decisions.

Some cases may require *second-order structural analysis,* which involves the recognition and analysis of complex ego states. The Parent, for example, includes both mother and father elements, with each of these having Parent, Adult, and Child components. The Child ego state includes Parent, Adult, and Child components, the last of which is an archaic ego state within the total Child ego state.

IMPLEMENTATION AND TECHNIQUES

There are three injunctions, or slogans, as Berne calls them, for the therapist, which are taken from the field of medicine.

1. *Primum non nocere:* Above all, the therapist should do no harm. Intervention should be made only when necessary and only to the extent necessary.
2. *Vis medicatrix naturae:* The organism has a built-in drive toward health, which applies to the psychological as well as to the physical realm. The therapist's function is to remove the blocks to natural healing and growth.
3. *Je le pensay, Dieu le guarit:* The therapist treats the patient, but it is God who cures the patient; or, the therapist provides the best treatment possible, avoiding hurting or injuring the patient, and nature does the healing.[41]

Therapy is preceded by an agreement or a contract. The patient is asked why he or she has come to the therapist. When the patient can express clearly what he or she wants, the therapist states what he or she can offer or suggests that the patient come for a few sessions to evaluate the therapist and what he or she has to offer. The first goals stated by the patient and accepted by the therapist may be symptomatic relief or social control. The therapist may have another ultimate goal, but this is reserved for the appropriate time when the contract may be amended. The contract is thus not usually agreed on before therapy can start but arises in the process and is changed as therapy progresses.

The methods and techniques of transactional analysis, however, are not very clear. There is no systematic discussion by Berne. The method is illustrated by case summaries or brief excerpts, which, however, are not verbatim transcripts but reconstructions after the interview. There is an emphasis on individualization of treatment. Berne writes, "It is, unfortunately, difficult to offer more than a few general suggestions as to how to deal with people who are by definition the epitome of individuality."[42]

The general method appears to consist of (1) identifying, pointing out, and labeling the origins of behavior in terms of ego states or their contamination and decontaminating them through explanation (structural analysis), and (2) identifying, pointing out, and labeling transactions, pastimes, games, and scripts (transactional analysis). This involves teaching: for example, the patient "was educated to distinguish the reactions of his Parent, his Adult, and his Child, respectively, to what the therapist and others said to him."[43] Patients are taught the essentials of the theory and concepts of ego states, games, and so on, directly in the early interviews.

Berne provides some therapeutic hints for the beginning therapist, which include the following:

1. First learn to differentiate the Adult from the Child; the Parent will become clear later.
2. Wait until the patient has provided at least three examples or diagnostic illustrations before introducing the system's concept that is applicable.
3. Later diagnosis of the Parent or the Child must be confirmed by actual historical material.
4. Realize that the three ego states are to be taken literally, as though the patient were three people. The therapist also must recognize *his* or *her* own three ego states and their influence on the therapy.
5. Every patient is assumed to have an Adult; the problem arises in cathecting it or in "plugging it in."
6. The Child is not childish but childlike and possesses potentially valuable qualities.
7. The patient must experience the Child ego state, not simply recall its experiences (regression analysis).
8. Pastimes and games are not habits, attitudes, or occasional occurrences; they constitute most of the patient's activities.
9. "The ideal intervention is the 'bull's-eye,' one which is meaningful and acceptable to all three aspects of the patient's personality, since all three overhear what is said."[44] It is recognized by all three ego states.
10. The beginner is likely to experience a negative reaction toward the terminology, but this is an expected part of learning a new system.

The therapist must be a keen observer, using all the senses, particularly hearing and sight. "Observation is the basis of all good clinical work, and takes precedence even over technique."[45] The therapist notes the incipient stages of blushing, palpitation, sweating, tremors, tension, excitement, rage, weeping, laughter, and sexuality by being sensitive to carriage, posture, movements, gestures, facial mimicry, twitches of single muscles, arterial pulsations, local vasomotor and pilomotor phenomena, and swallowing. Facial expressions and gestures may reveal "hidden" thoughts by their inconsistency with verbalization or with one another.

Visual observation should be accompanied by auditory observation, which involves listening to the accompaniments of the content of the patient's talking: coughing, gasping, weeping, or laughing. More subtle auditory observation may require the suspension of visual observation, in order that the therapist be allowed to concentrate on pitch, timbre, rhythm, intonation, and vocabulary. Patients have three voices, depending on whether their Parent, Adult, or Child is talking.

These observations are basic and prior to techniques. In addition, personal interest and concern for the patient and the patient's welfare takes precedence over techniques.

Therapeutic Operations

In his exposition of group treatment, Berne considers eight categories of therapeutic operations or basic techniques of transactional analysis. Each is accompanied by caveats. The first four are classified as simple *interventions*. The others are *interpositions,* which attempt to stabilize the patient's Adult by placing something between it and the Parent and Child to make it more difficult for the patient to slip into Parent or Child activity.

Interrogation

Interrogation is used to document clinically important points. It should be used when the therapist is confident that the patient's Adult will respond. It should rarely be used to obtain more information than is immediately necessary, or it could lead to the patient playing the game of "Psychiatric History."

Specification

Specification attempts to fix certain things in the patient's mind by the therapist assenting to or reiterating (reflecting on) what the patient has said or informing the patient of it. It is used to help prevent the patient from denying that he or she said or meant something or as preparation for explanation.

Confrontation

In confrontation, the therapist uses information previously elicited and specified to point out an inconsistency. Its purpose is to cathect the uncontaminated part of the patient's Adult. If it is successful, the patient will respond insightfully. It is used when the patient is playing "Stupid" and when the patient is incapable of recognizing the inconsistency.

Explanation

Explanation is used in the attempt to recathect (strengthen), decontaminate, or reorient the patient's Adult. It should be used when the patient has been prepared and the Adult is listening; it may be used when the patient is wavering between playing games and facing up to himself or herself. Explanations should be concise, or the game of "Psychiatry—Transactional Type," may develop.

Illustration

"An illustration is an anecdote, simile, or comparison that follows a successful confrontation for the purpose of reinforcing the confrontation and softening its possible undesirable effects."[46] Illustrations may immediately follow a confrontation or may be remote or delayed "from ten minutes to ten weeks" to allow the patient to settle down, so that then he or she can be given an additional push. Illustrations should be light, lively, or humorous and should be intelligible to the Child as well as to the Adult of the patient. Thus they are used when the Adult is listening and when the Child also will hear and when the therapist is sure that the Parent will not take over. They can also be used to let the patient know that therapy is not always solemn. Caution should be used so that the therapist is not the only one laughing at the joke.

Confirmation

As the patient's Adult becomes more stabilized, the patient offers material to confirm his or her confrontation, which the therapist then reinforces by confirmation. It should be used only when the patient's Adult is established strongly enough to prevent the Parent from using it against the Child or the Child from using it against the therapist. It should not be used if the previous confrontation and illustration were not successful.

Interpretation

If the techniques considered so far have been successful in cathecting and decontaminating the Adult so that it is strong and competent, the therapist can enter the terminal phase of pure transactional analysis by crystallizing the situation and providing symptomatic relief and social control for the patient. Even though the Child has not been deconfused, the patient can continue improvement as long as the Adult maintains the executive position, or the therapist can postpone crystallization until the Child is deconfused by the psychodynamic interpretation of orthodox psychoanalysis. Still another alternative is that this may be postponed until the Adult becomes stabilized, and then it can be undertaken. The last may be preferred, since the patient can function well in daily life while bringing up a family. Psychoanalysis postpones improved functioning until it is completed.

Interpretation "deals with the pathology of the Child. The Child presents its past experiences in coded form to the therapist, and the therapist's task is to decode and detoxify them, rectify distortions, and help the patient regroup the experiences.

In this an uncontaminated Adult is the most valuable ally."[47] The Child resists, and the Parent also exerts an influence against interpretation as the Child's protector. Interpretation should be used only when the patient's Adult is on the therapist's side, when the Adult is in the executive position, and when the therapist is not directly opposing the Parent and not asking too much of the Child. It must be the therapist's Adult that is talking, and the therapist must be using his or her intelligence instead of intellectualizing.

Crystallization

"The technical aim of transference analysis is to bring the patient to a point where crystallizing statements from the therapist will be effective. A crystallization is a statement of the patient's position from the Adult of the therapist to the Adult of the patient."[48] In effect, it says to the patient that he or she can stop playing games or function normally if the patient chooses to do so. The choice is still the patient's, however. The Child and the Parent must be prepared. The Child and the Adult are on good terms, so the Child accepts the crystallization. The Parent may resist seeing the Child become healthy, and this resistance must be handled. The patient cannot be pushed; if the patient is pushed, he or she may get well psychologically but develop somatic symptoms or even a broken leg. Transactional analysis is completed with crystallization, whether or not interpretation has been used.

In using all these therapeutic operations, the therapist is advised to stay three steps behind the clinical material and never to get ahead of it. While the therapist should never miss a real chance to forge ahead, he or she should "never push against resistance except for testing purposes based on a well-thought-out concrete hypothesis."[49] In addition, in all his or her operations (except in certain types of confrontation), the therapist should avoid crossed transactions; that is, the therapist should direct the intervention at the patient's ego state that is most likely to respond.

With most patients, the therapist functions as his or her Adult, although the patient may perceive or wish the therapist to function as a Parent. The therapist occasionally may function as a Parent in giving the patient permission to engage in desirable activities or in assigning the patient particular tasks, thus freeing the patient from undesirable Parental injunctions or prohibitions. When the therapist functions as an Adult, the patient can accept the therapist in place of his or her own Parent. When the patient can accept his or her own Adult, the patient no longer needs the therapist's Adult, and therapy is completed.

With schizophrenics, modifications of treatment are required. The therapist may have to function as a Parent rather than as an Adult during much, if not most, of the treatment. As a Parent, the therapist will offer *support* (which may be simply stroking), *reassurance, persuasion,* and *exhortation.*

Child interventions (where the therapist functions as the patient's Child) are appropriate only in treating children; they should not be used as trickery. "No transactional analyst should allow himself to use any form of deception or dissimulation, for that amounts to deliberately starting a game with the patient."[50]

In all these situations, whether the therapist is operating from the Adult, the Parent, or the Child, he or she is not playing a role.

If the therapist plays the role of a therapist, he will not get very far with perceptive patients. He has to *be* a therapist. If he decides that a certain patient needs Parental reassurance, he does not play the role of a parent; rather he liberates his Parental ego state. A good test of this is for him to attempt to 'show off' his Parentalism in the presence of a colleague, with a patient toward whom he does not feel parental. In this case he is playing a role, and a forthright patient will soon make clear this difference between being a reassuring Parent and playing the role of a reassuring parent.[51]

Regression Analysis

In addition to these eight therapeutic operations, regression analysis sometimes may be useful. "The optimal situation for the readjustment and reintegration of the total personality requires an emotional statement from the Child in the presence of the Adult and the Parent."[52] This requires that all three ego states be in the state of awareness; thus hypnosis and drugs are ruled out when the therapist obtains the Child's statement. In psychoanalysis, the analyst interprets indirect expressions of the child, which is not satisfactory. In transactional analysis, there is an appeal to the Child in the waking state. "Reasoning and experience leads to the belief that a child expresses himself most freely to another child."[53] Regression analysis utilizes this belief. The material produced is then available for detailed examination with the patient.

RESULTS

Berne reports some early results. From September 1954 to September 1956, 75 patients were treated, 23 of whom were prepsychotic, psychotic, or postpsychotic. Of these, 2 (10 percent) were failures, voluntarily entering a hospital; 3 (12 percent) showed little or no change; and 18 (78 percent) improved. Of 42 other patients, none were failures; 14 (33 percent) showed little or no change; and 28 (67 percent) improved.[54] From 1956 to 1960, about 100 people gave the treatment a fair trial (at least 7 consecutive weeks, and up to 2 to 3 years), of whom 20 were prepsychotic, postpsychotic, or psychotic. "In the majority of cases the treatment ended with the patients, their families, and the therapist all feeling better. Three cases were outright failures, being hospitalized voluntarily. All had had previous hospitalizations."[55] Berne considers that these results compare favorably with those of other approaches. He expresses skepticism about evaluating results because of the difficulty of defining criteria.

EXAMPLE[56]

The patient, who complained of "depressions" of sudden onset and of difficulty in handling her adolescent son, had had three previous forms of therapy: Alcoholics Anonymous, hypnosis, and psychotherapy combined with Zen and Yoga. "She showed a special aptitude for structural and transactional analysis, and soon began to exert social control over the games which went on between herself and her husband, and herself and her son. The formal diagnosis is best stated as schizo-hysteria." The following material presents Berne's summaries and comments on the therapy sessions. Dr. Q refers to Berne, the therapist.

1. April 1

The patient arrived on time for her initial interview. She stated she had been going to other therapists but had become dissatisfied and had called a municipal clinic, and after some discussion with a social worker had been referred to Dr. Q. She was encouraged to proceed and at relevant points appropriate questions were asked in order to elicit the psychiatric history. She stated that she had been an alcoholic for ten years and had been cured by Alcoholics Anonymous. She dated the onset of her drinking from her mother's psychosis when she was 19. She said that her depressions began at the same time. The nature of her previous psychiatric treatment was discussed. The preliminary demographic information was obtained so that she could be placed as a native-born, 34-year-old, once-married Protestant housewife, a high school graduate, whose husband was a mechanic. Her father's occupation, the length of her marriage, her sibling position in years and months, and ages of her children were noted. A preliminary search for traumatic events elicited that her father drank heavily and that her parents separated when she was 7 years old.

The medical history revealed headaches and numbness of one arm and leg, but no convulsions, allergies, skin afflictions, or other physical disorders with common psychiatric implications. Her age at the time of all operations, injuries, and serious illnesses was noted. Her childhood was explored for gross psychopathology, such as sleep-walking, nail-biting, night terrors, stammering, stuttering, bed wetting, thumb sucking, and other pre-school problems. Her school history was reviewed briefly. Chemical influences such as medications and exposure to noxious substances were also noted. A cautious exploration of her mental status was undertaken, and finally she was asked to relate any dream that she could remember. Recently she dreamed: "They were rescuing my husband from the water. His head was hurt and I started to scream." She mentioned that she often heard inner voices exhorting her to health, and once, two years ago, an "outer" voice. This satisfied the requirements for preliminary history taking, and the patient was then allowed to wander as she pleased.

Discussion

The history taking was carefully planned so that at all times the patient seemed to have the initiative, and the therapist, at most, was curious rather than formal or openly systematic in gathering information. This means that the patient was allowed to structure the interview in her own way as far as possible and was not required to play a game of psychiatric history taking. Because of her complaint of numbness, she was referred to a neurologist for examination.

2. April 8

The neurologist suspected cervical arthritis, but did not recommend any specific treatment. The patient conducted this interview as a kind of psychological survey. She spontaneously mentioned wanting approval and rebelling "like a little girl," as some "grown-up part" of her judged it. She said the "little girl" seemed "childish." It was suggested that she let the "little girl" out, rather than try to clamp down on her. She replied that that seemed brazen. "I like children, though. I know I can't live up to my father's expectations, and I get tired of trying to." This also includes her husband's "expectations." Such expectations were generalized for her as "parental expectations," since she had practically said as much herself. She sees the two most important "parents" in her life as her husband and her father. She is seductive toward her husband and recognized that she was the same with her father. When her father and mother separated she thought (age 7): "I could have kept him." Thus she has not only a conflict about compliance, but also an attitude of seductiveness toward parental figures.

Discussion

The patient's special aptitude for structural analysis is already evident. She herself makes the separation between "the little girl" and "a grown-up part" and recognizes the compliance of "the little girl" toward certain people whom she relates to her parents. It was only necessary, therefore, to reinforce this trichotomy in a nondirective way. With many other patients this might not have been undertaken until the third or fourth session, perhaps even later.

3. April 15

She resents people who tell her what to do, especially women. This is another reaction to "parents." She mentions a feeling of "walking high." It is pointed out that this is the way a very small girl must feel, that this is again the Child. She replied: "Oh, for heaven's sake, that's true! As you said that I could see a little child . . . it's hard to believe, but that makes sense to me. As you say that, I feel I didn't want to walk: a little girl in rompers. . . . I feel funny now. They pull you up by your right shoulder and you're outraged . . . yet I do the same to my own son. I disapprove while I'm thinking 'I don't disapprove, I know just how he feels.' It's really my mother disapproving. Is *that* the Parent part you mentioned? I'm frightened a little by all this."

It was at this point that it was emphasized that there was no mysterious or metaphysical aspect to these diagnostic judgments.

Discussion

The patient has now experienced some of the phenomenological reality of the Child and has added to the behavioral, social, and historical reality she established in the previous interviews. The indications, therefore, are favorable for treatment with transactional analysis.

4. April 22

"This week I've been happy for the first time in fifteen years. I don't have to look far to find the Child, I can see it in my husband and in others too. I have trouble with my son." The game with her son was clarified in an inexact but timely and illustrative way in terms of Parent (her disapproval and determination), Child (her seductiveness and her sulkiness at his recalcitrance), and Adult (her gratification when he finally did his work). It was hinted that an Adult approach (good reason) rather than a Parental approach (sweet reason) might be worth a try.

Discussion

The patient is now involved in transactional analysis proper, and the idea of social control has been suggested.

5. April 28

She reports that things work better with her son. Regression analysis is attempted to find out more about the Child. She relates: "The cat soils the rug and they accuse me and make me wipe it up. I deny that I did it and stammer." In the ensuing discussion she remarks that both Alcoholics Anonymous and the Anglican Church require confession to "messes." For this reason she gave them both up. As the session ends she asks: "Is it all right to be aggressive?" Answer: "You want *me* to tell you?" She understands the implication that she should decide such things on Adult grounds rather than asking Parental permission, and replies: "No, I don't."

Discussion

During this session some of the elements of her script are elicited. It can be anticipated that she will try to repeat with the therapist in some well-adapted form the cat situation. Her question "Is it all right to be aggressive?" is perhaps the first move in this adaptation. This gives the therapist an opportunity to decline to play and to reinforce her Adult. The patient has made such good progress in understanding structural and transactional analysis that she is already considered adequately prepared for fairly advanced group therapy. The group she is to enter consists largely of women.

6. May 4

A dream. "I look at myself and say: 'That's not so bad.' " She liked the group but it made her uncomfortable during the rest of the week. She relates some memories, including homosexual play during childhood. "Oh! That's why I didn't like AA. There were two homosexual women there and one of them called me sexy." She complains of vaginal itching. "My mother and I slept together and she bothered me."

Discussion

The manifest content of her dream is taken to be Adult and indicates the possibility of a good prognosis. The experience in the group has activated sexual conflicts, and this is the first indication of their nature.

7. May 11

She felt highly excited on leaving the group meeting. "Things are moving quickly. Why did they make me laugh and blush? Things are better at home. I can kiss my son now and my daughter for the first time came and sat on my lap. I can't be a good lover when things are monotonous."

Discussion

The analysis of her family games . . . has resulted in the establishment of some Adult social control. It is evident that this improved control has been perceived by her children and for the first time in a long while they have the feeling that she can maintain her position and they react accordingly. Her excitement in the group and her statement that she can't be a good lover when things are monotonous indicate that she is involved in a sexual game with her husband.

An experience in the group later this week rather clearly showed her need for parental figures in some of her games. There was a new patient in the group, a male social worker, and she was very much impressed by his occupation. She asked him what they were supposed to do there. It was pointed out that she knew more than he did, since it was his first meeting and her third. She says she resents it when people tell her what to do; yet peasant-like, in spite of her superior experience, she asks a novice for instructions because she appears to be impressed by his education: evidently an attempt to set up a game. This interpretation strikes home. She recognizes how she "cons" a likely candidate into being parental and then complains about it.

8. May 18

She was upset by regression analysis in the group. It made her think of her fear of insanity, and of her mother in the state hospital. Her own production was of some elegant gates leading into a beautiful garden. This is a derivative of a Garden of Eden fantasy from before the age of five. The material indicates that the garden has become adapted to the gates of the state hospital where she visited her mother many years ago. This experience in the group offered a timely opportunity to mention to her that she might want to be hospitalized and so relieved of responsibility.

She has visited her mother only once in the past five or six years and it was suggested that it might be advisable for her to do that again. This suggestion was very carefully worded so as to be Adult rather than Parental. Any implication that she was a bad girl for not visiting her mother had to be avoided. She was able to understand the value of such a visit as an exercise for her Adult and as a means of preventing future difficulties between her Parent and her Child if her mother should die. The good reception of this suggestion was manifested by her bringing up new information. Her husband never washes his hair and always has a good excuse, which she accepts. He has not washed it for many months. She says it doesn't bother her too much. The therapist said she must have known that when she married him. She denied it.

9. May 25

She said she has always been more afraid of sick animals than of sick people. This week her cat was sick, and for the first time she was not afraid of him. Once when she was little her father hit her and her dog jumped on him, whereupon he gave the dog away. She told her children that her mother was dead. Whenever she would think of her mother she would start to drink. One time she was told that when her mother was eight months pregnant, her father tried to poison her. They saved the patient and thought her mother was a goner, but then she was revived. The aunt who told her this story says: "Your life has been a mess since birth."

Discussion

The import of this is not clear. It is evident, however, that she is working through some rather complex conflicts concerning her mother. Her maintenance of social control with the sick cat is evidence that a visit to her mother may be possible in the near future.

10. June 1

"Frankly, the reason I'm afraid to visit my mother is that I might want to stay there myself." She wonders: "Why do I exist? Sometimes I doubted my existence." Her parents' marriage was a shotgun wedding and she has always felt that she was unwanted. The therapist suggested that she get a copy of her birth certificate.

Discussion

The patient is now involved with existential problems. Her Adult has evidently always been shaky because her Child has implanted doubts about her existence, her right to exist, and the form in which she exists. Her birth certificate will be written evidence that she does exist, and should be particularly impressive to her Child. As social control is established and she learns that it is possible for her to exist in a form which she herself chooses, her desire to retreat to the state hospital should diminish.

11. June 8

She describes her husband's alcoholic game. At AA she was told that she should bless him and comfort him, and that made her sick. She tried something different. "One day I said I would call the ambulance for the hospital, since he didn't appear to be able to take care of himself, so he got up and didn't drink again." He said he was only trying to help her stay sober by drinking himself. This comes up because he was drinking heavily last week and she had pain in her shoulders and wanted to hit him, but told him off instead.

It appears from this that their secret marriage contract is based partly on the assumption that he will drink and she will function as a rescuer. This game was reinforced by AA to her benefit. When she refused to continue as a rescuer and became a persecutor instead, the game was thrown off and he stopped drinking. (Evidently it was reinstituted due to her insecurity of the past week.)

This outline was presented to her. She first said: "It couldn't have been part of our marriage contract, because neither of us drank when we met." A little later in the interview she suddenly said: "You know, I remember I did know when we were married that he didn't wash his hair, but I didn't know that he drank." The therapist said that the unkempt hair was also part of the secret marriage contract. She looked skeptical. Then she thought a minute and said: "By golly, yes, I did know he drank. When we were in high school we used to drink together all the time."

It now appears that in the early years of their marriage, they played a switchable game of alcoholic. If she drank, her husband didn't; and if he drank, she stayed sober. Their relationship was originally based on this game, which they later interrupted, and must have exerted considerable effort to forget about.

Discussion

This session helped to clarify for the patient the structure of her marriage, and also emphasized the amount of time and effort which is required to keep marital games going, and equally, the amount of energy involved in their repression without conscious control.

12. July 6

There has been an interval of a month for summer vacation. The patient returns with a sore shoulder. She has been to the state hospital and her mother sent her away. This made her feel hopeless. She has some olfactory illusions. She thinks she smells gas in the office, but decides it is clean soap. This leads into a discussion of her mental activity. During her recent Yoga training, she developed imagery which was almost eidetic. She would see gardens and wingless angels with sparkling clarity of color and detail. She recalled that she had had the same kind of imagery as a child. She also had images of Christ and her son. Their complexions were clear and lively. She sees animals and flowers. As a matter of fact, when she walks through parks she likes to talk secretly but aloud to trees and flowers. The longings expressed in these activities are discussed with her. The artistic and poetic aspects are pointed out, and she is encouraged therefore to write and to try finger painting. She has seen her birth certificate and her existential doubts are less disturbing.

Discussion

These phenomena and the auditory manifestations she has previously mentioned, are not necessarily alarming. They point to childhood restitutive tendencies related to a deeply distrubed relationship between her and her parents. The conventional approach would be to give her "supportive" treatment and help her repress this psychopathology and live on top of it. Structural analysis offers another possibility which requires some boldness: to allow this disturbed Child to express herself and profit from this resulting constructive experiences.

13. July 13

She went to her internist and he gave her Rauwolfia because her blood pressure was high. She told her husband she was going to finger-paint and he got angry and said: "Use pastels!" When she refused, he started to drink. She recognizes what happened here as a game of "Uproar" and feels some despair at having been drawn into this. She says, however, that if she does not play "Uproar" with him then he will feel despair, and it is a hard choice to make. She also mentions that the gate on the beautiful garden is very similar to the gate on the day nursery where her mother used to send her when she was very small. A problem now arises: How to distinguish the effect of psychotherapy from the effect of Rauwolfia. She is eager to help with this.

14. July 20

She is losing interest and feels tired. She agrees it is possible that this is an effect of the medication. She reveals some family scandals she has never mentioned to anyone before, and states now that her drinking did not begin after her mother became psychotic, but after these scandals.

At this session a decisive move was made. During her therapeutic sessions, the patient habitually sits with her legs in an ungainly exposed position. Now she complains again about the homosexual woman at AA. She complains that the men also made passes at her. She doesn't understand why, since she did nothing to bring this on. She was informed of her exposed position and expressed considerable surprise. It was then pointed out to her that she must have been sitting in a similar provocative way for many years, and what she attributes to the aggressiveness of others is probably the result of her own rather crudely seductive posture. At the subsequent group meeting she was silent most of the time, and when questioned she mentioned what the doctor had said and how this had upset her.

Discussion

This is a crucial session. At the price of sacrificing the possibilities of a normal family life, the patient has obtained a multitude of gains, primary and secondary, by playing games with her husband and other men and women. The primary external gain is the avoidance of pleasurable sexual intercourse. If she can relinquish these gains, she may be ready to undertake a normal marital relationship whose satisfactions should more than repay her for her abdication. The schizoid elements in her Child are clear from her symptomatology. The hysterical elements are most clearly manifested in her socially acceptable game of "Rapo." Hence the diagnosis of schizo-hysteria.

In her case, the naming of the game is avoided since she is still too softboiled to tolerate such bluntness. It is simply described to her without giving it a name. In very sophisticated groups, however, it is known technically as "First-degree Rapo." It is the classical game of hysterics: crude, "inadvertent," seductive exhibitionism, followed by protestations of surprise and injured innocence when a response is forthcoming. (As previously noted, "Third-degree Rapo," the most vicious form, ends in the courtroom or the morgue.) The therapeutic problem at the moment is whether her preparation has been adequate and the relationship between her Child and the therapist sufficiently well-understood to make this confrontation effective. In a sense, her life and those of her children hinge on the therapist's judgment in these matters. If she should decide to become angry and withdraw from treatment, psychiatry might be lost to her for a long time afterward, perhaps permanently. If she accepts it, the effect could be decisive, since this particular game is her chief barrier to marital happiness. The therapist, naturally, has not ventured to bring the matter up without considerable confidence of success.

15. August 10

The therapist returns after a two-week vacation. The confrontation has been successful. The patient now describes an assault by her father in early puberty while her stepmother pretended to be asleep. He also molested other children, but her stepmother used to defend him. She relates this "assault" to her own seductiveness. This situation she discusses at some length, eliciting her feeling that sex is dirty or vulgar. She says she has always been very careful sexually with her husband because of this feeling and has tried to avoid sex with him for this reason. She understands that the games she plays with him are an attempt to avoid sex, as she feels she cannot let go enough to enjoy it and it is merely a burden to her.

Discussion

The patient is evidently shocked at the therapist's directness, but is gratified because it lays bare still further the structure of her marriage and indicates what could be done about it.

16. August 17 (Terminal Interview)

The patient announces that this is her last session. She no longer fears that her husband will think she is dirty or vulgar if she acts lusty. She never asked him if he thought so but just assumed that he did. During the week, she approached him differently and he responded with gratified surprise. For the last few days he has come home whistling for the first time in years.

She also realizes something else. She has always felt sorry for herself and tried to elicit sympathy and admiration because she is a recovered alcoholic. She recognizes this now as a game of "Wooden Leg." She feels ready at this point to try it on her own. She also feels different about her father. Maybe she contributed even more than she thought to the seduction. The remark about her skirts being too short shocked her but helped her. "I would never admit I wanted sex. I always thought I wanted 'attention.' Now I can admit I want sex." During the week she visited her father who was ill in another city in a hospital. She was able to observe her visit with considerable objectivity. Now she feels that she has divorced him and doesn't want him any more. That is why she was able to proceed sexually with her husband. She feels the transfer was accomplished through the intermediary of the therapist, who took her father's place for a while at first; but now she doesn't need him any more. She can talk freely to her husband about sexual repression causing her symptoms, and about her sexual feelings for him. He said he agreed with her and reciprocated her feelings. After she thought all this out, following the last visit, she had a dream that night in which there was a beautiful, feminine, peaceful woman, and it made her feel really good inside. The children are different too; they are happy, relaxed and helpful.

Her blood pressure is down and her itching is gone. The therapist thought the improvement might be due to the medicine. She replied: "No, I don't think so, I would know the difference, I've taken it before. The medicine makes me feel tired and nervous when it's taking hold, but this is an entirely new feeling."

She reports that she is drawing instead of finger-painting, doing what she wants; she feels this isn't wrong, it's like learning to live. "I don't feel sorry for people any more, I feel they ought to be able to do this too if they went about it right. I no longer feel I'm below everyone although that feeling isn't completely gone. I don't want to come to the group any more, I'd rather spend the time with my husband. It's like we're starting to go with each other again when he comes home whistling, it's wonderful. I'll try it for three months and if I feel bad I'll call you. I don't feel so 'neurotic,' either: I mean having psychosomatic symptoms and guilt feelings and my fear of talking about sex, and like that. It's a miracle, is all I can say. I can't explain my feeling of being happy, but I feel we [you and I] worked together on it. There's more closeness and harmony with my husband and he's even taking over the children like he's becoming the man of the house. I even feel a little guilty about AA because I used them in my game of 'Wooden Leg'."

She was asked directly whether structural analysis helped and whether game analysis helped, and in each case replied: "Oh, yes!" She added: "Also the script. For example, I said my husband had no sense of humor and you said 'Wait a minute, you don't know him and he doesn't know you because you've been playing games and acting out your scripts, you don't know what either of you is really like.' You were right because now I've discovered that he really has a sense of humor and that not having it was part of the game. I'm interested in my home and I'm grateful for that. I can write poetry again and express my love for my husband. I used to keep it in." At this point the hour was drawing to a close. The therapist asked: "Would you like a cup of coffee?" She replied: "No thanks, I've just had some. I've told you now how I feel, that's it, that's all, it's been a great pleasure to come here and I enjoyed it."

General Discussion

There is no need to regard this gratifying improvement with either skepticism, alarm, or pursed lips, in spite of the apparent raggedness of the above extracts. The patient herself has already answered many of the questions which might occur to an experienced reader.

A few days short of the three-month trial period she had suggested, the patient wrote the therapist as follows: "I feel fine. I don't have to take any pills and have been off those blood pressure pills for a month now. Last week we celebrated my thirty-fifth birthday. My husband and myself went away without the children. The water was beautiful, and the trees. Gosh, if only I could paint them. We saw a huge porpoise, the first time I have ever seen one, and it was beautiful to watch, so graceful in movements. . . . My husband and I are getting along so nicely. Night and day such a difference. We have become closer, more attentive, and I can be me. That's what seemed to stump me most of the time. I always had to be polite, etc. He still comes whistling up the stairs. That does more good for me than anything. I am so glad you suggested drawing. You have no idea what that alone has done for me. I am getting better and I might try paints soon. The children think they are very good and have suggested that I exhibit some of them. Next month I am going to take swimming lessons, no fooling, something I would never have been able to do. As the time gets closer I am a little afraid but I have made up my mind I am going to learn. If I can learn to put my head under water, that alone will be a great thrill for me. My garden looks so nice. That's another thing you helped me with. By golly, I go out there at least twice a week now for several hours and no one objects. You know I think they like me better this way.

"I didn't intend to ramble on this way but it seemed I had so much to tell you. I'll write and let you know how my swimming progresses. Love from all of us in Salinas."

This letter reassured the therapist of two things:

1. That the patient's improvement persisted even after the medication for her blood pressure was discontinued.
2. That the improvement in the patient's husband and children persisted even after psychotherapy was discontinued.

It should be added that the husband now washes his hair. The most pessimistic thing which can be said about this case so far is that it represents a flight into a healthy family life. The only clinical demand that can legitimately be placed on transactional analysis is that it should produce results which are as good as or better than those produced by any other psychotherapeutic approach, for a given investment of time and effort. The improvement was still maintained on a one-year follow-up.

SUMMARY AND EVALUATION

Transactional analysis divides the personality into three ego states: the Parent, the Adult, and the Child. The Child is derived from actual experiences in childhood, and the Parent represents the actual parents—their behaviors and their influence, in terms of both prohibitions and encouragements. The Adult represents reality testing and regulates and mediates between the Parent and the Child. All behavior can be related to one of these ego states. Early in life, the child solves certain problem situations in a way that leads to a decision about the self and a position toward life. The Child's life becomes a process of justifying or defending this position and warding off influences that threaten it. There are four major positions involving the individual and others:

1. I am OK; you are OK.
2. I am OK; you are not OK.
3. I am not OK; you are OK.
4. I am not OK; you are not OK.

The individual, unless he or she withdraws from social contact, uses social intercourse to satisfy stimulus hunger, including the need for contact, recognition, and structure to occupy and organize the use of time. These contacts involve activities, rituals, simple transactions, pastimes, and games. All are influenced by the individual's position and life script or plan, which derives from a decision made as a child under the influence of the parents. The autonomous individual is able to rise above games and live in intimacy with one or more others.

Psychopathology involves disorders in ego states and their interrelations, which are derived from a tragic life script. Psychotherapy or transactional analysis attempts to resolve these disorders and free the individual from this tragic script by structural analysis (analysis of ego states), transactional analysis, game analysis, and script analysis.

This summary suggests that transactional analysis is quite simple. Berne emphasizes its simplicity and its specialized vocabulary of only five terms—*Parent, Adult, Child, games,* and *scripts*—which can be taught to patients in two or three sessions.

This apparent simplicity is, however, the biggest problem and handicap in transactional analysis achieving recognition as a serious professional method of psychotherapy. Its presumed simplicity has led to its wide popularity. Literally hundreds of practitioners have been spawned from short-term workshops and training courses that teach the simplified terminology and concepts, but they have little understanding of Berne's actual theory and practice. The simplistic form of transactional analysis has become to many a therapy for the masses, who can easily acquire its terminology. While this is viewed by many as a desirable situation, it is unfortunate in at least two respects. First, many of its practitioners, who apparently lack a real understanding of Berne, are usually highly controlling and manipulative in their activities. In effect, transactional analysis as too frequently practiced is the biggest game on the street, whose stakes, or payoffs, are financial returns to the practitioner or the consultant. Perls wrote, "The real game they play, the compulsive pigeonholing of each sentence as belonging to parent and child, remained unnamed."[57] Second, in popular practice, practitioners appear to be teaching subjects how to play the game of "Psychiatry—Transactional Analysis Type," which consists of labeling their own and other people's behavior in terms of Parent, Adult, or Child and in terms of the games that it involves. This labeling process can be a handicap to or even preclude any real understanding or therapeutic gain.

This popularization of transactional analysis has resulted in its rejection by many professionals. Carson, for example, in a brief review of a collection of papers presented at an international conference on transactional analysis writes, "The curious mixture of pop psychology, autistic argot, intellectual superficiality, graphic overkill, and fun-and-games ambience that has characterized this 'movement' from its inception is again displayed here. . . . One can only wonder at the success of an organization now claiming 12,000 members and replete with various ranks and certifications that stands on such flimsy and amateurish foundations."[58]

This is perhaps an unfair and unjustified criticism of transactional analysis as it was developed by Berne. Berne's system is highly complex, so much so that it is one of the most difficult theories to summarize adequately in a limited space. His theory and practice are difficult to master. It is not a quick and easy approach, as it may appear from its popular practice. Berne cautions against oversimplification: "Transactional theory is simpler and more scientifically economical than many other psychotherapeutic theories, but its clinical use requires conscientious study, and in the advanced stages where it begins to overlap with psychoanalytic and existential therapies it takes on increased complexity."[59]

Berne's lack of attention to specification of techniques has no doubt been in part responsible for the proliferation of techniques used by individuals who claim to practice transactional analysis, particularly those who are lacking in a thorough knowledge of Berne's theory. It is also true that those who have had training with Berne have departed from his methods or added to them, so that there is a great variety of techniques now being used by those who identify themselves with transactional analysis, ranging from some psychoanalytic techniques to psychodrama and Gestalt techniques.

Berne had the benefit of years of training in and practice of psychoanalysis as a basis for his work with patients. He was obviously cautious and careful in his interventions (although his clinical intuition led him to interventions that would appear to be rash if done by others), quite unlike many of the current popular practitioners. He was genuine and authentic in his relations with his patients. And he was clearly concerned and caring. He observed, listened, and followed the productions of his patients, responding to them perhaps more frequently than initiating interventions and directing them; although as he gained experience, he apparently became more active.

Yet Berne's penchant for popular terminology and his use of myths and metaphors, along with his claim for simplicity, opened the way for abuse and misuse of his approach through oversimplification and the use of its terminology as jargon. Its terminology actually goes far beyond the five words listed above. In his book on group treatment, Berne includes a glossary of 127 terms (there are almost 100 listed in *What Do You Say After You Say Hello?*), many of which are common words but with other than their standard meanings. There are numerous terms or phrases, often metaphors, which are called colloquialisms. All of this, plus the catchy names given to games, leads to the development of a whole language that has meaning only to the initiates who have mastered it. Thus while it can be claimed that there is no technical terminology, there is an extensive jargon, which is used to replace technical (often psychoanalytic) and sometimes common terms.

Because of this, it is difficult to evaluate Berne's contribution. Is transactional analysis anything more than psychoanalysis clothed in a new terminology? Does the new terminology contribute to understanding? And does the terminology aid or improve the practice of psychotherapy? Each of these questions will now be addressed.

1. Berne acknowledges his agreement with the basic theories and concepts of psychoanalysis. His system, however, is not simply a translation of psychoanalysis into a new terminology. There is a relationship between Parent, Adult, and Child ego states and Freud's superego, ego, and id, but they are not the same. Although Freud recognized the importance of early experiences in infancy and childhood on later life, he did not detail the mechanisms of the influence. Berne does this. His concept of the life script also goes beyond psychoanalysis. Also, Berne's concern with interpersonal behavior rather than only intrapersonal factors is an addition to psychoanalysis.

2. The use of a new vocabulary and terminology to apply to old concepts has both advantages and disadvantages. Berne's writing is easier to understand than much of Freud's and other psychoanalysts', and it is certainly more interesting, as indicated by its popularity. The use of myths, metaphors, and analogies can be enlightening. The analysis of social behavior in terms of rituals, pastimes, and games is helpful for an understanding of much that goes on in social intercourse. The comparison of a life plan and its implementation to a script is also useful. His dramatic and theatrical vocabulary often throws light on the behaviors with which he is concerned.

    However, analogies and metaphors may come to be accepted for what they stand for, and labels and classifications of behavior have a way of becoming substitutes for the understanding of the specific and unique aspects of individual behavior and of leading to stereotypes. Much of current practice in transactional analysis appears to consist of the use of the terminology as jargon. The clothing of valid, significant, and important ideas in simple language is desirable, but when this language is a newly created, popular language, it may become a substitute for ideas and concepts. Individuals and their behaviors are forced into the Procrustean bed that has been prepared for them. Berne was perhaps too successful with his terminology, maybe in part because his metaphors and analogies were so good; he notes how closely "real" games parallel the social games. Yet there is a difference between the map, no matter how perfect it is, and the territory it depicts.

    Berne was convinced that he had a contribution to make. He placed particular importance on the concept of the life script and the script matrix, which diagramatically illustrate the origins of an individual's script in his or her forebears. "Even if the origins . . . of the script directives vary in individual cases, the script matrix nevertheless remains one of the most useful and cogent diagrams in the history of science, compressing as it does, the whole plan for a human life and its ultimate destiny into a simple, easily understood, and easily checked design, which also indicates how to change it."[60] Further, "Script analysis is then the answer to the problem of human destiny, and tells us (alas!) that our fates are predetermined for the most part, and that free will is for most people an illusion."[61] (He does note, however, that the script is more flexible than the genetic apparatus, is influenced by outside factors and life experiences, and can be changed by psychotherapy.) Yet he admits that "since psychiatric script analysis is itself only a few years old, there is in fact not a single example of clinical observation of a complete life script."[62]

3. As for the contribution to practice of Berne's theory, there is no evidence that transactional analysis is more effective or more efficient than any other therapy. Berne appears to have been an effective therapist, but there is no way to demonstrate that this was because of his theory. He claimed that on the basis of a brief diagnostic evaluation, but utilizing his theoretical concepts, he could predict future behaviors of his patients. "Some apparently trivial incident," he writes, "lasting only a few seconds, may reveal to a perceptive therapist the whole story of the patient's life."[63] Perhaps this is true. Berne was a perceptive and highly intuitive therapist. Too often, however, predictions come true or are "verified" by patients because they are made to come true, through the way therapists perceive and interpret what they see and hear and through suggestion. Transactional analysis teaches patients how to label, analyze, and interpret their behavior and that of others by using the vocabulary and concepts of the system. It is perhaps not surprising that they support the expectations of the therapist. How much is validation of the theory and how much is getting out what is put in is thus questionable. Patients of therapists of any persuasion have a way of supporting their therapists' theories. Berne makes a point of the everyday language of his system, but it is not the everyday language of people who have not been exposed to the system.

People feel better when they are able to rationalize or conceptualize their behavior according to a system or theory, regardless of the theory's validity or lack of validity. In this respect, transactional analysis differs from—and has an advantage over—most other theories in that it openly teaches the concepts and labels. In its simplest form, it is also perhaps clearer and thus more appealing and useful, at least for temporary results. Berne also notes that patients enjoy transactional analysis in groups. Patients may enjoy it more, but whether they get more out of it has not been demonstrated.

Serious students, as well as practitioners of psychotherapy, should not be turned off by the popular psychology or the popular literature on transactional analysis; they should go directly to Berne's writings. They will find the writings more interesting than the popular versions. Berne had a scholarly and highly productive mind. He was a keen observer of people and their behaviors and possessed a strong clinical intuition. Many of his observations are not couched in the terminology of the system but in ordinary language. Whether he employed the terminology or not, what he had to say is well worth reading.

REFERENCES

1. Berne, E. *The mind in action.* New York: Simon & Schuster, 1947; *A layman's guide to psychiatry and psychoanalysis.* (3rd ed.). New York: Simon & Schuster, 1968.
2. Berne, E. *Transactional analysis in psychotherapy.* New York: Grove Press, 1961. Copyright © 1961 by Eric Berne. Reprinted by permission of Random House, Inc.
3. Berne, E. *The structure and dynamics of organizations and groups.* Philadelphia: Lippincott, 1963.
4. Berne, E. *Principles of group treatment.* New York: Oxford University Press, 1966.
5. Berne, E. *Games people play: The psychology of human relationships.* New York: Grove Press, 1964.

The summary provided here attempts to integrate the earlier and the later Perls in a clear, systematic presentation.

BACKGROUND AND DEVELOPMENT

Perls's exposure to a wide variety of influences is reflected in his development of Gestalt therapy. His basic training was in psychoanalysis. He credited psychoanalysis and Freud with having provided the foundation on which he could build, although mainly by reacting to and changing psychoanalytic theory. He replaced the sex instinct with the hunger instinct as the major instinct, for example. While still a psychoanalyst, he was influenced greatly by Wilhelm Reich's views, including Reich's emphasis on affect, body involvement in neurosis, form rather than content (including the nonverbal in behavior), confrontation as a method in treatment, and techniques tailored to the individual patient. He was influenced by the existential emphasis on individual responsibility for thoughts, feelings, and actions and on the immediate experience—the now, the I–Thou relationship, and the what and how, rather than the why of experience and behavior.

Perls declares that Gestalt therapy is one of the three existential therapies, together with Frankl's logotherapy and Binswanger's daseinanalysis. Again, before Perls's rejection of psychoanalysis, Gestalt psychology exerted its influence through his experiences with Goldstein and his reading of Lewin. The meaning of the German word *Gestalt* as "whole, configuration, integration, pattern, or form" occupies a central place in Perls's theory. The Gestalt figure–ground concept is basic also to Perls's theory of needs and their satisfaction in the drive toward self-actualization, a term first used by Goldstein. The idea of organismic regulation derives from Gestalt psychology, as does the concept of closure, or completion, in Gestalt formation, which Perls used in his concept of unfinished business. Gestalt, in Perls, thus refers to the wholeness of completed acts, as well as to the integration of split-off parts of the personality into a self-actualizing whole. Perls extended the Gestalt treatment of perception to include not only perception of the external world, but also perception of bodily processes and of feeling and emotions.

Perls was also influenced by the general semantics of I. A. Richards and A. Korzybski, in relation to the clear and explicit use of language. Finally, there is the influence of Zen Buddhism and Taoism, with regard to the principle of opposites (the Yin and the Yang) and the recognition that human beings can transcend themselves only by becoming what they are—their true nature.

All of these and other concepts were incorporated into Gestalt therapy by Perls. While the theory has not yet been developed or stated in a clear, systematic form, the work of Perls provides the basis for such an integrated statement.

PHILOSOPHY AND CONCEPTS

Perls was more interested in action and experience than in philosophy. He recognized the importance of philosophy, but he was ambivalent about developing a systematic philosophy, one "that hopefully will encompass the human *and* the all."[8] Yet, whether they are explicit or implicit, there are assumptions about the nature of humanity and experience in Gestalt therapy as in every other therapy; many of its concepts are philosophical.

Perls rejected the belief that human beings are determined and controlled by external and/or internal factors; this was one of his differences with psychoanalysis. This rejection is reflected in two of his basic ideas: (1) that human beings are responsible for themselves and their lives and living, and (2) that the important question about human experience and behavior is not "Why?" but "How?" Implicit in these assumptions is the belief that human beings are free and have the potential for change.

In agreement with Gestalt principles, Perls rejected the dualities of mind and body, body and soul, thinking and feeling, thinking and action, and feeling and action. This rejection of dualities is inherent in the concept of holism.

The Nature of the Organism

The Holistic Principle

Perls quotes Wertheimer's formulation of Gestalt theory: "There are wholes, the behavior of which is not determined by that of their individual elements, but where the part-processes are themselves determined by the intrinsic nature of the whole."[9] Human beings are unified organisms and always function as wholes. There is not an *I,* which *has* a body, a mind, and a soul, but *we* who exist *as* organisms. The healthy organism is a feeling, thinking, and acting being. Emotions have thinking and acting (physiological) as well as feeling aspects. "Mental activity seems to be activity of the whole person carried on at a lower energy level than those activities we call physical . . . the mental and physical sides of human behavior [are] not . . . independent entities which could have their existence apart from human or from one another. . . ."[10] Body, mind, and soul are aspects of the whole organism.

The Dialectic Principle of Homeostasis

Perls was influenced by the philosopher Sigmund Friedlander, whose book *Creative Indifference* develops the concept of differential thinking, or thinking in opposites (dialectics). Opposites (polarities) come into being by differentiation from a zero point of undifferentiation.

> [E]very event is related to a zero-point from which a differentiation into opposites takes place. These *opposites* show *in their specific context* a great affinity for each other. By remaining alert in the center, we can acquire a creative ability of seeing both sides of an occurence and complete an incomplete half. By avoiding a one-sided outlook we gain a much deeper insight into the structure and function of the organism.[11]

Opposites relate to each other more than to any other concepts (compare with Kelly). "Thinking in opposites is deeply rooted in the human organism. Differentiation into opposites is an essential quality of our mentality and of life itself."[12]

A specific case of the general concept of opposites is the concept of *organismic balance,* or *homeostasis.* The basic tendency of every organism is to strive for balance.

The organism is faced at every moment with factors that disturb this balance, either external (a demand from the environment) or internal (a need). A countertendency arises to restore the balance; the process of restoration of the balance constitutes organismic self-regulation. In the process, the organism creates an image or a reality of the satisfaction of the need; in effect, it selects its world or creates a figure–ground situation. The satisfaction of the need decreases tension, restores the balance, and completes the situation. Homeostasis is thus the process by which the organism satisfies its needs. It is a continuous process, since the balance, or equilibrium, is constantly being upset. The process applies in the satisfaction of psychological needs as well as of physiological needs; indeed, the two processes cannot be separated. In relation to the external environment, the individual may adjust his or her behavior to the environment (autoplastic behavior) or may adjust (adapt) the environment to his or her (alloplastic) behavior.

In terms of Gestalt psychology, the awareness of a need becomes the figure against the background. The unmet need constitutes an incomplete Gestalt that demands completion. Sensorimotor activity is stimulated, and the environment is contacted to meet the need. "When a need is met, the gestalt it organized becomes complete, and it no longer exerts an influence—the organism is free to form new gestalten."[13] Balance is achieved, and the situation is changed. "[T]he dominant need of the organism, at any time, becomes the foreground figure, and the other needs recede, at least temporarily, into the background."[14]

Consciousness is not the searching for or the finding of the problem or the imbalance; it is identical with the problem or the disequilibrium; that is, the dominant need's development into the figure, or the foreground, and its organization of the functions of contact with the environment to achieve reduction of tension constitute consciousness.

What determines which need becomes dominant is the need's relevance to the organism's need for self-preservation and its need to grow or to actualize its potential. "Every individual, every plant, every animal has only one inborn goal—to actualize itself as it is."[15]

Instincts

Freud rightly recognized the importance of the sex instinct, which is necessary for the preservation of the human race, but he overlooked the existence of another instinct, which is necessary for the preservation of the individual. This is the hunger instinct. The numerous specific instincts may all be classified under these two basic instincts.

The stages of the hunger instinct are the prenatal, the predental (suckling), the incisor (biting), and the molar (biting and chewing). The understanding of these stages in their normal and abnormal aspects leads to an understanding of behavior that the sex instinct does not clearly or easily provide. These stages are related to psychological characteristics: the predental to impatience, the incisor to destruction and aggression, and the molar to assimilation. The vicissitudes of hunger and its satisfaction appear to be an analog for all psychological behaviors, as will become apparent later. In his later writings, Perls does not emphasize this parallel, as he does in his earlier writings, although allusions are made to it.

Aggression and Defense

Aggression is an important concept in Perls's early theory. Aggression is neither an instinct nor an energy, although it is a biological function. It is the organism's means of contacting its environment to satisfy its needs and of meeting resistance to the satisfaction of its needs. Its function is not destruction but overcoming the resistance, leaving the object as intact as possible so it can be used for satisfaction. Aggression is similar or analogous to the biting and chewing of food to satisfy hunger: "The use of the teeth is the foremost biological representation of aggression."[16] Destruction does not leave the object intact but destructures it—as in biting and chewing—so that a new structure or intactness develops in its assimilation. "Mankind suffers from suppressed individual aggression and has become the executor and victim of tremendous amounts of released collective aggression. . . . *The re-establishment of the biological function of aggression* is, and remains, the solution to the *aggression problem.*" Sublimation (letting off steam in aggressive sports and physical work) provides helpful outlets. "But they will never equal dental aggression, the application of which will serve several purposes: one rids oneself of irritability and does not punish oneself by sulking and starving—one develops intelligence, and has a good conscience, because one has done something 'good for one's health.' "[17] (This statement appears to be inconsistent with the previous contention that aggression is not an instinct or an energy that seeks discharge.)

Defense is an instinctive self-preservative activity. Defenses are mechanical (shells in animals, character-armor [Reich] in humans) and dynamic, either motoric (flight), secretoric (snake poison), or sensoric (scenting).

Reality

Since the organism is not self-sufficient, it is continuously interacting with its environment. In the process of striving for a balance in relation to environmental demands, the organism is not a passive receptor or simply a reactor but an active perceiver and organizer of its perception. "For our purposes we assume that there is an objective world from which the individual creates his subjective world; parts of the absolute world are selected according to our interest, but this selection is limited by our tools of perception, and by social and neurotic inhibitions. . . . the reality which matters is the reality of interests—the *internal* and not the *external* reality."[18] Reality thus changes with the changing interests and needs of the organism. Through interests and needs, the environment is organized into figure and ground as they emerge and are satisfied, as noted above. An important aspect of this organization of the environment is that individuals cannot perceive or respond to their entire environment at the same time but only to one aspect of it, the figure, which relates to current interests and needs. It is apparent that Perls's concept of reality is phenomenological.

The Contact Boundary

The organism and the environment exist in a mutual, or dialectic, relationship. The organism must find the satisfaction of its needs in the environment. It reaches out toward the world to do so, through the sensory process of orientation and the motor process of manipulation. The point of interaction between the individual and the environment is the *contact boundary*. "The study of the way the human being functions in his environment is the study of what goes on at the contact boundary between the individual and his environment. It is at this contact boundary that the psychological events take place. Our thoughts, our actions, our behavior, our emotions are our way of experiencing and meeting these boundary events."[19]

Those objects or persons in the environment that provide satisfaction of needs acquire a positive cathexis (Freud's term), while those that hinder or threaten satisfaction acquire a negative cathexis. The individual seeks contact with the first kind of objects and persons and withdraws from the second. When the first kind of object is appropriated (assimilated), the Gestalt is closed. Similarly, when the second kind of object is annihilated (avoided or rejected), the Gestalt is closed. The individual is in a situation in which he or she can concentrate on another need as it comes into figure. We live by the dialectical process of contacting and withdrawing from objects and persons in the environment as they are discriminated as positive or negative. Activity is energized by the basic excitement inherent in the living organism, which is transformed into specific emotions according to the situation.

The Ego

"The ego is neither an instinct, nor has it instincts; it is an organismic function."[20] It is not a substance with either finite or even changing boundaries. Rather, the boundaries, the places of contact, constitute the ego. "Only where the self meets the 'foreign' does the ego start functioning, come into existence, determine the boundary between the personal and impersonal 'field.' "[21] It is thus the system of responses or contacts of the organism with the environment, involving identification or alienation. Awareness of the self and the nonself constitutes the ego.

The ego performs an integrative or administrative function in relating the actions of the organism to its needs: "it calls, so to speak, upon those functions of the organism which are necessary for the satisfaction of the *most urgent* need."[22] It identifies with the organism and its needs and alienates itself from other needs or demands to which it is hostile. It then structures the environment (the field) in terms of the organism's need. If the organism is hungry, food becomes the figure in the Gestalt, but if the food can be obtained only by stealing, and the person would rather die than steal, the ego alienates the taking of the food.

Growth and Maturity

Growth occurs through assimilation from the environment, both physically and mentally. The organism experiences a need, contacts its environment, and satisfies the need by assimilating energy from the environment. The healthy organism is in a continuous process of need $\longrightarrow$ disequilibrium $\longrightarrow$ aggressive contact with the environment $\longrightarrow$ need satisfaction through assimilation $\longrightarrow$ equilibrium, and so forth. "Life is practically nothing but an infinite number of unfinished situations—incomplete gestalts. No sooner have we finished one situation than another develops."[23] The healthy individual successfully finishes each situation, completes each incomplete Gestalt, and, in the process, grows.

Psychological growth is not an unconscious process but occurs through aware-ness. Sensing, excitement, Gestalt formation, and contact are accompanied by or cha-racterized by awareness in the normal individual. "Contact as such is possible without awareness, but for awareness contact is indispensable. . . . Sensing determines the nature of awareness, whether distant (e.g., acoustic), close (e.g., tactile) or within the skin (proprioceptive). . . . Excitement . . . covers the physiological excitation as well as the undifferentiated emotions. . . . Gestalt formation always accompanies awareness. . . . The formation of complete and comprehensive Gestalten is the condition for mental health and growth."[24]

The normal organism functions as a whole. Its behavior is in tune with its organismic needs, not with external demands, or "shoulds." The total organism is involved, with no parts isolated or cut off. The ego—self-awareness—incorporates all organismic needs and functions.

Frustration, rather than preventing growth, fosters it. Frustration challenges the individual and enables the individual to discover his or her potential and to learn to cope with the world. "Without frustrations there is no need, no reason, to mobilize your resources, to discover that you might be able to do something on your own, and in order not to be frustrated, which is a pretty painful experience, the child learns to manipulate the environment."[25]

Through growth, the child matures. Maturation is the transformation from envi-ronmental support to self-support. The child becomes independent rather than remain-ing dependent on others. The child who does not learn to overcome frustration, perhaps because he or she is spoiled or overprotected by the parents, does not grow up. Dependent on others, the child manipulates the environment for support by being helpless, stupid, or compliant. The point at which the child starts to manipulate the environment is when the child cannot get support and cannot yet provide his or her own support; it is called the *impasse*.

Normal growth and development is not without problems, as the difficulty of achieving maturity illustrates. *Anxiety* is also an accompaniment of learning. It is "the gap between the now and the later. Whenever you leave the sure basis of the now and become preoccupied with the future, you experience anxiety."[26] It is like stage fright, which when the action begins becomes the excitement that stimulates a good perform-ance. In his later formulation, Perls appears to use *dread* as a synonym for *anxi-ety;* dread is a vague, undifferentiated sense of danger, which becomes fear when there is an object with which to cope.[27]

There are also other problems related to or analogous to the hunger instinct. Although in his later writing, Perls discusses these under the topic of neurosis, the earlier recognition that they are present to some extent in normal development also seems to continue to be accepted. They are, therefore, considered here rather than in the discussion of neurosis.

The process of assimilation does not always proceed smoothly but encounters certain kinds of difficulty. There is a similarity or parallel in physiological and mental functioning. "Our attitude towards food has a tremendous influence upon intelligence, upon the ability to understand things, to get a grip on life and to put one's teeth into the task at hand. Anyone not using his teeth will cripple his ability to use his destructive functions for his own benefit."[28] Such people are excessively modest and lack backbone, but there is a greed behind their apparent lack of interest in food. Another character type of a similar parasitic nature is the person who lives in permanent unconscious fear of starvation and seeks financial security in life. These represent disturbances in the contact boundary between the individual and the environment.

Another form of such disturbance consists of *resistances* related to oral development, including the hunger strike in the form of lack of appetite: "I just can't swallow a bite." Analogous is the inability to swallow unpalatable information. *Disgust,* the nonacceptance or emotional refusal of food, is another resistance. Disgust at an object is a reaction to it as though it were in the stomach. There are four other major boundary disturbances that will be considered in more detail: introjection, projection, confluence, and retroflection.

"*Introjection* means preserving the structure of things taken in, whilst the organism requires their destruction"[29] for assimilation to occur. The introject, not having been "chewed" but having been "gulped down," remains intact as a foreign body in the system. Introjection is the natural form of eating in the suckling stage. Its persistence relates to disturbances in the development of the biting and the chewing stages. Oral aggression (biting) has been blocked, but food is forced into the child. The oral aggression becomes displaced, in part against other persons. Forced feeding also leads to disgust with food, which is repressed, and the food is swallowed whole or in chunks. In introjection, the organism reacts to an object or situations as it does to food by "swallowing it whole" but then being unable to "stomach it."

Psychologically, introjection is the uncritical acceptance on authority of concepts, standards of behavior, and values. The person who habitually introjects does not develop his or her own personality. The introjection of conflicting or incompatible concepts or values results in personality disintegration. In introjection, the boundary between the self and the world is so far inside the self that there is little real self left.

Projection is the placing in the outside world of those parts of one's personality with which one refuses (or is unable) to identify oneself (or to express). "The projecting person cannot satisfactorily distinguish between the inside and outside world."[30] Feelings of guilt lead to the projection of blame onto someone or something else. Projections are usually onto the outside world but can take place within the personality—for example, onto the conscience. Projection gives temporary relief but prevents contact, identification, and responsibility.

In projection, the boundary between the self and the world is extended into the world, so that aspects of the self that are unacceptable are displaced outside the self into the world. The projected aspects are unacceptable because they are inconsistent with introjected attitudes and values.

Confluence exists when the individual feels no boundary between the self and the environment. This condition is present in the newborn infant and in adults in moments of ecstasy or extreme concentration and on ritualistic occasions. A continuous state of confluence, when the individual cannot distinguish between the self and others, is pathological. In states of confluence, the person cannot tolerate differences; everyone must be alike.

"*Retroflection means that some function which originally is directed from the individual towards the world, changes its direction and is bent back towards the originator.*"[31] Narcissism is an example. Suicide, a substitute for murder, is another.

Aggression and hatred are reversed and directed toward the self. Such behavior is a reaction against meeting hostility and frustration. Inhibiting or suppressing emotions and behavior is sometimes necessary, but it can become habitual and lead to neurotic repression. There is a resulting split in the personality between the self as doer and the self as receiver.

The person who retroflects treats his or her self as he or she wants to treat others. Energies are directed inward toward the self, which is substituted for the environment, rather than outward toward the environment to satisfy needs.

> The retroflector knows how to draw a boundary line between himself and the environment, and he draws a neat and clean one right down the middle—but he draws it down the middle of himself. *The introjector does as others would like him to do, the projector does unto others what he accuses them of doing to him, the man in pathological confluence doesn't know who is doing what to whom, and the retroflector does to himself what he would like to do to others.*[32]

Introjection, projection, confluence, and retroflection function "to interrupt mounting excitement of a kind and degree with which the person cannot cope. . . . These mechanisms constitute neurosis only when they are inappropriate and chronic. All of them are useful and healthy when they are employed temporarily in particular circumstances."[33]

Neurosis

Neurosis is an interruption or a stagnation of growth; it is thus a "growth disorder" or a "disturbance in development."[34] This disturbance involves the individual's relation to society, which is a conflict between the needs and the demands of the individual and those of society. The individual is caught in the conflict between the biological needs of humanity and the social (ethical and moralistic) requirements of society, which may be against the biological laws of self-regulation. "Often enough, however, the socially required self-control can only be achieved at the cost of devitalizing and impairing the functions of large parts of the human personality—at the cost of creating collective and individual neurosis."[35] Yet there is no inherent conflict between the individual, with his or her basic drives, and society. The individual is not antisocial but has a need for social contact. The difficulties are those of growing up, maturing, and realizing one's nature and potentialities in the face of deprivations and frustrations.

Neither the individual nor the society can be blamed; each is part of a whole, and a causal relationship cannot exist between parts of a whole. Both are ill or disturbed. Yet

> man seems to be born with a sense of social and psychological balance as acute as his sense of physical balance. Every movement he makes on the social or psychological level is a movement in the direction of finding that balance, of establishing equilibrium between his personal needs and the demands of his society. His difficulties spring not from a desire to reject such equilibrium, but from misguided movements aimed towards finding and maintaining it.[36]

When, in the search for the contact boundary, the individual impinges too heavily on society, the individual becomes a delinquent or a criminal. When the search leads the individual to draw back, so that society impinges too heavily on her or him, neurosis develops. The neurosis is a defensive maneuver against the threat of an overwhelming world. It is an effort to maintain balance and self-regulation in a situation in which the odds are very much against the individual.

Thus the neurotic is unable to satisfy any needs and to organize his or her behavior in accordance with a hierarchy of needs. The neurotic cannot see his or her needs clearly, cannot separate and order them so that they can be dealt with one at a time. Thus there is no continuous sequence in which needs come clearly into awareness in order of urgency and the environment is searched for relevant satisfaction, so that the Gestalt is completed and destructed to make way for the next higher need. The neurotic is unable to distinguish between those objects or persons that have a positive cathexis and those that have a negative cathexis; the neurotic does not know whether to contact or to withdraw. The latter tendency is stronger. As a result, the neurotic is characterized by avoidance of contact.

The mechanisms of introjection, projection, confluence, and retroflection in extreme or pathological forms are characteristic of the neurotic's defenses. In whichever of these forms the neurosis is primarily shown, it is a confusion of identification between the self and the other, resulting in disintegration of the personality and incoordination of thought and action. Behavior is rigid and compulsive rather than spontaneous. The neurotic's efforts are deflected from the actualization of the self to the actualization of a self-image that is the neurotic's (unrealistic) concept of what he or she should be like. The neurotic is not whole, since parts of the self that are inconsistent with the self-image are disowned or alienated. Perls refers to these (missing) parts as "holes."

Neurotic anxiety is the basic, common symptom of all neuroses. It is exemplified in anxiety attacks, and in individuals in whom it may not be felt, it is manifested by excitement or restlessness and difficulty in breathing. The physiological concomitants of excitement are increased metabolism, increased heart activity, quickened pulse, and increased breathing. If the excitement is inhibited or its expression is suppressed by the restricting of breathing, the insufficiency of oxygen leads to difficulty in breathing. "In a state of anxiety an acute conflict takes place between the urge to breathe (to overcome the feeling of choking), and the opposing self-control. . . . *Anxiety equals excitement plus inadequate supply of oxygen.*"[37] The neurotic inhibits or suppresses excitement and suffers anxiety.

Guilt develops when, instead of contacts with others by means of interacting at the boundaries, there is a confluence between persons, "with no appreciation of a boundary between them" and "no discrimination of the points of difference or otherness that distinguishes them." There is, then, no figure–ground distinction, no awareness, and no contact. Confluence as a result of contact is healthy. It is unhealthy when it prevents contact. A healthy confluence can exist between persons who are close, as in marriage and old friendships. When a confluence is interrupted, guilt or resentment arises—guilt if the person feels responsible for the interruption and resentment if the person believes that the other is responsible.[39] Guilt is also aroused when a person feels unable to question what he or she has been told to believe and what he or she feels compelled to accept as what he or she ought to do but is unable to assimilate and accept. Guilt is thus projected resentment.[40]

To the question as to what it is in the organism–environment field that leads to neurosis, Perls writes:

> It seems to me that the imbalance arises when, simultaneously, the individual and the group experience differing needs, and when the individual is incapable of distinguishing which one is dominant. The group can mean the family, the state, the social-circle, co-workers—any or all combinations of persons who have a particular functional relationship with one another at a given time. The individual, who is part of this group, experiences the need for contact with it as one of his primary psychological impulses. . . . But when, at the same time, he experiences a personal need, the satisfaction of which requires withdrawal from the group, trouble can begin. In the situation of conflict of needs, the individual has to be able to make a clear-cut decision. If he does this . . . neither he nor the environment suffers any severe consequences. But when he cannot discriminate . . . he can neither make a good contact nor a good withdrawal, and both he and the environment are affected.[41]

Psychosis

In his later writings, Perls has little to say about psychosis. Thus his earlier writings are drawn on here.

Neurosis is a disturbance in the self-function, or the ego, while psychosis is a disturbance of the id functions.[42] In neurosis, there is conflict within the self or between individual needs and social demands; in psychosis, the individual is out of touch with reality and is incapable of distinguishing fantasy from reality and thus hallucinates or is deluded. Little consideration is given to the nature of psychosis in the Gestalt approach, except for paranoid conditions.

The manic–depressive cycle involves aggression. "In the manic period the unsublimated, but dentally inhibited aggression is not retroflected as in melancholia but is directed in all its greediness and with most violent outbursts against the world. A frequent symptom of cyclothymia is dipsomania which is on the one hand a sticking to the 'bottle' and on the other a means of self-destruction."[43]

In the paranoiac character, *"repressed disgust plays an essential part."*[44] In *paranoiac aggression,* there is "an attempt to re-digest projections," which is experienced "not as dental aggression, as belonging to the alimentary sphere, but is directed as personal aggression against another person, or against a collection of individuals, acting as screens for the projections."[45] Introjection is a part of a *paranoiac pseudometabolism.*

"The healthy character expresses his emotions and ideas, the *paranoid character projects them."*[46] "The paranoiac character exhibits what is called 'pseudo-metabolism.' " Material is introjected rather than assimilated, is felt as something strange to the self (as indeed it is), and then projected. The introjection represents the "swallowing" without tasting to avoid disgust. The material cannot be brought up to be rechewed because this would involve vomiting (disgust). It is, therefore, ejected (projected). The paranoiac thus treats as outside material, with attack and aggression,

what is really a part of the self. Reintrojection may occur, and the total process may repeat itself.

Every paranoid exhibits the megalomania–outcast or the superiority–inferiority complex. "In the period of introjection—of identification with the faeces—the paranoid character feels himself as dirt; in times of projection—of alienation—he thinks himself superior and looks upon the world as dirt."[47] The obsessional neurosis has a psychotic or paranoid nucleus. The continual washing attempts to undo the feeling of being dirty.

THE GOALS OF THERAPY

"The man who can live in concernful contact with his society, neither being swallowed up by it nor withdrawing from it completely, is the well-integrated man. . . . He is the man who recognizes the contact boundary between himself and his society, who renders unto Caesar the things that are Caesar's and retains for himself those things which are his own. The goal of psychotherapy is to create just such men."[48]

If pathology is the disturbance of the organismic balance, "the object of every treatment, psychotherapeutic or otherwise, is to facilitate organismic balance, to reestablish optimal functions."[49] Persistent imbalance is characterized by avoidance of various kinds, including avoidance of emotions and excitement, often under the inhibiting influence of shame. Thus therapy must deal with these avoidances by bringing them to awareness. *The awareness of, and the ability to endure, unwanted emotions are the conditio sine qua non for a successful cure.*"[50]

In terms of the relationship of the organism to its environment, the purpose of therapy is to reestablish contact and normal interaction and to replace abnormal retroflection, introjection, projection, and confluence by assimilation. "Only by reestablishing the destructive tendency towards food as well as toward anything that represents an obstacle to the individual's wholeness, by re-instating a successful aggression, the re-integration of an obsessional, and even a paranoid, personality takes place."[51]

From the point of view of pathology as a disturbance in the ego function, then, restoration of the integrative function of the ego is the object of therapy. "So what we are trying to do in therapy is step-by-step to *re-own* the disowned parts of the personality until the person becomes strong enough to facilitate his own growth. . . ."[52] The wholeness of the organism must be restored.

As neurosis is an arrest or a stagnation of growth, so therapy fosters growth. The focus on organismic control makes it possible for the individual to actualize *the self* rather than to attempt to actualize a *self-image.* As the neurotic is immature and dependent on others, so therapy fosters maturation, independence, and the transition from environmental support to self-support.

Basic to all these objectives is the attainment of awareness: *"awareness per se— by and of itself—can be curative."*[53] The healthy person "is completely in touch with himself and with reality."[54] Awareness leads to organismic self-regulation based on "the wisdom of the organism" in contrast to "the whole pathology of self-manipulation, environmental control and so on, that interferes with this subtle organismic control."[55] When awareness is present, "the organism can work on the healthy gestalt principle: that the most important unfinished situation will always emerge and can be dealt with.''[56] This occurs in therapy, so the therapist does not have to dig because unfinished situations will come to the surface.

Therapy, like living, is in the here and now. "Nothing exists except in the here and now."[57] The past exists only as it is represented in present memory, and the future exists only in present expectation and anticipation. The past affects the individual and persists as unfinished situations.

THE PROCESS OF THERAPY

The patient seeks therapy because he or she is in an existential crisis: psychological needs are not being met. The patient is thus motivated but comes with certain expectations and with neurotic—and unsuccessful—ways of attempting to get the environment to do the work for her or him. The patient expects the therapist to provide environmental support and uses techniques in an attempt to manipulate the therapist to do so by "putting on the appearance of the good child."

Although Gestalt therapy gives the patient much of what the patient wants (exclusive attention, for example), it does not give the patient all that he or she expects (answers that the patient thinks are necessary, admiration, and praise). Thus while the patient does get some satisfaction, he or she is also frustrated.

Gestalt therapy is not concerned with the whys of the patient's behavior, derived from the patient's past history, unconscious, or dreams. It rejects the doctrine of single causes. In addition, the whys explain very little and can lead to projection of responsibility. Gestalt therapy focuses on present characteristics of the patient's behavior of which he or she is unaware. The unaware is broader than the unconscious, including not only material that has been repressed, but also material that has never come into awareness, that has faded, or that has been unassimilated; it "includes skills, patterns of behavior, motoric and verbal habits, blind spots, etc."[58] Thus awareness and unawareness are both mental activities and sensory and motor activities.

Dreams are useful because they represent an attempt to find a solution to an apparent paradox. They are not interpreted by the therapist. Rather, the therapist uses them to help the patient discover the paradox, represented by two inconsistent strivings. All the parts of the dream—objects as well as persons—represent projected and disowned parts of the personality, which must be reowned and integrated.

The neurotic's problems are not in the past but in the present. Therapy must, therefore, deal with present behaviors and concerns through the development of here-and-now awareness. The solving of present difficulties will resolve any residual of past problems, which are also current problems. Through therapy, the patient learns how to live in the present by living in the here-and-now therapy situation.

Since it focuses on present problems and concerns, Gestalt therapy is an experiential therapy. The patient is asked and forced to experience as much of himself or herself as possible—gestures, breathing, voice, and so on. As the patient experiences the ways in which he or she has blocked or "interrupted" the self, the patient becomes more aware of what that self really is. The focus on the *I* as the self, or person who experiences or is aware, places the responsibility on the patient for feelings, thoughts, and actions. The patient becomes aware of relationships between feeling and behavior in different areas, is thus able to integrate the dissociated parts of his or her personality, and can establish an adequate balance and appropriate boundaries between the self and the environment.

The patient's unfinished or interrupted past business must be experienced or relived, not simply recounted, so that it can be resolved in the here and now. An intellectual explanation or understanding (insight) is not enough. The therapist requires the patient to focus or concentrate on each specific area of unfinished business. In contrast to the free-association method of psychoanalysis, Gestalt therapy emphasizes concentration. (Perls called his method "concentration therapy" before adopting the name Gestalt therapy.) Free association leads to avoidance, to a flight of ideas, or to "dissociation." Concentration involves focusing on the figure rather than the ground.

Even though the patient is disturbed and confused, there is always something in the foreground—some Gestalt formation—however muddy or fragmental it may be. Whatever is there appears because it represents the most important need for survival at that time. It usually represents a need for security and support from the therapist, accompanied by resistance to being self-supporting. In the "safe emergency" of therapy, unfinished situations (or problems) can emerge into clearer figure. Concentration is necessary in order to overcome resistances. As each piece of unfinished business is resolved or completed, a Gestalt is completed and then destructed, so that the patient is then ready to go on to another piece of unfinished business. A point is reached at which the patient no longer interrupts himself or herself and the process of assimilating and destructuring.

Therapy, then, by focusing on the recognition and awareness of interests and needs, attempts to reinstate the normal process by which these interests and needs can come into figure and be dealt with, either by seeking and obtaining satisfaction from them in the environment or by effecting a clear, deliberate withdrawal that closes the Gestalt. Thus the homeostasis, or self-regulation, process can continue without interruption and accumulation of unfinished business or incomplete Gestalts. Since the goal of therapy is not to solve the patient's problems but to help the patient learn to solve his or her own problems, therapy is not a problem-solving process. Following therapy, the patient should be in a position to solve his or her own current problems and to prevent, minimize, or resolve future problems alone.

IMPLEMENTATION AND TECHNIQUES

There is no systematic presentation of the methods and techniques of Gestalt therapy. Specific exercises are presented in *Ego, Hunger and Aggression* and more systematically in *Gestalt Therapy.* However, since neurosis is a symptom of growth stagnation, the remedy is not therapy but a method of reinstating growth. This is what the exercises accomplish. The object is to discover the self, which is achieved not through introspection but through action.

Even the average person is lacking in awareness. The first half of *Gestalt Therapy* consists of exercises that help the individual develop awareness of his or her functioning as an organism and as a person. The first set of exercises is for everyone and is directed toward (1) contacting the environment by becoming aware of present feelings, sensing opposed forces, attending and concentrating, and differentiating and unifying; (2) developing awareness of self through remembering, sharpening the body sense, experiencing the continuity of emotion, listening to one's verbalizing, and integrating awareness; and (3) directing awareness by converting confluence into contact and changing anxiety into excitement. Another set of exercises deals with processes that are chronic in organismic malfunctioning and is directed toward changing malfunctioning processes through (1) retroflection, by investigating misdirected behavior, mobilizing the muscles, and executing the re-reversed act; (2) introjection, by introjecting and eating, and dislodging and digesting introjects; and (3) projection, by discovering projections and assimilating projections. These exercises are aspects of therapy.

One of the reasons for the absence of systematic discussion of techniques is no doubt the fact that the emphasis is on the unique ways in which patients attempt to manipulate their environments (and the therapist as well) to gain environmental support. Thus therapy is improvised as it develops. Methods vary with each patient and with each session by means of techniques invented to meet each situation. "Anything goes if it contributes to the patient's awareness."[59] Yet there are some consistencies among therapists, although therapists may vary in methods as well as style. "Gestalt therapy is done in as many ways as there are Gestalt therapists."[60] Still, there are some common, if not standard, techniques. They focus on developing the patient's awareness in the here and now. They are often referred to as *experiments* in directed awareness.

Much, if not most, Gestalt therapy takes place in groups, either of the workshop type, which Perls developed, in which the therapist works with an individual in the group setting, or of the somewhat more traditional group-therapy type, in which the therapist usually focuses on one individual at a time. In his 1969 introduction to *Ego, Hunger and Aggression,* Perls states his conviction that individual and long-term therapy is obsolete, with individual sessions being the exception rather than the rule. The group format has led to the development of techniques that are called games.

The Role of the Therapist

Paradoxically, the therapist is not a helper. But the patient wants to depend on the therapist for support. The therapist who provides help is driven by the patient to give more and more help, or if the therapist does not or cannot help, the therapist is made to feel inadequate by the patient. Helping means providing support, and the patient's demand for support is his or her problem. Goodman phrased it well: "The very worst thing you can do for people is to help them."[61] To provide help is not helpful. Rather, the function of the therapist is to frustrate the demands for support and help from the patient so that the patient can learn that the resources for resolving problems are in himself or herself. "[W]e frustrate the patient in such a way that he is forced to develop his potential. We apply enough skillful frustration so that the patient is forced to find his own way, discover his own possibilities, his own potential, and discover that *what he expects from the therapist, he can do just as well himself.*"[62] The energy that is misdirected toward attempting to obtain environmental support can be used to actualize the self rather than to try to actualize a self-image. The patient has to learn this alone; teaching, conditioning, information giving, and interpreting cannot do it for him or her.

The patient resists this frustration and avoids facing the "holes" and the disowned parts of his or her personality. The patient is phobic and develops a scotoma; he or she cannot see the obvious. The therapist frustrates the patient "until he is face to face with his blocks, with his inhibitions, with his way of avoiding having eyes, having ears, having muscles, having authority, having security in himself."[63]

At this point, where the patient is unable to manipulate the environment (the therapist) into helping her or him and where the patient does not feel capable of self-support, is the *impasse*. The patient is stuck. The awareness of *how* he or she is stuck can lead to recovery. The patient discovers that the impasse is mostly a matter of fantasy, that he or she has the resources to get through it but only believed that he or she could not or that he or she was prevented from using these resources by imagining catastrophic outcomes.

The therapist must, however, provide a situation in which the patient feels accepted and not threatened. Frustration is not of a hostile, sadistic kind. The therapist is sympathetic, concerned, and caring about the patient and frustrates the patient in the context of this sympathy because it is the only way the therapist can really help the patient.

The therapist provides a "safe emergency," in which the patient can engage in the process of becoming self-supporting. The therapist is the facilitator of the process, but he or she is an active and pushing if not a leading facilitator. The therapist is an expert at directing the process by which the patient comes to the impasse, breaks it, and then achieves awareness and independence. The therapist must be sensitive, aware, and able to experience the patient's total communication, especially the nonverbal communication, since "verbal communication is usually a lie."[64]

Here-and-Now Awareness

The slogan for Gestalt therapy is "I and Thou, Here-and-Now." "Now" is the zero point between the past and the future, neither of which exists; only the now exists. The neurotic is not a person who had a problem in the past but one who has a problem now, which may also have been a problem in the past. The past influences behavior only as it is represented in the present. If the patient "can become *truly aware* at every instant of himself and his actions on whatever level—fantasy, verbal or physical—he can see how he is producing his difficulties, he can see what his present difficulties are, and he can help himself to solve them in the present, in the here and now."[65] Any past problems will also be taken care of, since they are part of the present problems.

The present, the here and now, is the therapy situation itself. The patient lives the problem in the interview. It is not necessary that the therapist probe or get a personal history. It is not even necessary that the patient verbalize the problem, because it will express itself in nonverbal behavior. The patient is not allowed to talk "about" problems in the past tense or in terms of memories; the patient is asked to reexperience them now. More generally, the patient is asked to experience now as much and as fully as possible his or her breathing, gestures, feelings, emotions, and voice. The manner of expression, not the content or the words, is what is important.

> [L]isten to what the voice tells you, what the posture tells you, what the image tells you. If you have ears, then you know all about the other person. You don't have to listen to *what* the person says: listen to the sounds. . . . [T]he voice is there, the gesture, the posture, the facial expression, the psychosomatic language. . . . [I]f you

use your eyes and ears, then you can see that everyone expresses himself in one way or another.[66]

The basic sentence that the patient is required to repeat is "Now I am aware. . . ." The present tense is required. Variations of this request are "What are you aware of now?" "Where are you now?" "What are you seeing? feeling?" "What are you doing with your hand? foot?" or "Are you aware of what you are doing with your . . . ?" "What do you want?" "What do you expect?"

The function of the therapist is to call the patient's attention to his or her behavior, feelings, and experiencing, not to interpret them. The purpose is not to discover why but how—how the patient is preventing awareness of interrupted or unfinished business, of the "holes" or missing parts of his or her personality, or the rejected or dissociated aspects of his or her personality. Awareness cannot be forced; the formation of Gestalts is an autonomous process. Thus if the patient resists dealing with material that the therapist calls the patient's attention to, the therapist does not push it. There will be other times when the patient may be ready to work on it.

Awareness itself can be curative, since it leads to contact with the unfinished business, which can then go to completion. The objective of all the techniques of Gestalt therapy, not only the here-and-now method, is to create awareness in the patient, so that the patient can integrate the disowned parts of his or her personality.

Making the Patient Responsible

The responses of the patient to awareness questions, both verbal and nonverbal, provide indications of the total personality; they are all expressions of the self. The therapist observes these responses and asks further questions.

The patient's responses often are avoidance responses or questions to the therapist, or they contain other indications of an attempt to shirk responsibility for behavior. "To him responsibility is blame, and as he is afraid of being blamed, so is he ready to blame. 'I'm not responsible for my attitudes, it's my neurosis that's at fault,' he seems to say."[67] Or the patient projects responsibility onto other people—parents—or early experiences. The patient also may dissociate himself or herself from nonverbal responses, referring to his or her body or its parts as "it" or to his or her actions as "they."

The therapist requires the patient to restate questions as statements, thus making the patient responsible for these statements. The therapist requires the patient to use *I* instead of *it* when referring to body parts and activities. "The therapist's primary responsibility is not to let go unchallenged any statement or behavior which is not representative of the self, which is evidence of the patient's lack of self-responsibility."[68] The patient is thus led to take responsibility for himself or herself and for his or her behavior, here and now, and becomes more aware of what and who he or she is.

Drama and Fantasy Work

Although the awareness technique alone is curative, it is slow. The therapist can speed up the process by initiating a number of other techniques that involve dramatic activity (role taking) and fantasy by the patient.

The therapist can work with the patient's behavior and experience in fantasy as well as in actuality. This approach is particularly useful if the patient is blocked in dealing with reality. Fantasy, through the use of symbols, reproduces reality on a diminished scale, although it is still meaningfully related to reality. Fantasy can be verbalized, written down, or acted out in various forms with the therapist, with other members of a group, or in *monotherapy.* In monotherapy, the patient creates and directs the entire production, playing all the parts. Fantasy involves acting out in therapy the neurotic tendencies, which then can be handled. Fantasy work may involve a number of different dramatic techniques.

Perls was influenced in the use of drama both by his early interest and some experience in the theater and by Jacob Moreno, who developed psychodrama as a method of treatment for hospitalized patients. However, unlike Moreno, Perls did not involve others in the dramatic production. Rather, he had the patient play all the parts alone. He utilized various techniques or situations to facilitate the role playing on the part of the patient.

The Shuttle Technique

The *shuttle technique* involves directing the patient's attention back and forth from one activity or experience to another. In one form, the patient shuttles between talking and listening to himself or herself. The therapist may facilitate the process by calling the patient's attention to what has been said or how it has been said, for example, by asking "Are you aware of this sentence?"

The patient also may shuttle between reliving a past experience in fantasy and in the here and now. The reliving evokes proprioceptions, which when brought to awareness lead to filling in of blanks related to the experience and to completion of the unfinished business that it represents.

The shuttle technique is also involved in other techniques, such as the topdog–underdog dialogues and the empty-chair technique.

Topdog–Underdog Dialogue

Neurotic conflicts involve opposite or opposing traits or aspects of the personality. When the therapist becomes aware of such a split in the personality, the patient is asked to experiment by taking each part of the conflict in turn by means of a dialogue. The most common split is between two aspects or two selves in the personality, which Perls called *the topdog* and *the underdog.* The topdog is the equivalent of Freud's superego. It represents the "shoulds" that are introjected by the individual, usually mainly from the parents. It is righteous, perfectionistic, authoritarian, bullying, and punishing. The underdog represents the id, or the infraego, to use Perls's term. It is primitive, evasive, "yes but," excusing, and passively sabotaging the demands of the topdog and usually succeeding. This success, however, does not resolve the conflict; the conflict can be resolved only by an integration of the two aspects of the personality by the patient. The process of integration is achieved when the patient becomes aware of both the topdog and the underdog by entering into a dialogue in which he or she alternately takes the part of both.

The Empty Chair

One of the most widely used Gestalt techniques is the *empty chair*. Essentially, it is a method of facilitating the role-taking dialogue between the patient and others or between parts of the patient's personality. It is usually used in a group situation. Two chairs are placed facing each other: one represents the patient or one aspect of the patient's personality (for example, the topdog), and the other represents another person or the opposing part of the personality (for example, the underdog). As the patient alternates the roles, he or she sits in one or the other chair.

The therapist may simply observe as the dialogue progresses or may instruct the patient when to change chairs, suggest sentences to say, call the patient's attention to what has been said or how it has been said, or ask the patient to repeat or exaggerate words or actions. In the process, emotions and conflicts are evoked, impasses may be brought about and resolved, and awareness and integration of polarities may develop —polarities or splits within the patient, between the patient and other persons, or between the patient's wants (underdog) and social norms (represented by topdog).

The empty-chair technique is frequently used in a group situation where the therapist works with a member of the group on a one-to-one basis. The person being worked with occupies the "hot seat" and faces the empty chair in front of the group.

Confusion

In *The Gestalt Approach and Eyewitness to Therapy,*[69] Perls introduced the technique of dealing with confusion without giving it a designation. All patients demonstrate confusion, which is manifested in hesitation between contact and withdrawal, the latter representing the neurotic's real need. Since confusion is unpleasant, the patient attempts to get rid of it by avoidance, blanking out, verbalism, and fantasy. All of this shows as "faded motoric behavior" in the therapy situation. The therapist must help the patient to become aware of, to tolerate, and to stay with this confusion. When it is not avoided or interrupted and is allowed to develop, it will be transformed into a feeling that can be experienced and can lead to appropriate action. An attempt to develop an intellectual understanding of it, on the contrary, does not resolve it, but constitutes an interruption—a premature arresting of development.

Blankness is a correlate of confusion. The patient cannot visualize anything clearly when asked; his or her fantasy images are hazy, as in a fog. If the patient can stay with it, it will clear up, and an image will form. A complete blank or blackness, like a black velvet curtain, may be another manifestation of confusion. The patient can be asked in fantasy to open the curtain, often revealing what he or she was hiding.

Confusion also may be dealt with by the patient's "withdrawal into a fertile void," which is an eerie experience similar to a hypnogogic hallucination before falling asleep. This can lead to an "aha!" experience, in which confusion is transformed into clarity.

Dreamwork

Freud referred to the dream as the royal road to the unconscious. Perls states that it is the royal road to integration. Whereas the psychoanalyst works with associations to the individual elements of the dream and interprets them, the Gestalt therapist attempts to have the patient relive the dream in the present, in the therapy situation, including acting it out. Interpretation is avoided, as it leads only to intellectual insight. The interpretation is left to the patient. "The more you refrain from interfering and telling the patient what he is like or what he feels like, the more chance you give him to discover himself and not to be misled by your concepts and projections."[70]

The dream represents or contains in some form an unfinished, unassimilated situation. "The dream is an existential message. It is more than an unfinished situation; it is more than an unfulfilled wish, it is more than a prophecy. It is a message of yourself to yourself, to whatever part of you is listening. The dream is possibly the most spontaneous expression of the human being."[71] The different parts are projections of different and conflicting sides of the self. In principle, the dream contains all that is essential for the cure, if all its parts are understood and assimilated. "Everything is there. . . . We find all we need in the dream. . . . Understanding the dream means realizing when you are avoiding the obvious."[72] The forms change, but everything is in every dream. "A dream is a condensed reflection of our existence."[73]

Dreams reveal missing personality parts and the methods of avoidance used by the patient. Patients who do not remember dreams (everyone dreams) are refusing to face what is wrong with their existence; they "*think* that they have come to terms with life."[74] Such patients are asked to talk to the missing dreams: "Dreams, where are you?"

In dreamwork, the patient is asked to play the part of the various persons and objects. In doing so, the patient identifies with the alienated parts of the self and integrates them. Difficulty in or resistance to playing the alienated parts indicates that the patient does not want to reown or take back rejected parts of the self. The use of the empty-chair technique, in which the patient changes his or her seat during interaction with a dream person, object, or part of the self, facilitates the process.

Homework

"We ask all of our patients to try doing some homework and many are capable of speeding up their therapy in this way."[75] Not all patients are able to carry out their assignments, however, and they may go to great lengths to avoid doing so. The homework involves the patient reviewing the session by imagining himself or herself back in it. If there are blocks in reexperiencing it, the patient must try to find out if something disturbing occurred, such as something that could not be expressed in the therapy. If so, can the patient now say it? The focus is on becoming aware of avoidance and interruption of total expression.

Integration

These techniques (awareness, responsibility giving, drama and fantasy work, confusion, dreamwork, and homework) do not operate in isolation, by focusing on specific actions, feelings, experiences, or awareness per se. All are directed toward integration into a whole person.

In Gestalt therapy, the focus is on integrating rather than, as in psychoanalysis, on analyzing. Those things that are projected and resisted must be reowned, reassimilated. "Everything the person disowns can be recovered, and the means of this recovery is understanding, playing, becoming these disowned parts. And by letting him play and discover that he already has all this (which he thinks only others can give him) we increase his potential. . . . So what we are trying to do in therapy is step-by-step to *re-own* the disowned parts of the personality until the person becomes strong enough to facilitate his own growth."[76]

The achievement of integration can be fostered by having the patient deal with any of the parts of the total person (the body, emotion, thinking, or speech) and the physical and social environment, since all are related and exist in a functional unity. However, if any one is dealt with exclusively,

> the effects will not spread sufficiently to those areas which the particular method neglects. If any partial approach is pursued, in isolation from the others, the unaware resistances in other components of the functioning will increase to such a degree as either to make further progress in the selected approach impossible unless or until other kinds of material are admitted or else to achieve a "cure" in terms of a new, arbitrary pattern.[77]

The basic rule of psychoanalysis—that the patient should say everything that comes to mind—is broadened. In addition to expressing thoughts and emotions, the patient is expected to express everything that is felt in his or her body, including not only major physical symptoms, but also unobtrusive sensations. Also, since when the patient forces himself or herself to say everything, the patient suppresses embarrassment by "either wording the embarrassing material in a noncommittal manner, or by bracing himself and deadening his emotions . . . we have to impress upon the patient that he must neither suppress nor force anything, and that he must not forget to convey to the analyst every bit of conscious resistance such as embarrassment, shame, etc."[78] Shame and embarrassment

> are the primary tools of repressions. . . . Endurance of embarrassment brings the repressed material to the surface . . . and helps the patient to accept previously refused material via the amazingly relieving discovery that the fact behind the embarrassment may not be so incriminating after all, and may even be accepted with interest by the analyst. . . . *The awareness of, and the ability to endure, unwanted emotions are the sine qua non for a successful cure;* these emotions will be discharged once they have become Ego-functions. This process, and not the process of remembering, forms the *via regia* to health.[79]

Thus therapy is not a pleasant or an easy experience for the patient. The facing and dealing with avoidance is not painless. As a result, most of those who begin therapy do not continue or complete it. The patient who persists, however,

> learns that the hard work is not mere drudgery. However far removed it may at first seem from what he thinks is urgent and therefore the place to start, he gradually gains orientation and perspective. He comes to see particular symptoms as merely surface manifestations of a more general and complicated system of malfunctioning which

underlies and supports them. Though now, in a way, the job looks bigger and will obviously take longer than originally supposed, it does begin to make sense.[80]

The therapist is more considerate than relatives or friends in leading the patient to face what the patient wishes to avoid. Nevertheless, the patient, usually following a "honeymoon" period at the beginning of therapy, becomes critical of therapy and the therapist or enters into what the Freudians call a "negative transference" period. If the patient can openly express and discuss this resentment, therapy continues and is accelerated; if the patient cannot or does not discuss it, therapy slows down and is likely to be terminated by the patient.

The development of awareness is directed toward repression. However, unlike psychoanalysis, which focuses on recovering what is repressed, Gestalt therapy emphasizes awareness of the existence of repression or avoidance and how it is being done. The blocked impulse will come out by itself. In retroflection, the impulse whose expression is being directed against the self instead of toward the environment is expressed toward its natural object in the environment. This is not easy or rapid. There is a long process in which the patient must first become aware of the retroflection, the repression, the repressed impulse, its acceptance, its redirection (possibly after modification), and its appropriate expression. The reintegration of dissociated parts is painful; "it always involves conflict, destroying and suffering."[81]

In contrast to the treatment of retroflection, which involves the acceptance and integration of dissociated parts of the self, the treatment of introjection involves becoming "aware of what is not truly yours, to acquire a selective and critical atttitude towards what is offered you, and, above all, to develop the ability to 'bite off' and 'chew' experience so as to extract its healthy nourishment."[82]

The chronic drinker is anchored in the suckling stage. He or she wants to drink in the environment and to enter into confluence with others without real contact. The alcoholic accepts social reproaches uncritically as coming from himself or herself. Then the alcoholic may silence the self-aggressive conscience in alcohol; but afterward, its vindictiveness is redoubled. "Since his aggression is not used in attacking his food or his problems, the surplus which is not invested in his conscience often turns outward in surly, irrelevant fights."[83] The sexually promiscuous person is also an introjector who seeks immediate sexual satisfaction without the development of a relationship through real contact. Introjection leads to the formation of an ego that is a collection of unassimilated traits and qualities taken over from authorities without understanding. Becoming aware of eating habits of gulping, swallowing whole, greed, and disgust is the first step. The next step is to remobilize or reinstate the experience of disgust in eating by chewing a bite of food until it is fully liquefied; then a bit of reading matter or a difficult sentence is thoroughly analyzed and "chewed up." In therapy, that which has been swallowed whole must be brought back up to be rejected, or chewed, so it can be assimilated. Catharsis is not enough; the patient must learn not to introject. The "working through" of psychoanalysis does this, but with only limited aspects of behavior.

If projections are to be dealt with, they must be discovered or recognized. Projections are encouraged by our language, which attributes our behavior to external causes. The process of alienation must be reversed by changing our language and thinking from *it* (or id) language to the responsible *I*. "The aim is to come to realize again that you are creative in your environment and are responsible for your reality—not to blame, but responsible in the sense that it is you who lets it stand or changes it."[84] Once projections are recognized, they must be accepted as aspects of oneself and assimilated or modified.

Rules and Games

The rules and games of Gestalt therapy have been collected by Levitsky and Perls.[85]

The rules include the *principle of the now* (using the present tense), the *I and thou* (addressing the other person directly rather than talking about the person to the therapist), *using* I *language* (substituting *I* for *it* in talking about the body and its acts and behaviors), *using the awareness continuum* (focusing on the *how* and *what* of experience rather than on the *why*), *no gossiping* (addressing the person directly when he or she is present rather than making statements about the person), and *asking the patient to convert questions into statements.*

The games are mainly techniques used in groups. They are defined briefly as follows:

1. *Games of Dialogue*   The patient takes the parts of aspects of the split personality and carries on a dialogue between them. These parts include the topdog (superego or shoulds) versus the underdog (passive resistant), aggressive versus passive, nice guy versus scoundrel, masculine versus feminine, and so forth.
2. *Making the Rounds*   The patient extends a general statement or a theme (for example, "I can't stand anyone in this room") to each person individually, with additions pertinent to each.
3. *"I Take Responsibility"*   The patient is asked to follow each statement about himself or herself or feelings with ". . . and I take responsibility for it."
4. *"I Have a Secret"*   Each person thinks of a personal secret involving guilt or shame and, without sharing it, imagines how he or she feels others would react to it.
5. *Playing the Projection*   When a patient expresses a perception that is a projection, the patient is asked to play the role of the person involved in the projection to discover his or her conflict in this area.
6. *Reversals*   The patient is asked to play a role opposite to his or her overt or expressed behavior (for example, to be aggressive rather than passive) and to recognize and make contact with the submerged or latent aspect of himself or herself.
7. *The Rhythm of Contact and Withdrawal*   The natural inclination toward withdrawal is recognized and accepted, and the patient is permitted to experience the security of withdrawing temporarily.
8. *Rehearsal*   Since much of thinking is rehearsal in preparation for playing a social role, group members share rehearsals with one another.
9. *Exaggeration*   Exaggeration is also a repetition game. When the patient makes an important statement in a casual way, indicating that he or she does not recognize its importance, the patient is required to repeat it again and again with increasing loudness and emphasis.

10. *"May I Feed You a Sentence?"*   The therapist suggests a sentence for the patient to repeat that the therapist feels represents something significant to the patient, so that the patient can try it on for size. This often involves interpretation.

EXAMPLES

These examples are from workshops, which were Perls's major activity in therapy. These workshops were not therapy groups; rather, participants volunteered to "work with" Perls on an individual basis. The group was involved only when a volunteer came to a therapeutic realization and was asked to express it in interaction with other participants in the procedure or game called "making the rounds."

Linda[86]

LINDA: I dreamed that I watch . . . a lake . . . drying up, and there is a small island in the middle of the lake, and a circle of . . . porpoises—they're like porpoises except that they can stand up, so they're like porpoises that are like people, and they're in a circle, sort of like a religious ceremony, and it's very sad—I feel very sad because they can breathe, they are sort of dancing around the circle, but the water, their element, is drying up. So it's like a dying—like watching a race of people, or a race of creatures, dying. And they are mostly females, but a few of them have a small male organ, so there are a few males there, but they won't live long enough to reproduce, and their element is drying up. And there is one that is sitting over here near me and I'm talking to this porpoise and he has prickles on his tummy, sort of like a porcupine, and they don't seem to be a part of him. And I think that there's one good point about the water drying up, I think—well, at least at the bottom, when all the water dries up, there will probably be some sort of treasure there, because at the bottom of the lake there should be things that have fallen in, like coins or something, but I look carefully and all that I can find is an old license plate . . . That's the dream.

FRITZ: Will you please play the license plate?

L: I am an old license plate, thrown in the bottom of a lake. I have no use because I'm no value—although I'm not rusted—I'm outdated, so I can't be used as a license plate . . . and I'm just thrown on the rubbish heap. That's what I did with a license plate, I threw it on a rubbish heap.

F: Well, how do feel about this?

L: (quietly) I don't like it. I don't like being a license plate—useless.

F: Could you talk about this? That was such a long dream until you come to find a license plate; I'm sure this must be of great importance.

L: (sighs) Useless. Outdated . . . The use of a license plate is to allow—give a car permission to go . . . and I can't give anyone permission to do anything because I'm outdated . . . In California, they just paste a little—you buy a sticker—and stick it on the car, or the old license plate. (faint attempt at humor) So maybe someone could put me on their car and stick this sticker on me, I don't know . . .

F: Okeh, now play the lake.

L: I'm a lake . . . I'm drying up, and disappearing, soaking into the earth . . . (with a touch of surprise) *dying* . . . But when I soak into the earth, I become a part of the earth—so maybe I water the surrounding area, so . . . even in the lake, even in my bed, flowers can grow (sighs). New life can grow . . . from me (cries) . . .

F: You get the existential message?

L: Yes. (sadly, but with conviction) I can paint—I can create—I can create beauty. I can no longer reproduce, I'm like the porpoise . . . but I . . . I'm . . . I . . . keep wanting to say I'm food . . . I . . . as water becomes . . . I water the earth, and give life—growing things, the water—they need both the earth and water, and the . . . and the air and the sun, but as the water from the lake, I can play a part in something, and producing—feeding.

F: You see the contrast: On the surface, you find something, some artifact—the license plate, the artificial you—but then when you go deeper, you find the apparent death of the lake is actually fertility . . .

L: And I don't need a license plate, or a permission, a license in order to . . .

F: (gently) Nature doesn't need a license plate to grow. You don't have to be useless, if you are organismically creative, which means if you are involved.

L: And I don't need permission to be creative . . . Thank you.

Jane[87]

JANE: The dream I started on, the last time I worked, I never finished it, and I think the last part is as important as the first part. Where I left off, I was in the Tunnel of Love—

FRITZ: What are you picking on? (Jane has been scratching her leg)

J: Hmmm. (clears throat) . . . I'm just sitting here, for a minute, so I can really be here. It's hard to stay with this feeling, and talk at the same time . . . Now I'm in the intermediate zone, and I'm—I'm thinking about two things: Should I work on the dream, or should I work on the picking thing, because that's something that I do a lot. I pick my face, and . . . I'll go back to the dream. I'm in the Tunnel of Love, and my brother's gone in the —somewhere—and to the left of me, there's a big room and it's painted, kind of a drab green, and to the left of me there are bleachers. I look over and there are all people sitting there. It looks as though they are waiting to get on the ride. There's a big crowd around one person, Raymond. (financé) He's talking to them and he's explaining some- thing to them and they're all listening to him. And he's moving his finger like this, and making gestures. I'm surprised to see him. I go up to him, and it's very obvious that he doesn't want to talk to me. He's interested in being with all these people, entertaining all these people. So I tell him that I'll wait for him. I sit three bleachers up and look down, and watch this going on. I get irritated and I'm—pissed off, so I say, "Raymond, I'm leaving. I'm not gonna wait for you any more." I walk outside the door—I stand outside the door for awhile—I get anxious. I can feel anxious in my dream. I feel anxious now, because I don't really want to be out here. I want to be inside, with Raymond. So I'm going inside. I go back through the door—

F: Are you telling us a dream, or are you doing a job?

J: Am I telling a dream—

F: Or are you doing a job?

J: I'm telling a dream, but it's still—I'm not telling a dream.

F: Hm. Definitely not.

J: I'm doing a job.

F: I gave you only the two alternatives.

J: I can't say that I'm really aware of what I'm doing. Except physically. I'm aware of what's happening physically to me but—I don't really know what I'm doing. I'm not asking you to tell me what I'm doing . . . Just saying I don't know.

F: I noticed one thing: When you come up to the hot seat, you stop playing the silly goose.

J: Hm. I get frightened when I'm up here.

F: You get dead.

J: Whew . . . If I close my eyes and go into my body, I know I'm not dead. If I open my eyes and "do that job," then I'm dead . . . I'm in the intermediate zone now, I'm wondering whether or not I'm dead. I notice that my legs are cold and my feet are cold. My hands are cold. I feel—I feel strange . . . I'm in the middle, now. I'm—I'm neither with my body nor with the group. I notice that my attention is concentrated on that little matchbook on the floor.

F: Okeh. Have an encounter with the matchbox.

J: Right now, I'm taking a break from looking at you, 'cause it's—it's a—'cause I don't know what's going on, and I don't know what I'm doing. I don't even know if I'm telling the truth.

F: What does the matchbook answer?

J: I don't care if you tell the truth or not. It doesn't matter to me. I'm just a matchbox.

F: Let's try this for size. Tell us, "I'm a matchbox."

J: I'm just a matchbox. And I feel silly saying that. I feel, kind of dumb, being a matchbox.

F: Uhhm.

J: A little bit useful, but not very useful. There's a million like me. And you can look at me, and you can like me, and then when I'm all used up, you can throw me away. I never liked being a matchbox . . . I don't—I don't know if that's the truth, when I say I don't know what I'm doing. I know there's one part of me that knows what I'm doing. And I feel suspended, I feel—steady. I don't feel relaxed. Now I'm trying to understand why in the two seconds it takes me to move from the group to the hot seat, my whole—my whole *person* changes . . . Maybe because of—I want to talk to the Jane in *that* chair.

   She would be saying, (with authority) well *you* know where you're at. You're playing dumb. You're playing stupid. You're doing this, and you're doing that, and you're sucking people in, and you're—(louder) not telling the truth! and you're stuck, and you're dead . . .

   And when I'm *here,* I immediately—the Jane here would say, (small, quavery voice) well, that's—I feel on the defensive in this chair right now. I feel defensive. I feel like for some reason I have to defend myself. And I know it's not true. So who's picking on you? It's *that* Jane over there that's picking on me.

F: Yah.

J: She's saying . . . She's saying (briskly) now when you get in the chair, you have to be in the here and now, you have to do it *right,* you have to be turned on, you have to know everything—

F: "You have to do your job."

J: You have to do your job, and you have to do it *right.* And you have to—become totally self-actualized, and you have to get rid of all your hangups, and along with that—it's not —it's not mandatory that you do this, but it's nice if you can be entertaining along the way, while you're doing all that. Try to spice it up a little bit, so that people won't get bored and go to sleep, because that makes you anxious. And you have to *know* why you're in the chair. You can't just go there and not know why you're there. You have to know *everything,* Jane.

   You really make it hard for me. You really make it hard. You're really putting a lot of demands on me . . . I don't know everything. And that's hard to say. I don't know everything, and on top of that, I don't know what I'm doing half the time . . . I don't know —I don't know if that's the truth or not. I don't even know if that's a lie.

F: So be your topdog again.

J: Is that—

F: Your topdog. That's the famous topdog. The righteous topdog. This is where your power is.

J: Yeah. Well—uh—I'm your topdog. You can't live without me. I'm the one that—I keep you noticed, Jane. I keep you noticed. If it weren't for me, nobody would notice you. So you'd better be a little more grateful that I exist.

Well, I don't want to be noticed, *you* do. You want to be noticed. I don't want to be noticed. I don't want . . . I don't really want to be noticed, as much as you do.

F: I would like you to attack the righteous side of that topdog.

J: Attack—the righteous side.

F: The topdog is always righteous. Topdog *knows* what you've got to do, has all the right to criticize, and so on. The topdog nags, picks, puts you on the defensive.

J: Yeah. . . . You're a bitch! like my mother. You know what's good for me. You—you make life *hard* for me. You tell me to do things. You tell me to be—*real.* You tell me to be self-actualized. You tell me to—uh, tell the truth.

F: Now please don't change what your hands are doing, but tell us what's going on in your hands.

J: My left hand . . .

F: Let them talk to each other.

J: My left hand. I'm shaking, and I'm in a fist, straining forward, and (voice begins to break) that's kind of—the fist is very tight, pushing—pushing my fingernails into my hand. It doesn't feel good, but I do it all the time. I feel tight.

F: And the right hand?

J: I'm holding you back around the wrist.

F: Tell it why you hold it back.

J: If I let you go you're gonna hit something. I don't know what you're gonna hit, but I have to—I have to hold you back 'cause you can't do that. Can't go around hitting things.

F: Now hit your topdog.

J: (short harsh yell) Aaaarkh! Aarkkh!

F: Now talk to your topdog. "Stop nagging—"

J: (loud, pained) Leave me alone! [F: Yah, again.] Leave me alone [F: Again.] (screaming it and crying) *Leave me alone!* [F: Again.] (she screams it, a real blast) LEAVE ME ALONE! I DON'T HAVE TO DO WHAT YOU SAY! (still crying) I don't have to be that good! . . . I don't have to be in this chair! I don't have to. You make me. You make me come here! (screams) Aarkkh! You make me pick my face, (crying) that's what you do. (screams and cries) Aarkkh! I'd like to kill you.

F: Say this again.

J: I'd like to kill you. [F: Again.] I'd like to *kill* you.

F: Can you squash it in your left hand?

J: It's as big as me . . . I'm strangling it.

F: Okeh. Say this, "I'm strangling—"

J: (quietly) I'm gonna strangle you . . . take your neck. Grrrummmm. (Fritz gives her a pillow which she strangles while making noises) Arrghh. Unghhh. How do you like *that!* (sounds of choked-off cries and screams)

F: Make more noises.

J: Hrugghhh! Aachh! Arrgrughhh! (she continues to pound the pillow, cry and scream)

F: Okeh. Relax, close your eyes . . . (long silence) (softly) Okeh. Come back to us. Are you ready? . . . Now be that topdog again . . .

J: (faintly) You shouldn't have done that. I'm gonna punish you for that . . . I'm gonna punish you for that, Jane. You'll be sorry you did that. Better watch out.

F: Now talk like this to each one of us . . . Be vindictive with each one of us. Pick out something we have done . . . Start with me. As this topdog, for what are you going to punish me?

J: I'm gonna punish you for making me feel so stupid.

F: How are you going to punish me?

J: (promptly) By being stupid. Even stupider than I am.

F: Okeh. Do this some more.

J: Raymond, I'm gonna punish you for being so dumb. I'll make you feel like an ass . . . I'll make you think I'm smarter than you are, and you'll feel dumber and I'll feel smart . . . I'm really scared. I shouldn't be doing this. (cries) It isn't nice.

R: Say this to him. Turn it around, "You should not—"

J: You sh—you shouldn't—you shouldn't—you shouldn't be doing—hooo—you shouldn't be doing—you shouldn't be so dumb. You shouldn't play so dumb. Because it isn't nice.

F: You're doing a job again.

J: Yeah, I know. I don't wanna do it. (crying) I—I know how I punish you. (sigh) I'll punish you by being helpless.

RAYMOND: What are you punishing me for?

J: I'll punish you for loving me. That's what I'll punish you for. I'll make it *hard* for you to love me. I won't let you know if I'm coming or going.

F: "How can you be so low as to love somebody like me?" Yah?

J: *I* do that.

F: I know. How can you love a matchbox? . . .

J: Fergus, I'm gonna punish you for being so slow—in your body, but so quick in your mind. The way I'm gonna do that—I'm gonna excite you, try to excite you, and it's the truth. I'll punish you for being sexually inhibited. I'll make you think I'm very sexy. I'll make you feel bad around me . . . And I'll punish you for pretending to know more than you do.

F: What do you experience when you are meting out the punishment?

J: (more alert, alive) It's a very strange experience. I don't know that I've ever had it before, for such a long time. It's kind of—it's a feeling I used to get when I—when I got back at my brothers for being mean to me. I'd just grit my teeth and think of the *worst* thing I could do—and kind of enjoy it.

F: Yah. This is my impression; you didn't enjoy this here.

J: Mm.

F: Okeh. Go back and be the topdog again, and enjoy punishing Jane—pick on her, torture her.

J: You're the only one I enjoy punishing . . . When you're too loud—when you're too loud, I'll punish you for being too loud. (no sound of enjoyment) When you're not loud enough, I'll tell you that you're too inhibited. When you dance too much—when you dance too much, I'll tell you that you're trying to sexually arouse people. When you don't dance enough, I'll tell you that you're dead.

F: Can you tell Jane, "I'm driving you crazy"?

J: (cries) I'm driving you crazy. [F: Again.] I'm driving you crazy. [F: Again.]

I'm driving you *crazy*. . . . I used to drive everybody else crazy, and now I'm driving *you* crazy . . . (voice drops, becomes very faint) But it's for your own good. That's what my mother would say. "For your own good." I'll make you feel *guilty* when you've done bad things, so you won't do it again. And I'll—I'll pat you on the back when you do something good, so you'll remember to do it again. And I'll keep you out of the moment. I'll—I'll keep you planning—and I'll keep you programmed, and I won't let you live—in the moment. I won't let you enjoy your life.

F: I would like you to use this: "I am relentless."

J: I—I am relentless. [F: Again.]

I *am* relentless. I'll do anything—especially if somebody dares me to do something. Then I've gotta tell you to do it, Jane, so you can prove it, so you can prove yourself. You've *gotta* prove yourself—in this world.

F: Let's try this. "You've got a job to do."

J: (laughs) You've gotta job to do. You're gonna quit fuckin' around, and—you've been doin' nothin' for a long time—

F: Yah. Now, don't change your posture. The right arm goes to the left and the left arm goes to the right. Say the same thing again and stay aware of this.

J: You've been doing nothing for a long time. You gotta do something, Jane. You've gotta be something . . . You've gotta make people proud of you. You've got to grow up, you have to be a woman, and you gotta keep everything that's bad about you hidden away so nobody can see it, so they'll think you're perfect, just perfect . . . You have to lie. I make you lie.

F: Now take Jane's place again.

J: You're—you're (cries) you are driving me crazy. You're picking on me. I'd really like to strangle you—uh—then you'll punish me more. You'll come back—and give me hell for that. So, why don't you just go away? I won't—I won't cross you up any more. Just go away and leave me alone—and I'm not begging you! Just go away! [F: Again.]

 Just go away! [F: Again.]

 Go away! [F: Change seats.]

 You'll be just a half if I go away! You'll be half a person if I leave. Then you'll really be fucked up. You can't send me away, you'll have to figure out something to *do* with me, you'll have to *use* me.

 Well then—then I—I would change your mind about a lot of things if I had to.

F: Ah!

J: And tell you that there's nothing I could do that's bad . . . I mean, if you'd leave me alone, I wouldn't do anything bad . . .

F: Okeh. Take another rest.

J: (closes eyes) . . . I can't rest.

F: So come back to us. Tell us about your restlessness.

J: I keep wondering what to do with that. When I had my eyes closed I was saying, "Tell her to just relax."

F: Okeh. Play *her* topdog, now.

J: Just relax.

F: Make her the underdog and you're the topdog.

J: And you don't have to do anything, you don't have to prove anything. (cries) You're only twenty years old! You don't have to be the queen . . .

 She says, O.K. I understand that. I know that. I'm just in a *hurry*. I'm in a *big* hurry. We've got so many things to do—and now, I know, when I'm in a hurry you can't be now, you can't—when I'm in a hurry, you can't stay in the minute you're in. You have to keep —you have to keep hurrying, and the days slip by and you think you're losing time, or something. I'm *much* too hard on you. I have to—I have to leave you alone.

F: Well, I would like to interfere. Let your topdog say, "I'll be a bit more patient with you."

J: Uh. I'll be—I'll be a bit more patient with you.

F: Say this again.

J: (softly) It's very hard for me to be patient. You know that. You know how impatient I am. But I'll—I'll try to be a bit more patient with you. I'll try—I'll *be* a bit more patient with you. As I say that, I'm stomping my foot, and shaking my head.

F: Okeh. Say, "I *won't* be patient with you—"

J: (easily) I won't be patient with you, Jane! I won't be patient with you. [F: Again.] I won't be patient with you. [F: Again.] I won't be patient with you.

F: Now say this to us . . . Pick a few.

J: Jan, I won't be patient with you. Claire, I won't be patient with you. Dick, I won't be patient with you. Muriel, I won't be patient with you. Ginny, I won't be patient with you . . . And June, I won't be patient with you, either.

F: Okeh. How do you feel, now?

J: O.K.

F: You understand, topdog and underdog are not yet together. But at least the conflict is clear, in the open, maybe a *little* bit less violent.

J: I felt, when I worked before, on the dream, and the dream thing, that I worked this out. I felt good. I keep—I keep—it keeps—I keep going back to it.

F: Yah. This is the famous self-torture game.

J: I do it so *well.*

F: Everybody does it. You don't do it better than the rest of us. Everybody thinks, "I am the worst."

SUMMARY AND EVALUATION

There are two basic principles underlying Gestalt therapy as it was developed by Perls: (1) the holistic principle that persons are organized wholes, and (2) the dialectic principle of opposites, including the principle of homeostasis. The experiencing of a need leads to an imbalance, or disequilibrium, in the organism. The organism as a whole responds in an attempt to restore the balance by satisfying the need. In Gestalt terms, the need emerges out of the background and becomes the figure. The organism engages in sensory and motor behavior in interaction with its environment to obtain satisfaction for the need. When the need is met, completing the Gestalt, the Gestalt dissolves or destructs, leaving the organism ready for the emergence of another dominant need. The continuing process of awareness of emerging needs causes disequilibrium, is followed by aggressive contact with the environment and need satisfaction through assimilation from the environment with resulting momentary equilibrium, and then leads to growth and development.

The disturbance of this process constitutes neurosis or psychosis. The disturbed individual is not aware of any needs, is unable to organize his or her needs into a hierarchy, or is unable to obtain satisfaction of his or her needs and resorts to a pathological degree to introjection, projection, confluence, and/or retroflection.

Therapy consists of reinstating the growth process by enabling the patient to become aware of unmet needs—unfinished business, or incomplete Gestalts—so that the patient can resolve or complete them and then begin to satisfy current needs. Gestalt therapy does not attempt to recover the past by analysis. The unfinished business of the past manifests itself in the present, particularly in nonverbal behavior and dreams. Therapy focuses, then, on behavior in the here and now, which leads to awareness of unresolved conflicts with others and within the self. With awareness, the patient is then able to resolve the conflicts or reintegrate alienated parts of the self.

The Gestalt approach offers a provocative theory. It overcomes the restriction of psychoanalysis to the individual and the intrapersonal and of Sullivan's interpersonal theory, with its neglect of the individual. It goes beyond those theories that concentrate on reason and the intellect to the neglect of affect and emotion and beyond those theories that may include both but neglect the body and motor activity. It does not, however, limit itself to the latter, as do some approaches, such as Reichian therapy and Lowen's bioenergetics. The concept of the whole organism in the environment incorporates all of these. The Gestalt concept of the self as the system of and the awareness of the contact boundary with the environment is a major addition to the psychoanalytic concept of the ego. The distinction between the actualization of the self rather than the actualization of a self-image is useful. The Gestalt concept of motivation is a unitary concept, almost identical with that of Combs and Snygg[88] and of Rogers.[89] Its recognition that needs emerge as they take priority in the process of self-actualization overcomes the problem posed by Maslow's hierarchy[90] in the same way as that proposed by me.[91] Like the client-centered approach, Gestalt therapy is phenomenological in its orientation. It recognizes that the individual creates a subjective (and effectively real) world according to interests and needs. Internal, not external, reality is the only reality that matters.

A further similarity to the client-centered approach is the parallel between organismic self-regulation and Rogers's concept of the organism as a whole reacting to the phenomenal field.[92] There is also a parallel with Rogers's concept of the fully functioning person as one who is open to all experiences, able to symbolize those experiences in awareness, and able to experience himself or herself as the locus of evaluation, with the valuing process being organismically based rather than environmentally based. Perls's concept of introjection of values (the topdog of the ego) is similar to Rogers's concept of incongruence as a result of the change in the locus of evaluation from the self in infancy to outside the self with the imposition by others (parents) of conditions of worth. Finally, there appears to be a close similarity between client-centered therapy and Gestalt therapy in their goals: awareness in the client leading to the process of self-actualization.

A minor theoretical difficulty involves the concept of homeostasis. This is essentially a physiological concept, which was accepted for a time by many psychologists but is now seldom referred to. It does not allow for change, growth, or development. "The principle of homeostasis represents conservation but not construction."[93] Allport calls it "a stay-put conception. It is static, unprogressive, allowing inadequately for either change or growth. The picture is one of a semiclosed system, not a system fully open to the world, capable of expanding and becoming more than it is." A person, Allport states, "is not a homeostatic creature. He does not seek equilibrium within himself and with the environment."[94] This difficulty with the concept of homeostasis is not important, however, since the concept is not essential for Perls's, or Gestalt, theory. It is not necessary for the concept of wholes; the concept of growth and self-actualization; the process of Gestalt formation, closure, and destruction; or the existence of opposites, or polarities.

Thus the theory is appealing; there is little in it that one can reject or greatly disagree with. Questions that arise have to do with the application of the theory: Are the methods and techniques of Gestalt therapy necessary derivations from the theory, and are they the necessary and the most effective and efficient methods for achieving the goals of Gestalt therapy without undesirable side effects? There is considerable doubt that this is the case.

Much of the problem inheres in the fact that there is no systematic discussion of Gestalt therapy, particularly as it derives from theory. In the absence of systematic discussion and of complete taped, filmed, or printed case presentations, a person must depend on description of methods and on excerpts and examples. Much of this material derives from workshops conducted by Perls. However, as the Polsters note: "When the master works, it is hard to discriminate between what is his *style* and what is the theory which supports his style."[95] It becomes difficult, if not impossible, to separate the method from the man, the essence from the style. Perls was, as he admitted, a showman. In his autobiographical book, he writes, "I feel best when I can be a prima donna and can show off my skill of getting rapidly in touch with the essence of a person and his plight."[96] Perls was superbly egotistical: "I believe I am the best therapist for any type of neurosis in the States, maybe in the world. How is that for megalomania. The fact is that I am wishing and willing to put my work to any research test."[97] Unfortunately, there is little more than testimonials to support his claim. The brief demonstrations are often impressive. They, as well as brief examples given by others, sometimes seem little short of miraculous, but there is no validating evidence of the value or any lasting effects of the high emotional experience or insights felt by the subjects. Those who knew Perls and saw him operate acknowledge that he was effective. Kempler, for example, writes that "his skill consisted of a remarkable ability to perceive and influence behavior. His own behavior was provocative, evocative, and inspiring. To meet him and come away feeling more complete in oneself was not at all unusual."[98] Yet Perls himself apparently had some doubts about his effectiveness. Immediately following the statement about his effectiveness as a therapist, he says, "At the same time I have to admit that I cannot cure anybody, that those so-called miracle cures are spectacular but don't mean much from the existential point of view."[99]

Shepherd cautions against assuming that Gestalt therapy offers "instant cure" on the basis of the sometimes dramatic effects observed in the short time of the demonstrations.[100]

It is also not clear what the source is of the effects that are achieved. The combination of Perls's personality, reputation, self-assurance, and techniques, together with the attitudes and expectations of his subjects, or "patients," as he called them, makes for a powerful placebo effect. Kempler, who knew Perls, writes,

> "In no way could Perls' behavior be called 'I' [in the I and Thou context]. He was the puppeteer, the manipulator, the director, and that was how it had to be. Any remark inviting Perls to look at his own behavior met with the invitation for the subject to look at *his* own motives in making the suggestion. There is no doubt that Perls did his job well but there was always something missing. And it was the personal Perls."[101]

It must also be remembered that the "patients" with whom he worked in his demonstrations were often professional people. They represent perhaps the kind of persons for whom Gestalt therapy is claimed to be most effective: "overly socialized, restrained, constricted individuals—often described as neurotic, phobic, perfectionistic, ineffective, depressed, etc.—whose functioning is limited or inconsistent, primarily due to their internal restrictions, and whose enjoyment is minimal";[102] in other words, essentially "normal" but inhibited, intellectually controlled individuals.

In many instances, results seem to be provoked or created by the therapist—in part by suggestion—rather than produced spontaneously by the patient. There is a sense of artificiality, of a forced nature, of patients attempting to divine what Perls wanted and then complying. Perls sometimes does not appear to be listening to the patient but to be waiting for the patient or maneuvering the patient into a split so that an empty-chair dialogue can be set up. This tends to give an aura of technique to the performance. Perls eschewed "gimmicks" and games, yet his demonstrations come dangerously close to these. In his review of the collection of papers published under the title *Gestalt Therapy Now,* Stone notes that "the most unappealing aspect of Perls' therapy is that he and his followers sometimes seem to be playing games on people rather than with them."[103] While I would not go as far as that, it does appear in many cases that the therapist is playing games—often a guessing game—with the patient.

In the absence of a clear, systematic statement of therapeutic procedure, together with a tendency to imitate the master, emphasis on techniques is to be expected. Perls was justified in his concern about the trend toward techniques without adequate grounding in theory. It is the Gestalt techniques that have spread, picked up by those with no particular theoretical orientation or added to another theoretical orientation, especially Berne's transactional analysis. Kempler notes that "the greatest hazard to the movement is the gimmick therapist, the tactician. . . . [M]any disciples, eager to learn and clever with mental gymnastics, became enamored of the tactics, learn to confront people by using the tactics initiated by Perls and consider themselves Gestalt therapists."[104]

There would appear to be some inconsistency between theory and practice. The theory emphasizes an existential encounter between equals and the responsibility of patients to make their own interpretations and achieve their own insights. Patients should be responsible, independent, and take the initiative; the therapist should not provide interpretations, advice, or support. Yet, the therapist in practice does function as an expert and conveys to patients that he or she is an expert. The therapist directs the patients' attention, verbalizations, and dramatic activities. The patients follow the directions of the therapist. The very use of the word *patients* indicates an attitude of the therapist. The net result is that patients view the therapist as an expert and are susceptible to suggestions from the therapist. Perls recognizes that the therapist's role of frustrator and asker of questions makes her or him a power figure rather than simply another human being. "Admittedly it is not easy," he writes, "to find the way through this inconsistency, but once the therapist has resolved the psychotherapeutic paradox of working with *support* and *frustration* both, his procedures will fall correctly into place."[105] It is doubtful if the therapist ever does resolve this paradox.

Unlike the developers of some of the other theories included in this book, Perls makes no broad claims for the success of Gestalt therapy. To the question "Where is your proof?" Perls replied in 1951: "Our standard answer will be that we present nothing that you cannot *verify for yourself in terms of your own behavior,* but if your psychological make-up is that of an experimentalist . . . , this will not satisfy you and you will clamor for 'objective evidence' of a verbal sort, *prior* to trying out a single non-verbal step of the procedure."[106] Such evidence does not yet exist. It is puzzling that there is little, if any, definitive research involving such a widely used method of therapy.

The demonstrations have in them the elements of the fallacy of personal validation.[107] In one of Perls's seminars, one of the participants raised this question:

Dr. Perls, will you—as you've been formulating and experiencing what has come out as Gestalt Therapy, I want to be reassured. I want to hear you say it, it seems like a process of discovery. Yet I think that people can arrange themselves to fit the expectations of the therapist, like, I sit here and watch person after person have a polarity, a conflict of forces, and I think I can do it too. But I don't know how spontaneous it would be, although I think I would feel spontaneous. You've experienced people over a long time; are we fitting you or have you discovered us?

To which Perls replied, "I don't know."[108]

REFERENCES

1. Perls, F. S. *Ego, hunger and aggression: The beginning of Gestalt therapy.* New York: Random House, 1947, 1969. (Paperback published by Orbit Graphic Arts, 1966)
2. Perls, F. S., Hefferline, R. F., & Goodman, P. *Gestalt therapy: Excitement and growth in personality.* New York: Julian Press, 1951. (Paperback published by Dell, 1965)
3. Perls, F. S. *Gestalt therapy verbatim.* Lafayette, Calif.: Real People Press, 1969.
4. Perls, F. S. *In and out of the garbage pail.* Lafayette, Calif.: Real People Press, 1969.
5. Perls, F. S. *The Gestalt approach and eyewitness to therapy.* Palo Alto, Calif.: Science and Behavior Books, 1973.
6. Baumgardner, P., & Perls, F. S. *Legacy from Fritz. Book One: Gifts from Lake Cowichan; Book Two: Legacy from Fritz.* Palo Alto, Calif.: Science and Behavior Books, 1975.
7. Fagan, J., & Shepherd, I. L. (Eds.). *Gestalt therapy now.* Palo Alto, Calif.: Science and Behavior Books, 1970. (Republished in two volumes, *What is Gestalt therapy?* and *Life techniques in Gestalt therapy.* New York: Harper & Row, 1971); Stephenson, F. D. (Ed.). *Gestalt therapy primer: Introductory readings in Gestalt therapy.* Springfield, Ill.: Thomas, 1975; Smith, W. L. (Ed.). *The growing edge of Gestalt therapy.* New York: Brunner/Mazel, 1976; Hatcher, C., & Himmelstein, P. (Eds.). *The handbook of Gestalt therapy.* New York: Aronson, 1976. Other books include Latner, J. *The Gestalt therapy book.* New York: Julian Press, 1973; Simkin, J. S. *Gestalt therapy mini-lectures.* New York: Brunner/Mazel, 1974; Zinker, J. *Creative process in Gestalt therapy.* New York: Brunner/Mazel, 1977. An issue of the journal *The Counseling Psychologist* [1974, *4* (4)] was devoted to Gestalt therapy.
8. Perls, *In and out of the garbage pail,* n. p.
9. Perls, *Ego, hunger and aggression,* p. 27.
10. Perls, *The Gestalt approach and eyewitness to therapy,* pp. 13, 14.
11. Perls, *Ego, hunger and aggression,* p. 15.
12. Ibid., p. 18.
13. Perls, F. S. Theory and technique of personality integration. *American Journal of Psychotherapy,* 1948, *2,* 565–586.
14. Perls, *The Gestalt approach and eyewitness to therapy,* p. 8.
15. Perls, *Gestalt therapy verbatim,* p. 31.
16. Perls, *Ego, hunger and aggression,* p. 114.
17. Ibid., pp. 116, 117.
18. Ibid., pp. 38, 40.
19. Perls, *The Gestalt approach and eyewitness to therapy,* p. 16.
20. Perls, *Ego, hunger and aggression,* p. 36.
21. Ibid., p. 143.
22. Ibid., p. 146.
23. Perls, *Gestalt therapy verbatim,* p. 15.

24. Perls, Hefferline, & Goodman, *Gestalt therapy,* pp. viii–ix.
25. Perls, *Gestalt therapy verbatim,* p. 32.
26. Ibid., p. 30.
27. Perls, *The Gestalt approach and eyewitness to therapy,* p. 19.
28. Perls, *Ego, hunger and aggression,* pp. 114–115.
29. Ibid., p. 129.
30. Ibid., p. 157.
31. Ibid., pp. 119–120.
32. Perls, *The Gestalt approach and eyewitness to therapy,* pp. 40–41.
33. Perls, Hefferline, & Goodman, *Gestalt therapy,* pp. 211, 212.
34. Perls, *Gestalt therapy verbatim,* p. 28.
35. Perls, *Ego, hunger and aggression,* p. 61.
36. Perls, *The Gestalt approach and eyewitness to therapy,* p. 27.
37. Perls, *Ego, hunger and aggression,* p. 77.
38. Perls, Hefferline, & Goodman, *Gestalt therapy,* p. 118.
39. Ibid., pp. 118–123.
40. Perls, *Gestalt therapy verbatim,* p. 48.
41. Perls, *The Gestalt approach and eyewitness to therapy,* p. 28.
42. Perls, Hefferline, & Goodman, *Gestalt therapy,* p. 432.
43. Perls, *Ego, hunger and aggression,* p. 133.
44. Ibid., p. 113.
45. Ibid., p. 116.
46. Ibid., p. 157.
47. Ibid., p. 170.
48. Perls, *The Gestalt approach and eyewitness to therapy,* p. 26.
49. Perls, *Ego, hunger and aggression,* p. 69.
50. Ibid., p. 179.
51. Ibid., p. 136.
52. Perls, *Gestalt therapy verbatim,* p. 38.
53. Ibid., p. 16.
54. Ibid., p. 46.
55. Ibid., p. 17.
56. Ibid., p. 51.
57. Ibid., p. 41.
58. Perls, *The Gestalt approach and eyewitness to therapy,* p. 54.
59. Enright, J. B. An introduction to Gestalt therapy. In Stephenson (Ed.), *Gestalt Therapy primer,* pp. 13–33.
60. Latner, *The Gestalt therapy book,* p. 38.
61. Glasgow, R. Paul Goodman: A conversation. *Psychology Today,* November 1971, pp. 62–96.
62. Perls, *Gestalt therapy verbatim,* p. 37.
63. Ibid., p. 39.
64. Ibid., p. 53.
65. Perls, *The Gestalt approach and eyewitness to therapy,* p. 62.
66. Perls, *Gestalt therapy verbatim,* pp. 53–54.
67. Perls, *The Gestalt approach and eyewitness to therapy,* p. 78.
68. Ibid., p. 79.
69. Ibid.
70. Perls, F. S. Four lectures. In Fagan & Shepherd (Eds.), *Gestalt theory now,* p. 29.
71. Ibid., p. 27.

72. Perls, *Gestalt therapy verbatim,* p. 70.

73. Ibid., p. 147.

74. Ibid., p. 120.

75. Perls, *The Gestalt approach and eyewitness to therapy,* p. 82.

76. Perls, *Gestalt therapy verbatim,* pp. 37, 38.

77. Perls, Hefferline, & Goodman, *Gestalt therapy,* pp. 112–113.

78. Perls, *Ego, hunger and aggression,* p. 74.

79. Ibid., pp. 178, 179.

80. Perls, Hefferline, & Goodman, *Gestalt therapy,* p. 141.

81. Ibid., p. 166.

82. Ibid., p. 191.

83. Ibid., p. 194.

84. Ibid., p. 216.

85. Levitsky, A., & Perls, F. S. The rules and games of Gestalt therapy. In Fagan & Shepherd (Eds.), *Gestalt therapy now,* pp. 140–149.

86. Perls, F. S. *Gestalt therapy verbatim,* pp. 81–82. Perls is one of the therapists in the film *Three approaches to psychotherapy* (Shostrom, E. [Ed.]. Santa Anna, Calif.: Psychological Films, 1965).

87. Ibid., pp. 264–272.

88. Combs, A. W., & Snygg, D. *Individual behavior: A perceptual approach to behavior* (Rev. ed.). New York: Harper & Row, 1959.

89. Rogers, C. R. *Client-centered therapy.* Boston: Houghton Mifflin, 1951.

90. Maslow, A. H. *Motivation and personality* (2nd ed.). New York: Harper and Row, 1969.

91. Patterson, C. H. A unitary theory of motivation and its counseling implications. *Journal of Individual Psychology,* 1964, *20,* 17–31.

92. Rogers, *Client-centered therapy,* pp. 484–492.

93. Kluckhohn, C., & Murray, H. A. *Personality: In nature, society and culture.* New York: Knopf, 1950. P. 16.

94. Allport, G. W. *Pattern and growth in personality.* New York: Holt, Rinehart and Winston, 1961. Pp. 89, 558; see also Allport, G. W. The open system in personality. In Allport, G. W. *Personality and social encounter: Selected essays.* Boston: Beacon Press, 1960.

95. Polster, E., & Polster, M. *Gestalt therapy integrated: Contours of theory and practice.* New York: Brunner/Mazel, 1973. P. 286.

96. Perls, *In and out of the garbage pail,* n.p.

97. Ibid.

98. Kempler, W. Gestalt therapy. In R. Corsini (Ed.), *Current psychotherapies.* Itasca, Ill.: Peacock, 1973. Pp. 251–286.

99. Perls, *In and out of the garbage pail,* n.p.

100. Shepherd, I. L. Limitations and cautions in the Gestalt approach. In Fagan & Shepherd (Eds.), *Gestalt therapy now,* p. 236.

101. Kempler, Gestalt therapy.

102. Shepherd, Limitations and cautions in the Gestalt approach, p. 235.

103. Stone, A. A. Play: The "now" therapy. (Review of *Gestalt therapy now,* edited by J. Fagan & I. L. Shepherd). *Psychiatry and Social Science Review,* 1971, 5, 12–16.

104. Kempler, Gestalt therapy.

105. Perls, *The Gestalt approach and eyewitness to therapy,* pp. 76–77.

106. Perls, Hefferline, & Goodman, *Gestalt therapy,* p. 7.

107. Forer, B. R. The fallacy of personal validation: A classroom demonstration of gullibility. *Journal of Abnormal Social Psychology,* 1949, *4,* 118–123.

108. Perls, *Gestalt therapy verbatim,* pp. 214–215.

chapter 14

Client-Centered Therapy: Rogers

The approach to counseling that was at first called nondirective but is now called client-centered is still best represented by the writing of its originator or first expositor, Carl Ransom Rogers (b. 1902). Rogers received his B.A. from the University of Wisconsin in 1924 and his M.A. and Ph.D. from Columbia University in 1928 and 1931, respectively. From 1928 to 1938, he was a psychologist at the Child Study Department of the Society for the Prevention of Cruelty to Children in Rochester, New York, and from 1931 on, he was the department's director. The department became the Rochester Guidance Center in 1939; Rogers remained as director for a year and then went to Ohio State University, where he was professor of clinical psychology from 1940 to 1945. During 1944 and 1945, he served as director of counseling services of the USO. In 1945, he became professor of psychology and executive secretary of the Counseling Center at the University of Chicago, leaving in 1957 to become professor of psychology and psychiatry at the University of Wisconsin. In 1962 to 1963, he was a fellow at the Center for Advanced Study in the Behavioral Sciences at Stanford, and in 1963, he joined the staff of the Western Behavioral Sciences Institute (WBSI) at La Jolla, California, as a resident fellow. In 1968, he joined with others in forming the Center for Studies of the Person in La Jolla, where he is a resident fellow. He is a Diplomate in clinical psychology of the American Board of Professional Psychology.

Rogers is the author of *The Clinical Treatment of the Problem Child* (1939), *Counseling and Psychotherapy* (1942), *Client-Centered Therapy* (1951), *On Becoming a Person* (1961), and, with Stevens, *Person to Person* (1967). He has edited, with Dymond, *Psychotherapy and Personality Change* (1954); with Gendlin, Kiesler, and Traux, *The Therapeutic Relationship and Its Impact* (1967); and, with Coulson, *Man and the Science of Man* (1968).

During the period at WBSI, Rogers became involved in the group movement and extended his theory to the basic encounter group: in 1970, he published *Carl Rogers on Encounter Groups.* He also became interested in the application of his theory to education and wrote *Freedom to Learn* (1969). *Becoming Partners: Marriage and Its Alternatives* (1972) was the result of his interest in the marriage relationship. *Carl Rogers on Personal Power* (1977) extended his theory to interpersonal relationships in general. At the 1977 Convention of the American Psychological Association in San Francisco, Rogers's seventy-fifth year was recognized with three programs of special papers. His work had been recognized earlier by the American Psychological Association when in 1956, he had been the recipient of one of the first three Distinguished Scientific Awards, and in 1972, he had received its first Distinguished Professional Contribution Award.

BACKGROUND AND DEVELOPMENT

During the period spent in Rochester, Rogers became dissatisfied with the commonly accepted approaches to psychotherapy and began to develop an approach of his own. The traditional, highly diagnostically oriented, probing, and interpretive methods did not appear to be very effective. His own experience in practicing therapy led to a recognition of an orderliness in the experience. The views of Rank, brought into the Rochester group by individuals whose training was influenced by them, had an impact on the development of Rogers's therapeutic methods.

The emerging principles of therapy were subjected to critically minded graduate students in clinical psychology at Ohio State University, and it was recognized that rather than being a distillation of generally accepted principles, as Rogers at first considered them, they constituted a new development. *Counseling and Psychotherapy*[1] represented the attempt to present the new approach.

The stimulation of teaching and research at Ohio State and the University of Chicago and the continuing experience in practicing psychotherapy resulted in the development of Rogers's approach, in theoretical formulations of the nature of therapy, and in a tentative theory of personality. In 1951, in *Client-centered Therapy,*[2] a current view was presented, together with its application in play therapy (by Elaine Dorfman), group-centered psychotherapy (by Nicholas Hobbs), group-centered leadership and administration (by Thomas Gordon), and student-centered teaching. Also included was a theory of personality and behavior. The point of view continued to be developed in many papers and articles, some of which were brought together in *On Becoming a Person.*[3] The theory of personality was revised and expanded and was presented in 1959 in *Psychology: A Study of Science.*[4]

Certain basic convictions and attitudes underlie the theoretical formulations:[5]

1. Research and theory are directed toward the satisfaction of the need to order significant experience.
2. Science is acute observation and careful and creative thinking on the basis of such observation, not simply laboratory research involving instruments and computing machines.
3. Science begins with gross observations, crude measurements, and speculative

hypotheses, and progresses toward more refined hypotheses and measurements.

4. The language of independent-intervening-dependent variables, while applicable to advanced stages of scientific endeavor, is not adapted to the beginning and developing stages.
5. In the early stages of investigation and theory construction, inductive rather than hypothetico-deductive methods are more appropriate.
6. Every theory has a greater or a lesser degree of error; a theory only approaches the truth, and it requires constant change and modification.
7. Truth is unitary, so that "any theory, derived from almost any segment of experience, if it were complete and completely accurate, could be extended indefinitely to provide meaning for other very remote areas of experience."[6] However, any error in a theory, if projected in a remote area, may lead to completely false inferences.
8. Although there may be such a thing as objective truth, people live in their own personal and subjective world. "Thus there is no such thing as Scientific Knowledge, there are only individual perceptions of what appears to each person to be such knowledge."[7]

PHILOSOPHY AND CONCEPTS

The Nature of Human Beings and of the Individual

The common concept of human beings is that they are by nature irrational, unsocialized, and destructive of themselves and others. The client-centered point of view sees human beings, on the contrary, as basically rational, socialized, forward moving, and realistic.[8] This is a point of view developing out of experience in therapy rather than preceding it. Antisocial emotions—jealousy, hostility, and so on—exist and are evident in therapy, but they are not spontaneous impulses that must be controlled. Rather, they are reactions to the frustration of more basic impulses—love, belonging, security, and so on. Human beings are basically cooperative, constructive, and trustworthy, and when they are free from defensiveness, their reactions are positive, forward-moving, and constructive. There is, then, no need to be concerned about controlling their aggressive, antisocial impulses; they will become self-regulatory, balancing their needs against one another. The need for affection or companionship, for example, will balance any aggressive reaction or extreme need for sex or for other needs that would interfere with the satisfactions of other persons.

As individuals, human beings possess the capacity to experience, in awareness, the factors in their psychological maladjustment and have the capacity and the tendency to move away from a state of maladjustment toward a state of psychological adjustment. These capacities and this tendency will be released in a relationship that has the characteristics of a therapeutic relationship. The tendency toward adjustment is the tendency toward self-actualization. Psychotherapy is thus the liberating of an already existing capacity in the individual. Philosophically, the individual "has the capacity to guide, regulate, and control himself, providing only that certain definable conditions exist. Only in the absence of these conditions, and not in any basic sense, is it necessary to provide external control and regulation of the individual."[9] When the individual is provided with reasonable conditions for growth, the individual will develop his or her potential constructively, as a seed grows and becomes its potential.

The Philosophical Orientation of the Counselor

The basic philosophy of the counselor is represented by an attitude of respect for the individual, for the individual's capacity and right to self-direction, and for the worth and significance of each individual.[10] The orientation follows from these concepts of the nature of humanity.

Definitions of Constructs

The theory of therapy and personality makes use of a number of concepts, or constructs. These are briefly defined prior to their use in the theory.[11]

> *Actualizing Tendency* "the inherent tendency of the organism to develop all its capacities in ways which serve to maintain or enhance the organism."
>
> *Tendency Toward Self-actualization* the expression of the general tendency toward actualization in "that portion of experience of the organism which is symbolized in the self."
>
> *Experience (Noun)* all that is going on in the organism at a given time, whether in awareness or potentially available to awareness, of a psychological nature; the "experiential field" or the "phenomenal field" of Combs and Snygg.
>
> *Experience (Verb)* the receiving "in the organism of the impact of sensory or physiological events which are happening at the moment."
>
> *Feeling, experiencing a feeling* "an emotionally tinged experience, together with its personal meaning."
>
> *Awareness, Symbolization, Consciousness* the representation of some portion of experience.
>
> *Availability to Awareness* the capability of being symbolized freely, without denial or distortion.
>
> *Accurate Symbolization* the potential correspondence of symbolization in awareness to the results of the testing of the transitional hypothesis that it represents.
>
> *Perceive, Perception* "a hypothesis or prognosis for action which comes into awareness when stimuli impinge on the organism." Perception and awareness are synonymous, the former emphasizing the stimulus in the process. Perceiving is becoming aware of stimuli.
>
> *Subceive, Subception* "discrimination without awareness."
>
> *Self-experience* "any event or entity in the phenomenal field discriminated by the individual as 'self,' 'me,' 'I,' or related thereto."
>
> *Self, Concept of Self, Self-structure* "the organized, consistent conceptual gestalt composed of perceptions of the characteristics of the 'I' or 'me' and

the perceptions of the relationships of the 'I' or 'me' to others and the various aspects of life, together with the values attached to these perceptions."

Ideal Self   "the self-concept which the individual would most like to possess."

Incongruence Between Self and Experience   a discrepancy between the perceived self and actual experience, accompanied by tension, internal confusion, and discordant or incomprehensible (that is, neurotic) behavior resulting from conflict between the actualizing and the self-actualizing tendencies.

Vulnerability   "the state of incongruence between self and experience," with emphasis on "the potentialities of this state for creating psychological disorganization."

Anxiety   "phenomenologically a state of uneasiness or tension whose cause is unknown. From an external frame of reference, anxiety is a state in which the incongruence between the concept of the self and the total experience of the individual is approaching symbolization in awareness."

Threat   "the state which exists when an experience is perceived or anticipated (subceived) as incongruent with the structure of the self"; an external view of what is phenomenologically anxiety.

Psychological Maladjustment   the state that exists when the organism denies or distorts significant experience in awareness, resulting in incongruence between the self and experience; incongruence viewed from a social standpoint.

Defense, Defensiveness   "the behavioral response of the organism to threat, the goal of which is the maintenance of the current structure of the self."

Distortion in Awareness, Denial of Awareness   Denial or distortion of experience that is inconsistent with the self-concept, by means of which the goal of defense is achieved; the mechanisms of defense.

Intensionality   the characteristics of the behavior of the individual who is in a defensive state—rigidity, overgeneralization, abstraction from reality, absolute and unconditional evaluation of experience, and so on.

Congruence, Congruence of Self and Experience   the state in which self-experiences are accurately symbolized in the self-concept—integrated whole, genuine.

Openness to Experience   absence of threat; the opposite of defensiveness.

Psychological Adjustment   complete congruence; complete openness to experience.

Extensionality   perception that is differentiated, dominated by facts rather than concepts, with awareness both of the space-time anchorage of facts and of different levels of abstraction.

Mature, Maturity   an individual is mature "when he perceives realistically and in an extensional manner, is not defensive, accepts the responsibility of being different from others, accepts the responsibility for his own behavior, evaluates experience in terms of the evidence coming from his own senses, changes his evaluation of experience only on the basis of new experience, accepts others as unique individuals different from himself, and prizes others"; the behavior exhibited by an individual who is congruent.

Contact   the minimal essential of a relationship, in which each of two individuals "makes a perceived or subceived difference in the experiential field of the other."

Positive Regard   perception of some self-experience of another that makes a positive difference in one's experiential field, resulting in a feeling of warmth, liking, respect, sympathy, and acceptance toward the other.

Need for Positive Regard   a secondary or learned need for love, affection, and so on.

Unconditional Positive Regard   perception of the self-experiences of another without discrimination as to greater or lesser worthiness; prizing, acceptance.

Regard Complex   "all those self-experiences, together with their interrelationships, which the individual discriminates as being related to the positive regard of a particular social other."

Positive Self-regard   "a positive attitude toward the self which is no longer directly dependent on the attitudes of others."

Need for Self-regard   a secondary or learned need for positive self-regard.

Unconditional self-regard   perception of the self "in such a way that no self-experience can be discriminated as more or less worthy of positive regard than any other."

Conditions of Worth   the valuing of an experience by an individual positively or negatively "solely because of . . . conditions of worth which he has taken over from others, not because the experience enhances or fails to enhance his organism."

Locus of Evaluation   the source of evidence as to values—internal or external.

Organismic Valuing Process   "an on-going process in which values are never fixed or rigid, but experiences are being accurately symbolized and continually and freshly valued in terms of the satisfactions organismically experienced"; the actualizing tendency is the criterion.

Internal Frame of Reference   "all of the realm of experience which is available to the awareness of the individual at a given moment"; the subjective world of the individual.

Empathy   the state of perceiving "the internal frame of reference of another with accuracy, and with the emotional components and meanings which pertain thereto, as if one were the other person, but without ever losing the 'as if' condition."

External Frame of Reference   perceiving "solely from one's own subjective frame of reference without empathizing with the observed person or object."

A Theory of Personality

Characteristics of the Human Infant

The infant perceives experience as reality; for the infant, experience is reality. The infant is endowed with an inherent tendency toward actualizing his or her organism. The infant's behavior is goal directed, or directed toward satisfying the need for actualization in interaction with his or her perceived reality. In this interaction, the infant behaves as an organized whole. Experiences are valued positively or negatively in an organismic valuing process in terms of whether they do or do not maintain this actualizing tendency. The infant is adient toward (approaches) positively valued experiences and is abient toward (avoids) negatively valued experiences.

The Development of the Self

As a result of the tendency toward differentiation (which is an aspect of the actualizing tendency), part of the individual's experience becomes symbolized in awareness as self-experience. Through interaction with significant others in the environment, this self-experience leads to a concept of self, a perceptual object in the experiential field.

The Need for Positive Regard

With awareness of the self, the need for positive regard from others develops. The satisfaction of this need is dependent on inferences regarding the experiential fields of others. Satisfaction is reciprocal in human beings in that the individual's positive regard is satisfied when the individual perceives himself or herself as satisfying another's need. The positive regard of a significant social other can be more powerful than the individual's organismic valuing process.

The Development of the Need for Self-Regard

A need for self-regard develops from the association of the satisfaction or frustration of the need for positive regard with self-experiences. The experience or loss of positive regard thus becomes independent of transactions with any social other.

The Development of Conditions of Worth

Self-regard becomes selective as significant others distinguish the self-experiences of the individual as more or less worthy of positive regard. The evaluation of a self-experience as more or less worthy of self-regard constitutes a condition of worth. The experience of only unconditional positive regard would eliminate the development of conditions of worth and lead to unconditional self-regard, to congruence of the needs for positive regard and self-regard with organismic evaluation, and to the maintenance of psychological adjustment.

The Development of Incongruence Between Self and Experience

The need for self-regard leads to selective perception of experiences in terms of conditions of worth, so that experiences in accord with the individual's conditions of worth are perceived and symbolized accurately in awareness, but experiences contrary to the conditions of worth are perceived selectively or distortedly or are denied to awareness. This presence of self-experiences that are not organized into the self-structure in accurately symbolized form results in the existence of some degree of incongruence between the self and experience, in vulnerability, and in psychological maladjustment.

The Development of Discrepancies in Behavior

Incongruence between the self and experience leads to incongruence in behavior, so that some behaviors are consistent with the self-concept and are accurately symbolized in awareness, while other behaviors actualize those experiences of the organism that are not assimilated into the self-structure and have thus not been recognized or have been distorted to make them congruent with the self.

The Experience of Threat and Process of Defense

An experience that is incongruent with the self-structure is subceived as threatening. If this experience were accurately symbolized in awareness, it would introduce inconsistency, and a state of anxiety would exist. The process of defense prevents this because it keeps the total perception of the experience consistent with the self-structure and the conditions of worth. The consequences of defense are rigidity in perception, an inaccurate perception of reality, and intensionality.

The Process of Breakdown and Disorganization

In a situation in which a significant experience demonstrates the presence of a large or significant incongruence between the self and experience, the process of defense is unable to operate successfully. Anxiety is then experienced to a degree depending on the extent of the self-structure that is threatened. The experience becomes accurately symbolized in awareness, and a state of disorganization results. The organism behaves at times in ways consistent with the experiences that have been distorted or denied and at times in ways consistent with the concept of the self, with its distorted or denied experiences.

The Process of Reintegration

For an increase in congruence to occur, there must be a decrease in conditions of worth and an increase in unconditional self-regard. The communicated unconditional positive regard of a significant other is one way of meeting these conditions. In order to be communicated, unconditional positive regard must exist in a context of empathic understanding. When this regard is perceived by the individual, it leads to the weakening or dissolving of existing conditions of worth. The individual's own unconditional positive regard is then increased, while threat is reduced and congruence develops. The individual is then less susceptible to perceiving threat, less defensive, more congruent, has increased self-regard and positive regard for others, and is more psychologically adjusted. The organismic valuing process becomes increasingly the basis of regulating behavior, and the individual becomes more nearly fully functioning. The occurrence of these conditions and results constitutes psychotherapy.

A Theory of Interpersonal Relationships[12]

The Conditions of a Deteriorating Relationship

"A person, Y, is willing to be in contact with person X, and to receive communications from him. Person X desires (at least to a minimal degree) to communicate to and be in contact with Y. Marked incongruence exists in X among the following three elements: his experience of the subject of communication with Y; the symbolization of this experience in his awareness, in its relation to his self-concept; his conscious communicated expression (verbal and/or motor) of this experience."

The Process of a Deteriorating Relationship

Under the above conditions, the following process occurs:

"The communication of X to Y is contradictory and/or ambiguous, containing expressive behaviors which are consistent with X's awareness of the experience to be communicated [and] expressive behaviors which are consistent with those aspects of the experience not accurately symbolized in X's awareness. Y experiences these contradictions and ambiguities. He tends to be aware only of X's conscious communication. Hence this experience of X's communication tends also to be incongruent with his awareness of same [and] . . . his response tends also to be contradictory and/or ambiguous. . . . Since X is vulnerable, he tends to perceive Y's responses as potentially threatening."

Thus he tends to perceive Y's responses in a distorted way, congruent with his own self-structure. He also perceives Y's internal frame of reference inaccurately and therefore is not empathic. As a result, he cannot and does not experience unconditional positive regard for Y. Y thus experiences the receipt of, at most, a selective positive regard and an absence of understanding and empathy. He is thus less free to express his feelings, to be extensional, to express incongruence between self and experience, and to reorganize his self-concept. As a result, X is, in turn, even less likely to empathize and more likely to have defensive reactions. "Those aspects of experience which are not accurately symbolized by X in his awareness tend, by defensive distortion of perception, to be perceived in Y": Y then tends to be threatened and to show defensive behaviors.

The Outcome of a Deteriorating Relationship

The process of deterioration leads to increased defensiveness on the part of X and Y. Communication becomes increasingly superficial. Perceptions of self and others become organized more tightly. Thus the incongruence of self and experience remains in status quo or is increased. Psychological maladjustment is to some degree facilitated in both X and Y.

The Conditions of an Improving Relationship

"A person, Y', is willing to be in contact with Person X', and to receive communication from him. Person X' desires to communicate to and be in contact with Y'. A high

evolution of the species. These directions include, according to Rogers, being real rather than presenting a façade, valuing one's self and self-direction, valuing being a process rather than having fixed goals, valuing sensitivity to and acceptance of others, valuing deep relationships with others, and, perhaps most important, valuing an openness to all one's inner and outer experiences, including the reactions and feelings of others. In other words, the older values of sincerity, independence, self-direction, self-knowledge, social responsivity, social responsibility, and loving interpersonal relationships appear to have a universality arising out of the nature of human beings as they become, under conditions that have been found to be effective in psychotherapy, fully functioning persons. The characteristics of the fully functioning or self-actualizing person include the conditions for the development of such persons.

Several implications of this concept are of interest:

1. *The Fully Functioning Person Is a Creative Person*   Such a person could be, notes Rogers, one of Maslow's "self-actualizing people," one of whose characteristics is creativeness. His or her sensitive openness and existential living would foster creativeness through allowing awareness of relationships not observed by others. He or she is not a conformist and perhaps not always "adjusted" to the culture but is able to live constructively and satisfy basic needs. "Such a person would, I believe, be recognized by the student of evolution as the type most likely to adapt and survive under changing environmental conditions. He would be able creatively to make sound adjustments to new as well as old conditions. He would be a fit vanguard of human evolution."[17]

2. *The Fully Functioning Person Is Constructive and Trustworthy*   The basic nature of individuals is good, individually and socially, when they are functioning freely. When we are able to free individuals from defensiveness, so that they are open to the wide range of their own needs, as well as the range of environmental and social demands, their reactions may be trusted to be positive, forward-moving, and constructive. We do not need to ask who will socialize them, for one of the deepest needs that each person has is affiliation with and communication with others. When people are fully themselves, they cannot help but be realistically socialized. We do not need to ask who will control the individual's aggressive impulses, for when an individual is open to all of his or her impulses, the need to be liked by others and the tendency to give affection are as strong as impulses to strike out and seize for the self. The individual will be aggressive in situations in which aggression is realistically appropriate, but there will be no runaway need for aggression. When a person is open to all experience, then his or her total behavior in these and other areas is balanced, and realistic behavior is appropriate to the survival and enhancement of a highly social animal.

3. *The Fully Functioning Person's Behavior Is Dependable but Not Predictable*   Since the particular pattern of inner and outer stimuli at each moment is unique, fully functioning people are not able to predict their behavior in a new situation, but they appear dependable to themselves and are confident that their behavior is appropriate. On later analysis by another person, a scientist, for example, the fully functioning person's behavior will appear lawful; the scientist can postdict but not predict it. Science cannot collect and analyze all the necessary data, even with a computer, before the behavior has occurred. This suggests that the science of psychology, when it deals with the fully

functioning person, will be characterized by understanding (of the lawfulness of behavior that has occurred) rather than by prediction and control.

4. *The Fully Functioning Person Is Free and Not Determined*   Science has shown that we live in a world in which cause and effect operate. Behavior can be controlled by external, or environmental, conditions and events. Yet the individual can be free to choose how to act. Rogers reports his experiences with clients in therapy who in the process have made decisions and choices that have changed their behaviors and their lives. He says: "I would be at a loss to explain the positive change which can occur in psychotherapy if I had to omit the importance of the sense of the free and responsible choice on the part of my clients. I believe that this experience of freedom to choose is one of the deepest elements underlying change."[18]

This freedom is an inner freedom, an attitude or a realization that people have of an ability to think their own thoughts and to live their own lives, choosing what they want to be and being responsible for themselves. Such freedom is phenomenological rather than external. It is not a contradiction to the cause and effect apparent in the psychological universe but a complement to such a universe. "Freedom rightly understood is a fulfillment by the person of the ordered sequence of his life. The free man moves out voluntarily, freely, responsibly, to play his significant part in a world whose determined events move through him and through his spontaneous choice and will."[19] It exists in a different dimension from external cause and effect.

Individuals differ in the extent to which they are free from influence and control by others and external events. Rogers cites the findings of several studies in which subjects who yielded or conformed or were susceptible to control in psychological experiments differed from those who did not conform. They panicked under stress, showed feelings of inadequacy and personal inferiority, were lacking in openness and freedom in emotional processes and in spontaneity, and were emotionally restricted and inhibited. The nonconformists, on the contrary, were able to cope effectively with stress, were more self-contained and autonomous in their thinking, had a sense of competence and personal adequacy, and were more open, free, and spontaneous. Thus the sense of personal freedom and responsibility makes a difference in behavior.

The ideal fully functioning person does not exist. There are persons who can be observed moving toward this goal in therapy, in the best family and group relationships, and in good educational experiences.

THE THERAPY PROCESS

The counseling process is outlined in the theory of therapy discussed above. More detailed consideration of the process may be approached from two frames of reference: (1) the phenomenological frame of reference, or the client's frame of reference; and (2) the external frame of reference, or an observer's frame of reference.

The Process as Experienced by the Client

In Chapter 3 of *Client-Centered Therapy,*[20] there is a description of the therapeutic relationship as experienced by the client. A somewhat more recent description appears in Chapters 5 and 6 of *On Becoming a Person.*[21]

The client's perception of the process is important, since it is on his or her perception of the experience and of the counselor's personality, attitudes, and techniques that therapeutic change depends.

The Client's Experience of the Counselor and the Counseling Situation

The client's perceptions are initially influenced by what the client expects of the counselor and the counseling situation. These expectations vary and include feelings ranging from fear to eager anticipation, but an ambivalent, fearful feeling seems most characteristic. Progress is facilitated when both client and counselor perceive the relationship in the same way. Verbal structuring of the relationship by the counselor, which was earlier considered desirable, does not necessarily lead to a common perception of the relationship, however.

When the counselor is perceived favorably as helpful, it is as someone with warmth, interest, and understanding. At first, client-centered methods often appear frustrating to the client, but they are later perceived as leading to self-exploration and understanding. The therapy hour becomes a stable, accepting experience in an otherwise unstable life and is thus experienced as supportive, although the counselor is not supportive in the usual sense of the term.

How Therapy is Experienced by the Client

The experiencing of responsibility   The client soon discovers that he or she is responsible for himself or herself in the relationship, and this may lead to various feelings, including a sense of being alone, annoyance, or anger, and a growing sense and acceptance of responsibility.

The experiencing of exploration   As therapy develops, the client explores his or her attitudes and feelings. The client reacts with both fear and positive interest as inconsistencies and contradictions are discovered in the client's self. Honesty in facing this self develops in the nonthreatening counseling relationship. The verbal exploration that takes place in the interview is less than the unverbalized exploration that goes on during and outside the interviews.

The discovery of denied attitudes   As a result of exploration, attitudes that have been experienced but denied to awareness are discovered. Both positive and negative attitudes arise. Experiences inconsistent with the self-concept, formerly denied or distorted, become symbolized in awareness.

The experiencing of reorganizing the self   The bringing of denied experiences into awareness necessitates the reorganization of the self, which begins with a change in perception of and attitude toward the self. The client views himself or herself more positively, as a more adequate person; the client's acceptance of himself or herself increases. This changed perception of the self must begin before the client can become aware of and accept denied experiences. The permitting of more experiential data to enter awareness leads to a more realistic appraisal of the self, relationships, and the environment and to an acknowledgment of the basis of standards within himself or herself. The change in the self may be great or small, with more or less accompanying pain and confusion. More or less disorganization may precede the final organization, and the process may fluctuate up or down. The emotions that accompany the process, although fluctuating, appear to be mainly those of fearfulness, unhappiness, and depression; they are not consistent with actual progress, so that a deep insight may be followed by strong despair.

The process of reorganizing the self, of becoming oneself, or becoming a person, includes various aspects.[22] One may be termed "getting behind the mask." In the atmosphere of freedom of the counseling relationship, the client begins to drop false fronts, roles, or masks and tries to discover something more truly himself or herself. The client is able to explore the self and its experience, facing the contradictions that he or she discovers and the façades and fronts behind which he or she has been hiding. The client may discover that he or she seems to have no individual self but exists only in relation to the values and demands of others. There is, however, a compelling need to search for and become oneself.

A part of being one's real self is the experiencing of feelings to their limits, so that the person *is* his or her fear, anger, love, and so on. There is a

> free experiencing of the actual sensory and visceral reactions of the organism without too much of an attempt to relate these experiences to the self. This is usually accompanied by the conviction that this material does not belong to, and cannot be organized into, the self. The end point of the process is that the client discovers that he can *be* his experience with all of its variety and surface contradiction; that he can formulate himself out of his experience instead of trying to impose a formulation of self upon his experience, denying to awareness these elements which do not fit.[23]

In the experiencing of these elements of the self, a unit, harmony, or pattern emerges. All these experiences are a part of the potential self, which is being discovered.

The result of the reorganization of the self is not merely acceptance of the self, but also a liking of the self. It is not a bragging, self-assertive liking but a "quiet joy in being one's self, together with the apologetic attitude which, in our culture, one feels it is necessary to take toward such an experience."[24] It is a satisfying, enjoyable appreciation of oneself as a whole and functioning person.

The process of therapy is not the solving of problems; it is the experiencing of feelings, leading to the being of oneself. It "is a process whereby man becomes his organism—without self-deception, without distortion."[25] Rather than acting in terms of the expectations of others, a person acts in terms of his or her own experiences. It is the full awareness of these experiences, achieved in therapy, that makes it possible for the person to come to *be* (in awareness) what he or she *is* (in experience)—a complete and fully functioning human organism.

The experiencing of progress   Almost from the beginning, the client feels that progress is being made. This progress is felt even when confusion and depression are present. The facing and resolving of some issues and the reconstructing of a segment of personality represent progress and give the client confidence in continuing to explore himself or herself, even though the exploration continues to be upsetting.

it. So I mean, it doesn't . . . I knew that it was a good thing, see. And I think I clarified it within myself . . . what it has to do with this situation, I don't know. But I found out, no, I don't love, but I do *care* terribly.

TH: Um-hum. Um-hum. I see . . .

CL: It might be expressed better in saying I care terribly what happens. But the caring is a . . . takes form . . . its structure is in understanding and not wanting to be taken in, or to contribute to those things which I feel are false and . . . it seems to me that in . . . in loving, there's a kind of *final* factor. If you do that, you've sort of done *enough.* It's a . . .

TH: That's *it,* sort of.

CL: Yeah. It seems to me this other thing, this caring, which isn't a good term . . . I mean, probably we need something else to describe this kind of thing. To say it's an impersonal thing doesn't mean anything, because it isn't impersonal. I mean, I feel its very much a part of a whole. But it's something that somehow doesn't stop. . . . It seems to me you could have this feeling of loving humanity, loving people, and at the same time . . . go on contributing to the factors that make people neurotic, make them ill . . . where, what I feel is a resistance to those things.

TH: You care enough to want to understand and to want to avoid contributing to anything that would make for more neuroticism, or more of that aspect in human life.

CL: Yes. And it's . . . *(pause)* Yes, it's something along those lines. . . . Well, again I have to go back to how I feel about this other thing. It's . . . I'm not really called upon to give of myself in a . . . sort of on the auction block. There's nothing final. . . . It sometimes bothered me when I . . . I would have to say to myself, "I don't love humanity," and yet, I always knew that there was something positive. That I was probably right. And . . . I may be all off the beam now, but it seems to me that, that is somehow tied up in the . . . this feeling that I . . . I have now, into how the therapeutic value can carry through. Now, I couldn't tie it up, I couldn't tie it in, but it's as close as I can come to explaining to myself, my . . . well, shall I say the learning process, the follow-through on my realization that . . . yes, you *do care* in a given situation. It's just that simple. And I hadn't been aware of it before. I might have closed this door and walked out, and in discussing therapy, said, yes, the counselor must feel thus and so, but, I mean, I hadn't had the dynamic experience.

CL: I have a feeling . . . that you have to do it pretty much yourself, but that somehow you ought to be able to do that with other people. *(She mentions that there have been "countless" times when she might have accepted personal warmth and kindness from others.)* I get the feeling that I just was afraid I would be devastated. *(She returns to talking about the counseling itself and her feelings toward it.)* I mean there's been this tearing through the thing myself. Almost to . . . I felt it . . . I mean I tried to verbalize it on occasion . . . a kind of . . . at times almost not wanting you to restate, nor wanting you to reflect, the thing is *mine.* Course all right, I can say resistance. But that doesn't mean a damn thing to me now. . . . The . . . I think in . . . relationship to this particular thing, I mean, the . . . probably at times, the strongest feeling was, it's *mine.* I've got to cut it down myself. See?

TH: It's an experience that's awfully hard to put down accurately into words, and yet I get a sense of difference here in this relationship, that from the feeling that "this is mine," "I've got to do it," "I am doing it," and so on, to a somewhat different feeling that . . . "I could let you in."

CL: Yeah. Now. I mean, that's . . . that's that it's . . . well, it's sort of, shall we say, volume two. It's . . . it's a . . . well, sort of, well, I'm still in the thing alone, but I'm *not* . . . see . . . I'm . . .

TH: Um-hum. Yes, that paradox sort of sums it up, doesn't it?

CL: Yeah.

TH: In all of this, there is a feeling, it's still—every aspect of my experience is mine and that's kind of inevitable and necessary and so on. And yet that isn't the whole picture either. Somehow it can be shared or another's interest can come in and in some ways it is new.

CL: Yeah. And it's . . . it's as though, that's how it should be. I mean, that's how it . . . has to be. There's a . . . there's a feeling, "and this is good." I mean, it expresses, it clarifies it for me. There's a feeling . . . in caring, as though . . . you were sort of standing back . . . standing off, and if I want to sort of cut through to the thing, it's a . . . a slashing of . . . oh, tall weeds, that I can do it, and you can . . . I mean, you're not going to be disturbed by having to walk through it, too. I don't know. And it doesn't make sense. I mean . . .

TH: Except there's a very real sense of rightness about this feeling that you have, hm?

CL: Um-hum.

CL: I'm experiencing a new type, a . . . probably the only worthwhile kind of learning, a . . . I know I've . . . I've often said what I know doesn't help me here. What I meant is, my acquired knowledge doesn't help me. But it seems to me that the learning process here has been . . . so dynamic, I mean, so much a part of the . . . of everything, I mean, of me, that if I just get that out of it, it's something, which, I mean . . . I'm wondering if I'll ever be able to straighten out into a sort of acquired knowledge what I have experienced here.

TH: In other words, the kind of learning that has gone on here has been something of quite a different sort and quite a different depth; very vital, very real. And quite worthwhile to you in and of itself, but the question you're asking is: Will I ever have a clear intellectual picture of what has gone on at this somehow deeper kind of learning level?

CL: Um-hum. Something like that.

Liking Oneself[54]

CL: One thing worries me—and I'll hurry because I can always go back to it—a feeling that occasionally I can't turn out. Feeling of being quite pleased with myself. Again the Q technique. I walked out of here one time, and impulsively I threw my first card, "I am an attractive personality"; looked at it sort of aghast but left it there, I mean, because honestly, I mean, that is exactly how it felt . . . a—well, that bothered me and I catch that now. Every once in a while a sort of pleased feeling, nothing superior, but just . . . I don't know, sort of pleased. A neatly turned way. And it bothered me. And yet —I wondered—I rarely remember things I say here, I mean I wondered why it was that I was convinced, and something about what I've felt about being hurt that I suspected in . . . my feelings when I would hear someone say to a child, "Don't cry." I mean, I always felt, but it isn't right; I mean, if he's hurt, let him cry. Well, then, now this pleased feeling that I have. I've recently come to feel, it's . . . there's something almost the same there. It's . . . We don't object when *children* feel pleased with themselves. It's . . . I mean, there really isn't anything vain. It's maybe that's how people *should* feel.

TH: You've been inclined almost to look askance at yourself for this feeling, and yet as you think about it more, maybe it comes close to the two sides of the picture, that if a child wants to cry, why shouldn't he cry? And if he wants to feel pleased with himself, doesn't he have a perfect right to feel pleased with himself? And that sort of ties in with this, what I would see as an appreciation of yourself that you've experienced every now and again.

CL: Yes. Yes.

TH: "I'm really a pretty rich and interesting person."

CL: Something like that. And then I say to myself, "Our society pushes us around and we've lost it." And I keep going back to my feelings about children. Well, maybe they're richer than we are. Maybe we . . . it's something we've lost in the process of growing.

TH: Could be that they have a wisdom about that that we've lost.

CL: That's right. My time's up.

Discovering that the Core of Personality is Positive[55]

CL: I think I'm awfully glad I found myself or brought myself or wanted to talk about self. I mean, it's a very personal, private kind of thing that you just don't talk about. I mean, I can understand my feeling of, oh, probably slight apprehension now. It's . . . well, sort of as though I was just rejecting, I mean, all of the things that western civilization stands for, you see. And wondering whether I was right, I mean, whether it was quite the right path, and still of course, feeling how right the thing was, you see. And so there's bound to be a conflict. And then this, and I mean, now I'm feeling, well, of course that's how I feel. I mean, there's a . . . this thing that I term a kind of a lack of hate, I mean, is very real. It carried over onto the things I do, I believe in . . . I think it's all right. It's sort of maybe my saying to myself, well, you've been bashing me all over the head, I mean, sort of from the beginning, with superstitions and taboos and misinterpreted doctrines and laws and your science, your refrigerators, your atomic bombs. But I'm just not buying, you see, I'm just, you just haven't quite succeeded. I think what I'm saying is that, well, I mean, just not conforming, and it's . . . well, it's just that way.

TH: Your feeling at the present time is that you have been very much aware of all the cultural pressures—not always very much aware, but "there have been so many of those in my life—and now I'm going down more deeply into myself to find out what I really feel" —and it seems very much at the present time as though that somehow separates you a long ways from your culture, and that's a little frightening, but feels basically good. Is that . . .

CL: Yeah. Well, I have the feeling now that it's okay, really . . . Then there's something else —a feeling that's starting to grow, well, to be almost formed, as I say. This kind of conclusion, that I'm going to stop looking for something terribly wrong. Now I don't know why. But I mean just . . . it's this kind of thing. I'm sort of saying to myself now, well, in view of what I know, what I've found . . . I'm pretty sure I've ruled out fear, and I'm positive I'm not afraid of shock . . . I mean, I sort of would have welcomed it. But . . . in view of the places I've been, what I learned there, then also kind of, well, taking into consideration what I don't know, sort of, maybe this is one of the things that I'll have to date and say, well, now, I've just . . . I can't find it. See? And now without any, without, I should say, any sense of apology or covering up, just sort of simple statement that I can't find what at this time appears to be bad.

TH: Does this catch it? That as you've gone more and more deeply into yourself, and as you think about the kind of things that you've discovered and learned and so on, the conviction grows very, very strong that no matter how far you go, the things that you're going to find are not dire and awful. They have a very different character.

CL: Yes, something like that.

Openness to Experience[56]

CL: It doesn't seem to me that it would be possible for anybody to relate all the changes that you feel. But I certainly have felt recently that I have more respect for, more objectivity toward my physical makeup. I mean, I don't expect too much of myself. This is how it works out: It feels to me that in the past I used to fight a certain tiredness that I felt after supper. Well, now I feel pretty sure that I really *am tired*—that I am not making myself tired—that I am just physiologically lower. It seemed that I was just constantly criticizing my tiredness.

TH: So you can let yourself *be* tired, instead of feeling along with it a kind of criticism of it.

CL: Yes, that I shouldn't be tired or something. And it seems in a way to be pretty profound that I can just not fight this tiredness, and along with it goes a real feeling of I've got to slow down, too, so that being tired isn't such an awful thing. I think I can also kind of pick up a thread here of why I should be that way in the way my father is and the way he looks at some of these things. For instance, say that I was sick, and I would report this, and it would seem that overtly he would want to do something about it, but he would also communicate, "Oh, my gosh, more trouble." You know, something like that.

TH: As though there were something quite annoying really about being physically ill.

CL: Yeah, I'm sure that my father has the same disrespect for his own physiology that I have had. Now, last summer I twisted my back, I wrenched it, I heard it snap and everything. There was real pain there all the time at first, real sharp. And I had the doctor look at it and he said it wasn't serious, it should heal by itself as long as I didn't bend too much. Well this was months ago . . . and I have been noticing recently that . . . hell, this is a real pain and it's still there—and it's not my fault.

TH: It doesn't prove something bad about you . . .

CL: No—and one of the reasons I seem to get more tired than I should maybe is because of this constant strain, and so . . . I have already made an appointment with one of the doctors at the hospital that he would look at it and take an X ray or something. In a way I guess you could say that I am just more accurately sensitive—or objectively sensitive to this kind of thing. . . . And this is really a profound change, as I say, and of course my relationship with my wife and two children is . . . well, you just wouldn't recognize it if you could see me inside—as you have—I mean . . . there just doesn't seem to be anything more wonderful than really and genuinely . . . really *feeling* love for your own children and at the same time receiving it. I don't know how to put this. We have such an increased respect—both of us—for Judy and we've noticed just—as we participated in this—we have noticed such a tremendous change in her . . . it seems to be a pretty deep kind of thing.

TH: It seems to me you are saying that you can listen more accurately to yourself. If your body says it's tired, you listen to it and believe it, instead of criticizing it; if it's in pain, you can listen to that; if the feeling is really loving your wife and children, you can feel that, and it seems to show up in the differences in them too.

An Internal Locus of Evaluation[57]

CL: Well, now, I wonder if I've been going around doing that, getting smatterings of things, and not getting hold, not really getting down to things.

TH: Maybe you've been getting just spoonfuls here and there rather than really digging in somewhere rather deeply.

CL: Um-hum. That's why I say . . . *(slowly and very thoughtfully)* well, with that sort of foundation, well, it's really up to me. I mean, it seems to be really apparent to me that I can't depend on someone else to give me an education. *(very softly)* I'll really have to get it myself.

TH: It really begins to come home—there's only one person that can educate you—a realization that perhaps nobody else can give you an education.

CL: Um-hum. *(long pause—while she sits thinking)* I have all the symptoms of fright. *(laughs softly)*

TH: Fright: That this is a scary thing, is that what you mean?

CL: Um-hum. *(very long pause—obviously struggling with feelings in herself)*

TH: Do you want to say any more about what you mean by that? That it really does give you the symptoms of fright?

CL: *(laughs)* I, uh . . . I don't know whether I quite know. I mean . . . well, it really seems like I'm cut loose *(pause),* and it seems that I'm very—I don't know—in a vulnerable position, but I, uh, I brought this up and it, uh, somehow it almost came out without saying it. It seems to be . . . it's something I let out.

TH: Hardly a part of you.

CL: Well, I felt surprised.

TH: As though, "Well for goodness sake, did I say that?" (both chuckle)

CL: Really, I don't think I've had that feeling before. I've . . . uh, well, this really feels like I'm saying something that, uh, is a part of me really. *(pause)* Or, uh, *(quite perplexed)* it feels like I sort of have, uh, I don't know. I have a feeling of *strength,* and yet I have a feeling of . . . realizing it's so sort of fearful, of fright.

TH: That is, do you mean that saying something of that sort gives you at the same time a feeling of, of strength in saying it, and yet at the same time a frightened feeling of what you have said, is that it?

CL: Um-hum. I am feeling that. For instance, I'm feeling it internally now—a sort of surging up, or force, or outlet. As if that's something really big and strong. And yet, us, well, at first it was almost a physical feeling of just being out alone, and sort of cut off from a . . . a support I had been carrying around.

TH: You feel that it's something deep and strong, and surging forth, and at the same time, you feel as though you'd cut yourself loose from any support when you say it.

CL: Um-hum. Maybe that's . . . I don't know . . . it's a disturbance of a kind of pattern I've been carrying around, I think.

TH: It sort of shakes a rather significant pattern, jars it loose.

CL: Um-hum. *(pause, then cautiously, but with conviction)* I, think . . . I don't know, but I have the feeling that then I am going to begin to do more things that I know I should do. . . . There are so many things that I need to do. It seems in so many avenues of my living I have to work out new ways of behavior, but—maybe—I can see myself doing a little better in some things.

SUMMARY AND EVALUATION

Client-centered therapy hypothesizes that human beings are rational, socialized, constructive, and forward moving and that each individual has the potential for growth and self-actualization. Counseling or psychotherapy releases the potentials and capacities of the individual.

The maladjusted or disturbed individual is characterized by incongruence between the self and experiences, which are threatening. This individual reacts defensively, denying or distorting experiences that are inconsistent with the self-concept. Counseling offers a relationship in which incongruous experiences can be recognized, expressed, differentiated, and assimilated, or integrated into the self. The individual becomes more congruent, less defensive, more realistic and objective in his or her perceptions, more effective in problem solving, and more accepting of others—in short, the individual's psychological adjustment is closer to the optimum.

This process and these outcomes are facilitated when the counselor manifests unconditional positive regard for the client, evidences empathic understanding of the client, and is successful in communicating these attitudes to the client in a relationship in which the therapist is congruent, or genuine. The relationship is one in which threat is reduced, thereby freeing the client for experiencing, expressing, and exploring his or her feelings.

Client-centered counseling developed out of Rogers's experience as he engaged in counseling or psychotherapy with many clients over more than 30 years. The theory grew out of experience, the results of which were not anticipated; indeed, Rogers's experience led to radical changes in the theoretical point of view that he had held early in his professional life.

Rogers's development of a theory of therapy preceded the development of a theory of personality. The theory of therapy emerged as a way of giving order to the phenomena experienced in therapy. This theory involved personality change, which led to the evolution of a theory of personality that deals with the nature of normal and abnormal personality and its development.

The theory of personality has been called self-theory because of the central importance of the self, or self-concept, in it. More broadly, however, both the theory of therapy and the theory of personality constitute a perceptual theory, or, more specifically, a phenomenological theory. The phenomenological nature of this theory is clearly represented by Combs and Snygg in *Individual Behavior: A Perceptual Approach to Behavior.*[58]

Phenomenology assumes that although a real world may exist, its existence cannot be known or experienced directly. Its existence is inferred on the basis of perceptions of the world. These perceptions constitute the phenomenal field, or the phenomenal world, of the individual. Human beings can know only their phenomenal world, never any real world. Therefore, they can behave only in terms of how they perceive things, or how things appear to them.

Rogers thus accepts or adopts a phenomenological point of view when he utilizes the internal frame of reference, or the subjective world of the individual, as a basis for empathizing with and understanding the individual. It is also apparent in his theory of personality when he postulates that the individual perceives his or her experience as reality—that, indeed, the individual's experience *is* his or her reality—and when he defines experience as the phenomenal field of the individual. In counseling or therapy, it is the *perception* that the client has of the therapist that is important, not what the therapist actually is or may be trying to be. The process of therapy is seen as a reorganization of the client's perceptions about himself or herself and his or her world. "The essential point about therapy . . . is that the way the client perceives the objects in his phenomenal field—his experiences, his feelings, his self, other persons, his environment—undergoes change. . . ."[59] Rogers quotes, with approval, Snygg and Combs: "We might, therefore, define psychotherapy from a phenomenological point of view as: the provision of experience whereby the individual is enabled to make more adequate differentiation of the phenomenal self and its relationship to external reality."[60]

The outcomes of therapy also include self-direction and the perception of the

variables, and their relationship to the client's progress and change have been demonstrated. However, the descriptions of these concepts are broad and general, with little, if any, consideration of how they are manifested by the counselor in the counseling process. This lack of specification is an example of the increasing emphasis on attitudes, with consequent deemphasis or neglect of techniques. Rogers states: "I believe the quality of my encounter is more important in the long run than is my scholarly knowledge, my professional training, my counseling orientation, the techniques I use in the interview."[70] While this may be so, the quality of the relationship is not independent of the other factors, including techniques. The beginning counselor, especially, needs some help in going about the process of implementing the basic attitudes, but the impression is sometimes given that techniques are entirely incidental. Gendlin, for example, states that "many different orientations, techniques, and modes of therapist response could manifest these attitudes. . . . An unlimited range of therapist *behavior* might implement and communicate these *attitudes.*"[71] This, of course, cannot literally be true; there are some limits—some techniques are inconsistent with the attitudes. Other client-centered writers give more attention to techniques, however, including Porter[72] and Patterson.[73]

An important question concerning the client-centered approach is whether the conditions presented by Rogers are the necessary and sufficient conditions for counseling or psychotherapy. Rogers states that when these conditions are present, therapeutic personality change invariably and inevitably occurs. However, the conditions are presented, not as final, but as a theory, a "series of hypotheses which are open to proof or disproof, thereby clarifying and extending our knowledge of the field."[74]

Ellis challenges these conditions, questioning whether they are necessary or sufficient, although he concedes that they may be desirable.[75] He notes that personality change does occur without psychological contact with another through experiences of reading or listening. It may be questioned, of course, whether, although there is no direct *personal* contact, there is not *psychological* contact, even though certain experiences may not involve any individual. Ellis also notes that individuals who were not incongruent, but basically congruent and unanxious, have improved their personalities significantly through life experiences and reading. He points out that he has seen clients helped by therapists who were emotionally disturbed and incongruent. Whether such therapists were congruent in the therapy relationship, which is Rogers's point, Ellis does not discuss, however. Commenting on unconditional positive regard, Ellis states that he has seen at least one client who benefited appreciably when treated by theapists who "do not have any real positive regard for their patients, but who deliberately try to regulate the lives and philosophies of these patients for the satisfaction of the therapist's own desires."[76] Ellis feels that the presence of empathic understanding is the most plausible condition, but he contends that clients whom he has helped by pointing out their self-defeating behavior and showing them alternative methods of behavior—after seeing their problems from their own frame of reference—have then helped friends and relatives by dogmatically and arbitrarily indoctrinating them without any empathic understanding. Finally, Ellis claims that he has disproved in his own therapy the necessity for the client's perceiving the therapist's acceptance and empathy, in the case of paranoid patients who insisted that they were not understood but who finally accepted the therapist's frame of reference.

Ellis concludes, therefore, that while very few individuals significantly restructure their personalities when all six conditions are absent, some do. He feels that there is probably no single condition that is absolutely necessary for constructive personality change. There are a number of alternative conditions that might lead to this same result.

It might be pointed out that, as has been indicated several times in this chapter, it is not the presence of these conditions as perceived by an external observer that is necessary, but their presence as perceived by the client. Nevertheless, Ellis raises some question as to whether any one or all of the conditions are necessary.

A possible solution of this issue, which appears to be consistent with the general client-centered approach, is that the only necessary—but not sufficient—condition of constructive personality change is that the individual's potential for growth, as manifested in the drive for maintenance and enhancement of the self, is operating and has not been destroyed by severe organic or psychological trauma. The degree of this motivation varies, of course. When it is strong, the conditions that Rogers lists need be present in only very minimal degrees, perhaps hardly observable by an external observer but present from the viewpoint of the client. When the basic motivation for change is weak or when it is inhibited or threatened, the external conditions must be present in greater degrees. They may vary in the degree to which they are present, and it may be possible that not all the conditions need be present, although there appears to be a positive relationship among the conditions that relate to the therapist, so that if one is present, the others are likely to be present, at least to some extent. Or it may be that the only other necessary condition, which, with the client's motivation, constitutes the sufficient conditions, is the perception by the client of congruence, empathy, and unconditional positive regard in the therapist.

Thus whether the conditions posited by Rogers are necessary is not yet known. However, that they are sufficient for positive personality and behavior change appears to have been demonstrated in the extensive research that was carried out over some 30 years and that involved a wide variety of clients with a wide variety of problems, including hospitalized patients diagnosed as schizophrenic. Truax and Carkhuff, almost 20 years ago, summarized the research as follows:

> These findings suggest that the person (whether a counselor, therapist or teacher) who is better able to communicate warmth, genuineness and accurate empathy is more effective in interpersonal relationships no matter what the goal of the interaction (better grades for a college student, better interpersonal relationships for the counseling center outpatient, adequate personality functioning and integration for the seriously disturbed mental patient, socially acceptable behavior for the juvenile delinquent, or greater reading ability for the third-grade reading instruction student).[77]

Subsequent research has supported and strengthened this conclusion.

Client-centered therapy has been a developing and changing approach. Cognitive concepts, especially information-processing theory, have been used to describe and analyze the therapy process, particularly the client's activity in the process of self-exploration. Information-processing theory appears to be particularly congenial to client-centered therapy, since it shares the phenomenological approach and the assumption of the presence of a drive within the individual toward active learning by constructing and organizing, or experiencing, the world. Thus it is congruent with the emphasis on empathic understanding as the only way to understand another person's experiencing. These developments in client-centered therapy retain and elaborate the essence of the approach.

REFERENCES

1. Rogers, C. R. *Counseling and psychotherapy: Newer concepts in practice.* Boston: Houghton Mifflin, 1942.
2. Rogers, C. R. *Client-centered therapy: Its current practice, implications and theory.* Boston: Houghton Mifflin, 1951.
3. Rogers, C. R. *On becoming a person: A therapist's view of psychotherapy.* Boston: Houghton Mifflin, 1961.
4. Rogers, C. R. A theory of therapy, personality, and interpersonal relationships, as developed in the client-centered framework. In S. Koch (Ed.), *Psychology: A study of science.* Study 1: *Conceptual and systematic.* Vol. 3: *Formulations of the person and the social context.* New York: McGraw-Hill, 1959. Pp. 184–256.
5. Ibid., pp. 188–192.
6. Ibid., p. 191.
7. Ibid., p. 192.
8. Rogers, *On becoming a person,* pp. 90–92, 194–195.
9. Rogers, A theory of therapy, personality, and interpersonal relationships, p. 221.
10. Rogers, *Client-centered therapy,* pp. 20–22.
11. Rogers, A theory of therapy, personality, and interpersonal relationships, pp. 194–212.
12. Ibid., pp. 236–240. Passim.
13. The theory of therapy was developed first, and the theories of personality and interpersonal relationships grew out of it, in part as generalizations from it. For our purposes in this chapter, the presentation is reversed, going from the more general to the more specific. The theory of therapy is an expansion of the process of reintegration outlined earlier.
14. Rogers, A theory of therapy, personality, and interpersonal relationships, p. 216.
15. Ibid., pp. 218–219.
16. Rogers, C. R. *Freedom to learn.* Columbus, Ohio: Merrill, 1969. Pp. 279–297.
17. Ibid., p. 290.
18. Ibid., p. 268.
19. Ibid., p. 269.
20. Rogers, *Client-centered therapy.*
21. Rogers, *On becoming a person.* (Chap. 5 originally published in O. H. Mowrer (Ed.), *Psychotherapy: Theory and research.* New York: Ronald Press, 1953.)
22. Ibid., Chap. 6.
23. Ibid., p. 80.
24. Ibid., p. 87.
25. Ibid., p. 103.
26. Ibid., Chap. 7.
27. Ibid., p. 132.
28. Ibid., p. 133.
29. Ibid., p. 135.
30. Ibid., p. 138.
31. Ibid., p. 150.
32. Ibid., p. 153.

33. Rogers, *Client-centered therapy,* p. 14.
34. Rogers, *On becoming a person,* Chap. 2.
35. Ibid., Chap. 3. (originally published in *Personnel and Guidance Journal,* 1958, *37,* 6–16.)
36. Rogers, C. R. The necessary and sufficient conditions of therapeutic personality change. *Journal of Consulting Psychology,* 1957, *21,* 95–103.
37. Rogers, *On becoming a person,* p. 284.
38. Ibid., p. 35.
39. Rogers, C. R. Personal communication, November 13, 1964.
40. Rogers, C. R. The process equation of psychotherapy. *American Journal of Psychotherapy,* 1961, *15,* 27–45.
41. Hart, J. T., & Tomlinson, T. M. (Eds.). *New directions in client-centered therapy.* Boston: Houghton Mifflin, 1970.
42. Truax, C. B., & Carkhuff, R. R. *Toward effective counseling and psychotherapy.* Chicago: Aldine, 1967; Carkhuff, R. R., & Berenson, B. G. *Beyond counseling and therapy.* New York: Holt, Rinehart and Winston, 1967 (2nd ed., 1977); Carkhuff, R. R. *Helping and human relations.* Vol. I: *Selection and training.* Vol. 2: *Practice and research.* New York: Holt, Rinehart and Winston, 1969.
43. Patterson, C. H. *Relationship counseling and psychotherapy.* New York: Harper & Row, 1974. Revised as *The therapeutic relationship.* Monterey, Calif: Brooks/Cole, 1985.
44. Wexler, D. A., & Rice, L. N. (Eds.). *Innovations in client-centered therapy.* New York: Wiley, 1974.
45. Wexler, D. A. A cognitive theory of experiencing, self-actualization and therapeutic process. In Wexler & Rice (Eds.), *Innovations in client-centered therapy,* pp. 49–116.
46. Rice, L. N. The evocative function of the therapist. In Wexler & Rice (Eds.), *Innovations in client-centered therapy,* pp. 289–311.
47. Butler, J. M. The iconic mode in psychotherapy. In Wexler & Rice (Eds.), *Innovations in client-centered therapy,* pp. 171–203.
48. Gendlin, E. T. Client-centered and experiential psychotherapy. In Wexler & Rice (Eds.), *Innovations in client-centered therapy,* pp. 211–246; Gendlin, E. T. Existentialism and experiential psychotherapy. In Hart & Tomlinson (Eds.), *New directions in client-centered therapy,* pp. 70–94 (originally published in C. Moustakas (Ed.), *Existential child therapy.* New York: Basic Books, 1966); Gendlin, E. T. A theory of personality change. In Hart & Tomlinson (Eds.), *New directions in client-centered therapy,* pp. 129–173 (originally published in P. Worchel & D. Byrne (Eds.), *Personality change.* New York: Wiley, 1964).
49. Rogers, C. R. Empathic: An unappreciated way of being. *Counseling Psychologist,* 1975, *5,* (2) 2–10.
50. Rogers, A theory of therapy, personality, and interpersonal relationships, p. 184.
51. Wexler, A cognitive theory of experiencing, self-actualization and therapeutic process, p. 112.
52. Rogers, *On becoming a person,* pp. 77–78. This and the following three excerpts are from the same client.
53. Ibid., pp. 81, 82–84, 84–85, 85–86.
54. Ibid., pp. 87–88.
55. Ibid., pp. 100–101.
56. Ibid., pp. 116–117.
57. Ibid., pp. 120–122. A film with Rogers as the therapist is included in Shostrom, E. (Producer). *Three approaches to psychotherapy.* Santa Ana, Calif.: Psychological Films, 1965.
58. Combs, A. W., & Snygg, D. *Individual behavior: A perceptual approach to behavior* (rev. ed.). New York: Harper & Row, 1959. Revised by Combs, A. W., Richards, F., & Richards, A. *Perceptual psychology.* New York: Harper & Row, 1976.

59. Rogers, *Client-centered therapy,* p. 142.

60. Ibid., p. 146.

61. Rogers, *On becoming a person,* p. 154.

62. Combs & Snygg, *Individual behavior,* p. 20.

63. Beck, C. E. *Philosophical foundations of guidance.* Englewood Cliffs, N.J.: Prentice-Hall, 1963. Pp. 66–67. The quote is from Snygg, D., & Combs, A. W. *Individual behavior: A new frame of reference for psychology.* New York: Harper & Row, 1949. Pp. 130–131n.

64. Malcolm, N. Behaviorism as a philosophy of psychology. In T. W. Wann (Ed.), *Behaviorism and phenomenology.* Chicago: University of Chicago Press, 1964. P. 107.

65. Rogers, Toward a science of the person. In J. W. Wann (Ed.), *Behaviorism and Phenomenology.* Chicago: University of Chicago Press, 1964, p. 135.

66. Ibid.

67. Rogers, *On becoming a person,* p. 193. See also Rogers, C. R. Freedom and commitment. *Humanist,* 1964, *24,* 37–40.

68. Ibid., p. 392. See also Rogers, C. R. Two divergent trends. In R. May (Ed.), *Existential psychology.* New York: Random House, 1961.

69. Ford, D. H., & Urban, H. B. *Systems of psychotherapy.* New York: Wiley, 1963. P. 439.

70. Rogers, C. R. The interpersonal relationship: the core of guidance. *Harvard Educational Review,* 1962, *32,* 416–429.

71. Gendlin, E. T. Client-centered development in work with schizophrenics. *Journal of Counseling Psychology,* 1962, *9,* 205–212.

72. Porter, E. H., Jr. *An introduction to therapeutic counseling.* Boston: Houghton Mifflin, 1950.

73. Patterson, C. H. *Counseling and psychotherapy: Theory and practice.* New York: Harper & Row, 1959; Patterson, *Relationship counseling and psychotherapy.*

74. Rogers, C. R. The necessary and sufficient conditions of therapeutic personality change.

75. Ellis, A. Requisite conditions for basic personality change. *Journal of Consulting Psychology,* 1959, *23,* 538–549. (Originally published in A. Ellis. *Reason and emotion in psychotherapy.* New York: Lyle Stuart, 1952. Pp. 110–119.)

76. Ibid., p. 114.

77. Truax, C. B., & Carkhuff, R. R. *Toward effective training in counseling and psychotherapy.* Chicago: Aldine, 1967. Pp. 116–117.

five

EXISTENTIAL PSYCHOTHERAPY

In our presentation of varying approaches to counseling or psychotherapy, we have been moving from a conception of therapy as a rational or mainly cognitive problem-solving process to a conception of it as concerned with attitudes, feelings, and affects, with resulting or concomitant changes in methods or techniques. That is not to say that human beings are essentially irrational or that counseling or psychotherapy is irrational in its approach. It is to say that human beings are more than just intellect and that counseling or therapy must therefore be psychological rather than logical. The emphasis is placed increasingly on the counseling relationship rather than on techniques for influencing the client. The content becomes the current experiencing of the client, rather than the client's "problem." The therapist's concern is with understanding the experiencing of the client. The therapist must see and know the client as a unique, specific individual. The therapist must see and know the world in which the client exists —his or her real world, which is unique and different from the objective world, or the so-called world of reality.

The concern with understanding the client as he or she exists in his or her world is at the basis of an approach or approaches to counseling or psychotherapy to which the adjective *existential* has been attached. The general name existential psychotherapy is applied to these approaches. Although they have much in common, they differ in some respects, so that it is not possible to refer to *the* existential method but only to existential approaches. The general approach was developed independently in various parts of Europe. A number of psychiatrists, many of whom were trained in Freudian psychoanalysis, have been concerned with the relation of existential concepts to psychotherapy. They include Binswanger,[1] Boss,[2] Frankl,[3] Marcel,[4] and Sonneman.[5] In this country, Rollo May[6] has been perhaps the foremost exponent of an existential approach to psychotherapy, although others, such as Lefabre,[7] Van Dusen,[8] and van Kaam[9] have contributed.

The development of existentialism has been sketched by May.[10] It is in part an outgrowth of the phenomenological movement in philosophy,[11] with Husserl's[12] phenomenology influencing it particularly.[13] Mainly, phenomenology contributed the method of approach to the person and his or her world. Existential philosophy, the second major contributor, had its origins in the work of Kierkegaard[14] and Jaspers.[15] Later existential philosophers, such as Heidegger,[16] Marcel,[17] and Sartre,[18] were influenced by the phenomenology of Husserl. Existential philosophy is concerned with the nature of humanity, with its existence in the modern world, and with the meaning of this existence to the individual. Its focus is on the individual's most immediate experience, his or her own existence and the experiencing of this existence.

Existentialism is defined by May as "the endeavor to understand man by cutting below the cleavage between subject and object which has bedeviled Western thought and science since shortly after the Renaissance. . . . It arose specifically just over a hundred years ago in Kierkegaard's violent protest against the reigning rationalism of his day, Hegel's 'totalitarianism of reason,' to use Maritain's phrase."[19] The individual is not a substance or a mechanism but an emerging, becoming, or *existing* being, and *exist* means literally "to stand out; to emerge." Existence has been opposed to essence, which is an abstraction and which has been the concern of traditional science. However, the opposition has been reconciled unwittingly, as Tillich[20] notes, by Sartre's denial of it in his statement "Man's essence is his existence"; that is, the essence of a human being is his or her power to create himself or herself.

The human being as the subject can never be separated from the object that the human being observes. The meaning of objective fact depends on the subject's relationship to it. Human beings exist in a world of which they are a part—beings-in-the-world. Existentialism focuses on the individual's experience—particularly the nonintellectual modes of experience—and on existence in its total involvement in a situation within a world. It makes an individual's experience the center of things; its "frame of reference is in man as he exists inside, in the full range of his fears, hopes, anxieties, and terrors. . . . The fundamental contribution of existential therapy is its understanding of man as being. . . . The fundamental character of existential analysis is, thus, that it is concerned with *ontology,* the science of being, and with *Dasein,* the existence of this particular being sitting opposite the psychotherapist."[21]

Nor is there a single existential psychotherapy; rather, there are numerous approaches. None of them is at present a systematic approach, and little attention is given to techniques. Sartre's analysis is a philosophy rather than a clinical practice. Binswanger's analyses[22] are, as van Kaam notes, not examples of how to do therapy but only suggestions that "the therapist has to foster a participation of the whole human existence of the patient in the existence of others in order to overcome his anxiety."[23]

Existentialist philosophers do not constitute a single school. There are differences and conflicts among them. Van Dusen sees them on a continuum, with some, such as Sartre, emphasizing the nonbeing end and with Marcel emphasizing the being end of the range of human experiences. One end is characterized by pessimism—darkness and death—and the other by optimism—light and life.[24]

While there is thus no single theory or approach, there are perhaps some common aspects or elements basic to all existential approaches to psychotherapy. These may include the following themes:[25]

1. The distinctive character of human existence is *dasein,* the being who is there, who has a there in that the being knows he or she is there and can take a stand with reference to that fact. Human beings differ from all other animals in their capacity for being aware of (conscious of) themselves, as well as of the events that influence them and of the past, present, and future as a continuum. This makes possible choices and decisions. A person is thus responsible because he or she can choose. "Self-consciousness itself—the person's potential for aware-ness that the vast complex, protean flow of experience is his experience—brings in inescapably the element of decision at every moment."[26]

    A person is thus free and is what he or she makes of himself or herself; heredity, environment, upbringing, and culture are alibis. External influences are limiting but not determining. "Man is the being who can be conscious of, and therefore responsible for, his existence. It is this capacity to become aware of his own being which distinguishes the human being from other beings. The existential therapists think of man not only as 'being-for-itself.' Binswanger and other authors . . . speak of Dasein choosing this or that, meaning 'the person who-is-responsible-for-his-existence choosing.' . . ."[27]

2. Existentialists share the "conviction that it is impossible to think of the subject and the world as separate from each other."[28] Terms such as *participation, encounter, presence,* and *dasein* express this conviction. Human beings live in three worlds simultaneously, the *Umwelt,* or the biological world, without self-awareness; the *Mitwelt,* or the world of interrelationships or encounters with other persons, involving mutual awareness; and the *Eigenwelt,* or the world of self-identity or being-in-itself.

3. Thus the human being is not a static entity but is in a constant state of transition, emerging, becoming, evolving, that is, *being.* The human being actualizes himself or herself, or fulfills inner potentialities by continuous par-ticipation in a world of things and event and always in encounters or dialogue with other people. Some qualities of being can be distinctly developed only in relation to another person. Therapy is an encounter or a dialogue in which the client is enabled to develop certain human qualities. Being is thus not some-thing given once and for all but is constantly developing. The future is, therefore, the significant tense for human beings.

4. Human beings also know that at some future time, they will not be. Being implies the fact of nonbeing, and the meaning of existence involves the fact of nonexistence. Existentialism holds that death gives life reality; it is the one absolute fact of life. Human beings are aware of the fact that they must die; and they must confront this fact. They are also capable of choosing not to be at any instant. They are conscious of isolation, nothingness, loss of individual significance or identity, alienation, or emptiness.

5. The threat of nonbeing is the source of "normal" anxiety, hostility, and aggression—normal because the threat is always present in all individuals. This anxiety (sometimes called existential anxiety) is "an ontological charac-teristic of man, rooted in his very existence as such."[29] Anxiety strikes at the core of the individual's self-esteem—the sense of value as a self; it is the threat of dissolution of the self, the loss of existence itself. It involves a conflict

between being and nonbeing, between the emerging potentiality of being, on the one hand, and the loss of present security, on the other. It is a concomitant of freedom. Guilt accompanies the failure to fulfill one's potentialities.

6. Being is not reducible to the introjection of social and ethical norms. The self-esteem based on a sense of being is not simply the reflection of others' views of the individual. Although it involves social relatedness, it presupposes *Eigenwelt,* the "own world" of a sense of self-identity or being-in-itself. Each individual, then, is not a carbon copy cut from social pressures and norms but is unique, singular, and irreplaceable—and thus significant.

7. Human beings have the capacity to transcend the immediate situation, to rise above the past, to transcend themselves. This capacity is inherent in the term *exist.* Human beings exemplify transcendence in their concept of the possible, in bringing the past and the future to bear on the present, in thinking in symbols, in seeing themselves as others see them, and perhaps most characteristically in the capacity to be aware that they are the ones who are acting— to see themselves as both subject and object at the same time. "Self-conscious implies self-transcendence."[30] The capacity for transcendence is the basis of freedom, since it opens up possibilities for choice. There are, however, limits to life and to being that must be accepted.

8. The modern person, "normal" as well as neurotic, is characterized by alienation from the world and from the community. Psychiatrists and counselors are no longer presented with the symptoms with which they were presented while Freud was developing his theories. Increasingly, the symptoms or complaints are loneliness, isolation, depersonalization, and detachment. The person has lost his or her world; he or she is homeless and a stranger in a world that he or she not only did not make, but also is no longer a part of.

Ellenberger[31] selects three concepts of existential psychotherapy as especially significant: (1) the concept of *existential neurosis* (derived from Frankl),[32] according to which emotional disturbances are a result of an inability to see meaning in life rather than of repressed drives or trauma, a weak ego, or life stress; (2) the concept of the therapeutic relationship as an encounter or a new relationship opening up new horizons, rather than a transference relationship, repeating the past; and (3) the concept of *kairos,* critical points when the patient is ready for therapy and when rapid change and improvement are possible.

While these elements and concepts seem to characterize most, if not all, existential therapies, they are not sufficient to develop *an* existential psychotherapy. May feels that it would be a mistake for a special school of existential psychotherapy to be developed. Indeed,

there cannot be any special existential psychiatry. . . . Existentialism is an *attitude,* an approach to human beings, rather than a school or group. Like philosophy, it has to do with *presuppositions* underlying psychiatric and psychoanalytic techniques. The existential approach is not a system of therapy—though it makes highly important contributions to therapy. It is not a set of techniques—though it may give birth to them. It is rather a concern with understanding the structure of the human being and his experience, which to a greater or lesser extent should underlie *all* technique.[33]

In addition to the fact that existential therapy is relatively new and there has not been time for a systematic approach to develop, May feels that concern about techniques is undesirable, since "it is precisely the overemphasis upon techniques, an overemphasis which goes along with the tendency to see the human being as an object to be calculated, managed, 'analyzed,'" that blocks the understanding that existentialism seeks. "The central task and responsibility of the therapist is to seek to understand the patient as a being and as being in his world."[34] Technique follows rather than precedes understanding.

Many existential therapists, particularly those who have been influenced by Binswanger, appear to use the techniques of psychoanalysis. Binswanger essentially sees existential analysis as an "anthropological type of scientific investigation,"[35] rather than as a method of psychotherapy for which psychoanalysis is indispensable. His discussions are concerned with the analysis of cases in terms of existential concepts instead of being discussions of a therapeutic approach.

While existential therapists appear to use many of the techniques common to other approaches, however, particularly psychoanalysis, certain aspects or emphases seem to characterize existential therapies and to distinguish them as a group from other approaches. May discusses six characteristics:[36]

1. Existential therapists evidence considerable variability of technique. They are flexible and versatile, "varying from patient to patient and from one phase to another in the treatment of the same patient," depending on what appears to be necessary "to best reveal the existence of this particular patient at this moment of his history" and "what will best illuminate his being-in-the-world."[37]

2. Existential therapists, particularly those with a psychoanalytic background, utilize psychological dynamisms such as transference, repression, and resistance but always in terms of their meaning for the existential situation of the patient's own immediate life.

3. Emphasis is placed on *presence,* or the reality of the therapist–patient relationship, in which the therapist is "concerned not with his own problems but with understanding and experiencing so far as possible the being of the patient"[38] by entering and participating in the patient's field. This emphasis is shared by therapists of other schools who see the patient as a being to be understood rather than as an object to be analyzed. "Any therapist is existential to the extent that, with all his technical training and his knowledge of transference and dynamisms, he is still able to relate to the patient, as 'one existence communicating to another,' to use Binswanger's phrase."[39] The patient is not a subject but an "existential partner," and the relationship is an encounter or "being-together" with each other in genuine presence.[40] The concern of the therapist is to provide a meaningful relationship as a mutual experience, not a relationship in which the therapist influences the patient.

4. The therapist attempts to avoid behavior that would impede or destroy the existence of full presence in the relationship. Since full encounter with another person can be anxiety producing, the therapist may tend to protect himself or herself by treating the other person as "only a patient" or as an object or by focusing on behavior mechanisms. Technique may be used as a way of blocking presence.

5. "The aim of therapy is that the patient *experience* his existence as real. The purpose is that he become aware of his existence fully, which includes becoming aware of his potentialities and becoming able to act on the basis of them."[41] Interpretation of mechanisms or dynamisms, as a part of existential therapy, will "always be in the context of this person's becoming aware of his existence."[42] Therapy "proceeds *not* merely by showing the patient where, when and to what extent he has failed to realize the fullness of his humanity, but tries to make him *experience* this as radically as possible. . . ."[43] This is important because it is one of the characteristics of the neurotic process in our day that the individual has lost a sense of being and, in an attempt to be objective about himself or herself, has come to view himself or herself as an object or a mechanism. Simply to give the individual new ways of thinking of himself and herself as a mechanism structures the neurosis, and therapy that does this only reflects and continues the fragmentation of the culture that leads to neurosis. Such therapy may result in the loss of symptoms and of anxiety, but it does so because the patient conforms to the culture and constricts his or her existence, giving up his or her freedom.

6. Existential therapy helps the patient develop the attitude or orientation of commitment. Such an attitude involves decisions and actions but not decisions and actions for their own sake. It is, rather, commitment to some point in the patient's own existence. Such commitment is necessary before knowledge is possible: "The patient cannot permit himself to get insight or knowledge until he is ready to decide, takes a definite orientation to life, and has made the preliminary decisions along the way."[44]

A seventh characteristic might be added: in the therapeutic situation, existential psychotherapy focuses on the here and now. The past and future are involved insofar as they enter into the present experience. The here and now includes not only the patient's experiences outside therapy, but also the patient's relationship with the therapist. The patient's life history may be investigated but not in order to explain it in terms of any school of psychotherapy. Instead, it is understood as a modification of the total structuring of the patient as being-in-the-world.[45]

These aspects or emphases of existential psychotherapy are hardly enough on which to base a practice. The underlying concepts are, of course, of first importance, and it is significant that the object of concern or focus of existential therapy—existence as it is experienced rather than symptoms—differs from that of most conventional therapies. However, it is necessary that the concepts be implemented by methods, and it would be supposed that a theory such as existentialism differs enough from other theories in its concepts and principles that it would lead to somewhat different methods. However, there is nowhere a thorough, systematic statement of the nature and procedures of existential psychotherapy, particularly as the procedures may differ from those of other approaches to psychotherapy. Lyons suggests that there is little that is new or different from other therapies.[46] However, he agrees that the approach has had an influence on the field of psychotherapy as a corrective to psychoanalysis and, as Alexander states it, as a counterbalance to the psychoanalytic trend toward concentration on techniques.[47]

We must still ask how the existential therapist operates, how the therapist interacts with clients, and how the therapist participates in the therapeutic relationship. If the therapist uses essentially psychoanalytic techniques, how does he or she use them, and how, then, does existential therapy differ from psychoanalytic therapy or psychoanalysis? If the therapeutic relationship is defined as an encounter, what does this mean? What does it mean to say that the therapist is authentic? If the therapist is concerned with the mode of being-in-the-world of the client, how does he or she gain access to this world? When the therapist understands the client's mode of being-in-the-world, what does he or she do with this understanding? Does the therapist interpret in terms of existential concepts? Is existential therapy an interpretative psychotherapy, then, that uses another theoretical system as a basis for approaching, understanding, and finally interpreting the experiences of the client? Hora contends that special interpretations are not required, in existential psychotherapy, since "that which is speaks for itself, provided it is understood phenomenologically rather than interpreted in accordance with certain theoretical presuppositions. That which is understood needs no interpretation. That which is interpreted is seldom understood."[48]

Binswanger appears to reject any attempt to systematize the approach.[49] He rejects theory because he feels that it leads the therapist to try to make the client's behavior fit his or her theories and that it may result in the therapist's attending only to those behavioral phenomena that fit his or her categories of analysis, thus obstructing a full understanding of the client. However, can a therapist enter into a relationship with a client without being influenced by his or her own concepts, ideas, hypotheses, theories, or values? If the therapist is to be authentic, does not his or her own view of the world, and his or her own being-in-the-world enter into the relationship? Can a person enter the world of another person and view it from that person's point of view? Can a person view things as they are or as they manifest themselves without bias or without a prior assumption (Husserl's method of pure phenomenology)?

It remains true that those who profess to engage in a form of psychotherapy that has been influenced by existentialism have not faced the problem of methods. If they feel that techniques must be subordinated and must not interfere with the authenticity of the relationship, they should be concerned with avoiding involvement with techniques and with defining how they function in order to do so. They not only have not dealt with this problem as a problem, but also have not provided illustrations or demonstrations of how they function so that a person could attempt to understand or learn their methods and procedures. These methods and procedures must exist and, therefore, must be given attention, unless the approach is to be considered entirely intuitive.

Although, as Lyons points out, a number of existential therapists have published articles or books on existential therapy, "as a full scale exposition of theory and practice, there is next to nothing from any of the major European figures in this movement."[50] Such a situation poses a problem in terms of the presentation of this approach. However, as Lyons also notes, there is one exception—Viktor Frankl. Frankl is possibly not typical (if anyone is) of the existential approach. While earlier he used the term *existenzanalysis,* he later adopted the word *logotherapy* to distinguish his approach from Binswanger's existential analysis, or daseinsanalysis, and its related approach to psychotherapy. Frankl's work is more accessible to students and is less obtuse than that of most other existential writers. For these reasons, his approach has been selected for inclusion here.

May and van Kaam note that a number of American psychiatrists and psychologists have held existential viewpoints (including William James, Adolph Meyer, Harry Stack Sullivan, Gordon Allport, Carl Rogers, Henry Murray, and Abraham Maslow). They go on to say that "what has been lacking . . . has been a consistent underlying structure which would give unity to the work of these psychiatrists and psychologists who are concerned with man and his immediate existence." They continue: "We propose here that the existential approach, recast and re-born into our American language and thought forms, can and will give this underlying structure."[51]

This recasting, though, has not yet occurred. May perhaps has come closest to being an American existential therapist. More recently, Bugental has developed an existential approach that is built on a psychoanalytic base. He has described his methods in a series of case studies. A wide range of techniques is included. While he provides a discussion of his philosophy and rationale, it is not a systematically developed theory. It appears that the various methods are used on an intuitive basis.[52]

It might be argued that this is the nature of existential therapy—that it is, on the one hand, the technique of no technique and, on the other hand, the use of any and all techniques—but this is not necessarily the case.

There is an increasing similarity between existential concepts and client-centered therapy. It must have been evident to the reader that many, if not most, of the concepts discussed above characterize client-centered therapy, which has been increasingly emphasizing the immediate experiencing of the psychotherapist. The phenomenology represented in existentialism is fundamental to and is implemented in client-centered therapy—with its focus on the client's perceptions and the necessity of the therapist's entering into the client's frame of reference—more than in any other systematic approach to psychotherapy. It would appear that client-centered therapy has been moving toward existentialism; van Kaam, in "Counseling from the Viewpoint of Existential Psychology," differs very little from exponents of the client-centered approach.[53] May recognizes the existential nature of client-centered therapy,[54] and Wolf notes its similarity to existentialism.[55]

Therefore, it should not be too surprising that a therapist trained in the client-centered approach should have developed an existential approach. Gendlin has focused on the immediate felt experiencing of the client (see Chapter 14, on developments in client-centered therapy). He writes that "psychotherapy generally, with any type of population, seems to involve not only verbalization, but more fundamentally, the client's inward reference to and struggle with his directly felt experiencing. The individual's inward data, concretely felt, seem to be the actual stuff of psychotherapy, not the words. . . ."[56] The therapist, however, must be able to understand and respond to the client's felt experiencing. Gendlin has come to grips with this in the development of what he calls experiential psychotherapy, which is essentially an extension or an elaboration of client-centered therapy in an existential direction. As noted in Chapter 14, experiential psychotherapy focuses on the basic method of client-centered therapy—the empathic response—as the way of encountering the felt experiencing of the client. Gendlin's systematic formulation of this approach may well become the American existential psychotherapy.[57]

REFERENCES

1. Binswanger, L. Existential analysis and psychotherapy. In F. Fromm-Reichmann & J. L. Moreno (Eds.), *Progress in psychotherapy: 1956.* New York: Grune & Stratton, 1956. Pp. 144–148 (also in H. M. Ruitenbeek (Ed.), *Psychoanalysis and existential philosophy.* New York: Dutton, 1962. Pp. 17–23); Binswanger, L. The existential analysis school of thought. In R. May, E. Angel, & H. F. Ellenberger (Eds.), *Existence.* New York: Basic Books, 1958. Pp. 191–213.
2. Boss, M. "Daseinsanalysis" and psychotherapy. In J. H. Masserman & J. L. Moreno (Eds.), *Progress in psychotherapy: 1957.* New York: Grune & Stratton, 1957. Pp. 156–161. (Also in Ruitenbeek (Ed.), *Psychoanalysis and existential philosophy,* pp. 81–89.)
3. Frankl, V. E. *The doctor and the soul* (2nd ed.). New York: Knopf, 1965.
4. Marcel, G. *The philosophy of existence.* London: Harvill, 1948; Marcel, G. *Homo Victor.* Chicago: Regnery, 1951.
5. Sonneman, U. *Existence and therapy.* New York: Grune & Stratton, 1954.
6. May, R. The origins and significance of the existential movement in psychology. In May, Angel, & Ellenberger, (Eds.), *Existence,* pp. 3–36; May, R. Contributions of existential psychotherapy. In May, Angel, & Ellenberger (Eds.), *Existence,* pp. 37–91; May, R. The emergence of existential psychology. In R. May (Ed.), *Existential psychology.* New York: Random House, 1961. Pp. 11–51; May, R. Dangers in the relation of existentialism to psychotherapy. *Review of Existential Psychology and Psychiatry,* 1963, *3,* 5–10 (also in Ruitenbeek (Ed.), *Psychoanalysis and existential philosophy,* pp. 179–184); May, R., & van Kaam, A. Existential theory and therapy. In J. H. Masserman (Ed.), *Current psychiatric therapies* (Vol. 3). New York: Grune & Stratton, 1963. Pp. 74–81.
7. Lefabre, L. B. Existentialism and psychotherapy. *Review of Existential Psychology and Psychiatry,* 1963, *3,* 271–285.
8. Van Dusen, W. The theory and practice of existential analysis. *American Journal of Psychotherapy,* 1957, *11,* 310–322. (Also in Ruitenbeek (Ed.), *Psychoanalysis and existential philosophy,* pp. 24–40.)
9. van Kaam, A. The impact of existential phenomenology on the psychological literature of western Europe. *Review of Existential Psychology and Psychiatry,* 1961, **1,** 62–91; van Kaam, A. Counseling from the viewpoint of existential psychology. *Harvard Educational Review,* 1962, *32,* 403–415.
10. May, The origins and significance of the existential movement in psychology, pp. 3–36.
11. Spiegelberg, H. *The phenomenological movement: A historical introduction* (2 vols). The Hague: Martinus Nijhoff, 1960.
12. Husserl, E. Phenomenology. In *Encyclopaedia Britannica* (Vol. 17). (14th ed.). 1929. Pp. 699–702.
13. Spiegelberg, H. Husserl's phenomenology and existentialism. *Journal of Philosophy,* 1960, *57,* 62–74.
14. Kierkegaard, S. A. *Either/or: A fragment of life.* Princeton, N.J.: Princeton University Press, 1944; Kierkegaard, S. A. *Fear and trembling.* New York: Doubleday, 1954; Kierkegaard, S. A. *The sickness unto death.* New York: Doubleday, 1954.
15. Jaspers, K. *Reason and existence.* New York: Noonday, 1955.
16. Heidegger, M. *Being and time.* London: SCM Press, 1962; Heidegger, M. *Existence and being.* Chicago: Regnery, 1949.
17. Marcel, *The philosophy of existence.*
18. Sartre, J. P. *Existential psychoanalysis.* New York: Philosophical Library, 1953.
19. May, The origins and significance of the existential movement in psychology, p. 11.
20. Tillich, P. Existentialism and psychotherapy. *Review of Existential Psychology and Psy-*

chiatry, 1961, *1,* 8–16. (Also in Ruitenbeek (Ed.), *Psychoanalysis and existential philosophy,* pp. 3–16.)

21. Van Dusen, The theory and practice of existential analysis.
22. Binswanger, The existential analysis school of thought, pp. 191–213.
23. van Kaam, The impact of existential phenomenology on the psychological literature of western Europe.
24. Van Dusen, The theory and practice of exisenial analysis.
25. May, The origins and significance of the existential movement in psychology, pp. 3–36; van Kaam, The impact of existential phenomenology on the psychological literature of western Europe; Braaten, L. J. The main themes of existentialism from the viewpoint of a psychotherapist. *Mental Hygiene,* 1961, *45,* 10–17.
26. May, & van Kaam, Existential theory and therapy, p. 78.
27. May, Contributions of existential psychotherapy, p. 41.
28. van Kaam, The impact of existential phenomenology on the psychological literature of western Europe.
29. May, Contributions of existential psychotherapy, p. 50.
30. Ibid., p. 74.
31. Ellenberger, H. F. A clinical introduction to psychiatric phenomenology and existential analysis. In May, Angel, & Ellenberger (Eds.), *Existence,* pp. 92–124.
32. Frankl, *The doctor and the soul.*
33. May, Dangers in the relation of existentialism to psychotherapy.
34. May, Contributions of existential psychotherapy, pp. 76–77.
35. Binswanger, The existential analysis school of thought, p. 191.
36. May, Contributions of existential psychotherapy, pp. 37–91.
37. Ibid., p. 78.
38. Ibid., p. 80.
39. Ibid., p. 81.
40. Binswanger, Existential analysis and psychotherapy.
41. May, Contributions of existential psychotherapy, p. 85.
42. Ibid., p. 86.
43. Binswanger, Existential analysis and psychotherapy.
44. May, Contributions of existential psychotherapy, p. 87.
45. Binswanger, Existential analysis and psychotherapy.
46. Lyons, J. Existential psychotherapy: Fact, hope, fiction. *Journal of Abnormal Social Psychology,* 1961, *62,* 242–249.
47. Alexander, F. Impressions from the Fourth International Congress of Psychotherapy. *Psychiatry,* 1959, *22,* 89–95.
48. Hora, T. Existential psychiatry and group psychotherapy. *American Journal of Psychoanalysis,* 1961, *21,* 58–70. (Also in Ruitenbeek (Ed.), *Psychoanalysis and existential philosophy,* pp. 130–154.)
49. Binswanger, The existential analysis school of thought, pp. 191–213.
50. Lyons, Existential psychotherapy.
51. May, & van Kaam, Existential theory and therapy, p. 75.
52. Bugental, J. F. T. *The search for authenticity: An existential-analytic approach to psychotherapy.* New York: Holt, Rinehart and Winston, 1965; Bugental, J. F. T. *The search for existential identity: Patient–therapist dialogues in humanistic psychology.* San Francisco: Jossey-Bass, 1976; Bugental, J. F. T. *Psychotherapy and process: the fundamentals of an existential-humanistic approach.* Reading, Mass: Addison-Wesley, 1978; see also Yalom, D. *Existential psychotherapy.* New York: Basic Books, 1980.
53. van Kaam, Counseling from the viewpoint of existential psychology, p. 75.

54. May, Contributions of existential psychotherapy, pp. 37–91.

55. Wolf, W. *Values and personality.* New York: Grune & Stratton, 1950.

56. Gendlin, E. T. Client-centered developments and work with schizophrenics. *Journal of Counseling Psychology,* 1962, *9,* 205–212; see also Gendlin, E. T. *Experiencing and the creation of meaning.* New York: Free Press, 1962.

57. Gendlin, E. T. A theory of personality change. In J. T. Hart & T. M. Tomlinson (Eds.), *New directions in client-centered therapy.* Boston: Houghton Mifflin, 1970. Pp. 129–173 (originally published in P. Worchel & D. Byrne (Eds.), *Personality change.* New York: Wiley, 1964); Gendlin, E. T. Existentialism and experiential psychotherapy. In Hart & Tomlinson (Eds.), *New directions in client-centered therapy,* pp. 70–94 (originally published in C. Moustakas (Ed.), *Existential child therapy.* New York: Basic Books, 1966); Gendlin, E. T. Client-centered and experiential psychotherapy. In D. A. Wexler & L. N. Rice (Eds.), *Innovations in client-centered therapy.* New York: Wiley, 1974; Gendlin, E. T. Experiential psychotherapy. In R. Corsini (Ed.), *Current psychotherapies.* Itasca, Ill.: Peacock, 1973.

chapter 15

Logotherapy: Frankl

Viktor E. Frankl (b. 1905) was born and educated in Vienna and received his M.D. (1930) and Ph.D. (1949) from the University of Vienna. He founded the Youth Advisement Centers in Vienna in 1928 and headed them until 1938. He was on the staff of the Neuropsychiatric University Clinic from 1930 to 1938. From 1936 to 1942, he was specialist in neurology and psychiatry and then head of the Neurological Department at Rothschild Hospital in Vienna. He became head of the Neurological Policlinic Hospital (in Vienna) in 1946. In 1947, he was appointed associate professor of neurology and psychiatry at the University of Vienna and became professor in 1955. He was visiting professor at Harvard University summer school in 1961, and in 1964 and 1965, visiting professor at the Chicago Psychiatric Foundation. From 1942 to 1945, he was imprisoned in German concentration camps, including Auschwitz and Dachau. His mother, father, brother, and wife died in the camps or gas chambers.

Frankl has written a number of books in German, some of which have been translated into Polish, Japanese, Dutch, Spanish, Portuguese, Italian, Swedish, and English. He has made many lecture tours in South America, India, Australia, Japan, the United States, and Europe.

BACKGROUND AND DEVELOPMENT

Frankl began his professional career in psychiatry with a psychoanalytic orientation, having been a student of Freud. However, he became influenced by the writings of existential philosophers, including Heidegger, Scheler, and Jaspers, and began developing his own existential philosophy as well as an existential psychotherapy. In 1938, he first used the terms *existenzanalysis* and *logotherapy* in his writings. In order to avoid confusion with Binswanger's existential analysis, Frankl has concentrated on the term *logotherapy.* The name existential analysis has continued to be used, however, and appears to refer to a different aspect of Frankl's theory and method than does logotherapy. Tweedie, who attempts to summarize Frankl's approach, notes that "these terms are nearly synonymous and refer to two facets of the same theory. While Existential Analysis is more indicative of the anthropological direction in which this theory is developed, Logotherapy is more descriptive of the actual therapeutic theory and method."[1] He goes on to say that "Logotherapy proceeds from the spiritual, while Existential Analysis proceeds toward the spiritual."[2] Later he writes that "Logotherapy . . . seeks to bring to awareness the unconscious spiritual factors of the patient's personality, while Existential Analysis is the endeavor to enable the patient to become conscious of his responsibility" and quotes Frankl: "By definition Existential Analysis aims at 'being conscious of having responsibility' *(Bewusstsein des Verantworkunghabens).*"[3] He goes on to another quotation from Frankl: "Beyond this it is the task of logotherapeutic endeavor to stimulate concrete meaning possibilities; this, however, requires an analysis of the concrete human existence (Dasein), the personal existence of the patient in question, in a word, existential analysis."[4] It appears that existential analysis refers to the analysis of the individual's existence, while logotherapy refers to the actual treatment. The name logotherapy seems to be more generally used, however, to include both aspects, and will be so used in this chapter.

This philosophy and therapy, developed in clinical practice and teaching, was tested and strengthened in Frankl's concentration camp experiences. He saw the truth so often expressed by poets and writers, that love is the ultimate and highest goal of human beings and that "the salvation of man is through love and in love."[5] He became convinced that there was one ultimate purpose to existence.

Frankl recorded his experiences in a book published in German in 1946 and in English in 1959 under the title *From Death Camp to Existentialism.* A revised edition, with the added section "Basic Concepts of Logotherapy," is called *Man's Search for Meaning* (1962). A revised paperback edition appeared in 1968. This little book is one of the main sources for the present chapter. Another source is *The Doctor and the Soul,* a translation of *Ärzliche Seelsorge* (1946). A second, expanded edition, with revisions and an added chapter, was published in 1965. This book brought together materials published in German prior to 1946, some of which had been published in the 1930s. Frankl has written a number of books in German since then.

PHILOSOPHY AND CONCEPTS

Introduction

In spite of the apathy of the prisoners in concentration camps, which resulted from both physical and psychological causes, Frankl found that "man *can* preserve a vestige of spiritual freedom, of independence of mind, even in such terrible conditions of psychic and physical stress."[6] Opportunities for choice were many, and there were examples of heroic choices to help others rather than to preserve oneself. "The sort of person the prisoner became was the result of an inner decision, and not the result of camp influences alone. Fundamentally, therefore, any man can, even under such circumstances decide what shall become of him—mentally and spiritually. He may retain his human dignity even in a concentration camp. . . . It is this spiritual freedom—which cannot be taken away—that makes life meaningful and purposeful."[7] If there is a meaning to life, Frankl reasoned, there is a meaning to suffering, since suffering, like death, is an ineradicable part of life; without them, life cannot be complete.

Only a few prisoners resisted falling victim to the prison camp's degenerating influences. The lack of any future goal or hope caused many to overlook existing opportunities to make something positive of camp life. Unusually bad external situations can also give a person the opportunity to grow beyond himself or herself spiritually. To do this, however, the person must have faith in the future. Without it, he or she gives up and has no will to live. With no aim, no purpose, no sense or meaning in life, there is no point in carrying on. Frankl asked his fellow prisoners who said that they expected nothing more from life "whether the question was really what we expected from life. Was it not, rather, what life was expecting from us?"[8] Life sets tasks for each person, and in meeting them, the person defines the meaning of his or her life. The tasks are different for each, and each situation is different, requiring a unique response. Sometimes a person is required to accept fate or to suffer. Each person's suffering is unique, and opportunity for growth lies in the way the person bears it.

The Nature of the Person

An individual is a unity with three aspects or dimensions: the somatic, or physical; the mental, or psychological; and the spiritual.[9] The first two are closely related and together constitute the "psychophysicum." They include inherited and constitutional factors, such as the innate drives. Psychoanalysis, through Freud, Adler, and Jung, has contributed to the understanding of these dimensions, particularly the psychological, but has neglected the spiritual, the distinctively human dimension.

Logotherapy emphasizes the third dimension, the spiritual. Spirituality is the first of three characteristics of human existence that distinguish people from animals. Spirituality is revealed phenomenologically in immediate self-consciousness, but it is derived from the "spiritual unconscious." "Unconscious spirituality is the origin and root of all consciousness. In other words, we know and acknowledge, not only an instinctive unconscious, but rather also a *spiritual unconscious,* and in it we see the supporting ground of all conscious spirituality. The ego is not *governed* by the id, but the spirit is *borne by the unconscious.* "[10] Spirituality is the chief attribute of the individual, and from it derives conscience, love, and aesthetic conscience.

The second characteristic of human existence is freedom. "But what is man? He is the essence which always decides. And he again and again decides what he will be in the next instant."[11] Freedom means freedom in the face of three things: (1) the instincts, (2) inherited disposition, and (3) environment. Although human beings are influenced by all of these, they still have freedom to accept or reject and to take a stand toward these conditions. Thus human beings do not simply exist; they decide what their existence will be. Since they can rise above biological, psychological, and sociological conditions, on which predictions can be based, they are individually unpredictable.[12]

The third factor in the individual's existence is responsibility. The individual's freedom is not only freedom *from,* but also freedom *to* something, which, according to Frankl, is the individual's responsibilities. The individual is responsible to himself or herself, to his or her conscience, or to God. "Logotherapy tries to make the patient fully aware of his own responsibilities; and therefore it must leave to him the option for what, to what or to whom, he understands himself to be responsible."[13]

Psychoanalysis is concerned with individuals becoming conscious of their repressed experiences or drives. Individual psychology is concerned with persons accepting responsibility for their symptoms. Each is one-sided and complements the other. "One might in fact state it as a basic theorem that *being human means being conscious and being responsible.* Both psychoanalysis and individual psychology err in that each sees only one aspect of humanity, one factor in human existence—whereas the two aspects must be taken jointly to yield a true picture of man."[14] Logotherapy goes beyond both to add the realm of the spiritual *(Geistig).* Responsibility is related to consciousness through conscience.

Although each individual is unique, he or she would have no meaning alone. "The significance of such individuality, the meaning of human personality, is, however, always related to community."[15] In the community, each individual, because he or she is unique, is irreplaceable. This is the difference between the community and the "mass," which is composed of identical units. "The community needs the individual existence in order for itself to have meaning," but also "the meaning of individuality comes to fulfillment in the community. To this extent, then, the value of the individual is dependent upon the community."[16] The mass, however, submerges the individual: "by escape into the mass, man loses his most intrinsic quality: responsibility."[17] But by becoming a part of the community, which is in itself a choice, the individual adds to his or her responsibility.

Motivation

Homeostasis, tension reduction, or the psychoanalytic pleasure principle cannot adequately account for human behavior. The status drive of individual psychology is also an insufficient explanation, as are self-expression, self-fulfillment, and self-actualization. These, according to Frankl, are effects rather than intentions, and the same is true for pleasure. In fact, "only when the primary objective orientation is lacking and has foundered, does that interest in one's self arise, as it is so strikingly manifested in neurotic existence. Therefore the striving for self-fulfillment is in no way something primary, rather, we see in it a deficient mode and a reduced level of human existence."[18]

The primary motivation in the individual is not what Frankl calls the will to pleasure or the will to power, but the will to meaning. It is this that "most deeply inspires man," that is "the most human phenomenon of all, since an animal certainly never worries about the meaning of its existence."[19]

Meaning is not invented by human beings, as Sartre claims, but, according to Frankl, is "discovered" by them. "Men can give meaning to their lives by realizing what I call *creative values,* by achieving tasks. But they can also give meaning to their lives by realizing *experiential values,* by experiencing the Good, the True, and the Beautiful, or by knowing one single human being in all his uniqueness. And to experience one human being as unique means to love him."[20] Even when these experiences are impossible, "a man can still give his life a meaning by the way he faces his fate, his distress."[21]

Human beings realize values by their attitude toward their destined, or inescapable, suffering. These are *attitudinal values,* as Frankl calls them, and the possibility for their realization exists until the last moment of life. Suffering thus has meaning.

The will to meaning is not a driving force in the psychodynamic sense. "Values do not drive a man; they do not *push* him, but rather *pull* him."[22] They involve choices or decisions. "Man is never driven to moral behavior; in each instance he decides to behave morally." He does so, not to satisfy a moral drive or to have a good conscience, but "for the sake of a cause to which he commits himself, or for a person whom he loves, or for the sake of his God."[23]

The meaning of life is not an abstraction.

> Ultimately, man should not ask what the meaning of life is, but rather he must recognize that it is *he* who is asked. In a word, each man is questioned by life; and he can only answer to life by *answering for* his own life; to life he can only respond by being responsible. . . . This emphasis on responsibleness is reflected in the categorical imperative of logotherapy, which is: 'So live as if you were living already for the second time and as if you had acted the first time as wrongly as you are about to act now!'[24]

The meaning of life is thus unique for each individual and varies with time.

Existence is transitory, but on its transitoriness hinges its responsibleness, since individuals are constantly faced with choices among the current potentialities. "Man constantly makes his choice concerning the mass of present potentialities." Once potentialities are actualized, "they are rendered realities; they are saved and delivered into the past, wherein they are rescued and preserved from transitoriness. For, in the past, nothing is irrecoverably lost, but everything is irrevocably stored."[25] Potentialities that are not chosen, however, are lost.

The Existential Vacuum and Existential Frustration

A common complaint of patients today is that their lives are meaningless. "They lack the awareness of a meaning worth living for. They are haunted by the experience of their inner emptiness, a void within themselves; they are caught in that situation which I have called the 'existential vacuum.' "[26] Frankl explains it as follows: with no instincts to guide their behavior and with the disappearance of traditions to guide their choices but faced with the necessity of making choices, people do not know what to do or what they want to do. "This existential vacuum manifests itself mainly in a state of boredom. . . . In actual fact, boredom is now causing, and certainly bringing to psychiatrists, more problems to solve than distress."[27] One manifestation is the "Sunday neurosis," which is "that kind of depression which afflicts people who become aware of the lack of content of their lives when the rush of the busy week is over and the void within themselves becomes manifest."[28]

The frustration of the will to meaning is "existential frustration," as Frankl calls it. This frustration is sometimes "vicariously compensated for by a will to power. . . . In other cases, the place of frustrated will to meaning is taken by the will to pleasure. That is why existential frustration often eventuates in sexual compensation. We can observe, in such cases, that the sexual libido becomes rampant in the existential vacuum."[29]

Existential frustration is not pathological or pathogenic per se. "Not every conflict is necessarily neurotic . . . suffering is not always a pathological phenomenon. . . . I would strictly deny that one's search for a meaning to his existence, or even his doubt of it, in every case is derived from, or results in, any disease. . . . A man's concern, even his despair, over the worthwhileness of life is a *spiritual distress* but by no means a *mental disease.*"[30] Philosophical conflicts and problems involving a person's view of the world are psychologically, biologically, and sociologically "conditioned but not caused." It is the fallacy of psychologism "to analyze every act for its psychic origin, and on that basis to decree whether its intellectual content is valid or invalid."[31] Even if there is pathology in the individual, his or her philosophy or world view cannot necessarily be labeled as pathological. Psychologism, however, tends to devaluate; "it is always trying to unmask," is forever bent on debunking, is constantly hunting down extrinsic—that is, neurotic or culturo-pathological—motivations. "Everywhere, psychologism sees nothing but masks, insists that only neurotic motives lie behind these masks."[32]

The search for meaning may lead to tension rather than to equilibrium, but such tension is not pathological; it is, rather, " an indispensable prerequisite of mental health . . . mental health is based on a certain degree of tension, the tension between what one has already achieved and what one still ought to accomplish, or the gap between what one is and what one should become."[33] What the individual needs in the first place is not the discharge of tension—a homeostasis, or equilibrium—but " 'Noödynamics,' i.e., the spiritual dynamics in a polar field of tension where the pole is represented by a meaning to be fulfilled and the other pole by the man who must fulfill it."[34]

The Nature of Neuroses and Psychoses

Although existential conflicts may exist without neurosis, every neurosis has an existential aspect. Neuroses are "grounded in the four basically different layers (or 'dimensions') of man's being": the physical; the psychological; the societal; and the existential, or spiritual.[35] The physiological bases are the constitutional (including neuropathy and psychopathy) and the conditioned (for example, the shock of a traumatic experience). The conditioned bases are probably precipitating factors. The various types of neuroses differ in terms of the relative importance of each of the four dimensions. The physiological bases cannot be reached by psychotherapy but only by drugs, and when the physiological component is great, there is little that psychotherapy can do.[36]

Noögenic Neuroses

Noetic refers to the spiritual dimension. "Noögenic neuroses do not emerge from conflicts between drives and instincts but rather from conflicts between various values; in other words, from moral conflicts, or, to speak in a more general way, from spiritual problems. Among such problems, existential frustration often plays a large role."[37] The disturbance is not in the spiritual dimension as such but is manifested in the psychophysicum. "Noögenic neuroses are illnesses 'out of spirit' *(aus dem Geist),* but they are not illnesses 'in the spirit' *(im Geist).* "[38]

The Collective Neurosis

Although our age is often called the age of anxiety, it is doubtful that anxiety is more prevalent now than in other times. There are, however, certain characteristics of the modern person that are "similar to neurosis" and may be designated as the collective neurosis. "First, there is the planless, day-to-day attitude toward life," with no long-term planning, which seems to be related to the uncertainty of life since the Second World War and the development of the atomic bomb.[39] "The second symptom is the fatalistic attitude toward life. This, again, is a product of the last war."[40] It is the attitude that it is not possible to plan one's life. The third symptom is collective thinking.

> Man would like to submerge himself in the masses. Actually, he is only drowned in the masses, he abandons himself as a free and responsible being. The fourth symptom is fanaticism. While the collectivist ignores his own personality, the fanatic ignores that of the other man. . . . Only his own opinion is valid. . . . Ultimately, all these four symptoms can be traced back to man's fear of responsibility and his escape from freedom.[41]

Education and mental hygiene, rather than psychotherapy, are required to cure the collective neuroses.

The Neuroses

Noögenic neuroses and the collective neuroses are included under the neuroses in the broad sense of the term. In a more restricted sense, neurosis involves primarily the psychic dimension of the person. "Neurosis is no noetic, no spiritual illness, no illness of man merely in his spirituality. Much more it is always an illness of man in his unity and wholeness."[42] Psychological complexes, conflicts, and traumatic experiences, however, are manifestations, rather than causes, of neurosis, which is more closely related to a developmental defect in the personality structure. Anxiety is a common factor, although it is not the cause of neurosis; however, it sustains the neurotic circle. Anticipatory anxiety is a more basic element. A fleeting symptom or a momentary failure in functioning may become the focus of attention. A fear of the recurrence of the symptom arises, which reinforces the symptom, beginning a neurotic circle that includes anticipatory anxiety.

There are two major types of neurosis.

Anxiety neurosis   Anxiety neurosis involves a malfunctioning of the vasomotor system, a disturbance of endocrine function, or a constitutional element. Traumatic experiences act as precipitating agents by focusing attention on the symptoms, but behind neurotic anxiety is an existential anxiety. This existential anxiety is the "fear of death and simultaneously the fear of life as a whole."[43] It is the result of a guilty conscience toward life, a sense of not having realized one's own value potentials. This fear becomes focused on a particular organ of the body or becomes concentrated on a symbolic concrete situation in the form of a phobia. A patient suffering from fear of open places described her anxiety as "a feeling like hanging in the air," which aptly described her whole spiritual situation, of which her neurosis was an expression.[44] The neurosis, existentially, is a mode of existence.

Obsessional neurosis   Obsessional neurosis, like all other neuroses, includes a constitutional, dispositional factor as well as a psychogenic factor. However, there is also an existential factor, represented by the choice or decision of the individual to go on to a fully developed obsessional neurosis. "The patient is not responsible for his obsessional ideas," but "he certainly is responsible for his attitude toward these ideas."[45] The obsessional neurotic is not able to tolerate uncertainty, the tension between what is and what ought to be. His or her world view is that of "hundred-percentness," or a search for the absolute, a striving for "absolute certainty in cognition and decision."[46] Since it is impossible for this person to achieve his or her total demands on life, he or she concentrates on a specific area; but even so, the person can succeed "only partially . . . and only at the price of his naturalness, his 'creaturalness.' Thus all his strivings have an inhuman quality."[47]

The Psychoses

In the neuroses, both the symptoms and the etiology are psychological. In the psychoses, the etiology is physical and the symptoms are psychological.

Melancholia   Melancholia, or endogenous psychosis, also involves psychogenetic and existential aspects, or a "pathoplastic" factor, which refers to the freedom to shape one's destiny and to determine one's mental attitude toward the disease. Thus "even psychosis is at bottom a kind of test of a human being, of the humanity of the psychotic patient."[48] With freedom of mental attitude goes responsibility. The anxiety present in melancholia has a physiological basis, but this does not explain the anxiety or the guilt, which are caused primarily by fear of death and of conscience and represent a mode of existence or of experiencing.[49] "Conscientious anxiety can be understood only . . . *as the anxiety of a human being as such: as existential* anxiety,"[50] not in physiological terms. Although an animal can suffer from anxiety, human psychoses involve a crucial element of humanity—of existentiality—above and beyond the organic condition.

In melancholia, the physiological basis or "psychophysical insufficiency is experienced in uniquely human fashion as tension between what the person is and what he ought to be," between "the need and the possibility of fulfillment."[51] This insufficiency is felt as inadequacy and appears in various forms, bringing out fears that were present in the premorbid condition: fears of inability to earn sufficient money, of inability to attain one's life goals, of "Judgment Day." The melancholiac "becomes blind to the values inherent in his own being" and later to the values outside himself. First "he feels himself as worthless and his own life as meaningless,"[52] and then the world itself is seen in the same light. Guilt arising from the individual's feeling of insufficiency and "resulting from his intensified existential tension can swell to such a point that he feels his guilt to be ineradicable."[53] Life then assumes colossal dimensions.

Schizophrenia   In schizophrenia, the phenomena of feelings of being influenced, observed, or persecuted are all forms of the "experience of pure objectness. . . . The schizophrenic experiences himself as the object of the observing or persecuting intentions of his fellow men."[54] The schizophrenic experiences himself or herself as though he or she were transformed from a subject into an object. An "experiential passivity" is evidenced in the language of schizophrenics by their use of the passive mood. "The schizophrenic person experiences himself as so limited in his full humanity that he no longer feels himself as really 'existent.' "[55] Both consciousness and responsibility are affected.

THE THERAPY PROCESS

Patients repeatedly present problems concerning the meaning of their lives, that is, philosophical or spiritual problems. These problems may or may not be a sign of disease or neurosis. Neuroses and psychoses, including the organic psychotic processes, have an existential aspect as well as constitutional and psychogenetic aspects. They involve both a freedom of spiritual attitude toward the constitutional and psychological factors and a mode of existence. Therefore, treatment must be more than medical and more than psychological; it must include consideration of the existential aspects, too.

Logotherapy is directed toward such problems. The word *logos* has the twofold definition of "the meaning" and "the spiritual." Logotherapy thus deals with the existential and spiritual nature of the person.

Diagnosis

Proper diagnosis is the first step in psychotherapy and an important one. All emotional disturbance or mental illness involves physical, psychological, and spiritual factors: "there are really no pure somatogenic, psychogenic, or noögenic neuroses. There are merely mixed cases, cases in which, respectively, a somatogenic, psychogenic, or noögenic moment moves into the foreground of the theoretical object and the therapeutic objective."[56] The purpose of diagnosis is to determine the nature of each factor and which is the primary factor. When the physical factor is the primary one, the condition is a psychosis; when the psychological factor is the primary one, it is a neurosis; and when the spiritual factor is the primary one, it is a noögenic neurosis.

Therapy involves the whole person, however, and may include physical (or medical) treatment, psychotherapy, and logotherapy, together or consecutively. According to Frankl, it is "not the aim of logotherapy to take the place of existing psychotherapy, but only to complement it, thus forming a picture of man in his wholeness—which includes the spiritual dimension." It focuses explicitly on meanings and values. A psychotherapy "which is blind to values"—for "there is no such thing as a psychotherapy unconcerned with values"[57]—is inadequate to deal with these problems.

General Nature of Logotherapy

Whereas the aim of psychoanalysis is to make the unconscious conscious and the aim of individual psychological therapy (Adler) is to make the neurotic accept responsibility for his or her symptoms, the aim of logotherapy is to make the person consciously accept responsibility for himself or herself. "For the aim of the psychotherapist should be to bring out the ultimate possibilities of the patient. Not to penetrate his deepest secrets, but to realize his latent values. . . ."[58] Logotherapy fills a gap in psychotherapy;

it "operates, as it were, beyond the fields of the Oedipus complex and the inferiority complex . . . beyond all affect-dynamics." It is "a form psychotherapy which sees beneath the psychic malaise of the neurotic his spiritual struggles."[59]

Philosophical and existential, or spiritual, problems cannot be avoided, nor can they be disposed of by focusing on their pathological roots or consequences—physical or psychological.

> What is needed here is to meet the patient squarely. We must not dodge the discussion, but enter into it sincerely. We must attack these questions on their own terms, at face value. Our patient has a right to demand that the ideas he advances be treated on the philosophical level. . . . A philosophical question cannot be dealt with by turning the discussion toward the pathological roots from which the question stemmed, or by hinting at the morbid consequences of philosophical pondering. . . . If only for the sake of philosophical fairness, we ought to fight with the same weapons.[60]

Psychotherapy cannot deal with philosophical questions. The neurotic's world view may be wrong, but correcting it is the function of logotherapy rather than of psychotherapy. If the neurotic's world view were right, psychotherapy would be unnecessary. Philosophical questions cannot be reduced to psychological terms. "Psychotherapy as such is exceeding its scope in dealing with philosophical questions. . . . Logotherapy must *supplement* psychotherapy."[61]

In actual practice, however, psychotherapy and logotherapy cannot be separated, since the psychological and the philosophical or spiritual aspects of the individual are indissolubly joined and can be separated only logically. Nevertheless, in principle, they represent different realms. Psychotherapy uncovers the psychological background of an ideology, while logotherapy reveals the flaws in the improper bases for a world view.

With some patients, it is wise to begin with the spiritual level, even though the genesis of the problem may be in the lower layers. With others, logotherapy follows psychotherapy of psychoses or neuroses.

Logotherapy and the Noögenic Neuroses

Logotherapy is the specific therapy for existential frustration, existential vacuum, or the frustration of the will to meaning. These conditions, when they result in neurotic symptomatology, are called *noögenic neuroses*.

Logotherapy is concerned with making people conscious of their responsibility, since being responsible is an essential basis of human existence. Responsibility implies obligation, and obligation can be understood only in terms of meaning—the meaning of human life. The question of meaning is an intrinsically human one and arises in dealing with patients suffering from existential frustration or conflicts.[62] Thus logotherapy is concerned with problems that involve meaning in its various aspects and realms.

The Meaning of Life and Death

The normal individual can escape from a responsible life only in situations such as festivals and intoxication. The neurotic seeks a permanent refuge from everyday society. The melancholiac seeks it through suicide. If questioned, the melancholiac will deny such thoughts.

> [W]hereupon we ask him . . . why he does not have (or no longer has) ideas of committing suicide. A melancholiac who really is not harboring such intentions or has overcome them, will answer without hesitation that he must consider his family, or think of his work, or something of the sort. The man who is trying to fool his analyst, however, will immediately fall into a typical state of embarrassment. He is actually at a loss for arguments supporting his "phony" affirmation of life. Characteristically, such dissimulating patients will try to change the subject, and will usually bring up their naked demand to be released from confinement. People are psychologically incapable of making up counterfeit arguments in favor of life, or arguments for their continuing to live, when thoughts of suicide are surging up within them.[63]

We can grasp the meaning of the universe best in the form of a "supermeaning" to indicate that the meaning of the whole goes beyond what is comprehensible. However, "belief in a supermeaning—whether as a metaphysical concept or in the religious sense of Providence—is of foremost psychotherapeutic and psychohygienic importance. . . . To such a faith there is, ultimately, nothing that is meaningless."[64]

The individual, of course, not only, or perhaps even primarily, is concerned with the meaning of the universe, but also is concerned with the meaning of his or her own life. Patients often assert that the meaning of life is pleasure, "that all human activity is governed by the striving for happiness, that all psychic processes are determined exclusively by the pleasure principle. . . . Now, to our mind the pleasure principle is an artificial creation of psychology. Pleasure is not the goal of our aspirations, but the consequence of attaining them."[65] Pleasure cannot give meaning to life. If pleasure were the source of meaning, life would have little to offer, since unpleasant sensations outnumber pleasant sensations in life. "In reality, life is little concerned with pleasure or unpleasure. . . . Life teaches most people that 'we are not here to enjoy ourselves.' "[66] Those who are bent on the search for pleasure and happiness fail to find them, because of their concentration on them.

The basic skepticism and nihilism of these patients has to be countered. "But it often becomes necessary in addition to disclose the full richness of the world of values, and to make clear the extent of its domain."[67] If the patient bewails his life for its lack of meaning, "since his activities are without any higher value . . . this is the point at which we must reason with him, showing him that it is a matter of indifference what a person's occupation is, or at what job he works. The crucial thing is how he works, whether he in fact fills the place in which he happens to have landed."[68]

In the case of a would-be suicide, the question is "whether the sum of [a] balance sheet can ever turn out so negative that living on appears incontrovertibly without value." Such a conviction is subjective and may be unjustified.

> "We can therefore risk the generalization that suicide is never ethically justified. . . . it is our duty to convince the would-be suicide that taking one's own life is categorically contrary to reason, that life is meaningful to every human being under any circumstances. We believe this can be done by objective argument and analysis of the problem on its own terms—by the methods of logotherapy, that is. . . . Where

no psychopathological basis of motivation can be shown, and where, therefore, psychotherapy in the narrower sense of the word can find no point of departure, logotherapy is the indicated method.[69]

Even in suicide "man cannot escape his sense of responsibility. For he commits the act of suicide in freedom (assuming, of course, that he is still sane)."[70]

The aim of logotherapy is to help patients "find an aim and a purpose in their existence" and to help them "achieve the highest possible activation" of their lives.[71] In addition to being led to experience existence as a constant effort to actualize values, patients must be shown the value of the conviction of responsibility for a task—a specific task. "The conviction that one has a task before him has enormous psycho-therapeutic and psychohygienic value. We venture to say that nothing is more likely to help a person overcome or endure objective difficulties or subjective troubles than the consciousness of having a task in life."[72]

"The factors of uniqueness and singularity are essential constituents of the mean-ingfulness of human existence." The patient must be shown that every life has a unique goal, which is reached by a single course. If the patient does not know his or her unique potentialities, then the patient's primary task is to discover them. "Existential analysis is accordingly designed to help the individual comprehend his responsibility to accom-plish each of his tasks";[73] the fulfillment of these assignments gives meaning to life.

The finiteness of existence also gives meaning to life. Death does not render life meaningless; rather, the temporality of life gives it meaning. If life were not finite, everything could be postponed; there would be no need for action, choice, or decisions, and thus no responsibility. "The meaning of human existence is based upon its irreversi-ble quality."[74] In logotherapy, this aspect of life must be put before the patient to bring the patient to consciousness of his or her responsibility. The patient may be encouraged to imagine that he is reviewing "his own biography in the declining days of his life," and as he comes to the "chapter dealing with the present phase of his life . . . by a miracle he has the power to decide what the contents of the next chapter shall be. He is to imagine, that is, that it still lies within his capacity to make corrections, as it were, in a crucial chapter of his unwritten inner life story."[75] The categorical imperative of logotherapy applies here: "live as if you were living for the second time and had acted as wrongly the first time as you are about to act now."[76] Once a patient does this, the patient will realize the great responsibility for the next hour and the next day.

Every person has a unique destiny, which, like death, is a part of life. "What we call destiny is that which is essentially exempt from human freedom, that lies neither within the scope of man's power nor his responsibility."[77] Destiny has meaning, and to quarrel with it is to overlook its meaning. Without the restrictions imposed by destiny, freedom would have no meaning.

Freedom without destiny is impossible; freedom can only be freedom in the face of a destiny, a free stand toward destiny. . . . Freedom presupposes restrictions, is contingent upon restrictions. . . . If we wanted to define man, we would have to call him that entity which has freed itself from whatever has determined it (determined it as biological-psychological-sociological type); that entity, in other words, that tran-scends all these determinants either by conquering them and shaping them, or by deliberately submitting to them.[78]

The past is part of a person's destiny, since it is unalterable, but the future is not exclusively determined by the past. The mistakes of the past can serve as lessons for shaping the future. A person's disposition, or biological endowment, is part of the destiny, as is the person's situation, or external environment, and psychic attitude, to the extent that it is unfree. The constant struggle between the person's inward and outward destiny and his or her freedom is the intrinsic nature of life.

Logotherapy sees destiny as "the ultimate testing ground for human freedom."[79] Biological, psychological, and sociological destiny obstruct human freedom, but the way in which the same handicaps and barriers are meaningfully incorporated into a person's life varies widely among individuals, as does the attitude or position taken toward them. Neurotics exhibit a morbid acceptance of fate and destiny, but such neurotic fatalism is only a disguised form of escape from responsibility. Patients cannot be allowed to blame childhood educational and environmental influences for what they are or for determining their destinies. This practice and that of blaming their neuroticism for their faults are ways of avoiding responsibility. Even the patient with an organic disorder is responsible for his or her spiritual attitude toward his or her condition.

The Meaning of Suffering

A person's responsibility is to actualize values. The three categories of values (already mentioned) are those that are actualized by doing; those that are realized by experiencing the world; and attitudinal values, which "are actualized wherever the individual is faced with something unalterable, something imposed by destiny. From the manner in which a person takes these things upon himself, assimilates these difficulties into his own psyche, there flows an incalculable multitude of value-potentialities. This means that *human life can be fulfilled not only in creating and enjoying, but also in suffering.*"[80] Life can obtain its ultimate meaning not only in sacrificing it, as a hero, but in the very process of facing death. Trouble and suffering guard a person from apathy and boredom; they result in activity, thus leading to growth and maturity.

The destiny a person suffers is "to be shaped where possible, and to be endured where necessary." Only when a person "no longer has any possibility of actualizing creative values, when there is really no means at hand for shaping fate—then is the time for attitudinal values to be actualized. . . . The very essence of an attitudinal value inheres in the manner in which a person resigns himself to the inevitable; in order therefore for attitudinal values to be truly actualized, it is important that the fate he resigns himself to must be actually inevitable."[81] Thus every situation offers the opportunity for the actualization of values, if not for creative or experiential values, then for attitudinal values. "Cases may arise where existential analysis is called upon to make a person capable of suffering—whereas psychoanalysis, for instance, aims only at making him capable of pleasure or capable of doing. For there are situations in which man can fulfill himself only in genuine suffering, and in no other way."[82]

The Meaning of Work

Responsibility to life is assumed by responding to the situations that it presents. "The response should be given not in words but in acting, by doing."[83] Consciousness of responsibility arises out of awareness of a unique concrete personal task, a "mission."

The realization of creative values usually coincides with a person's work, which generally represents the area in which the person's uniqueness can be seen in relation to society. This work as a contribution to society is the source of the meaning and the value of the person's uniqueness. It is not the particular occupation on which fulfillment depends. "The job at which one works is not what counts, but rather the manner in which one does the work."[84] Neurotics who complain that a different occupation would offer fulfillment must be shown this. It is not the occupation itself but the expression of the person's uniqueness and singularity in the work or beyond the required duties that gives meaning to the occupation.

For some, work seems to be only a means to the end of obtaining money to live, and life seems only to begin with leisure. There are also those whose work is so exhausting that there is no time for leisure, but only for sleep. Some devote all their time to the pursuit of wealth as an end in itself. Work can be misused as a means to a neurotic end. The neurotic also may sometimes attempt to escape from life in general by taking refuge in work. When the neurotic is not working, he or she feels at a loss, and the poverty of meaning in the neurotic's life is revealed. "These people who know no goal in life are running the course of life at the highest possible speed so that they will not notice the aimlessness of it. They are at the same time trying to run away from themselves—but in vain. On Sundays, when the frantic race pauses for twenty-four hours, all the aimlessness, meaninglessness, and emptiness of their existence rises up before them once more."[85] Commercialized entertainment provides a refuge for these Sunday neurotics.

The existential importance of work is seen in what Frankl calls the "unemployment neurosis." The most prominent symptom in the unemployed person is apathy, the feeling of uselessness and emptiness. "He feels useless because he is unoccupied. Having no work, he thinks life has no meaning."[86] In neurotics, unemployment becomes an alibi for all their failures and wipes out all responsibility to others and to themselves, as well as to life. However, the unemployment may be a result of the neurosis rather than the neurosis being a result of unemployment.

Unemployment is not an unconditional fate to which a person must succumb by developing an unemployment neurosis. There is an alternative to surrendering physically to the forces of social destiny. It is possible to engage in various other activities, to use time constructively, and to take an affirmative attitude toward life. Work is not the only way to give life meaning. The individual can decide what his or her attitude will be, whether positive and hopeful or apathetic.

Unemployment neurosis can be treated psychotherapeutically, but only by logotherapy, since it is a problem related to the meaning of existence. Logotherapy "shows the jobless person the way to inner freedom in spite of his unfortunate situation and teaches him that consciousness or responsibility through which he can still give some content to his hard life and wrest meaning from it."[87]

The Meaning of Love

The community is a rich field of human experience. The intimate community of the self with another is the area in which experiential values are especially realizable.

> Love is living the experience of another person in all his uniqueness and singularity. . . . In love the beloved person is comprehended in his very essence, as the unique

and singular being that he is; he is comprehended as a thou, and as such is taken into the self. As a human person he becomes for the one who loves him indispensable and irreplaceable without having done anything to bring this about. . . . Love is not deserved, is unmerited—it is simply grace. . . . It is also enchantment.[88]

Enchantment reflects on the world and on a person's values. There is a third factor that enters into love—"the miracle of love," that is, the entrance into life of a new person, a child.

The individual as lover can react differently to the three layers of the human person—the physical, the psychic, and the spiritual. The most primitive attitude is the sexual, which is directed toward the physical layer. The erotic attitude (commonly called infatuation) is directed toward the psychic layer. Love is the third attitude, directed toward the loved one's spiritual layer. This layer constitutes the uniqueness of the loved one, which, unlike the physical and psychological states, is irreplaceable and permanent.

"Love is only one of the possible ways to fill life with meaning, and is not even the best way. Our existences would have come to a sad pass and our lives would be poor indeed if their meaning depended upon whether or not we experienced happiness in love. . . . The individual who neither loves nor is loved can still shape his life in a highly meaningful manner."[89] The absence of love may be due to a neurotic failure rather than to destiny. Outward physical attractiveness is relatively unimportant, and its lack is not sufficient reason for being resigned to renunciation of love. Renouncing love engenders resentment, since it implies either overvaluing or devaluing love.

Emphasis on appearance or external beauty leads to devaluation of the person as such. Sex appeal is impersonal. Relationships based on sex are superficial; they are not love. Nor do those involved in such relationships want love, which includes responsibility. True love is experienced as valid forever. A person can mistake infatuation for love, but it can turn out to be error only later on.

Neurotics may fear the tensions of unhappy, unrequited love and so avoid opportunities for love. Such persons must be reeducated to be ready and receptive, to wait for the single happy love affair that may follow nine unhappy ones. Psychotherapy must bring the flight tendency into the open.

Psychosexual maturing, which begins in puberty, is subject to three kinds of disturbance, resulting in different sexual neuroses. One type occurs at the final stage of sexual maturing, when the physical sexual urge is becoming an erotic tendency directed toward a person. It may happen, perhaps after some disappointment in love, that a young person believes that he or she will never find someone that he or she can at the same time respect and desire sexually. This person then plunges into sexuality without emotion or love, reverting to a lower level of psychosexual development. This is, according to Frankl's terminology, the "resentment type." The second type is represented by persons who have never progressed beyond sexuality to an erotic attitude and do not expect to experience love. This is the "resignation type." Such individuals maintain that love is an illusion; they include the Don Juan. The third type, the "inactive type," shuns the other sex entirely. The sexual instinct is expressed only in masturbation. This group also includes young people who suffer from sexual frustration, which is the expression of a more general psychological distress. Such sexual frustration in a young person is "an indication that his sex instinct is not yet (or is no longer) subordinated to an erotic tendency and so integrated into the total system of his personal strivings."[90]

The so-called sexual frustration of youth is not solved by sexual activity but by maturation to love. "The therapy is of the simplest. It suffices to introduce the young person in question into a mixed company of people of his age. There the young man will sooner or later fall in love—that is, he will find a partner—in the erotic and not in the sexual sense"[91] and will progress to the erotic stage of development. Crude sexuality and frustration will disappear. The person meanwhile matures, so that if and when a serious sexual relationship does develop, its sexuality will assume the appropriate form, as an expression of love. "Now, under the dominance of the erotic tendency, he can build up an erotic relationship within the framework of which sexual relations can then be considered. . . . The young man's sense of responsibility has meanwhile matured to the point where he can decide on his own and his partner's behalf whether and when he ought to enter into a serious sexual relationship with her."[92] The therapist's position on sexual intercourse between young people is that he or she must veto it if possible whenever it is not a part of real love. In no case, however, can the therapist recommend it, since this is a personal moral problem and it is the responsibility of the person to decide. The therapist's task is to teach the person to be responsible.

Logotherapy is the specific therapy for the noögenic neuroses because it directs itself toward the primary problem—their basic nature, the existential frustration or vacuum, or the lack of meaning in life and its various aspects. The therapeutic goal is to eliminate the frustration by filling the vacuum, by helping the patient achieve meaning in life. This is accomplished by helping the patient to understand and accept the existential or spiritual nature of life and to assume responsibility for himself or herself and for the actualization of values by responding to the demands or tasks that life presents.

Logotherapy as a Nonspecific Therapy of Neuroses

In the treatment of psychogenic neurotic reactions, logotherapy directs itself neither to the symptoms nor to their psychogenesis, but to the patient's attitudes toward the symptoms. Logotherapy has developed two specific techniques for dealing with neuroses. These are described below.

In addition, general logotherapy, as applied in the noögenic neuroses, is applicable to the treatment not only of the specific neuroses, but also of psychoses, in relation to the existential or spiritual problems that are present.

In dealing with neurotics, logotherapy is not a symptomatic treatment. It is concerned instead with the patient's attitude toward his or her symptoms. "Insofar as logotherapy does not treat the symptom directly, but rather attempts to bring about a change of attitude, a personal reversal of attitude toward the symptom, it is truly a personalistic psychotherapy."[93]

IMPLEMENTATION: TECHNIQUES OF LOGOTHERAPY

Logotherapy places emphasis on the relationship between the patient and the therapist. "This relationship between two persons is what seems to be the most significant aspect of the psychotherapeutic process, a more important factor than any method or technique."[94] With the diversity of patients and therapists, "the psychotherapeutic process consists of a continuous chain of improvisations."[95] The relationship requires a balance between the extremes of human closeness and scientific detachment. "This means that the therapist must neither be guided by mere sympathy, by his desire to help his patient, nor, conversely, repress his human interest in the other human being by dealing with him in terms of technique."[96]

Because it is concerned with existential, spiritual, or philosophical problems, logotherapy engages in discussion of these problems. The method is not an intellectual or strictly rational one, however. "Logotherapy is as far removed from being a process of 'logical' reasoning as from being merely moral exhortation. Above all, a psychotherapist—and the logotherapist included—is neither a teacher nor a preacher. . . ." The maieutic dialogue in the Socratic sense may be used; "it is not necessary, however, to enter into sophisticated debates with the patients."[97]

The concern with existential or spiritual questions is "fraught with intricate problems, for it then becomes necessary for the doctor to take a stand on the question of values. The moment the doctor commits himself to such a 'psychotherapy' . . . his own philosophy necessarily comes to the fore—whereas previously his outlook remained hidden behind his role as doctor."[98] The logotherapist must "beware of forcing his philosophy upon the patient. There must be no transference (or, rather, countertransference) of a personal philosophy, of a personal concept of values, to the patient."[99] This is because the concept of responsibility implies that the patient is responsible for himself or herself. The logotherapist only brings the patient to experience this responsibility; the logotherapist does not tell the patient to what—conscience, society, God or another higher power—or for what—the realization of values, the fulfillment of personal tasks, the particular meaning of life—he or she is responsible.

Two logotherapeutic techniques, paradoxical intention and dereflection, are designed to deal with conditions met in cases of the anxiety and obsessive–compulsive neurosis. Anxiety neuroses and phobic conditions are characterized by anticipatory anxiety, which produces exactly the condition that the patient fears. According to Frankl, the occurrence of the condition then reinforces the anticipatory anxiety, creating a vicious circle, until the patient avoids or withdraws from those situations in which he or she expects the fear to recur. This withdrawal Frankl calls "wrong passivity," which is one of the "four patterns of response" he describes.[100] The patient suffering from obsessive–compulsive neuroses engages in "wrong activity" when he or she fights obsessive ideas and compulsions. "Wrong activity" also occurs in sexual neuroses, in which the patient, striving for competent sexual performance, which the patient feels is demanded of him or her, engages in responses that are inappropriate to the situation. Excessive intention makes the performance of the desired function impossible. In such cases, there is also frequently an excessive attention and a compulsive self-observation.

In cases involving anticipatory anxiety, and obssessive-compulsive and phobic conditions, the logotherapeutic technique called paradoxical intention is useful. This technique requires or encourages the patient to intend, if only momentarily, that which is anticipated with fear. The obsessive-compulsive patient stops resisting obsessions and compulsions, and the phobic patient stops fighting fears, breaking the vicious circle of anticipatory anxiety. This is a reversal of the patient's attitude toward the situation. In addition,

> it is carried out in as humorous a setting as possible. This brings about a change of attitude toward the symptom which enables the patient to place himself at a distance from the symptom, to detach himself from his neurosis. . . . if we succeed in bringing the patient to the point where he ceases to flee from or to fight his symptoms, but on the contrary, even exaggerates them, then we may observe that the symptoms diminish and that the patient is no longer haunted by them.[101]

"Paradoxical intention is effective irrespective of the underlying etiologic basis: in other words it is an intrinsically nonspecific method. . . . This is not to say that it is a symptomatic therapy, however, for the logotherapist, when applying paradoxical intention, is concerned not so much with the symptom in itself but, with the patient's *attitude* toward his neurosis and its symptomatic manifestations."[102]

Paradoxical intention is sometimes successful in severe and longstanding cases. It is particularly effective in short-term treatment of phobias with underlying anticipatory anxiety. Seventy-five percent of the patients treated have been cured or have improved, according to Frankl. It is not a superficial method; it appears to affect deeper levels. It is "essentially more than a change of behavior patterns; rather, it is an existential reorientation *(existentielle Umstellung).* "[103] It is logotherapy in the truest sense of the word, "based on what is called in logotherapeutic terms psychonoëtic antagonism . . . which refers to the specifically human capacity to detach oneself, not only from the world but also from oneself."[104]

Excesses of attention, intention, and self-observation are treated by another logotherapeutic technique, which is called dereflection. Dereflection is particularly useful in cases of male sexual impotence and female inability to reach a climax. Hyperintention and hyper-reflection inhibit performance. Dereflection diverts attention from the act and from the self to the partner, and removes the demand for performance.

> Such ignoring, or de-reflection, however, can only be attained to the degree to which the patient's awareness is directed toward positive aspects. De-reflection, in itself, contains both a negative and a positive aspect. The patient must be de-reflected from his anticipatory anxiety *to* something else. . . . Through de-reflection, the patient is enabled to ignore his neurosis by focusing his attention away from himself. He is directed to a life full of potential meanings and values that have a specific appeal to his personal potentialities.[105]

Paradoxical intention substitutes "right passivity" for "wrong passivity," Dereflection substitutes "right activity" for "wrong activity."

EXAMPLES

The following case is reported by Frankl.[106]

Paradoxical intention is also applicable in cases more complex than those involving monosymptomatic neurosis. The following will demonstrate that even instances of severe obsessive-compulsive character neurosis (in German clinical terminology referred to as anankastic psychopathic character structure) may be appropriately and beneficially treated by means of paradoxical intention.

The patient was a sixty-five-year-old woman who had suffered for sixty years from a washing compulsion of such severity that she was admitted to our clinic for a period of observation in order that I might certify her for a leucotomy (which I expected to be the only available procedure for bringing relief in this severe case). Her symptoms began when she was four years of age. When she was prevented from indulging her washing compulsion, she would even lick her hands. Later on she was continually afraid of being infected by people with skin diseases. She would never touch a doorknob. She also insisted that her husband stick to a very complicated prophylactic ritual. For a long time the patient had been unable to do any housework, and finally she remained in bed all day. Nevertheless, even there she persisted in scrubbing things with a cloth for hours, up to three hundred times or more, and having her husband repeatedly rinse out the cloth. "Life was hell for me," she confessed.

In the hope of avoiding brain surgery, my assistant, Dr. Eva Niebauer, started logotherapeutic treatment by means of paradoxical intention. The result was that nine days after admission the patient began to help in the ward by mending the stockings of her fellow patients, assisting the nurses by cleaning the instrument tables and washing syringes, and finally even emptying pails of bloody and putrid waste materials! Thirteen days after admission she went home for a few hours and upon her return to the clinic, she triumphantly reported having eaten a roll with soiled hands. Two months later she was able to lead a normal life.

It would not be accurate to say that she is completely symptom-free, for frequently obsessive-compulsive ideas come to her mind. However, she has been able to get relief by ceasing to fight her symptoms (fighting only serves to reinforce them) and, instead, by being ironical about them; in short, by applying paradoxical intention. She is even able to joke about her pathologic thoughts. This patient still kept in contact with the outpatient clinic, for she continued to need supportive logotherapy. The improvement in her condition persisted however, and thus the leucotomy, which previously had seemed unavoidable, had now become unnecessary.

The following case report is taken from a report of seven cases by an American psychiatrist who applied the method of paradoxical intention to twenty-four cases with successful results.[107]

A. V., aged forty-five, married mother of one sixteen-year-old son, has a twenty-four-year history of a grave phobic neurosis consisting of severe claustrophobia such as fear of riding in cars. She had fear of heights, of riding in elevators, of crossing bridges, of collapsing, of leaving the house (when forced to do so, she would hang on to trees, bushes, anything). She also had a fear of open spaces, being alone, and becoming paralyzed. She was treated for her phobic neurosis over the past twenty-four years by various psychiatrists and received, repeatedly, long-term psychoanalytically oriented psychotherapy. In addition, the patient was hospitalized several times, received several series of electroconvulsive treatments (ECT), and finally lobotomy was suggested. During the four years before I saw her, she had been hospitalized continuously on a disturbed ward in a state hospital. There she received ECT and intensive drug therapy with barbiturates, phenothiazines, monoamine oxidase inhibitors, and amphetamine compounds—all to no avail. She had become so paralyzed by her numerous phobias that she was unable to leave a certain part of the ward which surrounded her bed. She was constantly in acute distress in spite of receiving large doses of tranquilizers. Her tension was so great that her muscles hurt intensely. She tried constantly "not to collapse," "not to get nervous," and "not to become panicky." Diagnoses of her illness, made by private psychiatrists, ranged from psychoneurosis to schizophrenic reaction, schizo-affective type. Diagnosis at the hospital, just a few months before I treated her, was schizophrenic reaction, pseudo-neurotic type, with phobic anxiety and depressive manifestations. While in the hospital, she had been treated for a year and a half with "intensive analytically oriented psychotherapy" by an experienced clinical psychologist.

On March 1, 1959, all medication was discontinued and I began treatment with Paradoxical Intention. The technique was fully explained to her and we worked together, symptom by symptom and fear by fear. We started off first with removing the smaller fears, such as the one of not being able to sleep. The patient was removed from the disturbed ward and was instructed to "try to pass out and become as panicky as possible." At first, she said angrily, "I don't have to be afraid! I am afraid! This is ridiculous. You are making me worse!" After a few weeks of struggle, the patient was able to remain on a ward located on the third floor and "unsuccessfully" tried hard to pass out and become paralyzed. Both the patient and I went to the elevator to ride to the fifth floor. The patient was instructed to walk into the elevator and ride up with the strong intention of passing out and showing me "how wonderfully she can become panicky and paralyzed." While on the elevator, I commanded her to pass out, but at this she laughed and replied: "I am trying so hard—I can't do it. I don't know what is the matter with me—I can't be afraid anymore. I guess I'm trying hard enough to be afraid!" Upon reaching the fifth floor, the patient was proud and overjoyed as well. This seemed to be the turning point in the treatment. From then on, she used Paradoxical Intention any time she needed it. For the first time in many years, the patient walked outside alone around the hospital without fear, but "constantly trying hard to become panicky and paralyzed." After five months of this therapy, she was symptom-free. She returned home for a week-end visit and enjoyed her stay without any phobias for the first time in twenty-four years. When she returned to the hospital from this trip, she was contented and stated that there was only one fear left, namely that of crossing bridges. The same day we went together in my car and crossed a bridge. While crossing, I ordered her to pass out and become panicky, but she only laughed and said, "I can't! I can't!" Shortly thereafter, she was released from the hospital. Since then she has seen me every two to three months for a check-up "because of gratefulness." It is important for me to emphasize that quite purposefully I did not familiarize myself with her past history, nor with the underlying psychodynamics.

Two months ago she wanted a special appointment. When I saw her, she was quite tense, expressing anticipatory anxiety about getting sick again. Her husband had been out of work for several months and also had been suffering from a neurological disorder which was in the process of clearing. At the same time the patient was menstruating. This pressure caused her to become anxious and she was just beginning to slide back into the vicious cycle of her previous illness. In one session, however, she was able to understand what had happened and to avoid a re-establishment of the destructive pattern of her phobias. This patient has been out of the hospital and living a full and happy life with her family for two and a half years. Recovery was brought about with no attempt on my part to "understand" the patient's symptoms in terms of psychoanalytic theory and "depth psychology."

The question might well be asked: what really goes on in the sessions? Therapy is begun with taking the case history, recording symptomatology, etc., explaining to the patient the basic principles of Paradoxical Intention, and discussing case histories of my own and some of the typical cases reported by Frankl, Niebauer, and Kocourek. This usually takes between one and a half and two hours. This will do two things for the patient: he will learn to understand what we are trying to do and he will gain confidence that this therapy is effective. I have, for instance, found it very valuable to have a patient who has been cured with this type of treatment meet with the one who is starting in therapy, both in hospital and private practice. This can be done very well individually, and also is valuable in the group psychotherapy setting. I do not deny that this sort of thing has suggestive value, but, may I ask, what doctor or psychiatrist can treat his patients without this factor? As far as the technique itself is concerned, it must not be confused with suggestion. In fact, Paradoxical Intention represents just the opposite. It does not tell the patient as Coué did, "everything will get better and better," but it instructs the patient to *try intentionally to get worse.* The logotherapist asks the patient himself to wish that the feared thing will happen to him. Frankl says very specifically that "Paradoxical Intention is most genuine logotherapy. The patient shall objectivize his neurosis by distancing himself from his symptoms. The spiritual in man shall detach itself from the psychic within him, and the patient shall call on the *Trotzmacht des Geistes,* man's spiritual capacity to resist, and by his inner freedom choose a specific attitude in any given situation."

The following comments are from a practitioner of logotherapy in America.[108]

When I feel that the patient thoroughly understands the mechanism involved in the technique, we apply and practice it together in my office. For instance, the patient who is afraid he might lose consciousness is asked to get up and try to "pass out." To evoke humor in the patient I always exaggerate by saying, for example, "Come on; let's have it; let's pass out all over the place. Show me what a wonderful 'passer-out' you are." And, when the patient tries to pass out and finds he cannot, he starts to laugh. Then I tell him, "If you cannot pass out here on purpose, intentionally, then you cannot pass out any other place if you try." So together we practice Paradoxical Intention in the office over and over again; but also, if necessary, in the patient's home or wherever his neurotic symptoms appear. Once the patient has successfully used Paradoxical Intention on one of his phobias, he enthusiastically applies the technique to his other symptoms. The number of therapy sessions depends largely on how long the patient has been sick. When the illness is acute, and duration has been of only a few weeks or months, most patients respond to this therapy within about four to twelve sessions. Those who have been sick for several years, even as long as twenty years or more (in my experience I had six such cases, although more have been reported in the literature), need six to twelve months of biweekly sessions to bring about recovery. It is necessary during the course of treatment to repeatedly teach and encourage the patient to use the technique according to his specific symptoms. Since the nervous system in itself is well known for its repetitious qualities, and since our feelings are carried and expressed through nerve tissue, namely the autonomic nervous system, a once-established neurotic feeling pattern will tend to repeat itself and become a sort of reflex, even when the causes of the neurotic symptoms have been resolved and removed. Because of this repetitious quality of the nervous system, it is also absolutely essential in therapy to repeat the application of Paradoxical Intention over and over . . .

Initially, patients show very good response to Paradoxical Intention but during the course of therapy, particularly in chronic cases, patients will repeatedly suffer little setbacks. This is caused by the fact that as soon as patients *try to get better,* they enter the vicious cycle again, trying for health and providing the neurosis with new fuel. In other words, they "forget" to apply Paradoxical Intention and become worse by Coué's method of suggestion. This failure of the patient to continue to practice the technique is precisely because of the above-mentioned repetitive neurotic behavior patterns. ("I have tried to fight my neurosis for so many years the wrong way. It is hard to re-learn.") But there is another element involved here: the therapist demands from the patient tremendous courage, namely to do the things he so much fears. For instance, the patient who has the fear of blushing when in a group, is asked to do just that. Here, we appeal to the personal pride of the patient and his inner freedom in his spiritual dimension, and thus practice logotherapy in its true meaning. For all these reasons the therapist must never tire of encouraging the patient to continue to use Paradoxical Intention over and over—just as his neurosis produces the symptoms over and over. Then, finally, the neurotic symptoms will "become discouraged" and disappear. Only too often "they try to come back" but then Paradoxical Intention strangles them. "When they saw that they could not get anywhere with me anymore, they gave up completely."

SUMMARY AND EVALUATION

Logotherapy is an existential approach to aiding the individual with problems of a philosophical or a spiritual nature. These are problems of the meaning of life—the meaning of death, of suffering, of work, and of love. Problems in these areas result in existential frustration or a sense of meaninglessness in life.

The meaning of life is not found by questioning the purpose of existence. It arises from the responses that a person makes to life, to the situations and tasks with which life confronts the person. Although biological, psychological, and societal factors influence a person's responses, there is always an element of freedom of choice. The person cannot always control the conditions with which he or she is confronted, but the person can control his or her responses to them. The person is thus responsible for his or her responses, choices, and actions.

Existential frustration may exist without neurosis or psychosis, but it may lead to neurosis, and neuroses and psychoses always have existential aspects. Logotherapy is directed toward existential frustration and the existential aspects of neurosis and psychosis. Thus it is not a substitute for but is complementary to psychotherapy. Logotherapy is not concerned with psychodynamics or psychogenesis, but deals with the patient's philosophical and spiritual problems. Its aim is to bring out the ultimate possibilities of the patient, to realize the patient's latent values, not to lay bare his or her deepest secrets. Self-actualization is not accepted as an end in itself. Fulfillment of the self is possible only to the extent that the person has fulfilled the concrete meaning of his or her personal existence. Self-actualization is thus a by-product.

Two specific techniques are described: paradoxical intention and dereflection. The former appears to be quite similar to Knight Dunlap's negative practice. Some other aspects of Frankl's method also resemble deconditioning. However, Frankl relates these techniques to existentialism and emphasizes effects beyond symptom removal. Nevertheless, there appear to be some similarities and parallels between the cases described by Frankl and those presented by Salter and by Wolpe. Paradoxical intention deals with symptoms. The method encourages the patient to enter or expose himself or herself to feared situations but without the expected results occurring, thus breaking the vicious cycle and leading to extinction of the fear or the anticipatory anxiety. Frankl, however, emphasizes the attitudinal aspects of the situation. It is the patient's attitude rather than the command, urging, or encouragement of the therapist that leads the patient to put himself or herself in a situation where extinction can take place. It may be that at the bottom, it is the changing of the patient's attitudes that is also the effective or necessary condition of other methods that lead to deconditioning or extinction, such as those of Salter and of Wolpe.

For Frankl, the spiritual aspect is a separate dimension of the individual, different from the psychological. This is probably a result of the lack of concern for, or even rejection of, meanings and values by psychology. However, it should not be necessary to consider meanings and values as constituting an independent aspect of the individual; they should be included as part of his or her psychological aspect. Nevertheless, Frankl has recognized and dealt with the concerns and the distress of the modern person by admitting them into psychotherapy as legitimate objects of treatment, rather than ignoring them or treating them as symptoms of unconscious or repressed intrapsychological impulse conflicts. His concept of attitudinal values is also a contribution. Ungersma feels that with this concept Frankl "has made a profound and unique contribution to psychotherapy of all orientations . . . an insight that transcends the profoundest of Freud's contributions."[109]

While other approaches to counseling or psychotherapy emphasize self-actualization, self-fulfillment, or self-enhancement as the goal of therapy, Frankl subordinates this goal to that of the achievement of meaning. One might argue that it is the significance of events, situations, tasks, values, attitudes, and so on for self-realization that gives them meaning; they have no meaning in and of themselves but only as they relate to the development of the individual.

It is probably unfair to judge logotherapy (or existential psychotherapy) on the basis of the techniques of paradoxical intention and dereflection. They appear to be specific techniques for rather specific symptoms or neurotic conditions. They would hardly be generally applicable for the other major disturbances with which existential psychotherapy is concerned—existential frustration and loss or lack of meaning in life.

Logotherapy does deal with these philosophical or spiritual problems. The discussion of methods is inadequate and disappointing, however. Logotherapy often appears to be combined with general psychotherapy and to utilize common techniques. Frankl denies that his approach involves teaching or preaching or that it is an intellectual or a rational approach. Yet it often appears to be essentially a discussion of philosophical or spiritual problems with just these characteristics. Terms such as *reasoning, convincing, instructing, training, leading,* and so forth occur in the discussion of cases. Suggestion, persuasion, and reasoning appear to be part of the process.

Weisskopf-Joelson makes the relevant point that logotherapy is a faith, a philosophy of life, or a secular religion, rather than a science or a school of psychotherapy in the usual sense. Frankl's writings are not limited to the preparation of logotherapists but are useful to clients as well. Weisskopf-Joelson suggests that therapy sessions are essentially devoted to teaching the values and philosophy of logotherapy rather than using techniques. It has only one technique—paradoxical intention. The first part of the technique, the accepting rather than the fighting of neurotic symptoms, is consistent with the philosophy. The second part, the magnification of symptoms, she regards as a gimmick. It is this that she feels is overemphasized by those therapists who are seeking for techniques, although it is inconsistent with the philosophy. Frankl, she says, is "a mixture of prophet, guru and preacher disguised as a psychiatrist who disseminates his message in a language to which men and women of the twentieth century are likely to listen, the language of psychology. But the world, and perhaps the man himself, has taken the disguise too seriously and has become oblivious to the prophetic person who stands behind the psychiatric cloak."[110]

There seems to be no question about Frankl's concern, sincerity, and dedication. He neither prescribes the meanings of life for nor specifies the responsibilities of his clients, but he does appear to exert considerable influence in leading them to define and analyze their problems and to accept responsibility.

What, then, is the value of logotherapy? Perhaps its major value is the frank and open acceptance of philosophical problems involving goals and values as being of concern to the counselor or the therapist. There is increasing evidence that the modern person is troubled by problems of values and goals, the meaning of existence, and questions about freedom and responsibility. While other therapists show some peripheral concern about this area of human experience, Frankl makes it the center of his approach. This is the general center of interest of existentialism as manifested in the work of other existentialists, but Frankl's work has some advantages for students of counseling. It is not as obscure and as difficult to read as are most of the writings in existentialism, even though it is unsystematic, lacks organization, and is somewhat repetitious. It is not as abstract or as mystical in its orientation, nor is it characterized by the morbidity or pessimism of other existentialist approaches. While Frankl uses the word *spiritual* as a key concept, he is not using it as a synonym for *religious.* In addition, although he seems to use *spiritual* interchangeably with *intellectual* or *mental,* it goes beyond these, or beyond their rational aspects. Perhaps *philosophical* is the closest synonym.

While the approach of logotherapy is rather vague, and neither the theory nor the technique has been systematically developed or presented, it is of value to the student as an indication of the growing concern with aspects of life that are not considered or not emphasized in most other approaches to counseling or psychotherapy. It is possible that these aspects—related to values, goals, and the meaning of life —are today more frequently the source of problems and so-called neuroses than was true in the past. Contemporary civilization and society perhaps have changed the nature of the problems of people. If so, counseling and psychotherapy should reflect this changing or differing content. Changing conditions have brought to light a different view of the individual that should be considered by those interested in counseling or psychotherapy.

REFERENCES

1. Tweedie, D. F., Jr. *Logo-therapy and the Christian faith.* Grand Rapids, Mich.: Baker Book House, 1961. P. 27.
2. Ibid., p. 30.
3. Frankl, V. E. *Logos und Existenze.* Vienna: Amandus-Verlag, 1951. P. 39. Quoted (and translated) in Tweedie, *Logo-therapy and the Christian faith,* p. 129.

4. Frankl, V. E. *Das Menschenbild der Seelenheilkunde.* Stuttgart: Hippokrates-Verlag, 1959. P. 53. Quoted (and translated) in Tweedie, *Logo-therapy and the Christian faith,* p. 129.

5. Frankl, V. E. *Man's search for meaning* (rev. ed.). New York: Washington Square Press, 1963. P. 59.

6. Ibid., p. 104.

7. Ibid., pp. 105–106.

8. Frankl, V. E. *The doctor and the soul* (2nd ed.). New York: Knopf, 1965. P. xi.

9. It must be emphasized that by "spiritual," Frankl does not mean "religious."

10. Frankl, V. E. *Handbuch der Neurosenlehre und Psychotherapie.* Vienna: Urban & Schwarzenberg, 1957. P. 674. Quoted (and translated) in Tweedie, *Logo-therapy and the Christian faith,* p. 57.

11. Frankl, *Logos and Existenze,* p. 7. Quoted (and translated) in Tweedie, *Logo-therapy and the Christian faith,* p. 60.

12. Frankl, V. E. Existential dynamics and neurotic escapism. *Journal of Existential Psychiatry,* 1963, *4,* 27–42.

13. Frankl, *Man's search for meaning,* p. 173.

14. Frankl, *The doctor and the soul,* p. 5.

15. Ibid., p. 70.

16. Ibid., pp. 70, 71.

17. Ibid., p. 72. See also Frankl, V. E. Logotherapy and the collective neuroses. In J. Masserman & J. L. Moreno (Eds.), *Progress in psychotherapy* (Vol. 4). New York: Grune & Stratton, 1959.

18. Frankl, V. E. On logotherapy and existence analysis. *American Journal of Psychoanalysis,* 1958, *18,* 28–37.

19. Frankl, *The doctor and the soul,* p. x.

20. Ibid., p. xiii.

21. Ibid.

22. Frankl, *Man's search for meaning,* p. 157.

23. Ibid., p. 158.

24. Ibid., pp. 172, 173.

25. Ibid., pp. 190–191.

26. Ibid., p. 167.

27. Ibid., p. 169.

28. Ibid.

29. Ibid., p. 170.

30. Ibid., pp. 162–163.

31. Frankl, *The doctor and the soul,* p. 15.

32. Ibid., pp. 18–19.

33. Frankl, *Man's search for meaning,* pp. 164, 165–166.

34. Ibid., p. 166.

35. Frankl, *The doctor and the soul,* pp. 176–177.

36. Ibid., p. 177.

37. Frankl, *Man's search for meaning,* p. 160.

38. Frankl, V. E. *Theorie und Therapie der Neurosen.* Vienna: Urban & Schwarzenberg, 1956. P. 125. Quoted (and translated) in Tweedie, *Logo-therapy and the Christian faith,* p. 95.

39. Frankl, *The doctor and the soul,* p. xvi.

40. Ibid., p. xvi.

41. Ibid., pp. xvi–xvii. See also Frankl, Logotherapy and the collective neuroses.

42. Frankl, *Theorie und Therapie der Neurosen,* p. 125. Quoted (and translated) in Tweedie, *Logo-therapy and the Christian faith,* p. 99.

43. Frankl, *The doctor and the soul,* p. 180.

44. Ibid.
45. Ibid., p. 188.
46. Ibid., p. 191.
47. Ibid., p. 193.
48. Ibid., p. 200.
49. Ibid., p. 201.
50. Ibid.
51. Ibid., p. 202.
52. Ibid., p. 204.
53. Ibid., p. 205.
54. Ibid., pp. 208–209.
55. Ibid., p. 210.
56. Frankl, *Theorie und Therapie der Neurosen,* Foreword. Quoted (and translated) in Tweedie, *Logo-therapy and the Christian faith,* p. 75.
57. Frankl, *The doctor and the soul,* pp. xi, xii.
58. Ibid., p. 8.
59. Ibid., p. 11.
60. Ibid., p. 13.
61. Ibid., p. 17.
62. Ibid., p. 26.
63. Ibid., pp. 30–31.
64. Ibid., p. 33.
65. Ibid., pp. 34–35.
66. Ibid., pp. 36, 38.
67. Ibid., p. 42.
68. Ibid., pp. 42–43.
69. Ibid., pp. 50, 51, 52.
70. Ibid., p. 53.
71. Ibid., p. 54.
72. Ibid.
73. Ibid., pp. 55, 58.
74. Ibid., p. 64.
75. Ibid.
76. Ibid.
77. Ibid., p. 78.
78. Ibid., pp. 75–76.
79. Ibid., p. 82.
80. Ibid., pp. 105–106.
81. Ibid., pp. 111–112.
82. Ibid., pp. 113–114.
83. Ibid., p. 117.
84. Ibid., p. 118.
85. Ibid., pp. 127–128.
86. Ibid., p. 121.
87. Ibid., p. 126.
88. Ibid., pp. 132–133.
89. Ibid., p. 141.
90. Ibid., p. 170.
91. Ibid., pp. 170–171.
92. Ibid., p. 172.

93. Frankl, V. E. *Der Unbedingte Mensch.* Vienna: Verlag Franz Deuticke, 1947. P. 34. Quoted (and translated) in Tweedie, *Logo-therapy and the Christian faith,* p. 106.

94. Frankl, V. E. Paradoxical intention: A logotherapeutic technique. *American Journal of Psychotherapy,* 1960, *14,* 520–535. (Reprinted in Frankl, V. E. *Psychotherapy and existentialism: Selected papers on logotherapy.* New York: Washington Square Press, 1967. P. 144.)

95. Ibid.

96. Ibid.

97. Frankl, V. E. Logotherapy and the challenge of suffering. *Review of Existential Psychology and Psychiatry,* 1961, *1,* 3–7. (Reprinted in Frankl, *Psychotherapy and existentialism,* pp. 57–58.)

98. Frankl, *The doctor and the soul,* p. 11.

99. Ibid., p. xv.

100. Frankl, Paradoxical intention. (Reprinted in Frankl, *Psychotherapy and existentialism,* pp. 161–162.)

101. Ibid., p. 147.

102. Ibid., pp. 152, 153.

103. Ibid., pp. 156–157.

104. Ibid., p. 157.

105. Ibid., pp. 160, 162.

106. Ibid., pp. 153–154.

107. Frankl, V. E. Seminar on logotherapy conducted at Harvard University Summer School, 1961.

108. Gerz, H. O. The treatment of the phobic and the obsessive–compulsive patient using paradoxical intention sec. Viktor E. Frankl. *International Journal of Neuropsychiatry,* 1962, *3,* 375–387. (Reprinted in Frankl, *Psychotherapy and existentialism,* pp. 199–221.) Reprinted here by permission of *Journal of Neuropsychiatry* Vol. 3, No. 6. Brief summaries of other cases are in Frankl, V. E. Paradoxical intention and dereflection. *Psychotherapy: Theory, Research, and Practice,* 1975, *12,* 226–237.

109. Ungersma, A. J. *The search for meaning.* Philadelphia: Westminster, 1961. P. 28.

110. Weisskopf-Joelson, E. Logotherapy: Science or faith? *Psychotherapy: Theory, Research, and Practice,* 1975, *12,* 238–240.

six

ECLECTIC PSYCHOTHERAPY

Eclecticism in counseling and psychotherapy has been subjected to extensive criticism, falling into disrepute among many writers and theorists who hold to a particular school of thought. Rogers has referred to the attempt to reconcile various schools of thought as "a superficial eclecticism which does not increase objectivity, and which leads nowhere"[1] and has noted a "confused eclecticism," which "has blocked scientific progress in the field" of psychotherapy.[2] Snygg and Combs write that "an eclectic system leads directly to inconsistency and contradiction, for techniques derived from conflicting frames of reference are bound to be conflicting."[3] Thus from the point of view of research and of practice, eclecticism has been considered undesirable. In research, "it is only by acting consistently upon a well-selected hypothesis that its elements of truth and untruth can become known,"[4] In practice, a consistent frame of reference is desirable.

Nevertheless, eclecticism has gained adherents over the past 30 years. Thorne pointed out in 1972 that in 1945, no members of the Division of Clinical Psychology of the American Psychological Association identified themselves as eclectics, whereas by 1970, more than 50 percent so identified themselves.[5] Garfield and Kurtz reported that in 1973, 55 percent claimed to be eclectic.[6] In 1982, Smith reported a survey of 422 members and fellows of the Divisions of Clinical Psychology and of Counseling Psychology of the American Psychological Association. Forty-one percent identified their orientation as eclectic. In the same year, Norcross and Prochaska reported that 30 percent of their sample of members of the Division of Clinical Psychology professed an eclectic orientation,[8] and a year later, they reported a survey of 410 members and fellows of the Division of Psychotherapy, 30 percent of whom professed an eclectic orientation.[9] It is not yet clear whether there has been an actual decline in the number of eclectics since 1970. And, to be sure, a substantial number of clinicians still adhere to theoretical positions: psychoanalytic-psychodynamic systems claimed 10.8 percent in Smith's study, and 26.5 percent and 30 percent in Prochaska and Norcross's two surveys. No other theoretical approach claimed more than 15 percent of those surveyed. However, when those who identified themselves as eclectics in Prochaska and Norcross's surveys were asked to select one of four theoretical perspectives underlying their eclectic approach (all admitted to having one), 17.5 percent selected behavioral; 24.6 percent, humanistic; 45 percent, psychodynamic; and 12.8 percent, other.

It is thus difficult to know just what eclecticism means. While most eclectics may not be antitheoretical, they appear to be atheoretical. They seem to have little in common; they do not subscribe to any common principles or system. Thus there seem to be as many eclectic approaches as there are eclectic therapists. Each operates out of his or her unique bag of techniques; on the basis of his or her particular background of training, experience, and biases; and case by case, with no general theory or set of principles for guidance. Essentially, it amounts to flying by the seat of one's pants.

Since no body of theory or knowledge can be called eclectic psychotherapy, it cannot be taught; it can be developed only on the basis of individual experience. Thus the beginning therapist is in an unenviable and, more significantly, untenable position —scientifically, theoretically, and practically. Garfield's statement puts it simply: "Eclecticism is perceived as the adherence to a nonsystematic and rather haphazard clinical approach."[10]

True eclecticism, however, is neither nonsystematic nor haphazard. English and English define eclecticism as follows.

> Eclecticism. n. in *theoretical system building,* the selection and orderly combination of *compatible* features from diverse sources, sometimes from incompatible theories and systems; the effort to find valid elements in all doctrines or theories and to combine them into *a harmonious whole.* The resulting system is open to constant revision even in its major outlines. . . . Eclecticism is to be distinguished from *unsystematic and uncritical combination,* for which the name is syncretism. The eclectic seeks as much *consistency* as is currently possible; but he is unwilling to sacrifice conceptualizations that put meaning into a wide range of facts for the sake of what he is apt to think of as an unworkable over-all systematization. The formalist thus finds the eclectic's position too loose and uncritical. For his part, the eclectic finds formalism and schools too dogmatic and rigid, too much inclined to reject, if not facts, at least helpful conceptualization of facts.[11]

Eclecticism thus is, or should be, a systematic, integrative, theoretical position. It appears that the atheoretical, unsystematic approach to which the term *eclecticism* has been applied is syncretism, rather than true eclecticism.[12]

Eclecticism differs from the theoretical positions of schools or cults in that, on the one hand, it is more comprehensive, attempting to integrate or synthesize the valid or demonstrated elements of these narrower or more restricted theories, and, on the other hand, it is a more open ended, loose, or tentative theoretical position. There is, however, no sharp line between eclecticism and any other theoretical or systematic approach to counseling or psychotherapy. Many adherents of schools would insist that they are not rigid or dogmatic but that they recognize the tentativeness of their approach. They are not formalists. They would feel that they are seeking a "maximum of understanding (with some loss of tightness of organization)," as English and English describe the eclectic, rather than a "maximum of rational order and over-all consistency (with resulting temporary loss in inclusiveness and explanatory power)," as they describe the formalist.[13]

The true eclectic thus is not syncretistic but systematic; he or she is not atheoretical but theoretical. Woods notes that "if there were no theoretical positions, there would be no eclecticism."[14] Eclecticism is simply a more comprehensive, loosely organized theory than a formal theory and attempts to be all-inclusive. If there is an underlying consistency and integration of the phenomena encompassed by an eclectic position, then, as the position or stance is developed or becomes supported by research and experience, it becomes more systematic and more tightly organized. In other words, it becomes a formal theory. Most of those who call themselves eclectics are actually syncretists.

The basis for eclecticism has been delineated by many writers as the idea that different problems require different treatment. Ford and Urban note:

> Most of the theories which have guided psychotherapy during the last half century have characterized all behavior disorder as resulting from a common nucleus, whether it was an Oedipus complex (Freud), a conflict between strivings for independence and dependence (Rank), strivings to overcome inferiority (Adler), or conflicts between learned and organismic evaluations (Rogers), to name only a few. If the cause of all disorder is basically the same, it follows that one psychotherapeutic approach will suffice for all. The trend now is clearly to reject this view.[15]

In a later publication, Ford and Urban write that the task of the field of psychotherapy is "to articulate the conditions under which specific tactics are appropriate for particularized sets of problems. . . . the discovery of which set of procedures is effective for what set of purposes when applied to what kinds of patients with which sets of problems and practiced by which sorts of people."[16]

This theme has been echoed by other writers. Paul writes, "In all its complexity, the question toward which all outcome research should ultimately be directed is the following: *what* treatment, by *whom,* is most effective for *this* individual with *that* specific problem, and under *which* set of circumstances?"[17]

Strupp and Bergin, following their review of research in counseling and psychotherapy, make a similar statement: "We have become convinced that the therapy of the future will consist of a set of specific techniques that can be applied under specifiable conditions to specific problems, symptoms or cases. . . . We feel that the problem of psychotherapy research in its most general terms, should be reformulated as a standard scientific question: what specific therapeutic interventions produce what specific changes in specific patients under specific conditions?"[18]

The answer to this question would require (1) a taxonomy of client problems or of psychological disorders (a reliable, relevant diagnostic system); (2) a taxonomy of client personalities; (3) a taxonomy of therapeutic techniques or interventions; (4) a taxonomy of therapists; (5) a taxonomy of circumstances, conditions, situations, or environments in which therapy is provided; and (6) principles or empirical rules for matching all these variables.

Such a solution is far from the possibility of achievement. Moreover, while it would provide an empirical basis for treatment, it would lack a theoretical foundation and would be more syncretic than eclectic.

Several writers have proposed eclectic approaches to psychotherapy, modeled on this solution, with varying degrees of theoretical integration. The most detailed of these approaches is that of Thorne, who attempts to develop a true eclecticism. Arguing that all the major theories or approaches are incomplete, he tries to incorporate them into an all-inclusive method, utilizing "the contributions of all recognized schools and systems of psychology according to their indications and contraindications."[19]

The development of an eclectic position requires the availability of a number of theoretical positions that, while lacking in comprehensiveness, have demonstrated validity in terms of experience and/or research. That such theoretical systems exist some would doubt, but one cannot or should not wait for complete validation of limited or partial theories before attempting to go beyond or to integrate them. Few have dared to attempt such an integration. Indeed, there has been only one such attempt—the eclectic system of counseling and psychotherapy developed by Thorne.

Thorne was one of the first persons in the field of clinical psychology and counseling or psychotherapy to espouse the eclectic point of view in terms of a systematic position. His articles in the *Journal of Counseling Psychology,* beginning in 1945, presented this position, which was definitively stated in *Principles of Personality Counseling* (1950). His contribution has been inadequately recognized.

Thorne's system is highly detailed and complex, and it is unlikely that any therapist adheres to it very closely. A search for a simpler, more practical eclectic system to replace that of Thorne in this edition ended in failure, however, and Thorne's approach was retained. Three candidates were carefully considered before being rejected. Two of them specifically purport to present an eclectic psychotherapy. Garfield's *Psychotherapy: An Eclectic Approach*[20] is more of a syncretism. It brings together many methods organized under standard topical areas but does not make an attempt to provide a theoretical base or integration, although common elements among various theories are pointed out.

Beutler's *Eclectic Psychotherapy: A Systematic Approach* claims to be "an effort to describe a systematic eclectic psychotherapy."[21] Beutler does adapt a simplified version of the model described above and is, indeed, more systematic than Garfield. The focus is on matching therapists and their methods with patients in order to maximize the persuasiveness of the therapist in changing the patient's beliefs, attitudes, and values. Patients are classified into four groups, and various techniques are suggested —or listed—as appropriate for each group. The resulting matches are, as Beutler acknowledges, speculative and hypothetical. The concept of psychotherapy as a persuasive process, which is discussed in Chapter 16, is not actually used as a basis for theoretical integration.

Similarly, Lazarus's multimodal therapy[22] lacks a theoretical foundation and integration. Lazarus "has yet to provide a systematic evaluation of his position, nor has he fully integrated and operationalized the multi-methods of treatment."[23] His approach is purely empirical and pragmatic; Lazarus accepts any technique, regardless of theoretical origins or basis or of lack of such, as long as he thinks that it has some empirical support or that it works for him.

The most stimulating, if not entirely satisfying, of the attempts to develop an eclectic psychotherapy is that of Hart.[24] While his approach is pragmatic and includes a wide variety of techniques, it is also theory based. It is included in this edition as, in the writer's judgment, the most promising new development in therapy.

A final word should be said about the kind of eclecticism that could be developed. The model presented above is not the only possible model for eclecticism in psychotherapy. It is based, as Ford and Urban note, on the assumption of multiple emotional disorders that have multiple causes. But the theory of unitary emotional disturbance, while unpopular in the present *Zeitgeist,* is not dead. If emotional disturbance is unitary, then, as Ford and Urban point out, there would be one psychotherapy for all.

Theories of emotional disturbance as having a common core have persisted over the past century or more. As Ford and Urban note, all the major theories of psychotherapy are actually based on this concept. The only exception is behavior therapy. A number of writers have espoused the unitary concept, although they differ in their identification or labeling of the single basic cause of emotional disturbance. Angyal[25] was among the earliest holistic psychiatrists or psychologists to take this view. Menninger and his associates began to write of a unitary concept of mental illness in 1958,[26] and in a later book, they note that many psychiatrists were coming to the conclusion that there is but one type of mental disturbance.[27] Patterson has proposed this view in several publications.[28]

The recognition of common elements in all the major systems of psychotherapy supports the concept of a common etiology of all emotional disturbance and the possibility of one most effective psychotherapy. These ideas lead to a different concept of an eclectic psychotherapy, in which the common elements would provide the core. Such an approach is suggested in Chapter 19 of this book.

REFERENCES

1. Rogers, C. R. *Client-centered therapy: Its current practice, implications and theory.* Boston: Houghton Mifflin, 1951. P. 8.
2. Rogers, C. R. Client-centered therapy: A current view. In F. Fromm-Reichmann & J. L. Moreno (Eds.), *Progress in psychotherapy: 1956.* New York: Grune & Stratton, 1956. P. 24.
3. Snygg, D., & Combs, A. W. *Individual behavior: A new frame of reference for psychology.* New York: Harper & Row, 1949. P. 282.
4. Rogers, Client-centered therapy: A current view.
5. Thorne, F. C. Personal communication, January 22, 1972.
6. Garfield, S. L., & Kurtz, R. M. A survey of clinical psychologists: Characteristics, activities and orientation. *The Clinical Psychologist,* 1974, *28,* 7–10; Garfield, S. L., & Kurtz, R. M. Clinical psychologists in the 1970s. *American Psychologist,* 1976, *31,* 1–9.
7. Smith, D. Trends in counseling and psychotherapy. *American Psychologist,* 1982, *37,* 802–807.
8. Norcross, J. C., & Prochaska, J. O. A national survey of clinical psychologists: Affiliations and orientations. *The Clinical Psychologist,* 1982, *35,* 1–6.
9. Prochaska, J. O., & Norcross, J. C. Contemporary psychotherapists: A national survey of

characteristics, practices, orientations and attitudes. *Psychotherapy: Theory, Research and Practice,* 1983, *20,* 161–173.

10. Garfield, S. L. Eclecticism and integration in psychotherapy. *Behavior Therapy,* 1982, *13,* 610–623.

11. English, H. B., & English, A. C. *A comprehensive dictionary of psychoanalytic terms.* New York: McKay, 1958. (Italics added)

12. Woods, J. E. Letter to the editor. *Rehabilitation Counseling Bulletin,* 1964, *8,* 18–20.

13. English & English, *A comprehensive dictionary of psychoanalytic terms,* p. 168.

14. Woods, Letter.

15. Ford, D. H., & Urban, H. B. Psychotherapy. *Annual Review of Psychology,* 1967, *18,* 340.

16. Ford, D. H., & Urban, H. B. Some historical and conceptual perspectives on psychotherapy and behavior change. In A. E. Bergin & S. L. Garfield (Eds.), *Handbook of psychotherapy and behavior change: An empirical analysis.* New York: Wiley, 1971. P. 20.

17. Paul, G. L. Strategy of outcome research in psychotherapy. *Journal of Consulting Psychology,* 1967, *31,* 111.

18. Strupp, H. H., & Bergin, A. E. Some empirical and conceptual bases for coordinated research in psychotherapy. *International Journal of Psychiatry,* 1969, *7,* 68, 19–20. Also reported in Bergin, A. E. and Strupp, H. H. *Changing frontiers in the science of psychotherapy.* Chicago: Aldine/Atheton, 1972.

19. Thorne, F. C. *Integrative psychology.* Brandon, Vt.: Clinical Psychology Publishing, 1967. P. 347.

20. Garfield, S. L. *Psychotherapy: An eclectic approach.* New York: Wiley, 1980.

21. Beutler, L. E. *Eclectic psychotherapy: A systematic approach.* New York: Pergamon Press, 1983. P. xi.

22. Lazarus, A. A. *Multimodal therapy.* New York: McGraw-Hill, 1981.

23. Kendall, P. C. Integration: Behavior therapy and other schools of thought. *Behavior Therapy,* 1982, *13,* 559–571.

24. Hart, J. T. *Modern eclectic therapy: A functional orientation to counseling and psychotherapy.* New York: Plenum, 1983.

25. Angyal, A. *Foundations for a science of personality.* New York: Commonwealth Fund, 1941.

26. Menninger, K., Ellenberger, H. F., Pruyser, P., & Mayman, M. The unitary concept of mental illness. *Bulletin of the Menninger Clinic,* 1958, *22,* 4–12.

27. Menninger, K., Mayman, M., & Pruyser, P. *The vital balance.* New York: Viking Press, 1963.

28. Patterson, C. H. Is psychotherapy dependent on diagnosis? *American Psychologist,* 1948, *3,* 155–159; Patterson, C. H. Diagnosis and rational psychotherapy. *Journal of Nervous and Mental Disease,* 1949, *109,* 440–450; Patterson, C. H. *Counseling and psychotherapy: Theory and practice.* New York: Harper & Row, 1959; Patterson, C. H. *Relationship counseling and psychotherapy.* New York: Harper & Row, 1974.

chapter *16*

Functional Eclectic Psychotherapy: Hart

Joseph Truman Hart (b. 1937) was born in Portland, Oregon. He received his B.A. in psychology from Lewis and Clark College in 1958, M.S. in clinical psychology from the University of Wisconsin in 1961, and Ph.D. in experimental and consulting psychology from Stanford University in 1965. During his graduate years at Wisconsin, he studied with Carl Rogers and participated in the psychotherapy research project with schizophrenics conducted by Rogers.

From 1965 to 1979, Hart was associate professor in the School of Social Sciences at the University of California at Irvine. Between 1976 and 1980, he was clinical director of the Center for Functional Counseling and Psychotherapy. In 1980–1981 he was visiting associate professor of psychology at the University of Southern California. Since 1983 he has been affiliated with California State Polytechnic University in Pomona, California, as director of counseling and testing services, and with Hart and Associates in Los Angeles.

Hart is author of "Beyond Psychotherapy—The Applied Psychology of the Future" and of "Looking Back and Ahead: A Conversation with Carl Rogers," both in *New Directions in Client-Centered Therapy* (1970), which he edited with Tomlinson.

Hart has studied at the Jungian Institute in Zurich, at the Esalen Institute, and at other growth centers in the United States. He is a member of the Divisions of Consulting Psychology, Health Psychology, and Psychotherapy of the American Psychological Association, and a member of the American Association for Counseling and Development.

BACKGROUND AND DEVELOPMENT

Functional eclectic therapy, or clinical functionalism, derives from the functional psychology of William James and its applications to psychotherapy by Janet, Burrow, Taft, and Thorne.

The Functional Psychology of William James

The functional psychology of William James underlies current eclecticism in psychotherapy.

1. The emphasis on conscious as well as unconscious determinants of personality change derives from James's definition of psychology as the study of mental processes and their resulting behaviors.
2. The belief of therapists that clients' behavior and self-statements determine their feelings derives from James's theory of emotion. To change people's feelings, one must first persuade them to change their actions, perceptions, and thoughts.
3. The importance of choice, will, and purposiveness in behavior change was one of the emphases in the psychology of James.
4. James's language was always that of everyday discourse, the language used by clients and therapists. His theories are thus in a language appropriate for everyday use as well as for cutting across various techniques and theories clothed in technical language. "At the functional level of discourse if individuals cannot understand or use an idea, that idea is not true for them—even though the concept may explain their behavior!"[1]
5. The eclectic emphasis on doing what works is an example of James's pragmatism—that the truth of a concept is in its practical consequences—applied to a human situation.
6. The emphasis of therapists on inner attentiveness derives from the "stream of consciousness" of James.
7. The concern for positive mental health is related to James's emphasis on psychological experience, the development of positive habits, and the perfectability of the personality.

James's functional psychology "is the greatest single unrecognized influence on the attitudes of the majority of today's psychotherapists and counselors. . . . Indeed, I believe, in the United States today the functional orientation to psychotherapy *is* psychotherapy."[2]

The Clinical Eclecticism of Pierre Janet

James was a philosopher-psychologist; Janet was a clinician-philosopher. Pierre Janet's contributions to eclectic psychotherapy are therefore more direct and specific than are those of James. Janet collected detailed observations on more than 5000 patients. He used a wide variety of techniques, including hypnotic suggestion, "automatic writing" and "automatic talking" (similar to Freud's free association), corrective abreaction, identification of subconscious ideas, moral reeducation, religious instruction, and rest cures. To Freud's analysis, Janet added synthesis. He developed a comprehensive theory that permitted him to use such a wide range of techniques.

Janet defined neuroses as arrested development; symptoms represent restricted functioning of normal psychological processes. Understanding normal development and behavior is thus necessary for understanding abnormal behavior. Janet developed a hierarchy of functions of the organism that included nine tendencies grouped in three levels: (1) the lower tendencies (reflexive tendencies, perceptive tendencies, sociopersonal tendencies, basic intellectual tendencies); (2) the middle tendencies (immediate actions and assertive beliefs, actions and beliefs); and (3) the higher tendencies (rational tendencies, experimental tendencies, progressive tendencies). The higher tendencies are lost first in the development of the neuroses.

Janet, like James, emphasized feelings as regulators of actions; in abnormal states, regulation is disorganized. "Janet defined psychological strengths by perfection of action and psychological weakness by the imbalance of feelings and the mediocrity of actions."[3] The higher mental operations allow human beings to grasp the reality of the present in the stream of consciousness. In psychotherapy, there are gaps in consciousness that limit voluntary action and attention.

Janet's "progressive tendencies" are dispositions to action at a high moral level; they involve intentionality—choosing, willing, and planning. "Morality consists of choosing one's duty."[4]

Janet was concerned with what came to be called ego psychology and self psychology in psychoanalysis. He anticipated aspects of cognitive therapy and humanistic psychology and therapy.

The Iconoclastic Eclectism of Trigant Burrow

Although Trigant Burrow published widely—4 books and about 70 papers between 1909 and 1950—he is virtually unknown to present-day psychologists and psychotherapists.

Burrow developed the concept of primary identification, the identification of the infant with the mother prior to its earliest objective relations with its surroundings. The continuation of this primary identification into childhood and adulthood leads to "introverted mental states"—the inability to perceive the real mother (rather than the mother image), the self, and the world—a narcissistic state.

Burrow observed a universal "social neurosis," in which the social image represented by the community is as unreal as the mother image in the individual. Group analysis was developed to remedy the social neurosis.

Burrow focused on the immediate moment in therapy. He considered gaps in consciousness, which he attempted to fill in therapy, as the interference of self-images in the stream of thought; loss of awareness of the immediate moment is replaced by perception of a fantasy world. Burrow considered feeling as central in life. What he called phyloanalysis is essentially a science of feelings. He pioneered in the psychophysiological study of feelings and was able to distinguish between defending and nondefending states.

Burrow worked outside traditional psychology and therapy. His work and ideas were against the *Zeitgeist,* which was dominated by Freud's psychoanalysis in the field of psychotherapy. As a result, he was attacked and ostracized by many professionals, being dropped from membership in the American Psychoanalytic Association, of which he had been a founder and president, in 1933.

Burrows' work, although not acknowledged, appears to have influenced that of other therapists, including Fromm, Horney, and Kohut. "[T]he modern shift toward eclecticism among therapists is likely to bring about a reassignment of historical weightings so that Trigant Burrow, who is now largely unknown and ignored, will be reappraised and found to be of great significance for contemporary therapy."[5]

The Functional Therapy of Jessie Taft

Jessie Taft was influenced by the functional psychology of John Dewey and George H. Mead during her doctoral work at the University of Chicago from 1908 to 1913. She was the first to apply this approach to psychotherapy and developed the functional school of social casework with Virginia Robinson at the University of Pennsylvania School of Social Work in the 1930s. She was also influenced by Otto Rank.

Taft referred to her approach to psychotherapy as relationship therapy, to differentiate it from psychoanalysis and to emphasize the immediacy of the therapy experience. "One might fairly define relationship therapy as a process in which the individual finally learns to utilize the allotted time from beginning to end without undue fear, resistance, resentment or greediness."[6] Relationship therapy works to release the growth forces in the individual, which are blocked by fear, thus preventing the operation of conscious, willful choices. Success in therapy depends on the personal qualities of the therapist—what the therapist is rather than what the therapist knows. Therapy is not a rational or an intellectualized process but a feeling process: "The therapist must be able to be, what the patient is not for a long time, spontaneous and aware of his own slightest feeling response."[7] Taft's relationship therapy is clearly related to client-centered therapy as developed by Rogers a decade later.

The Systematic Eclecticism of Frederick Thorne

Frederick Thorne is at the opposite pole from Taft in his role as an applied scientist seeking to diagnose and treat. He was highly systematic in developing his detailed eclectic system. Influenced by Adler, he also drew from psychoanalysis, behaviorism, humanism, and existentialism. He emphasized the individual person as a whole, existing in and meeting his or her environment, including other persons, in an ongoing stream of states, or "personality statuses." The goal of therapy is psychological health or fitness, involving full humanness and self-actualization. Thorne's range of techniques included all possibly useful methods to achieve various specific objectives.

Conclusion

Although there are many specific differences among the functional therapists considered above, they (and others) share six characteristics in their approaches.

1. The clinical focus is on the immediate moment; gaps in the ongoing consciousness are important.

2. Feelings are the conscious regulators of behavior.
3. The self and the self-concept, with its related images, are of basic concern.
4. Choices, plans and intentions, and philosophical and moral concerns are included in psychotherapy.
5. Psychological growth and health are as important as psychopathology.
6. Therapy is a pragmatic process that involves the use of any effective technique or idea.

PHILOSOPHY AND CONCEPTS

A Paradigm for Modern Functional Eclecticism

"The field of psychotherapy and counseling is too underdeveloped for comprehensive theory building. . . . Therapy theories (such as psychoanalytic theory and cognitive behaviorism) are more accurately described as orientations or paradigms rather than explanatory theories."[8] A paradigm suggests a direction of exploration. The paradigm for modern functional eclecticism suggests several directions. "James provided the background metatheory for modern eclecticism," which "should be combined with other functional eclectics such as Janet, Burrow, Taft, and Thorne."[9]

The paradigm for functional eclecticism is that of multiple role models. The usual role models for psychotherapy are limited: doctor–patient, scientist–subject, teacher–student. But many other role models should be considered and used, including coach–athlete, employer–employee, minister–church member, master artist–artist, engineer–project client, parent–child, and so on. The recognition of other role models opens up therapy to contributions from other areas, such as organizational psychology. The precursors of eclectic therapy—James, Janet, Burrow, Taft, and Thorne—used many role models for therapy in their work. "Genuine functional eclecticism *begins* with a plurality of role models."[10]

The Goals of Therapy

Most therapies follow the medical model of cure and relief of symptoms. Functional therapy and the humanistic therapies derived from the functional school "argue that therapy is a search for growth rather than a cure for illness."[11] The focus is on health as a model, rather than on pathology to be remedied. Eclectic therapy is concerned about symptoms, but it gives equal weight to better functioning as a goal of therapy. Both negative and positive factors in functioning must be considered, and the preponderance of the positive over the negative should be striven for in therapy.

Psychological Fitness: A Model for Personality Exercise and Change

The model of psychological fitness is based on five premises.

1. As physical exercise is necessary for physical fitness, so psychological exercise is necessary for psychological fitness.
2. The personality must change and grow over a lifetime.
3. Positive personality change comes about by emphasizing strengths as well as by improving on weaknesses.

4. Psychological fitness requires satisfying contacts with other people.
5. Planned periods of psychological exercise involving change in activities or in modes of personality functioning enhance positive emotions and reduce negative emotions.

"Psychological fitness is the attainment and maintenance of a self-defined high quality of life. Psychological exercise is any activity that enhances the individual's psychological fitness."[12] In psychologically fit individuals, positive self-evaluations outweigh negative self-evaluations; psychological exercises build up positive and diminish negative self-evaluations in different life areas.

"[*T*]*o be psychologically fit a person must be sensitive to inner experiences and take actions in response to this inner sensitivity.*"[13] The individual must take responsibility for his or her own psychological fitness. The person acts from personal meanings and intentions, which enables him or her to persist in beneficial psychological activities.

In promoting psychological fitness, the therapist's role model is that of a coach or trainer rather than of a physician or healer.

THE THERAPEUTIC PROCESS

The goal of functional eclectic therapy is personality change. However, not all who come for therapy are candidates for such change. "For some clients support, reassurance, and a return to their previous level of less-distressed personality functioning is the real goal of the therapist."[14] Among those who want personality change, some will progress under the fitness-and-growth model, with no necessity to deal with areas of dysfunction, while others will require a therapy that deals directly with resistances and defenses; "a therapist *must* work with dysfunctioning when the client is unable to make positive changes"[15] under the fitness-and-growth approach. The first group fits the integration model; the second group requires a disintegration–reintegration model.

The Integration Model

There are four steps in the integration model.

1. *Need Step*   The Need step involves the identification of a need or want. The satisfaction of needs and wants is a main function of the personality. The viewing of a need not as a problem but as a personal declaration makes possible personality development. The therapist helps the client identify and verbalize a need or want.
2. *Choice Step*   The Choice step involves the assumption of responsibility for satisfying needs and wants; it is an affirmation of personal needs. The therapist encourages the client to make this affirmation.
3. *Action Step*   The Action step fulfills a need by taking action. The therapist may teach the client new behaviors or act as a sounding board for the effectiveness of the behaviors the client tries out.
4. *Image Step*   The Image step is a recognition of a new personality image, a new self-definition. The therapist helps the client to reorganize the dysfunctional old image and to develop the new image.

This integration process repeats itself during therapy as new needs are recognized. This is the most fundamental of all psychological exercises.

The Disintegration–Reintegration Model

The failure to grow indicates dysfunction. The refusal to become aware of and to choose and act on wants and needs is a manifestation of resistance and defensiveness. Old personality images persist and determine choices and actions.

Disintegration involves the breakdown of personality images. It can be positive when it leads to growth. Dabrowski has developed the concept of positive disintegration, in which psychological symptoms and personality breakdown are regarded as signs of efforts toward growth.[16] The therapist can foster a positive, controlled disintegration that leads to a reintegration at a higher level of personality organization.

There are four steps in the process of reintegration, although some steps may be skipped in the process.

1. *Counteraction*   Personality images become dysfunctional when they fail to meet current needs and wants, thus blocking the affective or feeling system. Defenses and resistances lead to the substitution of acceptable feelings and expressions for unacceptable ones. In therapy, the client displays discrepancies between what he or she says and what he or she is experiencing. The therapist can counteract the dysfunctional image by confronting the client with the discrepancies. The counteractive process undermines the image, leading to stress in the client or to a temporary disintegration when the client expresses ideas that are inconsistent with the old image prior to the development of a new image.
2. *Catharsis*   The counteractive process may lead to a catharsis in which emotions that have been held in by the old personality image are expressed. The therapist and the client then have to explore the differences between the past environment, which required the old image, and the new environment, which requires a new image.
3. *Proaction*   In proaction, the client "is helped to explore new feelings and develop new expression skills that eventually will lead to new personality images. . . . The client moves from a focus on reexpressing feelings that were blocked in the past to *the expression of similar or related feelings with the therapist in the present.*"[17]
4. *Reintegration*   The reintegration step puts the person where he or she would have been if the personality image had not become distorted and prevented growth. The person is now open to new wants and needs and to thinking, feeling, and acting in new ways. The "process of reintegration is necessarily an emotional process. The feelings and emotions that emerge may be mild or intense but they will be real and involving."[18]

The process of integration occurs in normal adult development. The full process of reintegration usually occurs only in the therapeutic setting. The crucial element in functional therapy is the facilitation of expression. The process of bringing incomplete feelings to expression is the same whether the problem is with defenses holding back feelings or with impulses promoting feelings: the identification of feeling moments, using dynamics of expression, and shifting levels of personality dynamics.

The Feeling Moment

Feelings and emotions are a cause not only of pathology, but also of growth and creativity. Functional eclectic psychotherapy emphasizes feelings and emotions. In psychotherapy, the rule is not "You must make intellectual sense," but "You must make emotional sense." "By changing the rules of communication and varying the dynamics of expression the therapist can create *feeling moments*. A feeling moment is created whenever a therapist detects a mismatch between *what* is said and *how* it is expressed and brings this to the client's attention."[19] The art of therapy consists of being aware of these mismatches, selecting those to react to, and helping the client to become aware of and explore them. It involves what is called "intuitive listening," "empathic listening, "listening with the third ear," or "seeing with the third eye." The mismatches and the gaps revealed by them are the *visible* unconscious. "There is no presumption, within functional theory, that the content of gaps or feeling moments is repressed or suppressed. Basically what is *in* a feeling gap is simply unknown, whether the gap represents an emergent feeling or a pushed-down feeling or some combination is not known."[20] Feeling moments are the smallest units of the therapeutic process.

The reduction of gaps or affective incongruities is important because there appears to be a drive toward clear and complete emotional communication. "Gaps and mismatches leave the organism affect deprived just as surely as the gaps and mismatches of perception leave the organism cognition deprived. As we come to know what we mean by talking, so do we come to know what we feel by expressing. *Talking about* feelings is not the same as expressing feelings."[21]

The Dynamics of Expression

Dealing with gaps and mismatches involves more than using words. Besides expressive words, expressive gestures and postures are part of the therapy process. "[I]f the therapist detects that there is a mismatch between what is said and what is felt the best way to elucidate the hidden emotional content is to work with the dynamics of expression (have the person repeat the statement, say it louder, change the gestures, say it softer, etc.) rather than ask the individual to explain."[22] Other ways to bring out emotional meanings are to ask the client to speak faster or slower, to stress different words, to assume different postures, to change position—moving closer or farther away.

Dealing with feeling moments is "the working level of functional therapy. At times it is possible to think about each therapy session as 'nothing but' a series of feeling moments. The therapist working at this level does nothing but follow the stream of consciousness wherever it goes and uses expression dynamics to further the flow whenever it become narrowed, diverted, or affectively inconsistent."[23] This is the molecular level of therapy. It does not provide an understanding of "how feeling moments and expression dynamics are organized into molar personality characteristics that can be targeted for therapeutic intervention. . . . [A] theory of personality organization and change must then be added."[24] The functional theory of dreaming yields this understanding.

A Functional Theory of Dreaming

"[T]he way a person dreams provides a very clear picture of how effectively he or she expresses and experiences feelings."[25] Dreams are less influenced by environmental or situational circumstances than is everyday waking life; the dreamer exerts greater control over dreams than does the environment. In addition, affective experiences predominate over cognitive processing in dreams. Dreams do not give access to the unconscious, but to feeling consciousness.

"The basic thesis of functionalism is that dreams are attempts to complete feelings that were left incomplete. . . . The focus is on *how* the dreamer functioned in his dream and in his life not on what caused the dream."[26] Symbolic dreams are only a partial expression of incomplete feelings. Nonsymbolic dreams represent completed feelings; they are evidence that the person is living his or her feelings. Progress in therapy, then, is indicated by movement from symbolic to nonsymbolic dreaming. "The argument is that undisguised dreams are natural and that what are usually called normal adult dreams are disordered. . . ."[27]

Dream analysis consists of having the client assess how he or she functioned in the dream on the basis of five personality dynamisms. A dynamism is a fluctuating personality characteristic related to emotional perceptiveness and expressiveness. The dynamisms are expression, activity, clarity, feeling, and contact. The client then decides which might be increased or decreased. Parallels between functioning in the dream and in waking life are then considered. "To change dream functioning the dreamer must change waking functioning."[28]

TECHNIQUE: A FUNCTIONAL MANUAL

The Manual for Functional Therapy (a 124-page concluding section of Hart's book) presents "one set of procedures among the many that are potentially available" for implementing the functional approach.

PURPOSIVENESS AND ADULT GROWTH

Moments, crises and expressions of feeling are hardly sufficient to sustain and organize personality change. Eventually in therapy, the crises of consciousness and feeling must arrive at some superordinate, real-life involvement that is personally meaningful. Inner meanings and outer meanings must come together.[29]

The question of personal meaning introduces the concept of teleology. In Jamesian psychology, an essential function of consciousness is to provide a superordinate, guiding purpose to the individual's life. The functional therapist is

. . . obligated to inquire about what dominant purposes or symbols the client is using to guide his or her life. Consciousness raising as a goal of therapy involves helping the individual to examine what makes life meaningful. A sense of coherence or purposiveness in one's life is the strongest counter to dissociation.[30] The program, which attempts to provide a middle ground between directed therapy and undirected therapy, "is to be used to organize the client's and therapist's activities and to provide some direction of movement within a session and across sessions."[31] Although each session is programmed, it can be changed or delayed to adapt to the client. Each client and therapist goes through the program in different ways.

The manual outlines a 12-month program of 4 sessions a month as follows:

Month	Sessions	Themes
1	1–4	Orientation to therapy—feeling moments and psychological fitness
2	5–8	The expression dynamism
3	9–12	The activity dynamism
4	13–16	The clarity dynamism
5	17–20	The feeling dynamism
6	21–24	The contact dynamism
7	25–28	Reorientation—images and growth
8	29–32	Relationships
9	33–36	Sex
10	37–40	Play and recreation
11	41–44	Work
12	45–48	Ending the therapy

Each session is built on questions and topics to be explored. The formats of the sessions are highly specific. They include tests, exercises, and the use of various techniques including Gestalt techniques.

Different sessions call for the therapist to take on different role models. These range from the most general person-to-person role to specific coach–athlete, doctor–patient, hypnotist–subject, and teacher–student roles that are used for special sessions and objectives. . . . The functional therapist is willing to use whatever technique might achieve desirable results. . . . The one common idea that runs through all of these guidelines is an emphasis on the form or process of emotional functioning.[32]

A "technical eclecticism" is guided by the concepts of psychological fitness, feeling moments, integration and reintegration, expression dynamics, and personality dynamics.

EXAMPLE[33]

Here is a short sample of therapeutic work with a dream from an experienced client, who had been exposed to the functional approach to dreams for several months. . . . The therapist helped the client increase his feeling level by first allowing him to express the defensive feeling and then the wanting or direct feeling. The interweaving of work with feeling moments, expression dynamics, and personality dynamisms emerges very easily in this dream.

THERAPIST: Tell me the dream.
CLIENT: It's still vivid: I was wandering around on the street with no particular direction in mind. There were many other people around; I could see them but was only vaguely aware that they were around. I was in a state of general malaise. J. stopped me and talked to me about being lost and directionless. He talked directly to me, looking intently into my eyes. I noticed being there with him, being on the street and seeing other people around, and feeling my body and particularly my feet on the ground. As J. talked to me I got increasingly more feeling, mostly sadness. I felt drawn to him and moved toward him. I became even more sad and started crying and telling him how it is for me just to wander around. I felt very settled by his talking to me, soothed by his voice and the words he was saying to me. Then he said, "You need this a lot. You need someone to talk to you like this all the time." I stayed with J. for a long time listening to him and enjoying my sad feeling.
TH: How do you feel telling me the dream now?
CL: I get the same sad feeling I had in the dream.
TH: What would happen if you let this sad feeling increase?
CL: I don't know . . . I'd feel more I guess.
TH: Go ahead, remember the dream feeling and let it increase.
    (The client is silent for a few minutes and then speaks.)
CL: I don't like feeling lost and vague!
TH: Go ahead and say that again.
CL: I don't like feeling lost and vague!
TH: Do you feel sad?
CL: Well, underneath, on top I just feel lost and vague.
TH: Go underneath. What would you say to me from underneath?
CL: I do feel sad. I need someone to talk to before I can feel it.
TH: Say that—"I need someone to talk to."
CL: I need someone to talk to . . . (crying)
TH: That's right, K., you can't feel much unless you have someone to share the feeling. You tell yourself that in the dream very clearly.

SUMMARY AND EVALUATION

Functional eclectic psychotherapy draws on the functional psychologists, including James, Janet, Burrow, Taft, and Thorne, for its theoretical concepts. These concepts include focus on the immediate moment in therapy; on feelings; on the self and self-images; on intentions, choices, and plans; on psychological growth and fitness; and on the conscious rather than the unconscious. Techniques to implement these concepts include anything that works, in a pragmatic process. This approach is thus a technical eclecticism. The therapist functions in many different roles, including those of coach and teacher.

Hart's eclectic approach is, as are other recent eclectic formulations, limited. It does not attempt to identify elements that are common to all major theories. Its theoretical concepts are derived from functional psychology, to the neglect of other systems, although Hart does attempt to show that some of them are shared with other systems, such as humanistic psychology. Although the concepts are not well integrated into a theoretical system, they are directly incorporated into the practice of functional eclectic psychotherapy.

Hart notes that "A good theory of practice acts like an instructional set: the therapist is set to respond in certain ways but not in other ways and does not need to reflect distractingly and deliberate before each response." He continues, "At any point in a therapy session where a therapist does not 'know what to do' it means either: 1) that the theory does not provide therapeutic instruction for the phenomenon at hand or 2) that the therapist does not fully understand these instructions. In either case the theory, considered as a set of instructions, must be revised."[34]

Hart's system attempts to meet these potential difficulties in the Manual for Functional Therapy. The manual is highly specific and detailed, with each session being structured and focusing on one of the theoretical concepts. Although the program is said to be flexible, it would seem that more than a few minor changes would disrupt the whole program. While the therapist at times, usually at the beginning of a session, is urged to listen to the client, the session soon becomes focused on the scheduled topic, with the client responding to the therapist. It would seem that the changes in roles by the therapist might be confusing to the client. However, most roles are directive, and the client no doubt soon looks to the therapist for direction. There appears to be a conflict between Hart's need for structure and his recognition that therapy cannot be highly structured: "It would be misleading if the format of the therapy manual (repetitive instructions, exercises, charts, and assignments) conveyed the impression that going for therapy is much like taking one's car for a tune-up." Yet that is the clear impression, which is supported by other parts of the book besides the manual. The process is clearly a highly cognitive, didactic teaching process.

The didactic, cognitive nature of the process, in spite of the emphasis on feeling moments, poses another problem. Although Hart notes the difference between talking about and expressing feelings, he seems to follow one of the common recommendations of textbook writers—that the therapist focus on feelings by asking the client such questions as "How did you feel then?" "How did that make you feel?" "How do you feel now?" or "What are you feeling now?" Answers to such questions are expressions not of feelings, but of thoughts about feelings. That is, such questions change the level of the client's responses from spontaneous expression of feelings to cognitions about feelings.

Hart emphasizes pragmatism. "The practical test of a therapeutic approach is not how well it explains but how well it works."[35] Hart does recognize a limitation to functional eclectic therapy. "Clients who cannot pay attention to feeling moments or who cannot learn to notice mismatches and work toward expressing fully what they feel and mean should be taught how to do so."[36] But he notes that if that is not possible, then functional therapy should be abandoned and something else tried. Two questions must be raised, however.

1. What is the evidence that it works?
2. If it works, why does it work?

Hart does not offer evidence to answer the first question, and he disregards the second. The test of a good theory *is* how well it explains: Does it work for the reasons that it is claimed to work? Pragmatism is not enough; we must be concerned with why something works.

Hart's approach is not a finished system. It does, however, seem to offer more potential than do other attempts at formulating an eclectic approach to psychotherapy. It contains many new and stimulating ideas and concepts that should be considered in the development of a systematic, theoretically based eclecticism.

REFERENCES

1. Hart, J. T. *Modern eclectic therapy: A functional orientation to counseling and psychotherapy.* New York: Plenum, 1983. P. 21.
2. Ibid., pp. 16, 17.
3. Ibid., p. 23.
4. Quoted in Ey, H. Pierre Janet: The man and his work. In B. Wolman (Ed.), *Historical roots of contemporary psychology.* New York: Harper & Row, 1968. P. 193.
5. Hart, *Modern eclectic therapy,* p. 59.
6. Taft, J. *The dynamics of therapy in a controlled relationship.* New York: Dover, 1962. P. 17. (Originally published, 1933.)
7. Ibid., p. 118.
8. Hart, *Modern eclectic therapy,* p. 95.
9. Ibid., p. 96.
10. Ibid., p. 98.
11. Ibid., p. 146.
12. Ibid., p. 179.
13. Ibid., p. 168.
14. Ibid., pp. 187–188.
15. Ibid., p. 188.
16. Dabrowski, K. *Positive disintegration.* Boston: Little, Brown, 1964; Dabrowski, K. *Personality-shaping through positive disintegration.* Boston: Little, Brown, 1967.
17. Hart, *Modern eclectic therapy,* p. 196.
18. Ibid.
19. Ibid., p. 112.
20. Ibid., pp. 112–113.
21. Ibid., p. 114.
22. Ibid., p. 116.
23. Ibid., p. 124.
24. Ibid.
25. Ibid., p. 125.
26. Ibid., p. 130.
27. Ibid., p. 134.
28. Ibid., p. 145.
29. Hart, J. Functional eclectic therapy. In J. Norcross (Ed.) *Handbook of eclectic psychotherapy.* New York: Brunner/Mazel, 1985.
30. Ibid.
31. Hart, *Modern eclectic therapy.* pp. 208, 209.
32. Ibid., pp. 216, 217.
33. Ibid., pp. 138, 139.
34. Ibid., p. 325, 326, 328.
35. Ibid., p. 207.
36. Hart, *Functional eclectic therapy.*

chapter *17*

Eclectic System of Clinical Practice: Thorne

Frederick Charles Thorne (1909–1978) received his B.A. at Columbia College and his M.A. (1931) and Ph.D. (1934) at Columbia University, all in psychology. Unable to obtain the clinical experience he desired in psychology, he turned to medicine and obtained his M.D. in 1938 at Cornell University. From 1939 to 1947, he was director of the Brandon State School in Brandon, Vermont. In 1947, he entered private practice. He was associated with the Department of Psychiatry of the University of Vermont College of Medicine as part-time assistant professor of psychiatry from 1941 to 1953. In 1945, he founded the *Journal of Clinical Psychology,* which he edited and published. He was a Diplomate in Clinical Psychology of the American Board of Professional Psychology.

Thorne wrote *Principles of Personality Counseling* (1950), *Principles of Psychological Examining* (1955), *Clinical Judgment* (1961), *Personality: A Clinical Eclectic Viewpoint* (1961), and *How to Be Psychologically Healthy: Tutorial Counseling* (1965), as well as the books on which this chapter is mainly based: *Integrative Psychology* (1967) and *Psychological Case Handling* (1968), Volume 1: *Establishing the Conditions Necessary for Counseling and Psychotherapy* and Volume 2: *Specialized Methods of Counseling and Psychotherapy.* The latter constitute a revision of *Principles of Personality Counseling,* which was the basis for the chapter "Thorne's Personality Counseling" in the first edition of this book.

BACKGROUND AND DEVELOPMENT

Thorne states that his interest in personality counseling originated in his search at the age of 15 for an explanation of the stammer he had had since the age of 5. He entered

Columbia University in 1926 to major in psychology and continued through the Ph.D. His decision to attend medical school was a result of his frustration with the experimental and theoretical emphasis in psychology. He was impressed by the integration of the basic medical sciences into the eclectic system of practice, in comparison with the "ideological confusion of the psychological sciences in which there were almost as many schools and viewpoints as there were 'masters' who could win recognition."[1] He determined to attempt "to collect and integrate all known methods of personality counseling and psychotherapy into an eclectic system which might form the basis of standardized practice."[2] Beginning with the first volume of the *Journal of Clinical Psychology* in 1945 and in other journals, Thorne published articles directed toward this objective. In 1950, these became part of his *Principles of Personality Counseling*.

The two volumes of *Psychological Case Handling* are based on the system of personality developed in *Personality*[3] and *Integrative Psychology*[4] and on the diagnostic system of psychopathology developed in *Principles of Psychological Examining*,[5] and are to be used within the system of clinical practice presented in these books, as well as in *Clinical Judgment*[6] and *How to Be Psychologically Healthy.*[7]

Thorne's eclectic position was no doubt influenced by the many teachers he had and by others he was exposed to during his professional education and development. They included H. L. Hollingsworth, an associationist; K. M. Dallenbach, a psychophysicist; Adolph Meyer and W. H. Sheldon, psychobiologists; Alfred Adler and H. L. Ansbacher, Adlerians; Prescott Lecky and C. R. Rogers, self psychologists; Mortimer Adler, an objectivist; and William A. Marston, an integrative psychologist. He also made a personal study of Freudian psychology. His Ph.D. was taken with Robert S. Woodworth, an objectivist who was also an admitted eclectic, from whom Thorne developed the idea of applying the eclectic method to clinical science in psychology following the pattern of Sir William Osler in medicine. He found that no single system had the complete answer and set out to develop an integration.

PHILOSOPHY AND CONCEPTS

Thorne attempts to be "rigidly scientific and eclectic" in his approach.[8] A true eclecticism is not "(a) a 'hodgepodge' of disconnected facts, (b) largely torn from context, (c) unrelated to any unifying structure, (d) lacking global perspective, (e) unsupported by valid theoretical models, and (f) barren as to research-stimulating hypotheses."[9] It is, in fact, the opposite, since it utilizes theoretical unifying principles from various schools to interrelate and integrate pertinent facts from all sources. It is inductive rather than deductive. "Instead of starting with theoretical preconceptions and then checking the fit of the facts to the model, the eclectic usually proceeds inductively, gathering and analyzing the data, and only later attempting to construct explanatory theories. . . . The main problem in all clinical work is to discover the organizational dynamics of the person under study rather than to invent one out of possible theories."[10]

While drawing on many theorists and schools (including Meyer and Lecky), Thorne's work is not a "compilation of all standard theories" but an original contribution. He "determined to make a fresh start right from the beginning, accepting nothing on authority alone, and to formulate an eclectic system integrating all pertinent scientific information available, at this time and place."[11] The model was that of Sir William

Osler's work in medicine, which integrated the data of the medical sciences into an eclectic system of practice.

Recognizing that

many methods of case handling are discussed which have not been scientifically validated to date . . . at this early stage in the development of clinical psychological science, the most profitable approach appears to be to attempt an eclectic collection and evaluation of all known methods in terms of empiric experience. . . . Our main objective is to simply present an eclectic collection of methods which may be applied rationally according to their indications and contraindications. To us, this is all that clinical science can ever do. How these methods are combined and used is a function of the art of clinical practice.[12]

Philosophical presuppositions or foundations are not dealt with directly. The psychological nature of the individual is discussed in detail however, in *Personality* and in *Integrative Psychology*.

A Clinical Eclectic Viewpoint of Personality

In *Personality,* Thorne does not present a single theory of personality. He attempts instead to bring together all observations and empirical data on personality. This eclectic view is not, however, unsystematic, unorganized, or a "rag-tag collection of miscellaneous theories and methods, resulting in a patchwork of observations and data," but an integrated and systematic approach because personality itself is an integrated whole, and its study leads to "an inductively derived theory of personality which is rooted in empiric observations and methods."[13] (It should be noted here that, as indicated in the beginning of the next section, the concept and term *personality* have been replaced in Thorne's system by *person* or *behavior.* Where *personality* occurs in this section, then, the reader should substitute *behavior* to be consistent with Thorne's later position.)

Thorne presents his point of view, or system, in 97 postulates. It is obviously impossible to do justice to his approach in a limited space. We can only attempt to present the core or essence of his concept of personality.

Personality consists of the changing states of the total, or whole, individual living organism as it copes with the experience of interacting with its environment in the unique, individual ways that differentiate it personally and socially from others. Personality is thus a process of changing or becoming, and it is its *givenness,* existentially, that must be apprehended and that constitutes the raw data of personality. Personality can be studied only by observing the individual person in action in specific situations and through the phenomenological method by entering into his or her world and experiencing it with him or her. The case history supplements observation by providing information about what the person has been. Since the individual is perceived differently by various other people, the results of a personality study depend on the viewpoints or perceptual biases of the persons who are supplying the information or of the approach used. The competent clinical scientist is in a position to provide the most valid and reliable, or "real," picture of the individual. The scientist does this by an eclectic method, utilizing all existing approaches to personality, since they are complementary or supplementary rather than competing or conflicting.

A system or theory of personality must provide an explanation for the whole range of behavior of human beings. The clinical eclectic viewpoint is the only method that does this. Eclecticism is a theoretical system involving "the selection and orderly combination of compatible features from diverse sources, even from otherwise incompatible theories and systems," into a "mutually consistent whole."[14] At the present time, "valid methods of sufficient complexity have not been developed to permit a multivariate analysis of the inconstant qualities and quantities of factors actually determining personality status."[15] Nevertheless, the eclectic approach utilizes all existing methods, including the method of trained introspection applied in the clinical encounter. Since a personality state or status is an organized, unified whole, it can be grasped in its totality only by phenomenological methods, that is, by directly experiencing its issues and meanings.[16]

Personality dynamics involves a series of drives. There is a drive for higher organization, which includes a person's need to maximize himself or herself, to achieve perfect functioning, and to organize his or her expanding experience into meaningful wholes. There is also a drive to achieve and maintain stability of organization, which includes self-preservation, homeostasis, habit systems, ideological controls, life goals and purposes, roles and statuses, and life style. A third drive is to integrate opposing functions in order to resolve imbalance (but not necessarily to avoid tensions). Personality integration is the dynamic process in which the organism strives to organize and unify all elements of the behavior field of the moment or of the organizational status that the organism has been able to achieve. The organism strives to maintain the highest possible level of integration at all times and at all levels of functioning, from the lower psychophysiological functions to the highest psychosocial interactions. There is a "constant striving for unity manifesting itself in efforts to maintain the unity of the system of organization self-consistently."[17] Unification is a general, or master, motive.

An individual's life style consists of characteristic ways of attempting to achieve unification or a "distinctive offensive-defensive strategy of satisfying needs and coping with reality by use of mechanisms and expressive styles."[18] Although there is a constancy of life style in personality, there is also constant change and flux, with multivariate etiological factors entering the hierarchical systems that underlie the personality status at any particular time and place.

Consciousness is the central datum of psychology, and conscious experiences are "primary behavior data whose existential reality cannot be denied."[19] Although consciousness can be studied by objective methods, it can be apprehended only by a subjective reporter who is in a conscious state. Consciousness acts as a master sense organ or integrating function in which stimuli or momentary experiences are presented in awareness as a unified whole. "Consciousness is considered the main organizing, integrating, and unitizing mechanism determining and making possible higher level personality functioning."[20] It is the essence of being—the most unique characteristic of human beings. Consciousness is the locus of the self and of self-awareness. The contents of consciousness determine mental status, and disturbances in consciousness result in disturbances in behavior. Behavior processes that can be brought into consciousness are potentially susceptible to self-control after appropriate analysis and practice.[21] Although there are nonconscious aspects of behavior, "they should not be postulated routinely but only when indicated by the evidence elicited in the specific case. Depth psychology should be investigated only when the possibilities of utilizing hypotheses concerning normal conscious mental life have been exhausted."[22]

The self develops in consciousness around feelings of personal identity and the experiencing of what is happening to the self. "The *self image* is the self one *thinks* oneself to be . . . the self concept . . . is the evaluative core concept of one's own self particularly as we think it appears to others."[23] The ego is the executive function of the self and includes the awareness of itself, evaluation of itself, regard for itself, and control of itself. The cumulation of self-knowledge and experience results in a self-apperception mass, which provides the basis for the continuity of the self and of its state of morale, or self-respect. Perceptions of personal identity and of the physical body constitute the core of the self-apperception mass.[24]

The conscious self participates in all the functions of personality and, therefore, becomes the organizational center of the personality. "Thus, the self becomes able to regulate the whole organism and to cause it even to do things which are against its instincts and interests, such as to kill itself in suicide."[25] In abnormal states the self may not be aware of, or able to control, certain functionings. The self-concept is important because "it operates as the functional core of being."[26]

Ideally, the individual does not react mechanically to external stimuli or constitutional determinants but exercises self-direction, acting purposefully, shaping his or her own life, and accepting responsibility. The striving for unity operates in consciousness toward self-consistency and elimination of conflicts.

Personality evolves in an irreversible sequence of statuses in the process of becoming self-actualized. Continuity exists and is present in awareness as the stream of consciousness or the stream of experience (life). Thus while it is possible to speak of personality traits, it is more important to consider the ongoing acts of the individual in terms of the existential concept of doing something with his or her life. While past experience places limits on what personality can be, "man is able to transcend the nature of his past and present existences through his ability to imagine and shape the future."[27] The self constantly strives for meaning, that is, the understanding of its experiences. There is a basic drive to organize experience into meaningful wholes: one of the highest values in life is to have meaning in one's personal existence. Meanings are determined by the whole organismic reaction of the person to experiences. Although most meanings are acquired by social conditioning, "self-consistency theory would stress that each person should do what is best for him in terms of his own health, maturity, and growth rather than because of any artificial social meaning which may be attached."[28]

Since reason is a person's greatest hope for becoming healthier and better, logical thinking is the best weapon in the existential struggle against blind emotion and irrationality. Therefore, "the ultimate value of man, both personally and socially, is a function of the quality of his cognitive functioning."[29]

Personality development is influenced by constitutional-biological factors, cultural factors, and self-actualization. The last includes self-determination; thus individuals are not entirely mechanically determined. The drive for self-actualization is one of the most powerful human motives and involves a dissatisfaction with self and a working toward self-improvement or perfection. The awareness of alternatives and the existence of decision making are evidences of freedom from mechanistic determination. The need to make choices introduces the need for a value system and for responsibility for one's actions. "Human living reaches its most outstanding peaks in the moments of the highest self-actualization and self-transcendence."[30] This, or the striving toward it, constitutes positive mental health.

The basic units of personality are the acts performed by the individual. These acts are organized in terms of the various roles that the individual plays, which are defined by his or her concepts of the physical and social world, perceived with himself or herself as the center.

"From the eclectic viewpoint, personality development is regarded as a struggle to transcend affective-impulsive-unconscious determination of behavior by learning and perfecting rational-logical-voluntary control of behavior."[31]

Integrative Psychology

In his book *Personality,* Thorne achieved the "break-through of postulating that behavior occurs naturally only in the form of psychological states and that these are the only proper raw data for clinical study." *Integrative Psychology* expands the theory of the psychological state, developing the psychology of integration and its clinical diagnostic implications. This psychology consists of "a basic theory of the psychological nature of man."[32] In this book, personality is regarded as "a theoretical artifact . . . a semantic abstraction . . . an abstract generalization describing the individuality of the person."[33] Because of its vagueness and lack of clarity, the word should be avoided; the unit of study is the psychological state of being in the lives of people. The focus of concern is the person in his or her world, with all his or her situational and existential concerns.

"The basic problem of psychology is the study of factors organizing the pattern of any integration of integrates—the psychological state . . . of any particular moment."[34] The whole existence and meaning of a person could be understood if we could study the person's life pattern of psychological states. In general, the individual's basic goals, needs, and motivations organize the sensations, perceptions, learning, memory, feeling, and thinking that constitute a person's psychological state. Integrative psychology is thus holistic.

Behavior is integrated on many levels, from low-level physiological functions to high-level psychosocial interactions. The organism strives to maintain the highest possible level of integration in accordance with the master motive, the homeostatic principle. Behavior is integrated by a variety of organizing principles at the different levels of the hierarchy. The more biologically primitive, lower level functions tend to be prepotent, although higher level functions may establish a transitory prepotence.

At the psychological level, the master motive is the principle of unification, leading to self-consistency. The individual's "internal consistency is preserved by the selective assimilation of compatible ideas and values and the selective resistance to assimilation of inconsistent values."[35]

Organizing factors at many levels of behavior operate at the same time. It is postulated that organizers at all levels are integrated to support the dominant activity at the moment, so that the organism as a whole functions in a unified manner. Unifica-

Postulate 45 In a normal person, the contents of consciousness largely determine mental states. . . .

Postulate 46 Introspective reporting is the prime method for objectifying mental status and the contents of consciousness. . . .

Postulate 47 Every act in the waking state can be held in the focus of consciousness, so as to be sensed, perceived, evaluated, weighted, manipulated associatively, and considered in relation to past, present and future factors. . . .

Postulate 48 Any behavior process which can become conscious is potentially susceptible to self-control after suitable operational analysis of the necessary steps and adequate practice. . . .

Postulate 49 The self is the continuing conscious awareness of being a separate person. . . .

Postulate 50 The experiential background of the self is provided by the self apperception mass consisting of the accumulated experiential context of the self with itself. . . .

Postulate 51 Perceptions of personality identity constitute the core of the self apperception mass. Perceptions of the physical body are particularly important. . . .

Postulate 52 Instead of hypothesizing a variety of "selves" performing different functions, it is more valid to regard the self as participating in all integrative functions. . . .

Postulate 53 The importance of the self concept is that it operates as the functional core of being. . . .

Postulate 54 The validity of self-evaluatory functioning is an important determiner of psychological health. It is measured in the psychiatric concept of insight. . . .

Postulate 55 Under ideal conditions, to some degree, the self is capable of determining what it can become by imagining some future status and then acting to accomplish it. . . .

Postulate 56 Ego functioning relates to the awareness and concerns of the self with itself, i.e., with the self experiencing itself and dealing with itself. . . .

Postulate 57 The striving for unity operates on levels of conscious self-awareness in terms of the need to be self-consistent, i.e., positively to eliminate conflict and, negatively, not to create problems for one's self. . . .[38]

Therapeutic Implications of Integrative Psychology

Since all psychopathological or disturbed states involve disorders of integration, the objective of all methods of counseling or psychotherapy is to strengthen and improve the quality of the integrative process, thus fostering higher levels of self-actualization. Since the level of integration is manifested in the current psychological state of the client, the specific phenomenological goal of all case handling is to alter the existing psychological state. The focus is, thus, the person in the present situation, or "the psychological state of the-person-running-the-business-of-his-life-in-the-world."[39] Once the therapist determines that the client has sufficient resources for accepting the responsibility for his or her own life, the therapist gives the client this responsibility.

The focus on integration and the principle of unification direct clinical attention to the *integrative milieu,* or the psychological field of forces that are causative factors in the psychological state. The client's behavior in therapy reflects his or her psychological state and provides the data for understanding this state and its causes. Such understanding comes from the therapist's empathizing with the client from the phenomenological frame of reference of the client. Since any psychological state represents the client's attempt to achieve maximum self-actualization through maximum integration, the primary question is: What and how is the client doing in managing self-actualization? This effective management involves adequate or optimum control of his or her life, particularly his or her affective-impulsive life. Therapy involves the training, reeducation, or rehabilitation of the client in acquiring the controls necessary for self-regulation. Sometimes it is necessary for the client to experience a *positive disintegration* before reorganization or reintegration can occur.

Underlying every psychological state is an etiological equation (see below), which organizes the pattern of integration represented by the state. This etiological equation provides the indications or contraindications for specific interventions. Psychotherapy attempts to modify the equation or the causes of disabling behavior. The eclectic approach treats each case individually. Rather than fitting the case (deductively) to a particular theory, it operates inductively from the specific case data. Specific methods of therapy, including pharmacotherapy and those of the various schools or systems, are appropriate for specific levels of disintegration. Eclectic therapy utilizes each of them on the basis of the level of disintegration presented by the client.

PSYCHOLOGICAL CASE HANDLING

The term *psychological case handling* is used in preference to *psychotherapy* for two reasons. First, the effectiveness of psychotherapeutic methods has not yet been demonstrated, so that "most parsimoniously, every clinician should be regarded as only a case handler."[40] Second, the term is broad enough to include not only all methods of psychotherapy, but also "all the operations conducted by competent psychologically trained personnel in helping clients to get along better in life."[41]

Elements of psychological case handling are (1) adequate diagnostic study, (2) detailed knowledge of limitations of treatment methods, their indications and contraindications, (3) treatment of basic causes rather than symptoms, (4) an individual plan of treatment, (5) choice of methods on the basis of specific indications, (6) use of single methods where possible, so that effectiveness can be evaluated, (7) evaluation of results, (8) use of scientific methods in analysis of data, (9) recognition that there are no panaceas or universally applicable methods, and (10) eclecticism recognized as the keynote of modern science.[42]

Objectives of psychological case handling include (1) prevention of worsening of the condition, (2) correction of etiological factors, (3) palliation, (4) systematic support, (5) facilitating growth, (6) reeducation, (7) expression and clarification of emotional attitudes, (8) resolution of conflict and inconsistencies, (9) catalysis of maturation and growth, (10) acceptance of what cannot be changed, (11) attitudinal reorganization, and (12) maximization of intellectual resources.[43] These may be summarized as catalyzing self-actualization by improving integrational status.

Psychological case handling includes personality counseling, marriage counseling, psychotherapy, psychoanalysis, pastoral counseling, child guidance, special education, vocational and educational guidance, psychiatric social work, group therapy, and hypotherapy. It also includes educative and advisory activities, as well as administrative activities and modification of the client's environment or removal of the client from a pathogenic environment.

Since the clinician has training and experience in all known methods,

> the basic responsibility for the *direction* of all stages of case handling lies with the therapist even though some responsibility may be delegated to other persons, including the client himself. The possibility of a completely nondirective method is nonexistent, since by the very nature of the clinician–client relationship (a) the client comes to a person considered to be of superior experience and training, which establishes a relationship of dominance through prestige, (b) the case handler determines the method to be used. . . . One of the principal characteristics of the maladjusted or disordered person is the inability to resolve problems unaided. Although self-direction is the highest democratic goal and evidence of integration, the maladjusted person either asks for help spontaneously or is induced to do so for his own good. Until such time as the person demonstrates his ability to regulate his behavior within the limits of what is socially acceptable, he is subjected to varying degrees of direction or regulation from the environment. . . . While recognizing the dangers of over-regulation and over-interpretation, failure to institute degrees of direction in more serious cases may constitute grave error since the case handler has the obligation to protect the interests of the client when the client is unable to do so himself. . . . It is assumed that training and experience will provide the knowledge concerning when to be directive or relatively nondirective.[44]

But

> proper case handling can make counseling and psychotherapy an interesting voyage of client discovery in which the case handler operates as a catalyst to help the client to greater insight, knowledge and competency in achieving a more individualistic life. The case handler does not have to adopt authoritarian roles to influence the client. More properly, the case handler operates as a friendly adviser. . . . primarily concerned with helping the client to work out his own problems.

If he must take control when the client is unable to control himself, "the goal must always be to return ultimate control of the situation back to the client himself."[45] Since many clients are not familiar with the different case-handling methods and their objectives, it may be necessary to structure the objectives in terms of the concepts of integrative psychology.

The referents of psychological case handling are (1) the client, (2) the life situation of the client, particularly in relation to important others, and (3) the clinical encounter between the client and the case handler. The first two have been noted in the summary of integrative psychology above.

Factors Determining the Choice of Case-Handling Methods

Case handling should be based on an individual, rational plan for each client. The plan should include appropriate measures for beginning the relationship and discovering the problem, for dealing with pathognomonic symptoms and etiological factors, for utilizing all available methods, and for terminating the relationship.

> In general, actual direction or interference in the life of another person should be rigorously limited to the absolute minimum necessary to protect health and welfare. This implies that passive methods of counseling and psychotherapy are the techniques of choice unless definite indications exist for more active methods. Apart from this general rule, the plan of therapy will be determined by the indications of the specific situation.[46]

Some of the factors or criteria that determine the method of choice are:

Specificity of Action   A specific method acts directly on the etiological factors in the disorder. There is little evidence for the specificity of action of various methods, and the therapist must depend on clinical experience.

Economy of Action   The method that is most quickly and economically effective (yet safe) is preferred.

Natural History of the Disorder   The pattern of development of the disorder must be understood for the most effective choice of treatment methods. In the prodromal stage, which is vague, treatment should be supportive or palliative, using nondirective methods. In a syndromal stage without client insight, efforts are directed toward getting the client to recognize that he or she is maladjusted and to accept treatment. In a syndromal stage with client insight, the therapist has more freedom of action. Specific methods need to be applied at the optimum time in order to achieve maximum effects.

The Distributive Principle   In distributive treatment, the counselor directs the treatment actively and according to a plan, adapting to the course of treatment and the client's progress. Problems and questions based on the information obtained from the client are submitted to the client to assist him or her in developing insight and reaching solutions in selected areas.

Total Push   Every possible influence and treatment should be brought to bear in a concentrated manner.

Failure of Progress   When a client fails to respond to treatment, more drastic methods are applied. When no rational prescription is possible or when plans have failed, every possible method is used. While unscientific, this procedure is expedient.

Case Handling as an Adaptive Process   The case handler must be adaptable to the needs of each client as they develop and must evaluate the indications

    H. Neoplastic
    I. Presenile deterioration
    J. Undifferentiated
  II. If the disorder appears to be functional, is it a
    A. Reaction of physiological deficit
      1. Schizophrenic reaction
      2. Affective disorder
      3. Convulsive disorder
      4. Somatization reaction
      5. Psychoneurotic reaction
    B. Reaction of psychological deficit
    C. Conditioned behavior disorder
    D. Attitudinal disorder
    E. Situational maladjustment

Step Two: Identification of a Specific Etiologic Agent or Syndrome   If the disorder is organic, what is the specific etiologic agent and the extent and the location of the lesion? If the disorder is functional, what are the primary etiologic factors? Differentiate between primary and secondary (precipitating) factors.

Step Three: Measurement of Specific Defects or Abnormal Dynamisms   In organic disorder, measure the degree of defect in mental functioning, that is, memory defect. In functional disorders, measure emotional reactions, attitudinal factors, and so forth.

Step Four: Evaluation of Personality Reactions to the Disorder

Step Five: Evaluation of Situational Factors   How does the disorder affect the total situation of the person-meeting-the-environment?

Step Six: Formulation of a Diagnosis   Explain the integrative dynamics of the case in terms of all factors identified.[55]

This procedure is an ideal, since it is rarely possible to obtain complete data. At present, objective diagnostic methods are inadequate, so that major dependence must be placed on clinical judgment and intuition.

The Case History in Diagnosis

The case history consists of the direct examination of the client and any other information obtained from legitimate sources relating to the client's past and present status. Information from other sources is necessary because of the unreliability and invalidness of the statements of persons with psychological disorders. The client may be unable to reveal all his or her problems because of unconscious repression and resistance and distortion of reality. Deliberate suppression or falsification by the client may also occur. "Actually, no statement or behavior pattern should be taken at face value, whether the person is normal or abnormal, except with confirmatory evidence from external sources" because of "misperceptions of the client or informants due to different phenomenological viewpoints."[56]

The case history is useful in developing the steps in diagnosis listed above. It contributes to valid diagnosis by providing accurate information and thus avoiding diagnostic errors based on inadequate information. When other persons are involved, it includes their side of the story. The dynamics of interpersonal and situational disturbances can be discovered. It uncovers misinformation and irrational thinking in the client. It aids in differentiating between organic and functional complaints. "An adequate case history is the most reliable source of information upon which reliable predictions of future behavior can be based."[57]

The taking of the case history can be therapeutic in itself. It assists in the building up of rapport. It provides catharsis and abreaction, as well as desensitization. It offers reassurance by impressing the client with the carefulness and interest of the clinician. In some cases, the client's relating of his or her history to an understanding clinician is sufficient for carrying the client over temporary difficulties. Further, the eliciting of a good case history may lead to the development of insight. Finally, interpersonal misunderstandings may be resolved in the process of obaining a case history from the client and those involved with the client, particularly in a group discussion.

When blocking, resistances, or an impasse occurs during the therapy process, the case history may provide leads for exploration. When progress has not occurred after many interviews, the case history can be reviewed and even returned to for deeper exploration.

The Technique of History Taking

"The therapist would do well to assume a passive, non-directive attitude during the initial contacts, interjecting only enough to elicit a coherent history."[58] The client should not be hurried. Questions should be nondirective: How? When? Where? Why? Significant or representative samples of the client's statements should be recorded verbatim. Information on the client's use of time should be obtained. The clinician should find out how the client thinks and feels about significant happenings in his or her life and what the client thinks the trouble is. An outline is useful to avoid overlooking significant areas. Areas to be covered should include birth and develomental history, medical history, educational history, emotional development, sex life, social development, work history, family life, personal habits, attitudes toward self, and socioeconomic status.

The Etiological Equation

"An *etiologic equation* is a formal statement describing all classes of causal factors and indicating their relationship." It "differentiates between primary, secondary, predisposing, precipitating, preexisting and situational factors and attempts to weigh the contribution of each."[59] The equation is based on the diagnosis and provides the basis for treatment. Principles of primacy assert that genetic factors command priority over other factors, followed by biologically primitive factors and developmental factors. Organic factors have primacy over functional factors. Temporally, earlier factors have primacy over later factors. Lower level integrations have priority over higher level integrations. The etiological equation must represent the integrational milieu, including both internal and external, or organismic and situational, factors. Since both the internal and the external milieus are constantly changing, the etiological equation must be constantly revised.

Twelve classes of etiological equations are identified, in terms of the prepotent determining factor: (1) biogenetic determination, (2) constitutional determination, (3) pathological-physiological determination, (4) affective or emotional-conflict determination, (5) cognitive-behavior determination, (6) conditioned mental-context determination, (7) role-playing and social-status determination, (8) self-concept and ego-structure determination, (9) life-style determination, (10) interpersonal-transactional determination, (11) existential-status determination, and (12) social-environmental determination. Characteristic etiological equations are given in each class. As an example, the equations under (8) are as follows:

1. Low self-concept + lack of confidence = poor performance = inferiority complex (Adler)
2. Low self-concept + anxiety over failure = defensive reaction formations = existential anxiety
3. Weak ego functioning + high stress = personality disintegration caused by breakdown of controls
4. Self-damaging errors + ego deflation = lowered self-concept and guilt
5. Self-anger + frustration and aggression directed inwardly = depression and suicide
6. Lack of self-consistency + conflictual actions = neurosis (Lecky, Thorne)

These classes are related to integrative levels and to different theories and hypotheses concerning psychopathology. Direct examination is necessary to determine etiological equations; psychological tests are not adapted to the measurement of changing psychological states and are not available to measure factors in the higher level integrations.

Every psychological state is the result of psychological fields of forces in which are represented the interactions of heredity and environment, constitutional and acquired factors, drives, needs, affective impulses, past conditioning, imaginings of the future, and various forms of self-determination. The etiological equation for the state expresses all these factors. "The equation is given naturally, in the state, and the problem is to discover what it is."[60] The process is inductive. The clinician's task is to analyze the natural data and develop an etiological equation based on hypotheses concerning the determination of the psychological state. "Clinical judgment is the only tool available for differentiating, evaluating and weighing all the various classes of factors etiologic to a psychological condition."[61]

The Clinical Encounter

"In the existential sense, every interview should be a genuine *clinical encounter* in which clinician and client *experience* each other and themselves more completely and meaningfully. . . . It is now well established that all productive case handling depends upon the creation of positive, accepting interpersonal relationships between counselor and client."[62] Factors that contribute to a therapeutic relationship include personal warmth and liking, unconditional positive regard, nonjudgmentalism, nonimposition, permissiveness, empathy, and genuineness. These factors reduce defensiveness and provide a safe environment in which the client can be and experience himself or herself more completely and constructively.

The client usually has had no previous experience in counseling or psychotherapy and often has a different viewpoint from the case handler's. Although it is only by experiencing the process that the client can come to know what it involves, some structuring can reduce differences in viewpoints. The client, impatient for quick relief of symptoms and to find happiness and success, can be helped to understand that it is necessary to discover and modify basic etiological causes, which may require weeks or months of hard work.

Most clients are ambivalent about coming for help. They do not know what to expect. Some orientation is necessary for obtaining the client's cooperation. "The permissive nondirective relationship is desirable if it works, but unfortunately many clients are so disturbed that they may not remain in the situation unless external pressures are brought to bear."[63] Once contacts are initiated, a relationship usually can be developed.

Communication must be established at the client's level. Rapport, which is defined as *"the harmonious relationship and mutual responsiveness which results from heightened suggestibility and emotional transference occurring where people have confidence, trust and esteem for each other,"*[64] involves a number of factors. The client expects help and ascribes prestige to the counselor, who responds with warmth, acceptance, permissiveness, respect, genuineness, empathy, and self-disclosure. Rapport is maintained by the counselor's avoidance of criticism, moralism, judgmental attitudes, insincerity, and any suggestion of ulterior motivation. Rapport creates a sense of security in the client, which is conducive to learning.

The counseling relationship develops most favorably when the counselor is passive at the beginning, while the client becomes familiar with the situation at his or her own rate. However, with clients who are doubting, negative, and resistant, more active methods may be necessary.

Terminating Case Handling

Ideally, counseling concludes naturally, with the client gradually resuming independent self-regulation. In many instances, however, factors enter that either terminate counseling before the desired objectives have been reached or prolong it.

The closing phase of counseling is characterized by the achievement of an understanding of the nature and origin of the maladjustment, the reduction of tension and defensive reactions, and the development of a rational approach to dealing with the maladjustment or problems. The client is freed from affective-impulse behavior and is able to use intellectual resources in problem-solving behavior. Clients with good intellectual resources may be able to arrive at solutions by themselves, and counseling may terminate before specific solutions have been reached. With clients of lower intelligence, counseling may continue, with the counselor contributing more actively or directively to the solution of problems. The first and longer part of counseling consists of release and clarification of emotional problems, with the counselor in a passive and nondirective role. In the second and shorter part of the counseling process, the counselor participates more directively in the intellectual problem-solving process.

Most counseling relationships come to a natural termination by mutual consent. The client begins to feel capable of getting along by himself or herself and may skip an appointment to try out this new independence, or the counselor may suggest that the client is now capable of becoming independent and should try to get along on his or her own.

Although the counselor should respect the client's feelings and wishes about terminating counseling, the counselor has a responsibility to prevent premature discontinuance of counseling. Some clients desire to terminate counseling after experiencing symptomatic relief but before getting at the etiological factors. Other clients want to terminate when they experience the discomfort of facing painful memories or insights. Clients may also desire to terminate prematurely when the counseling reaches the point where they must take action on new insights, which the clients may not be ready to accept or to implement. Clients may also want to discontinue counseling because of external problems, such as financial difficulties or changes in residence. Finally, poor handling by the counselor—including inability to establish rapport (which may not, however, always be the counselor's fault), failure to structure adequately, overdirectiveness, and improper handling of the transference—may lead to premature termination.

Whether the counselor should take action to prevent premature termination depends on the nature of the individual case. In some cases, the client may be told simply that the counselor feels that treatment should continue, but persuasion or threat should not be used. The counselor should handle resistance by accepting, reflecting, and clarifying the client's feelings. A client who is known to be at an acute crisis of conflicts must not be allowed to terminate treatment until all resources fail. When termination is due to incompatibility of the client and the counselor, referral should be attempted.

The counselor must be concerned about premature termination, which results in undertreatment, because of possible serious consequences to the client. When a client develops further difficulties, which presumably might have been avoided with adequate treatment, the counselor may be blamed for poor clinical judgment, with consequent damage to his or her reputation and future effectiveness. The counselor should, therefore, be very careful about abandoning treatment too easily. He or she should be sure that all pathological processes have been recognized and handled. The counselor should abandon passive methods for more active methods when the former are ineffective and should not be afraid to attempt drastic treatment methods. The counselor should follow up clients to see that they carry out instructions and take appropriate actions.

While counseling may continue for long periods of time, sometimes for years, some clients would continue indefinitely if they were allowed to. The counselor should avoid overtreatment of such clients. There are also cases where the counselor holds clients in treatment for unnecessarily long periods. The financially insecure counselor in private practice may become dependent on the fees of a client and keep the client longer than necessary. Sometimes the counselor may be overconscientious or overanxious and may lack confidence in the client's ability to become independent. While it is desirable to prevent undertreatment, this danger may be minimized by follow-up checks, and overtreatment should be avoided.

The closing phase of counseling involves the termination of a transference relationship if it has developed. This termination sometimes occurs spontaneously, but with dependent clients, separation may become a problem. Such clients may attempt to delay termination. The counselor may bring the relationship to a close by interpreting the transference and indicating why termination is desirable.

Counseling should be concluded with some type of summary of the process and its accomplishments. Counseling is a slow and gradual process, with many small gains or insights. Bringing these together gives an overview and clarifies what has gone on for the client. With verbal clients, it may be desirable to ask them to summarize. This enables the counselor to evaluate the accuracy of the client's conclusions. Some clients are unable to make an interpretive summary, however, and the counselor must summarize. Such summarizing is useful at various points in counseling as well as at its conclusion.

METHODS OF PSYCHOLOGICAL CASE HANDLING

Dealing with Presenting Complaints and Symptoms

While psychotherapy or counseling is directed toward removing or remedying the causes of the client's disturbance, it is desirable to give the client relief from symptoms and to improve the client's general condition by supportive therapy and reassurance. In general, symptomatic and supportive therapy are used when deep psychotherapy is not indicated or is not possible. While the methods are superficial and are not major methods of therapy, they are useful either when other methods are not possible or in conjunction with other methods.

Symptomatic Therapy

Symptoms deserve attention because, to the client and to those who are concerned about the client, they constitute the complaint and may be their only concern. If symptoms do not improve or disappear, treatment may not be considered useful or successful.

Many maladjustments or disorders terminate spontaneously with the passage of time. Palliative methods—that is, methods of reducing the client's suffering by relieving the symptoms—are useful while the natural recuperative processes are functioning. In addition, these methods are useful in the absence of more specific methods. Although symptoms may disappear with other methods of treatment, such as nondirective methods, they should be dealt with directly. Such treatment of symptoms does not interfere with more specific treatment directed to the etiological factors.

Indications for palliative methods include the following.

1. *Major Crises in Adjustment* Clients sometimes are in a state in which they are unable to approach their problems constructively because the are too excited or agitated. Their behavior may only make their condition worse. In such situations, palliative actions alleviate the condition until other approaches can be used.
2. *Minor Periods of Instability* Most people have periods of difficulty that re-

solve themselves spontaneously. During those periods, palliative measures help the client until the period passes or the environmental conditions improve. In periods of temporary instability or indecisiveness, plans or actions may be suggested to the client, or the client may be supported in postponing decisions or actions until conditions change or the client is sure of what he or she wants to do.

3. *Insoluble Problems*   When reality prevents any satisfactory solution, support may be provided to give the client relief.
4. *Distressing Symptoms*   It may be desirable or necessary for the therapist to palliate distressing symptoms before dealing with the basic problems.
5. *Dangerous Symptoms*   Symptoms of organic disorders, symptoms of desperation and panic, suicidal threats, uncontrollable sexual impulses, homicidal ideas, and paranoid delusions must be dealt with actively to safeguard the client and society.

Techniques of symptomatic therapy include the following.

1. *Structuring the Process*   Structuring the process consists of leading the client to understand the relation of the symptoms to causes, the distinction between symptomatic and specific therapy, and the results to be expected from symptomatic therapy.
2. *Avoiding Symptom Fixation*   Encouraging the client to action that antagonizes symptom formation or that enables the client to control the symptoms may prevent the fixation of symptoms.
3. *Maintaining Morale*   Attention, sympathy, and encouragement provide the emotional support and hope that may be necessary in order for the client to continue, and they thus make possible more specific therapy. They may also make bearable an insoluble problem.
4. *Masterful Inactivity*   Masterful inactivity is a technique that involves the postponement of action without disturbing rapport or losing the client's confidence. In effect, it consists of putting the client off with plausible excuses, explanations, or vague assurances of later action.
5. *Suggestion*   Suggestion has long been used, and although it has been widely criticized, it has a use in certain situations, such as dealing with functional or psychogenic symptoms.
6. *Nondirective Methods*   While nondirective methods are primarily suited for counseling normal people, they may be used also for palliative purposes with neurotics, psychotics, and mental defectives, pending the application of more suitable active methods, including hospitalization.

Supportive Therapy

Supportive therapy consists of nonspecific techniques used for their constitutional or psychological effects and includes both physical and psychological methods. The former were used in early psychiatry, illustrated by Weir-Mitchell's rest cure, but have come into disrepute. Nevertheless, they may be useful in restoring or building up the organism, so that it may function adequately in everyday living and develop resistance to disturbances.

Among the factors involved are the natural functions of the body, including eating and sleeping; economic support; and satisfaction in work, family relationships, social activities, and recreation. The correction and improvement of these factors may increase the client's threshold of personality disorder.

Physical methods of supportive therapy include medical treatment, rest, improved nutrition, physiotherapy, hydrotherapy, chemotherapy, material (financial) security, and hospitalization. It is desirable that every client who exhibits any psychosomatic symptoms have a complete physical examination, and the counselor should consult with a physician at frequent intervals. When a medical examination indicates no organic disease, this information may help the client to recognize the psychological nature of his or her disturbance.

Psychological supportive therapy includes healthy habit routines, environmental manipulation, occupational therapy, diversional therapy, bibliotherapy, changing attitudes in the environment, and reassurance, suggestion, and advice.

Reassurance is an important supportive method. Reassurance strengthens positive attitudes and healthy behavior by acting as a reward. It is an antidote for fear, worry, doubt, uncertainty, and insecurity and is one of the oldest and most widely used methods of psychotherapy. Even though it may be superficial and its effects, transient, it is a valuable method of treatment, although it is sometimes misused. Reassurance is indicated in treating cases of mental deficiency, in combating anxiety, in dealing with feelings of inferiority and inadequacy, in reinforcing new adjustment patterns, and in counseling children. It is contraindicated when it is necessarily false and the client knows the truth, when it allows the client to shift responsibility to the counselor, and when it may lead to overconfidence or aggressiveness.

Reassurance is of several types. There may be reassurance that the client is not unique or unusual, that the nature of the client's condition is known and has a cause, that the symptoms may be annoying but not dangerous, that something can be done, that the condition will not lead to insanity, that relapses occur and are not an indication that the condition is getting worse, and that the condition does not indicate sinfulness or blame.

Reassurance may be freely used when it is true; if it is used too freely or too early, however, it may give premature and superficial relief, which may block further progress. The client should first be allowed to express fears, and the counselor should recognize, accept, and clarify the need for reassurance before reassurance is given. Reassurance may be either verbal or behavioral. The counselor should use both, and they should be used consistently.

High fees, impressive surroundings, an air of confidence, and pomp and ceremony are reassuring in that they meet the client's need of feeling that he or she is getting the best treatment from a competent therapist. "An effective personality and a quick, dignified mode of speaking and acting are very reassuring to most patients. Successful clinicians inspire such utter confidence that their clients are reassured that they are receiving the best possible treatment."[65] These methods may be justified, even though they have no direct effect on the therapeutic outcome, in persuading the client to continue treatment until other techniques become effective.

Reassurance is most effective when it involves factual information rather than opinions. When a client raises questions about which he or she could be reassured by one of the methods listed above, being nondirective and telling the client nothing may increase the client's anxiety and lead the client to conclude that his or her condition must really be bad if the counselor cannot tell him or her about it. Yet when the condition or prognosis is actually serious or unfavorable, this should not usually be revealed to the client.

Conditioning and Behavior Therapies

"The whole process of case handling must be regarded as a learning situation in which suitable conditions for reconditioning are provided for the client to unlearn maladaptive behaviors and acquire more healthy patterns."[66] The specific methods of the behavior therapies, however, "treat the patient like a mindless animal organism which is subjected to an authoritarian reconditioning instigated by a directive therapist who assumes the responsibility of knowing what is wrong with the patient and what should be done for him without securing his permission or even his cooperation."[67] Whether any changes in personality integration or life styles occur is yet to be demonstrated.

When the affective component of a disorder is primary, it must be dealt with first, and learning methods are not effective. When the affective component is secondary or reactive, learning and training methods may be effective. Moreover, since motivation is necessary for learning, the client's need systems and motivational status must be studied in order to determine effective incentives and rewards.

Tutorial counseling, in which specific problem areas are discriminated and formulated in psychological terms that the client can understand, followed by tutoring and training exercises in the solution of the problems, utilizes retraining involving conditioning methods.

Life-Management Analysis and Tutoring

Many simple adult maladjustments are situational. Some situations contain pathogenic factors that stimulate maladaptive reactions in even "normal" persons. The case handler must have knowledge of such situations, particularly those of a local nature. Analysis of the extent of situational factors in maladjustment is part of diagnosis.

Observation and operational analysis of the client's behavior in the situation should be made. The observation should involve empathically living through situations with the client. The client's role-playing skills in the major roles of student, worker, financial manager, sex and marriage partner, parent, and social person in the community should be evaluated.

After the counselor has diagnosed what the client is doing wrong in the situation, the counselor communicates it to the client with techniques of situational adjustment and carries on intensive tutoring in the requisite skills. Tutorial counseling is dealt with in detail by Thorne in *Tutorial Counseling.*[68]

Circular and chain reactions may occur. Thus in addition to strengthening the person's ability to deal with situations whenever possible, the counselor should deal with or modify the external factors. This is particularly relevant in treating problems of childhood, cases of mental deficiency, marriage and family problems, and problems of the aged.

"Failure to recognize the situational determination of many simple adult maladjustments may constitute an important source of diagnostic and therapeutic errors."[69]

Methods of Therapeutic Influence

Methods of directly and actively influencing the client have been in disrepute, but this is mainly because they have been abused. They appear to be ineffective because they have not been used in accordance with specific indications and because they are inconsistent with the prevailing orientation of psychotherapy. Nevertheless, many clients are unable to move toward goals by their own efforts and require active intervention and direction on the part of the counselor.

Suggestion

Suggestibility is a universal phenomenon and enters into all psychogenic disorders and all therapy. Therapeutic results are often ascribed in error to other factors when in actuality they are the result of suggestion. Suggestion is the influence of the ideas, feelings, or actions of another without direct command or appeal to intellectual functions. Hypnotism appears to be based on suggestibility, and suggestibility is related to positive transference.

Suggestive techniques are indicated to achieve limited objectives, such as (1) antagonizing the effects of negative suggestions, (2) stimulating positive attitudes, (3) catalyzing desirable actions by the client, and (4) removing symptoms known to have been produced by suggestion. Suggestion is effective with children, mental defectives, and immature personalities. It should not be used when it is not likely to succeed or to result in symptom disappearance.

The technique of suggestion may be facilitated if (1) it is kept to a minimum and used only when indicated, (2) it is not used too early or too often, (3) positive ideas are emphasized, (4) negative suggestions are avoided, (5) benevolent rather than dictatorial authority is used, (6) suggestions are repeated often, (7) the client is prepared to accomplish the suggestion, (8) the truth (but not necessarily all the truth) is adhered to, and (9) the counselor is cheerfully reassuring. Reflections of the client's feelings may provide suggestion if the counselor selects elements and word responses in a suggestive manner.

Persuasion and Advice

Persuasion appeals to reason and intelligence. It involves a counselor–client relationship in which the counselor is wiser and more mature than the client, whom the counselor teaches or advises. Advice consists of opinions or recommendations to the client, usually on the assumption that the counselor knows what to do better than does the client. Persuasion and advice imply client dependence and lack of responsibility. These methods have fallen into disrepute because they are limited to symptom removal and ignore emotional elements. However, when some directive action is indicated, persuasion and advice may be useful in obtaining the cooperation of all concerned. When an immediate, clear solution is available, persuasion and advice are methods for influencing clients in the simplest, quickest way. They are indicated, therefore, in mild conditions where intellect is intact and rapport and cooperation are easy to obtain, in emergency situations, and to secure limited objectives such as symptom removal. They should be used for client-centered purposes and should be avoided when they might interfere with major psychotherapy.

Techniques of persuasion include pointing out the facts of the situation to the client, explaining causal relationships, showing why the client should change his or her attitudes or habits, pointing out future consequences of maladaptive behavior, substituting knowledge for emotions, outlining rules of mental health, encouraging the facing of reality and the practice of problem-solving techniques, and introducing alternatives for action.

Since clinical judgment is generally unreliable and invalid, "persuasion and advice should not be used indiscriminately but only after intensive case study when specific etiologic findings indicate specific directive advice. . . . Too early application may destroy rapport and transference. Too frequent application may stimulate undesirable reactions of negativism or dependency."[70] They are justified in dealing with life-management situations for which outcomes can be predicted statistically by the case handler.

Pressure, Coercion, and Punishment

Although early treatment of mental patients included punishment, the pendulum has swung to the opposite extreme of rejecting any punitive methods. Nevertheless, there appear to be situations in which the suppressive methods of pressure, coercion, and punishment are useful. Such techniques are to be used with a firm, kind, understanding authoritarianism.

Restraints and punishment are necessary in dealing with the behavioral excesses of immature and asocial personalities. Absolute permissiveness leads to excesses. In psychotherapy, pressure and coercion are used to achieve therapeutic objectives of training or retraining or of correction or control of unacceptable or dangerous behavior, which have not been achieved in the home or the school. The therapist may have thrust on him or her the task of making a plan to control deviant behavior. It is desirable that the therapist accept the role of a reasonable, paternalistic authority, so that the client can learn to accept limits and authority.

The indications for the use of pressure and coercion include dependent persons who need a "push"; persons who are "spoiled"; persons who are escaping reality; persons who are constitutionally inadequate; clients who are domineering; persons who are creating an intolerable or dangerous emergency situation; persons who are temporarily emotionally uncontrolled; clients who will not or cannot act by themselves; clients who are indecisive, wavering neurotics; sociopaths; and the failure of other methods.

These methods probably have been misused more than any other methods of influencing behavior, and they may have lost their effects with some clients; they may lead others to react negatively or in other unconstructive ways, such as with anxiety, defiance, hostility, or aggression. Such clients require careful handling, and more coercion or punishment will not be effective. "In general, the use of pressure, coercion and punishment is contraindicated unless there are specific reasons for its use."[71] The

5. *Termination of Treatment* When resistance cannot be modified, counseling may have to be terminated, or the client may be referred to another counselor, who may not be the object of such strong resistance. The client may break off the relationship because of resistance.

Frustration and Conflict Resolution

Conflict normally provides a motive for change, but excessive conflict either blocks integration or produces disintegration. Conflict is a cause of frustration. In such cases, disabling conflicts involve two incompatible reactions, which are intense and approximately equal in strength. An objective of case handling is conflict resolution.

The disintegrating effects of frustration induced by conflict can be neutralized by increasing the client's frustration tolerance through training in tolerating tension and in rejecting immediate need gratification and by learning through conditioning to "take punishment."

A first step in conflict resolution is to bring the conflict and its opposing forces into consciousness through interpretation. Then plans can be formulated for coping with the forces and helping the client carry out the plan through tutorial counseling.

The Therapeutic Use of Conflict

Normal conflict is a motivating or corrective factor that stimulates creativity and achievement and leads to desirable changes in behavior; the absence of conflict may be pathological. Thus it may be desirable for the clinician to create conflict, so that the client can recognize the need for change and be motivated toward change.

Conflict may be induced by bringing into consciousness inconsistent and conflicting attitudes. When the client becomes aware of the inconsistency, he or she will be motivated to resolve it. The desirable effects of punishment may be the result of induced conflict.

> The use of induced conflict as a technique in therapy must be handled with great caution. Conflict should not be used promiscuously or indiscriminately. . . . It must be emphasized that the efficacy of the technique depends upon the clinical sagacity of the case handler, who must be able to guide the therapeutic process in positive directions, keep the conflict focused on inconsistencies in the client's attitudes, and avoid any attempt of the client to introduce interpersonal conflicts which would conceal the real issue.[76]

Maximizing Intellectual Resources

Education attempts to develop intellectual resources by improving sensory functions, perceptual training, memory training, and semantic training. Defects of sensation, perception, memory, learning, and the use of verbal symbols may be important causes of maladjustment and may be remedied by retraining methods. These methods are aimed at training the client to think straight and to correct illogical thoughts that are the basis of maladaptive behavior. It cannot be assumed that the client can resolve problems logically or intellectually simply by the removal of emotional blockages. The client needs direct assistance or formal training in intellectual problem solving.

general approach is for the therapist to begin with permissiveness in order to see how much responsibility the client can take in controlling his or her behavior and then, as is necessary, to progress to pressure (suggestion), coercion (requirement), and finally punishment.

Pressure and coercion may be necessary to make clients conform to the limits of the counseling situation or to keep them in treatment. Punishment, as such, is rarely, if ever, used in psychotherapy, but as an incentive to learning, it may be effective. However, it should be used only when rewards have proved ineffective. In emergency situations, shock methods, withdrawal of love, withdrawal of privileges, and rejection and ostracism may be used, not by choice but for want of better methods.

Drastic methods of coercion and punishment are indicated only for the protection of the client and of society.

Dealing with Emotional Factors in Maladjustment

> Much of behavior is determined by subconscious emotional factors which must be dealt with first before the higher mental functions can be released in problem-solving behavior. . . . There is no attempt to slight or minimize the importance of emotional behavior, particularly on subconscious or unverbalized levels. On the contrary, we reaffirm that the handling of emotional factors constitutes one of the most important problems in all psychotherapy because of the significant role played by early childhood conditionings in later maladjustments.[72]

However, "affective-impulsive factors are not the only, or even necessarily the most important, cause of disorder."[73] Although emotional factors constitute only one kind of primary etiological factor, clinical experience indicates that they usually should be dealt with first. Methods for dealing with affective-impulsive factors are derived primarily from psychoanalysis and nondirective therapy, with the addition of conditioning methods.

A distinction is made between *primary emotional states* and *secondary emotional reactions.* The former are related to temperament and are largely constitutionally determined, and thus are not usually modifiable by psychotherapy. Secondary emotional reactions result from frustration, conflict, and stress; they may be prevented by preventing these causes and can be modified by reconditioning. There are different types of emotional disorders, and thus there is no single therapeutic method that is suitable for all. Emotional reactivity constitutes a continuum from overexpressiveness to underexpressiveness, with different methods being required to deal with the extreme patterns.

Emotional Conditioning and Reconditioning

"Since most reactive emotional patterns are acquired by known principles of learning, they may be modified by appropriate methods of retraining."[74] Emotional retraining utilizes various methods to create situations in which the client may learn new emotional responses to replace neurotic responses to stimuli. Affective reconditioning be like if he or she could have the feelings or emotions that he or she is lacking.

12. *Active Techniques of Emotional Release*   Although encouraging the client to engage in social, recreational, and other activities is widely advocated, this method is usually not successful, since the client is generally unable to concentrate on such activities.

The objective of these methods is to prevent affectivity from becoming isolated and from blocking higher levels of integration.

Transference and Resistance Phenomena

While personality counseling, unlike psychoanalysis, does not foster the development of transference, the counselor must have an understanding of transference, since a transference relationship that is intensive and of long duration may develop in counseling. Transference is the projecting onto the therapist of emotional attitudes originally directed toward significant figures in early life. Positive attitudes result in positive transference, and negative attitudes result in negative transference.

The fact that many clients have strong unmet needs for love and affection and that they find the therapist accepting and noncritical often leads to emotional attitudes toward the therapist that create problems in counseling. The counselor must be careful to prevent the development of unhealthy emotional attachments in the client. Similarly, counselors must be prepared to handle reactions of fear, hate, hostility, and anger resulting from negative transference.

Since those without psychoanalytic training are not competent to resolve the transference, they should not allow a classical transference to develop. However, the counselor must terminate the dependency relationship that develops.

Resistance is the natural defense of the client against the pain and unpleasantness of recognizing and accepting insight and change. Resistance may be manifested in various ways: negative attitudes toward therapy and the therapist, failure to keep appointments and attempts to avoid or end treatment, lack of production or irrelevant productions, intellectualization, failure to carry out prescriptions, failure to pay for treatment, emotional blocking, and demands on the counselor to attempt to control the situation.

Methods of handling resistance include the following:

1. *Passive Listening*   Expressions of resistance and hostility tend to be self-limiting and tend to dissipate when they are allowed expression in a nonthreatening atmosphere.
2. *Acceptance, Reflection, and Clarification*   When resistances continue, they may be openly recognized and responded to by acceptance, reflection, and clarification.
3. *Neutral Conversation*   When resistance is too open or strong or leads to an impasse, temporarily leading the counseling away from sensitive areas may be desirable.
4. *Analysis of Resistance*   Analysis and interpretation of the causes of resistance may help the client face the nature of the resistance.

Sensory Problems and Complaints

The remedying of organic sensory defects is not a function of the personality counselor, but he or she should be alert to their occurrence and make appropriate referrals. Personality reactions may, however, require counseling. In addition, there are sensory complaints or peculiar sensory experiences that have a functional basis. They include frequent headaches, eyestrain, and hypersensitivity to light, noise, and other stimuli; muscular and joint aches and pains; cardiac palpitation and arhythmias; "nervous stomach"; and so forth. Diagnosis of these difficulties and differentiation from organic disorders is a medical function.

These sensory experiences are present in the normal individual, but the individual has learned to accept or ignore them or to become less concerned about them than the psychoneurotic. The counselor must accept the reality of the symptoms. Reassurance may be given that they are not dangerous, that they are due to emotional disturbance, and that they can be treated. Psychosomatic information and explanations may be given. Peculiar sensations may be ignored or treated symptomatically, since they will disappear with psychotherapy directed at the etiological factors. Behavior therapy may be used for desensitization and elimination of symptoms diagnosed as functional.

Perceptual Retraining

> Perception is organized by and makes its relevant contribution to the functional needs of the prevailing psychological state. . . . Clinically, we are interested in the study and remediation of factors interfering with the normal processing and integration of sensory input. . . . Pathologically, disorders or defects of information processing at perceptual (discriminatory) levels produce disturbances of reality testing and other perceptual errors. Since informational input is essential to keeping abreast of the times, perceptual disorders are an important cause of psychopathology.[77]

When the client's misperceptions become evident, attention is called to them, with an explanation of their nature. "When defects in reality testing in the client become apparent, it may be indicated to conduct diagnostic studies to discover their origin so that they may be corrected. Standard types of perceptual errors may be explained to the client with appropriate demonstrations as to how they may be corrected. The client may be tutored in more systematic reality testing by routinely analyzing maladaptive perceptual sets."[78] The client's perceptual field can often be reoriented by introducing new elements.

The client's perceptions of himself or herself are important in his or her perceptions of the world and of others and thus must be systematically evaluated. Delusional thinking and paranoid ideas can be corrected in their early stages by "pointing out their erroneous nature to the client, explaining the underlying projection mechanisms, and admonishing the client to try to correct such thinking himself."[79] Full-fledged paranoid complexes do not usually respond to counseling, however.

The Improvement of Memory Functioning

Memory deficits and pathological forgetting impair integration by preventing past experiences from entering into the process. Memory deficits due to incomplete learning may be corrected by the use of remedial learning methods (increasing motivation, grouping of materials into meaningful combinations, spaced practice, overlearning, special cues, and verbalization during learning). Pathological forgetting may be treated by the psychoanalytical methods of free association, dream analysis, and symptom analysis.

The intrusion of undesirable memories and minutia may interfere with adequate functioning. Ventilation through repeated catharsis and deliberate recalling of traumatic experiences are standard methods for reducing the affective charge of such experiences.

Semantic Reeducation

General semantics is concerned with the use of language and symbols in the thinking process. Semantic disorders include vague, fuzzy, and illogical thinking and inaccurate and unclear use of language, which interferes with communication.

The case handler should evaluate the client's language functioning from the beginning and undertake semantic reorientation through careful definition of psychological terms, which often are not understood clearly by clients.

Informal semantic reeducation consists of correcting semantic errors as they occur in counseling, thus helping the client to become clearer, more accurate, and more articulate in the use of language. Clients who are highly intelligent and verbal and who have basic emotional stability may be given formal semantic training, which may include reading and doing exercises that are aimed toward the objective of dealing with their problems logically and scientifically. Semantics underlies all methods of improving intellectual resources and is relevant to methods of developing emotional release and clarification, which may be regarded as preparation for intellectual problem-solving behavior.

Methods of Ideological and Attitudinal Reorientation

Ideas and attitudes integrate the highest levels of human behavior. Many disorders are the result of lack of knowledge, erroneous knowledge, and logical or semantic failure to use symbols validly. It is thus necessary to evaluate the client's ideological beliefs and values. The neurotically or emotionally determined ideas and values that are involved require deep psychotherapy. Most ideas are acquired normally, and ideological disorders then reflect a pathological environment rather than pathology in the person. Methods of ideological reorientation are then necessary.

Imparting Psychological Information

The counselor has a responsibility to provide helpful psychological information to the individual who needs it for more efficient functioning or problem solving. The giving of psychological information is indicated when it is lacking and when it will be necessary or useful to the client. It is contraindicated when it would have threatening or destructive effects and when there are unhealthy motives for seeking it. The kinds of information that may be given include material concerning the nature and prognosis of the disorder, alternative courses of action, the forestalling of unwise action, and the attitudes of others toward the client. In some cases, when scientific knowledge is not available, opinions may be offered.

Information should be given, not in the form of a lecture, but as needed and in relation to the problems of the client. The language should be adapted to the client's background. References to books and other sources may be used. Information should be selective and presented objectively in a manner that does not intimidate or threaten the client. The counselor should check to see whether the client has understood or assimilated the material.

Systematic psychological tutoring may be provided to impart the latest basic scientific psychological information. The book *How to Be Psychologically Healthy*[80] may be assigned to clients when appropriate; in selected cases (clients who are too directive and authoritarian or who have to deal with authoritarian people), study of the theory and practice of nondirective methods can be valuable.

The Method of Interpretation

One of the major goals of psychotherapy is the development of insight by the client. The method of interpretation, which is one of the most widely used and misused techniques of psychotherapy, is the most specific and most simple method of transmitting insights from the therapist to the client. Interpretations are attempts to provide understanding of the nature and the origin of the maladjustment.

Indications for interpretation are difficult to specify; mature clinical judgment must be relied on. In general, there must be reason to believe that the client can use the interpretation constructively. Interpretation is indicated when the client is unable to reach the insight alone and when therapy would be speeded up by the providing of an insight long before the client could achieve it alone. Interpretations should not be used when, although true, they are threatening, the client is unable to do anything about them, they may create more conflicts than they solve, and the client is unable to comprehend them.

Interpretations should be made cautiously and sparingly, at the optimum moment (not too soon), and tentatively, even though the counselor will make an interpretation only when he or she is convinced that it is valid. The counselor must be truthful, nonjudgmental, and simple in making interpretations. Methods of interpretation include sympathetic or understanding comments, reflective comments, focusing comments, facilitating comments, comforting comments, and connecting comments. The interpretation of symbols in psychoanalytic terminology should be avoided in general. The counselor should make certain that the client understands the interpretations by having the client reformulate or summarize them.

Ideological and Attitudinal Reorientation

Many normal people have adjustment problems that are related to unhealthy or untenable attitudes acquired in the normal learning process. Disorders of this kind are called *attitudinal psychopathies* and consist of a constellation of pathological attitudes. They are differentiated from the psychoneuroses and psychoses, in which pathological attitudes are secondary to an underlying disorder. Pathological attitudes are those that are so deviant, erroneous, or untenable that they cause maladjustment.

Reorientation requires first the analysis of the constellation of attitudes and the identification of core attitudes. Reorganization is achieved through the introduction of conflicting (healthy) attitudes, which require the reduction of inconsistency. Repetition is necessary, as is emotional and intellectual reinforcement of the new attitudes. The process of change is usually slow, often with resistance, so the counselor should be prepared for a long-term process. However, sudden and complete changes can occur when a nuclear, or core, attitude is displaced.

Caution must be used in attempting to reorganize the attitudes of older people and of those whose whole way of life is based on questionable beliefs, such as certain religious beliefs.

The Self

Many client complaints relate to perceived disorders of self-functioning. Self-functioning represents the highest level integrations. Positive mental health and complete self-actualization depend on the normality of self-functioning.

The Self and Its Status

The evaluation of self-functioning is an important part of the examination of the client's mental status. The client constantly reveals self-status throughout case handling. The Q sort provides an objective measure. Dissatisfaction of the client with the self-status is necessary for effective counseling, providing the motivation for change is there. Discrepancies between the concept of the self and that of the ideal self are the source of many adjustment problems, and important goals of case handling are to remove these discrepancies and to strengthen the self-concept.

The Ideal Self

Attempts to influence the client's concept of the ideal self are based on the argument that good character is essential for mental health. There are a number of systems of character building, including the theological. Spiritual counseling can be helpful for those who can accept its assumptions, and the case handler should utilize this as a referral resource.

Character rehabilitation is one objective of case handling. Moralistic judgments must be made in a nonauthoritarian and nonrejecting manner to avoid alienating the client. Psychological tutoring is one method of character rehabilitation.

When the ideal self is unattainably higher than the actual self, frustration is inevitable, until the ideal self becomes realistic and thus attainable.

Self-executive Functionings

The highest levels of integration are characterized by purposive, voluntary, and conscious integration. "It is also postulated that the ability to exert self-control, conscious volition or to utilize intellectual resources optimally is not instinctive or innate but is learned by training and experience."[81] Feelings and emotions exist involuntarily (unconsciously), but they may be controlled and channeled. Defects or disorders in learning control are involved in behavior disintegration from frustration and stress. Diagnosis of such disorders is thus important.

Factors contributing to control include emotional stability, the capacity for adequate discrimination of alternatives, adequate symbolic representation, a positive attitude or "mental set" toward control, ability to direct or withhold conscious attention selectively, acceptance of the possibility of self-control, and adequate self-signaling devices. These factors are integrated slowly in a learning process that is specific for differing situations.

"Many clients are completely undisciplined and out of control when they first come for help. . . . One of the first steps in case handling may be to persuade and train the client to adapt to the general requirements of cultural conformity. This may involve going back to the simplest exercises in self-control which should have been acquired in early childhood."[82] Clients in states of heightened affectivity must be taught how to deal with psychophysical reactions. With clients who have problems of interpersonal conflicts, tutoring in non-directive methods of handling hostility and aggression may be very effective.

Transactional Analysis and Social Psychiatry

Transactional analysis focuses on interpersonal relations. The integrational state of the person influences the person's social transactions. Berne's classification of ego states in the Child, the Parent, and the Adult is oversimplified, but it can be expanded to do justice to all the factors that organize integration levels. Games, following Berne, consist of a transactional unit or series of unified interactions with a beginning and an end, involving ulterior motives in the players, with a payoff for each. While games are only one kind of social transaction, they are important because of the effects on the loser. In addition, the person engaged in gamesmanship, even if a "winner," develops personally and socially unhealthy relationships.

"It is indicated to indoctrinate the client with a working knowledge of normal probabilities, gamesmanship and good sportsmanship to teach the client a philosophy of life which will support him in times of need."[83] The person who is being victimized can be taught to avoid victimization by refusing to play the game, by neutralizing moves with countermoves, or by withholding the payoff.

The Handling of Existential Problems

With the increasingly difficult conditions of living, more clients are seeking help with problems that are existential, that is, involving the meaning of life in a confusing world, in which values are being questioned and are often inconsistent. The counselor enters into the consideration of alternative values and their alternative consequences or costs with the client.

The primary existential motive is self-enhancement or self-actualization. Anxiety is the result of the threat or the actuality of failure to become actualized. An effort to cover up failure results in lack of authenticity and genuineness, with resulting anxiety. The case handler should have a pretty realistic understanding of what life can be expected to hold for any particular client. Clients with great unrealized possibilities for self-potentiation may be stimulated toward greater efforts and more aggressiveness in wresting for themselves what life has to offer. With clients of lesser potentialities, it may be necessary to discourage unreasonable expectations and to encourage acceptance of the status quo.

Maladjustments result from the failure to achieve a realistic and tenable *Weltanschauung.* The individual's *Weltanschauung* may be too rudimentary and incomplete; it may be inadequate to handle the inconsistencies of life; it may fail to evolve and thus become outdated; an adequate *Weltanschauung* may be insufficient to meet extreme adversity; or the individual may have insufficient experiential resources to build a satisfactory *Weltanschauung.* Although there are no objective methods for evaluating the client's *Weltanschauung,* it becomes apparent over a period of time. Misconceptions and unhealthy attitudes are dealt with realistically as they occur. Alternative attitudes may be discussed, but no attempt is made to argue the client out of his or her attitudes. When the client's *Weltanschauung* is the focus of concern, the case handler assumes the position of an educator who presents "the concentrated experience of mankind," so that the client does not have to learn by trial-and-error methods. The case handler

> attempts to overhaul and bring up-to-date the client's world conception in the light of the most advanced information. . . . Ideally, the client might be allowed to work through his problems nondirectively. . . . Practically, however, more or less direction is indicated, since the achievement of an adequate *Weltanschauüng* is [based] upon a broad cultural background which is beyond the education and experience of large segments of the population. The assumption of responsibility by the therapist for modifying a person's world conception assumes a genuine wisdom and years of experience.[84]

EXAMPLES

In *Psychological Case Handling,* Thorne includes many excerpts that illustrate the application of specific methods. However, he notes that "the case reports in this book are not exact transcriptions of any particular case but have been extensively edited and revised to describe general situations rather than specific cases."[85]

The following is an excerpt in which the counselor interprets resistance in terms of what had previously come out in counseling in an effort to prevent premature termination.[86]

CLIENT: I don't see as we are getting anywhere. Here I have been coming for almost five weeks and I don't feel any better than when we started. Sometimes I think maybe I feel worse.

COUNSELOR: Sometimes you get discouraged and feel that you are wasting your time.

CL: We . . . to be frank, yes. You just sit there listening to me and never say anything. I sometimes wonder if I wouldn't do better talking to the wall. You never answer any of my questions.

CO: It makes you mad because I don't tell you what to do, but just reflect the question back for you to solve for yourself.

CL: Why shouldn't I just talk this over with my husband? He says, "Why do you keep going there and seeing that doctor? He never seems to do anything for you."

CO: Sometimes you feel upset because you are wasting your time and money just talking things over when you feel that more should be done.

CL: I don't think I will come anymore. We seem to be at a standstill. I don't see where we are getting. I could use the money better somewhere else.

CO: I think we have discovered from these interviews that whenever we are coming to something important, you seem to become blocked emotionally and have trouble getting it out. You remember last time, it took you quite some time to express feelings of hostility toward your mother. It was so painful to you that you would almost rather break off the interview than talk about it. I wonder if your present feelings of discouragement are related to the fact that we are getting close to something else.

CL: What do you think it could be?

CO: I don't know. That is something you will have to discover for yourself. All I know is that as long as you continue to feel bad, your problems aren't solved. There was something you started to tell me last time but never got it finished. Do you remember? You started to tell me something that was upsetting you very much but somehow you couldn't bring yourself to.

CL: Oh, that. I don't see as that had anything to do with it. I am not sure I want to talk about it. I felt like talking for a minute and then it passed away.

CO: It's something which made you feel upset even to think about it.

CL: Yes, but it hasn't anything to do with this.

CO: How can we tell until we find what it is?

CL: I can't bring myself to say it. (cries) Sometimes I am afraid of myself.

CO: M'hm.

CL: You're going to think I'm awful.

CO: You're afraid I might reject you if you tell bad things about yourself.

CL: But this is bad.

CO: M'hm.

CL: I see you are going to get it out of me so I might as well tell it. Maybe you'll say I should be put away when you hear it. It's just this. The other night I had an impulse to choke my baby. It just came into my mind. It upset me so I didn't know what to do. There he lay, the dear little thing. Sleeping so peaceable. It was all I could do to keep from doing it. I had to run out of the room. I woke my husband and he said, "What's the matter anyway?" I was afraid to tell him, I just said I was lonely and would he love me a little bit. I guess people like me should be put away.

CO: Having such a thought frightened you.

CL: I'll say it did. I don't think I would have done anything but suppose I did. Do you think I am safe to have around?

CO: Have you ever had other thoughts like that?

CL: Once or twice I had funny thoughts. Knives bother me. I have had impulses to pick one up and stick it into somebody.

CO: Who?

CL: My mother for one. I don't understand it. She has done everything for me. Maybe too much. And I still feel like that.

CO: Sometimes people feel like this if they have unconscious resentments against people. They can love a person and hate them at the same time. It is all right to consciously admit that you love somebody, but most people don't want to face the fact that they have negative feelings to somebody they should love. It makes you feel guilty if you feel that way. Do you know what I mean?

CL: You mean that maybe I have hateful feelings way down inside me and they take this way of coming out. But why on my innocent child that I love so much?

CO: Probably most of the time you love him dearly but once in a while he upsets you. Maybe you are feeling tired or sick and it's just too much.

CL: Of course he does get on my nerves sometimes. I guess maybe I'm not a good mother.

CO: Again, it makes you feel guilty to have these thoughts. I want you to understand this and come to accept your own feelings. Probably if you could express what you feel more and not bury it deep inside you, it would not come out in these devious ways.

CL: Whew. It makes me feel better to get that out. Do you think I am safe to be around? I would be willing to go away if I thought anything would happen.

CO: I don't think there is any danger as long as you keep coming for a little to talk these things over. I want you to promise that you will come and talk with me anytime these things get to bothering you. Get them off your chest.

CL: All right, I will.

In the following excerpt, the client, a 20-year-old woman, is talking about her emotional feelings toward her mother. It is illustrative of semantic reorientation:[87]

CL: I suppose if I really faced the fact I would have to admit that I have never loved Mother. There is something about her which rubs me the wrong way. I think this has always been so. I can remember as a little girl being closer to my father. I know it's awful to say this but it's so.

CO: You have never felt easy with your mother.

CL: No. We never seem to understand each other. I know she tries her best to do things for me but I never know how to take her.

CO: In a way you are a little afraid of her.

CL: I wouldn't say that I was afraid of her, or am I? She can be quite cutting in her remarks. When I was a little girl I would try to be doing something and she would laugh at me.

CO: You were afraid that she would make fun of you.

CL: Sometimes she did. In a nice way, of course.

CO: It makes you feel guilty if you think bad thoughts about your mother.

CL: We-e-ll, anybody should be loyal to their mother. Think of all the things she has done for me.

CO: But still little hostile feelings come into your mind and then you feel guilty.

CL: I love my mother.

CO: I know you do. I didn't say anything about not loving her. I merely said that occasionally you feel upset by what she does and then you have hostile thoughts. That is perfectly natural. Nobody likes any other person 100 percent. We are all mixed in our feelings. There is a word for it—ambivalence. When you're ambivalent, you hold positive and negative feelings toward a person at the same time.

CL: You mean part of the time I love my mother and part of the time I don't like her so well. I never thought of it that way but I guess it's true.

CO: Many people are confused over these mixed feelings.

CL: I guess I've felt that way for some time.

CO: Can you remember when you first began to have mixed feelings toward her?

CL: I can remember there was always some jealousy and fighting with my brother. It seems that Mother always used to take his part and be on his side.

CO: It made you feel upset because you didn't feel she gave you an equal amount of attention.

CL: That's it. I remember that she used to let Bob get away with a lot of little things. Like when it came out that she had been giving him more spending money. I also used to notice that he got the best helpings of meat. She served him first.

CO: You felt resentful because he seemed to always get the best.

CL: Not always but most of the time. It didn't do any good for me to say anything, because if I did my mother would say, "You're just a jealous little girl."

CO: M'hm.

CL: And then if I said anything she would get mad. It seemed that she was always getting mad at me. Hardly a meal went by without her and I getting into a squabble. But it always ended up all right.

CO: Even now it upsets you to think about it.

CL: It still bothers me if it comes up. I live at home and he doesn't. When he comes to see us, Mother always makes a big fuss. You'd think he was something unusual. Of course he is something nice. I think a lot of him.

CO: You like your brother all right but it upsets you when your mother makes such a fuss over him. That is a very common situation. Most mothers are closer to their sons and fathers are closer to their daughters. That seems to be a natural thing in the world.

The following excerpt relates to "feelings of personal/social adequacy which tend to arise in every client and are handled within the eclectic method by the standard techniques of helping the client recognize and give up maladaptive defense mechanisms, to recognize and accept feelings of inadequacy, not to be incapacitated by anxiety reactive to fears of failure, and to learn new coping methods which promise some degree of success":[88]

CO: I see that you feel pretty bad today.

CL: Yes. Everything is awful. (cries)

CO: How is that?

CL: I have made a failure of everything. Now I can't go back.

CO: You feel terribly embarrassed and ashamed about things.

CL: I just feel terrible.

CO: Do you want to tell me about it?

CL: There's not much to tell. I just didn't make it up there. I made a terrible mess of things.

CO: H'hm.

CL: I was so happy and hopeful when the term started, but then the first two weeks were horrible. Things started to go bad. I went to class like a walking zombie. My body was there, but my mind was somewhere else. I just couldn't concentrate on anything. The instructor would ask a question, and my mind would just go blank. I must have seemed like a fool. They were all so kind, but I just knew they thought I was some kind of screwball. I started staying away from classes and going for long walks in the town. I just couldn't stand to face it. Then last weekend I just decided to give it all up and come home for good. I just couldn't take it anymore. If I try, I fear something terrible will happen.

CO: What is your worst fear about what might happen?

CL: Oh, I don't know. My head feels kind of funny, tight like, as if it might blow up. And I feel as in a daze, as if I was losing my mind. I was never like this before. What can be the matter with me? I don't understand myself. This is not me.

CO: This has shaken your confidence badly so you don't like yourself so much any more.

CL: Who would?

CO: How about before you got to college? Did you have much confidence in yourself?

CL: Oh, yes. I was always very popular and had a lot of dates and was considered one of the most popular girls. Most of the time it was very easy.

CO: How about the school work itself?

CL: I never had to work very hard. It all seemed to come very easy. I never studied too much —was always too busy having a good time. I would just listen in class. I have a good memory.

CO: But it was not so easy in college where you had to get the material yourself from outside readings?

CL: I couldn't seem to settle down and dig it out. I had several embarrassing experiences in class where I was supposed to know something and didn't. One instructor in particular seemed particularly tough. He went right after me and I felt like a fool.

CO: Your little ego has taken quite a beating, is that it?

CL: I guess so. I feel as if I have hardly any ego left.

CO: Well, you must understand this is an experience which many young people go through. In high school, you were a prima donna but now you find yourself in the big time where the competition is tougher. At first, it makes you anxious and discouraged, fearing that you haven't got the stuff. You develop an inferiority complex, and the easiest thing would be just to fold your tent and disappear.

CL: That's just what I did. I can't take it any more. I am developing a terrible inferiority complex.

CO: So what? You and everybody else. If you only knew it, most of your classmates in the freshman year are going through the same experiences. They all feel uncertain and shaky. Let me ask you something. Do you feel that it is best to do nothing rather than risk failure? Or, is it better to try and try again until you succeed?

CL: Right now, all I want is peace. I don't care whether I fail or not. I just want to be left alone. I'll just go somewhere and get a job on my own level.

CO: Well, you might do that but first, though, I want you to understand a few things about yourself. These terrible feelings you have are what we call anxiety, which is caused by fear of failing. You can't stand to mess up things, so, you get very upset emotionally, and then your mind does not work, and you feel like dropping out. You must believe that what you are experiencing is simply upset emotions. So what? Your emotions are upset, is that any reason to give up?

CL: But how can I go on like this? I can't trust myself. I might cry right in class.

CO: All right. So you feel bad a few minutes? So what? You can't give up on life whenever you feel bad. This is like the boys in the war who got combat fatigue. They felt just like you do. All to pieces and ready to give up. Those who gave up became neurotically disabled. Those who stayed in the situation and overcame their fears lived to become better men. Don't let the first big obstacle in your life stop you. I can assure you that nobody ever died from feeling upset emotionally. You may feel like it, but you won't.

CO: I am not going to ask anything superhuman of you, but simply that you regroup yourself and edge back into the situation. Go back up next Monday and resume as if nothing had happened. I will give you the name of a counselor you can look up, or you can always come back and talk to me if you get too upset.

CL: What will people think? What will the Dean say?

CO: She is a good friend of mine. I'll just call her up and tell her you got a little tense and worried about yourself and now you are going to settle down. Nobody will say anything to you. But suppose they did, what will you say?

CL: Oh, tell a lie and say that I had a date at home and act as if nothing happened.

CO: Why create more to feel defensive about? The best defense is no defense. Just tell the truth. Just say that you felt a little discouraged. That is true, isn't it?

CL: I hate to admit anything like that about myself.

CO: Why? Everybody has things they are sensitive about. The best defense is no defense. If you feel inadequate about something, don't hide it but instead come right out and admit it. Nobody is going to take advantage of you. They will like you just as much because they have things they are sensitive about too.

CL: I just don't think I can do it. The way I feel now, I just want to go to bed and stay there.

CO: I know it. But this is a key point in your life. You have got to lick this or it will lick you. My judgment tells me that you have the stuff to go back.

SUMMARY AND EVALUATION

The attempt to integrate all empirical psychological knowledge into an eclectic system is a tremendous undertaking. Some would consider it to be premature. The spotty, scattered, and inexact nature of psychological knowledge makes it a difficult, if not an impossible, task at the present time. Psychology is perhaps below the level of medicine in Osler's day as far as validated empirical knowledge is concerned. Thorne repeatedly admits the lack of experimental, empirical, or actuarial data regarding indications and contraindications for clinical methods or procedures. Thus it is not surprising that Thorne's system may leave one doubtful that he has convincingly demonstrated the relation of specific methods to specific problems. The system consists essentially of assumptions and opinions rather than of the integration of empirical facts or validated knowledge. In place of nonexisting empirically validated data, Thorne has used his wide clinical experience and extensive knowledge of various psychological systems and theories. Thorne is not, of course, responsible for the state of affairs in psychology. He must be admired for his courage in attempting the task of integration of all existing knowledge in psychology. The result is impressive. It is without doubt the most comprehensive system of behavior and its psychopathology and treatment in existence. Thorne would no doubt agree that it is only a first approximation to a final eclectic system.

Thorne's concept of clinical case handling goes beyond the usual definitions of counseling or psychotherapy. He is concerned with the entire range of disturbed, abnormal, or psychopathological behavior, from disturbed psychological states often classified as "no psychiatric disorder," emotional immaturity, or "simple adult maladjustment" to clear psychotic states. Also included are maladaptive attitudes and the existential problems of living. Thus Thorne visited at home those clients who had taken to bed for psychological reasons. Again, since many of his clients did not come on their own seeking help, he became involved in attempts to help or work with involuntary and resisting clients. This, of course, extends the range of methods of psychological case handling beyond the methods of office counseling or psychotherapy.

The range of disorders dealt with also lends support for a diagnostic system that attempts to classify clients or problems for more specific treatment. It may be questioned whether the detailed system of diagnostic classification developed by Thorne is particularly useful. Thorne himself, however, minimizes the value of a diagnostic classification system, and his methods of case handling are not organized on the basis of this classification. Rather, it is the etiological equation that is to be the basis of treatment, and the equation is unique to each client and is to be constantly revised on almost a moment-to-moment basis. Thus it is presumably etiological equations that are classified and related to treatment indications and contraindications. A broad or general classification of samples, or illustrations, of diagnostic equations is presented. It is not clear just how the equations are derived, except that it is a process of clinical judgment. This is, of course, the best that can be done at our present stage of knowledge. There is no specific instruction on assigning weights to the elements of the equations, although relative weights are assigned to different major kinds of etiological elements, as indicated above. Presumably, a client may have a complex problem or a number of different problems and thus require a number of etiological equations. Thorne appears to have selected a single—or what he considers the major—problem and worked on that, apparently moving on to other problems later. It is difficult to know just how the entire process of treatment might be handled, since the numerous case illustrations are brief and represent only a part of the total treatment. The impression of clear-cut discrete problems may be misleading, since the examples, as mentioned, are not actual cases but reconstructions. It should be noted, however, that this approach to diagnosis is not the standard method of psychiatric classification and is certainly an advance over that method. The concept of etiological equations, related not only to the unique individual, but also to changing psychological states, would appear to be a fruitful one.

The impression that one gets from reading the examples and illustrations is that Thorne's practice was highly didactic or tutorial. This approach is advocated for certain kinds of problems, but it seems to have permeated his treatment of all clients. The general approach to problems is a rational, logical problem-solving approach. To the criticism that rational elements are emphasized, Thorne replies that "it is only because we believe that reason is man's ultimate resource, and that only by maximizing rationality can man cope with an increasingly complex reality."[89] While this is no doubt true, the disturbed individual is in no condition to enter into a rational or logical problem-solving process. Thorne does, of course, recognize emotional factors in disturbance. While the goal is rationality, the cure for unreason may not be reason. Forcing the client to talk and think rationally may have some value, however, and Thorne apparently found it to be effective. Again, one must remember that the excerpts in his writings may not represent exactly how Thorne operated. They also, of course, do not and cannot present the personal, psychological context of the counseling.

This leads to a comment on the extent to which Thorne's eclectic system incorporates elements of the major schools of counseling or psychotherapy, or what is coming to be recognized as basic common elements of all systems or approaches. The three major elements, or "core conditions," as they are called by Carkhuff and his associates, are empathic understanding, respect and warmth, and genuineness. There is now considerable research that supports these conditions as necessary (and sufficient in many, if not all, cases) for successful counseling or psychotherapy. Thorne recognizes these conditions, but they do not receive the emphasis or attention that they appear to deserve. There is no doubt that they are present in Thorne's practice, and, in fact, it may be that his success is due more to the presence of these conditions and less to his specific techniques than he recognizes.

The emphasis on self-actualization, self-enhancement, and self-consistency as the primary dynamic motives underlying all of life and as the highest level of integration brings Thorne's position into agreement with perceptual-phenomenological-existential systems and with the Gestalt approach. This provides an organizing principle, which is necessary for a truly integrative system.

Thorne has attempted a herculean task, to use the phrase of one reviewer, who goes on to say:

He has brought together a large variety of methods and procedures and has offered what he believes is a comprehensive and organized system. However, it is this reviewer's opinion that the attempt, while valiant, is not quite successful. The reader does not really get a concise or integrated system for practice. The scheme offered tends to be abstract, and the diagnostic system and the methods of case handling are not tied together in a really functional way. While the author has attempted to meet previous criticism of his eclectic system by offering an attempt at an integrative theory or substructure, I do not believe the venture has succeeded. It still remains, essentially, a loosely tied together eclectic system, and one is not able to derive a formulation clearly and then to select the appropriate method of case handling.[90]

All this may be true. Yet I believe that Thorne's work is more than a valiant try. If our goal is to integrate all psychological knowledge into a comprehensive system—and, certainly, this is the goal of science and of psychology as a science—then Thorne was moving in the right direction. Certainly, proponents of and experts in various schools, such as psychoanalysis, client-centered therapy, Gestalt therapy, or existentialism, may feel that he did not adequately recognize or utilize their formulations. Certainly, the result of any integration in the near future will not be a completely satisfying or finished product. Perhaps no one person will ever achieve a complete integration, but Thorne set an example and put down a foundation on which others can continue to build.

REFERENCES

1. Thorne, F. C. *Psychological case handling.* Vol. 1: *Establishing the conditions necessary for counseling and psychotherapy.* Brandon, Vt.: Clinical Psychology Publishing, 1968. P. vi.
2. Ibid.
3. Thorne, F. C. *Personality: A clinical eclectic viewpoint.* Brandon, Vt.: Clinical Psychology Publishing, 1961.
4. Thorne, F. C. *Integrative psychology.* Brandon, Vt.: Clinical Psychology Publishing, 1967.
5. Thorne, F. C. *Principles of psychological examining.* Brandon, Vt.: Clinical Psychology Publishing, 1955.
6. Thorne, F. C. *Clinical judgment.* Brandon, Vt.: Clinical Psychology Publishing, 1960.
7. Thorne, F. C. *How to be psychologically healthy: Tutorial counseling.* Brandon, Vt.: Clinical Psychology Publishing, 1965.
8. Thorne, *Psychological case handling,* Vol. 1, p. v.
9. Thorne, *Personality,* pp. 42–43.
10. Ibid., p. 43.
11. Thorne, *Psychological case handling,* Vol. 1, p. v.
12. Ibid., pp. vi–vii.
13. Thorne, *Personality,* p. xiii.
14. Ibid., p. 40.
15. Ibid., p. 41.
16. Ibid., p. 54.
17. Ibid., p. 65.
18. Ibid., p. 68.
19. Ibid., p. 74.
20. Ibid., p. 92.

21. Ibid.
22. Ibid., p. 101.
23. Ibid., p. 102.
24. Ibid., p. 108.
25. Ibid., p. 110.
26. Ibid., p. 111.
27. Ibid., p. 141.
28. Ibid., p. 159.
29. Ibid., p. 163.
30. Ibid., p. 181.
31. Ibid., p. 184.
32. Thorne, *Integrative psychology,* p. vii.
33. Ibid., pp. 22–23.
34. Ibid., pp. 1, 2.
35. Ibid., p. 14.
36. Ibid., p. 20.
37. Ibid., p. 22.
38. Ibid., pp. 25–85, 158–185. Passim.
39. Ibid., p. 315.
40. Ibid., p. 350.
41. Thorne, *Psychological case handling,* Vol. 1, p. 23.
42. Ibid., pp. 11–12.
43. Ibid., pp. 12–13.
44. Ibid., pp. 30–31.
45. Ibid., p. 36.
46. Ibid., p. 59.
47. Ibid., p. 69.
48. Ibid., p. xi.
49. Ibid., p. 129.
50. Thorne, *Principles of psychological examining,* pp. 96–106.
51. Thorne, F. C. Diagnostic classification and nomenclature for psychological states. *Journal of Clinical Psychology,* 1941 (Monograph Supplement No. 17). (Also in Thorne, *Integrative psychology,* pp. 86–157.)
52. Thorne, *Psychological case handling,* Vol. 1, p. 46.
53. Ibid., p. 104.
54. Ibid., p. 111.
55. Ibid., pp. 130–131.
56. Ibid., p. 132.
57. Ibid., p. 139.
58. Ibid., p. 140.
59. Ibid., p. 81.
60. Ibid., p. 87.
61. Ibid., p. 99.
62. Ibid., p. 53.
63. Ibid., p. 152.
64. Ibid., p. 176.
65. Ibid., p. 221.
66. Ibid., p. 232.
67. Ibid., p. 238.
68. Thorne, *How to be psychologically healthy.*

69. Thorne, *Psychological case handling,* Vol. 1, p. 261.

70. Ibid., p. 292.

71. Ibid., p. 305.

72. Thorne, F. C. *Psychological case handling.* Vol. 2: *Specialized methods of counseling and psychotherapy.* Brandon, Vt.: Clinical Psychology Publishing, 1968. P. 347.

73. Ibid.

74. Ibid., p. 357.

75. Ibid., p. 373.

76. Ibid., pp. 452, 453.

77. Ibid., pp. 468–469.

78. Ibid., p. 477.

79. Ibid., p. 485.

80. Thorne, *How to be psychologically healthy.*

81. Thorne, *Psychological case handling,* Vol. 2, p. 615.

82. Ibid., p. 621.

83. Ibid., p. 640.

84. Ibid., p. 671.

85. Ibid., p. 346.

86. Thorne, *Psychological case handling,* Vol. 1, pp. 175–176.

87. Thorne, *Psychological case handling,* Vol. 2, pp. 402–403.

88. Ibid., pp. 585–587.

89. Thorne, F. C. Personal communication. Letter dated June 2, 1967.

90. Garfield, S. L. A valiant try. (Review of *Integrative psychology* and *Psychological case handling* by F. C. Thorne). *Contemporary Psychology,* 1969, *14,* 131–133.

seven

CONCLUSION: DIVERGENCES AND CONVERGENCE

This book has summarized a number of approaches to counseling or psychotherapy. Many more could have been included—such as the varied psychoanalytic and neoanalytic approaches—enough for another volume. As noted in the preface, summaries of most of these theories are available elsewhere.

The picture, at least on the surface, is one of diversity. The various approaches appear to differ from one another considerably, not only in their methods, but also in their goals, basic concepts, and philosophies. In the attempt to achieve uniqueness, theorists emphasize differences, often coining new terms for old concepts. Even if they do recognize the similarity of their approach to that of other theories, they may attribute the claimed effectiveness of their theory to its specific or unique methods.

In view of the apparent diversity, can all these theories be true or valid? Since all the approaches derive from the experience of capable and honest people dealing with the same general population—disturbed human beings—we should expect some agreement in the observation, even though they may be expressed in differing language or terminology.

Goldfried has provided a historical survey of the literature representing attempts to integrate varying approaches to psychotherapy over the past 50 years.[1] The major and most frequent contributions have been those of proponents of behavioristic approaches and of psychoanalysis. Beginning in 1932, this effort culminated in 1950, with the publication of Dollard and Miller's *Personality and Psychotherapy.* With the more recent development of behavior therapy, efforts in this direction have continued, as evidenced by the publication of numerous articles and several books that attempt to relate behavior therapy and psychodynamic approaches. Several articles have dealt with attempts at rapprochement between behavior therapy and humanistic approaches.

529

Behavior therapy has moved toward borrowing and incorporating elements of other approaches, notably the cognitive therapies. The additions to behavior therapy, however, have not been integrations so much as agglomerations; there has been little, if any, theoretical integration. This is also the case with recent eclectic approaches, which do not have a core of theory and principles on which a true eclecticism can be built.

Other writers, beginning with Rosenzweig,[2] have attempted to identify common factors among various psychotherapies. These factors usually are rather general and broad—therapist personality (undefined), for example—and are considered to be non-specific—therapists with a strong theoretical orientation have been loathe to give up their beliefs in the unique nature of their methods.

In 1967, Truax and Carkhuff[3] provided evidence that empathic understanding, respect or warmth, and genuineness were present, either explicitly or implicitly, in the major theories of psychotherapy. Since then, numerous writers have recognized these qualities as common elements and have assigned them considerable importance, some-times accepting them as necessary conditions for effective psychotherapy. However, they are still considered to be nonspecific conditions.

In this section, I will not attempt a detailed comparison of the various theories by listing similarities and differences. Rather, I will first consider some of the recent major divergent emphases in psychotherapy and then examine the common elements that have been identified. These common elements are divided into two groups. One group, consisting of the nonspecific or social-influence elements, is identified as the ubiquitous placebo. The other group includes those elements that are considered to be specific for therapeutic personality change. It is these common elements, or conditions, rather than the unique elements, that account for the effectiveness of differing approaches to psychotherapy. Some years ago, I suggested that "the differences among these approaches are accidental, at best irrelevant or at worst detrimental. An approach may be effective in spite of, rather than because of, its unique variables."[4]

The common specific relationship variables have been demonstrated to be related to positive outcomes in psychotherapy. They therefore form the core of any systematic eclectic psychotherapy.

REFERENCES

1. Goldfried, M. A. On the history of therapeutic integration. *Behavior Therapy,* 1982, *13,* 572–593. (I am indebted to Suzanne Brannon, then a doctoral student at the University of North Carolina at Greensboro, for providing me with a copy of this article.)
2. Rosenzweig, S. Some implicit common factors in diverse methods of psychotherapy. *American Journal of Orthopsychiatry,* 1936, *6,* 412–415.
3. Truax, C. B., & Carkhuff, R. R. *Toward effective counseling and psychotherapy.* Chicago: Aldine, 1967.
4. Patterson, C. H. *Relationship counseling and psychotherapy.* New York: Harper & Row, 1974. P. x.

chapter 18

Divergences

Twenty-five years ago, Rogers wrote, "The field of psychotherapy is in a mess."[1] He earlier had felt that therapists were talking about the same experiences but using different words and labels to describe them. By the time he wrote these words, he had come to believe that therapists differed at the basic level of personal experiences.

At about the same time, Ungersma wrote:

> The present situation in psychotherapy is not unlike that of the man who mounted his horse and rode off in all directions. The theoretical orientation of therapists is based upon widely divergent hypotheses, theories and ideologies. . . . Individual practitioners of any art are expected to vary, but some well-organized schools of therapy also seem to be working at cross-purposes with other equally well-organized schools. Nevertheless, all schools, given favorable conditions, achieve favorable results: the patient or client gets relief and is often enough cured of his difficulties.[2]

This apparently equal success of apparently widely differing approaches constitutes a problem that requires some explanation.

Almost 10 years later, Kanfer and Phillips noted that not only do clinicians disagree in the theories they hold, but also "their practices and beliefs reflect even deeper inconsistencies and contradictions." Limiting themselves to the behavior therapies, Kanfer and Phillips recommended that "instead of accepting the goal of more refinement of the numerous specific procedures, it may be useful to strive for their eventual integration into a more comprehensive behavior system. . . . The first step toward such a framework lies in efforts to find the common elements and the differences among the variety of techniques used."[3]

The recommendation went unheeded, both by behavior therapists and by therapists of other persuasions. An obstacle to the recognition and acceptance of common elements is the striving of theorists to be unique, even if only by the coining of different terminology. Differences are focused on and emphasized. The attempts to discover and define common elements[4] have not been favorably received, for reasons that will be noted in Chapter 19. As a result, we have seen the proliferation of new techniques, if not new theories: arica therapy, bio-energetics, primal therapy, autogenic therapy, reality therapy, psychosynthesis, direct-decision therapy, EST (not electroshock therapy, but Erhard Seminars Training), and even placebo therapy.[5] One writer discussed training in psychotherapy under the heading "the Tower of Babel."[6] The lead-in for an article by Parloff refers to 130 subschools of psychotherapy, although the article does not enumerate them.[7] The cover of the magazine has the headline "The Psychotherapy Jungle."

As a person immerses himself or herself in the study of the dozens of theories and approaches to counseling or psychotherapy, he or she indeed develops the feeling of being in a jungle. Differences, inconsistencies, and contradictions appear at all levels, from philosophy to techniques. Concepts relating to the nature of human beings and of emotional disturbance or abnormal behavior vary considerably, from the concept of the individual as determined by the environment to that of the person as capable of making choices and being free to do so. The goals and methods of therapy related to these concepts are different: the control and change of specific behaviors by manipulating consequences in terms of reward and punishment, in the first case, and the attempt to provide the conditions for the growth and development of the person's potential in the process of self-actualization, in the second case.

These divergent concepts of the human being and of behavior change provide the basis for distinguishing two major, distinct, if not incompatible, approaches that have taken shape over the past three decades. One is epitomized by behavior therapy, and the other, in its most extreme form, is epitomized by existential approaches to psychotherapy. The first is a technological approach; the second is a humanistic approach.

THE ERA OF BEHAVIOR THERAPY

Just as the 1950s was the era of client-centered therapy, the 1960s was the era of behavior therapy. Its appeal is that of technology, although it is couched in the terminology of science; that is, it claims to be based on learning theory (although there is no single accepted learning theory), on laboratory experiments (although its methods are extrapolations from animal experiments), and on the specificity of treatment methods for particular problems (although specificity has not been demonstrated). It has a logical appeal: first, the problem must be identified; second, a specific goal or solution to the problem must be formulated; and third, a specific technique—desensitization, reinforcement, aversive methods, modeling, assertiveness training, homework assignments, and so on—must be selected and applied. Therapy is simply a matter of technological operation; the therapist is a technician who arranges for the application of contingencies or other manipulations of the environment, in or out of the interview.

It is, in London's classification, an action therapy.[8] Action therapies are not concerned with talk but with actions or behaviors—or symptoms. The action therapist operates on behavior, and, as London expresses it, "he cares not a whit what the patient does or does not say about himself or even know about himself except insofar as such behaviors have concrete and demonstrable value for producing change."[9]

The therapist is an expert. Two characteristics of the action therapist, according to London, are: "1. The therapist assumes a much greater influence over the detailed conduct of the treatment sessions, and possibly over the outside life of the patient, than Insight therapists would. 2. The therapist is much more responsible for the outcome of the treatment, that is, for whatever changes take place in the patient, than are the Insight therapists."[10]

The behavioristic approach became very widespread in the late 1960s and the early 1970s. It adherents are strongly committed to it and highly persuasive in their arguments. They are convinced that they have *the* answer to understanding and controlling behavior and that behaviorism is *the* science of behavior. They have made wide claims for the effectiveness of their techniques and, indeed, have been able to offer considerable apparent support for their claims in terms of single cases and studies in highly controlled situations. The literature has burgeoned, with the publication of dozens of books on behavior therapy and behavior modification in various settings, including schools, mental hospitals, and correctional institutions. Several annual collections of articles are being published. Between 1963 and 1970, four journals were established for behavior therapists, who even founded their own association, the American Association for the Advancement of Behavior Therapy. In 1971, the first review chapter devoted to behavior therapy as distinct from psychotherapy appeared in the *Annual Review of Psychology.*[11]

THE DEMISE OF BEHAVIOR THERAPY

Two of the most significant developments in psychology in the 1970s were the death of behavioristic psychology in its orthodox, monolithic form and the rebirth of cognitive psychology. This is not the place for a full-scale critique of behaviorism; I have provided an extensive critique elsewhere.[12] Only a general review of the decline of behaviorism will be provided.

Behavior therapy has been subjected to numerous criticisms. One of the first was that of Grossberg in 1964, followed by that of Breger and McGaugh in the same year.[13] Criticisms continued into the 1970s.[14] These early critiques weathered, however, and behavior therapy continued to grow in popularity.

By the middle of the 1970s, the situation had begun to change. Yates, noting the growth of behavior therapy, wrote that "it is possible to discern a rising tide of criticism and dissent in relation to the ever-widening applications of behavior therapy."[15] The criticism included widespread public reaction against the use—and sometimes misuse—of behavior therapy and behavior modification techniques in institutions, including mental hospitals and prisons, in disregard of human rights.[16] Beyond this, there were questions about the effectiveness of behavior therapy and about the source of the effectiveness that was demonstrated. Those who read the recent literature on behavior therapy cannot help but realize that the early promise has not been fulfilled. Early reports were almost invariably of successful cases. More recent reports include the failures. Practitioners and writers have become more open and candid about limitations and failures. This follows the pattern of almost every new method of treatment. It suggests that part, if not much, of the source of the early successes lay in the attitudes of the practitioner, whose enthusiasm, optimism, and belief were transmitted to patients, who responded at least temporarily by feeling better and reporting improvement —in other words, the pervasive placebo effect.

If one were to date the onset of the terminal illness of behaviorism, Bandura's 1974 presidential address to the American Psychological Association might well be chosen. Bandura denied that the empirical facts of human behavior support the theory that behavior is completely and automatically controlled by conditioning—classical or operant or both—to the exclusion of inner cognitive and affective factors. "It is well documented," he writes, "that behavior is influenced by its consequences much of the time. . . . But the external consequences, influential as they often are, are not the sole determinants of human behavior, nor do they operate automatically."[17] The consequences of behavior provide information or feedback, which through thought serves to guide action. Consequences also motivate behavior because they enable the individual to represent possible outcomes symbolically. Individuals act or fail to act in order to gain anticipated benefits or to avert possible aversive consequences. "The widely accepted dictum that man is ruled by response consequences thus fares better for anticipated than for actual consequences."[18] When a fixed-ratio schedule is used, for example, with every fiftieth response reinforced, 96 percent of the responses are not reinforced; behavior is maintained in spite of the absence of reinforcement.

> As people are exposed to variations in frequency and predictability of reinforcement, they behave on the basis of the outcomes they expect to prevail on future occasions. When belief differs from actuality, which is not uncommon, behavior is weakly controlled by its consequences until repeated experience instills realistic expectations. Had humans been ruled solely by instant consequences, they would have long become museum pieces among the extinct species.[19]

Social factors also influence the effects of consequences in behavior. Behavior can be influenced by observed consequences (vicarious reinforcement) as well as by direct experience. Human beings also develop personal standards of conduct that lead to actions having self-reinforcing properties. These may be in conflict with external outcomes: if the consequences for the self-concept are negative, external influences are relatively ineffective.

Behavior in a social context is influenced by personal as well as social factors. "Personal control is clearly more complex and flexible than the theorizing implies."[20] Self-management or self-regulation of behavior involves self-control, and even though external variables are involved, self-influence (through internal or inner variables) is also involved. "The recognition of self-directing capacities represents a substantial departure from exclusive reliance upon environmental control."[21]

Bandura summarized:

> It is true that behavior is regulated by its contingencies, but the contingencies are partly a person's own making. By their actions, people play an active role in producing the reinforcing contingencies that impinge upon them. Thus, behavior partly creates

the environment, and the environment influences behavior in a reciprocal fashion. To the off-repeated dictum, change contingencies and you change behavior, should be added the reciprocal side, change behavior and you change the contingencies.[22]

He further noted that "a valid criticism of extreme behaviorism is that, in a vigorous effort to avoid spurious inner causes, it has neglected determinants of behavior arising from cognitive functioning. Proponents of this approach marshalled numerous reasons why cognitive events are inadmissable in causal analysis." He concluded: "A theory that denies that thoughts can regulate actions does not lend itself readily to the explanation of complex human behavior. Although cognitive activities are disavowed in the operant conditioning framework, their role in causal sequences simply cannot be eliminated."[23]

The title of a paper by Brewer, although extreme, is relevant: "There Is No Convincing Evidence for Operant or Classical Conditioning in Adult Humans."[24] A more moderate statement would be that very little of the behavior of adult humans is the result of operant or classical conditioning. Such behavior occurs only in highly controlled, restricted situations, such as experiments in the laboratory or in institutional settings.

Criticism of behaviorism also came from another source, neuropsychology. Sperry, noting that conceptual developments during the preceding decade provide a new interpretation of the conscious mind, wrote:

> In essence, our current modified concept of the mind–brain relation endorses the phenomena of conscious experience with an active causal role in brain processing, in direct contradiction to the central founding precepts of Watsonian behaviorism. . . . Conscious phenomena in our revised model are "different from, more than, and not reducible to" neural events. . . . We center in on the interpretation of consciousness as an emergent property of brain activity. . . . The emergent properties in the present view are not interpreted to be mere passive parallel correlates, aspects, or by-products of cortical events, but rather to be active, causal determinants essential to the control of normal cerebral processing. A conceptual explanatory model is provided, in principle, for the way mind can rule matter in the brain and exert causal influence in the guidance and control of behavior, on terms acceptable to neuroscience and without violating monistic principles of scientific explanation.[25]

Other criticism of behavioristic psychology could be cited. It no longer appears to be possible to maintain an orthodox behavioristic approach to human behavior, whether or not it is possible to do so in the case of animal behavior. While the behavioristic principles of conditioning may apply to certain, very limited aspects of human behavior or to human behavior in situations where the individual is prevented from behaving in any other way, they are inadequate to explain the great bulk of human behavior. Skinner and a few experimental psychologists whose work is limited to laboratory studies are essentially alone in adhering to an orthodox behaviorism. Behaviorism is not false; it is simply limited and inadequate as a theory of human behavior.

What does the death of behavioristic psychology mean for behavior therapy? This is a complex question because it is impossible to define behavior therapy. Lazarus and Wilson admit that behavior therapy has "no universally accepted definition, no consensus as to goals, concepts or underlying philosophy, no agreement as to its purview, no monolithic point of view, no overriding strategy or core technique, no single founding father, no general agreement about matters of training, and there is no single profession to which primary allegiance is declared."[26] Lazarus dissociates behavior therapy from behaviorism.[27] Yet many behavior therapists, including Eysenck, Rachman, and Wolpe, insist that behavior therapy is an application of behavioristic psychology.

Lazarus, following Franks and Yates, equates behavior therapy with an empirical scientific approach involving "due regard for scientific objectivity, extreme caution in the face of conjecture and speculation, a rigorous process of deduction from testable theories, and a fitting indifference toward persuasion and hearsay."[28] These characteristics, however, would not distinguish behavior therapy from some other approaches, as Lazarus himself notes, and would not warrant the use of the name behavior therapy. Lazarus appears to question the use of the name, not because of this lack of distinction, however, but because it and the name behavior modification (whose death Krasner has mourned in a satirical vein[29]) have become unpopular and because, "limited to principles and methods derived from research in experimental and social psychology, it can be seen as a small but significant part of a multimodal approach."[30]

Lazarus recognizes the limitations—even the erroneousness—of the orthodox behaviorist view of human behavior. It "cannot account for vicarious learning, semantic generalization, and other 'exclusively human functions' such as imagined response patterns and symbolic processes."[31]

In actuality, behavior therapy has never restricted itself to techniques derived from behavioristic psychology. Dollard and Miller included many "higher mental processes" and cognitive factors in their theory. Other behavior theories and therapists have used imaginal and symbolic, or cognitive, processes. Clients were never treated as rats or pigeons. Nevertheless, these cognitive elements were not acknowledged, and, more important, their contribution to the effectiveness of so-called behavior therapy was not recognized. Systematic desensitization is a cognitive method, not derived from conditioning research, that involves imagination and language.[32]

Recently, behavior therapists have begun to acknowledge the presence of cognitive elements and methods and to incorporate additional cognitive methods in their practice. O'Leary and Wilson, for example, note that "cognitive methods are increasingly being incorporated into the armamentarium of treatment techniques of the practicing behavior therapist."[33] Goldfried and Davison write that "perhaps as a reaction to the earlier insight therapists, the first developments in behavior therapy tended to downgrade the importance of human cognitive capacities," while more recent developments "emphasize the nature of cognitive processes. The result of these efforts has been, in essence, to make the consideration of cognitive processes a legitimate domain for behavior therapists."[34] We may wonder about the basis for making cognitive psychology a legitimate domain for behavior therapy. Apparently, the justification is a pragmatic one; behavior therapists have shown a willingness to try anything that works or that might work. Both O'Leary and Wilson, and Goldfried and Davison include cognitive techniques in their armamentaria.

A number of behavior therapists, among them Mahoney and Meichenbaum, have moved toward a highly cognitive approach, which they call cognitive-behavior therapy or cognitive-behavior modification.[35] Meichenbaum notes that "behavior therapy techniques, as originally conceptualized and implemented, have over-emphasized the importance of environmental events (antecedents and consequences), and, therefore, underemphasized and often overlooked how a client perceives and evaluates those events."[36]

As Lazarus puts it, "only a few diehards would not agree that the stimulus–response 'learning theory' basis of behavior therapy is passé and that a distinctively cognitive orientation now prevails."[37] Even Wolpe, who might be called a diehard behavior therapist, has acknowledged the presence and use of cognitive elements in his therapy.[38]

We must conclude that there is no such thing as behavior therapy if, as is generally believed, behavior therapy is the application of techniques derived from behavioristic psychology. Further, the presence of cognitive factors, as well as other factors (for example, relationship factors, which will be considered later), in so-called behavior therapy raises questions regarding the source of any effects that occur in behavior therapy.

COGNITIVE PSYCHOLOGY AND THERAPY

During the height of the influence of behavioristic psychology in the 1960s and early 1970s, cognitive psychology was overshadowed. However, extensive work was being done by Jean Piaget and Jerome Bruner, for example. The rebirth of cognitive psychology is one of the significant developments of the 1970s. The emphasis on cognition extends throughout various areas or fields of psychology and various aspects of human behavior and experience, although reference is frequently made to cognitive psychology as a distinct field.

The field of motivation was one of the areas that underwent the process of becoming cognitively oriented.[39] Zimbardo in 1969 clearly stated the basic principle of cognitive psychology: "Through utilizing cognitive controls (of virtually limitless potential) man gains freedom from the behavioral prescriptions—imposed by his history, physiology, and ecology. Indeed, thinking and believing can make it so!"[40] Five years later, Bolles, noting the trend in psychology from the mechanistic (behavioristic) to the cognitive, wrote, "There seems to be a widespread movement toward the position that cognitive processes intervening between the person's adaptive transactions with the environment and the emotional reaction (including the somatic consequences) are important determinants, though the empirical case for this position is still somewhat uncertain."[41] Dember, referring to the "cognitive revolution" in psychology, noted the "dissatisfaction among motivational theorists with the prevailing stimulus–response (S–R) behavioristic model that had characterized American psychology for several decades. . . . The motivational significance of information is by now firmly based in sound, empirical evidence."[42] He recognized, however, that cognitively oriented motivational models could not yet handle some motivational phenomena.

Lazarus, who considers himself to be a cognitively oriented psychologist, views biofeedback as involving cognitive factors: "emotional processes and their regulation are products of mediating cognitive appraisals about the significance of an event for a person's well-being."[43] Cognition enters into behaviorism in the concept of reinforcement, which is viewed not as an automatic process but as informational feedback.

Subjects interpret or perceive reinforcement differently: "Behavior therapy may be assumed to evoke complex cognitive and evaluative processes which are not comfortably handled by the Skinnerian model. To a greater degree than rats or chimpanzees, humans appear to impose meaning upon social situations."[44]

This is the position of Bandura, as suggested above. Clearly, although he is labeled a behaviorist, Bandura is a cognitive psychologist. Bandura states that empirical evidence, rather than supporting the behaviorist contention that cognitions are unnecessary in causal analysis, has shown the opposite.

> A large body of research now exists in which cognitions are activated instrumentally, their presence is assessed indirectly, and their functional relationship to behavior is carefully examined. Results of such studies reveal that people learn and retain behavior much better using cognitive aids that they generate than by reinforced repetitive performance. With growing evidence that cognition has causal influence on behavior, the arguments against the influence of internal determinants began to lose their force.[45]

Learning occurs by observing or modeling others (which is not a behavioristic technique, although behavior therapists claim it is), by reading about something, or by listening in situations where, by any strict definition of terms, there is no stimulus, no overt response, and no contingency. Modeling is effective without the presence of vicarious or direct reinforcement. It is facilitated by the imaginal or symbolic (through language) coding of the information derived from the behavior of the model.

While the overt movement of the more orthodox behavior therapists toward cognitive psychology is relatively new, cognitive therapy itself is not new. Insight-oriented therapists as well as what, for a better name, might be called commonsensical advising approaches to counseling or psychotherapy have been cognitively oriented. There are strong cognitive elements in the approaches of Adler, Dollard and Miller, Kelly, Rotter, and Thorne, among others, and, of course, Ellis's rational-emotive therapy is one of the oldest and strongest cognitive approaches. More recently, other cognitive therapies have been developing, including Raimy's approach, which is based on the misconception hypothesis,[46] and Beck's approach, which is directed at straightening out disorders or distortions in conceptual thinking.[47] Meichenbaum labels his approach cognitive-behavior therapy, but, as noted in the discussion of his theory earlier in this book, it is almost purely cognitive. While these approaches are interesting, there is, in my opinion, no well-developed, comprehensive cognitive therapy. Moreover, neither such a purely cognitive therapy nor the cognitive-learning approach suggested by Mahoney[48] would, in my opinion, offer the ultimate method of psychotherapy, since it would very likely emphasize cognition at the expense of affect (although it is possible that affective factors in learning could be included) and would appear to neglect or minimize the relationship between the therapist and the client (although, again, the importance of the relationship in learning might be recognized and integrated into the theory). To term such an approach cognitive therapy would, then, be a misnomer.

This brings us to a common aspect of behavior therapy and cognitive therapy. It was noted earlier that behavior therapy places the therapist in the role of an expert. The same is true of cognitive therapy. The therapist evaluates or assesses the client's problem in terms of cognitive deficits or disordered thinking and then proceeds to straighten out the client's thinking through direct or indirect instruction or training in personal or social skills (as is done in Meichenbaum's theory). Mahoney suggests that the cognitive-learning therapist must be knowledgeable in sociology, logic, neurology, nutrition, philosophy, cybernetics, pharmacology, medicine, and communication.[49] The relationship is vertical: the therapist is in a superior position, while the client is perceived as inadequate, incompetent, incapable, dependent, and in need of direction, guidance, instruction, and so forth. The client often is only too willing to assume this role and to strengthen the therapist's superior role. This concept of the therapist as an active interventionist goes beyond behavior therapy and cognitive therapy. It is characteristic of most of the newer approaches or techniques that have been flooding the literature. It appears that there is a trend (backward) toward the more directive, controlling, authoritarian, or "therapist-knows-best" approaches of the past.

THE UNFULFILLED PROMISE OF EXISTENTIAL THERAPY

Along with the development of behavior and cognitive therapies, although much less visible, has been the development of the existential approach. Whereas the behavior and cognitive therapies emphasize the assessment of specific problems or behaviors and the planned, structured application of specific methods by the therapist as an expert, the existential therapies take a different road: there is no diagnosis or assessment; there are few, if any, specific methods, or the therapist is free to use any technique that he or she feels is appropriate at a particular instant in therapy. Burton suggests that existential psychotherapy may be considered a technique of no technique.[50] There is little, if any, planning for therapy; which is a spontaneous encounter. Emphasis is on the experiencing of the client and the therapist in the encounter. The therapist is not an expert or a technician applying techniques; he or she is an equal with the client, engaging in a real, spontaneous encounter, and is with the client in his or her experience. It is, of course, true that the therapist and the client cannot be equals in every characteristic—the client usually places the therapist in a higher position in many respects. However, it is the attitude and the behavior of the therapist that are important. The existential and/or humanistic therapist respects the client as an equal as a human being. Burton noted "an increasing acceptance of the philosophy which says that a true encounter can only take place when patient and psychotherapist meet each other on an I–Thou basis."[51] A student of mine defined therapy as "a shared journey with no predetermined route."[52] It is a journey of discovery, for both the therapist and the client, with neither knowing at the outset just what will be discovered or where the journey will end.

The promise of existential psychotherapy has not been fulfilled. It has not prospered in terms of acceptance or widespread use, perhaps, in part, because of the competition of behavior therapy, with its "scientific" appeal. It is also handicapped by the diversity of practice encouraged by the emphasis on spontaneity and the absence of common methods. Thus it is difficult to teach or to learn existential psychotherapy. It is somewhat vague, if not mysterious. It opens the way for esoteric practices that are justified as being spontaneous and genuine reactions of the therapist, which may be more therapeutic for the therapist than for the client.

Nevertheless, the ideal of the existential relationship, although it may appear to be extreme, provides an alternative to cognitive therapy or to cognitive-behavior therapy. Philosophically and theoretically, these two approaches present a contrast that must be faced.

The existential-humanistic approach shares with a number of other approaches the minimization of active intervention or manipulation in the therapist–client relationship. Among these other approaches is client-centered therapy, with its emphasis on the potential of the client for growth, for working through and resolving his or her own problems, and for taking responsibility for himself or herself and his or her life. Almost unanimously, the major "traditional" therapists, from Freud through Jung and Rank to Rogers, have advocated minimal intervention. Surprisingly, considering the practices of some of their followers, Perls and Berne take this stance. But in view of the fact that most of these therapists were trained in medicine, it may not be surprising. Berne explicitly states the basic medical principles that (1) above all, the therapist must do no harm, and (2) the therapist must depend on the organism's drive toward health for cure. Every intervention involves a risk; the more powerful the intervention, the greater the risk. The responsible practice of medicine requires the minimization of intervention, or, as it is commonly expressed, the principle of conservative management. Psychological intervention also involves risks, and many therapists operate on the basis of these same principles.

THE SOCIAL-INFLUENCE MODEL: A FALSE HOPE

In 1961, Frank suggested that psychotherapy is a process of persuasion.[53] In 1966, Goldstein urged that research in psychotherapy be directed toward study of variables derived from research in social psychology, particularly the psychology of interpersonal attraction, and he, Heller, and Sechrest provided an analysis of relevant research in social psychology.[54]

Two years later, Strong picked up on this theme and proposed applying the concept of cognitive dissonance to the interpersonal-influence process in counseling or psychotherapy.[55] He suggested that the greater the extent to which counselors are perceived as expert, attractive, and trustworthy, the greater is their credibility and thus their power to influence clients.

There are three main therapist variables in the concept of psychotherapy as a social-influence process. The first is actually a loose cluster of variables that is designated as perceived expertness, or credibility, and that includes respect, perceived competence, and trustworthiness (often considered a separate variable). Contributing to the perception by the client of expertness are indications of status (degrees, diplomas, office decor and furnishings), prestige (reputation), power, and authority.

The second variable is perceived attractiveness, which includes therapist and client similarities in opinions, attitudes, beliefs, values, and background; therapist liking for the client; therapist likeability, friendliness, and warmth; and therapist self-disclosure.

The third variable is therapist expectations. Therapist self-confidence and/or confidence in the methods used leads to expectation of change or improvement in the client. This expectation is communicated to the client through various subtle, unintentional ways as well as through direct expressions of optimism, suggestion, and reassurance.

Strong's article stimulated a series of research studies, which has been reviewed by Beutler,[56] Strong,[57] and Corrigan, Dell, Lewis, and Schmidt.[58] Almost all the studies (68 of the 70 reviewed by Corrigan, Dell, Lewis, and Schmidt) are analogue studies, involving the presentation of audiotapes or videotapes or a single contrived interview with nonclients, usually college students, as subjects. Most of the research was concerned with correlates of or cues for therapist expertness and attractiveness. The measures or criteria used in outcome studies included subject reports, or self-ratings, of changes in attitudes or opinions, of improvement or satisfaction, or of likelihood of self-referral for counseling. The results of these studies have been varied, inconsistent among and within studies, and even directly contradictory. Beuter concludes that "it is not clear from these findings that credibility consistently produces attendant attitude change or persuasion in psychotherapy. . . . These persuader variables serve only as a basis for facilitating a therapeutic relationship and are not necessarily a direct contributor to therapeutic change."[59] In other words, they are nonspecific variables.

Strong, in spite of the mixed results and the fact that the studies reviewed were analogue studies and did not include outcome studies, states that "as a whole, these studies show that therapist credibility is an important variable in psychotherapy." This would seem to be an unjustifiable assumption. In regard to perceived therapist attractiveness, he concludes that "studies of the effect of client attraction to the therapist on the ability of the therapist to influence the client have obtained mixed and generally pessimistic results."[60]

Corrigan, Dell, Lewis, and Schmidt conclude that "the effects of expertness and attractiveness on counselors' ability to influence clients are, at best, unclear. . . . Those studies that successfully manipulated attractiveness failed to find differential effects on client change." Yet these authors recommend further research on these social-influence variables in counseling as "interesting and reasonable," although they admit that "the question of the utility of considering counseling as a social influence process remains."[61]

These conclusions, as negative as they are, appear to be too optimistic. It is difficult to understand the continued enthusiasm for social-influence theory and research. The reviewers, however, are among the major researchers in the field, and their commitment to and identification with the area probably influence their conclusions. A study published after these reviews might appear to offer support for the conclusions. This study, by LaCrosse,[62] was not an analogue study, but involved 36 clients on a drug-counseling program, whose counseling ranged from 4 to 31 sessions. Clients rated their counselors at the beginning and the end of counseling on an instrument devised to measure clients' perceptions of expertness, attractiveness, and trustworthiness. They also rated themselves for change following counseling. There was a significant relationship between the clients' ratings of their counselors and their self-ratings of outcomes. However, there is not only questionable validity and probable bias in the self-ratings of outcomes, but also the distinct possibility of a spurious element in the correlations, since both variables were ratings by the clients. In addition, only two of the clients sought counseling voluntarily, so there is a question about the relevance of the results to the usual voluntary counseling or therapy relationship.

These social-influence variables appear to constitute the "good guy" factor in psychotherapy.[63] LaCrosse and Barak[64] suggest that the common element in expertness, attractiveness, and trustworthiness is what is labeled "influence" by Strong, "persuasiveness" by Frank and by LaCrosse, and "power" by Strong and Matross and by Dell. They note that "these terms are also related to what might be described as 'charisma' or 'impressiveness.'" These words suggest an image of the counselor or therapist as a person exuding or projecting self-confidence, self-assurance, competence, power, and persuasiveness—a charismatic snake-oil huckster.

Although the social-influence model (like the cognitive theories and Beutler's eclectic therapy) is based on the concept of psychotherapy as a process of persuasion and draws its ideas and support from social psychology, the effectiveness of persuasion and of related cognitive factors in attitude change is far from having been demonstrated.[65] Not only is the social-influence model not supported by the research of its advocates, but its nonspecific variables actually constitute the placebo in psychotherapy, as will be shown in Chapter 19.

THE MOVE TOWARD ECLECTICISM

It remains to note a final sign of diversity in psychotherapy—the apparent trend toward eclecticism. As mentioned earlier, eclectics are a diverse group; indeed, no two are alike. Each author of a book purporting to present eclectic psychotherapy outlines a different approach. It is a classic example of the blind men defining an elephant, with one describing its trunk; another, its tail; yet another, its leg; and so on. The various approaches have little in common. We have yet to see a truly eclectic system of psychotherapy, which would integrate the valid elements of the major theories and practices.

CONCLUSION

We have reviewed trends in psychotherapy over the past 20 years. The resulting picture is one of diversity. Two major developments have been the decline of behavior therapy and the rise of cognitive therapy, with some attempts to marry the two, resulting in a somewhat unstable or incompatible union. There are some fundamental similarities in the philosophical and theoretical foundations of these two approaches, however. Both, in their current formulations, view the client as a person to be operated on by a therapist who possesses certain methods of changing behaviors, either covert or overt. The therapist is an expert technician, while the client is a relatively passive recipient of the therapist's knowledge and expertise.

In contrast to these relatively authoritarian approaches is the existential-humanistic approach, which differs from the cognitive-behavior therapies in some fundamental respects. It goes beyond a logical, rational, planned application of specific techniques to a view of psychotherapy as a spontaneous encounter of two equals. The relationship between therapist and client approximates a horizontal plane, rather than the vertical plane of the cognitive-behavior approaches. These positions appear to be inconsistent with, if not antagonistic to, each other. The problem of the future is to attempt to reconcile or integrate these divergent approaches, to define their respective areas of operation, and, through research, to demonstrate their relative effectiveness.

A recent interest has developed in what is known as the social-influence model of psychotherapy, which regards the therapy process as one of persuasion. The research by proponents fails to support the model; it appears that the approach is essentially placebo therapy.

Finally, the renewed interest in eclecticism has failed to produce agreement on a unified, theory-based eclectic system of practice.

REFERENCES

1. Rogers, C. R. Divergent trends. In R. May (Ed.), *Existential psychology.* New York: Random House, 1961.
2. Ungersma, A. J. *The search for meaning.* Philadelphia: Westminster, 1961. P. 55.
3. Kanfer, F. H., & Phillips, J. A. A survey of current behavior therapies and a proposal for clarification. In C. M. Franks (Ed.), *Behavior therapy: Appraisal and status.* New York: McGraw-Hill, 1969. Pp. 445–475.
4. Patterson, C. H. *Counseling and psychotherapy: Theory and practice.* New York: Harper & Row, 1959. Chap. 12.
5. For brief descriptions of these (except EST) and other approaches, see Harper, R. A. *The new psychotherapies.* Englewood Cliffs, N.J.: Prentice-Hall, 1975. A journalist's report on his EST experience appeared in *Time,* June 7, 1976, pp. 53–54.
6. Singer, J. *Imagery and daydream methods in psychotherapy and behavior modification.* New York: Academic Press, 1974.
7. Parloff, M. Shopping for the right therapy. *Saturday Review,* February 21, 1976.
8. London, P. *The modes and morals of psychotherapy.* New York: Holt, Rinehart and Winston, 1964.
9. Ibid., p. 78.
10. Ibid.
11. Krasner, L. Behavior therapy. *Annual Review of Psychology,* 1971, *24,* 483–532.
12. Patterson, C. H. *Foundations for a theory of instruction.* New York: Harper & Row, 1977. Pp. 240–266.
13. Grossberg, J. M. Behavior therapy: A review. *Psychological Bulletin,* 1964, *62,* 73–88; Breger, L., & McGaugh, J. L. Critique and reformulation of "learning theory" approaches to psychotherapy and neuroses. *Psychological Bulletin,* 1964, *62,* 338–358.
14. Weitzman, B. Behavior therapy and psychotherapy. *Psychological Review,* 1967, *74,* 300–317; Wiest, W. M. Some recent criticisms of behaviorism and learning theory with special reference to Breger and McGaugh and Chomsky. *Psychological Bulletin,* 1967, *67,* 214–225; Breger, L., & McGaugh, J. L. Learning theory and behavior therapy: A reply to Rachman and Eysenck. *Psychological Bulletin,* 1968, *65,* 170–173; Patterson, C. H. Relationship therapy and/or behavior therapy? *Psychotherapy: Theory, Research and Practice,* 1968, *5,* 226–233; Patterson, C. H. Some notes on behavior theory, behavior therapy and behavioral counseling. *Counseling Psychologist,* 1969, *1,* 44–56; Murray, E. J., & Jacobson, L. I. The nature of learning in traditional and behavioral psychotherapy. In A. E. Bergin & S. L. Garfield (Eds.), *Handbook of psychotherapy and behavior change: An empirical analysis.* New York: Wiley, 1971. Pp. 709–747.
15. Yates, A. J. *Theory and practice in behavior therapy.* New York: Wiley, 1975. P. 2.
16. Trotter, S., & Warren, J. Behavior modification under fire. *APA Monitor,* 1974, *5,* 1; Stoltz, S. B., Wienckowski, L. A., & Brown, B. Behavior modification: A perspective on critical issues. *American Psychologist,* 1975, *30,* 1027–1048; Patterson, C. H. Humanistic concerns and behavior modification: Toward a basis for ethical practice. In L. E. Beutler & R. Greene

(Eds.), *Special problems in child and adolescent behavior.* Westport, Conn.: Technomic Publishing, 1978. Pp. 187–205.

17. Bandura, A. Behavior theory and the models of man. *American Psychologist,* 1974, *29,* 859–869.

18. Ibid.

19. Ibid.

20. Ibid.

21. Ibid.

22. Ibid.

23. Bandura, A. *Social learning theory.* Englewood Cliffs, N.J.: Prentice-Hall, 1977. P. 10.

24. Brewer, W. There is no convincing evidence for operant or classical conditioning in adult humans. In W. Weimer & D. Palermo (Eds.), *Cognition and the symbolic processes.* New York: Halstead Press, 1974.

25. Sperry, R. W. Bridging science and values: A unifying view of mind and brain. *American Psychologist,* 1977, *32,* 237–245.

26. Lazarus, A. A., & Wilson, G. T. Behavior modification: Clinical and experimental perspectives. In B. B. Wolman (Ed.), *The therapist's handbook.* New York: Van Nostrand Reinhold, 1976. P. 153.

27. Lazarus, A. A. Has behavior therapy outlived its usefulness? *American Psychologist,* 1977, *32,* 550–554.

28. Ibid.

29. Krasner, L. On the death of behavior modification: Some comments from a mourner. *American Psychologist,* 1976, *31,* 387–388.

30. Lazarus, Has behavior therapy outlived its usefulness?

31. Ibid.

32. Wilkins, W. Desensitization: Social and cognitive factors underlying the effectiveness of Wolpe's procedure. *Psychological Bulletin,* 1971, *76,* 311–317; Locke, E. A. Is "behavior therapy" behavioristic? (an analysis of Wolpe's psychotherapeutic methods). *Psychological Bulletin,* 1971, *76,* 318–327; Brown, B. Cognitive aspects of Wolpe's behavior therapy. *American Journal of Psychiatry,* 1967, *124,* 854–859.

33. O'Leary, K. D., & Wilson, G. T. *Behavior therapy: Application and outcome.* Englewood Cliffs, N.J.: Prentice-Hall, 1975. Most of the recent books on behavior therapy have sections and chapters on cognitive techniques or methods, for example, Bellack, A. S., & Hersen, M. *Behavior modification: An introductory textbook.* New York: Oxford University Press, 1977; Walen, S. R., Hauserman, N. M., & Laven, P. J. *Clinical guide to behavior therapy.* New York: Oxford University Press, 1977; Redd, W. H., Porterfield, A. W., & Anderson, B. L. *Behavior modification: Behavioral approaches to human problems.* New York: Knopf, 1977; Phillips, E. L. *Counseling and psychotherapy: A behavioral approach.* New York: Wiley, 1977; Martin, G., & Pear, J. *Behavior modification: What it is and how to do it.* Englewood Cliffs, N. J.: Prentice-Hall, 1978.

34. Goldfried, M., & Davison, C. *Clinical behavior therapy.* New York: Holt, Rinehart and Winston, 1976. P. 5.

35. Mahoney, M. *Cognition and behavior modification.* Cambridge, Mass.: Ballinger, 1974; Meichenbaum, D. *Cognitive-behavior therapy: An integrative approach.* New York: Plenum, 1977.

36. Meichenbaum, *Cognitive-behavior therapy,* p. 108.

37. Lazarus, Has behavior therapy outlived its usefulness?

38. Wolpe, J. Review of *Behavior therapy and beyond* by A. A. Lazarus. *Professional Psychology,* 1972, *3,* 390–392; Wolpe, J. Reply by Wolpe, *Professional Psychology,* 1974, *5,* 111–112.

39. Zimbardo, P. G. (Ed.). *The cognitive control of motivation.* Glenview, Ill.: Scott, Foresman, 1969.
40. Zimbardo, P. The human choice. In W. Arnold & D. Levine (Eds.), *Nebraska symposium on motivation, 1969.* Lincoln: University of Nebraska Press, 1969. P. 240.
41. Bolles, R. Cognition and motivation: Some historical trends. In B. Weiner (Ed.), *Cognitive views of human motivation.* New York: Academic Press, 1974.
42. Dember, W. N. Motivation and the cognitive revolution. *American Psychologist,* 1974, *29,* 161–168. In the area of personality theory, see Mischel, W. Toward a cognitive social learning reconception of personality. *Psychological Review,* 1973, *80,* 252–283.
43. Lazarus, R. S. A cognitively oriented psychologist looks at biofeedback. *American Psychologist,* 1975, *30,* 553–561.
44. Davidson, A. R., & Steiner, I. D. Reinforcement schedules and attributed freedom. *Journal of Personality and Social Psychology,* 1971, *19,* 357–366.
45. Bandura, *Social learning theory,* p. 10.
46. Raimy, V. *Misunderstandings of the self.* San Francisco: Jossey-Bass, 1975.
47. Beck, A. T. *Cognitive therapy and the emotional disorders.* New York: International Universities Press, 1976.
48. Mahoney, M. J. Reflections on the cognitive-learning trend in psychotherapy. *American Psychologist,* 1977, *32,* 5–13.
49. Ibid.
50. Burton, A. *Modern humanistic psychotherapy.* San Francisco: Jossey-Bass, 1967, P. 6.
51. Ibid., p. 122.
52. Connie Nast.
53. Frank, J. D. *Persuasion and healing.* Baltimore: Johns Hopkins University Press, 1961.
54. Goldstein, A. P. Psychotherapy research by extrapolation from social psychology. *Journal of Counseling Psychology,* 1966, *13,* 38–45; Goldstein, A. P., Heller, K., & Sechrest, L. B. *Psychotherapy and the psychology of behavior change.* New York: Wiley, 1966.
55. Strong, S. R. Counseling: An interpersonal influence process. *Journal of Counseling Psychology,* 1968, *15,* 215–224; Strong, S. R., & Matross, R. Change processes in psychotherapy. *Journal of Counseling Psychology,* 1973, *20,* 25–37.
56. Beutler, L. E. Psychotherapy and persuasion. In Beutler & Greene (Eds.), *Special problems in child and adolescent behavior,* Pp. 119–159.
57. Strong, S. R. Social psychological approach to psychotherapy research. In S. L. Garfield & A. E. Bergin (Eds.), *Handbook of psychotherapy and behavior change: An empirical analysis* (2nd ed.). New York: Wiley, 1978. Pp. 101–135.
58. Corrigan, J. D., Dell, D. M., Lewis, K. N., & Schmidt, L. D. Counseling as a social influence process. *Journal of Counseling Psychology Monograph,* 1980, *27,* 395–441.
59. Beutler, Psychotherapy and persuasion, pp. 125, 129.
60. Strong, Social psychological approach to psychotherapy research, p.
61. Corrigan, Dell, Lewis, & Schmidt, Counseling as a social influence process, pp. 425, 437.
62. LaCrosse, M. B. Perceived counselor social influence and counseling outcomes: Validity of the Counselor Rating Form. *Journal of Counseling Psychology,* 1980, *27,* 320–327.
63. Muehlberg, N., Pierce, R., & Drasgow, J. A factor analysis of therapeutically facilitative conditions. *Journal of Clinical Psychology,* 1969, *25,* 93–95. The authors note that this term was proposed to them by Thorne in a personal communication.
64. LaCrosse, M. B., and Barak, A. Differential perception of counselor behavior. *Journal of Counseling Psychology,* 1976, *23,* 170–172.
65. Petty, R. E., and Cacioppo, J. T. *Attitudes and persuasion: classic and contemporary approaches.* Dubuque, Ia.: Brown, 1981; Petty, R. E., Ostrom, T. M., and Brock, T. C. (Eds.). *Cognitive responses in persuasion.* Hillsdale, N.J.: Erlbaum, 1981.

chapter **19**

Convergence

More than 10 years ago, I wrote, "The days of 'schools' in counseling and psychotherapy are drawing to a close."[1] At that time, I felt that there would soon be a convergence, based on common elements of the major theories, but I was premature. During the 1970s, divergence apparently increased. There was a proliferation of new techniques and strategies of intervention. Few, if any, of these methods warrant the designation of a school, however, and few, if any, have a theoretical basis.

Yet, in a sense, the days of narrow schools or multiple theories seem to have passed. Along with the proliferation of techniques was the abandonment of adherence to single theories and the increased interest in eclecticism, which has not, as yet, resulted in the development of a true eclecticism.

Yet there now exist the foundations for a truly integrative theory of psychotherapy. These foundations consist of the basic elements that are common to all the major systems of psychotherapy. In this chapter, we shall present these elements and consider both the objections that have been raised against them and the evidence for their acceptance and effectiveness.

COMMONALITIES IN PSYCHOTHERAPY

Implicit Commonalities

A number of characteristics of psychotherapy appear to be present in all theories or approaches but are seldom explicitly noted.

1. All approaches and all therapists agree that human beings are capable of change or of being changed; disagreement is on how best to bring about

change. Human beings are not predetermined; at any stage of development, they are still pliable. Learning theory approaches are based on this assumption. Skinner expresses it as follows: "It is dangerous to assert that an organism of a given species or age cannot solve a given problem. As a result of careful scheduling, pigeons, rats, and monkeys have done things in the last five years which members of their species have never done before. It is not that their forebears were incapable of such behavior; nature had simply never arranged effective sequences of schedules."[2] More dramatically, regarding the possibility of molding personality, he states: "Give me the specifications, and I'll give you the man."[3]

Other approaches may not be so optimistic about the changeability of personality or of behavior, but they clearly assume the possibility of change; otherwise there would be no point to engaging in counseling or psychotherapy.

2. There is agreement that some kinds of behavior are undesirable, inadequate, and harmful or result in dissatisfaction, unhappiness, or limitation of a person's potential and, therefore, warrant attempts at change. These behaviors may include cognitive or emotional disturbances or disorders, conflicts, unresolved problems, or those behaviors designated as neurotic or psychotic.

3. All therapies and therapists expect their clients or patients to change as a result of their particular techniques. This expectation may vary in its degree; in some instances, it approaches a highly optimistic or even enthusiastic expectation, while in others, it may be minimal, or minimal changes may be expected.

Every therapist believes in or has confidence in the theory and method that he or she uses. If the therapist did not believe that this approach was the best method, it would not be used; some other method would replace it. As in the case of belief in the ability of clients to change, therapists would not be engaged in the practice of therapy if they did not expect their clients to change and did not believe that their methods would lead to change. It might be hypothesized that success (or at least therapists' and perhaps clients' reports of success) bears a strong relationship to the degree of confidence that the therapist has in his or her approach. A common aspect of therapy thus appears to be the therapist's commitment to a particular theory or at least a particular method or set of techniques. The effect of this commitment, or the interaction of commitment and effectiveness of a method, is one of the problems in attempting to evaluate the effectiveness of a method apart from the therapist who uses it.

4. Individuals who enter and continue in therapy feel the need for help. They "hurt": they are suffering or are unhappy because of conflicts, symptoms, negative feelings or emotions, interpersonal problems or conflicts, inadequate or unsatisfying behaviors, and so on. They are, therefore, motivated to change. Therapists are not particularly interested in working with unmotivated or "involuntary" clients, even though such clients may obviously have problems. Persons who do not recognize their problems or do not feel any need for help do not often enter therapy, or if they do, they usually do not continue.

5. Clients also believe that change is possible and expect to change. Frank has emphasized the universality of this factor in clients.[4] Cartwright and Cartwright indicate that this is a complex factor: there may be a belief that improvement will occur, a belief in the therapist as the major source of help, or a belief in himself or herself as the major source of help.[5] Cartwright and Cartwright feel that it is only the last belief that leads to improvement in a

positive linear manner. The other beliefs are probably present to some extent in all clients, however. If the client did not feel that he or she would improve and that the therapist and the therapist's methods could effect such improvement, the client would not enter or continue in therapy.

6. All therapists appear to expect and insist that the client be an active participant in the process. The client is not a passive recipient, as is the physically ill patient who is being treated by a physician, even in those approaches that are most directive and active. All learning (behavior change) appears to require some activity (whether motor, verbal, or intellectual) on the part of the learner.

7. In addition to these general characteristics of all therapies, a number of more specific characteristics are shared by most, although not all, therapies or are present in differing degrees in the various therapies. They include suggestion, persuasion, encouragement, advice, support, instruction, and similar techniques.

The Relationship as a Common Element

The implicit commonalities underlie and/or enter into the relationship between the therapist and the client. More significant and more specific than the implicit elements, however, are a number of explicit elements that constitute the core of the therapeutic relationship. Therapy, by almost any definition, involves a personal contact between the therapist and the client. Many theories note the importance of the personal qualities of the therapist without, however, specifying their nature. But some qualities that enter into the relationship have been identified, defined, and even measured. A classic article by Rogers specified (as assumptions) the necessary and sufficient conditions for therapeutic personality change.[6] The focus was on the therapist's contribution to the relationship, although the client's contributions were also recognized.

1. All therapists manifest a real concern for their clients. They are interested in their clients, care for them, and want to help them. Rogers used the phrase unconditional positive regard. Others have referred to warmth or nonpossessive warmth, respect, prizing, valuing, and accepting. While client-centered therapists would include a respect for the client's potential to take responsibility for himself or herself and to resolve his or her own problems, some therapists would not include this. The client-centered nonevaluative, nonjudgmental attitudes also might not be shared by others, but a basic interest, concern, and desire to help another human being are common to all therapists and are a powerful aspect of the therapeutic relationship.

2. A second characteristic of all effective therapists is honesty, or a genuineness and openness. Rogers referred to it as therapist congruence—a consistency between the thoughts and feelings of the therapist and the therapist's expressions to the client. Therapists are sincere, authentic, transparent, and real persons. They are not engaged in trickery or deceit in their relations with their clients.

3. Empathic understanding is a third aspect of a therapeutic relationship. In some form or other, although it varies in terminology, all the major writers on counseling or psychotherapy refer to this characteristic of therapists as

being important. Theorists vary in the degree of emphasis they place on empathic understanding, and therapists of different persuasions vary in the degree to which they provide it, but no one seems to deny its desirability, if not its importance.

4. These attitudes or characteristics of the therapist lead to a therapeutic relationship only if they are recognized, perceived, or felt by the client. The therapist exists for the purpose of the relationship only as he or she is perceived by the client.

AGREEMENT ON THE RELATIONSHIP

The most widely known studies on the nature of the relationship as viewed by therapists are those of Fiedler,[7] who found that therapists from different schools of psychotherapy agree on the nature of the ideal therapeutic relationship. Factor analysis yielded one common factor of "goodness," whose items were concerned with empathy or understanding. Fiedler also concluded that a good therapeutic relationship as viewed by these therapists is similar to a good interpersonal relationship.

There is currently widespread, if not universal, agreement among theorists and therapists on the influence of the relationship in therapy or behavior change. Goldstein, reviewing the literature on therapist and patient expectations in psychotherapy, concluded: "There can no longer be any doubt as to the primary status which must be accorded the therapeutic transaction."[8]

Menninger and Holzman, in the second edition of *Theory of Psychoanalytic Techniques,* view the relationship as the "central focus of the therapeutic process."[9] Goodstein, reviewing a collection of papers published under the title *What Makes Behavior Change Possible?,* states that "among virtually all of the contributors there is an awareness of and attention to the therapeutic relationship as an essential ingredient of behavior change."[10] The 14 contributors included Frank, Strupp, Burton, Ellis, Raimy, the Polsters, Bandura, and Wolpe.

The behavior therapists, although admitting the presence of the relationship, have minimized its importance. Goldfried and Davison suggest that "perhaps one of the reasons that behavior therapists have tended to deemphasize the importance of the relationship is the fact that their techniques have been shown to be effective in their own right."[11] This is actually not a fact. The study that they and others cite as showing this effectiveness involved a laboratory study of fear modification that used an automated desensitization procedure.[12] Instructions for the desensitization process were taped, and subjects listened to the tapes instead of being involved with a therapist. However, the tapes were of a human voice, and the experimental situation involved relationship elements (personal and interpersonal elements). Furthermore, the possibility of the subjects anthropomorphizing the machine was not considered.[13] Indeed, the experimenters themselves may have done so—the device was designated as DAD (device for automatic desensitization). In addition, other research has shown that there is an influence of the relationship on conditioning. For example, Sapolsky showed that the effectiveness of reinforcement depended on the relationship between the experimenter and the subject. Subjects who were given instructions that pictured the experimenter as attractive conditioned well, while those who were led to perceive the experimenter as unattractive did not condition during the experimental period (although there was evidence of delayed conditioning). Also, subjects who were matched with experimenters for similarity (compatibility) on the basis of a personality test conditioned better than did those who were incompatible.[14] Similarly, "warm" experimenters were more effective than "cold" experimenters. There is considerable evidence that the rate and extent of conditioning are influenced by the personality and attitudes of the experimenter and the experimenter's relationship to the subject. As Ullmann and Krasner note, "Both the subject's and the examiner's expectancies, sets and so forth have a major effect on the individual's response to the situation." They go on to conclude that in therapy, "the best results are obtained when the patient and therapist form a good interpersonal relationship."[15]

Observers of Wolpe and of Lazarus (when he was associated with Wolpe) noted, as was indicated in Chapter 5, that relationship variables were present. Lazarus acknowledged this in his comment on the report: "Both Wolpe and I have explicitly stated that relationship variables are often extremely important in behavior therapy. Factors such as warmth, empathy and authenticity are considered necessary but often insufficient."[16] Subsequently, Wolpe has stated, "The more the patient feels a responsive warmth towards the therapist, the more likely to be inhibited are those of his anxieties that are evident during the interview."[17] Yet there are some who do not acknowledge the necessity or importance of the relationship. Gill, a psychoanalytically oriented therapist, has reviewed a book in which therapists representing three approaches (behavior therapy, Gestalt therapy, and psychoanalysis) discussed the same three cases. He wrote, "I confess that although I believe I understand why it is so, I remain astonished that so many therapists can remain blind to the fact that their allegedly specific methods of desensitization, rehearsing, and so on owe their effects to unacknowledged interpersonal interaction."[18]

Other relationship elements are or may be involved in psychotherapy. These variables are related to social, professional, and status differences between the therapist and the client—the concept of the therapist as an expert—and include professional authority, prestige, and status. "Bedside" manner, the manifestation of self-confidence and self-assurance, and the charismatic manner of the therapist are other examples. As indicated in Chapter 18, some approaches to psychotherapy emphasize this aspect, while others minimize it. To some extent, an element of authority is present in almost all therapeutic relationships. An authoritative role is usually assigned to the therapist by the client. Nevertheless, the degree of authority may vary tremendously, and it can be maximized or minimized in the relationship; it may be exploited or its explicit use may be avoided. More will be said about this aspect of the therapeutic relationship.

THE RELATIONSHIP: NECESSARY BUT NOT SUFFICIENT?

There is thus general, perhaps almost universal, agreement on the presence, importance, and even the necessity of a relationship between the therapist and the client that is characterized by empathic understanding, respect and warmth, and genuineness. Many, however, would question or deny the sufficiency of these qualities.

The problem of sufficiency involves the question of sufficiency for what. It has been argued that a relationship characterized by empathic understanding, respect, and therapeutic genuineness is the specific treatment for the absence of these conditions and leads to the development of these characteristics in clients through the powerful process of modeling plus the client's experiencing and participating in the relationship. There is evidence that this is the case.

What about other outcomes? What about client problems that involve lack of information or knowledge, or lack of skills of various kinds: are these deficiencies of a cognitive or a motor nature? Surely, with clients in whom these are lacking or inadequate, the providing of a relationship is not sufficient. Although it might appear to be a resort to specious reasoning, dealing with such problems would seem to be education (or reeducation), rather than therapy. While it may be difficult to draw a line between therapy and (remedial) teaching, there would seem to be some value in doing so. One difference might be that therapy is concerned with persons who are not lacking in knowledge or skills but who are unable for some reason to use their knowledge or skills. Their problem, in the distinction made by many learning theorists, is not one of learning, but of performance. Therapy as a relationship is sufficient for enabling them to do those things that they are capable of doing. But the relationship may not be sufficient with persons who demonstrate a lack or deficit. It is with such clients that the cognitive methods developed by Meichenbaum, for example, would be relevant and appropriate.

Two comments are in order, however. First, it is becoming increasingly recognized that learning is not simply a cognitive process, as Rogers and other writers on humanistic education have emphasized.[19] Cognitive therapists often appear to ignore or to be unaware of this. Second, the teacher–student interaction involves a personal relationship, and evidence is accumulating that the factors that lead to therapeutic personality change also facilitate cognitive learning. Indeed, in some teaching—perhaps in the best teaching—the creation of a suitable relationship may be sufficient for some kinds of learning by some learners.

In addition, evidence is accumulating that a therapeutic relationship characterized by empathic understanding, respect, and genuineness *without the addition of other techniques,* such as direct instruction, remedial teaching, or cognitive techniques, can lead to changes in a client's behavior beyond those related to the conditions themselves.

It might be expected that children with reading problems would benefit more from remedial instruction than from a therapeutic relationship or, if it is conceded that there are emotional factors involved, more from instruction and therapy than from either alone. Bills, in an early study, found that retarded readers who participated in play therapy improved their reading significantly during the therapy period compared with control periods preceding and following the experimental period.[20] In a later study, Lawrence found, contrary to his expectation, that poor readers who were provided with both counseling and remedial instruction did not gain as much as those who were provided with counseling alone.[21]

In light of research that indicates that the conditions of the therapeutic relationship alone are sufficient for a wide variety of outcomes, it becomes difficult to determine when other techniques or other kinds of help should be included. It would appear that a client who lacks information should be given the information or that a client who has inaccurate information should be provided with accurate information. But the client's responsibility might be increased if the client simply were told where to obtain the missing or the accurate information. Similarly, a client who lacks skills could be informed where he or she could learn those skills. Certainly therapists do not, and could not, provide instruction in all the kinds of skills in which their clients might be lacking or provide all the kinds of information that their clients need.

Not every client will improve in a relationship that includes the core conditions. There is, of course, the possibility that the conditions are not present at a high enough level for effectiveness. Even the best therapists encounter clients with whom they cannot fully empathize and to whom they not offer respect, warmth, or genuineness. Then there is always the possibility that in spite of the therapist's demonstrating these qualities, as rated by an outside observer, the client does not perceive them. It is difficult, and sometimes impossible, to break through to some clients, whose disturbance—for example, paranoia—may prevent it. They may be so threatened and defensive that they cannot perceive anyone as genuinely interested in them or cannot trust anyone. Finally, it is possible that even though the conditions may be present, they may be nullified by inconsistent and negative elements introduced by the therapist. Some therapists, after establishing a relationship, attempt to use it to manipulate, persuade, or guide the client, leading to the client's confusion or resistance.

An apparent reason for the wide variety of changes in clients who are provided a therapeutic relationship without direct instruction or specific training is found in one of the effects of the relationship conditions in the therapy process. The presence of the conditions leads the client to engage in self-exploration. Clients learn to take responsibility for themselves when they are expected to and allowed to do so. They make necessary choices and decisions, seek and obtain accurate information, and acquire training in essential or desirable skills.

Since therapy is effective with a wide variety of clients who have a wide variety of problems without use of specific methods beyond the relationship itself, a number of questions arise. When is the relationship not sufficient? Since results are obtained without the giving of information, advice, suggestions, interpretations, persuasion, and so forth, it is clear that none of these is necessary. The question then is: do these other techniques help when they are added to the relationship without undesirable side effects? When do they help? Finally, there is a question that has not been investigated: if the relationship is not only necessary, but also sufficient for so many outcomes, is it efficient?[22] Again, would other methods, if added to the relationship, increase the efficiency of therapy in achieving the same outcomes without undesirable side effects?

RESISTANCE TO ACCEPTANCE OF THE SUFFICIENCY OF THE RELATIONSHIP

It has been noted that there is general acceptance of the relationship as desirable or even necessary. The most effective therapists, whatever their orientation, describe themselves or are described as being warm, compassionate, genuine, optimistic, or respectful of their clients as persons who have potential for change. Almost universally, writers in the field of psychology have been converging in the recognition of the basic importance of a warm, concerned, empathic relationship. Yet, many qualify their acceptance with such caveats that the relationship is effective with only some clients or problems and that it frequently must be supplemented with specific methods or techniques—in effect, that its sufficiency is limited. There is considerable resistance to the acceptance of the relationship as sufficient for psychotherapeutic change. This idea is apparently a threat to many counselors and psychotherapists. The writings of Strupp and of Bergin have epitomized this attitude. Strupp writes,

> The trained therapist, whether he be a psychoanalyst or a behavior therapist, will reject as naive the suggestion that a large segment of the therapeutic influence—that is, the motive power for therapeutic change—might be encompassed by 'nonspecific' interpersonal factors. . . . On the basis of his clinical experience, he is deeply convinced that a good human relationship, which he might liken to the laying on of hands, sentimentality, moral treatment, or gross ignorance of the realities of therapeutic work, is severely limited in its therapeutic effects.[23]

For some years, Bergin and Strupp have been arguing that additional variables to the relationship are necessary in psychotherapy. In an extensive review of research in psychotherapy, although acknowledging the considerable evidence that supports the potency of personal qualities as therapeutic agents, they continually refer to the importance of "technical procedures," "mechanisms," "technical variables," and "technical skills," as being necessary.[24] Neither in this nor in other publications have these factors been identified or has evidence been presented for their importance.

The resistance to recognition of the interpersonal relationship as sufficient for therapeutic change is illustrated in a preliminary report of a study by Strupp. The results indicated that untrained college professors with reputations for warmth, trust, and interest in their students were as effective as trained therapists. It was expected that the latter would be more effective because of their mastery of technique. Strupp would not, or could not, accept these unexpected results. It was reported that members of the audience to whom the study was presented suggested "that the researchers take their own data more seriously and accept the conclusion that interpersonal factors alone can lead to psychological change."[25]

There are a number of apparent reasons for this resistance. The evidence that the relationship involving personal factors of the therapist is the necessary and sufficient condition for therapeutic personality change is threatening because of its implications of simplicity, therapist responsibility, and "nonprofessional" status.

First, the idea that the essence of psychotherapy is the relationship between the therapist and the client appears to be too simple. It is difficult to accept the fact that the relationship can have such profound effects on so many different problems and so many different kinds of clients. The idea that there must be different techniques for different problems and for different clients—indeed, for different therapists—appears to be more logical. It has been embraced by many writers. Paul's statement is frequently cited: "The question towards which all outcome research should ultimately be directed is the following: *What* treatment, by *whom,* is most effective for *this* individual with *that* specific problem, and under *which* set of circumstances?"[26] Krumboltz phrased it similarly: "What we need to know is which procedures and techniques, when used to accomplish which kinds of behavior change, are most effective with what kind of client when applied by what kind of counselor."[27] Bergin and Strupp concluded that "the problem of psychotherapy research in its most general terms, should be formulated as a standard scientific question: What specific therapeutic intervention produces specific changes in specific conditions?"[28]

This is an appealing view, even without identifying it with the scientific approach. If it is a scientific approach, it is purely empirical, unguided by theory. Its assumptions are questionable and its requirements, impossible to meet (see the Introduction to Part Six). Kisch and Kroll state the situation succinctly: "The compelling question of what aspects of therapy work for what kinds of therapists for what kinds of patients is probably empirically unanswerable because it is methodologically unsolvable."[29]

The preoccupation with this thinking seems to have led to the inability of some theorists to recognize or to accept the evidence for the power of the therapeutic relationship.

Second, the concept that the relationship is the essence of psychotherapy places responsibility squarely on the person of the therapist, who has no place to hide. The therapist cannot excuse himself or herself by disclaiming responsibility for ineffectiveness, blaming poor results on lack of suitable techniques, and arguing that more research is needed to discover specific effective techniques. There are frequent statements to the effect that the most important element in psychotherapy is the personality of the psychotherapist. As long as the nature of the personality characteristics are not stated or identified or it is implied that there are many different kinds of therapeutic personalities, this statement is innocuous or even meaningless. The research on the therapeutic relationship identifies and specifies those qualities that are therapeutic and provides evidence that high levels of these characteristics lead to therapeutic personality changes, while low levels do not.

Third, perhaps the most threatening implication of the relationship as the core of psychotherapy is that psychotherapy is not a profession. This threat is clearly reflected by Strupp: "If the contribution of a good human relationship to a specific therapeutic outcome is subtracted, what is left over? The development of psychotherapy as a set of theories and as a prestigious profession in the twentieth century, is predicated on the assumption that the residue is substantial."[30] He does not identify this residue; his statement is not supported by research. The emperor is without clothes.

Albee writes that "a *profession* must jealously guard its secrets! Historically, one of the hallmarks of a profession has been the *privacy* of its knowledge. If the knowledge of the professional, his techniques, and his skills are available to anyone, and could be performed by anyone, a profession would disintegrate. Secrecy and mystery are essential."[31]

If psychotherapy consists of providing a good human relationship, it cannot be the monopoly of a professional group; it can and should be disseminated throughout society. It does not require a medical or professional degree, many of the requirements of which are unnecessary or irrelevant—if not detrimental—to offering a therapeutic relationship. If, to paraphrase Miller,[32] psychotherapy is to be given away to the people, it cannot remain a profession.

To be sure, for a long time to come, there will be a need for those who are gifted or expert in providing a therapeutic relationship and whose time and commitment will be worth payments. Psychotherapy may be likened to the purchase of friendship, as Schofield noted,[33] but it is something more; to view it simply as bought friendship places the psychotherapist in the same category as taxi dancers, gigolos, and call girls. While it may not be a profession, psychotherapy is on a somewhat different level.

The concept of psychotherapy as a relationship is not a new idea. It is implicit, if not explicit, in the historical development of the medicine man and the witch doctor, who still exist and are effective in so-called primitive societies or cultures. It is not a simplistic view of psychotherapy. The therapeutic relationship is complex, and all its elements are not yet understood. Rather than be sidetracked in the study of techniques, research should build on what is already known about the relationship. There is a paradox involved, however. Research may be able to identify and to isolate the behaviors of an effective therapist or the ways in which the therapist implements the relationship, but the teaching and practice of these behaviors will not necessarily produce therapists. An example is the discovery that the empathic therapist maintains considerable eye contact with the client and tends to lean toward the client rather than push himself or herself back or maintain distance. Yet aside from the fact that we do not know how much eye contact is desirable (or when it is experienced by the client as staring) or what degree of trunk leaning is optimal, to teach a student of psychotherapy to maintain eye contact or to lean toward the client will not suffice to make him or her therapeutic. What is identified as characteristic behavior of an effective therapist cannot be used as a technique. It is not the behaviors that lead to effective therapy, but the effective therapist who tends to behave in certain ways in implementing his or her attitudes of concern, respect, and genuineness and who attempts to understand empathically. There is perhaps a wide range of behaviors by which different therapists implement these attitudes and which constitute different therapeutic styles. These differences often become the focus of study and cover over the basic commonality of the therapeutic relationship.

THE RELATIONSHIP AS A NONSPECIFIC ELEMENT

Many writers of diverse theoretical orientations view the total psychotherapeutic relationship as nonspecific. Frank[34] has long maintained this position. Bergin[35] and Strupp[36] also have emphasized the nonspecific nature of the relationship, repeatedly emphasizing the necessity of specific techniques in addition to the nonspecific relationship.

Behaviorists view the therapeutic relationship as nonspecific, in contrast to the specific techniques of behavior therapy. Wolpe, for example, has claimed that his method of reciprocal inhibition, as well as other behavioristic techniques, increases the improvement rate over that of the relationship alone, stating that "the procedures of behavior therapy have effects additional to those relational effects that are common to all forms of psychotherapy."[37] Such claims have been disputed and are not supported by any research that has controlled for the relationship.

Those who regard the relationship as nonspecific hold that it is not related directly to the treatment of any of the client's specific problems. It is the substrate from which the therapist operates, the setting or environment in which specific methods are used; some therapists view it as rapport or as the basis of the client's trust in the therapist, providing a power base for influencing the client in some way.

There are two arguments against this view.

First, if it is assumed that the source of many, if not most, of the problems of clients involves disturbed interpersonal relationships, then a therapeutic relationship that includes the characteristics of a good human relationship is a relevant, and specific, method of treatment. The therapist is a model for the client from whom the client can learn how to maintain a good relationship with others, and, at the same time, the client is helped by experiencing the relationship offered by the therapist. It is being increasingly recognized that good interpersonal relationships are characterized by understanding, honesty, openness, sincerity, and spontaneity. Psychotherapy is an interpersonal relationship that includes these characteristics. Indeed, therapy would be limited if it attempted to help the client develop better interpersonal relationships in the context of a different kind of relationship.

The evidence that the source of much, if not most, emotional disturbance is the absence of good human relationships is pervasive and generally acknowledged. Ford and Urban, in evaluating the theories or systems of psychotherapy presented in their book, state that "all of these theorists seem to agree that the situational conditions necessary for the development of behavior disorder are the ways other people behave toward the growing person."[38] Spitz's classic studies of institutionalized infants indicate that deprivation of attention, handling, and personal contact is deleterious not only psychologically, but also physiologically.[39] Love, which is the essence of a good human relationship, is necessary for survival. Burton writes that "the basic pathogen is, for me, a disordered maternal or care-taking environment rather than any specific trauma as such."[40] Many other writers and therapists have suggested that emotional disturbances or neuroses and psychoses are the result of lack of or inadequate love and acceptance (or unconditional positive regard) in childhood.[41] Burton notes that "after all research in psychotherapy is accounted for, psychotherapy still resolves itself into a relationship best subsumed by the word 'love.' "[42]

Second, there is evidence that the providing of a relationship as defined here without any additional techniques is effective with many clients who have many kinds of problems.

THE UBIQUITOUS PLACEBO

Related to the argument that relationship factors are nonspecific is the contention that such factors are placebos. Rosenthal and Frank[43] take this position, as do Krasner and Ullmann[44] and Wolpe.[45]

Shapiro, who probably has engaged in more intensive study of placebos than anyone else, and Morris give the following definitions:

A *placebo* is defined as any therapy or component of therapy that is deliberately used for its nonspecific, psychologic, or psychophysiological, effect, or that is used for its presumed specific effect, but is without specific activity for the condition being treated.

The *placebo effect* is defined as the nonspecific, psychologic, or physiologic effect produced by placebos.

A *placebo,* when used as a control in experimental studies, is defined as a substance or procedure that is without specific activity for the condition being evaluated.

The placebo effect is defined as the psychological or psychophysiological effect produced by placebos.[46]

Shapiro and Morris consider placebo effects in both medical treatment and psychotherapy, which are quite different situations. They note that "the placebo effect may have greater implications for psychotherapy than any other form of treatment because both psychotherapy and the placebo effect function primarily through psychological mechanisms. . . . *The placebo effect is an important component and perhaps the entire basis for the existence, popularity, and effectiveness of numerous methods of psychotherapy.*"[47]

The placebo as an inert substance does not exist in psychotherapy.[48] All the variables in the therapeutic relationship are psychological and active, having some specific or direct effects on the client.

In an earlier discussion of the placebo effect, Shapiro stated that he was presenting "an examination of psychotherapy as a placebo effect,"[49] thus suggesting that psychotherapy is nothing more than a placebo. However, Shapiro and Morris view the total psychotherapy *relationship* as a placebo. They refer to a review by Luborsky, Singer, and Luborsky[50] that found several types of psychotherapy to be about equally effective. Shapiro and Morris conclude that this equal effectiveness was related to the common therapist–patient relationship and point to this relationship as a demonstration of the placebo effect.

Rosenthal and Frank much earlier came to the same conclusion. Referring to the placebo effect as a nonspecific form of psychotherapy, they write, "The similarity of the forces operating in psychotherapy and the placebo effect may account for the high consistency of improvement rates found with various therapies, from that conducted by physicians to intensive psychoanalysis."[51] More recently, Pentony, in his extensive analysis of the placebo as a model of psychotherapy, suggests that "the placebo effect constitutes the most parsimonious explanation that would account for the apparently equal success achieved by each of the diverse collection of therapies practiced."[52]

This statement assumes that the total therapeutic relationship is a placebo. It is proposed here, however, that the relationship consists of two major classes of variables: specific variables; and nonspecific, or placebo, variables. We have already enumerated the major specific variables: empathic understanding, respect or warmth, and genuineness.

The nonspecific, or placebo, variables are the social-influence variables—perceived therapist expertness or credibility, trustworthiness, and attractiveness, and therapist expectations. These variables are among those listed by Shapiro and Morris[53] as variables through which the placebo operates. Indeed, they are the essence of what Fish boldly calls placebo therapy.[54]

Recognizing that "the social influence process has been considered the active ingredient in the placebo," Fish states that placebo therapy "denotes a broad frame of reference for considering all forms of human interaction, especially psychotherapy, in terms of social influence process."[55] The therapist does everything possible to establish himself or herself as an expert and an authority in the eyes of the client. The client's susceptibility to influence and persuasion is assessed. The impression is created that "once I know what is wrong with you I can cure you."

A treatment strategy is then formulated and communicated to the client in a plausible manner, tailored to the client's belief system. The major techniques used are those of behavior modification, together with suggestion and hypnosis. "Placebo therapy is a strategy for getting the maximum impact from such techniques regardless of their validity."[56] Placebo communications are used not because they are true, but because of their effects. The validity of the techniques, or the therapeutic ritual, to use Fish's term, is important only as it enhances the patient's faith—that is, how believable, impressive, or persuasive the technique is to the patient. The therapist "says things for the effect they will have rather than for his belief that they are true. Instead of speaking empathically because he believes that empathy cures, he does so because he sees that such statements add to credibility in the patient's eyes."[57] Further, "lying to a patient is desirable if the lie furthers the therapeutic goals, is unlikely to be discovered (and hence backfire) and is likely to be more effective than any other strategy."[58]

Pentony provides a critical evaluation of Fish's placebo therapy. He says that "it seems questionable whether a treatment based on suggestion [or persuasion] alone will be universally applicable," given the existence of strong resistance to change. He raises three other questions about placebo therapy: "1. Is it ethical to mislead the client in regard to the therapeutic strategy? 2. Will the therapist be convincing when he is not a true believer in the ritual he is carrying through? 3. If placebo therapy becomes general and clients become aware of its nature, will they lose faith in the healing rituals and hence render these ineffective?"[59] Fish's attempts to answer these questions are less than convincing. No attention is given to the problem of therapist genuineness and the client's detection of its absence in the therapist.

There are other problems with placebo therapy. Fish, who claims that it works, urges that the reasons be researched. There is probably no question that placebo therapy works with some clients some of the time. It is the basis for the success of charlatans and charismatics, who produce satisfied clients and testimonials.

There are three problems with the placebo as therapy, however. First, it is uncertain, or unreliable. Not all subjects are placebo reactors, and it is not possible to identify those who will respond positively to placebos. Fish attempts to determine who among his clients will be positive reactors. Although he notes that many are called, but few are chosen, he does not tell how many or what proportion are chosen. He refers to the problem client who expects and desires a different relationship with the therapist.

In Chapter 18, it was noted that the research on social-influence variables has yielded inconsistent and conflicting results. This is consistent with the hypothesis that these variables are essentially placebos.

Second, placebo effects are not dependable; that is, when they do exist, they usually are not durable, but tend to be transitory. None of the research on the social-influence variables has included long-term, or even short-term, follow-up of results.

Third, the possible side effects of placebo therapy are undesirable, including the fostering of dependence.

The social-influence variables and the specific-relationship variables probably are not completely independent. LaCrosse[60] found significant correlations between the Counselor Rating Form, which measures client perceptions of counselor expertness, attractiveness, and trustworthiness, and the Barrett-Lennard Relationship Inventory, which measures client perceptions of counselor empathic understanding, congruence, level of regard, and unconditional positive regard. Observer ratings were also highly correlated, although ratings by the counselors themselves were not, which raises some question about the presence of an artifact, such as the halo effect, in the client and observer ratings.

The presence of correlations between these two sets of relationship variables poses the question of which is primary, or which causes or leads to the others. That the core conditions are primary is suggested by studies that have shown them to be related to various therapy outcomes, while this has not been shown for the social-influence variables. Krumboltz, Becker-Haven, and Burnett[61] have indicated the direction of the relationship when they suggest, after reviewing the research, that "counselors who want to be seen as attractive should be empathic, warm and active." It also would appear, from LaCrosse's research, that counselors who want to be regarded as experts also should be empathic, respectful, warm, and genuine. Similarly, it might be suggested that counselors who want to be perceived as trustworthy should demonstrate the same qualities.

It appears that the complex therapeutic relationship cannot be prevented from being "contaminated" by placebo elements. Clients perceive therapists, to some extent at least, as authoritative and expert—regardless of the therapists' behavior. Clients normally trust their therapists. Therapists' belief in their theory is inextricable from their methods. If they did not have confidence in them, they would use other methods in which they did have confidence.

If placebo elements cannot be entirely eliminated from psychotherapy, they can be either maximized or minimized. If they are maximized, the therapist is engaging in placebo therapy, with the possibility that results may be limited, superficial, or temporary. The research on the social-influence variables has attempted to maximize the placebo effect in various ways, including favorable introductions of counselors to clients, display of degrees and diplomas and of professional books and journals, wearing of a white coat by the counselor, luxurious office furnishings, and cultivation of a self-confident, charismatic manner by the counselor. In spite of this, the research does not demonstrate the effectiveness of the variables.

If, on the contrary, placebo elements are minimized and specific-relationship variables are maximized, therapy is effective.

THE RELATIONSHIP AND COGNITIVE THERAPY

The development of the cognitive therapies has been noted as the strongest recent development in psychotherapy. It remains to attempt to reconcile this approach with the concept of the relationship as the core, or essence, of psychotherapy.

The reconciliation is not difficult. All therapies that focus on the relationship— for example, client-centered therapy—include cognitive elements. While the emphasis sometimes has been on noncognitive or affective elements, it is not possible to exclude cognitive factors from any relationship. In the client-centered relationship, the client examines his or her (irrational) beliefs (of Ellis) and (faulty) thought patterns (of Beck). Relearning occurs without didactic teaching. The fallacy of cognitive therapy is that learning requires direct instruction. The relationship itself is a learning experience, involving so-called discovery learning by the client. The client is the expert on the subject matter—himself or herself—although the therapist may think that he or she knows more. In this respect, the client is superior to the therapist. The client educates the therapist about himself or herself, and the therapist facilitates the client's self-exploration and self-learning. The relationship is horizontal rather than vertical. Therapy is not a one-way street, or if it is a one-way street in the sense that the client gains or learns more than does the therapist, it is on the level.

One of the difficulties in the movement toward the incorporation of cognitive elements in psychotherapy is analogous to the earlier concern with the application of learning theory to psychotherapy. Just as there are multiple theories of learning or learning psychologies, so there are multiple cognitive psychologies. The problem with the incorporation of cognitive elements in behavior therapy has been the absence of any theoretical integration. The problem with the newer cognitive therapies—of Meichenbaum and of Beck, for example—is their neglect of the relationship that conveys the techniques and their neglect, if not exclusion, of affective elements, which results in an attempt to develop a purely cognitive therapy, as some behaviorists attempt without success to develop a purely behavioristic therapy.

In contrast to these developments, the concern with cognitive factors in client-centered therapy has focused on the theoretical consistency and integration of cognitive elements. The cognitive theory that appears to be most consonant with client-centered theory is information theory, which views the individual as actively attending to, selecting, operating on, organizing, and transforming the information provided by the environment and by internal sources. Thus the individual defines stimuli and events and constructs his or her own world (compare Bruner's theory, for example[62]). In Wexler and Rice's words, "Like client-centered therapy, information-processing psychology is concerned with understanding the nature of internal events, and more particularly, processes occurring within the individual as he handles and organizes his experience."[63] This theory meets the two criteria for incorporation in (or consistency with) a client-centered relationship therapy: (1) it takes or accepts the internal frame of reference of the behaver or the client; (2) it keeps or leaves the initiative and the responsibility with the client.

THE RESEARCH EVIDENCE

It is not possible to review the tremendous amount of research on the effectiveness of empathic understanding, respect and warmth, and genuineness. A number of reviews are available.[64] However, the reviewers often are negatively biased, apparently influenced by the threat of the conclusion that the relationship is the essence of psychotherapy. Yet this is the inference that must be drawn from a review of the research. A detailed evaluation of the evidence has been attempted elsewhere.[65] Truax and Carkhuff summarized the results of the early research:

> These findings suggest that the person (whether a counselor, therapist or teacher) who is better able to communicate warmth, genuineness and accurate empathy is more effective in interpersonal relationships no matter what the goal of the interaction (better grades for college students, better interpersonal relationships for the counseling center outpatient, adequate personality functioning and integration for the seriously disturbed mental patient, socially acceptable behavior for the juvenile delinquent or greater reading ability for third grade reading instruction students).[66]

A later review by Truax and Mitchell discovered that the earlier findings

have been replicated, not only in several American studies, but also cross-culturally. Clearly, these findings are true of all human relationships, regardless of age, sex, degree of disturbance, or even cultural and language contexts. . . . [The findings] seem to hold up with a wide variety of therapists and counselors, regardless of their training or theoretic orientation, and with a wide variety of clients or patients, including college underachievers, juvenile delinquents, hospitalized schizophrenics, college counselors, mild to severe outpatient neurotics and the mixed variety of hospitalized patients.[67]

Recent reviewers, covering research that seems to warrant just as strong positive conclusions, are more reserved, even over cautious, in their statements. They question, but do not offer evidence to refute, the earlier findings. Their conclusions often do not follow from the results of the research reviewed or are equivocal, using extreme language and, in effect, setting up straw men to demolish. For example, Mitchell, Bozarth, and Krauft write that "it seems to us to be increasingly clear that *the mass of data neither supports the overriding influence of such variables as empathy, warmth, and genuineness in all cases. . . . The recent evidence, although equivocal, does seem to suggest that empathy, warmth, and genuineness are related in some way to client change, but their potency and generalizability are not as great as some thought.*"[68] Their conclusions were strongly influenced by a few studies whose flaws militated against obtaining positive results.

Again, Parloff, Waskow, and Wolfe use extreme language in the statement that they attempt to refute: "It must be concluded that the unqualified claim that 'high' levels (absolute or relative) of accurate empathy, warmth, and genuineness (independent of the source of rating or the nature of the instrument) represent the 'necessary and sufficient' conditions for effective therapy (independent of the outcome measure to conditions) is not supported."[69] No one makes such an extreme claim.

Orlinsky and Howard, reviewing much of the same literature, conclude that "the studies done thus far suggest that the positive quality of the relational bond, as exemplified in the reciprocal interpersonal relationship behaviors of the participants, is more clearly related to patient improvement than are any of the particular treatment techniques used by therapists."[70] Orlinsky and Howard reviewed studies of clients' perceptions of their therapists and of themselves, which were predominately positive in supporting the importance of the therapeutic relationship. Earlier, Gurman's review of research on clients' perceptions led him to the conclusion that "there exists substantial, if not overwhelming, evidence in support of the hypothesized relationship between patient-perceived therapeutic conditions and outcome in individual psychotherapy and counseling."[71]

Bergin and Lambert, presumably after reading the articles of the other contributors to Garfield and Bergin's *Handbook of Psychotherapy and Behavior Change,* write:

Interpersonal and nonspecific or nontechnical factors still loom large as stimulators of patient improvement. It should come as no surprise that helping people . . . can be greatly facilitated in an interpersonal relationship that is characterized by trust, warmth, acceptance and human wisdom. It appears that these personal factors are crucial ingredients even in the most technical [behavioral] therapies. This is not to say that techniques are irrelevant but that their power for change pales when compared to personal influence. Technique is crucial to the extent that it provides a believable rationale and congenial modus operandi for the change agent and the client.[72]

Not a surprise, perhaps, but greatly resisted. Interestingly, the statement about technique actually, although perhaps unwittingly, equates it with the placebo.

Considering the obstacles to research on the relationship between therapist variables and therapy outcomes and the factors that militate against achieving significant relationships,[73] the magnitude of the evidence for the effectiveness of empathic understanding, respect or warmth, and therapeutic genuineness is nothing short of astounding. The evidence for the necessity, if not the sufficiency, of these therapist qualities is incontrovertible. *There is little or no evidence for the effectiveness of any other variables or techniques or for the effectiveness of other methods or approaches to psychotherapy in the absence of these conditions.*

THE ECLECTIC INTEGRATION

The 1950s was the decade of affect (and client-centered therapy); the 1960s, the decade of behaviorism (and behavior therapy); and the 1970s, the decade of cognition (and cognitive therapy). The 1980s appears to be the decade of eclecticism and eclectic psychotherapy. The eclectic movement so far has failed to produce a truly integrative, systematic theory and practice of psychotherapy. All the purported eclectic approaches have virtually ignored the basic common elements just considered. Yet no systematic approach that claims to be eclectic can do so. Indeed, any eclectic psychotherapy must accept them as the essential core of its theory and practice.

CONCLUSION

In Chapter 18, we came to the conclusion that over the past decade or two, divergent approaches to counseling or psychotherapy have been developing. One stream, or extreme, was earlier represented by behavior therapy but now appears to be represented by cognitive therapy. In both approaches, the therapist is an expert who controls and directs the therapy process, ideally in a planned manner toward preconceived specific goals; the attitude is that the therapist knows best. The other stream, in its extreme form, is represented by existential psychotherapy. With its lack of structure or techniques, it tends to be rather vague and mysterious. The therapist is hardly an expert; rather, the therapist is a fellow traveler on a road for which neither he or she nor the client has a map or even a clear idea of the destination.

In this chapter, we have presented an alternative, somewhat middle-ground approach. It is based on the convergence of many theorists, researchers, and practitioners toward recognizing that the essence of psychotherapy is the relationship between the therapist and the client. If the therapist is an expert, he or she is an expert in human relationships—an expertise that the therapist does not and cannot retain for himself or herself but shares with nonprofessionals. Indeed, the therapist's goal is, in effect, to help the client become more expert in interpersonal relationships, which usually is the source of the client's difficulties. It is a sad commentary on our society that so many people must seek and pay for a good personal relationship, designated as psychotherapy, and that other people have to be educated and trained to provide such a relationship. The development of psychotherapy as a means of meeting the need of a large number of people for a good relationship institutionalizes the process as a profession, but with the recognition that psychotherapists do not have a monopoly on facilitative interpersonal relationships, psychotherapy will no longer be recognized as a profession. It may be that for some time, the direct teaching of good interpersonal relationships may continue as a professional activity.

The realization that psychotherapy cannot remain a distinct profession if it essentially consists of providing a good interpersonal relationship is a major source of resistance to acceptance of this conclusion. Yet it probably has as much, if not more, research support than any other conclusion in the psychology of human behavior.

The nature of the placebo in psychotherapy is considered. It is proposed that the social-influence variables are nonspecific and that the social-influence model of psychotherapy is the model for placebo therapy. While they probably cannot be eliminated from the therapy relationship, the placebo variables can be either maximized, as in placebo therapy, or minimized. Garfield writes that "one important step in the desired direction [toward integration in psychotherapy] is to delineate and to operationalize clearly some of the common variables which seem to play a role in most psychotherapies, and, perhaps, to regard them as a basis for a clearer delineation of psychotherapeutic principles and procedures. This may not be popular, but I think it will be worth the effort."[74]

This chapter is an effort in that direction. A more detailed and systematic discussion is provided elsewhere. The focus is on three variables that, although recognized by many writers as common elements, have not been given the importance they deserve, for reasons that have been suggested. Empathic understanding, respect or warmth, and therapeutic genuineness are specific variables whose effectiveness has been overwhelmingly demonstrated in hundreds of research studies. They cannot be ignored; they constitute the heart of any systematic eclectic approach to psychotherapy.

REFERENCES

1. Patterson, C. H. *Relationship counseling and psychotherapy.* New York: Harper & Row, 1974. P. ix.
2. Skinner, B. F. Reinforcement today. *American Psychologist,* 1958, *14,* 94–99.
3. Skinner, B. F. *Walden two.* New York: Macmillan, 1948. P. 243.
4. Frank, J. D. The dynamics of the psychotherapeutic relationship. *Psychiatry,* 1959, *22,* 17–39; Frank, J. D. *Persuasion and healing.* Baltimore: Johns Hopkins University Press, 1961; Rosenthal, D., & Frank, J. D. Psychotherapy and the placebo effect. *Psychological Bulletin,* 1956, *53,* 294–302.
5. Cartwright, D. S., & Cartwright, R. D. Faith and improvement in psychotherapy. *Journal of Counseling Psychology,* 1958, *5,* 174–177.
6. Rogers, C. R. The necessary and sufficient conditions of therapeutic personality change. *Journal of Consulting Psychology,* 1957, *21,* 95–103.
7. Fiedler, F. The concept of an ideal therapeutic relationship. *Journal of Consulting Psy-*

chology, 1950, *14,* 235–245; Fiedler, F. A comparison of therapeutic relationships in psychoanalytic, nondirective and Adlerian therapeutic relationships. *Journal of Consulting Psychology,* 1950, *14,* 436–445; Fiedler, F. Factor analyses of psychoanalytic, nondirective and Adlerian therapeutic relationships. *Journal of Consulting Psychology,* 1951, *15,* 32–38.

8. Goldstein, A. P. *Therapist–patient expectancies in psychotherapy.* New York: Macmillan, 1962, P. 105.

9. Menniger, K. A., & Holzman, P. S. *Theory of psychoanalytic techniques* (2nd ed.). New York: Basic Books, 1973.

10. Goodstein, L. D. Détente in psychotherapy. Review of *What makes behavior change possible?* edited by A. Burton. *Contemporary Psychology,* 1977, *22,* 578–579.

11. Goldfried, M., & Davison, C. *Clinical behavior therapy.* New York: Holt, Rinehart and Winston, 1976. P. 56.

12. Lang, P. J., Melamed, B. G., & Hart, J. T. A psychophysical analysis of fear modification using an automated desensitization procedure. *Journal of Abnormal Psychology,* 1970, *76,* 220–234.

13. Schwitzgebel, R. K., & Traugott, M. Initial note on the placebo effect of machines. *Behavioral Science,* 1968, *13,* 267–272.

14. Sapolsky, A. Effect of interpersonal relationship upon verbal conditioning. *Journal of Abnormal and Social Psychology,* 1960, *60,* 241–246.

15. Ullmann, L. P., & Krasner, L. (Eds.). *Case studies in behavior modification.* New York: Holt, Rinehart and Winston, 1965. P. 43.

16. Quoted in Klein, M., Dittman, A. J., Parloff, M. B., & Gill, M. M. Behavior therapy: Observations and reflections. *Journal of Consulting and Clinical Psychology,* 1969, *33,* 259–266; see also Ford, J. D. Therapeutic relationships in behavior therapy. *Journal of Consulting and Clinical Psychology,* 1978, *46,* 1402.

17. Quoted in Burton, A. (Ed.). *What makes behavior change possible?* New York: Brunner/Mazel, 1976. P. 66.

18. Gill, M. M. Three on a match but no light. Review of *Three psychotherapies: A clinical comparison,* edited by C. H. Loew, H. Grayson, & G. H. Loew. *Contemporary Psychology,* 1976, *21,* 291–292.

19. Rogers, C. R. *Freedom to learn.* Columbus, Ohio: Merrill, 1969; Patterson, C. H. *Humanistic education.* Englewood Cliffs, N.J.: Prentice-Hall, 1973; Patterson, C. H. *Foundations for a theory of instruction.* New York: Harper & Row, 1977.

20. Bills, R. E. Nondirective play therapy with retarded readers. *Journal of Consulting Psychology,* 1950, *14,* 140–149.

21. Lawrence, D. The effects of counseling on retarded readers. *Educational Research,* 1971, *13,* 119–124; see also Lawrence, D. The counseling of retarded readers by non-professionals. *Educational Research,* 1972, *15,* 48–52.

22. Ellis, A. The value of efficiency in psychotherapy. *Psychotherapy: Theory, Research and Practice,* 1980, *17,* 414–419.

23. Strupp, H. H. A reformulation of the dynamics of the therapist's contribution. In A. S. Gurman & A. M. Razin (Eds.), *Effective psychotherapy.* New York: Pergamon Press, 1977. Pp. 1–22.

24. Bergin, A. E., & Strupp, H. H. *Changing frontiers in the science of psychotherapy.* Chicago: Aldine, 1972; see also Strupp, H. H. Psychotherapy research and practice: An overview. In S. L. Garfield & A. E. Bergin (Eds.), *Handbook of psychotherapy and behavior change: An empirical analysis* (2nd ed.). New York: Wiley, 1978. Pp. 3–32; Strupp, H. H. The therapist's orientation: An overrated variable. *Psychotherapy: Theory, Research and Practice,* 1978, *15,* 314–317; Strupp, H. H. Humanism and psychotherapy: A personal statement of the therapist's essential values. *Psychotherapy: Theory, Research and Practice,* 1980, *17,* 396–480.

25. Albin, R. Therapy research: Still a way to go. *APA Monitor,* 1977, *8,* 11–12. A review of 42 studies comparing professionals and paraprofessions (Durlak, J. C. Comparative effectiveness of paraprofessional and professional helpers. *Psychological Bulletin,* 1979, *86,* 80–92) concludes that professional helpers are no more effective than nonprofessionals and notes that the reasons for this are not known. Strupp's study indicates that the reason lies in the relationship factors, thus supporting the thesis of this chapter.

26. Paul, G. L. Strategy of outcome research in psychotherapy. *Journal of Consulting Psychology* 1967, *31,* 109–118.

27. Krumboltz, J. D. Promoting adaptive behavior: New answers to familiar questions. In J. D. Krumboltz (Ed.), *Revolution in counseling.* Boston: Houghton Mifflin, 1966. Pp. 3–26.

28. Bergin & Strupp, *Changing frontiers in the science of psychotherapy,* p. 8.

29. Kisch, J., & Kroll, J. Meaningfulness versus effectiveness: Paradoxial implications in the evaluation of psychotherapy. *Psychotherapy: Theory, Research and Practice,* 1980, *17,* 401–413.

30. Strupp, A reformulation of the dynamics of the therapist's contribution.

31. Albee, G. W. The uncertain future of clinical psychology. *American Psychologist,* 1970, *25,* 1071–1080.

32. Miller, G. A. Psychology as a means of promoting human welfare. *American Psychologist,* 1969, *24,* 1063–1075.

33. Schofield, W. *Psychotherapy: The purchase of friendship.* Englewood Cliffs, N.J.: Prentice-Hall, 1964.

34. Frank, *Persuasion and healing,* 1973.

35. Bergin, A. E., & Lambert, M. J. The evaluation of therapeutic outcomes. In Garfield & Bergin (Eds.), *Handbook of psychotherapy and behavior change;* pp. 139–190.

36. Strupp, Psychotherapy research and practice.

37. Wolpe, J. *The practice of behavior therapy* (2nd ed.). New York: Pergamon Press, 1973. P. 9.

38. Ford, D. H., & Urban, H. B. *Systems of psychotherapy.* New York: Wiley, 1963. P. 649.

39. Spitz, R. Hospitalism: Genesis of psychiatric conditions in early childhood. *Psychoanalytic Study of the Child,* 1945, *1,* 53–74; see also Lynch, J. J. *The broken heart: The medical consequences of loneliness.* New York: Basic Books, 1977.

40. Burton, A. *Interpersonal psychotherapy.* Englewood Cliffs, N.J.: Prentice-Hall, 1972. P. 14.

41. Glasser, W. *Reality therapy.* New York: Harper & Row, 1965; Patterson, *Relationship counseling and psychotherapy.*

42. Burton, A. *Modern humanistic psychotherapy.* San Francisco: Jossey-Bass, 1967. Pp. 102–103.

43. Rosenthal & Frank, Psychotherapy and the placebo effect.

44. Krasner, L., & Ullmann, L. P. (Eds.). *Research in behavior therapy.* New York: Holt, Rinehart and Winston, 1965.

45. Wolpe, J. *Psychotherapy by reciprocal inhibition.* Stanford, Calif.: Stanford University Press, 1958; Wolpe, *The practice of behavior therapy.*

46. Shapiro, A. K., & Morris, L. A. The placebo effect in medical and psychological therapies. In Garfield & Bergin (Eds.), *Handbook of psychotherapy and behavior change,* pp. 369–410.

47. Ibid. (Italics added), p. 369.

48. Paradoxically, it appears that in medicine, the "inert" placebo may be an active and specific treatment for pain by triggering the release of endorphins in the brain; see Bolles, R. C., & Fanselow, M. S. Endorphins and behavior. *Annual Review of Psychology,* 1982, *33,* 87–102.

49. Shapiro, A. K. Placebo effects in medicine, psychotherapy and psychoanalysis. In Bergin, A. E., & Garfield, S. L. (Eds.), *Handbook of psychotherapy and behavior change: An empirical analysis.* New York: Wiley, 1971. Pp. 439–473.

50. Luborsky, L., Singer, B., & Luborsky, L. Comparative studies of psychotherapy. *Archives*

of General Psychiatry, 1975, *32,* 995–1008; see also Smith, M. L., & Glass, G. V. Meta-analysis of psychotherapy outcome studies. *American Psychologist,* 1977, *32,* 752–760; Smith, M. L., Glass, G. V., & Metler, T. I. *The benefits of psychotherapy.* Baltimore: Johns Hopkins University Press, 1980.

51. Rosenthal & Frank, Psychotherapy and the placebo effect.
52. Pentony, P. *Models of influence in psychotherapy.* New York: Free Press, 1981. P. 56.
53. Shapiro & Morris, The placebo effect in medical and psychological therapies.
54. Fish, J. M. *Placebo therapy.* San Francisco: Jossey-Bass, 1973.
55. Ibid., p. vi.
56. Ibid., p. vii.
57. Ibid., p. 32.
58. Ibid., p. 39.
59. Pentony, P. *Models of influence in psychotherapy,* pp. 8, 63–64.
60. LaCrosse, M. B. Comparative perceptions of counselor behavior: A replication and an extension. *Journal of Counseling Psychology,* 1977, *24,* 464–471.
61. Krumboltz, J. D., Becker-Haven, J. F., & Burnett, K. F. Counseling psychology. *Annual Review of Psychology,* 1979, *30,* 557–602.
62. Patterson, *Foundations for a theory of instruction,* Chap. 4.
63. Wexler, D. A., & Rice, L. N. Theory. In D. A. Wexler & L. N. Rice (Eds.), *Innovations in client-centered therapy.* New York: Wiley, 1974. Pp. 15–20.
64. Bergin, A. E., & Suinn, R. M. Individual psychotherapy and behavior therapy. *Annual review of psychology,* 1975, *26,* 509–556; Lambert, M. J., DeJulio, S. S., & Stein, D. Therapist interpersonal skills. *Psychological Bulletin,* 1979, *83,* 467–489; Mitchell, K. M., Bozarth, J. D., & Krauft, C. C. A reappraisal of the therapeutic effectiveness of accurate empathy, non-possessive warmth, and genuineness. In Gurman & Razin (Eds.), *Effective psychotherapy,* pp. 482–502; Orlinsky, D. E., & Howard, K. I. The relation of process to outcome in psychotherapy. In Garfield & Bergin (Eds.), *Handbook of psychotherapy and behavior change,* pp. 283–330; Parloff, M. B., Waskow, I. E., & Wolfe, B. E. Research on therapist variables in relation to process and outcomes. In Garfield & Bergin (Eds.), *Handbook of psychotherapy and behavior change,* pp. 233–283.
65. Patterson, C. H. *The therapeutic relationship: Foundations for an eclectic psychotherapy.* Monterey, Calif.: Brooks/Cole, 1985.
66. Truax, C. B., & Carkhuff, R. R. *Toward effective counseling and psychotherapy.* Chicago: Aldine, 1967. Pp. 116–117.
67. Truax, C. B., & Mitchell, K. M. Research on certain therapist skills in relation to process and outcome. In Bergin & Garfield (Eds.), *Handbook of psychotherapy and behavior change,* op. cit., pp. 330, 310.
68. Mitchell, Bozarth, & Krauft, A reappraisal of the therapeutic effectiveness of accurate empathy, non-possessive warmth, and genuineness, p. 483. (Italics in original)
69. Parloff, Waskow, & Wolfe, Research on therapist variables in relation to process and outcomes, p. 249.
70. Orlinsky & Howard, The relation of process to outcome in psychotherapy, p. 296.
71. Gurman, A. S. The patient's perception of the therapeutic relationship. In German & Razin (Eds.), *Effective psychotherapy,* pp. 503–543.
72. Bergin & Lambert, The evaluation of therapeutic outcomes, p. 180.
73. Patterson, *The therapeutic relationship;* Patterson, C. H. Empathy, warmth, and genuineness in psychotherapy: A review of reviews. *Psychotherapy,* 1984, *21,* 431–438.
74. Garfield, S. L. Eclecticism and integration in psychotherapy. *Behavior Therapy,* 1982, *13,* 610–623.
75. Patterson, *The therapeutic relationship.*

INDEXES

Index of Names

Index of Subjects

Abreaction, 11, 120, 246, 466, 511

Acceptance, 85, 90, 181, 185, 283–284, 298, 300, 396, 398, 511, 512, 548

Adult ego state, 312

Affective vs. rational approaches, 1–2, 56, 60, 419, 538

Aggression, 214, 241, 280, 281, 346, 347, 351, 353, 381, 392, 421, 500, 505

Alcoholism, 81, 244, 364

Alienation, 287, 348, 354, 364–365, 391, 421, 422

Ambiguity, 85, 292

Ambivalence, 239–240, 243

Anal stage, 216–217, 236

Anticipation, 35, 173, 272 *See also* Expectancy

Anticipatory responses, 78, 80

Anxiety, 25, 35, 110, 111, 118, 119, 151, 152, 175, 193, 198, 201, 213, 218–219, 220, 221, 239, 243, 279, 282, 300, 349, 352, 383, 386, 421, 437, 438, 447, 505, 519

Anxiety neurosis, 37, 219

Approach-avoidance conflict, 83, 85, 88, 102, 103

Assertive responses, 114–115, 123–127, 153, 236, 532

Attitudes and behavior change, 26, 40–41, 132, 305, 453

Attitudinal reorientation, 515–517

Attitudinal values, 435, 443, 453

Automatic thoughts, 34

Aversive therapy, 117–118, 121–122, 150, 159–161, 191, 200, 532

Awareness, 278, 354, 355, 358, 359, 382, 386, 394, 421, 424, 481, 485, 487

Barrett-Lennard Relationship Inventory, 558

Behavioral assessment, 148–149, 196–198

Behavioral equation, 141–144

Behavior potential, 173

Behavior therapy, xv, 33, 66–70, 107–135, 138–168, 506, 532–537
  demise of, 533–537
  evaluation of, 122–123, 129–135, 166–168

Bernreuter Self-Sufficiency Scale, 112

Carbon dioxide—oxygen treatment, 116, 118, 119

Case history in treatment, 112, 285–288, 498–499

Catastrophic reaction, 36

Catharsis, 182, 213, 281, 471, 511, 515

Cathexis, 214, 313, 348

Child ego state, 312–313

Choice, 273, 280, 393, 397, 412, 421, 422, 432, 467, 470, 483

Client
  dependence, 181, 283, 294, 539, 558
  expectations, 132, 133, 135, 152, 181, 283, 355, 547, 549
  faith in method, 548
  faith in therapist, 547
  motivation, 76–77, 173, 270, 415, 434, 481, 537, 547
  perceptions, 283, 394–396, 399, 400–401, 540–542, 549, 557, 559
  responsibility, 25, 397, 421, 433–444, 439, 440, 442, 454, 470, 483, 489
  selection, 28, 84, 130, 250–251
  self-exploration, 395, 402, 404, 552, 560